COL

Vladislav Zubok is Professor of International ~~History~~ ~~at the~~ London School of Economics and Political Science. He is the author of *A Failed Empire*, *Zhivago's Children* and *The Idea of Russia*.

Further praise for *Collapse*:

"The author seems to have read practically everything currently available, both published and unpublished, of relevance to his subject . . . [Zubok] writes very stylish and idiomatic English, which makes his work a real pleasure to read." Martin Dewhirst, *East-West Review*

"Such a huge event in world history as the collapse of the Soviet Union will undoubtedly be retold. When it is, Zubok's impressive book will have to be consulted." James Rodgers, *History Today*

"Using remarkably copious archival sources, which he has mastered with impressive thoroughness, Zubok presents an almost day-by-day, or even hour-by-hour, account . . . A powerful, detailed picture of puzzling events of great importance." Gary Saul Morson, *New Criterion*

"Meticulous . . . offers an impressive close-up of the hectic political and diplomatic activities between August 1991, the time of the failed Communist coup, and December of that year, when the Soviet Union formally ceased to exist." Maria Lipman, *Foreign Affairs*

"Zubok . . . has cutting insights on the 'who' and the 'what' and the 'where' and the 'when'." Gabriel Gavin, *Reaction*

"A drama of epic proportions, the Soviet collapse never looked so contingent on human courage and follies, accidents and missed opportunities, as in this book . . . The best narrative of the Soviet Union's end we have so far." Vladimir Pechatnov, co-editor of *The Kremlin Letters*

"This is a deeply researched indictment of Mikhail Gorbachev's timidity and mercurial policies that backfired. Zubok invokes George Kennan's hope at the dawn of the Cold War that the USSR would experience 'gradual mellowing'. Instead, Russia at the turn of the 21st century was ripe for the rise of Putin." Strobe Talbott, Former US Deputy Secretary of State and author of *The Great Experiment*

"A deeply researched, gripping account of the final Soviet unravelling: Gorbachev's growing weakness, infighting among his opponents, breakaways to independence by the USSR's constituent republics, including Russia itself, all in the face of growing reluctance of the Bush administration and the Western alliance to help Gorbachev salvage a democratic union." William Taubman, Pulitzer Prize-winning author of *Khrushchev: The Man and His Era*, and of *Gorbachev: His Life and Times*

COLLAPSE

THE FALL OF THE SOVIET UNION

VLADISLAV M. ZUBOK

YALE UNIVERSITY PRESS
NEW HAVEN AND LONDON

Copyright © 2021 Vladislav M. Zubok

First published in paperback in 2022

All rights reserved. This book may not be reproduced in whole or in part, in any form (beyond that copying permitted by Sections 107 and 108 of the U.S. Copyright Law and except by reviewers for the public press) without written permission from the publishers.

All reasonable efforts have been made to provide accurate sources for all images that appear in this book. Any discrepancies or omissions will be rectified in future editions.

For information about this and other Yale University Press publications, please contact:
U.S. Office: sales.press@yale.edu   yalebooks.com
Europe Office: sales@yaleup.co.uk   yalebooks.co.uk

Set in Minion Pro by IDSUK (DataConnection) Ltd
Printed in Denmark by Nørhaven

Library of Congress Control Number: 2021941540

ISBN 978-0-300-25730-4 (hbk)
ISBN 978-0-300-26817-1 (pbk)

A catalogue record for this book is available from the British Library.

10 9 8 7 6 5 4

To all reformers

CONTENTS

CONTENTS

CONTENTS

ILLUSTRATIONS

PLATES

1. Gorbachev at the funeral of his predecessor Konstantin Chernenko, 11 March 1985. Courtesy of Yuri Feklistov.
2. Gorbachev at the unveiling of Lenin's monument in Moscow, November 1985. Courtesy of Yuri Feklistov.
3. Popular Front activists in Estonia, fall 1988. Courtesy of Yuri Feklistov.
4. Andrei Sakharov as People's Deputy, June 1989. Author unknown / © The Yeltsin Foundation.
5. Boris Yeltsin displays his Russian charisma, March 1989. Vyacheslav Bakin / © The Yeltsin Foundation.
6. Gorbachev and Bush at the Malta summit, 2 December 1989. TASS / Contributor / Getty Images.
7. Gorbachev takes the oath to become the President of the USSR, March 1990. Dmitry Donskoy / © The Yeltsin Foundation.
8. Night rehearsal of the military parade on Red Square, early May 1990. Courtesy of Yuri Feklistov.
9. Gorbachev, Marshal Yazov, and Prime Minister Ryzhkov at Lenin's Mausoleum, 9 May 1990. Dmitry Donskoy / © The Yeltsin Foundation.
10. Grigory Yavlinsky, July 1991. Courtesy of Yuri Feklistov.
11. Yeltsin resigns his Party membership and walks away from the Party Congress, 12 July 1990. Anatoly Khrupov / © The Yeltsin Foundation.
12. Yeltsin and Leonid Kravchuk sign the Russian-Ukrainian "treaty," 19 November 1990. Author unknown / © The Yeltsin Foundation.
13. Democratic Russia rallies next to the Kremlin, 10 March 1991. Courtesy of Yuri Feklistov.
14. Vladimir Zhirinovsky speaks, May 1991. Dmitry Donskoy / © The Yeltsin Foundation.

ILLUSTRATIONS

MAPS

DRAMATIS PERSONAE

ABALKIN, Leonid (1930–2011): deputy head of the Soviet government, August 1989–December 1990

ADAMISHIN, Anatoly (1934–): Soviet ambassador to Italy, 1990–91

AFANASYEV, Yuri (1934–2015): deputy of the Supreme Soviet of the USSR; a leader of Democratic Russia

AGANBEGYAN, Abel (1932–): Soviet economist; architect of economic reforms in 1987–88 and September–October 1990

AKHROMEYEV, Sergey (1923–91): Marshal of the Soviet Union; Gorbachev's military advisor, December 1988–August 1991; member of the Emergency Committee, August 1991

BAKATIN, Vadim (1937–): Minister of the Interior of the Soviet Union, October 1988–December 1990; ran for the Russian presidency in 1991; the last head of the KGB, August–December 1991

BAKLANOV, Oleg (1932–): Party Secretary for Defense, 1988–August 1991; member of the Emergency Committee, August 1991

BERNSTAM, Mikhail (1940–): American economist; advisor to the RSFSR government, March–December 1991

BESSMERTNYKH, Alexander (1933–): Foreign Minister of the Soviet Union, January–August 1991

BOCHAROV, Mikhail (1941–2020): head of the Higher Economic Council of the RSFSR government, June 1990–September 1991

BOLDIN, Valery (1935–2006): Gorbachev's personal assistant, 1981–87; Gorbachev's chief of staff, 1987–91; member of the Emergency Committee, August 1991

BONNER, Yelena (1923–2011): dissident and wife of Andrei Sakharov; leading voice of the opposition and Democratic Russia

DRAMATIS PERSONAE

BRAITHWAITE, Rodric (1932–): British ambassador to Moscow, 1988–92

BURBULIS, Gennady (1945–): advisor to Yeltsin; organizer of Yeltsin's presidential campaign, April–June 1991; State Secretary of the Russian government, June–December 1991

CHERNYAEV, Anatoly (1921–2017): Gorbachev's aide for foreign policy, January 1986–December 1991

FOKIN, Vitold (1932–): Prime Minister of the Ukrainian Republic, November 1990–December 1991

GAIDAR, Yegor (1956–2009): economist; author of program of market reforms for the RSFSR; deputy head of the Russian government, 15 November 1991–December 1992

GERASHCHENKO, Viktor (1937–): Chairman of the State Bank of the USSR, July 1989–December 1991

IVANENKO, Viktor (1950–): Major-General of the KGB; head of KGB RSFSR, 5 August–26 November 1991; backed Yeltsin during the Emergency Committee rule in August 1991

KARIMOV, Islam (1938–2016): First Secretary of the Communist Party of Uzbekistan, 1989–91; "elected" by the Republic's Supreme Soviet as President of Uzbekistan in November 1990

KEBICH, Vyacheslav (1936–2020): Prime Minister of Belorussia, then sovereign Belarus, 1990–94

KHASBULATOV, Ruslan (1942–): Yeltsin's deputy in the Supreme Soviet of the RSFSR, June 1990–June 1991; head of the Supreme Soviet of the RSFSR, June 1991–October 1993

KORZHAKOV, Alexander (1950–): personal bodyguard and then head of Yeltsin's Presidential Security Service, 1989–96

KOZYREV, Andrei (1951–): Foreign Minister of the RSFSR, October 1990–December 1991

KRAVCHUK, Leonid (1934–): Chairman of the Supreme Soviet of Ukraine, July 1990–December 1991; first President of independent Ukraine, December 1991–19 July 1994

KRUCHINA, Nikolai (1928–91): chief administrator for economic affairs, central Party apparatus, 1983–91

KRYUCHKOV, Vladimir (1924–2007): Chairman of the KGB, October 1988–August 1991; ringleader of the Emergency Committee in August 1991

LANDSBERGIS, Vytautas (1932–): head of *Sajudis* (the Reform Movement of Lithuania) and the Parliament of Lithuania, 1989–August 1991

LIGACHEV, Yegor (1920–2021): Secretary of the Central Committee of the Communist Party of the Soviet Union, December 1983–July 1990; Politburo member, April 1985–July 1990

DRAMATIS PERSONAE

LUKIN, Vladimir (1937–): Deputy of the Supreme Soviet of the RSFSR; head of its Committee on International Affairs, June 1990–December 1991

LUKYANOV, Anatoly (1930–2019): Politburo member, September 1988–July 1990; Speaker of the Supreme Soviet of the USSR, March 1990–August 1991; collaborated with the Emergency Committee in August 1991

MASLIUKOV, Yuri (1937–2010): top economic planner in the Soviet government, 1982–November 1991; Chairman of Gosplan, 1988–November 1991

MATLOCK, Jack (1929–): US ambassador to the Soviet Union, 1987–August 1991

MEDVEDEV, Vadim (1929–): Politburo member, September 1988–July 1990

MOISEYEV, Mikhail (1939–): head of the General Staff of the USSR, December 1988–August 1991; briefly Minister of Defense, August 1991

MURASHOV, Arkady (1957–): Deputy of the Supreme Soviet of the USSR; organizer of Democratic Russia, January 1990–September 1991

NAZARBAYEV, Nursultan (1940–): Chairman of the Supreme Soviet of the Kazakh SSR, February–April 1990; elected as President of Kazakhstan by the Republic's Supreme Soviet, April 1990

PALAZHCHENKO, Pavel (1949–): interpreter for Soviet Foreign Minister Eduard Shevardnadze, July 1985–December 1990; interpreter for Mikhail Gorbachev, December 1985–December 1991

PANKIN, Boris (1931–): Minister of Foreign Affairs of the Soviet Union, August–November 1991

PAVLOV, Valentin (1937–2003): Minister of Finance of the USSR, July 1989–January 1991; head of the Cabinet of Ministers of the USSR, January–August 1991; member of the Emergency Committee, August 1991

PETRAKOV, Nikolai (1937–2014): Gorbachev's economic advisor, December 1989–December 1990; author of a program of radical market transition

POLOZKOV, Ivan (1935–): head of the Russian Communist Party, June 1990–August 1991

POPOV, Gavriil (1936–): economist; organizer of Democratic Russia; head of the City Council and then Mayor of Moscow, June 1990–December 1991

PRIMAKOV, Yevgeny (1929–2015): Gorbachev's advisor, March 1990–August 1991; head of the KGB's First Directorate (foreign intelligence), September–December 1991

PUGO, Boris (1937–1991): Minister of the Interior of the USSR, December 1990–August 1991; member of the Emergency Committee; committed suicide after the failure of the junta

RUTSKOY, Alexander (1947–): Major-General of Aviation, 1991; Vice-President of the RSFSR, June 1991–October 1993

DRAMATIS PERSONAE

RYZHKOV, Nikolai (1929–): Chairman of the Council of Ministers of the USSR, September 1985–December 1990; architect of Gorbachev's early economic reforms

SABUROV, Yevgeny (1946–2009): Minister of the Economy of the RSFSR, 15 August–15 November 1991

SAKHAROV, Andrei (1921–89): physicist, designer of nuclear weapons, dissident; winner of the Nobel Peace Prize, 1975; member of the Supreme Soviet of the USSR and opposition leader, May–December 1989

SAVISAAR, Edgar (1950–): co-founder of the Popular Front of Estonia, July 1988; Prime Minister of Estonia, August 1991–January 1992

SHAKHNAZAROV, Georgy (1924–2001): philosopher and sociologist; Gorbachev's aide, 1988–December 1991

SHAKHRAI, Sergey (1956–): Yeltsin's legal advisor; drafted the documents on the dissolution of the USSR on 7–8 December 1991

SHAPOSHNIKOV, Yevgeny (1942–2020): commander of the Soviet Air Force; Minister of Defense of the USSR, August–December 1991

SHATALIN, Stanislav (1934–97): economist; member of Gorbachev's Presidential Council, May 1990–January 1991

SHEBARSHIN, Leonid (1935–2012): head of the KGB's First Directorate (foreign intelligence), October 1988–August 1991; head of the KGB after the junta's fall in August 1991

SHEVARDNADZE, Eduard (1928–2014): Minister of Foreign Affairs of the Soviet Union, July 1985–December 1990 and November–December 1991

SHUSHKEVICH, Stanislav (1934–): Chairman of Belorussia's Supreme Soviet, August–December 1991; signed the documents to dissolve the Soviet Union on 8 December 1991

SOBCHAK, Anatoly (1937–2000): Mayor of St Petersburg, July–December 1991

STANKEVICH, Sergey (1954–): member of the democratic opposition, 1989–91; deputy head of the Moscow municipal government and advisor to Yeltsin, 1990–91

STAROVOITOVA, Galina (1946–98): Russian ethnographer; deputy of the Supreme Soviet of the USSR, May 1989–September 1991; deputy of the Supreme Soviet of the RSFSR, June 1990–93; advisor to Yeltsin, 1990–91

STEPANOV-MAMALADZE, Teimuraz (1934–99): aide and speechwriter to Foreign Minister Shevardnadze, July 1985–December 1990

VARENNIKOV, Valentin (1923–2009): commander of Soviet ground forces and Deputy Minister of Defense, 1989–August 1991; active in the Emergency Committee, August 1991

DRAMATIS PERSONAE

VOROTNIKOV, Vitaly (1926–2012): member of the Politburo, December 1983–July 1990; head of the Supreme Soviet of the RSFSR, October 1988–May 1990

VOSHCHANOV, Pavel (1948–): journalist; President Yeltsin's press secretary, July 1991–February 1992

YAKOVLEV, Alexander (1923–2005): member of the Politburo, 1985–July 1990; close associate of Gorbachev, July–December 1990 and September–December 1991

YAKOVLEV, Yegor (1930–2005): editor of *Moscow News*, 1986–91; head of Soviet television, August–December 1991

YAVLINSKY, Grigory (1952–): Soviet economist; author of the "400 Days of Confidence" program (which became "500 Days"), June–September 1990; author of the Grand Bargain, May–August 1991

ZASLAVSKY, Ilya (1960–): member of the parliamentary opposition and coordinator of Democratic Russia

ACKNOWLEDGMENTS

This book could not have been written without the encouragement, goodwill, advice, and support of my colleagues, librarians, archivists, and other individuals, as well as a number of organizations. The late Viktor Zaslavsky, a friend and a wonderful scholar of Soviet society and politics, urged me back in 2008 to write this book, while insisting that the Soviet Union had been doomed. I acted on his advice, but came to a different conclusion. My work on this book became possible largely because of an excellent academic environment, first in the Department of History at Temple University and then in the Department of International History at the London School of Economics and Political Science; there I worked in the company of Richard Immerman, William Hitchcock, Beth Bailey, Richard Farber, Ralph Young, Petra Goedde, Rita Krueger, Howard Spodek, Gregory Urwin, Jay Lockenouer, Matthew Jones, Piers Ludlow, David Stevenson, Kristina Spohr, Nigel Ashton, Svetozar Rajak, and Roham Alvandi, among others. I am deeply thankful to them for their advice, encouragement, and collegial interest. The generosity of several organizations in the United States and United Kingdom facilitated my access to the US archives and libraries, and allowed me to draft the first chapters of my book: a W. Glenn Campbell and Rita Ricardo-Campbell National Fellowship at the Hoover Institution, Stanford University; a public policy scholarship at the Kennan Institute of Russian studies; and a fellowship at the Woodrow Wilson Center in 2012 and 2014. A research grant by the Hoover Institution and Archive in 2018 allowed me to return to Palo Alto and do additional research there. At the Wilson Center I was consistently supported and encouraged by Christian Ostermann, Samuel Wells, Robert Litwak, Blair Ruble, Matthew Rojansky, and William Pomeranz. On the Stanford campus special thanks go to Norman Naimark, Eric Wakin, David Holloway, Gail Lapidus, Michael McFaul, and Anatol Shmelev. At the LSE, in

ACKNOWLEDGMENTS

2018 I received a grant from the Paulsen program, administered by Dominic Lieven and Janet Hartley; this money helped me conclude my research in the Moscow archives. My Department of International History also gave me the funds to do additional research and travel.

The book would not have happened without new evidence from Russia and the United States. My primary sources of material were in the Russian State Archive of Contemporary History (RGANI), the State Archive of the Russian Federation (GARF), the Hoover Institution Archives (HIA), the George H. W. Bush Presidential Library (GBPL), the National Security Archive at George Washington University (NSA), and the Seeley G. Mudd Library (SML) at Princeton University. I am thankful to the archivists who never lost patience with my many requests. The LSE librarian Paul Horsler always found ways to help me find the books and articles I was seeking. A number of individuals, mostly old friends and colleagues, shared their sources and ideas with me, among them Svetlana Savranskaya, Tom Blanton, Christian Ostermann, Hope Harrison, William Taubman, Mark Kramer, Arne Westad, Archie Brown, Timothy Colton, Diana Villiers Negroponte, Peter Ruggenthaler, Serhii Plokhi, Vladimir Pechatnov, Rudolf Pikhoia, and Oleg Skvortsov. Anna Kan showed me copies of BBC interviews and programs from 1991. Dr Natalya Kibita graciously shared with me documents at the Kiev-based State Archive for Public Organizations. Alexander Babkin from the Yeltsin Foundation advised me on visuals. Sir Rodric Braithwaite, the last British ambassador to the Soviet Union, provided a copy of his invaluable unpublished diaries. I also learned much about developments in the Baltic republics from the dissertation of Una Bergmane, whose book *Politics of Uncertainty: The US, the Baltic Question, and the Collapse of the USSR* is to be published by Oxford University Press.

In our age of electronic databases, I owe a great debt to those individuals who created the remarkably rich "electronic archives." These include the Archive of Yeltsin at https://yeltsin.ru/archive and another project of the Yeltsin Center, "Istoriia novoi Rossii," at http://ru-90.ru; the archive of Yegor Gaidar at http://gaidar-arc.ru; and the archive of interviews on Ukrainian independence, *Rozpad Radians'kogo Soiuzu. Usta istoriia nezalezhnoi Ukraiiny 1988–1991*, at http://oralhistory.org.ua/category/interview-ua. From those sources, which I could mine without leaving my apartment in national lockdowns during the pandemic, I learned more than I could have done as an individual researcher in "physical" archives.

As a result of my participation in unique "critical oral history" conferences, organized by the indomitable Janet Lang and Jim Blight, I was fortunate in being able to spend many hours, including informal and private conversations, with some major participants in the historical events described in this book. In

ACKNOWLEDGMENTS

particular, I was very influenced by my meetings and conversations with Mikhail Gorbachev's former aides Anatoly Chernyaev and Georgy Shakhnazarov, as well as Eduard Shevardnadze's former aide Sergey Tarasenko. In 1995, Chernyaev introduced me to Gorbachev; a few years later, Chernyaev shared with me his remarkable diaries, still unpublished at the time. In 1999, thanks to the creative energy of James Hershberg, I made a memorable trip to Georgia where I interviewed Shevardnadze. I met and talked with other men from the Soviet leadership, including Alexander Yakovlev, Yegor Ligachev, General Valentin Varennikov, the former Minister of Defense Dmitry Yazov, and the former head of the military-industrial complex, Oleg Baklanov. Among other individuals who appear in this book, I had a chance to meet with Leonid Shebarshin, the head of Soviet intelligence and briefly the head of the KGB, Boris Pankin, the last Minister of Foreign Affairs of the USSR, Gorbachev's interpreter Pavel Palazhchenko, the economist and politician Grigory Yavlinsky, Yeltsin's ally and then critic Vladimir Lukin, the diplomat Anatoly Adamishin, and Gorbachev's press secretary, Andrei Grachev. Gennady Burbulis, Yeltsin's top strategist in 1990–1, spent several hours with me online sharing his reminiscences and assessments of the Soviet collapse. I have learned much from my conversations with Andrei Kokoshin, Viktor Sheinis, Stanislav Shushkevich, Alexander Drozdov, Igor Malashenko, Andrei Zubov, Alexei Pankin, among others, who lived through the excitement and frustration of perestroika, crisis, and the Soviet collapse. My encounters and conversations with these individuals, which took place over the course of many years, were more than just formal interviews. We relived the history together, and this book amounts to a discussion with many of them.

The meetings and interviews that I had with Western politicians and other individuals were essential for me to fully comprehend the complexity and delicacy of the Western, particularly the American, "factor" in the story of the Soviet collapse. I am grateful to the former Secretary of State, James Baker, for an interview and permission to draw on his papers, when they were still restricted. I was privileged also to be able to meet and interview Robert Zoellick, Condoleezza Rice, Strobe Talbott, William Odom, Philip Zelikow, Francis Fukuyama, Michael Boskin, Rodric Braithwaite, and Jack Matlock. My meetings and interviews with Michael Bernstam, Professor Emeritus at the Hoover Institution, shaped my views, heretofore rather amorphous, on the nature of Soviet economic reforms and the ensuing crisis. He also shared with me his personal collections of documents from 1990–2 and spent countless hours with me at Hoover's cafeteria and in his office, reminiscing and explaining.

The manuscript benefited from the attention and suggestions of several readers, including Isaac Scarborough, Mikhail Bernstam, William Taubman,

ACKNOWLEDGMENTS

Georgy Kasyanov, Svetlana Savranskaya, Benjamin Nathans, Elizabeth Charles, Mark Kramer, and Rodric Braithwaite. The Alexander Dallin lectureship at Stanford University, the Institute of Slavic, East European, and Eurasian Studies at the University of Berkeley, the Davies Center for Russian and Eurasian Studies, the "kruzhok" of Russian-Soviet history at the University of Pennsylvania, and the NYU Abu-Dhabi gave me opportunities to share the preliminary conclusions of my research with a broad array of historians, sociologists, and political scientists. Marty Sherwin, Mark Kramer, Yuri Slezkine, Georgi Derluguian, and Victoria Zhuravleva organized seminars to discuss my project and asked probing questions. Sergey Radchenko organized an online workshop of Cold War history scholars at the height of COVID-19, where part of my draft was discussed. In my Department at the LSE, I benefited from questions posed by my colleagues at a research forum arranged by David Stevenson and Steve Casey. Last, but not least, students of my course on Soviet history, year after year have prodded me to clarify the puzzle of the sudden Soviet disintegration.

Joanna (Jo) Godfrey offered my book to the wonderful Yale University Press, and gently suggested how I might prune the oversized manuscript. She also gave me helpful editorial advice. The two anonymous reviewers were warmly supportive of the book, but they also induced me to improve its structure and focus. The book could not have had a more careful reader than the editor Richard Mason. James Williams suggested including a digital timeline, which should help readers, including students, follow the thread of my narrative without getting bogged down in the details. In the final stages of my research, Irina Podkolzina, Riccardo Cucciolla, and Isaac Scarborough assisted me in extracting more evidence from Moscow-based archives and libraries. And during the copy-editing phase, when COVID made travel difficult, Nelly Rylkova from the Russian Historical Library in Moscow generously checked the notes and verified my sources. This amazing array of help notwithstanding, all oversights, factual errors, warts and all remain entirely my responsibility.

Although the process of writing a book is a solitary exercise, I depended on friends and loved ones to keep me going, rebound from inevitable fits of self-doubt, and infuse faith that this project would succeed. During the unexpected pandemic, this "social bubble" was doubly important to keep the writer sane. My mother Liudmila Zubok, my wife Yelena Vitenberg, and my son Mikhail Zubok sustained me with their care and affection. They had asked me so many times when I would be done with this book, that finally I decided to complete it.

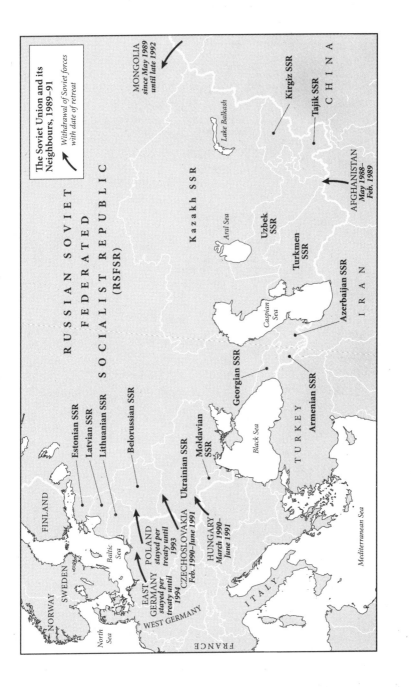

The Soviet Union and its
Neighbours, 1989–91

Withdrawal of Soviet forces
with date of retreat

NORWAY

SWEDEN

FINLAND

North
Sea

Baltic
Sea

EAST
GERMANY
stayed per
treaty until
1994

WEST GERMANY

POLAND
stayed per
treaty until
1993

CZECHOSLOVAKIA
Feb. 1990–June 1991

HUNGARY
March 1990–
June 1991

FRANCE

ITALY

Mediterranean Sea

Estonian SSR

Latvian SSR

Lithuanian SSR

Belorussian SSR

Ukrainian SSR

Moldavian
SSR

Black Sea

TURKEY

Georgian SSR

Armenian SSR

Azerbaijan SSR

Caspian
Sea

IRAN

Aral Sea

Turkmen
SSR

Uzbek
SSR

RUSSIAN SOVIET
FEDERATED
SOCIALIST REPUBLIC
(RSFSR)

Kazakh SSR

Lake Balkash

Kirgiz SSR

Tajik SSR

CHINA

AFGHANISTAN
May 1988–
Feb. 1989

MONGOLIA
since May 1989
until late 1992

North Sea

NORWAY

Arctic Ocean

Latvian SSR
28 July 1989

SWEDEN

Lithuanian SSR
18 May 1989

Estonian SSR
16 Nov. 1988

POLAND

FINLAND

Moldavian SSR
23 June 1990

Belorussian SSR
27 July 1990

Ukrainian SSR
16 July 1990
Referendum of 17 March 1991:
70.2 % voted "yes" for the reformed Union;
28 % voted "no."

The Republic of Crimea

Black
Sea

RUSSIAN SOVIET FEDERATED
(RSFSR)
12 June 1990

Georgian SSR
9 March 1990

TURKEY

Armenian SSR
23 August 1990

Nagorny Karabagh

Aral Sea

Kazakh SSR
25 Oct. 1990

Caspian
Sea

Azeri SSR
29 Nov. 1990

Uzbek SSR
20 June 1990

Lake Balkash

Turkmen SSR
22 Aug. 1990

I R A N

Tajik SSR
24 Aug. 1990

Kirgiz SSR
15 Dec. 1990

AFGHANISTAN

C H I N A

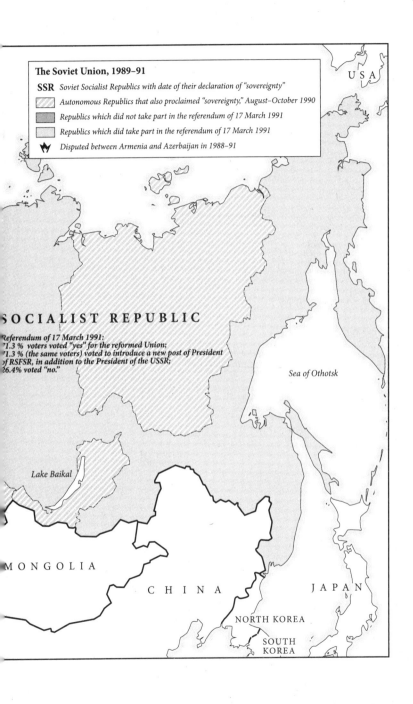

The Soviet Union, 1989–91

SSR *Soviet Socialist Republics with date of their declaration of "sovereignty"*

Autonomous Republics that also proclaimed "sovereignty," August–October 1990

Republics which did not take part in the referendum of 17 March 1991

Republics which did take part in the referendum of 17 March 1991

Disputed between Armenia and Azerbaijan in 1988–91

USA

...OCIALIST REPUBLIC

Referendum of 17 March 1991:
71.3 % voters voted "yes" for the reformed Union;
71.3 % (the same voters) voted to introduce a new post of President
of RSFSR, in addition to the President of the USSR;
26.4% voted "no."

Sea of Othotsk

Lake Baikal

MONGOLIA

CHINA

JAPAN

NORTH KOREA

SOUTH
KOREA

INTRODUCTION
A Puzzle

"They've finally got rid of him, that windbag." I heard this comment from fellow passengers on board an Aeroflot flight from Moscow to New York, which had just made a stop at Shannon, Ireland. It was the morning of 19 August 1991, and it took me a few minutes to realize that these people were alluding to the removal of Mikhail Gorbachev from power. They had learned the news from CNN during the refueling stop, and they clearly approved of what they heard. The plane was full of Russians: some of them were flying to conferences and diplomatic assignments; most were going on private business, to see émigré relatives, and for other reasons. I was flying to the United States with several projects in mind. A few months earlier I had begun working as a Russian aide for the journalist Strobe Talbott and historian Michael Beschloss, who were writing a book about the end of the Cold War. In my bag, I was carrying tapes recording my interviews with Soviet officials. I had also decided to write my own book about the Soviet experience of the Cold War. The prestigious Amherst College in Massachusetts had offered me a fellowship to start my project, far from the turmoil of Moscow where I was born and had lived all my life up to that point.

The news about Gorbachev's arrest was completely unexpected. As a young Moscow-based academic intellectual, I had been rooting for his reforms and liberalization in the Soviet Union. Gorbachev had evoked big expectations, yet since 1990, together with my friends, I had switched my allegiance to Boris Yeltsin, who sought a radical break with the old order. Nobody among the people I knew had any doubt that the old system, the Communist Party, centralized economic management, and the "socialist choice" were doomed. Still, no one wanted to storm the Kremlin and tear down the structures of the state; everyone hoped for reform, not revolution. With my friends, I took part in democratic rallies, avidly read the work of economists who discussed how to return from a command economy to a market economy, and supported independence movements in Lithuania and Georgia. After my plane arrived at New York's JFK airport, I bought a hefty copy of *The New York Times*. The newspaper informed me that Mikhail Gorbachev had apparently been ousted from power by the military and the KGB while on vacation in distant Crimea.

During the fall of 1991, I worked in the library and archives of Amherst College, but spent more time reading and watching the news from home. The immense relief when the coup failed and Gorbachev returned to the Kremlin quickly gave way to anxiety about the future. The Soviet economy was in free fall. Ukraine and other republics intended to leave the Union. My mind was exploding in cognitive dissonance: I found myself a citizen of a state that was collapsing and I could not share the excitement of American colleagues who joked that the USSR was now "the Union of Fewer and Fewer Republics." Fortunately, my wife and son were staying with me in Amherst. Life went on, and at the end of September my second son was born in a hospital in Northampton, Massachusetts. Yet a gnawing thought persisted: what sort of country would we be returning to?

We never got back to the USSR. On a return flight, my plane landed at Sheremetyevo, Moscow, on 31 December 1991, but by that time the leaders of the Russian Federation, Ukraine, Belarus, and other republics had dissolved the Soviet Union. Gorbachev had resigned. The dimly lit Sheremetyevo airport was empty: nobody to refuel the plane, nobody to operate a jet bridge, no customs officers, nobody even to check the passports and visas of arriving passengers. The new Russian state was the country of unprotected borders, without customs, with devalued currency, and empty stores. The immutable state structures seemed to have evaporated. The country that I had left just a few months ago in August had suddenly vanished.

For many years I wanted to write about the end of the Soviet Union. Yet I believed more time should pass before more dispassionate attitudes to this epic event could be formed. I waited in vain. As memories of 1991 faded, opinions and myths acquired a life of their own. What was a provisional insight became an established view, immutable just like the Soviet statehood had been before 1991. In the West, the Soviet collapse came to be universally accepted as predetermined and inevitable, something too self-evident to require further study.[1] When in 2005, Russian President Vladimir Putin called the Soviet collapse "the greatest geopolitical catastrophe of the century," most Western observers ridiculed him for his reactionary nostalgia. It was the time of Western liberal triumphalism and the enlargement of NATO to the East. This mood changed after Russia's war with Georgia in 2008 and the annexation of Crimea in 2014. Western commentators began saying that Russia wanted to restore its "lost empire." In 2019, the Polish head of the European Council, Donald Tusk, said that "the collapse of the Soviet Union was a blessing" for Central and Eastern Europe, for Georgians, Poles, and Ukrainians.[2] Only a few in the West recalled that the Russian Federation had been a leading actor in the Soviet dissolution. Mikhail Gorbachev remained the lonely hero in the West, since everyone acknowledged that he had set inevitable historical developments in motion. When Gorbachev supported Russia's annexation of Crimea, it was dismissed as an atypical pronouncement. In Russia, reactions to the Soviet collapse remain polarized. Liberal-minded people believe that the Soviet Union could not be reformed, and that even to write about its "autopsy" was a waste of time. Good riddance to the empire that could not give its people even "bread and entertainment"! Others feel nostalgia for Soviet greatness and think that Stalin was a great leader, while Gorbachev had sold out to the West. Some of them were not even born when the Soviet Union collapsed.

Scholars who studied the end of the Soviet Union identified several causes of the state's demise. Their conclusions can be summarized as follows. First, the superiority of the United States and its policies in the Cold War had made the USSR retreat and surrender. Second, Gorbachev's glasnost had discredited both communist ideology and doomed the Soviet system to failure. Third, the Soviet Union had died because its economy imploded. Fourth, the movements for national independence had led to the implosion of "the last empire." Finally, the most powerful Soviet elites had opposed Gorbachev's reforms and thereby inadvertently caused the demise of the USSR. In this book, I argue that none of those causes, when taken separately, could have destroyed the Soviet Union. And it took me some time to understand how all those threads had converged in a kind of a perfect storm, unleashed by the rule of Mikhail Gorbachev.

The literature about external Cold War pressures argues that the Soviet Union collapsed because it was overstretched: it lost the war in Afghanistan, carried the unbearable burden of military expenditures, and subsidized its clients around the world. The Soviet superpower, some scholars contend, could no longer compete, militarily and technologically, with the United States and its Western allies. Yet recently, scholars have concluded that US pressures had little to do with the fall of the Berlin Wall and the end of the Cold War. And, at least since 1987, Western governments were surprised and dismayed by the Soviet Union's destabilization, and then disintegration.[3] Recently, more nuanced studies of the Western, especially American, factor in the Soviet collapse have appeared.[4] This book explores the external factors as secondary to the internal causes. International factors became crucial for shaping the behavior of the Soviet elites and counter-elites, but only after the Soviet Union had entered its terminal crisis.

Glasnost (Gorbachev's policy of openness and transparency) and the media's attack on the communist past and ideology greatly contributed to the rise of anti-communist and nationalist movements. Yet it is not entirely clear what role ideological breakdown played in the disintegration of the Soviet statehood. For the Soviet elites, especially in Moscow, Stalin's crimes and repressions had long been known. And the majority of those in the Party ranks, especially younger cohorts, had long been imitating socialist rhetoric, while acting on their real interests in a parallel universe of coveted foreign goods, travel, Western rock music, and mass culture.[5] The Party's ideological legitimacy had long been eroded, yet this was not the main reason why the Party had ceded its economic and political levers of power in 1990–91. That was Gorbachev's decision, a voluntary and unprecedented devolution of power.

The Soviet economic crisis played a central and often underestimated role in the last three years of Soviet history. In conjunction with revelations of past communist crimes, it contributed to mass discontent and mobilization against the central authority. It is axiomatic that the Soviet economic system was wasteful, ruinous, and could not deliver goods to people. What happened to the Soviet economy, however, remains a bone of contention. The oft-repeated explanations about the resistance of the Party, the military-industrial complex, and other "lobbies," are not convincing. Scholars who studied the Soviet economy concluded that the Soviet economic system was destroyed not by its structural faults, but by Gorbachev-era reforms. The purposeful as well as unintended destruction of the Soviet economy, along with its finances, may be considered the best candidate as a principal cause of Soviet disintegration.[6] This book is the first study of the Soviet collapse that pays closest attention to the economic and financial factors within a larger historical narrative.

Some scholars wrote that the Soviet Union was "the last empire" bound to collapse along its multi-national seams, just like other empires did. One authoritative study explains that nationalist movements began in Soviet borderlands, but then created enough resonance to mobilize the Russians in the core of "the empire"; the idea of secession from the Soviet Union became imaginable, and then began to appear inevitable. Mark Beissinger concludes that "the multiple waves of nationalist revolt and inter-ethnic violence" overwhelmed the capacity of the Soviet state to defend itself.[7] The break-up of the Soviet Union into fifteen independent states, along the borders of its republics, made this explanation self-evident, yet deceptively circular. The paradigm of "empire" can be challenged: it exaggerates the role of the nationalist movements, especially in the Baltics and Ukraine, in the Soviet collapse. It also underplays the most crucial and amazing factor: the repeated failure of the central state to defend itself. And it gives a superficial explanation to the defection of the Russian Federation, the core of the Soviet Union.[8] This book offers a more comprehensive look, distanced from the imperial paradigm, at why so many Russians in Moscow wished away so fervently the Soviet statehood that in many ways had been their form of existence for decades.

Finally, there is the role played by the Soviet elites. Some scholars had already begun to question the old explanations of the "reactionary" and "hard-line" nomenklatura (the system whereby influential posts in industry and government were filled by Party appointees) that had allegedly opposed Gorbachev and obstructed his reforms. In fact, evidence shows that Soviet bureaucrats and officials were amazingly adaptive. Some scholars have written about "capitalist revolution" where Soviet nomenklatura abdicated the "socialist project" in order to grab national property for themselves. Others write about "uncivil society" and the crumbling of the centralized pyramid of patronage lines, crucial for state functioning. The attitudes of people in Soviet bureaucracies in fact varied from reactionary to liberal-democratic.[9] This book explores the changing outlook of the key Soviet elites in rapidly altering circumstances in a more fine-grained way than before. Above all, it dwells on their reactions to a failing economy, political anarchy, and ethno-national conflicts.

Many threads in the analysis of the Soviet collapse overlapped and created a widespread feeling of doom—with the result that ultimately the event became a self-fulfilling prophecy. Yet for a historian, this collapse presents a puzzle that does not quite click together. This puzzle became the main subject of this book.

Gorbachev lies at the center of this puzzle. The personality and leadership of the last Soviet leader helps to bring together many pieces in the story of Soviet dissolution. Scholars who sympathize with Gorbachev usually foreground his international policies and give short shrift to his domestic problems and failures, ascribing the latter to intractable historical and other factors, as well as to the resistance and treason of his enemies. This approach has been consistent in the books of Archie Brown, perhaps the most influential Western interpreter of Gorbachev's policies.[10] William Taubman, in his excellent biography of Gorbachev, finds faults in his hero, yet also refuses to call his reforms a failure. On the contrary, Taubman believes that Gorbachev "laid the groundwork for democracy" in the Soviet Union. "It is more the fault of the raw material that he worked with than of his own shortcomings and mistakes that Russian democracy will take much longer to build than he thought."[11] A leading Cold War historian, Odd Arne Westad, seems to agree. "The final drama of the Cold War became a purely Soviet tragedy," he concludes. Gorbachev could have preserved the country by force, but he "would rather see the union disappear . . ."[12]

The story of Gorbachev's best intentions and policies, however, begs for a realistic reassessment, with a more balanced exploration of social and economic dilemmas. After all, as wise people say, "foreign policy begins at home," and one cannot claim a foreign triumph against the background of domestic chaos. Was Gorbachev a world visionary who was too good for his own country? This book draws international and domestic processes that affected the fate of the Soviet Union into one narrative.

The book rethinks the inevitability of the Soviet collapse. It addresses questions: Which other policy options were available to the Kremlin? Could a smart use of coercion and incentives, resolute actions and a bit of luck, have made a difference? Were there other much earlier choices and contingencies that, in the light of new evidence, constituted the points of no return? Many skeptics, when they heard me raising these questions, reproached me: the Soviet Union was doomed, they said, so one should celebrate its collapse, not interrogate it. Those arguments reminded me of what one scholar wrote about the Soviet collapse in 1993: "We tend to confer the mantle of inevitability on accomplished facts, and arguing that what happened did not have to happen is likely to be dismissed as inventing excuses for the losing side."[13] My book is not an exercise in "how the evil empire could have been preserved." Rather it is an attempt to be intellectually honest about what happened. History is never a sequence of inevitabilities, and the Soviet demise was no exception: it was full of contingencies. Unpredictability and uncertainty are fundamental features of human, state, and world affairs. Social movements and ideological currents are not rational, and political wills propel history in unexpected directions. Finally, there are accidents that have huge consequences. This last point resonated with me especially as I was finishing this book during the pandemic.

The American diplomat George Kennan, author of the doctrine of containment, told his students at the National War College, Washington, in 1946 that the Soviet threat to the West could be removed by a "gradual mellowing of Soviet policy under influence of firm and calm resistance abroad." Yet this mellowing, he warned, would be "slow and never complete." Another, more radical option, Kennan wrote, was "internal dissension which would temporarily weaken Soviet potential & lead to [a] situation similar to that of 1919–20." Kennan did not consider this option likely, yet it describes quite well what happened to the Soviet Union in 1991.[14] Nobody, including the most sagacious observers, could predict that the Soviet Union, which had survived the epic assault of Hitler's armies, would be defeated from within, by its internal crises and conflict. During the three decades that followed World War II, the power of the USSR had grown immensely and seemed to prove its resilience. Western leaders and opinion-makers spoke about "a Soviet superpower," a rival of the United States in both economic and military potential. The CIA and many Western economists even forecast that the USSR would outpace the United

States. In fact, the Soviet Union had always suffered from its economic and financial inferiority relative to the US. Its access to superpower status was enabled by a system that allowed the state's phenomenal concentration of resources to achieve a global projection of military might. This worked, however, only as long as the military power could be backed by a convincing ideological message and/or economic capacities. In the 1980s, when severe internal problems at the heart of the Soviet economy, its ideology, and society became apparent, Western observers feared that the Soviet Union might get a second wind. It did not. Yet even in 1990, the majority of observers, in Moscow and elsewhere, did not assume that the Soviet Union was doomed. Gorbachev and even his critics admit that, without the "coup" of August 1991, the Soviet state would not have collapsed so quickly and thoroughly.[15]

In this book, I try to break free from the straitjacket of the dominant narrative that the Soviet collapse was inevitable—the narrative created in the West and within anti-communist circles inside the Soviet Union. That narrative is still in demand, but thirty years after the Soviet collapse, the audience has changed fundamentally: there are now as many people born after 1991 as those who had experienced and can remember the Soviet Union and the Cold War. Both audiences will find much that is new in this book. The history of the Soviet collapse was never a script, known in advance. It was a drama of human ideals, fears, passions, and unanticipated developments. In these pages the reader will find many "fly-on-the-wall" episodes, when Gorbachev and others in the Kremlin debated reforms, agonized over what to do with ethnic conflicts and seceding republics, and contested responsibility and power. To make the texture of the historical narrative authentic, I give preference to instantaneous reactions, rumors, and fears, rare moments of optimism and frequent fits of despair, that characterized those times.

The book, without de-centering Gorbachev, introduces more Soviet actors, voices, and initiatives. I argue that, taken together, they were much more than "the Greek chorus" to "a purely Soviet tragedy" hinging on Gorbachev's choices. Throughout the book, the cast of characters keeps widening and diversifying. As Gorbachev delegated central powers and replaced the old Soviet power hierarchy with an "all power to the Soviets" system, many people began to feel that they were not passive onlookers, but had become participants in history, if not its makers. And late Soviet politics was not just a duel between Gorbachev and his fateful rival Yeltsin. The book presents a broad array of Party stalwarts, reformers, economists, diplomats, parliamentary deputies, KGB officials, the military, captains of military-industrial corporations, budding entrepreneurs, journalists, the Baltic nationalists, the Ukrainian politicians, and many others.

INTRODUCTION

The book also reflects on the trajectory of the Western, and in particular the American, impact on the Soviet collapse, with government, non-governmental actors, and media playing an outsized role in Soviet imagination and politics. British and American sources, especially diaries and official dispatches, help to fill gaps and correct numerous imprecisions in Soviet records. Foreigners, just like at the outset of the Soviet regime, became both chroniclers of and participants in Soviet history. In 1990–91, the US administration, Congress, media, and non-governmental organizations became, willingly or unwillingly, participants in the radicalizing Soviet politics. The American factor loomed larger in the perceptions of those within the Soviet Union than Americans themselves ever suspected at the time. American soft power in the Soviet Union in 1990–91 was equal if not greater to what the United States had in Europe, when it introduced the Marshall Plan of 1947. This "American phenomenon" in Soviet politics was far more complex than political meddling or interference. Those in Russia who continue to speculate about an "American conspiracy to destroy the USSR" do not know what they are talking about. Many in the Soviet Union welcomed and invited the Americans to come and help transform Soviet society. It is remarkable how narrow-minded and unimaginative, albeit prudent, the American leadership was in wielding their enormous "soft power."

The sources for this book have been collected over at least three decades. They include personal observations, many conversations with senior Soviet politicians, diplomats, military, KGB officers, officials from the military-industrial complex, and people from diverse walks of Soviet life, the state, and society. Archives and libraries in Russia and other countries provided me with what individual memories could not. Contrary to common perceptions in the West, Russian sources on the end of the Soviet Union are extraordinarily open, rich, and widely available through a number of electronic databases. Particularly valuable for history are numerous stenographic records of what happened in the institutions of Soviet power, on parliamentary floors, at the meetings of the radical opposition, at numerous conferences of experts and pundits. There is also a tapestry of personal records, minutes, letters, and diaries that often allow one to reconstruct events with remarkable precision and sense the spontaneity of the moment. The second biggest treasure trove for this book were sources and interviews in the United States. They were often more insightful and analytically profound than Soviet accounts: after all, no one entity observed unfolding events in the Soviet Union more attentively than its superpower rival.

As I collected this evidence, I adjusted some of my pre-existing certainties and assumptions. I still believe, just like thirty years ago, that the central economy and Gorbachev's "socialist choice" were doomed, but I no longer have the same sense of inevitability about the Party's demise. In general, I was surprised how clearly many people saw the separate strands of the approaching crisis, yet could not imagine that the whole state construction would fall apart. It was also surprising to see how many historical actors radically changed their views within a few years, influenced by political passions, fears, ideological illusions or delusions, and personal ambitions. Those changes provided an unmistakable sign of revolutionary times.

Even well-known evidence looks different from a greater distance. The role of ideologies in the final phase of Soviet history looms larger to me now than when I was a witness to and participant in, the events. When I was young, I dismissed Gorbachev's neo-Leninist proclamations as mere rhetoric; the evidence reveals that it was absolutely genuine and heartfelt. Equally striking for me today is the explosive spread of ideological anti-communism and American-style liberalism, especially in economics. At the time, it looked "natural" and a "return to common sense." I also became stuck by the utopian nature of the home-grown projects and ideas of reforms that sprang from the democratic-minded intelligentsia in Moscow and elsewhere. What looked like "having no alternative" then, now appears to me as fanciful, naïve, and a prognosis of catastrophe. This is not to criticize the actors of history with the wisdom of hindsight, but to historicize their motives and passions. My biggest surprise, however, came from my realization of the decisive and implacable role of money in the Soviet demise—something, given my Soviet background of economic ignorance, that I completely missed.

At first, I wanted to start my account of the Soviet collapse in January 1991 and stay focused on month-by-month developments. Soon I realized, however, how crucial it was to explain to the reader, particularly the younger reader, the previous years of reforms, high hopes, mobilization of nationalism, impatience, and radicalization—before they gave way to the frustration, fears, and resignation of 1991. My narrative now begins with Yuri Andropov in 1983, when the ex-KGB leader and General Secretary of the Communist Party (1982–84) had tacitly revived the idea of reforms from above. The first part of the book, chapters 1–6, explains how Gorbachev and his reform-minded entourage transformed the conservative reforms from above into a revolutionary gamble and ultimately removed the critical props on which the Soviet system and state were resting. In this part I demonstrate how anti-systemic energy, accumulated by many years of Soviet one-party rule, had been magnified by Gorbachev's unsuccessful reforms, and released into the domain of public politics. The second part of the book, chapters 7–15, covers the collapse itself. The book revisits familiar aspects of this story, but adds much new information that will be unfamiliar to the reader.

I have completed this book with a conviction that the puzzle of the Soviet collapse is not a purely academic problem. In almost any conversation with

Russians or Westerners alike in the years since 1991, they have reacted to my topic vividly and with curiosity. Why had Gorbachev, a prophet of change abroad, some asked, become an epitome of failure and ineffectiveness at home? Was there back then really a threat of a new dictatorship? Did Gorbachev's project of a new voluntary union of democratic states stand a chance of success? Was the new Russia that emerged in 1991 doomed to return to authoritarianism or was there a missed opportunity? I hope this book will satisfy this curiosity and arm the reader with a much better understanding of a great geopolitical and economic upheaval, one that gave birth to a new world.

PART I

HOPE AND HUBRIS
1983–90

CHAPTER 1

PERESTROIKA

*The task is . . . to work out a system of logistical, economic, and moral
steps that would make old modes of work unprofitable, that would
encourage renovation of equipment and managers.*
Yuri Andropov, 15 June 1983[1]

We just can't go on living like this.
Mikhail Gorbachev, March 1985

THE KGB REFORMER

The idea of renovating the Soviet Union originated not with Mikhail Gorbachev,
but with his mentor Yuri Andropov. For years after the Soviet collapse, many
said wistfully: "If only Andropov had lived longer." They meant that under his
leadership the country could have been reformed yet be held together. In fact,
Andropov made the idea of renovation possible and left his heir apparent
Gorbachev with the task of promoting it.

Andropov was born in June 1914, two months before the outbreak of World
War I. His family origins are the subject of controversy.[2] He claimed to be of
Cossack descent, yet in reality he was born into the family of Karl Finkelstein, a
Jewish merchant from Finland, who had moved with his family to Moscow and
opened a jewellery shop on 26 Big Lubyanka street. Had Andropov been born a
few decades earlier, he might have become an entrepreneur or even a banker.
Instead, he concealed his origins, made a Party career during Stalin's terror, and
ended up in another office on Lubyanka street, as the head of the KGB (1967–
82). He was ruthless, clever, and resourceful. He cultivated influential sponsors
and transformed the KGB into a modern corporation specializing in surveillance, secrecy, and espionage.

Andropov was helpful to an aging Leonid Brezhnev, then General Secretary of the Communist Party, on many fronts: his KGB agents procured a secret channel to the West German leadership in 1969, which enabled the start of European détente; Andropov crushed dissent within the Soviet intelligentsia by consigning human rights defenders to mental asylums; he also proposed the forced emigration of dissidents and Jews from the Soviet Union, instead of oppressing them at home; he even provided the Soviet leader with foreign-made sedatives to combat his insomnia.[3] Andropov let Brezhnev down only once: in 1979 he convinced him to move Soviet forces into Afghanistan "to save the socialist regime." He promised it would be a short-term operation. Brezhnev forgave "Yura" this mistake. He wanted Andropov to be his successor. Shortly before his death, Brezhnev moved him from the KGB to the Party apparatus and asked Andropov to lead the Secretariat in his absence. This was the Soviet leader's final gift to his protégé. When Brezhnev died in his sleep in November 1982, Andropov succeeded him without a glitch.

The majority of Soviet people welcomed Andropov as a long-expected strong leader. The intelligentsia, however, oppressed and controlled by the KGB, shuddered at the prospect. Andropov's gaunt face and dour demeanor called to mind the Great Inquisitor from Fyodor Dostoyevsky's *The Brothers Karamazov*: the omniscient man without mercy. Andropov did not interview candidates for jobs in his personal entourage. When one man said to him: "Let me tell you about myself," Andropov replied without a touch of irony: "What makes you think that you know more about yourself than I know about you?"[4]

Andropov was in favor of controlled, conservative reforms.[5] The key to his approach was his experience as the Soviet ambassador in Budapest, Hungary, in 1956, the year when a huge protest erupted against the communist rulers. On 31 October, influenced by Andropov's reports, the Soviet leader Nikita Khrushchev and his Party colleagues launched "Operation Whirlwind": 6,000 Soviet tanks crushed the uprising and set up a puppet government. Andropov kept referring to "the unfortunate Hungarian events" for the rest of his life. It was perhaps his closest brush with violent death. His wife never fully recovered from her nervous breakdown.[6] From the carnage of Budapest emerged Andropov's political credo: deal with dissent ruthlessly, but cautiously; prepare reforms from above before it is too late; do not waver or flinch from the use of force when necessary.

From the early 1960s, when he worked in the Party apparatus in Moscow, Andropov surrounded himself with scholars and intellectuals. He wanted to know what the intelligentsia thought; he was also interested in the problem of modernization and renovation of Soviet economy. Andropov's intellectuals were people of the war generation, who believed in Marxist-Leninist socialism, were shocked by revelations of Stalin's crimes, and dreamed of reforms from above.[7] One of them, Georgy Shakhnazarov, a philosopher and sociologist, recalled a discussion between them: what could be a viable communist model that might replace the Stalinist model? Andropov invited his intellectual "consultants" to speak with absolute candor.[8]

Andropov posed Lenin's famous question: What is to be done? How to make the Soviet state function well as an instrument of socialism? Shakhnazarov responded: the problem was the stifling Party diktat. Without "socialist democracy" and genuine elections, the consultant argued, the Party bureaucracy would always act as a class with vested interests, and would not care about people's well-being. Andropov's face darkened. He cut Shakhnazarov off. In the past, he said, the Soviet system had accomplished fantastic, nearly impossible things. The Party bureaucracy, he acknowledged, had got "rusty," but its leadership was ready "to shake up" the economy. It would be a folly to dismantle the Party-State prematurely. "Only when people begin to feel that their life improves, then one can slowly loosen the yoke on them, give them more air . . . You, the intelligentsia folks, like to cry out: give us democracy, freedom! You ignore many realities."[9] "In some unfathomable way," Shakhnazarov recalled, "two different men co-existed in Andropov—a man of the Russian intelligentsia, in the common sense of this word, and a bureaucrat who saw his vocation as a service to the Party."[10]

In Andropov, the hard line always trumped reformism. In 1965–67, he supported the conservative economic reforms in the Soviet Union. Yet in 1968, he argued in favor of the Soviet military invasion of Czechoslovakia, where the Party reformers unleashed "socialist democracy." The occupation of Czechoslovakia turned, however, into a strategic defeat for the Andropovian vision of renovation. General Secretary Brezhnev shut down economic reforms; in fact, even the word "reform" became a taboo for fifteen years. The KGB under Andropov's command purged Party reformers, while careerists and corrupt officials, whom he despised, filled all nooks and crannies of the ruling nomenklatura.

When Brezhnev appointed him as his successor, Andropov knew that he would inherit huge problems. Soviet troops were in Afghanistan, détente with the West had failed, and Ronald Reagan was in the White House. In Poland, workers were demanding lower prices for food, and, with the help of dissident intellectuals, had created the Solidarity movement back in 1980. This time Andropov concluded that Soviet tanks could not help. The Polish state accumulated $27 billion of debt to Western banks, which came with high interest. The Soviet Union was unable to bail out its Eastern European client. In a conversation with the head of the East German secret police, the Stasi, Andropov informed him that the West was waging a financial war against the Soviet bloc. Washington had tried to block the construction of a new Soviet gas pipeline to Western Europe, a major source of currency for Moscow. Andropov added that

American and West German banks "have suddenly stopped giving us loans."[11] The Soviet Union could fall into the same financial hole in which Poland already found itself.

The first thing the new Soviet leader did was to destroy "the rust" in the Party-State apparatus. The KGB arrested several top men in the Soviet "shadow economy" that, some estimated, accounted for 20–25 percent of GDP. In the Moscow trade system, the top of the criminal pyramid, over 15,000 people were prosecuted, among them 1,200 bureaucrats. He also prosecuted corrupt clans in the Soviet republics; the largest case was the "cotton affair" in Uzbekistan, which had divested the Soviet budget of billions of rubles and involved the entire Party bureaucracy. Andropov also used police methods to restore work discipline across the country.[12]

All this was merely preparation for the next stage. Andropov now ordered the Economic Department of the CC CPSU (Central Committee of the Communist Party of the Soviet Union) to map out a road toward economic reforms. His choice to lead this effort was fifty-three-year-old Nikolai Ryzhkov, former director of a huge military plant, then the head of Gosplan (the State Planning Committee that set goals for the Soviet economy). Ryzhkov recalled Andropov's instructions: "Let the Party apparatus mind their business, and you should tackle the economy."[13] Ryzhkov recruited a team of economists and sociologists who had been involved in the economic reforms of the 1960s. (All of them will feature in subsequent chapters of this book.)[14] "For years," Ryzhkov remembered, "those people had been working in a vacuum, multiplying one abstract theory after another. And suddenly their 'heretical' thinking was in demand at the very summit of power."[15]

In January 1983, Andropov met with Shakhnazarov again, at a conference. The Soviet leader said to his former consultant, "You know, we have only begun to deploy reforms. A lot needs to be done. We should change things radically, fundamentally. You always had some interesting ideas. Come to see me. We should talk . . ."[16]

Andropov, just like Deng Xiaoping in China at the time, realized that modernizing the Soviet economy would require Western technology, know-how, and capital. He once asked Ryzhkov what he knew about the reforms of Lenin's New Economic Policy (NEP) in the 1920s. Was it possible, for instance, to lease Soviet economic assets to foreign companies? Ryzhkov said he knew nothing about this. Andropov responded: "Neither do I. Do research on this, and come back." Finally, somebody found a history thesis on this subject, buried in Moscow's central library.[17]

Andropov was keenly aware that the Cold War rivalry with the West, as well as the existing imperial burden, clashed with the Soviet need for renovation.

"The most complex problem," Andropov confessed to Erich Mielke, head of the Stasi, in 1981, "is that we cannot avoid the strains of military expenditures both for us and the other socialist countries." He also could not give up on Soviet clients, such as Vietnam and Cuba, as well as "progressive forces" in Laos, Angola, Ethiopia, and other countries. Without this burden, Andropov said, "we could solve all the other problems in two or three years." Also, Reagan's belligerent course in foreign policy remained the main challenge for Andropov's reforms. In March 1983, Reagan launched an ambitious Strategic Defense Initiative (SDI) to stop incoming Soviet missiles; the US military complex was flushed with money. American financial resources seemed unlimited. The NATO members, Japan, and the Arab states helped fund the American state debt and budget, including military expenses. The Cold War balance was shifting in favor of the United States.[18]

In contrast, Soviet revenues and finances were precarious. The problem, contrary to customary Western claims, lay not in the "crushing" defense outlays. The Soviet military, the military-industrial complex (MIC), and R&D were remarkably cost-effective; according to the best available estimates, they never exceeded 15 percent of GDP. A leading Western expert on the Soviet economy admitted, long after the Soviet collapse, that nobody in the leadership "saw the Soviet Union being crushed under an unbearable *military* burden." In economic terms, this expert acknowledged, "the Soviet Union had a revealed comparative advantage in military activities." It was not the military burden, significant yet small for a superpower, that endangered the Soviet economy and state.[19]

The problem was the growing Soviet engagement with the global economy and its own finances. The Soviet balance of trade depended entirely on high oil prices. The debonair Brezhnev, in contrast to Stalin, had never bothered to accumulate a stabilization fund, to save money for the future. At the Party Plenum of November 1982, Andropov denounced the growing Soviet import of grain, fats, meat, and other food products. "I don't want to scare anyone but I will say that over recent years we've wasted tens of billions of gold and rubles." Instead of using its oil profits to import Western technology, the Soviet Union used them to import food and subsidize its satellites. Poland at least could have expected the Soviets to help them out with Western debts. If the Soviet Union were to be engulfed in debt it too would be left to its own devices, and the United States would take advantage of this. Andropov spoke ominously about the "currency war" that the Americans were conducting against the Soviet bloc countries. The secret data on the imports and other profligacies of Brezhnev's rule were released to the Party activists of the key Soviet institutions.[20]

At the Politburo on 30 June 1983, Andropov returned to the topic of the newly vulnerable position of the Soviet Union vis-à-vis global economic and financial markets. "Our import has been growing, but we buy a lot of rubbish, instead of technologies. Western countries take our resources, but the rest of our products cannot compete." The Soviet leader ordered the Gosplan and ministries "to think" about increasing the export of machinery and oil products. Instead, the Soviet republics and state enterprises asked for more subsidies. "They do not count money, do not seek additional financial resources, they got into the habit of begging." Andropov proposed cuts in imports of foreign food. He also planned to gradually reduce Soviet subsidies to Eastern European countries, Mongolia, and Cuba. "This is not a community," he said with some emotion to Ryzhkov about the Soviet economic bloc. "This is a vulgar robbery."[21]

The preparations for reforms took place in complete secrecy. "Even deputies in the Gosplan did not know what we had been working at," recalled a member of Ryzhkov's team. "[Andropov] concluded that the old system of rigid planning from the top had exhausted itself ... We had to demonstrate to the bureaucracy that cooperatives, with their greater economic liberties, would make more profits than state enterprises. In the document we prepared we did not speak openly about private property, but we laid out an idea of having, next to state ownership, also cooperative ownership." Andropov backed those ideas.[22] A senior official of the State Bank remembered: "We understood that the enterprises needed more rights ... The situation when the center was responsible for everything ... throttled economic development." Andropov instructed the State Bank to shift from distribution of state investments to competition. "Other ministers should come to you," he said to the Minister of Finance, "crawling on their bellies, begging for money."[23] In July 1983, the Council of Ministers restated some notions of economic liberalization. In January 1984, with the approval of the Politburo, a pilot economic experiment was launched in some industries within Ukraine, Belorussia, and Lithuania. It was here where the reforms of 1965–68 had come to a standstill.[24]

Andropov had enough power, but he lacked the time necessary to carry out further reforms. In declining health, his kidneys failed completely in February 1983, so he was subsequently on dialysis. His last appearance at the Politburo was on 1 September 1983. Andropov went to a Black Sea resort and returned to Moscow only to be hospitalized. He died on 9 February 1984 from acute kidney failure.

Andropov's main contribution to Soviet reforms was the team of people and academics he had brought into the Politburo and the Soviet government. It took them a further two years to launch the reforms he had initiated. The key man whom the ex-KGB reformer had groomed to continue his policies was Mikhail Gorbachev.

PERESTROIKA

A LENINIST IN POWER

"We owe him everything," said Raisa Gorbacheva about Andropov. Her husband Mikhail Gorbachev had first met the KGB chief in April 1969. Andropov, who was already suffering from kidney problems, had come to Kislovodsk, a famous Soviet spa in the Stavropol region at the foot of the Caucasus. Gorbachev entertained Andropov on behalf of the regional Party leadership. They began to meet every summer thereafter. In 1978, also in Kislovodsk, Andropov set up a meeting to introduce Gorbachev to Brezhnev and his entourage. In September of that year, Gorbachev became the first man from the post-war generation to be promoted to the Politburo.

Andropov had discovered in Gorbachev his better alter ego. Mikhail Sergeyevich Gorbachev was born on 2 March 1931 to a Russian-Ukrainian family: both his father and mother farmed the land. They lived in the village of Privolnoye in the Stavropol region. This was Russian land with rich soil, which faced the majestic Caucasus mountains. Like Andropov, Gorbachev had been raised in the extremely humble conditions of farm life and grew up singing Cossack songs, yet he embraced the world of learning, sophistication, and high culture. Admitted to Moscow University in 1950 aged nineteen without having to sit exams— a reward for raising a record harvest—the young Gorbachev chose to study law. He found his match in Raisa Titarenko, a pretty Ukrainian from Siberia, a student of philosophy. They married in Moscow in 1953. Gorbachev joined the Party when he was a student and worked as an official in the Komsomol, the official youth organization. He was about to start work in Moscow, either in the Procurator's office or with the KGB. The state "distributed" graduates in a mandatory way to various locations and jobs across the Soviet Union, therefore the young couple had to go back to Gorbachev's home province in 1955.

Around that time Raisa had a nightmare that she shared with her husband. She dreamt that both of them fell to the bottom of a very deep, dark well. Then, with an enormous effort, cutting themselves and bleeding, they managed to climb up and drag themselves out of the well. A broad alley of trees then opened before their eyes, illuminated by the bright sun in which the alley seemed to be dissolving. Their hearts filled with anguish, flanked by dark shadows, they began to walk towards the sun ... The nightmare had a touch of Hollywood drama. Mikhail and Raisa interpreted it as a sign of predestination. They felt expelled from the cultural paradise of Moscow into the milieu of Party provincial hacks and peasantry in Stavropol. Nevertheless they were determined not to sink into this morass, but instead to advance culturally and intellectually. Raisa became the main engine behind this effort. They read and discussed books of history, sociology, and philosophy, as well as thick literary journals.

They took every opportunity in their occasional trips to Moscow to visit theaters and art galleries. Gorbachev was interested in both philosophy and political theory, reading them through the lens of Marxism-Leninism. All this turned him into a uniquely interesting interlocutor for Andropov.[25]

Andropov looked for Party reformers who would not become corrupt. Ryzhkov was one. Gorbachev was another. Unlike Andropov, Gorbachev's communist convictions were not darkened by years of terror, betrayal, and carnage. In the provincial Soviet nomenklatura, where men habitually drank, beat up their wives, and had extramarital affairs, Gorbachev was a paragon of virtue. His sparkling eyes, irresistible charm, unflagging optimism, and ebullient self-confidence contrasted with the atmosphere of cynicism and pessimism pervading in Moscow.

The Old Guard members of the Politburo were the last obstacle to Gorbachev's ascendancy. They ignored Andropov's wishes and elected Konstantin Chernenko as the next leader. Chernenko's brief tenure (1984–85), however, only made Gorbachev's candidacy that much stronger. Almost everyone yearned for a change after the decade of the ruling gerontocracy. Chernenko passed away on 10 March 1985, and all fingers then pointed at Gorbachev. Andropov's people in the Politburo and Secretariat lobbied hard for his election as leader. In addition to Nikolai Ryzhkov, this group included Yegor Ligachev, who was in charge of Party cadres in the Secretariat, the KGB chief Viktor Chebrikov, and the Politburo member for the Russian Federation, Vitaly Vorotnikov. Andrei Gromyko, the last key man of the Old Guard and Minister of Foreign Affairs, could not ignore this collective mood and nominated Gorbachev as the next Party leader. The Party Plenum voted for Gorbachev not out of a sense of duty and obligation, as they had for their recent leaders, but with apparent enthusiasm.

On the evening before his nomination at the Politburo, Gorbachev took his usual walk with Raisa. In his memoirs he claimed that his wife expressed her fears: "Do we really need this?" Those doubts were a comment on Gorbachev's career: he never fought for power, never had to remove his enemies, never used force to achieve his goals. It would hardly be possible to avoid asserting himself after assuming supreme Soviet power. Gorbachev reminded Raisa that, when he joined the Politburo, he believed he could help to change things in their country for the better. Yet he had in fact achieved nothing. "So if I really want to change anything, I have to accept the position ... *We just can't go on living like this.*"[26]

Many years later and with masses of archives mined, people still refuse to accept the sincerity of this phrase. One old practitioner wrote: "We know more about Gorbachev's actions than about his motivations and still lack a fully satisfactory explanation of his political evolution from 1985 to 1989 and beyond."[27]

William Taubman, the prize-winning American author of Gorbachev's authorized biography, begins his account with the phrase: "Gorbachev is hard to
understand." Taubman concluded that Gorbachev was a unique "tragic hero"
who attempted to change Russia, laid "the groundwork for democracy," but
predictably failed in constructing a new state, society, and economy. A Russian
biographer of Gorbachev writes about him as "a victim of a merciless caprice of
history . . . One of the most tragic figures in Russian history."[28]

Gorbachev certainly did not expect in 1985 to be remembered as the leader
who destroyed the country that he tried to change. The name he chose for
his course of action was "perestroika"—restructuring or renovation. After
Andropov's death, however, Gorbachev chose a revolutionary mentor, the man
who had destroyed Russia. This was Vladimir Lenin, the author of the Bolshevik
dictatorship that emerged in 1917, and the architect of the Soviet Union. For the
next five years, Gorbachev would invoke Lenin's name constantly, not only in
public speeches and at the Politburo meetings, but in private conversations with
his closest advisors. Gorbachev did not use Lenin's quotations, like his predecessors, to assert his legitimacy or outdo his rivals. He identified with Lenin. He
was the last true Leninist believer.[29]

As a student at Moscow University in the 1950s, Gorbachev looked at the
Bolshevik leader through a romantic lens. "Dear Ilyich" had opposed tyranny
and injustice, adopted mass terror only reluctantly, and died tragically early,
trying to remove Stalin. This myth became an ideology of Gorbachev's cohort:
Lenin was an ideal; Stalin was the flawed reality. The myth began to fade after
1968, yet it lived on in Russian provinces and reform-minded Party apparatchiks.[30] Gorbachev considered Lenin to be a genius of pure revolutionary
intuition. Lenin's authority, he believed, stemmed from theoretical insights, not
from the exercise of power, terror, and fear. Gorbachev's aide Anatoly Chernyaev
looked at Lenin through a similar lens. Gorbachev, he wrote in his diaries, "did
not play Lenin: he is like him by nature." Another close aide remembers that the
Soviet leader kept volumes from Lenin's collected works on his desk and "would
often pick one up in my presence and read aloud, comparing it to the present
situation and extolling Lenin's perspicacity." This veneration of Lenin, observes
Taubman, helped Gorbachev move with remarkable ease into the role of leader
of a superpower. Like the revolutionary prophet, he was on a mission not only
to change the Soviet Union, but also to transform the world. As Gorbachev
evolved, "his Lenin" evolved as well.[31]

The Soviet leader found soulmates who shared his neo-Leninist zeal. One of
them was Alexander Yakovlev, a Party ideologue who had been "exiled" during
Brezhnev's rule to become ambassador to Canada. Gorbachev met Yakovlev
during his visit to Ottawa in 1983. During a tour of Canadian farmlands, the

two officials, both peasants by birth, began to discuss the woes of Soviet agriculture and digressed into Marxist-Leninist theory in search of a theoretical key to understand what had gone wrong. They agreed that "everything" in the Soviet Union needed a revolutionary jump-start. Gorbachev managed to convince Andropov to bring Yakovlev to Moscow and appoint him director of IMEMO, a leading think tank. After Andropov's death, Yakovlev joined a small circle of individuals where Gorbachev discussed his ideas for reform. "We have been hibernating for fifteen years," Yakovlev said at a closed meeting of Party propagandists in August 1985. "The country weakens, and by the year 2000 we will become a second-rate power."[32]

In December 1985, Yakovlev sent Gorbachev a synopsis for future political reform. The leader's task, Yakovlev wrote, was to channel the pent-up frustration in Soviet society into radical change. The focus must be on political reforms. Yakovlev proposed to remove the Party from management of the economy. "Socialist democracy," decentralization, and glasnost (free discussion of problems) would liberate the USSR from the "dictatorship of bureaucracy." The pinnacle of the political reforms Yakovlev envisaged would be a democratic system of two parties, one Socialist, the other People's Democratic, with both holding regular elections. The supreme power would belong to the President of the USSR. Lenin's quotations peppered the memo. The ultimate goal, Yakovlev wrote, was "to transform every man [and woman] into a real master of the land."[33] The memo rejected the logic of conservative reformism and sided with the arguments Andropov had rejected many years before in his talk with Shakhnazarov.

Gorbachev read Yakovlev's memo; its ideas found a way into his speech to the Party Congress in February 1986, the first such gathering since Brezhnev's death. The Soviet leader had spent weeks, with Yakovlev and a few aides, brainstorming, drafting, and redrafting the text. Each workday lasted ten to twelve hours: Gorbachev had stamina that few could match. The date of the speech was highly symbolic: thirty years before, to the day, Khrushchev had denounced Stalin's crimes and urged all communists "to go back to Lenin." Gorbachev began to read his address on 25 February at 10 a.m. and—with breaks for coffee and lunch—spoke for five and a half hours. The mammoth document defined Brezhnev's period as "the time of stagnation" and included the key words from Yakovlev's memo: "democratization," "de-centralization," and "glasnost." Gorbachev also spoke about the need for "perestroika," a new code word for radical reforms, and about "the new thinking," which aimed to revise the ideological orthodoxy. He finished with a crescendo: "This is how we will be able to fulfill the farewell wishes of the great Lenin: with energy, unity of will, we will go higher and march forwards. We know no other destiny, and, comrades, how beautiful is this destiny!" Five thousand Party leaders and cadres stood up to applaud him. It is impossible to say how many of them acted sincerely. One man certainly did: Gorbachev himself.[34]

Despite his neo-Leninist rhetoric, Gorbachev could not decide on a strategy of reforms during his first two years in power. As an admirer of Lenin, he searched for some key leverage that could revive Soviet society and the economy. Yet he also heeded Andropov's conservative advice: before any radical political changes, suggested by Yakovlev, Soviet people should feel tangible improvements in the economy. Soon after coming to power, therefore, Gorbachev listed the economic and social problems he wanted to address: "1) Quality; 2) Struggle against drinking; 3) People in need; 4) Land for orchards and gardens; 5) Medicine."[35] Surprisingly, the list did not include the pressing issues that Andropov had raised about Soviet macroeconomic stability: the need to reduce the import of food, restore the balance of trade, crack down on the shadow economy, and discipline the labor force. Gorbachev's notes did not contain any diagnosis of the economic and financial problems plaguing the Soviet Union.

The Politburo discussions during Gorbachev's first two years in power revealed uncertainty about how to bolster the Soviet economy. Everyone agreed that it was vital to generate economic growth. The official slogan was "acceleration." But how to bring it about? At the same time, Gorbachev did not even include Ryzhkov and his reform-minded economists within his narrow circle of advisors. Nikolai Tikhonov, an old Brezhnev crony, remained as head of the Council of Ministers; Ryzhkov assumed this post only in late September 1985.

The biggest change that affected millions of Soviet people in 1985–86 was "the struggle against drinking." The idea had originated with Yegor Ligachev, another protégé of Andropov and now Gorbachev's deputy in the Politburo. Both men hated the Russian habit of binge drinking. The problem was that the tax on alcohol procured one-third of Soviet GDP. Andropov had also recognized this issue, but his solution was to fine and punish drunkards, not to ban alcohol. The Soviet Minister of Finance argued in vain to the Politburo that it would not be possible to replace the precious revenues from vodka with other products that people would buy, especially in towns and the countryside. A radical policy to cut alcohol consumption was implemented in May 1985. It was the third prohibition in Russian history: the first was in 1914, when the First World War broke out, and the second in 1941, when Germany attacked the USSR. The Party cadres, intimidated by Ligachev, overreacted: new breweries, purchased from Czechoslovakia, were left to rust; thousands of hectares of selection vineyards in Crimea were bulldozed; the makers of fine wine lost their jobs; some even committed suicide. The consumption of vodka, wine, and beer plummeted. In the longer term, hundreds of thousands of Soviet people would live a bit longer and healthier children would be born. Yet the budgetary disaster was immediate and long-lasting: the sales of vodka fell from 54 billion rubles in 1984 to 11 billion in 1986.[36] Another immediate casualty was Gorbachev's popularity. It plummeted and never fully recovered.[37]

Another unfortunate initiative in 1985–86, implemented later, was the struggle to improve the quality of Soviet goods. For decades, Soviet state enterprises had produced out-of-fashion clothing, poor shoes, badly manufactured TV sets. People refused to buy them and instead chased after quality imports; the unsold materials clogged numerous state warehouses. Soviet economists blamed the nature of centralized planning: the production from enterprises was measured in tons and numbers, not in sales figures. Gorbachev's Politburo ignored the economists. In May 1986, Gorbachev and Ryzhkov signed a decree that made all state enterprises subject to the State Inspection (*Gospriemka*), special teams of skilled specialists and workers. The influence of Lenin's works on this reform is striking. Shortly before his death, the Bolshevik leader had recommended the creation of "Worker's Inspection." Gorbachev, who knew Lenin's works by heart, was convinced that a new administrative tool staffed with "honest Soviet people" would make "socialist production" work better. In January 1987, 70,000 inspectors went to work.[38] This resulted in an immediate crisis of supply: most of the products from thousands of state enterprises, estimated to cost 69 billion rubles, were rejected for their poor quality. Even the best Soviet plants, built by Western companies in the 1960s, suddenly faced default. The end to the supply of many products, of whatever quality, affected entire economic chains of distribution: the lack of components and parts meant that many assembly lines came to a screeching halt. This was another example of how a sudden corrective measure, even well justified, could lead to inevitable economic collapse. Nobody knew what to do with failed enterprises and their workers. The former could not go bankrupt and the latter could not be laid off. After a few months of uncertainty, the economy returned to the old mode. Leninist ideas had failed.

Gorbachev's own priority in 1985–86 was the "acceleration of scientific-technical progress." When Andropov was the Soviet leader, he had put Gorbachev in charge of a team that worked on this issue. This was an attempt to plug a major hole in Gorbachev's biography: he joined the Politburo as "an agriculture expert" from the corn-growing Stavropol region, but he never had any experience dealing with machine-building industries and, most importantly, with the military industries. Gorbachev took on Andropov's assignment with the enthusiasm of a neophyte, and prioritized it after he assumed power. It resonated with his neo-Leninist beliefs. The role of science and technology in the expansion of socialism resonated with the thinking of many educated people of Gorbachev's generation. Smart machines, manned by educated, sober, and ideologically enthusiastic people, could overcome the Soviet Union's historic backwardness. The Party Congress in February 1986 approved Gorbachev's proposal to spend 200 billion rubles of state investment for the next five years implementing technological modernization and scientific innovation.

The expectations were that in five years the Soviet economy would be re-tooled and begin to produce quality goods to match the needs of consumers at home and to export abroad. In the past, Soviet modernization efforts produced the best results when the USSR had its new plants built by Western firms in the 1930s or the 1960s. New enterprises required newly trained engineers and workers, who willy-nilly emulated foreign practices and standards. In the absence of competition and other market drivers, this was the only way to leapfrog across antiquated processes and fossilized work habits. Instead, in 1986, the Gorbachev initiative invested the money in the re-tooling of existing state enterprises—a course of action that was bound to fail on a grand scale. The management and workers of the old plants acted conservatively and resisted innovations. Much of the expensive Western equipment was never put to use at the old plants and factories.[39]

Nobody could explain where the many billions in investments would come from. Gorbachev's expensive initiative was not matched by any measures to cut Soviet investments and expenditures elsewhere. Meanwhile, developments in Soviet trade and finances began to corroborate Andropov's fears of 1983. Soviet oil production had slightly declined in 1980–84, but had begun to grow under Gorbachev; yet world prices declined rapidly in 1986 from $27 per barrel to $10. This cost the Soviet economy $13 billion in export revenues. For the first time in decades, the USSR ended 1986 with a trade deficit of $14 billion. Soviet debt to Western banks in hard currency rose from $27.2 billion in 1985 to $39.4 billion in 1986. That was a bigger debt than Poland had in 1981. And it was an indicator of even worse things to come.[40]

Whatever calculations Gorbachev, Ryzhkov, and Soviet economists had made for the long term, the catastrophe at the Chernobyl nuclear plant wrecked everything. The explosion of one of its four reactors on 26 April 1986 in the northern part of Ukraine, not far from Kiev, took Soviet technicians, scientists, and bureaucrats completely by surprise. The flight of hundreds of thousands of people from Kiev, and mass panic elsewhere, was reminiscent of scenes from World War II. During the first month after the accident, the military, engineers, doctors, miners, and scientists risked their lives in an unprecedented operation to plug the source of radiation, evacuate 100,000 people from the nearby city, organize a 30-kilometer perimeter around the plant, remove the contaminated soil, secure rivers from radiation, take care of hundreds of thousands of children, provide necessary medicine, and more. The cost of the Chernobyl disaster to the Soviet budget during the first month alone was 3 billion rubles. In early 1989, Ryzhkov estimated the cost to be about 8 billion rubles. He recalled: "Chernobyl dealt a sudden and devastating blow to our convalescent economy."[41]

Raisa Gorbacheva, an atheist but a superstitious woman, considered Chernobyl a very bad omen; millions thought the same. Gorbachev's authority was badly tarnished. People surmised that "the stained leader" (they meant the birthmark on his forehead) brought misfortune. Aside from this nonsense, Gorbachev tarnished his authority again by not informing the people of the scale of the disaster until 14 May, when he finally made a televised address to the stunned country. And throughout the crisis, the top trouble-shooter and real hero was Ryzhkov, who spearheaded the massive efforts to tame the nuclear monster. The Prime Minister flew to Kiev and then to Chernobyl, to inspect the calamity for himself. Gorbachev went to Chernobyl, in the company of Raisa, only in February 1989, after the reactor had been covered by the concrete "sarcophagus."[42]

Gorbachev's insecurity about the nuclear accident came through with a vengeance. In June–July 1986 he scapegoated the Soviet atomic industry and its aged leaders, Anatoly Aleksandrov and Yefim Slavsky. Those men, then in their eighties, were the supreme brahmins of the Soviet defense establishment, the builders of the Soviet nuclear superpower and the atomic energy complex. In Gorbachev's harsh words, they embodied the worst qualities of the old elites. The atomic establishment, Gorbachev argued, "is dominated by servility, bootlicking, cliquishness, and persecution of those who think differently, by putting on a good show, by personal connections and clans. We are about to put an end to all this."[43] This was an unfair and inaccurate assessment: the Soviet nuclear science industry was one of the few that could demonstrate world-class achievements.

This reaction to Chernobyl was typical of Gorbachev, and was repeated in the years to come. The Soviet leader no doubt was angry, but he also re-enacted Lenin: he used the crisis to jump to sweeping conclusions: the entire old system was deeply sick and contaminated. The crisis demanded another revolution. His main message was that the USSR was a country on the brink; during the previous fifteen years the state and the people had lived beyond their means and learned awful habits. Either the Party should pull them out of this morass rapidly or the country would sink back into the "swamp" with lethal consequences. In September, speaking about the heroic efforts of tens of thousands of military and civilian "rescuers" at Chernobyl, Gorbachev said: "A Russian needs a mission impossible, so that he would send everything to [hell] . . . and do what is needed. A new Chernobyl should happen every day to make him wake up and move forward."[44]

William Taubman wrote that during 1986 Gorbachev underwent "the dual process of convincing himself and trying to convince his Kremlin colleagues that their initial strategy, or lack of strategy, had failed."[45] Gorbachev's rhetoric, however, pointed to different conclusions. Instead of taking stock of failures, the Soviet leader wanted his Politburo and government colleagues to abandon caution, and plunge headlong into the troubled sea of radical reforms without a road map. After all, he argued, this was what Lenin had done, as part of the normal revolutionary process. Huge costs and failures were part of the deal. "The main thing is not to retreat," Gorbachev said on 30 October 1986, "no matter how hard, difficult, painful it would be . . . there is no other way."[46]

During 1986, Gorbachev concluded that the Party apparatus was incapable of being the main instrument to pull the USSR from the swamp of "stagnation." After Lenin, Trotsky, and countless Party reformers, Gorbachev began to speak about the "bureaucratization" of the Party apparatus on all levels and in every district as being a major obstacle to his revolution. Shakhnazarov had told Andropov the same thing in the 1960s. And this was what Yakovlev preached. Gorbachev also took up another neo-Leninist slogan: "Bureaucracy cannot do anything . . . If we really want to develop democratic processes, the Soviets are the keystone."[47] In September 1986, Gorbachev told the Politburo: "When you read Lenin, you see how much he spoke, trying to explain the NEP . . . If we lived in a democracy, people would do anything. One war veteran wrote to me: you are the first after Lenin to call for democracy." Gorbachev implied that there was more support for reforms among common people than in the Party apparatus. The head of the KGB, Viktor Chebrikov, objected: "I am ready to take an oath on my Party membership card that the KGB harbors no opposition or doubts with regard to new policy."[48] The Party and state apparatus, while not revolutionary-minded enough, remained loyal and ready to follow its leader into uncharted waters.

MISGUIDED REFORMS

In early 1987, Gorbachev urged Ryzhkov and his economists to produce a radical comprehensive reform of the Soviet economy. Its essence was twofold. First, the resolution of a myriad of intractable economic problems had to be transferred from the hierarchical, conservative, ossified bureaucracy to the grassroots, to state enterprises and working collectives. Second, the Party had to be turned into a Leninist engine of revolutionary change. The Politburo discussed the proposals and consented. Even such stalwarts as Andrei Gromyko did not object.

The key reform was the Law on Socialist Enterprises. This document was the consummate product of the reformist cohort of Soviet economists, who sought to combine "socialism" with a state-regulated market.[49] Ryzhkov and his team of economists went back to the debates of the 1960s and formulated the policy of "three S's": self-accounting, self-financing, and self-governance. What did it mean in practice? The state would yield ownership to each enterprise to its management and "workers' collective"; they would then be responsible for the enterprise's assets. They could take credits from state banks and decide how to spend this money. Enterprises would have to deliver to the state a set amount of goods, according to a contract and the central plan of economic development. After this, they could work for profit and keep a part of this profit for themselves. Most importantly, the new law meant that the regional and local Party authorities would refrain from economic interference. Ryzhkov, who promoted this law enthusiastically, expressed the view of many "red directors" from the Soviet managerial class: they wanted the Party apparatus to be removed from their business.[50]

This was a radical transformation. In January 1987, Ryzhkov reported to the Politburo on the first draft of the Law. At the meeting Gromyko raised a core question: "In the report, the collective becomes the owner of the enterprise. Thus, factories and plants become the property of their collectives? This goes too far. The question of property had been solved in October 1917." Gorbachev too was confused. "The text is still hazy and confusing on basic notions," he admitted. Then he quickly added: "We cannot make mistakes."[51] The draft was sent back to the Council of Ministers. "Socialist" was dropped from the title in favor of "State Enterprises" to avoid the controversy. The collectives received the rights of *possession* over profits from enormous economic assets, while their responsibilities to the state, as the *owner*, remained legally ill-defined and unenforceable.

While ducking this key issue, Gorbachev and Ryzhkov doubled down on the effort to end the old "command-administrative system" whereby the Party dictated everything and the Gosplan calculated costs and benefits. The idea was to create something that never existed in history: an "economy of socialist democracy." The neo-Leninist vision assumed that possession of the means of production would make working people motivated and responsible for their output. Would it be enough to pull the Soviet people out of the swamp of corruption and indifference to output and quality? Gorbachev admitted that the passivity of people bothered him. Nobody could explain to him why, in those segments of the Soviet economy where self-financing and self-governance had been experimentally tried, production declined rather than increased. The Soviet leader argued with himself, as if responding to invisible critics: "In the West they tell us: 'In a society without fear, you cannot carry out any reform' because nobody has any interest in or fear of God.'" He also mentioned that most Russians had a safety net that enabled them to procure their basic needs. Many people began to feel that they did not need to work hard at all. "This is a grave problem," Gorbachev concluded.[52] Other members of the Politburo felt confused. Ligachev confessed: "We can't all flounder in economic affairs. We lack a scientific approach." Gorbachev, after reading more drafts of the Law, admitted: "I do not understand all of it."[53]

Nevertheless, under Gorbachev's pressure, the Politburo approved the Law. The Soviet leader was now full of revolutionary determination. In May 1987, when the Politburo agonized over the future of the new economic system, Gorbachev came up with a striking image: "We are moving forward as if in jungles with a machete. Everyone is blood-splattered, skin is torn and bruised, quarrels erupt. Yet we keep moving. And there are already clearings in the thick forest."[54] This was the image of David Livingstone struggling through the heart of Africa.

The Law on State Enterprises, approved by a special Party Plenum, came into force on 30 June 1987. The 11,000-word document redefined the structures of the Soviet economy for the first time since Khrushchev's ill-fated experiments thirty years earlier. In fact, "state enterprises" received more autonomy than they ever had since Lenin seized power in Russia. They acquired freedom of export, they could establish joint companies with foreign partners, and could have their own currency account. Ryzhkov told the Politburo that the goal was to connect the Soviet economy with the global market as much as possible, to bring profits in hard currency. "Let [the state enterprises] export everything and as much as they would be able to sell, except for strategic goods, like oil. It does not matter if [these goods] are in deficit domestically or not."[55]

Gorbachev pushed for even more decentralization than Ryzhkov: he now viewed the technocracy of the ministries as an obstacle to the initiatives from below. And he wanted to bypass a trial phase for the Law. It should be implemented immediately and across the board. In the past, he believed, the forces of conservatism had blocked similar reforms because they were piecemeal. At the Politburo he quoted Lenin, but also Sergey Witte, a reformist Prime Minister in the Tsarist government: reforms, in order to succeed, should be deep and swift. Turning to the drafters of the Law, the General Secretary said: "We must keep bombing [the old system] from all directions."[56]

The Law was enacted in January 1988. Its results, however, were opposite to what the reformers expected. The Law undermined the old stabilizing and controlling mechanisms of the Soviet economy, above all the role of the Party. For many decades the Party had exercised a controlling role in every major economic unit in the USSR. The enterprise leaders were members of the Party and its nomenklatura. From now on, the head of an enterprise was to be elected by "a collective" of workers and employees. He could no longer be fired from above.[57] At the same time the reform did not generate a true liberalization and revival of the economy. An economist from Stanford University, Mikhail Bernstam, a Soviet émigré, explained later that the Law was "de-centralization, and the erroneous one." The enterprises' collectives, represented by directors and trade union leaders, accumulated big profits but were not motivated to invest them in new equipment, to increase efficiency and quality of their production. Rather, they sought ways to pocket those profits, to maximize wages and salaries. They also stopped producing cheap consumer goods, which the vast majority of Soviet consumers wanted, and focused instead on the production of more expensive items.[58] In just a couple of years Gorbachev and Ryzhkov would become lost in the jungles of the Soviet economy, with no exit in sight.

Gorbachev's reforms also began to endanger the financial stability on which the economic and political unity of the Soviet Union rested. Gorbachev knew little about the Soviet budget, revenues, and financial mechanisms. When in 1983 he asked Andropov to have a look at the state budget, he received a firm "no." Meanwhile, the Soviet financial system was not an easy matter for a novice to grasp. It had no analogues in the world and was born of necessity—the product of wars, total mobilization, and absolute political dictatorship. In the Soviet Union, there were two kinds of money in circulation. One currency was virtual and was called *beznal*, which means "cashless." It was a completely virtual accounting system between the state and state enterprises. All investments, credits, and other big transactions in the Soviet economy were paid by *beznal*. This money resembled issue bills and letters of credit in a market economy, yet the Soviet *beznal* was never meant to be cashed. The second kind of money was in *nal* (cash): banknotes and coins issued by the State Bank. They were used to pay salaries and wages to Soviet people, to pay in state stores, and for goods and services of the "shadow economy" and on the black market. The total amount of *nal* was loosely related to the amount of production and the cost of labor.

Only a few professional bankers in the Soviet Union understood how this system worked. And meanwhile this unique system was vital for Soviet macroeconomic stability. The Soviet state could spend many billions of *beznal* money for financing big projects, and yet the inflation of cash—and prices of consumer goods and services—remained more or less under control. The profits from state enterprises could not be translated into cash. Even at the most difficult moments of history, such as during World War II, the Soviet financial system had not broken down.

Whereas the *beznal* money was completely under state control, however, cash was in people's hands. Cash in circulation, especially when it accumulated outside state-controlled personal savings accounts, generated inflation and macroeconomic instability. Stalin understood this danger: the Ministry of

Finance and Gosplan ensured there would be a watertight partition between the two kinds of Soviet money. All enterprises had to have double bookkeeping. They were strictly forbidden to use *beznal* allocations for salaries and wages. And they were not allowed to buy industrial equipment and raw materials with cash. Those had to be paid for only with *beznal* money provided from the central budget. Also, state leaders and institutions made sure that the accumulation of cash in savings accounts would not grow disproportionately; if it did, it would begin to chase goods, and people began to hoard them. In 1947 and in 1961, the Soviet state had to carry out secretly prepared monetary reforms to reduce the volume of money in circulation. Another painful measure could be to increase state-fixed prices.[59] This system of state control over capital allowed people's salaries and savings to increase gradually, but only so long as production increased and its efficiency improved.

During his long tenure, Brezhnev had avoided price hikes on basic consumer items. Meanwhile, investment in the military industries and research, instead of stimulating economic growth, drove up inflation. Subsidies to ineffective Soviet agriculture, the losses in agriculture, and the unsold poor-quality goods proved more costly than military expenditures. In a sprawling "shadow economy" illegal entrepreneurs accumulated billions of rubles. Oil revenues covered state deficits yet contributed to hidden inflation as well. Gorbachev had inherited highly troubled finances, yet he quickly made things much worse by his policy initiatives. The ban on alcohol aggravated this problem tremendously: people drank less, but in turn demanded quality goods they could spend their cash on.[60]

In early 1987, Ryzhkov warned his Politburo colleagues that, without price reform, the economy would not improve. There were two options available to the Soviet leadership: raise fixed prices to a "realistic" level by government action or prepare for their targeted deregulation. Gorbachev, however, appeared to be evasive. The Soviet leader remembered how Khrushchev had undermined his authority in 1962 by raising prices. This triggered workers' strikes and even a mutiny. In October 1986, Gorbachev said at the Politburo: "People still have not received any benefits from perestroika. If we raise prices . . . we will discredit perestroika."[61] Valentin Pavlov, head of the State Committee for Prices at the time, later recalled it was a missed opportunity. Gorbachev could have raised wholesale prices in *beznal*, yet maintain consumer prices at the lower level, and soak up "the money overhang" by 40 billion rubles.[62] In the end, economic reforms began with the hopelessly distorted system of prices inherited from Brezhnev's time.

The Law on State Enterprises initiated bank reform. Since the 1960s, Soviet reform-minded economists had been arguing that state enterprises should get money for development from state-controlled commercial banks. The enterprises would make a profit and pay back to the banks with interest. This scheme could replace the turnover tax as the main income for the state budget.[63] In 1985, a group of Soviet bankers adopted this idea. They traveled to Italy and West Germany, India, and communist Hungary and Yugoslavia. In China, they studied the financing of "free economic zones." In Japan, they looked at targeted investments and state-planned credits that redirected and modernized the economy. In June 1986, they presented their proposals to Ryzhkov. The State Bank, they wrote, would remain the monetary regulator. One needed, however, big "specialized" investment banks which would credit large industrial conglomerates. Smaller "innovative" banks under their control would credit small enterprises in consumer-oriented sectors. Mikhail Zotov, the man behind the initiative, was not a market liberal. He began his banking career under Stalin. "In our view," he remembered, the "time came . . . to make [banks] active and immediate actors, the agents of the economy." Ryzhkov supported the proposal. In July 1987, the Politburo allowed the establishment of four "specialized" banks with crediting functions.[64]

In May 1988, an even bigger change in the economic and financial system occurred. Ryzhkov's experts prepared and the Politburo enacted the Law on Cooperatives. "Cooperatives" had been touted in Lenin's times as "the road to socialism," but were largely defunct by the 1980s. All entrepreneurial energy gravitated to the shadow economy. Ryzhkov wanted to make cooperatives legal again and put them under state control. Gorbachev liked the idea. In China, he told the Politburo, "cooperatives" managed to feed one billion people in just a few years. He hoped they would do the same in the Soviet Union. The Law on Cooperatives, however, placed cooperatives and state enterprises under the same roof; the first could purchase from the latter; the latter could set up the former. The new law also allowed both cooperatives and state enterprises to create commercial banks, using their "surplus" money for the purpose of crediting others.

In 1987, Soviet bankers proposed tighter control over the total amount and circulation of both *nal* and *beznal* money. Instead, Ryzhkov and his experts opened visible loopholes in the partition between the two types of currency circulating in the financial system. Nobody in the Soviet government at the time understood the dire consequences of this for monetary affairs. The transactions that had been prohibited for decades were now legally sanctioned for cooperatives and commercial banks. People who began to launch cooperatives in 1988 immediately grasped new opportunities. Seven months after the law had come into force, forty-one commercial banks were registered. One year later the number of commercial banks in the Soviet Union would grow to 225. These banks created a major unregulated hole in the Soviet financial system.

Zotov wrote at the end of the 1990s: "What happened? . . . We dashed ahead in microeconomics: in practice we almost completely liberalized banks and monetary circulation."[65]

Cooperatives, credited by their own banks, began to buy resources and goods within the state economy from state enterprises at state-fixed prices. Then they sold those goods at higher market prices or exported them abroad, at a profit of 500 and even more percent. The state tax imposed on the cooperatives was only 10–13 percent. The commercial bankers created another profitable scheme: they would take help from state enterprises to transform their *beznal* assets into cash. The trickle turned into a torrent, inflating the monetary mass in people's pockets. By the end of 1989, neither the Politburo nor the State Bank would be in a position to control this flood.

SOCIALIST DEMOCRACY

Where did Gorbachev get the idea to democratize the Soviet Union? For Western readers, especially Americans, a course towards democracy and freedom was natural and positive. The General Secretary of the Communist Party, however, was not a liberal. And yet he decided to carry out far-reaching political liberalization *simultaneously* with radical economic reforms. Even thirty years later William Taubman could not conceal his amazement: "What possessed him to think he could overcome Russian political, economic, and social patterns dating back centuries in a few short years: tsarist authoritarianism morphing into Soviet totalitarianism . . . minimal experience with civic activity, including compromise and consensus, no tradition of democratic self-organization, no real rule of law?"[66]

Gorbachev had grown up in a society where liberties were secretly coveted by an idealistic and educated minority. For almost two centuries, the intelligentsia had daydreamed about a constitution and people's rights. The Bolsheviks and then Stalin made a travesty out of those dreams, yet they could neither fully suppress nor ignore them. Stalin's Constitution of 1936 solemnly guaranteed "socialist democracy" and "freedoms" of speech, conscience, and other civil rights. In 1948, the Soviet Union signed the UN Universal Declaration of Human Rights. In August 1975, Brezhnev signed the Helsinki Final Act. In 1977, parts of this act were included in the amended Soviet Constitution. Nobody in the Soviet Union ever thought that soon it would be taken seriously.[67] Indeed, such a thought could put a person into a mental asylum or make one a subject of interest to the KGB. Still, the notion of "socialist democracy" was not dead; it permeated mass consciousness as an ideal to be realized in the future. A group of young intellectuals, who published a *Samizdat* journal in the early 1980s in Moscow, concluded that "socialist democracy"—not liberal democracy—was the only slogan that could be understood by the majority of the Soviet population.[68]

Then came Gorbachev. His connections with the intelligentsia made him share their dreams of political liberalization. Gorbachev's personal discovery of the need for "social democracy" must have been nurtured in his conversations with his Czech friend Zdeněk Mlynář, a reform-minded communist who became an active participant in the "Prague Spring" of 1968. That was an era of socialist romanticism, when Andrei Sakharov, a nuclear physicist and soon to be a human rights defender, had famously proclaimed a link between economic progress, humanism, and intellectual freedom. It was natural for Gorbachev to accept what Andropov had totally rejected: Soviet people should have more say in their country's affairs; without "socialist democracy" people would remain alienated from the economy, continue to behave like lazy serfs, and economic modernization would be impossible. Yakovlev's memo of 1985 continued to be on his mind. Raisa probably reinforced her husband's aspirations to become an emancipator of Soviet society. She and Gorbachev shared a passion for big ideas, and liked to discuss them during their long strolls and when on vacation.

In August 1987, Gorbachev devoted his entire summer vacation to theorizing. At a dacha in Crimea, where Brezhnev and his Politburo cronies had played dominos, drank, and exchanged old jokes, Gorbachev read Lenin and for the first time "young Marx," his *1844 Economic and Philosophical Manuscripts.* The latter had been the most influential text from the late 1950s, "discovered" by left intellectuals in the West and discreetly studied in the 1960s by Soviet social scientists who had dreamed of de-Stalinization. From Crimea, Gorbachev also corresponded and talked with academics from the leading Moscow think tanks. The formal excuse was a contract with American publishers to write a book about perestroika. Instead of delegating this task to ghostwriters, Gorbachev plunged himself into writing and editing—a process that he enjoyed. He dictated the whole draft several times to Anatoly Chernyaev, who by that time had become his most trusted aide. Gorbachev even extended his vacation by one week. The title of the book was *Perestroika: New Thinking for Our Country and the World.* Gorbachev wanted to link his "revolution" to world affairs, just like Lenin had done seven decades before.[69]

The General Secretary also immersed himself in reading books and documents about the origins of Stalinism. The coming of the 70th anniversary of the Bolshevik revolution in November 1987 focused his mind. In July, before going on vacation to Crimea, Gorbachev asked his Politburo colleagues to read the materials on Stalin's crimes prepared on Khrushchev's order in 1961–62 but never released. Gorbachev, who had spent two decades in the province of

Stavropol, in the nomenklatura straitjacket, came to power holding the views of history that were popular in the 1960s. According to Chernyaev, he still believed that "if Lenin had not died in 1924, but at least ten years later, socialism in the USSR would have been developed nicely."[70] Now in 1987 he had access to all the information he wanted and attacked the historical turf with the fresh energy of a neophyte. He sought answers to the questions that troubled him: Why Stalin and his crimes? What "glitch" in the Leninist design led to tyranny and mass murder? How to avoid similar tragedies in the future? Those questions had been asked twenty years earlier by idealist Marxist-minded intellectuals of Gorbachev's generation.

The books he read proved to be ideological dynamite. Gorbachev was deeply impressed by them. He started sharing his ideas with a narrow circle of colleagues: he wanted to change "the whole system—from economy to mentality." Chernyaev recorded his words: "I would go far, very far." His biggest discovery was theoretical: "more socialism means more democracy."[71]

Instead of making speeches about Stalin's crimes, as Khrushchev had done, Gorbachev decided to dismantle the system of governance Stalin had built. With this goal in mind, he convened a special Party Conference for June 1988 to implement his policies. The last such conference was convened by Stalin in February 1941, to discuss preparations for inevitable war. Gorbachev had a similar urgency. As with his speech to the Party Congress in 1987, he turned to a group of close advisors. They included Yakovlev, an expert on "socialist democracy," Georgy Shakhnazarov, Chernyaev, the economists Vadim Medvedev and Stepan Sitaryan. The circle also included two old friends of Mikhail and Raisa from university days, the lawyer Anatoly Lukyanov and the philosopher Ivan Frolov. Valery Boldin, a former journalist and personal aide of both Gorbachevs, was in charge of logistics and communication. The working group commissioned dozens of memos from academic think tanks in Moscow. The moment for which the Soviet liberal-minded intelligentsia had been waiting for decades had finally arrived. The work on political reforms began in early 1988 and continued through the whole year.

Gorbachev, it turned out, had a concept of constitutional reforms in his mind even before the preparatory work began. Constitutional and legal issues were the areas where the Soviet leader felt strong, in contrast to economics and finances. His goal, Medvedev remembers, was "to turn the Soviets into permanently governing bodies."[72] The "Soviets" were revolutionary "Councils" or assemblies of workers, peasants, and soldiers, in whose name Lenin had seized power in Russia in 1917. Gorbachev's concept was breathtaking in its ambition: to return Russian socialism to square one, and reroute the great experiment in the direction of democracy. The starting point of political reforms would be a convocation, after national competitive elections, of a 2,250-member Congress of People's Deputies—an institution without parallels anywhere in the world. This Congress would represent all national republics and ethnic autonomies of the Soviet Union, all groups of its population, and all its major public institutions. The Congress would have supreme power: to change the constitution, to appoint a government, and to select a permanent law-making assembly, the Supreme Soviet. The first Bolshevik constitution, approved by Lenin, had a similar representation. A similar constitutional overhaul of political structures would be replicated on every level: republican, regional, and local. Gorbachev kept his colleagues in the Politburo out of the loop on his political reforms until the last moment, with the sole exception of Yakovlev. He was fully aware that the new constitutional order would put an end to the absolute power of the Politburo and the Party apparatus.

In Gorbachev's entourage, some believed the system was cumbersome and ultimately unmanageable. Yakovlev and Chernyaev favored a strong presidential system; Medvedev advocated a parliamentary system where a majority party forms the government, and the party head becomes the state leader. Gorbachev, who already had strong executive power, thanks to the Party dictatorship, did not consider strengthening it still further. And he refused to recreate strong executive components of the early Bolshevik governments. He only wanted to become chairman of the reformed Supreme Soviet. As Medvedev remembered, "it was hard, most likely impossible, to sway him."[73]

It was an inexplicable departure from the Soviet and Russian practice of governance. Had Gorbachev proposed the creation of stronger executive power—constitutional and delegated by the new representative assemblies—he could have had it without any problem. Nobody could have prevented the Soviet leader occupying two positions, as General Secretary and head of the Soviet's Supreme Executive Committee, simultaneously. Some historians claim that Gorbachev wanted to have an all-empowered legislature to balance off the omnipotent Party apparatus. Whatever his motives, Gorbachev's goal to "give all power to the Soviets" turned out to be a fundamental political error. Placing a super-parliament at the top of the political system during a period of fundamental reforms was risky and impractical. The Soviets, which had for decades only rubber-stamped the Politburo decisions, suddenly assumed both legislative and executive responsibilities—more than those institutions could possibly bear. Gorbachev also did not account for the pent-up populist energy that his political reforms would release. Ryzhkov later commented that Gorbachevian reform took him and other Politburo members by surprise. Without any experience of representative politics, they could not possibly anticipate what would be the consequences of such political reforms. When they did, it was too late. The two-tier Soviet system of representation would make the Soviet Union ungovernable. And after the Soviet collapse, the same system would place Russia on the brink of collapse; only the violent abolition of the Gorbachevian system of Soviets by Boris Yeltsin in October 1993 would stabilize the constitutional order.[74]

The preparations for political reforms revealed new facets of Gorbachev's personality and conduct. In 1988, the Soviet leader began to show signs of hubris. He could not avoid the effects of power on his ego. He was already in the limelight of the world's media, especially during frequent trips abroad, where he would meet Ronald Reagan, Margaret Thatcher, François Mitterrand, and other leaders. Gorbachev felt intellectually and politically superior to all his Kremlin colleagues. He told Chernyaev that they were "philosophically impoverished" and "lacking in culture." Even the hard-working Ryzhkov displeased him with his constant complaints and growing despondency regarding economic developments. At the Politburo, where the General Secretary presided, the nature of the discussions changed. "He really needed advice, the opinion of others," recalled the Politburo member Vitaly Vorotnikov, "yet only to the extent it allowed him to make [others] follow his position and his idea." Gorbachev had another peculiar trait: he often did not finish his arguments with a specific choice of action. This created an appearance of consensus-seeking, but also left room for later denial if there was too much dissent. Gorbachev was "permanently ready to dodge, to balance, to make a decision according to a situation."[75] He was proud of this quality. "Lenin also called himself opportunistic," he told Chernyaev in August 1988, "in order to save the revolution."[76] Gorbachev's hubris helped him steer an improbably radical set of political and economic reforms through a Politburo that was decidedly skeptical and Party elites who were increasingly concerned.

The key political moment for Gorbachev's grand design was the special Party Conference in late June 1988. Some 4,500 delegates gathered in the Kremlin. Gorbachev needed their approval for his radical course of action and he was remarkably successful. The conference, televised in full for the whole country to see, adopted the resolution "On the democratization of Soviet society and the reform of the political system." The conference also voted to make changes to the Soviet constitution, regarding the formation of a new political system by the fall of 1989. The new system would be implemented before the term of the old rubber-stamping Supreme Soviet was due to expire. Gorbachev felt, however, that the majority of delegates at the conference would not give him a blanket approval for all his reforms. He was right: most wanted some change, but they simply could not imagine that their General Secretary would move to dismantle the entire political system. At the very end of the conference, after four days of reports and speeches, almost as an afterthought, Gorbachev put to the vote a motion to delegate to the Politburo the task of reorganizing the Party apparatus before the end of the year. The motion was approved and gave Gorbachev the mandate he wanted. In Gorbachev's later estimate, this was "the start of genuine perestroika."[77] Eduard Shevardnadze a decade later would define Gorbachev's strategy as follows: "he used Stalin's power to dismantle the Stalinist system."[78]

After the conference Gorbachev embarked on a long vacation in Crimea, where a new luxurious villa had been finished for him near Foros. His aide Chernyaev, who accompanied him, was shocked by the opulence of the villa that did not chime with the image of a selfless Leninist reformer: "Why does he need it?" Chernyaev also noticed that Gorbachev had changed since the previous summer. Still spontaneous, he nonetheless preferred to pontificate and was cross when contradicted. As in the previous year, Gorbachev spent his vacation doing theoretical and historical research; he continued to pore over Bolshevik debates following Lenin's death. He began to dictate to Chernyaev a brochure on the evolution of "notions of socialism" from Marx to their own time. He noted that as one moved from the past to the present, clarity of thinking had disappeared. "Brains become so confused these days," Chernyaev commented, "that nobody knows any longer where socialism exists and where it does not, and what it is in general." Gorbachev did not want to admit it, but from now on his neo-Leninism ceased to provide him with guidance for his actions.[79]

Some scholars have speculated that in 1988 the General Secretary feared an internal Party coup to oust him. The conspiracy against Khrushchev in October 1964 emerged when he was vacationing at a Black Sea resort in Pitsunda. However, William Taubman has dismissed the speculation about a coup against Gorbachev, concluding that he did not fear such a conspiracy. The Soviet leader saw the Party as merely convalescing from its bureaucratic stupor and returning to its factional struggles, similar to the Bolshevik infighting back in the 1920s.

On the "left," in Gorbachev's view, stood Boris Yeltsin, whom Gorbachev had brought in to the Politburo and appointed to head a reorganization of the Party in Moscow in December 1985. A candidate member of the Politburo and former Party head of the Sverdlovsk region, Yeltsin was Gorbachev's political twin. Born in the village of Butka, Sverdlovsk, in the Urals in 1931 to a peasant family, which had suffered from Stalin's collectivization, Yeltsin had made his career in the provinces, with a larger-than-life ego and a remarkable memory for facts and names. Yeltsin was a good family man, just like Gorbachev. He also was a workhorse, free of corruption. In other ways, however, they were a study in contrasts. Yeltsin felt more comfortable among common people than intellectuals; he had never been spotted with a volume of Marx or Lenin in his hands. Yeltsin did not benefit from the university education and cultural polishing that Gorbachev had. His direct, working-class temperament differed from Gorbachev's suaveness and charm. Yeltsin owed his Party career mostly to his management of the giant industrial conglomerates in the Urals; he viewed Gorbachev as his inferior, not superior. He was poorly equipped to navigate the Byzantine corridors of the Old Square (the Communist Party headquarters in Moscow).

Gorbachev had given Yeltsin a truly Herculean assignment: to cleanse the Augean Stables of Moscow's corrupt individuals and institutions. This cleansing had already begun under Andropov, and Yeltsin continued it with great zeal: he fired corrupt officials, showed up with sudden inspections at stores, and found time to hear complaints from ordinary people. This garnered him populist fame among Muscovites. Yet the apparatchiks hated him for it and attempted to sabotage his activities. Naina, Yeltsin's wife, recalled that in Moscow she and her husband felt demoralized and ostracized.[80]

Yeltsin's "left" attack on perestroika began in October 1987 at the Plenary Meeting of the Party's Central Committee. A month before, in a state of stress, he had submitted a letter of resignation to Gorbachev. When his request was ignored, he addressed the Plenary Meeting. Gorbachev had chosen this occasion to deliver his first serious criticism of Stalin and map out his political views. Yeltsin inadvertently emerged as a spoiler of this historic occasion. Perestroika, he said, was drifting and he blamed the Party's apparatchiks, especially Ligachev, for this. The reaction was spontaneous and furious: one speaker after another denounced Yeltsin, after which he was ejected from the Politburo. Moscow was awash with rumors that Yeltsin had rebelled "against the bosses," and was a spokesman "for the people." Then the maverick from the Urals surprised everyone again: he experienced a nervous breakdown and even injured himself with a pair of scissors.[81]

In Brezhnev's time, a Politburo dissident would have been dispatched far away, perhaps as an ambassador to an African or a Central American country. Gorbachev chose not to do that. Instead, he subjected Yeltsin to enforced treatment in a Party hospital, where doctors treated him with powerful injections, as if he was in a psychiatric hospital. This was a traumatic experience that Yeltsin would never forgive or forget. He subsequently recovered from his breakdown. At the Party Conference in June 1988, he even humbly asked for forgiveness, but then once again criticized Gorbachev's perestroika for its lack of radicalism. He had acted as a spoiler for a second time and clearly stole the thunder from the Soviet leader. In November, Yeltsin delivered an iconoclastic lecture at the High School of Komsomol in Moscow on the need for a multi-party system and competitive presidential elections. His popularity in Moscow and the Russian provinces skyrocketed. Shakhnazarov recalled that some in Gorbachev's entourage urged him to exile Yeltsin, but Gorbachev categorically refused.[82]

On the "right" from Gorbachev was Yegor Ligachev, the ascetic deputy head of the Party Secretariat. He represented the ethos and interests of the Party provincial cadres, and people from poorer and agrarian Russian regions. For Ryzhkov and his team, Ligachev was the epitome of Party interference with their work. The Moscow intelligentsia demonized Ligachev as a neo-Stalinist and as a man who attempted to keep ideological censorship in place. Chernyaev urged Gorbachev to remove Ligachev. "You are in the situation of Lenin now," he wrote alluding to 1922, when Lenin had attempted to remove Stalin.[83] This comparison was absurd: Ligachev was not a scheming Stalin, but a dogmatic and loyal Party workhorse. And he was not a neo-Stalinist, but rather an advocate of the Andropov-style conservative reformism.

Ligachev lost his position as second in charge at the Politburo in March 1988, five months after Yeltsin. A group of Russian nationalist journalists had sent Ligachev an essay, allegedly based on a letter from Nina Andreyeva, professor of chemistry at Leningrad University. The essay, a crude resuscitation of Stalinist ideological campaigns, lashed out at "revisionists" in the Soviet media who were exploiting glasnost to "blacken" Soviet history. Ligachev approved of the article. It was published with the stamp of a Party-approved directive to ideological cadres. This episode can be considered as probably the last chance to reroute Soviet reforms in the direction envisaged by Andropov. The "Nina Andreyeva affair" alarmed the Moscow intelligentsia; the Western media speculated that perestroika was over. Gorbachev, however, had other plans. He viewed public discussion of the past and present, as well as support of the intelligentsia, as crucial factors for his future political reforms. With the support of Yakovlev, he easily put an end to the conservative "revolt." Ligachev and his supporters in the Politburo were cut down to size, humiliated and subdued. Yakovlev replaced Ligachev as the top Party ideologue, in charge of the state media. From then on, glasnost progressed by leaps and bounds.[84]

The main threat to Gorbachev in the fall of 1988 was not the Party elites. Instead, it came from a progressive failure of his economic reforms. The economic growth did not materialize, and disruptions to production lines and supply chains grew worse. Housing construction slowed down. Stores in most Soviet cities, even Moscow, were emptier than before, and the queues became longer. In early September 1988, during his stay in Crimea, Gorbachev went on an excursion to Sevastopol. A crowd of locals surrounded him, complaining about the lack of housing, unpaid pensions, and so on. Gorbachev spent three and a half hours with them. Finally, he exclaimed: "Who am I for you? The Tsar? Or Stalin?" He was clearly getting frustrated with Soviet people just as they were getting disheartened with him. He wanted them to elect their own representatives, solve their local problems, and get off his back. He also grew angry with local and regional Party officials. "He is quite worried," wrote Chernyaev in his diary. "The [Party] apparatus realized that his days were numbered, and they switched off the engine of the administrative system." Perhaps the Party officials had chosen to boycott perestroika, "to prove that all this is Gorbachev's crazy adventure."[85]

It was Gorbachev himself, in fact, who plotted a constitutional coup against his own Party. During his vacation in Crimea, he single-handedly decided to overhaul and cut the central Party apparatus, leaving behind only "revolutionary adepts of perestroika" to help him steer it in future. Between 800,000 and 900,000 Party officials would be sacked within a year: the biggest purge of Party cadres since Stalin, but this time a bloodless one. Chernyaev was the first person to see the draft of his proposals and comment on it. After Gorbachev returned from Crimea, he outlined his proposals to other aides. Twelve out of twenty departments of the central Party apparatus, the political brain of the entire Soviet political-economic system, were to be disbanded. Most of them supervised various parts of the economy. On 8 September 1988, the quiescent Politburo approved Gorbachev's program. Ligachev argued that the Party should continue to control the process of perestroika, yet he dared not criticize the General Secretary's pet project. Vitaly Vorotnikov asked who would be able to carry the burden of governance if the Party relinquished it. Gorbachev dodged the question. He spent the next two weeks summoning the old members of the Central Committee to him in person, one after another, and convinced each one to accept an honorable retirement.[86]

After securing his political goals at the Politburo, Gorbachev traveled to the Krasnoyarsk region of Central Siberia. He toured an enormous industrial area—the size of France and Spain combined—visiting plants that produced nickel, molybdenum, and platinum. The gigantic installations exhibited appalling inefficiency, everyday shortages of housing and food, and man-made environmental disasters. This trip confirmed Gorbachev's belief that the core problem lay in the Party's management of the economy. At a meeting in Norilsk with workers at the largest nickel-producing plant in the world, he urged them to elect leaders that they liked and trusted. One worker, he said, had sent him a letter urging him "to open fire on the headquarters." This was a slogan of Mao Zedong during the Cultural Revolution. Suddenly the audience roared enthusiastically: "That's right!" Gorbachev, taken aback by the mood of the crowd, explained that it would be disastrous to repeat China's experience. He returned to Moscow convinced that political reform was overdue. Only a frank discussion with the Congress of the problems facing the Soviet Union would help to redirect the huge levels of popular discontent into constructive channels.[87]

On 30 September, after just half an hour of discussion, the Party Plenum approved all his political reforms without even a shadow of dissent. The delegates, after some debates, sanctioned Gorbachev's right to become chairman of the future Supreme Soviet, while remaining head of the Party. The Party elite rubber-stamped the most radical shift of power since the time of Stalin.[88]

Gorbachev's radical reforms of 1987–88 originated from the failures of previous reforms, the frustration of the "people of the Sixties" with the Party-State bureaucracy, and from the ideological dreams of a few high-minded Party apparatchiks. Yet Gorbachev made a historic miscalculation. At the end of 1988, he moved to dismantle the Party apparatus as the only tool that could possibly keep reforms and the entire country under control. His diagnosis was incorrect. The Party bureaucracy, which he identified as the main obstacle to moderniza-tion and revitalization of the Soviet socialist project, preferred conservative and gradual reform, yet remained a tool in the hands of the top leadership. The misguided decentralization, together with other errors, threw a monkey wrench into the economy and finances. Moreover, "socialist democracy," just as Andropov had warned, was a highly dangerous enterprise. Gorbachevian perestroika, the way it was conceived, could not succeed. Instead, it exposed the Soviet Union to the demons of economic chaos, political populism, nationalism, and more.

CHAPTER 2

RELEASE

Experience teaches that the most critical moment for bad governments is the one which witnesses their first steps towards reform . . . Evils which are patiently endured when they seem inevitable become intolerable once the idea of escape from them is suggested.
Alexis de Tocqueville, *The Ancien Régime and the Revolution*, 1856

UNIVERSAL MISSION

On 7 December 1988, in New York, Gorbachev addressed the General Assembly of the United Nations. He announced the withdrawal of half a million Soviet troops from the countries of Eastern Europe. The Soviet Union also released almost all of its political prisoners. The main sensation, however, was the speech's ideological message. Gorbachev proposed a new world order based not on ideology, but on the "all-human interests" of cooperation and integration. This was a rejection of the Cold War order based on antagonism between the USSR and the USA and their respective allies. It was also a rejection of the Marxist-Leninist world view, based on "class struggle" and the inevitability of communist triumph. The General Secretary declared a principle of renunciation of any form of violence, any use of force in international affairs. Chernyaev, the main drafter of Gorbachev's UN address, considered it represented not only an ideological revolution, but also a possible farewell "to the status of a world global superpower."[1] In essence, the leader of the Soviet superpower proposed to the Western powers an end to the Cold War; the Soviet Union was ready to join all international organizations as a partner.

The address stemmed from what Gorbachev had been calling since 1986 a "new political thinking." It was a mix of his neo-Leninist hubris, breathtaking idealism, and abhorrence of nuclear confrontation. Against the background of Stalin's cynical Realpolitik, Khrushchev's brinkmanship, and Brezhnev's peace-through-strength détente, Gorbachev's project came as a complete break-through. It was not a clever camouflage for the start of Soviet geopolitical retrenchment and retreat, as some Western critics asserted. It was a deliberate choice of a new vision to replace the ideology of Marxism-Leninism and Soviet geopolitical power. As such, it was probably the most ambitious example of ideological thinking in foreign affairs since Woodrow Wilson had declared his Fourteen Points at the end of World War I. It was this vision that made Gorbachev, and not Ronald Reagan or other Western leaders, a truly key actor in ending the Cold War.[2]

Since early 1986, the Kremlin leader had been working to end the nuclear standoff with the United States and so reduce the terrifying threat of nuclear weapons. The Chernobyl disaster that April unexpectedly underscored this priority. As the enormity of nuclear catastrophe sank in, Gorbachev proposed to Reagan an emergency summit in Reykjavik, Iceland. This took place in October 1986 and Gorbachev surprised the US President by offering to cut half of the Soviet strategic nuclear arsenal in exchange for American cuts in nuclear weapons and a ban on Reagan's Strategic Defense Initiative (SDI). During 1986, Gorbachev also began to force the Soviet military to renounce the doctrine of pre-emptive nuclear strike and move to the principle of "strategic sufficiency."[3]

Dismantling the nuclear arsenals was a prerequisite for stopping the insane arms race. Like Andropov, Gorbachev realized that the Soviet Union could not be rebuilt and modernized without ending the Cold War confrontation. He had voiced the first draft of "new thinking" at his meeting with senior officials of the Soviet Foreign Ministry in May 1986. His main message was that the Reagan administration was trying to exhaust the Soviet Union in an expensive arms race. "Soviet foreign policy," he concluded, "must alleviate the burden" of mili-tary expenditures, must "do anything in its capabilities to loosen the vice of defense expenditures."[4] The Soviet leader expressed this concern many times, while arguing at the Politburo, the Defense Council, and to foreign leaders that the United States wanted "to exhaust the USSR" by a new arms race. His message was that it was time to stop worrying about the balance of power, and focus on internal reforms. In 1987, Gorbachev and Ryzhkov asked the leaders of Soviet military industries for the first time to begin this "conversion" to the production of consumer goods.[5]

The American pressures continued, however, to keep Soviet reformers hamstrung. The Reagan administration, unlike its predecessors, wanted to squeeze the economy and finances of the USSR to the maximum in order to stop Soviet expansionism. American belligerence, at least until the end of 1987, made it hard for Soviet reformers to reallocate resources from the military to the civilian economy. Reagan's SDI, if implemented, would mean an end to nuclear parity and stability; managers and scientific gurus of the Soviet military-industrial complex therefore demanded more billions from the budget to neutralize the American threat. Also, because of American sanctions, Soviet access to the resources of the world economy remained worse than in the 1960s. The US government used COCOM (Coordinating Committee for Multilateral Export Control), an informal network of Western countries and Japan established during the late 1940s, to deny the USSR Western equipment for finishing pipelines stretching from the new Soviet oil and gas fields in Eastern Siberia to Western Europe. In 1987, Washington cracked down on Toshiba, when in 1987 the Japanese corporation agreed to sell modern computer equipment to Moscow; the contract was canceled.[6]

Gorbachev's appointment of Eduard Shevardnadze in July 1985 to replace Andrei Gromyko as Soviet Foreign Minister was the first practical move to depart from the diplomacy of strength and quid pro quo. The Party head of Georgia, Shevardnadze was three years older than Gorbachev and another ex-Stalinist who had become a reform-minded communist. Shevardnadze experienced, like Gorbachev, the school of Komsomol idealism of the 1950s, and the frustration of the 1970s. He had made his career by his promise to defeat corruption in Georgia and by his effusive flattery of Brezhnev. He never managed the former and probably resented the latter. Shevardnadze performed a number of vital functions for Gorbachev: he implemented his ideas, projected a new smiling face of Soviet diplomacy abroad, and served as a lightning rod for the military, who found "new thinking" odd and incongruous.

Still, Gorbachev reserved the role of top negotiator for himself. He developed unique relationships with Western leaders, especially Ronald Reagan, François Mitterrand, Spain's leader Felipe González, Italy's Prime Minister Giulio Andreotti, Britain's Margaret Thatcher, and the West German Chancellor Helmut Kohl. Encounters with foreign leaders were important for all of Gorbachev's predecessors. Khrushchev was curious to explore the world and learn from capitalists how to build up socialism. Brezhnev carried the mantle of a peacemaker and used it to consolidate his stature at home. For Gorbachev, the relationship with foreigners, especially Western leaders, became a cultural and psychological necessity. The Russian scholar Dmitry Furman explained Gorbachev's desire for summits as a broader phenomenon: "For all Soviet people, including the higher echelons of the party," he wrote, "the West has always been an object of longing. Trips to the West were the most important status symbol. There is nothing you can do about this; it is 'in the blood,' in the culture."[7] Gorbachev, however, developed a strong need for more than this: an intellectual exchange with Western leaders and their feedback on his reformist initiatives. During frequent trips to the West, he began to discuss with his interlocutors how to change the Soviet Union.

One would expect that the General Secretary, bent on reforming the Soviet economy, would take with him on Western trips economists, planners, directors of military industries, bankers, and other technocrats. Instead, Gorbachev's huge entourage consisted mostly of journalists, social scientists, writers, theater directors, filmmakers, and other cultural figures. Most of them shared his fascination, admiration, and envy for things Western. They were encouraged to help Gorbachev prepare the Soviet people for radical reforms in all spheres of life, and they believed that the main sources of "real socialism" for which Gorbachev was searching all lay in the West.

Gorbachev introduced the "voices" of Western leaders, and what they discussed with him, into the debates at the Politburo. He also inserted the commentariat of the West into the ongoing debates about the nature and scope of Soviet reforms. At the Politburo, Gorbachev, helped by Yakovlev, Shevardnadze, and Medvedev, quoted from *The New York Times*, *The Financial Times*, *The Economist*, and other major Western sources of opinion. In this way, the Soviet leader acquired a semantic power, new formulas and arguments, fresh vocabulary and intonation—all to pit against his Politburo colleagues. This also opened the way for terms and concepts never before used in internal discourse. The Soviet Union could now be called "an empire"; the words "pluralism," "crisis," "totalitarianism," and "Stalinism" became acceptable. Gradually, the vocabulary imported from Western sources, as well as from the work of Soviet journalists, social scientists, and writers, would supplant the old Soviet vocabulary.

When Gorbachev began to develop his global world view, he was a dedicated neo-Leninist. In his discussions of foreign policy, at the Politburo and in his entourage, he used the metaphor of "Brest-Litovsk." This was the name of the town where the Bolshevik government had signed a treaty with the Kaiser's Germany in March 1918. The treaty allowed Lenin to trade land for time, and, against all expectations, to preserve the Soviet regime. For Soviet historians and Gorbachev, Brest-Litovsk became a metaphor that combined socialist idealism with pragmatism, and confirmed Lenin's genius. Gorbachev used this metaphor to argue the need for retreat and retrenchment, in order to focus on domestic reforms. The lessons of Brest-Litovsk for Gorbachev went beyond geopolitical concessions. He wanted to make an irresistible offer to his Cold War adversaries: to build together a new world order based on "common interests" and "common human values." Instead of complying with the playbook of Realpolitik, the Soviet leader announced a universal moral and idealistic vision. Gorbachev synchronized his offer with the launch of his economic and political reforms.

RELEASE

Gorbachev never connected, at least in public, his global vision to the future of Eastern Europe. He knew very well that the countries of this region, long held together by Soviet force, had considerable trouble making ends meet, and were drifting back into the Western economic and financial orbit. Gorbachev, like other reformers of his circle, had blamed this development on the Soviet policies of previous decades. It was, he and his entourage reasoned, Soviet intervention in 1968 in Czechoslovakia that had aborted much-needed democratization and the modernization of socialism, not only in Prague, but also in the Soviet Union and other socialist countries. With this lesson of history in mind, Gorbachev made a decision to draw a clear and principled line under the past. The USSR would never use force again and would stop telling its Eastern European allies what to do. The only way for Moscow to lead would be through the power of example: perestroika itself should convince those countries to follow the Soviet example and to emerge from their current quagmire towards a state of "genuine socialism." Vadim Medvedev, Gorbachev's appointee to the Politburo, remembers that his leader abided by this decision "to the point of squeamishness." It was pointless to propose anything that would be considered "interference into internal affairs" of the socialist countries. Even some in Gorbachev's entourage wondered about the logic of such a principled stance. After all, the Soviet leadership had helped to set up Stalinist regimes in Eastern Europe decades before and regularly intervened to keep them intact. Why not have "affirmative actions" to advance those who would have followed Gorbachev's example in 1986–87? In this light, some consider Gorbachev's visit to Czechoslovakia in April 1987 a missed opportunity. He did nothing to change the hard-line leader in that country, Gustáv Husák, and promote "a Czech Gorbachev."[8]

At first, Gorbachev paid special attention to political summits of the Warsaw Treaty Organization, the collective security alliance between Moscow and Eastern European satellites. The Soviet leader made an offer to deepen trade and economic cooperation and integration within the Council for Mutual Economic Assistance (CMEA), in an attempt to reflect the European Economic Community. Gorbachev was also aware that the European Community had signed the Single European Act, thereby starting the process of political union, and this piqued his curiosity: Lenin had prophesied that "the United States of Europe" was impossible under capitalism. Why then did socialist integration not work? The Soviet leader also hoped that East Germany, Czechoslovakia, Hungary, Bulgaria, and Poland would use their better access to Western information and technology to help with Soviet modernization. One of his pet ideas was an Eastern analogue to "Eureka," the EEC cooperative project for electronic and hi-tech industries. Those expectations brought few fruits. Eastern European countries gravitated towards Western countries, above all

West Germany, and had no desire to share what they obtained there with the Soviet "big brother."

Soviet ministers and economic managers had long known that their Eastern European partners regarded the Soviet Union only as a source of cheap energy and a market for goods that were not competitive on world markets. During Ryzhkov's visit to Warsaw in September 1986, the Polish leader General Wojciech Jaruzelski told him that the Polish economy was "handcuffed" by its $32 billion debt to Western banks. It was up to Moscow "to let Poland live or perish." In practice, it meant more subsidies in the form of cheap oil.[9] Since the Polish crisis, the Soviet leadership had acknowledged that it could not be responsible for Eastern Europe's economic and financial affairs, as well as the living standards of its peoples. In the fall of 1986, Gorbachev and Ryzhkov rejected the idea of a "common currency" for the Eastern bloc: it was obvious that the USSR would have to fund this currency without getting anything in return. In 1987, the Soviet leadership stopped advocating "deeper ties" with Hungary or "expanding cooperation" with East Germany. After his trip to Prague in April 1987, Gorbachev said: "I told them frankly that we will not carry out our perestroika at your expense, but you also should not count on living at our expense." As 1987 drew to a close, the Politburo became increasingly worried about the Soviet balance of payments: with extremely low oil prices the USSR would soon have to use up to two-thirds of its currency revenues to serve its foreign debt.[10] By 1988, Gorbachev began to think that Eastern European countries were a liability, not an asset, for his perestroika.[11]

As in his domestic reforms, the Soviet leader doubled down: he turned to Western Europe with a vision of a "Common European Home." Gorbachev's main inspiration was the Helsinki Final Act of 1975, the document signed by thirty-three European countries, including the Soviet Union, as well as the United States and Canada. The Act codified a common approach of the signatories to security, economic cooperation, and most importantly to human rights and cultural openness. Gorbachev acknowledged the Final Act as an expression of common values; "socialism" and "capitalism" were no longer important labels.[12] The Act also signified that the USSR's dependence on Eastern Europe as a "security buffer" was now an outdated notion. It recognized the realities of the nuclear age, but it was also a striking attempt to provide an argument for a future retreat of Soviet forces from Eastern Europe. In the light of common European values, the regimes in Eastern European countries were no longer considered to be socialist, but rather a parody of socialism. During their discussions in Moscow, Gorbachev, Shevardnadze, and other reformers began to declare exactly that.

And what should the Soviet leadership do if a violent uprising occurred in the Eastern bloc? In April 1988, Shevardnadze had already discussed this scenario with his deputies in the Foreign Ministry. "If we do not want violent anti-Soviet reaction," he said, "we should think about withdrawing [our] troops." Gorbachev shared similar concerns with his entourage.[13] In October 1988, Georgy Shakhnazarov warned him of another scenario: a probable chain reaction of financial bankruptcies in Eastern European countries and elsewhere, some of which "stand on the verge of payment crisis (Poland, Hungary, Bulgaria, Vietnam, Cuba, the GDR)." He wrote that Eastern Europe had become dependent on Western banks and that its political regimes might change. How should the USSR react to this course of events? And would the presence of Soviet troops in Eastern Europe "remain in Soviet interests"? Shakhnazarov himself seemed to know the answers to those questions. He and Chernyaev told Gorbachev that Eastern Europe was a "parasite" on the body of the Soviet economy; most leaders in the Soviet bloc were hostile to Gorbachev's radical reforms, and Soviet troops should leave the region as soon as possible. East Germany was the only exception: Soviet troops would remain there on the basis of the Potsdam accords of 1945, in the absence of a comprehensive peace agreement involving the great powers.[14]

In the fall of 1988, Gorbachev delegated to Alexander Yakovlev the task of creating a Politburo commission on the situation in Eastern Europe. Yakovlev turned to academic experts, whose views were virtually unanimous: all scenarios for the Soviet bloc were bad; the least harmful option for Moscow would be to pull out from Eastern Europe. In February 1989, in his subsequent report to Gorbachev, Yakovlev concluded that in the best possible scenario the communist regimes in the region would survive only through coalition with the opposition. The USSR should give up on the bloc and build relations with individual countries of Eastern Europe based on "balance of interests." Striking a more conciliatory tone, Yakovlev also said that, in the absence of a violent uprising, Eastern Europe might still remain "socialist" and even stay within the Warsaw Pact, "as a kind of security belt that creates strategic protection" for the Soviet Union "as the center of socialism." In the economic sphere, his report prudently stated, the USSR could not and should not hinder the economic reintegration of Eastern Europe into the West. This process could in fact be made compatible with Soviet economic interests. The Eastern bloc provided 40–50 percent of the goods for Soviet industries and consumers. In a sense, the Soviet economy would somehow be able to "return to Europe" on the coat-tails of the Eastern Europeans.[15]

In 1988, after endless Politburo debates, the Soviet leadership decided to pull out Soviet troops from Afghanistan unilaterally, having failed to reach with the United States an international agreement on the future of that country. The date for the final withdrawal was 15 February 1989. It was much more difficult for Gorbachev to announce an exit from Eastern Europe. The Soviet leadership hoped to synchronize this operation with progress on the scheme of a common European home. Gorbachev admitted to the Politburo that the Soviet Union did not have much time. The status quo in Eastern Europe had lasted only because many in the bloc still did not know how the USSR would react to the crumbling of its sphere of influence. The Soviet leader concluded: "They do not know yet that if they pull strongly on the leash, it would snap."[16] Still, nobody in Moscow expected this would happen in just a few months.

The UN address of 7 December 1988 was Gorbachev's attempt to accelerate détente with the United States. The Soviet leader wanted to present the Soviet withdrawals from Afghanistan and Eastern Europe as a triumph of his new principles, not as a geopolitical necessity or an admission of defeat. At first, he seemed to succeed. His speech was received with stormy applause and made Gorbachev hugely popular in Western Europe. It also impressed Reagan immensely; the US President became convinced that the Cold War was over. Yet, the public triumph concealed the fundamental fragility of Gorbachev's position. After the UN speech and at a meeting on Governors Island, Reagan innocently asked Gorbachev about the progress of perestroika. Gorbachev blushed, momentarily interpreting the question as an expression of mockery. There was in fact no progress to report, only grave problems.[17]

The incoming Bush administration deceived Gorbachev's expectations. George H. W. Bush had had an impressive Cold War career: ambassador to China, CIA director, member of the Ford administration, and then Vice-President in the Reagan administration. Whereas the Reagan team had been chaotic, wrangling, and inconsistent, Bush's team was steady, coherent, and prudent. The National Security Advisor Brent Scowcroft and Secretary of State James Baker were a powerful duo, next to the President, to steer US security and foreign policy respectively. They had lived through the attacks of the American right on the détente of the 1970s as being an "appeasement" of the Soviets. They regarded Gorbachev's initiatives and vision as dangerous "atmospherics." The Soviet nuclear arsenal was intact, Soviet armies still stood at the heart of Europe, and Moscow's arms and money propped up regimes in Afghanistan, Vietnam, Africa, Cuba, and Nicaragua. The Soviet military-industrial complex continued to build weapons, including chemical and biological, banned by international accords. Bush, Scowcroft, and Baker believed that Gorbachev had beguiled Reagan. The CIA's Robert Gates ascribed changes in Soviet foreign policy to the impact of Reagan's program for building a missile-defense system (SDI). That program, Gates reported to Bush, had allegedly convinced "even the most conservative members of the Soviet leadership" that the USSR would not be able to undertake such an incredibly expensive program itself and that "major internal changes were needed in the USSR." In a word, Gorbachev's "new thinking" was simply a child of necessity, a crafty strategy to seduce the West into the project of modernizing and re-energizing the Soviet economy—and resume Soviet expansion. Bush and his team wanted to press the Soviet leader more, into reducing his nuclear arsenal and unconditionally withdrawing from all parts of the Soviet "outer empire."[18]

In January 1989, the Bush administration declared "a reassessment" of relations with the Kremlin, which lasted for six months. During this time, Gorbachev's troubles escalated. The Soviet Union, in fact, became a different place, a whirlpool of political and economic turmoil. Even decades later, Gorbachev still nursed hard feelings about those in the West who had misjudged or ignored his good intentions. But he made an exception for Ronald Reagan.[19]

REVENGE OF THE PAST

Gorbachev's circle of reformers consisted mostly of ethnic Russians from the Russian Federation and intellectuals from Moscow. None of them had personal memories of bloody ethnic clashes or nationalist atrocities. All of them assumed that the vast majority of Soviet citizens identified themselves with their Soviet homeland. Gorbachev wrote about his own homeland of Stavropol as a "multiethnic milieu, in a remarkable poly-linguistic, multi-faceted, heterogeneous environment." For him and his entourage, the Leninist ideology of "internationalism" blended with the humanist, inclusive ethic of the Russian intelligentsia, at least those who sympathized with national liberation movements and considered xenophobia to be evil.[20] The reformers, as a result, were ill-equipped to deal with a load of national problems they had inherited from the past.

The Soviet Union was a minefield of nationalist grievances and aspirations. It had been forged by Bolshevik ideology, blood, and iron on the remnants of Tsarist Russia. The Bolshevik Party, an international band of revolutionaries, had developed a sophisticated policy on nationalities. Stalin and some other Bolsheviks had suggested that the country they occupied should be called the Russian Soviet Socialist Federation. Lenin, however, objected to this. His idea was to regard the "great Russians," the ethnic-cultural mainstay of the old empire, as "the oppressor nation" and all non-Russian nationalities along the periphery of the USSR as "the oppressed." He insisted that the country should be called the Union of Soviet Socialist Republics, a confederation of titular nationalities, with institutions and even the right of exit from the Union. Lenin's view prevailed. In December 1922 the Union was created as a constitutional accord of four republics: the Russian Soviet Federative Socialist Republic (RSFSR), Soviet Ukraine, Soviet Belorussia, and the Trans-Caucasian Soviet Socialist Republic.

The Bolsheviks subsidized and promoted non-Russian "nations," using resources and cadres from Moscow and St Petersburg to create their science academies, writers' unions, filmmaking studios, literary journals, etcetera.[21]

Following Lenin's death in 1924, in practice, Stalin governed the Soviet Union more and more as a unitary state. The "national" communist parties were held together by the iron grip of the Bolshevik Party (VKPb), later the Communist Party of the Soviet Union (CPSU). The Soviet army did not have "national" formations. The KGB had branches in the republics, yet they were all subordinate to Moscow. The commander-in-chief of both powerful institutions was the General Secretary of the CPSU. The State Bank of the USSR, located in Moscow, issued currency for all the republics and autonomous regions. Most of the big economic assets in the territories of every republic of the Union—factories, plants, energy utilities, gas and oil pipelines—were "Union property," controlled by the central ministries in Moscow. All those checks and balances against Russian nationalism continued to work well for decades, helping the regime to rule the multi-ethnic polity. Yet, the Soviet leadership remained a prisoner to the Leninist principle of "full independence" for the republics.[22]

In 1985, when Gorbachev came to power, the Czech Marxist historian Miroslav Hroch defined three phases of nationalism in Eastern Europe: phase A was the emergence of an idea of a nation by elite activists, usually historians, linguists, and other intellectuals who studied the past, languages, and cultures; phase B was the period of patriotic agitation; and phase C was the mass movement that leads to the creation of a nation state.[23] In the Soviet Union, however, and in just three or four years, this scheme would be collapsed into one phase. Some "nations" on its territory had already existed for centuries; others had been constructed by the Soviet dictatorship, even as anti-Soviet nationalists were being ruthlessly suppressed. A leading scholar of nationalism in the USSR, Mark Beissinger, observes that before Gorbachev people "simply never faced the opportunity or the necessity of choosing between loyalty to the Soviet order and loyalty to one's ethnic identity." He continues: "Despite the seriousness and complexity of Soviet nationality issues on the eve of perestroika, at the time Soviet ethnic problems appeared to most observers to be significant but hardly unmanageable."[24]

Andropov and the KGB had known, however, that "national" Party cadres and the "national" intelligentsia could become a nucleus of national movements in separate Soviet republics. Andropov, recalls his aide Arkady Volsky, was obsessed with the idea of downplaying the role of nationalities in the constitutional structures of the Soviet Union. He knew the power of nationalism and during his years as head of the KGB had received information that the republican branches of the Party were becoming increasingly ethnic-nationalist clans that barely camouflaged their true leanings under the veneer of communist "internationalism" in which they no longer believed. Andropov also realized that Russian and Ukrainian nationalism could be particularly dangerous for the Union. The General Secretary gave his aide a secret order: "Let's get rid of the national partition of the country. Present your ideas on the organization of states in the Soviet Union according to population and economic rationale, so that the title nationalities would be faded out. Draw me a new map of the USSR."[25] Volsky recalled that he drew up fifteen drafts, but Andropov rejected all of them. The devil was in reapportioning industrial objects across the states in such a way that the notion of "states" would make economic and budgetary sense. "I shudder, when I recall this mission," Volsky remembered. Andropov and his aide redrew the borders and reshuffled the lists of enterprises that "belonged" to one region or another. Volsky turned for help to his friend, the nuclear physicist Yevgeny Velikhov. "We came up with forty-one states. We finished the project, with all proper charts, but by that time [Andropov] got very ill." The idea of radical constitutional reform was shelved. Volsky was convinced that Andropov could have pushed reform down the throats of the republican elites, at least to a certain extent. "Had he had time to approve 'the project,' I can say with full confidence: Party secretaries who later would become heads of independent states would have applauded this wise decision of the Party."[26]

Could Andropov have undone seventy years of Soviet national construction? Would the potentates of the Soviet republics and autonomous regions, backed by their ethnic clans, have swallowed such a proposal? This proposition remains untested. Instead, under Gorbachev the Soviet confederated constitution became a minefield.

The first "alarm bell" about the growing power of nationalism rang for Gorbachev's Politburo in December 1986, when the Kazakh students in Alma-Ata, capital of the Kazakh republic, came out in an anti-Russian demonstration, protesting at the removal of the republican party boss Din-Muhammed Kunayev. The protests were repressed in predictable Soviet style, with 2,400 students arrested, over 450 injured, and two killed. For Gorbachev, Kunayev had been Brezhnev's appointee and belonged to the past. For students and the Kazakh intelligentsia, however, he was "the father of the nation." Even worse for them, Kunayev's replacement was an ethnic Russian, and this violated an unwritten rule: the republican boss belonged to a titular nationality.

At the Politburo, some members correctly concluded that the turmoil in the Kazakh republic originated with the "national" intelligentsia and the "national" party cadres. "Thank God," said Yakovlev, "they still do not talk about the destruction of the Soviet Union." Gorbachev unexpectedly objected: "Which god do you have in mind? For us Lenin is the only god in these matters. If he had managed to rescue the [correct policy] on nationalities from Stalin, we would not be in this situation." At the time of Lenin's death, the Soviet Union had 5,200 national territorial entities. In Gorbachev's eyes, the "national" intelligentsia were not a threat, but rather an important ally of his perestroika program. "Any punitive measures are very dangerous," he concluded. "Martyrs and saints immediately emerge." Those words would define Gorbachev's attitude to nationalism for the rest of his career. A multi-national polity, Gorbachev believed, could be harmonized only when Soviet institutions were fully empowered.[27]

This approach backfired most severely in South Caucasus. This area, surpassing the Balkans in ethnic complexity, was a pressure cooker for virulent local nationalisms. Created on the ruins of the Russian Empire in 1918–20, Georgia, Armenia, and Azerbaijan were pawns in the geopolitical games of the great powers. These territories were then conquered by the victorious Bolsheviks.[28] Also, as in the Balkans, old ethnic hatreds flared up over the region of Nagorny Karabagh, an autonomous territory within Azerbaijan. In February 1988, within a week, one million Armenians were out in the streets of Yerevan, demanding the transfer of the region to Armenia. The rally was peaceful, but the response to this demand in Azerbaijan was violent: a bloody pogrom in Sumgait, a working-class area near Baku, took the lives of thirty people. The Azeri police did not intervene.[29]

This conflict became the most serious test of Gorbachev's leadership since the disaster at Chernobyl. In Gorbachev's entourage, Shakhnazarov knew most about the long history of the Armenian-Azeri conflict. His family descended from the Karabagh's Armenian nobles and had taken an oath of allegiance to the Russian Tsars. Shakhnazarov was convinced that the feud between the two peoples "could be solved only by force." Moscow, he thought, had to stop the ethnic cleansing, and ensure security for both the Armenians and the Azeris. Yet Gorbachev and his Politburo colleagues were gripped by "the paralysis of will." After a few fatal days of delay, just like after the explosion at Chernobyl, Gorbachev finally decided to dispatch a military force from Russian regions to Azerbaijan. But it was ordered not to open fire and not to arrest those involved in the pogrom in Sumgait. While the Politburo procrastinated, a mass exodus of civilians shook both republics, and mass protests paralyzed the local Party authorities. Gorbachev was extremely reluctant to use force even after the horrific news emerged from Sumgait. He neither declared an emergency nor demanded an official investigation of the crisis.[30]

Instead, indecisive himself, Gorbachev went after the republican leaders, Armenia's Karen Demirchian and Azerbaijan's Kamran Baghirov, blaming them for their inaction. Gorbachev privately—and unfairly—blamed the two men for "provoking people against perestroika" in order to protect themselves.[31] He appealed for moderation to the Armenian intellectuals, who were the main agitators of the nationalist cause. At a confidential meeting with two of them, Gorbachev naïvely asked them not to raise the territorial issue; he promised that Moscow would find other ways to preserve Armenian cultural identity in the Karabagh region. His words fell on deaf ears. The attitude of Moscow intellectuals was no better: they supported Armenia in the conflict and criticized Gorbachev for not doing the same.[32]

One reason for Gorbachev's conduct was his personal aversion to violence—a feature that would later play a decisive role in his decision-making. Another was his fear of losing the momentum for his political reforms. Some members of the Politburo were already beginning to say that "a speedy democratization could jeopardize the unity" of the USSR.[33] Gorbachev dismissed those fears. He urged them to "engage fresh forces, including the intelligentsia of both republics."[34] In March 1988, he traveled to Yugoslavia, the socialist country where economic decentralization had created a constitutional and political crisis. After this trip, Gorbachev told the republican Party leaders: "What has happened to Yugoslavia should not happen to us."[35] His recipe, however, was to create "people's fronts," and informal associations of the "national" intelligentsia in the republics "to support perestroika."[36] The future would soon show that those "pre-emptive" initiatives amounted to adding oil to the fire.

In October 1988, as the Armenian-Azeri crisis raged on, Gorbachev had to admit to Chernyaev and Shakhnazarov that the "fresh forces" in the Party, as well as Armenian intellectuals, had failed his expectations. He was at a loss what to do next. "If I knew what to do, I would bypass any dogmas. But I don't know!"[37]

Shevardnadze's aide, Teimuraz Stepanov, half-Georgian and half-Russian, born in Moscow, blamed the architects of perestroika for starting a constitutional crisis. Those who "opened the sluices of perestroika had never seen a single live nationalist," he mused, and so were taken by surprise. Yet they had learned nothing from their discovery. After reading the draft of Gorbachev's report on the constitutional amendments and political reforms, Stepanov wrote that it completely undermined "two priority tasks—preservation of the Union's integrity and the personal authority of the General Secretary." Gorbachev had rushed ahead, Stepanov mused, without any regard for or fear of "personal and general catastrophe," as if his reforms were not putting the country "inside the ring of bloodless rebellions that shook the system to the core." Shevardnadze's aide feared a counter-revolutionary backlash and collapse of the system.[38]

In South Caucasus, the Azeri and Armenian nationalists continued to kill each other in great numbers; 50,000 refugees took flight in all directions; armed gangs robbed trains and villages. Even a disastrous earthquake that devastated a vast area of Armenia in December 1988 did not quell the nationalist fervor.[39]

Eventually, Gorbachev did authorize tough measures. The Armenian national-ists were arrested that month. In January 1989, the Supreme Soviet of the USSR declared martial law in Karabagh and removed it from the republican jurisdic-tion. Nothing was done, however, to punish those who had incited the pogrom in Azerbaijan.[40] This failure by the central authority to act sent a powerful nega-tive signal across the Soviet Union, to the "national" republican and local Party officials. The Pandora's box of problems, brimming with nationalist grievances, had suddenly opened.

Baltic nationalism also raised its head in 1988 and presented a grave and systemic challenge to the Soviet leadership. Three Baltic republics—Lithuania, Latvia, and Estonia—had become sovereign states in 1920, but twenty years later they had been absorbed by the Soviet Union in a kind of shotgun marriage. The Balts took advantage of Gorbachev's reforms to legitimize their nationalist discourse, organize nationalist movements, and ultimately "nationalize" the Party structures. Baltic nationalists also devised a strategy to address the funda-mentals of Soviet constitutional and territorial integrity.[41] During the all-Union debates on economic reforms, the Estonian historian and economist Edgar Savisaar, assisted by three colleagues, proposed the idea of republican "self-accounting." Savisaar had been born in a women's prison in 1950, after both his parents, an Estonian father and ethnic Russian mother, were arrested for an attempt to leave their collective farm. Later, however, Savisaar became a benefi-ciary of Soviet "affirmative action": he got a university degree in Tartu and began to work for Estonia's government as an economic planner. He knew the Soviet system inside out; his proposal was nothing short of a camouflaged bomb planted under the Moscow-centered pyramid of power. An idea similar to republican "self-accounting" was at the root of the demise of Yugoslavia. Surprisingly, Savisaar received the full support of both Gorbachev and Ryzhkov.

The Balts were the ones who gave Gorbachev the idea of "popular fronts" as a way to pre-empt ethnic conflicts and violence. In April 1988, Savisaar went on Estonian television to propose "a democratic movement in support of perestroika." In August, Yakovlev traveled to Vilnius and Riga and, to the great astonishment of local Party leaders, supported this idea. At that time, one expert concludes, "the balance of power in Moscow was still crucial for developments" in the Baltic republics. Yakovlev's intervention had in fact opened the gates and mobilized the Baltic nationalist cause.[42]

Yakovlev's appeasement of the Balts was fully backed by Gorbachev and stemmed from reformist zeal and neo-Leninist ideology. The Kremlin reformers viewed the Baltic republics as the best testing ground for economic reforms and wanted them to set an example for the rest of the Union. Like other educated Russians, they viewed the Baltics as "a window into Europe" that exhibited higher standards of civil consciousness. In his report to the Politburo, Yakovlev assured his colleagues that he was not able to detect in the Baltics "any single act of a nationalist, anti-Soviet, anti-Russian, anti-perestroika nature." He innocently believed that nationalism could be disarmed by the removal of "irritants," such as ecological damage caused by Soviet industrialization of the Baltics, reducing Russian migration to the Baltics, and constraints on national cultural and international activities. Yakovlev's claims were nonsense: Baltic nationalism was not a product of "irritants."[43] His colleagues would later accuse Yakovlev of treason. A clever man, had he really been deceived by a masquerade staged by his Baltic hosts? If so, he was not alone; most Western observers shared the illusion that the Balts merely wanted greater autonomy within the Soviet Union.[44]

Glasnost and the revelations of past crimes upended the precarious balance in the Baltic republics between the enemies of the Soviet state and those who defended it. Gorbachev appointed Yakovlev to be co-chair of a Politburo commission on the victims of Stalin's repressions, which began work in June 1988. The repressions carried out in the Baltic states after their incorporation into the Soviet Union were part of the story. Even the Baltic Party leaders, Karl Vaino in Estonia and Boris Pugo in Latvia, urged the Politburo "to give their political assessment" to the mass deportations from the republics in 1940 and 1949. The commission's investigations, just like Khrushchev's earlier efforts, revealed awful details of terror campaigns. Yakovlev did not expect, however, that the Balts would use the archival glasnost to question the Soviet annexation of Estonia, Latvia, and Lithuania. For the Baltic nationalists, the German-Soviet Non-Aggression Pact of 1939 was a secret deal that had sealed this annexation. The Soviet government had always denied it. Around 1988, however, Gorbachev discovered in Stalin's archives a copy of the German-Soviet secret protocols. He decided to keep this discovery under wraps. And he did not share the explosive secret even with Yakovlev.[45]

The Balts took full advantage of Gorbachev's gamble of radical political reform. During 1988, the old Party cadres in the Baltic Party organizations, loyal to the Party's central control, had been removed as backward-thinking enemies of reform; the new Party leaders, Algirdas Brazauskas in Lithuania and Anatolijs Gorbunovs in Latvia, were anti-Stalinist and nationalist-minded. The "national" intelligentsia used Soviet cultural institutions, such as the republican branches of the Union of Soviet Writers and the Academy of Sciences, to organize political movements: the Popular Front for Perestroika Support (*Rahvarinne*) in Estonia; the Latvian Popular Front in Riga; and the Reform Movement (*Sąjūdis*) in Lithuania. The scholars of Baltic independence viewed this moment as a point of no return in the mobilization for independence. In October 1988,

Sajudis elected as its chairman Vytautas Landsbergis, a musicologist and an intractable adversary of Gorbachev.

The leaders of pro-independence Baltic movements realized that the most viable strategy for them would be to promote the independence of *all* titular nationalities of the Soviet Union. They aimed their sights at Belorussia, Ukraine, and above all the Russian Federation, the Slavic core of "the socialist empire." They set up Russian-language media that promoted Baltic democracy as an example for other republics; they offered venues and logistics for the first gatherings of "popular fronts" and nationalist associations in Belorussia and Georgia, as well as in Moscow and Leningrad. In the following years their efforts would yield results that surpassed even their boldest imagination.[46]

In November 1988, a group of conservative Politburo members toured Estonia, Lithuania, and Latvia, and returned to Moscow horrified. Separatism, they reported, had become the new national consensus in the Baltics. The Baltic intelligentsia were playing a double game. They were telling visitors from Moscow tales of perestroika, but in the streets they were shouting: "Russians go home!" "The KGB, the Soviet Army and police—back to Moscow!" "Down with the dictatorship of Moscow!" "Immediate exit from the Union!" The Baltic nationalists agitated for the primacy of republican laws over the Union's constitutional order.[47] The head of the KGB, Viktor Chebrikov, said that no concessions would satisfy the Balts. Everyone expected Gorbachev to take a firm stand.

The Baltic challenge threatened to derail radical political reform on the eve of its emergence. Anatoly Lukyanov helped Gorbachev change the Soviet constitution and design the new institutions proposed to create a legal firewall to prevent probable Baltic secession. The exit of even one republic from the Union, Lukyanov said at the Politburo, could trigger a constitutional crisis. The way to proceed, he argued, was to turn the future Congress of People's Deputies into a powerhouse that would be able to cancel republican laws when they clashed with the Union laws. Yakovlev, Medvedev, and Gorbachev's aides all protested. Such a proposal, they argued, would lead to a unitary state and would be applauded by Russian chauvinists and Stalin's admirers. Gorbachev also objected. Perestroika, he said, should fulfill the Leninist promise of full rights for all nationalities. He and Ryzhkov wanted the Baltic republics to have economic autonomy and prove that economic decentralization could work. Lukyanov subsequently removed his proposal.[48]

At the end of 1988, just as Gorbachev's entourage argued about the political reforms, federation, and national republics, the Academy of Sciences ran a contest on the best constitutional project to reform the Soviet Union. Two young scholars from a Moscow-based academic think tank came up with a formula: a new Union could become a federation if it possessed a very strong center. The scholars were invited to the Party headquarters on the Old Square for a discussion. An official told them that the political line was different. "We need a strong center, but also strong republics." The scholars responded that it was only possible to have one or the other. Stronger republics meant a confederation and potential disintegration. They left the Party headquarters shaking their heads: "They don't understand a thing!" The absurd principle of "a strong center, but also strong republics" continued to frame Gorbachev's approach to nationalism, as well as to economic and political reforms.[49]

The constitutional changes, approved at the end of 1988, did not create a firewall against republican nationalism. Equally, it made the republican elites unhappy and defiant. According to the new political order, the republics would be given only a third of the seats in the forthcoming Congress of People's Deputies—instead of a half as during Brezhnev's time. Two-thirds of the seats would be eligible on the principle of "one person—one vote" or elected by "public organizations," most of which were located in Moscow. The Congress would be able to create ethnic autonomies within existing republics. Reacting to the reforms, Estonia's Supreme Soviet voted to make Estonian law capable of overriding Soviet laws, and claimed that all natural and economic resources on Estonian territory could no longer be controlled from Moscow.

Gorbachev argued for the transition of more economic rights and property to all Soviet republics, while simultaneously obstructing the exit of any republic from the USSR. He admitted that the Baltic nationalists had called his "bluff" and had begun to use political liberalization to prepare for their unilateral secession. Still, Gorbachev persevered in stating that perestroika would succeed and its economic results would help to solve the problem of nationalist unrest. In February 1989, he invited the Party and government leaders of the Baltic republics to Moscow. Vorotnikov, Chebrikov, and other Politburo conservatives told Gorbachev that his plans would lead to disaster. "The diktat of the center," said Vorotnikov, "may be replaced by a diktat of republics!" Chernyaev, in his private diary, feared that an open clash with the Baltic independence movements could have the same effect as Brezhnev's invasion of Czechoslovakia in 1968. Perhaps it would be better to let the Baltics secede, continue pushing ahead with perestroika, and start improving the lives of ordinary Russians.[50] Gorbachev was convinced that the deep integration of the Baltics into the Soviet economy, as well as the Slavic majority, would prevent Baltic secession. The center, he argued, would retain control over the military-industrial complex, pipelines, power plants and grids, communications, and other strategic assets. The Baltic leaders, as expected, eagerly embraced the offer of economic autonomy from the Kremlin and returned home.[51]

HOPE AND HUBRIS

In February 1989, Shakhnazarov wrote to Gorbachev that the only alternative to conflict in the Baltics was the incorporation of "people's fronts" into the emerging political system, as a check on the Party conservatives. He also pushed for a law that would make the exit of a republic from the USSR possible only after a popular referendum. Lithuania's nationalists, he argued, would not be able to pass this test. Such a constitutional change could have been approved at a special Party Plenum and stamped by the Supreme Soviet, before political reforms started and before the Congress of People's Deputies convened. One-third of the Soviet Constitution had been changed in exactly this way during 1988.[52] Inexplicably, Gorbachev waited for more than a year to implement Shakhnazarov's idea of an exit law.

INTO THE STORM

"My father thinks that Gorbachev is an idiot," said a son of Deng Xiaoping to an American journalist in 1990.[53] Deng, a loyal lieutenant of Mao Zedong, had started a new era in China in 1978 by lifting the communist ban on a market economy in the countryside, and then throughout the rest of the Chinese economy. Aside from the release of the productive energies of hundreds of millions of peasants, Deng opened "free economic zones" to foreign investment. Rapid economic growth caused social inequality, inflation, and discontent. In May 1989, crowds of Chinese students, along with many other young people and sympathizers, took to the streets of Beijing and occupied Tiananmen Square. They demanded a "return to socialist justice and equality," but also "democracy." By coincidence, Gorbachev had simultaneously arrived in Beijing for the first Soviet-Chinese summit since 1959. Students greeted Gorbachev as their hero and cited his neo-Leninist rhetoric of "socialist democracy." They also cheered Zhao Ziyang, a younger reformist member of the Chinese leadership, as a potential "Chinese Gorbachev." After days of embarrassment and hesitation, the Chinese leaders made a brutal decision: they sent the army to crush the protest, killing many students. Zhao Ziyang and other "liberalizers" among the Party ideologues were ousted from the leadership. Deng acted with the same logic that Andropov had expressed in 1983. He relied on the army, security services, and the ruling Party to stay in control and continue reforms. Two years later, Deng relaunched the market initiatives that resulted in three decades of unprecedented economic growth and prosperity for hundreds of millions in China. The Chinese leadership, scared by the collapse of the Soviet system, would never consider liberalization of the Party system.[54]

William Taubman, who quotes Deng Xiaoping's verdict on Gorbachev, concedes that Gorbachev put the cart (political reform) before the horse (radical economic reform). The Soviet leader's conservative colleagues in the Politburo thought so as well. Still, Gorbachev's biographer, as well as other scholars of perestroika, have dismissed Deng's verdict. The success of authoritarian reforms in China, they argue, was a unique case and could not be repeated under Soviet conditions.[55] China, although in many ways a communist clone of the USSR, had fundamentally different starting conditions for reforms. Gorbachev could not release the energy of the peasantry in the way Deng did: Soviet agriculture, no more than 20 percent of the total workforce, had long been a state-subsidized business. China could leave its old industries, 15 percent of the total economy, alone, while creating a new market industrial sector. The Soviet economy was industrialized to an absurd extent, and its mono-industrial cities had no chance of surviving under market conditions. China's economy tapped into peasants' savings and foreign investments. The Soviet budget was overloaded by a safety net of 100 billion rubles paid as pensions and social benefits to Soviet citizens, as well as subsidies to external clients and internal republics. Moscow was losing billions of rubles because of oil prices and ill-fated economic decentralization.[56]

More important, however, were Gorbachev's intentions. He never considered China a model for his reforms and, in contrast to Deng, pursued a global ideological mission. The Chinese, he said to Chernyaev, had not solved the main problem: how "to link personal interests with socialism," the problem "that preoccupied [Lenin]."[57] The Soviet leader believed the Soviet Union had human and scientific resources to reclaim a world leadership in new technologies. Democratization would tap into this potential. In May 1989, during his stay in Beijing, Gorbachev turned to his entourage of intellectuals: "Some of those present here have promoted the idea of taking the Chinese road. We saw today where this road leads. *I do not want the Red Square to look like Tiananmen Square.*" The Soviet leader believed that history had spoken in favor of the road he had taken.[58]

With this conclusion in mind, Gorbachev passed his own verdict on Deng Xiaoping. At his press conference in Beijing, Gorbachev declared: "We became convinced that we cannot succeed with reforms unless we dismantle the command-administrative system."[59] An emotional Chernyaev, Gorbachev's alter ego, had expressed the same sentiments a few months earlier: "The old regime must go, should be destroyed, and only then can society, acting on the instincts of self-preservation, resurrect itself from scratch." The Chinese communist leadership, which had just emerged from the shadow of the Cultural Revolution, preferred brute force to reclaim "the mandate of Heaven." Gorbachev, as his loyal aide Shakhnazarov recalled in 1992, "lacked the guts to have his Tiananmen. He only had to suppress the first stirrings of separatists and radicals, and the Soviet Union would have remained in good health. This, however, would have meant bidding farewell to his glorious dream of bringing democracy to our country and would have dealt an irrevocable blow to his personal prestige as a reformer."[60] Prestige among the liberal-minded intelligentsia and Western public, one should add.

Any historical comparisons are flawed. It is hard to find a case or a metaphor that captures what the Gorbachev leadership did during 1989. One thinks of the captain of a huge ship who suddenly decides to sail towards a distant Promised Land. He does so against the mood and instincts of his crew. He and his followers have no map; their compass is broken. They are under the impression that their ship is sailing westward, whereas in reality it is heading south. As the voyage becomes more and more difficult, the captain decides that his crew are unreliable saboteurs. So he turns to inexperienced passengers keen to take part in the voyage and lets them deliberate among themselves on the best ways to reach the Promised Land.

In the spring of 1989, the biggest cause of discontent was not yet nationalism, but the crisis of supply. Millions of Soviet citizens had long become accustomed to hardship and shortages. Perestroika gave them hopes for a better life, but instead it created more everyday troubles and problems. Those who remembered the late 1960s could not understand why stores had been well stocked then, and had become empty now? Soviet statisticians reported to the Politburo that Soviet people were consuming twice as much as twenty years before, and that Soviet farms had many more cattle, pigs, and cows. People took these statistics as a form of mockery. Money was increasingly chasing after goods; people began to hoard, sweeping anything available off the shelves in state-run stores. Even products that had been widely available in 1985, such as sugar, soap, and detergent, now disappeared from the shelves. The daily hunt for food items left people, especially women, standing in line for hours after work. One region after another introduced rationing of basic goods. Stores became barren in Moscow and Leningrad as well: state enterprises purchased food products directly from agro-farms or warehouses and distributed them among their employees. People were becoming exhausted and furious with the local bosses and top leadership.[61]

"1988 knocked us off," Nikolai Ryzhkov, head of the Council of Ministers, complained to his Politburo colleagues. The most alarming indicator was the budget deficit, projected to grow to 120 billion rubles by the end of 1989. It was one-third of the entire budget—an unprecedented situation since the end of World War II. On 5 January 1989, Ryzhkov convened a special meeting of the Council of Ministers to discuss why reforms were not working. He invited the economist Leonid Abalkin, director of the Institute of Economics in Moscow, to report on the situation.[62] Half a year prior to this, at the Party Conference, he had said publicly that perestroika in the economy was not working.[63]

The meeting lasted for six hours. Abalkin proposed austerity measures to balance the budget: cutting investment to costly long-term projects, ending the subsidies to unprofitable enterprises (60 billion rubles), and reducing allocations to the defense industries (8–10 billion rubles). It was the first admission that the reforms were beginning to take the Soviet state down the road to financial crisis. Abalkin was untrained in macroeconomic analysis: he did not identify the Law on State Enterprises and the Law on Cooperatives as a major source of the deficit. And he argued in favor of creating more commercial banks and credit, which would only further weaken monetary controls and undermine the austerity measures he proposed. One critic later said about Abalkin that it was a case of "the blind leading the blind." Ryzhkov closed the meeting with a paradox: "We see our errors and see the processes that to some extent went out of control." Yet, he added, "if we step back, we would damage economic reform."[64]

The fear of "stepping back"—the syndrome of 1968—entrapped the reformers. Gorbachev confessed as much in his speech to the young communist cadres: "Much of what we have been doing now," he said, "originated in the 1960s." There was also a lack of solid economics. Soviet economists, including Abalkin, remained caught between the realization that the Soviet economy was too complex to be managed from the top, and rejection of the idea of market deregulation. This left the Gorbachev leadership with the "third option": transferring power, responsibility, and resources to state enterprises, regions, and republics. "The shift of decision-making circles down the line is the correct way," said Gorbachev to the Indian leader Rajiv Gandhi. "Our society is mature enough for that culturally and educationally. People will solve their local problems themselves."[65] By recoiling from this experiment, Gorbachev and his economists feared, they would revert to the stagnation of the Brezhnev era.

The political moment on the eve of elections to the Congress of People's Deputies was also too awkward to make changes to the economic reforms that were only just under way. The Soviet leadership knew that most state enterprises simply boosted salaries instead of investing in modernization and production. Yet taking away those profits could lead to discontent and turmoil. For the same reason, it was the wrong moment to change the system of state-fixed prices. "We had to postpone price rises by 2–3 years," Ryzhkov explained to the Austrian chancellor Franz Vranitzky. "Otherwise—social explosion; the society was not prepared." Gorbachev was of the same opinion.[66]

Abalkin's austerity program quickly ran into a wall of departmental lobbyism. The agricultural sector employed 28 million people and included established, and hugely inefficient, conglomerates and chains of supply. A notorious case was the beef industry. It consisted of thousands of farms established during Brezhnev's time. Poorly equipped, with unskilled peasant personnel, they were monuments to waste and required annual subsidies and imports of wheat and additive vitamins from the West, in exchange for gold and hard currency. Gorbachev and Ryzhkov decided to give those farms more options, including the right of leasing and forming cooperatives, while continuing the subsidies. The utopian nature of this reform was obvious. Peasants, after two generations of being violently repressed by the state, just wanted to continue receiving their small salaries and pensions, keep their little plots, but they had no other ambition. Gorbachev was genuinely puzzled as to why peasants were not eager to embrace his "emancipation." Meanwhile, without coercion from the Party, farmers were not interested in transporting food to the cities at the low purchase prices fixed by the state. In the fall of 1988, Soviet farms failed to deliver to the state one-third of their harvest. They wasted or lost another third. Gorbachev's Politburo faced a dilemma: to raise purchase prices or import more food from abroad.[67]

The Politburo was badly split on this issue. Ligachev, supported by other colleagues, proposed to raise allocations in order to pay farmers more for the same output, in order to incentivize them. Ryzhkov objected furiously: he wanted to cut subsidies to the most inefficient collective farms and food-producing plants. Ligachev retorted that if that were to happen he would be unable to prevent food shortages in the cities. The two powerful officials could not conceal their mutual hatred. "The top leaders of the country," Chernyaev ruefully observed, "have been barking at each other over the issue: why this store lacks milk, and another lacks cream or kefir. Meanwhile, mountains of cabbage have been rotting in storage, and are not found in stores . . ."[68] Ligachev, however, had a point: without subsidies and higher purchase prices, without coordination and organization between the Party and state authorities, there would be no food on the shelves. Vorotnikov, another conservative, wrote in his diary about what happened: "Structures of agriculture were left disorganized, the party committees were removed from management, and the local councils had no power to act."[69]

Another obstacle to Abalkin's austerity program was the entangled problem with the military-industrial complex (MIC). In the Western imagination, the Soviet MIC was a sinister, powerful lobby that drained the country's resources, denied people decent living standards, caused Chernobyl and other man-made disasters, and stood as a reactionary wall against Gorbachev's reforms. In reality, it was a prize jewel of the Soviet economy consisting of seven huge ministries that commanded 1,500 plants, enterprises, and laboratories with 9.5 million employees and workers. It amounted to 7 percent of the total Soviet labor force.

RELEASE

The leadership of the MIC estimated its fixed assets, such as plants and equipment, at around 111 billion rubles—6.4 percent of the Soviet economy. Over half of these assets were located in Moscow and Leningrad; the other half were scattered across the Urals and Siberia, Ukraine and Kazakhstan, including dozens of "closed" cities with a strict governing regime, higher salaries, and a privileged lifestyle. The MIC had been the pet project of Stalin, and was vastly expanded under the rule of Khrushchev and Brezhnev. Its greatest achievements included the creation of nuclear weapons and the launch of Sputnik; its very greatest achievement was to reach strategic parity with the United States. The MIC expanded enormously during the Cold War, and all its plants, factories, and labs remained in "wartime" mode, in other words they maintained production capacities calculated as sufficient for a period of full-scale war.[70] In 1988, all Soviet leaders, even the most conservative, agreed that the Soviet Union should sharply reduce the costs of militarization and cut its defense budget.

The MIC, however, remained central to Gorbachev's dream of scientific-technical modernization of the Soviet Union. The Soviet leader was determined to have fewer guns but more butter in the future, yet he wanted to keep the MIC as a vehicle for taking the Soviet Union into the electronic-automatic age. "He was perplexed," one American scholar observed, "that one economic sector could accomplish so much that the rest of the economy seemed incapable of replicating . . . Much of his groping toward reform of the Soviet economy was based on an effort to resolve that paradox—to discover the 'secret' of the defense industry and apply it to the rest."[71] Much of the 200 billion in rubles earmarked in 1986 for "acceleration" was supposed to go toward the MIC structures. Between 1985 and 1988, state investments in electronics doubled. In November 1988, Gorbachev got another boost of confidence that those investments would pay off. The Soviet space program successfully launched, orbited, and landed a missile-shuttle called "Energy-Buran." The program employed about a million people from 1,200 enterprises across the whole Soviet economy. The budget was astronomical: $27 billion in today's prices. The 100-ton spaceship was similar to the US space shuttle and was able to land in a completely automatic manner, guided by computers. For the Soviet leader this was proof that, after a few years, the MIC would haul the rest of the Soviet economy out of its morass.[72]

So, investments into the MIC facilities and labs continued. The Ministry of Finance scrambled to find hard currency for Gorbachev's prize jewel. The defense complex also demanded and got more money to develop and produce modern equipment for the ailing industry of agriculture. The MIC took over the control of 250 plants that produced civilian goods, in an attempt to increase both their quantity and quality. Gorbachev authorized all those decisions. In January 1989, he proudly explained this to a group of the Trilateral Commission that included Henry Kissinger, David Rockefeller, President Valéry Giscard d'Estaing of France, and the former Prime Minister of Japan, Yasuhiro Nakasone. Some "ardent friends of perestroika" in the Soviet government, Gorbachev said, had urged him to "do anything to provide goods for the market" in order to avoid a "people's revolt." Gorbachev explained why he had rejected this proposal: "We have been thinking not about one or two years, but about creating an economy that would yield us what we need in the quantity and quality of required goods. For that, we need structural policies, the course towards [scientific-technical] progress. We made very big investments in this sphere."[73]

On 25 January 1989, Gorbachev left Moscow for a winter break. He flew with Raisa to Pitsunda, a government dacha on the Black Sea. It was the resort where Nikita Khrushchev had vacationed in October 1964, on the eve of the coup that deposed him. The KGB reported to Gorbachev that many in the Party ruling elite increasingly doubted the direction of perestroika. The number of discontents, judging by KGB estimates, reached 60–70 percent of the top Party elite: members of the Central Committee who, according to Party rules, could elect and dismiss the General Secretary. Gorbachev, however, was not afraid of a conspiracy. The political and constitutional changes had secured his position. Also, Gorbachev had his own appointee as the new head of the KGB, Vladimir Kryuchkov, appointed in October 1988. Having been Andropov's lifetime aide, Kryuchkov was a bureaucrat without political ambitions, and he apparently enjoyed the full trust of the General Secretary.[74]

The main concern for Gorbachev in Pitsunda was different: how to continue perestroika? As always, he turned to Lenin for a clue. Before leaving for Pitsunda, the Soviet leader found time to read "Lenin in Zurich," a documentary pamphlet written by the Russian anti-communist émigré Alexander Solzhenitsyn. It was published in 1975, after Solzhenitsyn was expelled from the Soviet Union at Andropov's suggestion. Solzhenitsyn's piece was a documentary study about the Bolshevik leader in 1916, on the eve of the Russian Revolution, when Lenin was living as a political émigré in Switzerland, was bored, and complained he would never live to see action again. The pamphlet tore to pieces the myth of a kind and humane Lenin. Solzhenitsyn used Lenin's correspondence with his lover Inessa Armand and other people to present a revolutionary fanatic who ranted and raved at his enemies and disciples alike. Solzhenitsyn also made a point that Russian nationalists had been making since 1917: Lenin viewed the Russian state and people as fuel for his world revolution. In the Soviet Union the pamphlet remained taboo; its reading was punished by imprisonment. Gorbachev's copy had been printed specially for the high Party nomenklatura. In a long monologue to Chernyaev after reading the pamphlet, Gorbachev admitted that Lenin was a destroyer: "And always alone against everyone." In front of his surprised aide, the excited Gorbachev began to impersonate Lenin, mimicking his style and gestures, his accent and favorite words, his acrimony and ire. This bizarre performance lasted for over an hour.[75]

Lenin's political loneliness resonated with Gorbachev. So did the unique ability of the Bolshevik leader to turn a seemingly intractable problem on its head, getting ahead of all others and seizing the political moment. Just as Lenin had dismissed all his critics as distractors, so Gorbachev viewed all doubters of perestroika as "conservatives," the "left" and "right" deviationists, "the ballast" for his idea of a revolution. Prompted by KGB reports, Gorbachev decided to purge the remaining Old Guard: about one hundred octogenarian members of the top state nomenklatura who had remained in the Party's Central Committee because of their past achievements and service. After his return to Moscow, he began to meet with the targeted stalwarts, apparently one to one, and convinced them to retire "voluntarily."[76]

After Pitsunda, Gorbachev distanced himself even more from discussion of economic and financial problems. He swung between Ryzhkov and the conservatives in the Politburo, but he was not interested in the nuts and bolts of reform. The Soviet leader never invited Abalkin or other economists to explain what was happening with the Soviet budget, supply and demand. Lenin's fixation was on a world revolution. Gorbachev became fixated on democratization. It was for him now even more than a precondition for successful modernization. Gorbachev convinced himself that he had a historic mission to guide the Soviet Union towards its social-democratic renewal.

Gorbachev's developing political views were powerfully affected by literary and historical revelations of glasnost. The second half of 1988 and early 1989 became a time of great cultural creativity in the Soviet Union: thick literary journals and mass circulation newspapers competed in publishing revisionist essays about history, novels and memoirs by banned authors, diaries and manuscripts buried for decades in secret archives. Writers and journalists rushed to bring out in print everything they had been accumulating over decades of their creative life. The cumulative effect was powerful. Not all publications had the power of Solzhenitsyn's pamphlet, yet each presented a fragment of Soviet history and culture that had defied and destroyed its literary canon and imaginative life. The dreary Party discourse was replaced by an effervescent intellectual feast of unexpected ideas, a baffling variety of ways of seeing and speaking. "How many ideas and talents in Russia," enthused Chernyaev in his diary. "What freedom! This alone is a great achievement that will make history forever, *even if nothing comes out of perestroika proper.*" Chernyaev, sensitive to the most minute motives of his boss, recorded a similar shift of perspective in Gorbachev. He "has been thinking about it and does not rule out failure," recorded Chernyaev after Pitsunda. "But he is entirely in a passionate surge . . ."[77]

The surge was genuine: Gorbachev had embarked on a mission to give his country and people "universal values" and freedoms they had never experienced before. He would continue to emancipate Soviet people, make them "masters of their factories and their land." He would take more power from the Party apparatus and give it to "the Soviets," the national republic, and local people's councils. The high-minded General Secretary was so fixated on this that he willingly overlooked history lessons apparent to those who had read widely on world and Russian history. Apparently, Gorbachev had never read about the Great Reforms in Russia during the period between 1861 and 1881. Tsar Alexander II had granted freedoms to peasants, and civil rights to broad groups of Russians and non-Russians. This had put Russia on the track of rapid modernization, but it also radicalized the educated youth and produced large numbers of radical intelligentsia; the non-Russian periphery of the empire (Poland) rebelled and a group of revolutionaries declared war on the Tsar and assassinated him in broad daylight in 1881. The British historian Dominic Lieven, a descendant of the aristocratic clan that had served the Russian monarchy, wrote in 1994 that "knowledge of Alexander II's goals, strategy and dilemmas allowed one to predict very accurately many of the problems Gorbachev was bound to face."[78]

Other great writers would have been instructive for Gorbachev, had he read them. Alexis de Tocqueville, the French conservative thinker, wrote about the fall of the French *ancien régime* in 1789 as follows: "Only a great genius can save a prince who undertakes to alleviate the lot of his subjects after a lengthy period of oppression. Evils which are patiently endured when they seem inevitable become intolerable once the idea of escape from them is suggested."[79] This was a powerful warning about the perils of a sudden release of mass emotion after decades of communist dictatorship. The developments of 1988 and early 1989, especially nationalist mobilization and economic discontent both in Eastern Europe and within the Soviet Union, provided early demonstrations of this phenomenon. Gorbachev could not ignore those signs of the gathering storm. And yet, he rushed headlong into the storm with remarkable confidence. In the spring of 1989, a revolution conceived by Gorbachev and his narrow circle of lieutenants took on a life all of its own. The ship had sailed; the time for "theorizing" had passed. In March 1989, Gorbachev's 400-page book, *Perestroika: Tested by Life*, was prepared for print. It was never published. Events soon overtook everything the Soviet leader had written or even imagined.

Gorbachev expected that the foreign policy of détente would end the danger of nuclear war and procure a more benign environment for his perestroika. He aimed to bring an end to the Cold War and open the Soviet Union to the West, to facilitate modernization and domestic reforms. Yet as 1989 began, he achieved none of those goals. Instead, his reforms began to undermine economic stability and triggered separatism. Gorbachev's attitude to reforms and power presented a major paradox. From Andropov, he had inherited awesome power, which allowed him to make radical changes. Continuing perestroika for him, however, meant devolving power "to the people." His reforms had passed economic levers from the central regulators to local enterprises. He then decided to pass political levers from the Politburo to the Congress of People's Deputies; from local Party organizations to local Soviets. In less than two years this course of action would destabilize the Soviet state, ruin its finances, and make the father of perestroika a "sorcerer's apprentice," unable to control the destructive forces he had unleashed.

CHAPTER 3

REVOLUTIONS

They that sow the wind, shall reap the whirlwind

Hosea 8:7

GOODBYE LENIN

On 26 March 1989, 172.8 million citizens of the Soviet Union cast their vote to elect the Congress of People's Deputies. For the first time since 1917, independent candidates opposed the Party candidates, and many of them won. It was the first contested elections in the communist world. With 2,550 seats, the Congress had five times more deputies than in the US Congress and over three times more than the Constituent Assembly of 1918, disbanded by Lenin.

The deputies were elected in three ways. The first group, one-third of all seats, were elected by direct vote across the land. The second one-third came from the "national-territorial" districts, representing the multi-national nature of the Soviet Union. The Russian Soviet Socialist Republic elected 403 deputies, the largest bloc among the republics of the USSR. The densely populated Ukraine followed with 143 seats. The small autonomies, such as Crimea and Tuva, elected one deputy each. The last group was elected by "public organizations" and represented the main segments of Soviet elites. The Communist Party, also considered a public organization, had a quota of 100 seats. Radical critics would soon speak about the "Red Hundred"—in reference to the violent "Black Hundred" movement that had supported Tsarism in the 1900s. They could not have been more wrong: Gorbachev selected the Party list and included in it many of his favorite intellectuals.[1]

In the Baltics, the nationalist movements won almost all twenty-two "national" seats, yet they also prudently supported the reformist Party leaders, among them Lithuania's Algirdas Brazauskas. The main electoral upheaval, however, took place in the Slavic core of the country: Party leaders lost their seats against completely unknown candidates in thirty-two major industrial regions of Moscow, Leningrad, the Urals, Siberia, and Donbass. In Leningrad and Moscow both workers and the intelligentsia voted against Party candidates: none of them got elected. In the "all-Moscow" elections, Boris Yeltsin ran as an independent against the Party-nominated director of a big automobile plant. Gorbachev unleashed the wave of people's wrath against "Party bureaucracy," and his rival rode this wave. Yeltsin projected resolve. His theatrical speeches, punctuated by movements of his big fist, had a mesmerizing effect. He received 89 percent of the ballot—over 5 million votes out of a total population of 8.8 million. Even state officials, including diplomats, the police, KGB officers, and the military, voted for Yeltsin in overwhelming numbers—and surprisingly, those votes were counted fairly.[2]

Gorbachev viewed the results of the elections as a trial by fire for the Party and concluded at the Politburo: "We must avoid intimidating people and ourselves." Shevardnadze and Yakovlev praised the triumph of democracy under a one-party system. Ryzhkov, a potential scapegoat for the poor Party performance, sided with Gorbachev.[3] The rest of the Politburo, however, refused to see black as white. Lukyanov urged Gorbachev to restore control over the press and television. He also proposed to delay the second phase of political reforms: the elections of similar congresses of deputies in the Russian Federation and other republics was scheduled within a year, in March 1990. Gorbachev dismissed both ideas.[4]

On 25 April, the Soviet leader faced the wrath of regional Party elites. The first Party Plenum after the elections began with a requiem for the Old Guard who now stepped down: this big group included managers and scientists who had begun their career under Stalin and turned the Soviet Union into a nuclear superpower. Their farewell speeches were calm and dignified. Then the storm broke. The new Party potentates from the industrial regions, promoted under Gorbachev, took the floor and lashed out against perestroika. Most vocal critics had just won competitive elections in their regions, yet they were convinced that the country was on the road to economic disaster and political turmoil. Several speakers from the Urals and Siberia said that the Law on Enterprises undermined productivity, prices, and management. The cooperatives were looting the market of cheap consumer goods. All critics were Russians, and they also raised questions about the Politburo's policies on national issues. Why did the leadership appease the Armenians and the Balts, giving them a greater share of economic resources? Why were glasnost journals and newspapers allowed to present the Party apparatus as the source of evil?

Did the Politburo really consider the regional Party cadres as the main enemies of reform?[5]

Gorbachev answered these questions with lengthy explanations, repudiating the accusations. Vorotnikov, a Politburo conservative, described Gorbachev's manner of address as "a stream of words, complicated, intricate phrases . . . In the end, all that verbiage confused the issue so much that people from different camps began to think that the general secretary actually supported its position." A Western scholar later interpreted this as a rhetorical skill to deflect the hardliners. Privately, Gorbachev spoke angrily of the Plenum as a coordinated attack against his course of action. He noticed that no one from the Politburo stood up against his critics, and this only reaffirmed his determination to transfer political power from the Party's elite to the Congress of People's Deputies.[6]

Gorbachev hoped that the Congress would empower the best forces within the Party and produce a new political elite. He was counting especially on the support of the Soviet intelligentsia, the educated class to which he and Raisa felt they belonged. The Soviet intelligentsia formed an impressive respresentation at the Congress: fifty-five writers, thirty-two theater directors and actors, fifty-nine journalists, sixteen artists, fourteen composers, and many people from scientific laboratories and institutes.[7] For Lenin, the Russian intelligentsia, especially people of culture, were "not brains, but the shit of a nation."[8] Gorbachev and Raisa, as students of the 1950s, believed the opposite. They venerated writers and scholars as a moral elite, a vanguard of modernization.

As in other aspects of perestroika, the Soviet leader was about to be deceived. One scholar of the Soviet intelligentsia aptly concludes: "If open discussion modeled on intellectual discourse had failed to produce a common political outlook among post-war intellectuals, how could it be expected to solve the crises of state socialism?"[9] In Moscow, the home of the Soviet intelligentsia, the educated elites had long stopped believing in the humane socialism that Gorbachev promoted.[10] The intellectuals split into two antagonistic camps: those who coveted political liberalization and Westernization, and the Russian nationalists with neo-Stalinist views. The Gorbachevs tried to curry favor on both sides—a hopeless exercise![11] In the spring of 1989, writers, scholars, and journalists—liberal-minded and nationalist alike—began to push political discourse far beyond what the architects of perestroika had deemed prudent and feasible. The barrage of publications in the Moscow media during those months attacked the foundations of Party rule. The sociologist Alexander Tsypko published a series of essays that questioned the revolutionary wisdom of Lenin. The well-known theater director Mark Zakharov urged on national television that the body of the Bolshevik leader should be removed from his Mausoleum. Before long, the sacral meaning of the Bolshevik Revolution itself would be up for fierce debate.[12]

REVOLUTIONS

The deputies elected from Moscow quickly formed an independent group. The Western media called them "liberals"; they called themselves "the first-wave democrats." Some in this group were intellectuals who had joined the Party during the Khrushchev Thaw (mid-1950s to mid-1960s) and dreamed of de-Stalinization; they worked in privileged academic institutions, and in 1986–88 they enjoyed the patronage of both Gorbachev and Yakovlev. Among them was Gavriil Popov, the editor-in-chief of the leading economics journal; Yuri Afanasyev, a historian of the French Revolution and board member of the Party's main theoretical journal *Kommunist*; and the prominent sociologist Tatiana Zaslavskaya.[13] There were younger deputies as well, who had grown up without communist illusions: the sociologist Galina Starovoitova, historian Sergey Stankevich, mathematician Ilya Zaslavsky, and physicist Arkady Murashov. The KGB's General Filipp Bobkov, whom Andropov had tasked in the 1970s with keeping the Soviet intelligentsia under control, wrote about such people as "a huge force" with "enormous brain-power," who could not claim status and income under the ossified Soviet system. This milieu, he concluded, produced nationalists in the Baltic republics, violent extremists in South Caucasus, and radical democrats in Moscow.[14] There was at least one element of truth in the general's crude estimate: "the democrats" believed that the Party system was ossified, but also obsolete, illegitimate, and criminal. They considered the anti-communist Solidarity movement in Poland as the model to emulate. In April 1989, the famous ophthalmologist Svyatoslav Fyodorov, whom Gorbachev elected to represent the Party at the Congress, proposed that all "democratic" deputies from Moscow should meet in his clinic to discuss common goals and tactics. Sergey Stankevich, then thirty-five, recalled that all of them were elated by their victory, yet also fearful. The forces of the Party nomenklatura still appeared to be overwhelming. The first instinctive desire was to look for allies: "We sent envoys and received guests . . . above all to the Leningraders . . . the Balts, the Ukrainians."[15]

The main authority within the group of "democrats" was Andrei Sakharov. He had designed the first Soviet nuclear weapons, but during the 1970s he became a world-famous human rights defender and received the Nobel Prize for his activities. He protested against the Soviet occupation of Afghanistan and spent 1980–86 in exile under KGB surveillance. Gorbachev allowed Sakharov to return to Moscow; in late 1988, with Yakovlev's assistance, Sakharov and other human rights defenders set up "Moscow Tribune," a discussion club of intellectuals, and "Memorial Society," a non-government organization to commemorate victims of Soviet repressions. When the elections to the Congress had been announced, the leadership of the Academy of Sciences of the USSR did not include Sakharov in the list of delegates. However, when hundreds of young scientists came forward to protest this decision, Sakharov was duly elected. At the meetings of Moscow democrats in the spring of 1989, Sakharov advocated a liberal-democratic agenda: the rule of law, civil society, and human rights. At one point, however, he said with disarming sincerity: "I am a freshly minted, one could say, young politician. But we do not know for how long this Thaw will last. A week, two weeks? Trust me: it can be snuffed out in an hour." The best tactic for the Russian democrats, he believed, was to reach for the sky: demand immediate and direct democracy, and tell millions from the podium as many "words of truth" as they would be allowed to say.[16] This was definitely not what Gorbachev expected or wanted.

Meanwhile other intellectuals, in South Caucasus, helped to produce another explosion of ethnic-territorial violence—and a new blow to Gorbachev's perestroika. The ethnic minority of Abkhazians, who had autonomy within the Georgian republic, were emboldened by the constitutional reforms and demanded that Abkhazia should become part of the Russian Federation. Abkhaz intellectuals from Moscow's academic institutions led the movement and wrote an appeal to the central authorities. In response, radical nationalists from the Georgian intelligentsia agitated for an immediate exit of Georgia from "the Russian empire." On 8–9 April 1989, the nationalist mobilization went out of control: in Tbilisi a huge rally occupied the central square. The Party leader of Georgia lost his nerve, fled into hiding, and called on troops, stationed in South Caucasus, to disperse the crowd. The officers and soldiers, mostly ethnic Russians, had no training to deal with civilians and did a hatchet job. Sixteen men and women died from beatings and a gas attack, trampled in the melee. Overnight the whole of Georgia erupted in a frenzy of anti-Russian, anti-communist revolt. Infuriated, Gorbachev ordered the Minister of Defense not to use force against peaceful gatherings under any circumstances. An emotional Shevardnadze was on the brink of resignation. Chernyaev was appalled that "a Christian people, much liked by Russians, with whom we had lived for two hundred years . . . want to leave the USSR." He began to envisage lying ahead "a collapse of the state and something like chaos."[17]

On 25 May 1989, the Congress of People's Deputies opened its first session in Moscow, to huge public expectations. The Politburo member Vadim Medvedev recalled the feelings of his colleagues: "It had become clear long before the Congress opened that we should expect something absolutely new and unprecedented." People noticed a historic coincidence: two centuries earlier, in 1789, in France, Louis XVI had convened the Estates General. Gorbachev, to everyone's surprise, was confident, almost "ecstatic." The Congress lasted for sixteen days, and during that time most activity in the Soviet Union was suspended. Millions of people stopped work and gathered in front of their television sets to watch the sessions: all of them were broadcast live and repeated across ten time zones.[18]

The opening ceremony of the Congress brought the first bombshell. A bearded deputy from Latvia ran up to a podium and shouted his demand to have a minute of silence to remember the victims of peaceful demonstrations in Tbilisi. He also shouted to set up a parliamentary inquiry into "the slaughter." This was the spontaneous act of a man who had participated in Stalin's time in the deportation of the Chechens by the secret police. Now this deputy sought justice and retribution. A few other deputies applauded him, then the majority joined in, under the impression that it was part of the script. Gorbachev, taken by surprise, applauded as well and stood for the minute of silence.[19]

Emotions were riding high at the Congress: fury, frustration, and memories of terror and injustice, pent up during many decades, broke loose. The Russian cultural historian Dmitry Likhachev was the oldest delegate at the Congress, and the atmosphere there reminded him of the first days of the Russian Revolution in March 1917. Then as now he saw people's faces and conduct changing in the same way. He told journalists: "The Congress liberated us from fear and taught us to speak the truth." But what would happen next? "Is it democracy or ochlocracy—a mob rule?" This was the question that Medvedev and other initiators of reforms had on their minds, as they observed from their seats the beehive of the Congress.[20]

Populist fury was on the rise beyond the Kremlin, in Moscow, Leningrad, and some of the Russian industrial regions. People responded with anger to revelations of the nomenklatura privileges: closed stores, exclusive resorts, special hospitals, and so on. Telman Gdlyan, a deputy from one of Moscow's districts, rode the tide of populism. He had grown up as a neo-Leninist believer and decided to become a prosecutor, to fight corruption. Under Andropov, he was sent to Uzbekistan to investigate the "cotton affair": a scam, when 4 billion rubles from the budget were paid to the republic for non-existing cotton production. Gdlyan's discoveries of corruption became a glasnost sensation and made him famous, a fighter against a sprawling Soviet "mafia." People approved of Gdlyan's KGB-style methods: his team arrested hundreds of officials and brutally interrogated them and their relatives. Gdlyan and his co-worker Nikolai Ivanov were elected to the Congress from Moscow and Leningrad respectively.[21]

Gorbachev was elected Chairman of the Supreme Soviet with all but eighty-seven votes of the assembly. This made him politically independent from the Party's elites. His power, however, was greatly diminished. The sociologist Max Weber had once formulated three types of authority: traditional, bureaucratic, and charismatic. Stalin's power had rested on all three, and was shrouded in mystery. Gorbachev inherited Stalin's authority to promote his revolution, while displaying the genuine charisma of a young, well-meaning leader. The Congress made political power transparent and electable, and thus destroyed its mystery. New charismatic figures took center stage: intellectuals, lawyers, and journalists, who became new national celebrities through their televised speeches. Gorbachev visibly struggled with his new role as a parliamentary leader. He would manipulate a discussion or cut off a microphone. He entered into altercations with others and had to endure insubordination. And he would soon face an opposition.[22]

Gorbachev's scheme of "democratic socialism" tolerated political factions. He allowed the Baltic and Moscow deputies access to the microphones; he cultivated his future antagonists. The Balts came to the Congress in force: almost a hundred pro-independence men and women. Their goal in Moscow was to agitate via the Soviet main media, cultivate allies and sympathizers, and do everything to delegitimize the use of force in domestic conflicts. They focused on denunciation of the "secret protocols" of the Molotov-Ribbentrop Pact of 1939, which they considered a basis for the Soviet annexation of Lithuania, Latvia, and Estonia. Many Party-State officials in those republics sympathized with this objective. In Lithuania, the Party leader Brazauskas and Vytautas Landsbergis, the nationalist leader of *Sajudis* (the Reform Movement of Lithuania), worked out a plan of action in Moscow, meeting out of earshot of the KGB.[23]

The independent-minded Moscow deputies, intellectuals who were grouped around Sakharov, declared that they wanted to support Gorbachev "conditionally," in other words only if he adopted their agenda. They interpreted Gorbachev's tolerance as weakness and his attempts to bring order to the discussions on the floor as an intolerable diktat. They aligned themselves with populist figures such as Gdlyan and Ivanov, and cultivated Yeltsin as a unique figure who had fallen from the pinnacle of the power system and now berated it for its corruption and privileges, to the delight of huge crowds of Muscovites. At the Congress, however, the "democrats" and populists were still a small minority. During the elections to the Supreme Soviet, the permanent ruling body of the land, the Moscow deputies, as well as Yeltsin and Sakharov, failed to get enough votes. This was not simply because of a conflict between "liberals" and "reactionaries," as the Western media described it. For years people from the provinces had been both envying and hating Moscow as a seat of power and privileges. Now the provincial deputies considered Moscow intellectuals, who posed as "democrats," as a pampered elite, and did not react well to their sermons. The Muscovite deputies exploded. Yuri Afanasyev, in an angry speech, denounced the "aggressive-obedient majority" who were allegedly blocking reforms that were expected by the people. It would become customary for the

Moscow intellectuals in politics to speak on behalf of "the people" against anyone who did not share their agenda.

The Politburo's Medvedev recalled: "I was in two minds: emotionally it was hard to suppress a feeling of revenge" against the self-righteous Moscow intellectuals. "At the same time, I realized very well that the Supreme Soviet would be unthinkable without [the elected Muscovites, Yeltsin, Sakharov, and other independent deputies], that a confrontation and their removal would . . . only aggravate the situation." Gorbachev felt the same way. Yeltsin, the leading rebel, kept a low profile and behaved reasonably. When his supporters proposed his candidacy for the leader of the Supreme Soviet, he prudently recused himself. After a series of procedural moves, however, and with the connivance of Gorbachev, the independents managed to get a seat for Yeltsin in the Supreme Soviet. Vorotnikov, an attentive conservative observer, wrote that Gorbachev "pulled Yeltsin inside . . ." and was clearly "relieved" when it happened.[24]

The group of independent-minded deputies, however, felt no gratitude towards Gorbachev. They announced they were forming an opposition to the Party called the "Inter-regional Deputies' Group" (Mezhregionalnaia Deputatskaia Gruppa, or MDG). They were joined by deputies elected as independents from Leningrad, the Urals, Siberia, Ukraine and Belorussia, the Baltic republics, and South Caucasus. This was the first political opposition in the country since 1927. The group's motives were diverse: the only common goal was to act against the existing system of power. Roy Medvedev, the historian and former Soviet dissident who attended the MDG meetings as an observer, recorded their contradictory demands: transition to "a free market"; a reduction in the production and export of raw materials for ecological reasons; a rapid increase in the construction of houses and apartments, hospitals, schools, resorts for the handicapped and veterans; and an increase in pensions. The opposition consisted of 250 deputies, over half of them non-Russian nationals. Its "coordinating board" included Sakharov, Popov, Afanasyev, Yeltsin, and a deputy from Estonia. "As a recent dissident," Medvedev recalled, "I felt sympathetic to many of these demands." What dismayed him, though, was the sense of haste. The MDG intellectuals, even Sakharov, operated on the "now or never" and "win or perish" principles.[25] Most of this first wave of democrats had no idea how to fix the economy and finances. Afanasyev said to a journalist: "If this feeling of freedom, which we all have now, means we have to wait a few years more to get a better economy, I am ready to pay this price."[26]

The image of an "aggressive-obedient" majority, however, consolidated the MDG ranks. At one point, Sakharov took the floor to denounce atrocities of the Soviet military in Afghanistan. In the huge hall, almost 2,000 people were suddenly united by a feeling of hatred towards this dissident who was questioning their Soviet patriotism. One deputy, a veteran of the Afghan war, where he had lost his legs, lashed out at Sakharov for his disrespect for the Soviet army. His speech ended with a slogan: "Great Power! Homeland! Communism!" Anatoly Sobchak, a member of the MDG from Leningrad, compared this moment to a political earthquake: everyone around him sprang to their feet in a patriotic frenzy. Sobchak felt as if some kind of powerful spring was trying to yank him from his chair, and he had to exercise great self-control in order to remain seated. Sakharov walked again to the podium to explain his stance, yet he was overwhelmed by the collective venom in the hall.[27]

Another pivotal moment occurred on the last day of the Congress. Sakharov asked Gorbachev to speak, but Sakharov himself took the floor and, with no regard for time, continued to talk about a new agenda for the future, apparently intent on detailing all of the opposition's demands. Gorbachev, reacting to the growing irritation of the majority in the hall, tried to stop him, and after twenty minutes he disconnected Sakharov's microphone. That merely served as a prop-aganda coup for the opposition. Sakharov was no great public speaker, but the sight of this old man on national television, moving his lips without sound because the audience were booing in disapproval, was the last impression that many people took away from the Congress. Many felt that Gorbachev repre-sented a political system that was silencing "the conscience of the intelligentsia."

Shakhnazarov wrote in 1992 that Gorbachev would go down in history as "the father of parliamentarianism" in Russia. Both admirers and critics agreed that his daring experiment would take an enormous amount of time and effort. The entire summer of 1989 was dedicated to the formation of committees on budgetary and economic reforms, taxation, and other issues. Those committees began to work only in the fall and then prepared their first bills: on land and property, labor conflicts, etcetera. Gorbachev was proud of his overhaul of the country's entire legal system. Yet, bills could only be voted into law at the next session of the Congress in December. By that time, the Soviet Union would already be in a full-blown economic and political crisis.[28]

The main message of the new Supreme Soviet, created by the Congress, was "down with the administrative-bureaucratic system." Much of the legislative work was inspired by the desire to create an economy that would be neither "totalitarian" nor capitalist. The newly minted parliamentarians, showing their zeal to the electorate, presented numerous costly requests to the government to expand the safety-net programs. But just how the necessary means and funds were to be procured was not their concern. Some committees began to act as clearing houses for new lobbies representing enterprises and cooperatives, as well as export-oriented interests. To those economic actors, the Supreme Soviet was prone to grant a higher share of profits and lower taxes. Abalkin, author of the government's austerity program, complained at the end of July 1989 that the

Supreme Soviet "has not passed a single bill to correct the [economic] situation," and thus contributed to the growing impression of "state impotence."[29]

In the old system, represented by the Politburo and the Council of Ministers, there were many flaws. Yet at least the Politburo could be used to deploy new policies and correct mistakes. After June 1989, however, the Politburo could no longer assume that its decisions would be passed by the Congress and the parliament. The Supreme Soviet asserted its control over all government ministries and agencies, using its power of appointment. The deputies confirmed Ryzhkov as Prime Minister but, acting on a populist whim, voted out over half of the Council of Ministers. Among them was a candidate to be Chairman of the State Bank, a well-respected professional called V. Gribov. As Ryzhkov hastily searched for an alternative candidate, his choice fell on Viktor Gerashchenko, a banker with many years of banking experience in the West. Gerashchenko knew his job would be hard as the Soviet financial system was being rapidly destabilized. He spoke with his father, who had been deputy director of the State Bank under Stalin, managed Soviet finances in extraordinary conditions of war and recovery, and lost his job when he criticized Khrushchev's profligate policies. Gerashchenko's father said to him: "Why the hell do you need this?" In the past, only the General Secretary of the CPSU could instruct the State Bank what to do. Yet now the chief banker of the Soviet Union had to respond to the people's deputies, who naïvely believed that "people's control" over the Bank would lead to prosperity for all. Gerashchenko took the job nonetheless, in the hope of limiting the damage to the country's finances.[30]

While the parliament sorted out its functions, discontent with Gorbachev's reforms broke out among the workers in Kuzbass, a big industrial zone in South-Central Siberia that depended on the centralized system of supply and delivery of goods and products across several time zones. This system had been suffering from decades of neglect, but Gorbachev's decentralizing reforms dealt it the final blow. Now even basic supplies were not being delivered; local cooperatives sold basic goods and food for high-end market prices. After watching the Congress on television, the miners sent a collective letter to the Supreme Soviet with a list of complaints and demands, but they got no reply. In July 1989, all across the Russian Federation and Ukraine, mining shafts were shut by their working collectives one after another: about 200,000 miners went on strike and formed striking committees. Strikers demanded a steady supply of consumer goods, food, more housing, new infrastructure and equipment in hospitals, and more medicines in drugstores. Local Party and state officials, after their initial shock and resistance, backed those demands.[31]

This was the first serious revolt of the Russian working class since 1962. Organized strikes remained illegal in the Soviet Union. Yet the Supreme Soviet acknowledged the strikers' demands were "fair and just" and allocated 10 billion rubles to purchase consumer goods and medicines. Throughout July and August, Ryzhkov, his deputies, and relevant ministries in the Council of Ministers negotiated with the miners. The state ministries imported the required goods. Those purchases had to be paid for with foreign credits or sales of gold from state reserves. The coal-mining ministry raised the miners' wages. The strikes began to abate. Their cost to the Soviet budget was at least 3 billion rubles; the estimate of total economic losses from strikes stood at 8 billion rubles. The Supreme Soviet continued its politics of economic populism by raising pensions, aid to the handicapped and war veterans, and so on. Gerashchenko at the State Bank had to find non-existing funds to pay for this. Abalkin's austerity plans were consigned to the dustbin; the state budget deficit grew and would soon be a staggering 100–120 billion rubles.[32]

"Is this capitulation by the rulers?" mused Shevardnadze's aide in his diary. "Or is this their alliance with the working class against the conservative 'swamp'?" Gorbachev in his memoirs called the miners' strike "a stab in the back" and "perhaps the most serious trial for perestroika." When he discussed reforms, he mentioned Margaret Thatcher. The "Iron Lady" had crushed the British miners' strikes in 1984–85; Gorbachev, by contrast, made concessions to them. The Soviet leader also delegated all trouble-shooting to Ryzhkov. In Chernyaev's diaries, usually so revealing, there is nothing about the events of this summer: Gorbachev's aide was too busy or too depressed to express his views. In his last entry before the summer break, Chernyaev predicted that Gorbachev would lose his authority among the Russian people, because he did not cut a strong figure as leader of the Soviet Union.[33]

Gorbachev was too self-confident to reveal any apprehensions. In July he met with workers from the Kirov factory (in 1917 their predecessors had taken part in the Russian Revolution), but returned visibly shaken. He had witnessed their rising anger against profiteers from the cooperatives; and the workers did not support his reforms. Gorbachev suspected that Moscow democrats were agitating the miners (they were not).[34] Now he no longer wanted to turn to Russian workers for their support. He felt more comfortable dealing with parliamentarians and intellectuals.

HISTORY ACCELERATES

In the spring and summer of 1989, another dramatic development occurred within the Soviet political elites: the Iron Curtain that prevented them from going abroad suddenly parted. This had revolutionary implications for Soviet politics, especially for the educated Moscow-centered intelligentsia. Since

REVOLUTIONS

Stalin's times, the West had been the forbidden fruit and the object of intense curiosity for Soviet citizens. The post-Stalin intelligentsia held an "imagined West" as a vital part of their identity, dreams, and cultural self-validation. Several educated cohorts had grown up with a veritable obsession with and idealization of Western culture and music, first jazz, then rock. Many of those people who learned to despise the Soviet system under Brezhnev felt uncritical admiration for all things Western.

In Leonid Brezhnev's household, the General Secretary and his wife had watched Soviet news and entertainment. Their grandchildren instead watched Western movies and cartoons on a large Sony TV screen with a video-cassette recorder (VCR). By 1989, VCRs, along with personal computers, became the most coveted object of social status, as well as an informational tool. Hundreds of new "cooperatives" began to import and sell them in great numbers on the Soviet market, a trade more lucrative than still illegal currency exchange. Yet nothing could be a substitute for the experience of crossing borders. "Trips to the West were the most important status symbol," wrote the Russian scholar Dmitry Furman. "See Paris, and die," was a popular joke, but also a dream for many in the Soviet Union. Scientists, artists, dancers, symphony orchestras, and many Soviet Jews lived in fear that they would not obtain clearance from "competent organs" to cross the Soviet borders—for no apparent reason other than that somebody higher up the pyramid of power questioned their loyalty or someone close to them informed on them. Memoirs from the post-Soviet period are replete with anger and drama regarding the abrogation of that clearance.[35]

In early 1989, the Soviet rules for foreign travel were radically relaxed. It was no longer necessary to grovel and conform to Soviet authorities, including the Party and the KGB, in order to obtain permission for a private trip abroad. During the first half of 1989, the number of approved applications for exit visas reached 1.8 million, three times more than two years earlier. During the same period about 200,000 people received official permission to emigrate, mostly to Israel and the United States.[36] The majority, however, applied for a foreign Soviet passport and a permit to leave the USSR and return—for the first time in their life. Bureaucrats and officials, directors of enterprises, cooperative managers, academic scholars, scientists, artists and actors rushed under the rising curtain. Performers went to perform, artists sold their art, intellectuals delivered talks. The glasnost journalists, academic scholars, government officials, especially those who knew some English and other foreign languages, were in high demand abroad. Western universities, the United States Information Agency (USIA), think tanks, fellowship programs, foundations all used their funds to invite Soviet visitors. Intellectuals were invited by Western foundations.

Scholars have studied this phenomenon exclusively as a factor in bringing the Cold War to an end.[37] Yet, it also delegitimized the Soviet system. Most Soviet diplomats, KGB officials, and military representatives abroad had become habituated to navigation between the West and their homeland; they lived in a kind of controlled schizophrenia. Gorbachev traveled abroad several times in the late 1960s and 1970s, and began to see a humiliating gap between the abundance in Western stores and a dearth of goods in Soviet ones.[38] Yet this was nothing compared with the shock that thousands of Soviet people experienced when they crossed Soviet borders and visited Western countries from early 1989 onwards—many of them for the first time. In May of that year, Shevardnadze's aide and speechwriter Teimuraz Stepanov wrote in his diary about West Germany: "The Devil took us to this Federal Republic, so groomed, preened, accurate, and caressed, where it is particularly painful to think about my beloved country—dirty and exhausted from futile efforts to overcome the utmost ugliness created by the most inhumane regime in the world." A few days later in Irkutsk, on the way to the Sino-Soviet summit, he wrote with even more bitterness: "Who said that my Motherland is less beautiful than the German Heimat . . .? It is, however, gutted [by the apparatchiks] armed with Party directives and a never-ending Marxist-Leninist world view."[39]

For first-time Soviet travelers to the West a visit to a supermarket produced the biggest effect. The contrast between half-empty, gloomy Soviet food stores and glittering Western palaces with an abundant selection of food was mind-boggling. Not a single Soviet visitor was prepared for the sight of pyramids of oranges, pineapples, tomatoes, bananas; endless varieties of fresh fish and meat, in lieu of a butcher cutting chunks from bluish hulks from a freezer; efficient cashiers with a smiling attitude, instead of rude saleswomen doling out greasy cans and jars to a long line of desperately hungry customers. And then actually to be allowed to touch, to smell, to savor! A severe aftershock awaited Soviet visitors upon their subsequent return to the Soviet Union, and to scenes of misery. This experience changed Soviet travelers forever. Western standards, unimaginable before, immediately became the new norm. Soviet realities, part of everyday habit, suddenly became "abnormal" and therefore revolting, unbearable.[40]

Most of the newly elected deputies of the Supreme Soviet traveled to the West in March–August 1989 for the first time at the invitation of Western parliamentarians, universities, non-governmental institutions, and émigré friends and relatives. Gennady Burbulis, elected to the Congress of People's Deputies, had grown up as an admirer of Lenin and joined the Party on his centennial in 1970. Because of his security clearance (he had served in strategic rocket forces during his obligatory draft), he never had a chance to travel outside the Soviet Union. In June 1989, however, he joined the MDG opposition in the

Supreme Soviet and traveled with a group of other deputies to Stockholm for a seminar on "Swedish socialism." Many years later he still recalled the shock from visiting a giant fish supermarket: a mile of stands and aquariums filled with fresh fish, oysters, calimari, shrimp, and other sea creatures. Equally amazing for Burbulis was the absence of long lines of customers. Burbulis left Stockholm as an enthusiast of "Swedish socialism" and an even more bitter enemy of the Soviet Party system.[41] Another member of this group, Nikolai Travkin, a construction worker and Soviet patriot, joined the MDG as a fan of "democratic socialism." His Soviet identity also crumbled in Stockholm. He returned to Moscow an angry man, convinced that the communists had been fooling Soviet people all along. In March 1990 he quit the Party and launched the Democratic Party of Russia in an attempt to seize power from the nomenklatura.[42]

The most consequential eye-opening experience occurred to Boris Yeltsin. In June 1989, he asked the American ambassador Jack Matlock to help him visit the United States. The idea came from Yeltsin's aides Lev Sukhanov and Pavel Voshchanov, who wanted to raise his international profile. Matlock's attempt to contact US Congressmen and their staff did not produce results; then Yeltsin's people discovered Gennady Alferenko, a remarkable cultural entrepreneur, founder of one of the first cultural NGOs of Gorbachev's era. Alferenko specialized in East-West public diplomacy and operated under KGB supervision. He contacted Jim Garrison from the Esalen Institute, an esoteric cultural center in Big Sur, California. The two worked out a ten-day lecture tour for Yeltsin across the United States; the proud Russian wanted to pay for all his expenses abroad. The tour began in New York on 9 September 1989 and covered eleven cities in nine states. This visit was more intense than Khrushchev's "discovery of America" in 1959. And it was to have even more impact on the fate of the Soviet Union.[43]

Available accounts of Yeltsin's journey vary from stories of drinking bouts, scandals, and gaffes to descriptions of his eye-opening experiences.[44] All of them were true. Yeltsin's political agenda was still to build a "democratic socialism," but without the Party monopoly on power. This was what he wanted to tell Americans and their leaders. He relished attacking Gorbachev on every occasion and in every interview. At the top of Yeltsin's list of engagements was a meeting with President George Bush. Jim Garrison knew Condoleezza Rice, who worked at the National Security Council on Soviet affairs, and contacted her. Ultimately, Yeltsin met instead Bush's National Security Advisor, General Brent Scowcroft. President Bush "dropped by" for a chat during that visit. The Russian and his aides left the White House in a triumphant mood. Sukhanov recalled: "Yeltsin was the first among the high-placed Soviet leaders who broke 'the seal' on the White House during the rule of Bush. Not Gorbachev, but Yeltsin."[45]

The United States was the first country that Yeltsin had ever visited outside the Soviet Union on his own rather than as part of an official Soviet delegation. He was feted and dined by wealthy Americans, flown by private jets, and stayed in the houses of American millionaires. Although he expected the lifestyle of the super-rich to be a never-ending feast, the real shock for him was his impromptu visit to Randalls discount supermarket, on the way to Houston Airport. As a regional party secretary, Yeltsin had spent years battling with lack of food supplies in his Sverdlovsk region. His greatest achievement had been to establish a system of poultry farms near Sverdlovsk that supplemented the meagre diet of workers in the industrial plants and factories. Randalls supermarket amazed him. This was an average place where the poorest American could buy what even the top Soviet nomenklatura could not back home. In the sweltering Texan desert Yeltsin and his entourage entered an air-conditioned paradise. The aides saw Yeltsin brooding, as if he was thinking: "Does this cornucopia exist every day for everyone? Incredible!"[46]

Yeltsin realized how stupid he must have appeared in the eyes of his American hosts when he repeated the slogans of "democratic socialism." He said to his aides: "What did they do to our poor people? Throughout our lives, they told us fairy tales, tried to invent the wheel. And the wheel already exists ... yet not for us." An aide wrote that "the last prop of Yeltsin's Bolshevist mentality decomposed" at this moment. After returning from his American trip, while speaking to journalists and his MDG colleagues, Yeltsin regaled them with details of his supermarket visit. He waxed lyrical about the "madness of colors, boxes, packs, sausages, cheeses," and rhapsodized that the average American family spent one-tenth or less of their salaries on food, while a Soviet family spent over half of their salaries on food, and more. Yeltsin decided that his mission now was to bring the "American dream" to the Russian people.[47]

The Congress of People's Deputies, the parting of the Iron Curtain, and liberalization in Eastern Europe had a spill-over effect on the Baltic nationalists. While the Supreme Soviet of the USSR sat in summer session in Moscow, Lithuanian deputies from *Sajudis* requested an official visit with the ambassador, Jack Matlock, and asked him point-blank whether the United States would recognize their independence. Matlock, stunned by their audacity and haste, explained that he and the American government were supportive of Baltic independence, yet sovereignty implied full control over the territory of a sovereign state. "So we're on our own?" one Lithuanian asked. Matlock felt stung by this question, but he had to confirm that if Soviet troops used force, the *Sajudis* nationalists would be as vulnerable as the Chinese students on

Tiananmen Square. The West would not even be able to provide economic aid, as long as the Soviet authorities were in control of all ports and communications.[48] Supporters of Baltic independence found no assistance forthcoming in Western Europe either, and even less sympathy.[49]

The Congress in Moscow created a special commission to investigate the German-Soviet talks in 1939; it was led by Yakovlev. The existence of a copy of the "secret protocols" was widely known in the West, where they had long been published. Yet the original documents remained locked away in Gorbachev's personal safe. He refused to acknowledge that Stalin's annexation of the Baltic states was a direct consequence of the deal between the Soviet leader and Hitler. "The unconditional denunciation [of the Pact] would have meant that we accept the main guilt for unleashing the Second World War," argued Vadim Medvedev at the Politburo. Gorbachev agreed. "Demagogues must be rebuffed. Otherwise, it looks like we waged the Second World War to acquire a miserable agrarian Lithuania!"[50]

The Balts took the matter into their own hands. The Russian miners' strikes emboldened them and strengthened their case. In August, Baltic nationalists decided to mobilize a massive protest on the fiftieth anniversary of the Molotov-Ribbentrop Non-Aggression Pact. Acting on the initiative of Estonia's Edgar Savisaar, on 23 August they staged a gigantic human chain that stretched all the way from Tallinn to Vilnius, some 600 kilometers. The media called it the "Baltic Way." The popular mood among the Balts was to break away from the Soviet Union as soon as possible. Millions of them did not believe that Gorbachev's program of liberalization would last. They therefore wanted to exit from the Union before this unique window of opportunity shut tight once again.[51]

In late July, Gorbachev proposed a new Union treaty that would transform the Soviet centralized state into a voluntary federation. Vladimir Shcherbitsky, long-time leader of the Ukrainian Communist Party, strongly objected: this would only open a can of worms. Eduard Shevardnadze was also pessimistic: he knew that Georgian nationalists, with the support of the masses, wanted full independence and demanded membership for Georgia in the United Nations. The reconstruction of a federation in turbulent times would only increase the risk of uncontrolled secession. Ryzhkov continued to push for an economic confederation, as long as the rights and property between the Center and the republics were delineated.[52] After the Baltic Way, Gorbachev shelved the proposal. He would, however, return to it one year later.

During the summer of 1989, the winds of independence spread to other national republics of the USSR. In Moldova, nationalists demanded independence. In Ukraine, a group of writers and intellectuals in Kharkov prepared the first conference of the People's Movement of Ukraine for Perestroika (*Rukh*). The authorization to set up this movement, along the lines of the Baltic popular fronts, had come from Gorbachev's office earlier. Shcherbitsky, leader of the Communist Party in Ukraine, strongly opposed this idea, but his days in power were numbered. The conference of Rukh opened on 8 September and lasted for three days. Most of the 1,200 delegates were Party members, but there was a minority of dissidents and former prisoners who demanded the restoration of an "organic" Ukrainian state that the Bolsheviks had disbanded in 1918.[53]

Among 500 guests at the conference were nationalist activists and intellectuals from the Baltics, South Caucasus, and delegates from the MDG. Eastern Europeans also came. The dissident members of Rukh were hugely impressed by the events in Poland, namely Solidarity's round-table discussions with the government and the quasi-free elections. Even more, they were inspired by the "Baltic Way." They vocally supported the Baltic denunciation of the German-Soviet Pact, although it was because of this agreement that Western Ukraine was annexed and became part of the Ukrainian Soviet Socialist Republic. The leadership of the Ukrainian Communist Party and the KGB were at the conference as well. Leonid Kravchuk, head of the agitation and propaganda department of the Ukrainian Party, was born in one of the regions that Stalin had annexed to the USSR in 1939. As Kravchuk listened to the nationalists, he concealed his emotions well. When someone pinned on his lapel a small blue-yellow flag—the colors of an independent Ukraine—Kravchuk took off his jacket just in case. But he did not remove the flag.[54]

In Moscow, independent deputies from the Supreme Soviet's MDG began to stage mass rallies in support of national movements within the Soviet republics. They did not want or expect a complete dissolution of the Soviet Union. On the contrary, Sakharov and his followers believed that complete and unconditional sovereignty and freedom of choice, based on the principle of national self-determination, was the only way to preserve the multi-ethnic country. Sakharov in particular was convinced that the Union forged by Lenin and Stalin had to be "reinvented" constitutionally as a voluntary "equal union of the sovereign republics of Europe and Asia," with a new constitution and a democratic central government. His constitutional project was to rebuild the country from the bottom up; to abolish small national-territorial districts and make republics the only subjects of the future Union. This was an intellectual utopia, but most of Sakharov's colleagues, Russian intellectuals, mimicked his folly. They believed that giving more power to the republics was an effective way to tame nationalism, or at least to bargain with separatists. In a sense, they were reaffirming the Leninist utopia.[55] The only exception was the ethnologist Galina Starovoitova. She worked for many months "in the field" in Abkhazia, Armenia, and Nagorny

Karabagh, and when the Armenian-Azeri conflict erupted, sided with the Armenian nationalists. Speaking at the meetings of the opposition in July 1989, Starovoitova said that, instead of the Soviet constitution of a future democratic federation, some republics should opt for full sovereignty and their own constitutions. "The reaction was negative," Starovoitova recalled. "Perhaps only Sakharov reacted positively." In September, she traveled to the United States for the first time, as a fellow of the Kennan Institute for Russian studies. She was surprised to find that American scholars, just like her colleagues at home, found her radical forecast of a Soviet break-up improbable. Only the scholars and activists of Baltic and West Ukrainian descent expressed their heartfelt approval.[56]

"REVOLUTION EQUALS INSTABILITY!"

In early August 1989, Gorbachev left Moscow for his customary Crimean vacation. In his luxurious villa, he dictated to Chernyaev a theoretical text for a long-delayed Party Plenum on national affairs. The text did not pan out. Instead, Gorbachev issued "a declaration of the Central Committee" that described the Baltic Way and separatist course of the Baltic popular fronts as a conspiracy of "anti-Soviet, de-facto, anti-national elements," who whipped up "nationalist hysteria," "full of venom towards the Soviet order, to the Russians, to the CPSU, to the Soviet Army." The document was so much at odds with the new political atmosphere in the country that the Balts suspected it had been concocted by Party hardliners behind Gorbachev's back.[57] Gorbachev's approach could be described in the form of a Russian fairy tale: A peasant wanted to transport a wolf, a goat, and a sack of cabbage in his boat across the river; but he did not know how to do this in one go and simultaneously keep his load intact. In trying to regain his balance amid a host of problems, Gorbachev was thinking out loud in the presence of Chernyaev, as if arguing with some conservatives: "Stabilization will be the end of perestroika. Stability is stagnation. Revolution equals instability!"[58]

Chernyaev believed his boss was now out of touch. Gorbachev's aide was now in agreement with those who wanted "to bury" Lenin. "They look into the core," he wrote. "For we cannot build our country on Leninism." Two weeks later, when observing the rising popular protests in East Germany, Chernyaev wrote that "the total dismantling of socialism as a global phenomenon was taking place" and concluded that it was probably "inevitable and good," because it meant "self-liquidation of a society that was alien to human nature and the natural course of things." Just as for other radicalized Party reformers, the liberal West began to look "natural" and "normal" to Chernyaev, in contrast to the "abnormality" of the Soviet Union. He had also got the bug of radical impatience. Why did

Gorbachev remain stuck with the old Politburo? Why did he not use his presidential status to get rid of the remains of the old political order? The only difference between Chernyaev and the opposition, which some of his friends joined, was his abiding loyalty to Gorbachev.[59]

Gorbachev refused to acknowledge that he was losing control over events, and over history. He composed speeches on Party unity and the harmonization of nationalities. In October 1989, he convened a conference of journalists and editors, where he, rather belatedly, accused the glasnost leaders of going too far, rocking the boat, and whipping up public passions. "People are at the end of their patience, we are sitting deep in kerosene," he complained, "and some of you carelessly throw matches." He singled out the sociologist Tatiana Zaslavskaya, who had predicted that the whole country would soon be on food rationing. He berated the economist Nikolai Shmelyov, who had published widely read articles about the failure of the Soviet economy. And he attacked one of the MDG organizers, Yuri Afanasyev, who had called for immediate freedoms and the right of republics to exit the Union. An editor of the hugely popular tabloid *Arguments and Facts* invoked Gorbachev's anger for publishing a ratings list in which Gorbachev was below Yeltsin. A witness recalled: "[Gorbachev] lectured us as if we were a class of naughty pupils . . . I saw him in a new light, an unfamiliar, ruffled man." The conference further diminished Gorbachev's authority: he managed to alienate those who respected him, but he did not use his power to oust any of them from their positions.[60]

The Soviet leader continued his course of reforming the Politburo. He eased out Shcherbitsky, who had questioned the wisdom of liberalization in Ukraine, and the ex-KGB leader Viktor Chebrikov, who had advocated the creation of an emergency apparatus of power under Gorbachev, to deal with separatism, economic recession, and rampant crime. Gorbachev took Chebrikov's proposal as a criticism of his method of governance. "I do not think we should create a parallel structure to implement decisions and to control their implementation," the General Secretary said. "We should co-opt people into our work. And this will not happen until people see improvements."[61] Those improvements never came.

Gorbachev filled the Politburo vacancies with his candidates: Yevgeny Primakov, an ambitious expert on the Middle East; Yuri Masliukov, Chairman of Gosplan, the State Planning Committee; and Vladimir Kryuchkov, the head of the KGB since the fall of 1988. Many historians and biographers wondered why Gorbachev elevated Kryuchkov, an apparatchik without any particular merits. Kryuchkov had been a lifelong aide to Yuri Andropov, and had transferred his unflagging loyalty to Gorbachev. The KGB chief promoted all the perestroika policies that Gorbachev wanted. The British ambassador commented on him: "Kryuchkov does a great imitation of an up-to-date and liberal police chief. But not all will be convinced."[62] Two years later, this baby-faced man would place his boss under house arrest.

In October and November 1989, Gorbachev's Politburo focused on the danger of the Lithuanian secession. They demanded that the Lithuanian leadership postpone a republican Party congress, which was expected to vote in favor of a political divorce of the Lithuanian Party from the CPSU. Their Party leader Brazauskas explained that it was impossible. Then Gorbachev sent a personal appeal to the Lithuanian "comrades": "Marching separately would take us into a blind alley," he wrote. "Only together, and only forward to a humane, democratic, prosperous society! With communist greetings, M. Gorbachev."[63] Everybody could see, however, that the Soviet Union was marching in quite a different direction. Discussing the Baltic separatists on 9 November, Gorbachev dropped a meaningful remark: "They have a new theme: 'We do not want to perish in the common chaos.' "[64]

THE WALL FALLS

Gorbachev's ambition was to synchronize domestic reforms with the construction of a "Common European Home." The Soviet leader, however, had a remarkably vague idea of what exactly this "home" would look like. He only knew that it was necessary for his ideological vision and for Soviet economic reforms. On 12 June 1989, he traveled to West Germany, this time with a large team of industrial specialists and managers. Gorbachev, just like Andropov, viewed Germans as key partners in the modernization of the Soviet economy. The Kremlin encouraged Soviet industries and enterprises to create "joint ventures" with West German firms: fifty-five such deals had already been reached. In Bonn, the Soviet delegation concluded eleven new agreements, many of them on economic cooperation.[65]

On 6 July, the Soviet leader was in France and delivered a speech to the Council of Europe in Strasbourg. In it he offered cooperation between the two parts of Europe that had long been divided. The Soviet Foreign Ministry, however, had not been informed about the content of the speech; Chernyaev had instructed a colleague, Vadim Zagladin, to draft the text: "Do not contact anyone or seek anyone's advice; do not disclose what you are working on." In Strasbourg, the speech received an ovation from socialist and social democratic deputies. In Gorbachev's address he implicitly supported the vision of France's President Mitterrand, of a Europe stretching from Vancouver to Vladivostok, but one that was also meant to check possible American attempts "to destabilize Eastern Europe." Gorbachev had a special request for Mitterrand; he asked him for his help to include the Soviet Union in the "world economy" and to include this issue on the agenda of the G-7 summit in Paris, 14–16 July 1989.[66]

During a one-on-one meeting in Bonn back in June, Helmut Kohl asked Gorbachev what would happen to Eastern Europe and East Germany. "With regard to our allies," the Soviet leader clarified, "we have a solid concept: everyone answers for himself." This was more than a renunciation of the Soviet right to intervene in Eastern Europe. It was in effect the end of any common policy within the Eastern bloc, a signal that each Eastern European country would be left to survive alone in the global economy. On 7–8 July, immediately after his triumph in Strasbourg, Gorbachev attended a political summit of the Warsaw Treaty Organization in Bucharest. There he pressed onto Eastern European leaders the same message he had delivered to Kohl. It was the moment when East Germany's Erich Honecker, Romania's Nicolae Ceaușescu, Bulgaria's Todor Zhivkov, and the Czechoslovak leadership finally realized that the Soviet Union was about to leave them to their own devices.[67]

There were numerous problems with Gorbachev's vision. Soviet economic reforms were not working; decentralization and changing rules on foreign trade were confusing potential Western partners. Lothar Späth, the Christian Democratic Union leader of the State of Baden-Württemberg, complained to Gorbachev that, in the past, Soviet ministries and other state agencies had signed contracts and provided financial and legal guarantees as to their completion. This system no longer worked; and the new system had not yet emerged. Soviet enterprises had the freedom on paper to engage in foreign transactions, yet their bosses did not know what they were allowed to do. "This complicates practical cooperation," concluded Späth.[68] Gorbachev ignored this important signal. Half a year later, however, this problem would bury Gorbachev's dream of modernizing the Soviet economy.

There was also the problem of timing. Left to its own devices, the communist nomenklatura in Eastern European countries began to realize that the keys to their future were no longer in Moscow but instead in Western capitals and banks.[69] This was especially true of Hungary and Poland. In both countries, the immediate prospect of default and bankruptcy pushed the leadership to co-opt the opposition into the government and hope the West would relent on their debts. This deal seemed to have worked at first in Poland: on 4 June 1989, the Poles voted in contested elections, second in the bloc after the Soviet elections, to elect their Senate and about one-third of the Sejm, the Polish Assembly. The opposition won the lion's share of the seats. At the same time, the opposition leaders still were not certain how far they could go without invoking a Soviet backlash. The bloody crackdown in China's Tiananmen Square, which happened so dramatically on the day of the Polish elections, restrained them considerably.

Still, the pro-Soviet leader of Poland, General Jaruzelski, was elected as the country's president by a majority of one vote. In Hungary, young people, including Viktor Orbán, then a democratic iconoclast, were eager to rock the boat of communist rule. And the Hungarian communist leaders followed this up, to test "the leash" that led to Moscow. In May, the communist Prime Minister Miklós Németh declared that, because of a shortage of funds, he would begin to remove the costly system of frontier installations with Austria, installed during the Cold War. Historians believe that this was the move that created a domino reaction: in September, East German refugees traveled to Hungary in order to cross the border into Austria, and then on into West Germany. This was the beginning of a terminal political crisis for the Honecker regime; in October, East Germany was already embroiled in a fever of popular revolution, with hundreds of thousands of people in Leipzig and other cities demanding economic and then political rights.[70]

Gorbachev, despite many warnings from Yakovlev and Soviet experts on Eastern Europe, was surprised by this acceleration of events. The Soviet internal crises affected the way Gorbachev, Shevardnadze, and their entourage viewed the accelerating changes in Europe. "It is clear that we will not intervene in Polish affairs," Teimuraz Stepanov confided in his diary on 19 August 1989. "We are stuck with our own disarray that we should fix. But how? Wherever you look—Hungary, the Baltics, or across the fence—everywhere there is disintegration of the order and the former state of things." Instead of a summer vacation, Stepanov accompanied Shevardnadze to Abkhazia in South Caucasus. The Foreign Minister of a superpower had to troubleshoot in his former bailiwick, and negotiate a truce between the Abkhazians and the Georgians. In the midst of this thankless mission, the news came from Moscow that in Poland the Sejm had elected the first non-communist Prime Minister, Tadeusz Mazowiecki, one of the Solidarity leaders. The Romanian ruler Ceauşescu requested an emergency meeting of the Warsaw Pact to deal with this matter. Stepanov reacted with fatalism: "In the key country [of the communist bloc] socialism is coming to an end calmly, without agony and painful convulsions."[71]

The real agony for Shevardnadze was not the future of Hungary, Poland, or even East Germany, but the tragedy taking place in his own homeland. The Georgian-Abkhaz inter-ethnic conflict grew worse by the day. Intellectuals and artists, who had been part of the Soviet intelligentsia all their life, became divided as mortal enemies, in the trenches of nationalism. There was no middle ground and violence spread fast. Andrei Sakharov, terrified by the vortex of hatred in South Caucasus, appealed to the Georgian intellectuals to respect the rights of ethnic minorities and defined the republic as a "mini-empire." This enraged Zviad Gamsakhurdia, the top nationalist behind Georgian rallies in Tbilisi in April. He blamed Sakharov for representing "Russian imperialism" and his wife, Yelena Bonner, for promoting "Armenian nationalism." Gamsakhurdia wanted "Georgia for Georgians" and had a fanatical mass following. In September 1989, 89 percent of Georgians believed their country should be independent of the USSR.[72]

The KGB, the GRU (the Soviet military intelligence service), and diplomats, stationed in Eastern Europe, bombarded Moscow in vain with their warnings about the political chaos in the region. The Soviet Embassy in the GDR proposed to interfere in the East German political crisis and work out political measures to regain the initiative. The leadership in Moscow ignored those messages. Finally, Gorbachev reluctantly agreed to take part in the commemoration of the fortieth anniversary of the GDR on 7 October 1989. He did not know what to say to the East German leaders. "Gorbachev goes to the GDR without a coherent policy," cabled the well-informed British ambassador from Moscow to London. "While he shuts his eyes and hopes that the German question will go away, events on the ground are overtaking him." Chernyaev quoted his boss saying that he wanted to go to Berlin "to support the revolution." It was a bizarre remark: the leader of the top communist country was about to express his solidarity with those in East Germany who demanded an end to the Soviet-run system. Yet Gorbachev was already on a mission to transform this system in his own country. He still believed he would make history, and not be regarded as someone who had merely bobbed on the surface of a revolutionary deluge.[73]

The Bush administration, on whose cooperation Gorbachev and other Soviet reformers had counted so much, watched with growing amazement the revolutionary developments inside the Soviet Union, and then in Eastern Europe. A junior member of the administration, Philip Zelikow, recalls that the White House was closely following how Gorbachev would react to the Polish elections. "That was the key test, and boy has he been passing it." And yet Bush and Scowcroft just could not believe that Gorbachev was letting Eastern Europe go. Scowcroft's deputy, Robert Gates, was convinced that Gorbachev's reforms would fail, and the Soviet Union would return to its belligerent ways. Secretary of Defense Dick Cheney thought that "the Soviets were as dangerous as ever, and despite its friendlier tone, communism remained just as evil as Reagan had once preached."[74]

In July 1989, Bush and his team toured Poland and Hungary, and then participated in the G-7 summit in Paris. He was impressed by the reforms in Poland and Hungary; the dismantling of the Iron Curtain moved him to tears; but the speed of change and the radicalism of anti-communist Eastern Europeans reminded him of the revolutions of 1956. He feared that this could lead once again to a Soviet backlash and intervention. All the US allies, above all President Mitterrand, believed that the Cold War was over, and that the American lack of communication with Gorbachev was intolerable. Bush tried to cool the enthusiasm of Western Europeans for Gorbachev's requests to bring the Soviet Union into the International Monetary Fund, World Bank, and the international talks on tariffs and trade (GATT), as well as to increase ties with the European Economic Community. The White House wanted to keep intact all structures that would allow the United States to continue waging the Cold War if necessary. Still, the trip to Europe had convinced Bush that the United States could not remain isolated from the process of rapid change. He therefore proposed to Gorbachev a "working meeting" in early December.[75]

As the fall of 1989 began, CIA analysts and the American Embassy reported to Bush and Scowcroft about potential disaster already developing *inside* the Soviet Union. During his visit, Yeltsin told them: "Perestroika is on the edge of collapse . . . There is a crisis in the economy and finances, with the Party, politics, nationalities."[76] On 21 September, Shevardnadze confirmed this message at his meeting with Bush and Scowcroft after the official talks.[77] Bush and Scowcroft ignored Yeltsin's words, but were struck by the candor of Shevardnadze's remarks. Still, the only scenario they could imagine was one like Tiananmen Square: the restoration of stability and order in the Soviet Union by the use of force.

Meanwhile, the popular movement in East Germany produced a spectacularly dramatic moment at the end of October, with mass demonstrations. In view of Gorbachev's deliberate refusal to get involved, the younger East German politicians scrambled to act themselves. They sent their aged leaders, the Party head Erich Honecker and the Stasi chief Erich Mielke, into retirement, and tried to put down the uprising by promising reforms. The new East German leader Egon Krenz knew that his state was bankrupt: the GDR had accumulated a large amount of debt that it owed to West Germany. Krenz rushed to Moscow to ask for Soviet assistance, but Gorbachev ignored his appeal: the Soviet budget was running low on foreign currency reserves. Scrambling for solutions, Krenz and his comrades promised East German citizens state-regulated travel to West Berlin. In the midst of their chaotic moves, an error by one confused official led to an unexpected release of pent-up tension: the opening of the Berlin Wall. On the night of 9 November 1989, a confused border guard let jubilant and stunned crowds of East Germans pass through formidable checkpoints and pour into West Berlin.[78]

During the rest of November, the communist regimes in Eastern Europe, led by Soviet clients, toppled one after another. The cautious Czechoslovaks followed in the footsteps of the triumphant East Germans and staged "a velvet revolution" demanding the end of Party rule and the withdrawal of Soviet troops. In Bulgaria, people did the same. Pragmatic people of the communist nomenklatura in those countries hurried to get rid of the compromised leaders, alter their political colors, and add "democratic" to the changed names of their parties. In Poland and Hungary, the ruling parties melted away like snow, while their leaders declared allegiance to political pluralism, democracy, and Western values.[79]

The revolutions of 1989, just like the radicalization in the Soviet Union during this year, was caused, among other factors, by a mass seduction of people by Western-style consumerism. While thousands of East Germans danced on the Berlin Wall in an ecstasy of freedom, hundreds of thousands swamped luxurious stores in West Berlin; they wanted to see, touch, and savor the forbidden fruit. "During the chaotic days of the Cold War's end in East Germany and throughout Eastern Europe," observed an American scholar, "capitalist-made consumer goods often seemed both the symbols and the substance of freedom." At the end of 1989, *Playboy* magazine claimed it was "exporting the American dream" as the first American consumer magazine published in Hungarian.[80]

"The post-Wall effect" now stood for a triumph of the West over the Soviet Union. William Taubman summed this up as follows: "The fall of the Berlin wall eventually changed almost everything. Until then, Gorbachev was the prime initiator of change . . . Afterward, he had to react to changes initiated by others—by masses of people on the ground in the GDR, by Eastern European politicians moving beyond Communism, by Western European and American leaders ignoring or challenging Gorbachev's vision."[81] Gorbachev himself, however, seemed unable to grasp the symbolic and political significance of what had happened. He was too busy with internal troubleshooting. On the night the Wall was breached, the Politburo retired late, following a long discussion about internal problems, above all Lithuania. Six days later, in a public speech, the Soviet leader rejected Margaret Thatcher's declaration about the "crumbling of the totalitarian socialist system" in Eastern Europe. He also told the British ambassador with breathtaking aplomb that events "are going in the right direction . . . Perestroika will reach out to you as well."[82] He refused to admit, perhaps even to himself, that his beautiful vision of a more open Soviet Union, gradually integrated into a "Common European Home," had become a victim of Eastern Europe's political stampede.

The Fall of the Berlin Wall and the domino-effect collapse of communist regimes in Eastern Europe heralded the greatest geopolitical opportunity presented to the West since 1945. President Bush suddenly had a formidable hand to play at his meeting with Gorbachev. Even the skeptical Brent Scowcroft realized that "suddenly everything was possible." The familiar Cold War framework had shattered and the emerging new world was "literally outside our frame of reference." Prudence, however, dictated to Bush and Scowcroft that they tread cautiously. Scowcroft also concluded that the revolutions in Eastern Europe made reversing the course of perestroika even more probable. In the end, Bush opted to be an optimist. Perhaps, he reasoned, the Soviet Union was "a ticking time bomb," but he wanted to engage the Soviet leader and take him up on his good words for as long as possible.[83] It was crucial to secure the revolutionary changes, and help the Soviet leader to manage his military forces and hardliners. The Baltic demands for independence were a special concern for Bush and Scowcroft in this respect. The Balts had support from the extremely active and well-organized Baltic Americans and their sympathizers on the Republican Right. The Baltic-American émigrés were actively involved in the independence movements: they brought recording and printing equipment, they funded the first foreign trips of the *Sajudis* leaders. They also played a significant role in key American states during elections.[84] At the same time Lithuanian secession could become a detonator of the Soviet conservative backlash, which could affect Eastern Europe and even East Germany, where Soviet troops still remained.

The meeting of Gorbachev and Bush on 2–3 December 1989 on the Soviet cruise ship *Maxim Gorky* near Malta attracted world attention. Gorbachev arrived at the meeting after his phenomenal diplomatic triumph in Italy. In Milan, he had been mobbed by people weeping with joy and showing quasi-religious veneration for the Soviet leader. For Gorbachev, the summit meant the psychological and political end of the Cold War.[85] On the US side of the talks the mood was very different: friendly, not warm, and sometimes tense. Bush had been seasick. The Soviet negotiating team was anxious, and Marshal Akhromeyev, Gorbachev's military advisor, was glum. On the Soviet side, only Gorbachev radiated energy and confidence, as if he had "won" rather than "lost" Eastern Europe. He beamed with pleasure when Bush said that he wanted to waive the Jackson-Vanik amendment to the US-Soviet Trade Act. This clause had been adopted in 1974 and linked American trade with the Soviet Union to freedom of emigration; it had helped to wreck Soviet-American economic relations and détente. Bush promised to "explore with Congress" the lifting of limitations on US export credits and guarantees, which prevented American businesses from operating in the Soviet Union. He also supported Soviet participation in GATT. He said nothing about Soviet membership of the IMF or World Bank.

The Soviet leader clearly needed money; he was frank about the problems at home and listed his unexpected deficits: 8–10 billion rubles from Chernobyl, 12–14 billion rubles from the Armenian earthquake, and more from the drop in oil prices. Some of his economists were singled out for blame—Gorbachev referred to the Soviet economist Nikolai Shmelyov who had advised him to spend

16–20 billion on imports, to satisfy Soviet consumers. Bush politely replied that he also had budgetary problems, cleaning up the $50 billion mess inherited from the Reagan administration. The US Secretary of State James Baker advised Gorbachev to use Soviet gold reserves to sell gold-backed bonds abroad.[86]

Bush set out the American demands. He pushed Gorbachev to halt assistance to Fidel Castro's Cuba and the communist Sandinistas in Nicaragua. This was top of the US list of priorities. The Soviet team was surprised. Gorbachev wanted to draw a "strategic and philosophical" line under the Cold War. On the second day of the summit he unveiled his surprise for the Americans—but it was not the one that Bush and Scowcroft feared. "I want to say to you and the United States," Gorbachev said solemnly, "that the Soviet Union will under no circumstances start a war. The Soviet Union is no longer prepared to regard the United States as an adversary." For the Soviet leader, this was a fundamental statement, a foundation for all future negotiations, but Shevardnadze and Chernyaev noted that Bush did not react. The Soviet offer was a hand extended, but without a handshake. The conversation dissipated into specific and familiar areas of discussion about arms control.

At the very end, the two leaders spoke about the Baltics. Gorbachev explained that he could not just let the Balts go unilaterally: the constitution required an equal treatment of all republics. If he just let Lithuania go, this "would bring out all sorts of terrible fires" in other parts of the Soviet Union. Bush replied: "But if you use force—you don't want to—that would create a firestorm." Gorbachev bristled at what he saw as a double standard: the US troops were in the process of intervening in Panama, where they would seize its ruler Manuel Noriega and put him in jail in the United States. Still, he did not give the usual Soviet rebuff about US meddling in internal Soviet affairs. Gorbachev was relieved that Bush refrained from triumphalism about Eastern Europe and the Berlin Wall. He was hopeful of a better future partnership.[87]

After the Malta meeting, Scowcroft flew secretly to Beijing, where he shook hands with "the butchers of Tiananmen" and assured the Chinese leaders that nothing would affect the Sino-American partnership. The Chinese accepted American reassurances almost indifferently. They were openly contemptuous of Gorbachev's policies. The Kremlin leader, said the Foreign Minister Qian Qichen, wanted to build a new order, but he could not maintain stability in his own country. Qian also shared some surprising news with Scowcroft: the Soviets had asked China, a very poor country, to lend them money.[88]

Inside the Warsaw Pact, people had even fewer illusions about where the wind was blowing. After his summit with Bush, Gorbachev returned to Moscow to meet with leaders of the Soviet bloc. Its fate was clear: half of the participants at the meeting were non-communists or anti-communists. The Polish Catholic

Prime Minister Tadeusz Mazowiecki sat next to the Polish President, General Jaruzelski. Romania's decidedly communist Ceauşescu sat apart, as if under quarantine. One senior Soviet diplomat said to Shevardnadze's aide Stepanov: "Half of these people will not be around at the next meeting." Stepanov replied: "If the next meeting ever happens." At Gorbachev's suggestion, the meeting approved a draft declaration that denounced the invasion of Czechoslovakia in 1968. Stepanov was surprised by the poor editing of the draft. "If all crucial questions are being decided in such a way, then it is clear why the country has reached such an impasse."[89]

On 16 December, the dictatorship of Ceauşescu in Romania, the last communist regime in Eastern Europe, began to fall. On that day, Shevardnadze visited the NATO headquarters in Brussels for the first time, to meet with its Secretary General Manfred Wörner. When the Soviet entourage arrived, the entire NATO staff came out and greeted the Soviet Foreign Minister with a standing ovation. Shevardnadze was visibly moved and muttered words of gratitude. Stepanov, however, viewed this spectacle through the lens of the Soviet domestic crisis. He, just like Shevardnadze, knew perfectly well that this standing ovation to Soviet foreign policy would only invoke the wrath of critics back home. "Only the well-nourished public in America and Europe," wrote Stepanov in his journal, "can afford to applaud their liberation from the fear of nuclear Apocalypse. This feeling is denied to the country, where hunger and misery cloud the light for people."[90]

The year 1989 witnessed many revolutionary transformations. In the spring and summer, Gorbachev's course of political liberalization produced significant radicalization, this time not in the national borderlands, but in the core of the country, above all in Moscow, Russian-speaking industrial regions, and within the ruling elites. The facade of communist ideology collapsed first, then came the turn of the external empire in Eastern Europe. The Fall of the Berlin Wall eclipsed Gorbachev's perestroika; it also became clear that the Warsaw Pact had no future. For the Soviet leaders and elites, however, the internal crisis began to overshadow external events. Gorbachev claimed abroad that the Soviet Union would join a "Common European Home." Yet his closest aides and advisors began to doubt whether the Soviet House would remain intact.

CHAPTER 4

SEPARATISM

The sovereignty of the RSFSR is a natural and necessary condition for the existence of the statehood of Russia, which has a history, culture, and traditions of many centuries.

From the Declaration on the State Sovereignty of the
Russian Soviet Federative Socialist Republic, 12 June 1990

RUSSIA WAKES UP

What to do with the Russians? That was another question that Gorbachev's reforms reopened. In 1989, according to the census and the nationality that people claimed, ethnic Russians numbered 145 million, over half of the Soviet population of 287 million. For decades they had been told that "their home" was the entire Soviet Union. Some 25 million of them lived and worked in Ukraine, Belorussia, the Baltic States, the Caucasus, and Central Asia. Most of them did not feel any special connection with the term "RSFSR" (Russian Soviet Federative Socialist Republic). And many of them had grown up thinking that the entire Soviet Union was historically "Russia." Indeed, the RSFSR was anything but a "Russian republic." It was the main body of the Soviet Union ruled by central Soviet institutions; its mass and resources held fourteen other Soviet republics together. From Stalin to Andropov, the RSFSR institutions, including the Supreme Soviet, remained decorative at best, and for a good reason: any "Russian" center of authority could become an inducement for Russian nationalism and represent a grave danger to the central Party-State.

In view of national movements in the Baltic republics, Ukraine, and elsewhere, however, the RSFSR began increasingly to look like the "home" of Russians. Russian journalists, politicians, and intellectuals began to call the

RSFSR "the Russian Federation" or simply "Russia." This then begged the question: if the Baltic republics were to become independent, could "Russia" also claim its constitutional right to be an independent sovereign state? Then what would remain of the Soviet Union?

The first rumblings of Russian secessionism were heard at the Congress of People's Deputies in June 1989. Valentin Rasputin, one of Gorbachev's favorite Russian writers, snapped at the Baltic and Georgian deputies who spoke about "Russian imperialism." If you want to bid farewell to the Soviet Union, said Rasputin, "perhaps Russia should leave the Union as well . . . Perhaps it would be better this way?" Rasputin implied that Russia should stop subsidizing other republics. Dmitry Likhachev, a famous cultural historian and another favorite of the Gorbachevs, said that the communist regime of the past "humiliated and robbed Russia so much, that Russians can hardly breathe." Russian nationalists within the Party apparatus and intelligentsia began to demand what other "nationalities" of the USSR had: a Russian branch of the Party, a Russian Academy of Sciences, a Russian writers' union, a preferential quota for Russians at the universities of Moscow and Leningrad.[1]

In July 1989, the Politburo concluded: the Russians would inevitably demand the same sovereign rights as the Balts, Georgians, Armenians, and other non-Russians. And this would mean the end of the Soviet Union. "To create a sovereign Russia," Vadim Medvedev warned, "is a pipe dream of the Balts." Nikolai Sliunkov, an ethnic Belorussian, proposed to break the RSFSR into six or seven parts, to make for a better balance among the republics of the Soviet Union. Ryzhkov proposed to divide the Russian Federation into several economic regions. Yakovlev was the only one in the Politburo who dismissed the Russian Question. Russians, he said, were not crazy enough to be willing to destroy the Union. Yakovlev's colleagues frowned at his false optimism. Ryzhkov remarked: "I feel that you want to disband everything. You must not be allowed to travel to the Baltics."[2] Everyone looked up to Gorbachev. "We cannot ignore the pressure of the Russian people," he said. One had to find a way to boost "the role of Russia in the Union," but without giving the Russian Federation greater sovereignty and without forming a separate Russian Communist Party within the CPSU. If that happened, he concluded, "this would remove the Union's backbone."[3]

Gorbachev never explained how this contradiction could be resolved: with his slogan of "stronger republics," it was impossible to discriminate among the individual states of the RSFSR. In the first half of 1990, Russian awakening and desire for separatism continued to gain momentum. Three forces, mutually hostile, promoted the idea of Russia's sovereignty. One was the Russian nationalists inside the Party and Soviet elites. The second was the democratic opposition that dominated Moscow politics. The third was the force of mass populism led by Boris Yeltsin.

Conservative Russian nationalism had been spreading inside the Party, state bureaucracy, and intelligentsia since World War II. The Brezhnev administration had been nourished more by chauvinism than communist internationalism. While many Georgians venerated Stalin as a great ethnic Georgian, many Russians admired the great tyrant as the builder of a "Russian superpower." This chauvinism was tempered by the realization of Russian demographic decline. A Party boss of a Russian region in 1979 recorded a typical diatribe in his private journal: "Russian people are being reduced before our eyes." The historical core of Russia "is getting empty."[4] The majority in the Party nomenklatura, the military, and the KGB sympathized with writers such as Valentin Rasputin, who bemoaned the destruction of the Russian peasantry. And in 1988–89, because of glasnost, they began to read the works of the previously banned Russian nationalists, such as Alexander Solzhenitsyn.

Gorbachev was a principled internationalist, but Chernyaev registered his "dangerous tilt towards Russians." Raisa Gorbacheva was on the executive board of the Soviet Cultural Foundation in Moscow that included Russian cultural historians, nationalist writers, and members of the Russian Orthodox Church. The foundation rediscovered the treasures of old Russian culture, published Russian pre-revolutionary thinkers and, as one of its leaders put it, "restored Russian dignity." Gorbachev donated to the foundation all his book royalties; many Party officials followed suit.[5] If Gorbachev hoped to keep Russian nationalists inside the Soviet tent, however, he was wrong. By the end of 1989, most of the Party and bureaucratic cadres from Russian regions considered Gorbachev's perestroika a disaster. They began to push for a "Russian" Communist Party, inside the CPSU, that could give them a "national" political base.

In October 1989, the Supreme Soviets of the RSFSR and the Ukrainian Soviet Socialist Republic—the two still unreformed and moribund bodies—convened in Moscow and Kiev to change the republican constitutions. The blueprints for reforms, agreed at the Politburo and announced by the media, prescribed that the Russian and Ukrainian republics would form new two-tiered representative institutions, just as had already been created at the Union level: a periodic Congress of People's Deputies and a permanent Supreme Soviet. In Kiev, the Ukrainian assembly diverged from the Moscow blueprint and just voted to hold elections for a new Supreme Soviet. In Moscow, many delegates, "elected" under the old rules, were anxious and resisted the change. They did not understand why the huge and complex republic, with many autonomous republics within it, should be plunged into political uncertainty. Anybody could see that the political experiment at the Union level had already produced rampant populism, unruly opposition, strikes, and economic troubles. The conservative deputies became even more defiant, when groups of

Moscow-based radicals accosted them with radical slogans on the route from the hotel to the Kremlin's Congress Hall.[6] Vitaly Vorotnikov, who chaired the assembly, carried out the Politburo decision and steered the Party conservatives to approve the new constitution. The pro-reform deputies proposed that all deputies should be elected by popular vote. This move was duly approved as well. In nine months, this reform would revolutionize Soviet politics.

Andrei Sakharov and other opposition intellectuals discussed the Russian Question from the liberal perspective of equality for ethnic minorities. Sakharov thought that Russians should not dominate in a future voluntary union. The RSFSR was too big and had to be broken up into several parts. This partition would make other smaller republics feel equal. On 27 November 1989, Sakharov delivered his constitutional proposals to Gorbachev.[7] The Soviet leader ignored them, however; he was too busy with current politics. This was when the Moscow opposition demanded the abolition of the Party's monopoly on power—codified by the Sixth Article of the Soviet Constitution. This issue was the focus of the second session of the Congress of People's Deputies of the USSR, held in Moscow between 12 and 24 December. Sakharov, Afanasyev, and other MDG leaders decided to call for an all-Union political strike to force Gorbachev and the Party to give up power. This effort fizzled out: most workers did not respond to the call of Moscow-based intellectuals. Then on 14 December, Sakharov suddenly died from a heart attack. The opposition buried him as a martyr to the cause.

Frustrated by the conservative majority in the Congress and the Supreme Soviet of the USSR, the Moscow opposition leaders shifted their energy to the forthcoming elections of the RSFSR Congress. Those elections—phase two of Gorbachev's design of "socialist democracy"—were originally scheduled for November 1989, but they were postponed until March 1990. This delay helped the opposition to organize itself more robustly. At a meeting in Moscow in January 1990, the opposition figures created a movement under a new name: Democratic Russia. The movement consisted of ex-dissidents, scientists, writers, academics, intellectuals, and other members of the intelligentsia. Most of them vowed to fight for "the ideas of Andrei Sakharov": freedom, democracy, the rights of man, a multi-party system, free elections, and a market economy. Democratic Russia excluded illiberal Russian nationalists. The journal *Ogonyok*, with its circulation of 4.6 million, published the appeal of Democratic Russia free of charge. The movement called for full sovereignty of the RSFSR; the Union would have only the powers that Russia and other republics voluntarily delegated to it.[8]

In the fall of 1989, Boris Yeltsin still struggled to find his own voice. It was a rough patch in his life: *Pravda* published an article from the Italian newspaper *La Repubblica* that described his drinking and uncouth conduct during his American trip. Shortly thereafter, Yeltsin was involved in an accident: his chauffeured car made an illegal U-turn in broad daylight and smashed into an oncoming car on Tverskaya street near the Kremlin. Yeltsin was uninjured but the driver of the other car suffered a heart attack. The next incident was even more embarrassing: police found Yeltsin in a brook, under a bridge, in the countryside near Moscow. He was soaking wet, holding two bunches of flowers. His first reaction was to ask the policemen not to report the incident; then he claimed some mysterious thugs had attacked him and thrown him off the bridge. Gorbachev held parliamentary hearings on the "attack on B. N. Yeltsin" which turned into a humiliating farce. Yeltsin said he did not want to talk about his "private life." The rumors spread that he had been visiting his mistress. Yeltsin's authority suffered tremendously.[9]

His misfortunes helped Yeltsin to make a momentous decision: to become a *Russian* politician. At first, he had leaned towards Russian conservative nationalism, yet his trip to the United States had converted him to a liberal agenda. In early December 1989, he announced that he would become "the President of Russia." His mission, Yeltsin declared, would be the "democratic, national, and spiritual resurrection of Russia." Yeltsin's "Russia" was not the entire Union; it was the RSFSR only. He wanted the core of the USSR to gain full sovereignty, get its own constitution, join the European Economic Community, and reach trade agreements with the United States, Japan, and Great Britain. Those were absurdly ambitious goals, yet they gave Yeltsin a radical populist agenda. He finally came out of the shade of Gorbachev's perestroika. His message to Russian nationalists was: "Russia is the only republic devoid of statehood, without economic, political, social, and scientific institutions that other republics had long possessed." For the Moscow intelligentsia his message was different: the RSFSR was a better target for the democrats. He brushed off accusations of separatism. He just wanted to reform the Soviet Union. If the opposition were to win elections to the Russian Congress and after "democracy wins in Russia, sooner or later it would win . . . on the Soviet Union's scale." And he promised his populist base that he would defeat the Party bosses and reallocate Russian resources for the benefit of Russian people.[10]

The Yeltsin phenomenon found a new traction: he became a contender for the empty seat of the Russian Tsar. The Russian people forgave their hero all his misdemeanors. Cab drivers and plumbers, industrial workers and peasants were absolutely certain that Yeltsin had been framed by the KGB and Party bosses. Very few people realized at the time that Yeltsin's new agenda would not reform but in fact destroy the Soviet Union. They longed nevertheless for a new course and decisive actions. Yeltsin ran an aggressive populist campaign. At numerous rallies with workers and peasants in Moscow and in the Urals, he called for a resurgence of Russia and urged the Russians who lived in other republics "to return to Russia." In his ghostwritten memoirs, he described his humble origins and presented himself as a defender of the common Russian people against the Party bosses. The book also criticized the luxurious lifestyle of Mikhail and Raisa Gorbachev, describing their opulent villas near Moscow and in Crimea. This luxury, Yeltsin wrote, would be normal in a well-to-do country, but not in Russia, where men and women had to endure food lines and empty stores.[11] This excerpt was picked up by the Western media, who wrote reviews and articles about Yeltsin's memoirs that had been translated and published in the West. Chernyaev informed Gorbachev about this with the comment: "Libellous and dirty." True, but Yeltsin's allegations affected many Russians. Chernyaev in his diaries feared that Russian intellectuals and ordinary people might unthinkingly support Yeltsin, just like their ancestors had supported the demagogues in 1917.[12]

On 4 March 1990, at the elections to the RSFSR Congress of People's Deputies, Yeltsin ran a campaign on his home turf of Sverdlovsk in the Urals and won with a 70 percent majority. He immediately traveled to Western Europe on a book tour. In Spain, Italy, the United Kingdom, and France the elites received him with guarded curiosity, as a nationalist demagogue without a positive program. In Paris, Yeltsin took part in a popular talk show, debating against the Russian philosopher Alexander Zinoviev. The latter had been evicted from the Soviet Union in the 1970s and had just published *Catastroika*, a satire on Gorbachev's reforms.[13] Unexpectedly, the Russian dissident attacked Yeltsin as a populist and demagogue. When Yeltsin argued that a multi-party system in Russia would bring social justice, Zinoviev objected: "You can create one thousand political parties in the Soviet Union, and all of them would degenerate into political mafias!" The anchorman asked Yeltsin: "How do you view the future of the USSR?" Yeltsin responded that people would choose young and energetic leaders, who would fix everything, but "without a super-authoritarian power." Zinoviev replied that Russian people had already seized power in 1917, but this had merely resulted in Stalin's dictatorship. Yeltsin, he said, would kill the USSR, and the West would applaud him. In several years, however, Russian society would slide back to authoritarianism, and people would feel nostalgia for Brezhnev's "golden age." The host asked Yeltsin whether he wanted to replace Gorbachev as President of the USSR. Yeltsin replied with a smirk: "No. The future belongs to Russia."[14] Yeltsin lived up to his words, but Zinoviev's verdict turned out also to be prophetic.

GORBACHEV'S PRESIDENCY

In January 1990, Gorbachev was worn down by economic and nationalist problems, yet he believed that he had pushed the Soviet Union from its totalitarian moorings. Raisa privately encouraged her husband to retire; she doubted that he could sustain much more stress. But Gorbachev did not leave, not in 1990 and not even a year later. He repeated to his aides that he did not like power for power's sake. Yet he was convinced that he was the only person who could steer perestroika forward. The problem was that with every month the sense of chaos and crisis in the country increased.[15]

The attempted "harmonization" of nationalities, utopian from the start, was a fiasco. In December 1989, despite all efforts of the Kremlin to stop it, the Lithuanian Communist Party declared its secession from the CPSU and its course towards complete national independence. Gorbachev convened the Party Plenum in Moscow, where many angrily demanded that he use force to stop the secession. The Party emissaries went to Lithuania for negotiations and returned empty-handed. In January 1990, Gorbachev flew there himself and appealed to "healthy forces." He blamed Stalin for turning the Soviet Union into a totalitarian unitary state and invited the Balts to take part in a genuine federation of republics, with rules for secession. He even accepted the idea of a multiparty state. All those offers, one observer noted, "had a stronger impact on the foreign journalists than on the Lithuanians." The latter saw that they now had a golden opportunity to exit the Soviet Union.[16]

Some historians later claimed that, had Gorbachev offered the Balts the possibility of a meaningful exit, he could have detached the Baltic fuse from the ticking bomb of separatism inside the rest of the Soviet Union.[17] This was yet another intellectual speculation. Gorbachev's main problem was not Lithuania, it was about the Russians. When speaking at an industrial plant in Vilnius, Gorbachev said to the workers, most of them ethnic Russians, that some people were peddling a ludicrous idea "that if Russia secedes from the Union, in four years it will be the most prosperous state in the world." Suddenly, the crowd began to applaud, clearly in approval of what Gorbachev deemed absurd. He snapped: "Do not applaud, better listen to me." Gorbachev's mood during his trip darkened "from fury and confusion." He returned to Moscow in a somber frame of mind.[18]

That same month, January 1990, the Politburo had to use military force in Azerbaijan. The Party there had disintegrated, and nationalists of "the people's front," many of them from the "national" intelligentsia, had taken over. The Soviet border with Iran, where ethnic Azeris had lived for centuries, was breached by a jubilant mob, echoing the opening of the Berlin Wall the previous year. This time, however, Soviet motorized and airborne divisions crushed the Azeris' desire for "sovereignty" and restored the state border of the USSR. In Baku over a hundred locals and up to twenty military personnel were killed. The crackdown in Azerbaijan, of course, was not a solution, it was just a means to buy time.[19] Raisa recalled that she barely recognized her husband the day after the military operation in Baku. His face was gray, he had aged visibly, as if he suffered "a split in his soul." This was yet another instance of Gorbachev's visceral aversion to the use of force.[20] An admirable moral quality in an individual, this was a huge political flaw in the leader of a country with a tragic history and facing a rising wave of toxic nationalism. In January 1990, the Kremlin leader faced a dilemma: to use force and keep the existing state intact or continue on his course of devolving power to the republics. Ultimately, Gorbachev chose the second path.

In Moscow, the Russian democratic opposition did not know about Gorbachev's moral pangs. Afanasyev, Gavriil Popov, Sergey Stankevich, and other leaders of Democratic Russia held a huge rally on 4 February, attended by half a million people, in support of "democracy" and Lithuanian independence. They also protested against Russian "fascism." Hundreds of rallies and protests took place in industrial areas of the RSFSR. Following Yeltsin's example, the opposition shifted gears and tapped into the popular wrath of the Party-State leaders and bureaucracies. Emboldened by their success, Afanasyev and his colleagues promised another massive rally in Moscow on 25 February, the anniversary of the Russian Revolution of 1917. The opposition counted on a million people attending, but the numbers in fact fell far short of that goal. The protesters carried banners against the Party nomenklatura and Ryzhkov's government, but also chanted, for the first time, "Down with Gorbachev!" Popov and Afanasyev demanded a round-table discussion with the opposition and "a democratic government of national salvation." The Moscow media, including the widely popular newspapers *Arguments and Facts* and *Moscow News*, even program producers and journalists at the state television station, still controlled by the Kremlin, rooted for the opposition.[21]

Lenin had famously defined three conditions for a Russian revolution: the paralysis of power; people's loss of fear of and growing contempt for the authorities; and a deterioration of living conditions. In January 1990, the situation was stacked against Gorbachev on all three counts. And yet the Soviet leader, who knew Lenin's formula by heart, remained optimistic. At a meeting with miners in early February 1990, he said that he counted on two important qualities of the Russian people: their patriotism and "great patience and endurance."[22] Gorbachev was not the first Soviet leader to think of the Russians as the last reserve. The majority of Russians, however, wanted Gorbachev to use his power, not to devolve it; and Gorbachev's reluctance to use that power appeared to many as weakness. The Soviet leader also suffered from an accumulating crisis of confidence: his long-winded explanations, in contrast to Yeltsin's more succinct populist style, no longer appealed to the majority who felt cheated and disillusioned.

The Soviet leader still convened regular Politburo meetings. But instead of setting policies there for the Party apparatus, he would waste time in endless discussions. The conservative reformers concealed their skepticism of his leadership. Ligachev thought the abdication of power by the Party was a huge political mistake. Vorotnikov demanded Gorbachev's resignation. Ryzhkov, responsible for the failing economic reforms, circled the wagons and bristled at any criticism. On the liberal side, Shevardnadze and Yakovlev also felt alienated and on their own. Gorbachev's self-isolation progressed. He kept asking naïve questions: Why do people forgive Yeltsin for everything? Why do the problems in Moscow and Leningrad get worse? What have we done wrong? He did not expect any answers. His colleagues merely wondered what kind of an isolationist bubble the General Secretary lived in.[23]

Everyone in the Politburo could now see that the political system created in 1989 was terribly ineffective. The double-tiered representative assemblies could not govern the country in a crisis; they were part of that crisis. The conservative reformers believed that the country needed strong executive power. The Politburo liberals feared a reactionary rollback and the end of "socialist democracy." Yakovlev urged Gorbachev "to seize power before it is too late," to become the President of the USSR and sideline the Politburo, the Party elites, and even the Supreme Soviet. In Yakovlev's scenario, Gorbachev should appeal directly to the people in Leninist fashion, offering land to peasants, factories to workers, a real Union of states to the republics, a multi-party politics for the democrats. He should also purge the army and central apparatus, dispatch Ryzhkov's government, liquidate central ministries, pull troops out of Eastern Europe, ask the West for big loans, and implement some kind of "urgent measures in the economy." Even Chernyaev was taken aback by this neo-Leninist radicalism. "Where could one find the new elites?" asked Gorbachev's aide. Yakovlev replied: "There are plenty. One should only have the courage to call on them, in the spirit of revolution!"[24]

The Soviet leader wanted to guide the country by his vision, not by force. In January 1990, Gorbachev began to write up a new ideological "platform" for a future Party Congress. After endless amendments, the document proclaimed "a humane, democratic socialism" as a new mission for the reformed Party. Three months later, Gorbachev began to work with great passion on "A Word about Lenin," an article for the Soviet press to commemorate the birthday of the leader of world communism on 22 April. He confessed to Chernyaev and Shakhnazarov that he admired his own text. "When I read a genuinely talented thing," he said, "it is not the content that captures my imagination, but the language, the words. I can ponder a single phrase for hours."[25]

His "theoretical" work induced Gorbachev to undertake more constitutional amendments. In December 1989, he had been against abolishing the Sixth

Article of the Soviet Constitution. But at the end of January 1990, he suddenly changed his mind and ambushed the Politburo with two ideas. First, the Party, he now thought, could reform itself only *after* rescinding its monopoly on power. Second, a new institution of the Presidency should replace the old hierarchical power structure. Ligachev was predictably upset: "The presidential rule is very important," he said. "But the main political force is the Party. In the final analysis, only the Party is capable of enforcing everything . . ." He and Ryzhkov agreed on the idea of a president, as long as the Party Plenum nominated and approved a candidate for this post. However, Gorbachev chose a middle way: he would be nominated by the Party, yet also elected at the Congress. Nobody had even mentioned openly democratic elections.[26]

Gorbachev proposed several specific constitutional amendments: on the exit of republics from the Soviet Union; on the sovereignty of the autonomous territories; on the creation of a Presidential Council and a Federation Council (the body consisting of the heads of republican Supreme Soviets); and on the right of the President to issue decrees. All those changes, approved by the Politburo, would be adopted at the extraordinary Congress of People's Deputies in mid-March, without a national referendum. After this, work should begin on a new Union Treaty. This document would legitimize a compact between the center and the republics, define their rights, responsibilities, economic assets, and finances.[27] This was a heavy workload, but Gorbachev threw himself into legislative work with his customary energy.

In early February, Gorbachev convened the Party Plenum to approve the changes. To dilute the quorum of regional Party bosses, he invited 500 "guests": workers, scientists, the military. The Party regional secretaries, mostly Russians, pressed their complaints. Vladimir Brovikov, former head of Belorussia's Party organization and now ambassador to Poland, harangued: "We brought our mother [Russia] down to such a poor state, turned it from a power the world admired into a state with a failed past, mirthless present and murky future." Supporters of Gorbachev defended his foreign policy, but they were out of their depth on domestic issues.[28] Gorbachev was furious, but he allowed his critics to vent their anger. The Plenum's sessions lasted until midnight. When the audience became exhausted, the General Secretary announced his own conclusions and obtained the agreements he wanted.[29]

On 12 March 1990, over 2,000 deputies came to the Kremlin Hall for the opening of the third session of the Congress of People's Deputies. The removal of the Sixth Article was already predetermined, meaning an end to the Party's monopoly. The discussion of the presidency, in contrast, turned into a political drama that lasted for two days. On 13 March, the democrats moved an amendment banning the President from occupying any other political position.

Almost twice as many delegates voted for it than against it. Had this amendment passed, Gorbachev would have been forced to step down as the Party leader, with unpredictable consequences. The Moscow opposition insisted on a clear division between the state and the Party. More shockingly, many conservative Party officials, above all Russians, supported this division. Gorbachev faced a deadly synergy between resentful Russian conservatives and democratic populists. The middle ground was dwindling. Yeltsin did not even attend, but his supporters at the Congress voted against Gorbachev's presidency.[30]

Fortunately for the Soviet leader, a number of delegates rallied behind him. Anatoly Sobchak, a deputy from Leningrad, evoked the image of China's Tiananmen Square in the event of political chaos. Another deputy from Leningrad, Dmitry Likhachev, compared the current moment with 1917, which he had witnessed as a child. Division between the Party and the state, he said, would lead to a dual power in the country and to civil war. The Congress voted to pass the Law on the Presidency; it became part of the Constitution. The Congress also approved the President's prerogatives to introduce an emergency or presidential rule in any republic of the Union "while respecting its sovereignty and territorial integrity." The President had powers of the commander-in-chief and could, with consent and advice of the Supreme Soviet, appoint the government, declare mobilization, and respond to an armed attack. After the law was passed, the Party Plenum, held in another hall inside the Kremlin, supported Gorbachev's candidacy. Then the Congress took a secret vote: 1,329 delegates voted to make Gorbachev the President of the USSR. Some 500 delegates, among them many radical democrats, voted against; over 300 abstained or were absent. Yeltsin was among them.[31]

From now on, Gorbachev presided over three institutions: the Politburo, the Presidential Council, and the Council of Federation. It took only a few weeks, however, to recognize that the main problem remained the same: it was not the lack of power in Gorbachev's hands, but his lack of an idea what to use this power for—along with his principled refusal to use force. He did not form a new government. Instead, he had endless consultations on who would replace him as the head of the Supreme Soviet. Yakovlev clearly wanted the job, but Gorbachev opted for Lukyanov, a skillful parliamentarian. Gorbachev also moved his cabinet: from the Party headquarters to the Old Square to the Kremlin. The Presidential Council included the KGB's Kryuchkov, Marshal Yazov, and other key ministers. As an indication of future economic moves, Gorbachev elevated two economists: Stanislav Shatalin and Nikolai Petrakov, both supporters of a market economy. The other members were intellectuals, writers, and even one "intelligent worker." Abalkin, the State Bank's Gerashchenko, the Minister of Finance Pavlov, and captains of big state corporations were not invited. All meetings took place in Gorbachev's offices, one in the Party headquarters, another in the Kremlin. Even rituals remained the same. During long sessions, at Gorbachev's signal, servants would bring cups of tea with small pastries. If the meetings lasted until long after lunch, as they usually did, participants would be offered small sandwiches. After many hours, fatigue would set in. The room lacked fresh air, because Gorbachev ordered the air-conditioning to be turned off, for fear of rheumatism.[32]

Having dismantled the Party Secretariat, Gorbachev did not create a presidential administration. Instead, he relied on his chief of staff Valery Boldin, who was in charge of all correspondence, stenography, archives, and secretarial duties. A former journalist, Boldin had no particular talent except punctuality. He was part of Gorbachev's inner circle from Andropov's time and enjoyed Raisa's complete trust. However, Gorbachev's biographer writes that Boldin was "secretly seditious," conspiring against his boss by filtering information that arrived on his desk. At the same time, Gorbachev did not translate any information—including from the lengthy meetings he chaired—into executive decisions. Most Politburo meetings, and later sessions of the Presidential Council, ended in "resolutions," the texts prepared for the media, rather than specific instructions for the bureaucracy. Officials learned to interpret the resolutions in the way they wanted, or simply ignored them.[33]

Gorbachev's presidency had other unintended consequences. Nursultan Nazarbayev, the fifty-year-old Party head of the Kazakh Soviet Socialist Republic, who had effusively supported Gorbachev, suddenly announced he would become the President of Kazakhstan. Two weeks later, the Party head of Uzbekistan, Islam Karimov, said the same. Gorbachev reacted with genuine surprise: "How come? Without any advice and consent . . . I thought we had agreed . . . that there would be only one president in the country." Karimov calmly replied: "It is the wish of the people." Nazarbayev intoned: "People in Kazakhstan also say: can't we have a president too?" Gorbachev then lamely agreed. Thus, he had recognized the right of the republican potentates to change the republican constitution in the same way the Kremlin had done.[34]

GERMANY AND LITHUANIA

On 26 January 1990, Gorbachev convened in his office a select group to discuss German reunification. The meltdown of the GDR had ruined his timetable for construction of the "Common European Home"; it became clear that German reunification would take months, not years. Everyone at the meeting understood the historical meaning of this development for the security and geopolitical future of the Soviet Union. Shevardnadze's older brother had died at

Brest-Litovsk during the first days of the German invasion in June 1941; Chernyaev, Yakovlev, Shakhnazarov, and Marshal Akhromeyev had all fought in the Great Patriotic War as junior officers and soldiers; Ryzhkov's family had to flee from the advancing German troops; Gorbachev had lost three of his uncles and had grown up under German occupation.

The discussion on the German Question was remarkably calm and pragmatic. Chernyaev spoke first and said the Kremlin could not prevent the reunification of Germany, therefore the only viable option was to cooperate with Chancellor Kohl and negotiate a settlement with three Western powers, who still had the occupational authority within the Potsdam framework of 1945. Gorbachev agreed that the Soviet Union had "no moral right" to oppose the German striving for unity, but insisted that German unification must be synchronized with the creation of a common European home, which would include the USSR. "Nobody should consider," he said, "that a unified Germany could join NATO. The presence of our troops would preclude it. And we can withdraw them if [the] Americans withdraw—and they will not do so for a long time."[35]

The Americans, however, played a different game. The danger, Brent Scowcroft recalled, was that Gorbachev "might make an offer to Kohl that Kohl would feel he could not refuse." Years later Scowcroft wondered: "I still don't know why Gorbachev didn't do it."[36] This was the danger behind Germany's neutrality—which would have entailed the collapse of NATO and the withdrawal of US troops from Europe. After the Malta summit between Bush and Gorbachev in early December 1989, the American President met with Kohl and offered him his full backing for German reunification in exchange for the Chancellor's unwavering support in preserving NATO. The two leaders agreed that their common goal would be to get Soviet troops out of Eastern Europe and East Germany. To achieve this, they had to tread judiciously and keep Gorbachev in power for as long as possible.[37]

On 5 February, Kohl offered the GDR a monetary union, which would take effect on 1 July. Disregarding the huge costs of such an endeavor, the chancellor promised to pay for the exchange of all devalued Eastern Marks into Deutschmarks at the rate of one to one. This amounted to the biggest bribe in modern times and it changed the balance of power in Central Europe. Even Soviet troops in East Germany, the Soviet main asset, succumbed to the Deutschmark. All of a sudden Gorbachev faced another dilemma: to find hard currency to pay for the maintenance of Soviet forces there or to withdraw them. The second option would be humiliating and politically disastrous. The first option was impossible, as Soviet currency reserves were approaching zero.

On 9 February, Secretary of State James Baker flew to Moscow, to inform Gorbachev about the Western line on German unification. What would be better for Soviet security, he asked rhetorically, a non-aligned and unstable Germany, or Germany within NATO? The Secretary of State promised, to sweeten the bitter pill, that NATO's jurisdiction and military presence would not "move even an inch in the direction of the East." Gorbachev later claimed this pledge was the nucleus of a future deal on Germany. At the time, however, he simply remarked: "Of course, the expansion of the NATO zone is unacceptable."[38] Later, numerous critics would blame the Soviet leader for his failure to capitalize on Baker's pledge. Gorbachev, however, knew better the weakness of his negotiating position.

Kohl also flew to Moscow and met with Gorbachev the next day. The Soviet leader delighted him by declaring that the future of Germany should be decided by Germans themselves "in the context of realities," including German neutrality, the recognition of existing German borders, the European situation as a whole, and Soviet economic interests. Kohl accepted all these "realities," except for German neutrality: a unified Germany would stay in NATO. Deftly, he offered Gorbachev a special relationship: "If you have any problems, I would be ready to meet you at the first sign, at several hours' notice."[39] This was the offer that the struggling father of perestroika badly needed.

Baker and Kohl knew that the Soviet balance of payments was in a pre-default situation. Soviet oil and gas industries, the main providers of hard currency, were projected to have a downturn in production and therefore in profits. As of December 1989, Western banks for the first time had refused to accept the Soviet Union's requests for commercial credits. Even its old partners, such as the Deutsche Bank and the Austrian banks, had closed off Soviet access to Western money markets. The main reason for this was Soviet political instability and the impending shift of power from the center to the republics. Western bankers wanted to know who exactly would be paying them back in a few years. Meanwhile, the export revenues of state enterprises, associations, and cooperatives were flowing into offshore accounts via ingenious schemes, instead of into the Soviet budget. And yet the volume of Soviet imports kept growing. Faced with this credit crunch, the State Bank of the USSR arranged "swap" operations, with a collateral of gold and diamonds in exchange for foreign currency. This did not help; the hole in the balance of payments kept growing. Cargo ships that brought grain and other imported goods to Soviet ports had to wait there for weeks for freight payments to be made.[40]

Kohl and Bush met again at Camp David toward the end of February 1990 to compare notes. Western sources in Moscow reported that "the loss" of East Germany and the specter of NATO moving eastwards might enrage the Russians and lead to Gorbachev's overthrow. Bush and Scowcroft were particularly concerned about the mood of the Soviet military. The President and the

Chancellor agreed to act cautiously, protecting Gorbachev's prestige and standing. Still, Bush argued, the Soviets were up against the wall. "This may end up as a matter of cash. They need money." Because of Kohl's monetary union, Gorbachev had to find a solution before July. He might accept the Western position on Germany and NATO at the next summit in Washington scheduled for the end of May.[41]

The Lithuanian crisis was also a huge problem for Gorbachev. On 11 March, after the republican elections that ended in triumph for the nationalists, the Lithuanian parliament issued its declaration to restore the sovereignty and constitution of the old Lithuania. They also approved about eighty laws and resolutions that restored "the state of Lithuania." The Lithuanian nationalists did precisely what Bush and Kohl wanted to avoid: they painted Gorbachev into a corner. They also elected the former professor of the Vilnius Conservatory, Vytautas Landsbergis, as chairman of the national assembly. The Soviet leadership agonized: the head of Gosplan, Yuri Masliukov, wanted to make an offer to Lithuania: it could leave the Union, but without the territories of Vilnius (Vilno) and Klaipeda that had become attached to Lithuania after the German-Soviet Non-Aggression Pact of 1939. Ryzhkov and Vorotnikov warned that such an offer would trigger into action Ukrainian and Russian nationalists. Suddenly, Ryzhkov recalled Andropov's old project: a new Union should abolish national autonomies and dilute republican sovereignties.[42] The same Congress that had made Gorbachev the President also declared Lithuanian independence as "illegal" and empowered Gorbachev "to ensure the interests and rights of the USSR, as well as allied republics" on Lithuanian territory.[43]

Gorbachev sent to Lithuania the commander of Soviet ground forces, Valentin Varennikov, to ensure that the vital objects of the economy and communications assets stayed under Moscow's control. Varennikov returned to Moscow to propose presidential rule for Lithuania, which meant that the military could take over power from the elected parliament. The Politburo discussed this option on 22 March. Ligachev and the Minister of Defense, Marshal Yazov, urged immediate military action: they feared that time was on the side of the separatists. Ryzhkov demurred. The main danger, he said, was not Lithuanian, but Russian separatism. If Yeltsin and those from the Moscow opposition came to power in the RSFSR, Ryzhkov argued, "they will effortlessly destroy the Soviet Union, overthrow the party and government leaders." Yakovlev kept silent; his appeasement of the Balts in the past had compromised him. Gorbachev listened but did not take a stand. Chernyaev left the Politburo meeting in a depressed state, haunted by memories of Czechoslovakia in 1968. If Gorbachev "carries out a massacre in Lithuania," he wrote in his diary, "I am not only going to resign . . . I will probably do something more."[44] A few days later, the Supreme Soviet of Estonia declared the power of the USSR in the republic to be illegal and "restored" an independent Estonian state.[45]

The Supreme Soviet of the USSR finally passed a law on the exit of republics from the Union. It was a laborious process, which could only happen after two-thirds of a republic's voters approved of secession in a referendum. Other republics and the Congress of the USSR also had to approve the secession. The Balts regarded it as a ruse to block their path to independence.[46] Still, legally, it was another step towards the constitutional devolution of powers to the republics.

On 9 April, Gorbachev summoned the Presidential Council to discuss Lithuania again. The KGB's Kryuchkov and the Minister of the Interior, Vadim Bakatin, reported their findings. Kryuchkov prevaricated; he wanted to use force, but knew that Gorbachev would not be in favor. Bakatin did not tiptoe around the issue. The crisis, he said, "can only be solved by force—we have no other levers." He proposed to take Lithuania's main economic assets into Moscow's control, cut off the delivery of oil and gasoline to Lithuania, and prevent Lithuanians from reselling Soviet goods abroad. Moscow should also ask Western leaders to encourage the Lithuanians to cooperate. Bakatin's proposal of economic pressure stole the thunder from Varennikov. This angered the Minister of Defense, Yazov: "For how long we can wait? We can fix this in three, five days, maximum a week." Ryzhkov objected: "This may end up in . . . a civil war."[47]

On 13 April, the Soviet government informed the Lithuanian authorities that they must rescind their unilateral measures within two days or pay for the goods delivered from other republics in "freely convertible currency."[48] This document did not demand the repeal of the Lithuanian declaration of independence. The nationalists in Vilnius refused to negotiate. On 18 April, delivery of oil to Lithuania almost stopped. Many wrote about "a blockade" and "strangulation" of Lithuania, yet it was not true. Lithuania had enough gasoline to last until June, and it continued to receive one-fifth of its usual supply of gas. The agrarian republic had no shortage of food. It could even arrange deliveries of "exportable" goods from other republics via cooperatives and enterprises, which bypassed the ruling of Moscow.[49]

On 6 April, Shevardnadze met with Bush in the Oval Office and asked him to support Moscow in the constitutional conflict with Lithuania. Bush let him know that only the use of force "or the perceived crushing of Lithuania would be a problem." "We are caught in fifty years of history," mused the US President, who then called for "a dialogue."[50] A few days later, talking to the Canadian Prime Minister Brian Mulroney, Bush admitted that a conflict between Lithuania and the USSR worried him enormously. Gorbachev, he said, was under severe criticism for "losing Eastern Europe and Germany," and now facing "the possible breakup of the Soviet Union." He also hinted that, if a crackdown in Lithuania happened, the US administration would do little to punish the USSR. Even in the worst-case scenario, Bush mused, "we would have to figure out how to get things back on track afterwards."[51]

Landsbergis also suspected that the US government would not stand by him. He spoke about "another Munich," meaning Western appeasement of Gorbachev. The Baltic Americans and some members of Congress demanded immediate US recognition of Lithuanian independence and economic sanctions against the USSR. This rattled Bush and Scowcroft. The latter recalled that "the Balts were pouring gasoline on a flame . . . The reality was that the only way the Baltic States could achieve lasting independence was with acquiescence of the Kremlin. Our task was to bring Moscow to this point." Bush and Scowcroft met with the Baltic Americans and tried to convince them that Lithuania's independence hung on keeping Gorbachev in power. The Baltic Americans insisted: the freedom of Lithuania would pave the way for the freedom of Russia, and Western firmness would constrain Soviet hardliners.[52]

Western European governments also thought that the Lithuanian separatists were acting rashly. The Soviet leader had to be given more time to negotiate a new stable framework in Europe and a new Union at home. "Lithuania," said the German Foreign Minister, Hans-Dietrich Genscher, in a conversation with Bush, "happened 6 to 12 months too early for Gorbachev."[53] President Mitterrand intoned at his meeting with Bush: "We should encourage the Lithuanians to be wise." If other dominoes in the Soviet Empire began to fall, he continued, then "Gorbachev is gone; a military dictatorship would result." This became a common Western position.[54] Mitterrand and Bush agreed to communicate to more moderate Lithuanians the suggestion that they delay their declaration of independence, as a way of breaking the impasse with the Kremlin. On 24 April, Mitterrand and Kohl sent a joint letter to the Lithuanian leadership arguing to this effect.

On 26 April, the Lithuanian worker Stanislovas Žemaitis died by setting himself on fire in Moscow, in front of the Bolshoi Theater, as a form of protest. Most Lithuanians, however, were not ready to make the ultimate sacrifice. Western refusal to recognize Lithuania and Gorbachev's resolve sobered the Lithuanian parliamentarians as well. On 4 May, the Latvian Supreme Soviet joined Lithuania and Estonia and declared the restitution of the pre-1940 independent Latvian state. Yet in Latvia and Estonia, half of the population were Russian speakers. The leaders of those republics decided to negotiate with Moscow.[55]

This was the moment when Shakhnazarov proposed that Gorbachev convene a round-table discussion with all republican leaders to discuss a new Union Treaty. Those who wanted independence could sign the treaty, while those who did not would get an associated status within the Union and pay full price for energy resources. In this way Gorbachev could also constrain Georgian, Armenian, and Azeri separatists. That was the only way, Shakhnazarov concluded, to defuse the Baltic bomb.[56] This was Sakharov's logic without Sakharov; yet Shakhnazarov counted on Gorbachev's presidential powers to bring the republican rulers inside the one tent.

Gorbachev, however, concentrated on Lithuania, as if this was the main problem plaguing the Soviet state. He thundered: "I will press [Lithuanian separatists] all against the wall!" On 18 May, he met with the Lithuanian Prime Minister Kazimira Prunskienė, a more moderate, reasonable alternative to Landsbergis. Gorbachev wanted Prunskienė to go to Vilnius and convince the parliament to freeze their declaration of independence. Prunskienė left the Kremlin under the impression that Gorbachev had caved in to the military; she appealed to Western diplomats for help against the Moscow hardliners. The Lithuanian crisis and the Soviet embargo continued.[57]

GERMANY AND RUSSIA

During the celebrations of 1 May, the international day of proletarian solidarity, Gorbachev stood on the podium of the Lenin Mausoleum, flanked by his usual entourage. The new face next to him was the head of Moscow City Council, Gavriil Popov, elected in March on the platform of Democratic Russia. Popov had advised Gorbachev to allow "an alternative" demonstration of political parties, clubs, and associations, which on the day mushroomed thanks to liberalization. Liberal Democrats, Christian Democrats, anarchist-syndicalists, and other "independent political parties and clubs" came to the celebrations under different colors. Some brought red flags with the hammer and sickle ripped out. About a hundred of the demonstrators stopped in front of the Mausoleum and began to chant: "Socialism? No, Thanks!"; "Communists: You Are Bankrupt!"; "Down with the Fascist Red Empire!"; "Freedom to Lithuania!"; "Down with the Politburo!"; "Down with Gorbachev!"; "Resign! Resign!! Resign!!!" Most of the crowd were ethnic Russians. The nationwide television broadcast was halted, but cameras captured the stony-faced Kryuchkov and Yazov, who stared above the crowd with blank eyes. In August 1968, when eight dissidents had come out on Red Square protesting against the Soviet invasion of Czechoslovakia, they were beaten and arrested by the KGB. This time, the ranks of KGB officers stood motionless, without instructions on how to behave. The May Day stampede lasted for twenty-five minutes. Finally, Gorbachev turned around and left the Mausoleum, followed by other leaders. The mob shouted at their backs: "Shame!"[58] In the corridors of the Kremlin, Ligachev approached Gorbachev, his face crimson from humiliation: "Look what a deplorable state the country is in!"[59]

Gorbachev dismissed the protesters as "hooligans" and "thugs," and blamed Popov for the idea of including them in the festivities. Yet he was also insulted and humiliated. His authority was damaged for all to see. He was falling into a deep hole between the radicalizing "democrats" of Democratic Russia, who fomented political anarchy, and enraged conservatives in the Party and state security. The latter could read him the riot act at the approaching Party Congress, now less than three months away. The Lithuanian secession and the inclusion of East Germany within NATO were already bad enough and could cost Gorbachev his Party leadership.

On 3 May, the Politburo discussed a new negotiating position on German unification. The policy draft, prepared by Chernyaev and signed by Shevardnadze, Kryuchkov, Yazov, and Yakovlev, proposed a unified Germany in NATO in exchange for Western concessions and guarantees. Suddenly, however, Gorbachev dismissed the draft with a burst of patriotic rhetoric. If the West continued to insist on Germany within NATO, he said, we should pull out from talks on the reduction of conventional forces in Europe, and from the START talks with the United States on strategic arms reductions. The Politburo fell silent, and only Ligachev looked satisfied. Even Gorbachev's loyal aide did not understand: why these theatrics?[60] Chernyaev pleaded with his boss to reconsider. "Our real security was defined at the Soviet-American negotiations ... The USSR needs, as never before, Western support of perestroika."[61] Chernyaev had hit the nail on the head. Gorbachev required tangible proof that the Soviet Union and the West would begin to converge on the road towards a new world order, Gorbachev being one of the key architects. And Gorbachev knew that his position was weakening by the day. He still held the keys to a German settlement, but the keys to Western cash flows were in Bonn and Washington.[62] At this point, Kohl made another deft gesture: he offered Gorbachev cash to help him out. In mid-May, he sent his personal aide Horst Teltschik to Moscow, accompanied by two officials from the Deutsche Bank. Gorbachev told them that the Soviet Union needed "oxygen" to the tune of a minimum 15–20 billion rubles in long-term credits, in order to survive the transition to a market economy. A few days later, the Soviet leader mentioned the same amount in his talks with James Baker. It was the first time that Gorbachev had signaled he expected the West to lend him money.[63]

On 16 May 1990, the RSFSR Congress of People's Deputies opened in Moscow and lasted for seven long weeks. All deputies were elected by direct vote, and in general the electoral campaign was remarkably free and well contested. Most deputies came from the provincial Russian bureaucracy and middle classes, as well as from the intelligentsia in big cities. Some 87 percent of them were Party members. In contrast to the Congress of the USSR, there were only a few workers and peasants from collective farms. On the conservative flank were the nomenklatura people from the Russian provinces, Party and state officials. There was also a sizable group of KGB and police officers, who ran with the promise to combat rising crime and economic insecurity with an "iron hand."[64] On the liberal flank was the Democratic Russia movement, which gained one-fifth of the seats. Its electorate was predominantly from cultural and educational institutions in Moscow, Leningrad, the industrial cities of the Volga and the Urals, and the "closed cities" of the military-industrial complex.[65] Many Moscow-based "democrats of the first wave" from the Supreme Soviet of the USSR ran as candidates for the Russian Assembly as well and won election. Their optimism soared. With the exception of the television censors, the Russian media was overwhelmingly on their side. The number of independent newspapers and regular political bulletins in Moscow, Leningrad, and other cities of the Russian Federation had grown from 245 in 1988 to 920 in 1989, and it reached 1,642 in 1990.[66] Their circulation reached an all-time peak. Viktor Sheinis, a scholar from a Moscow academic think tank and an author of the electoral platform for Democratic Russia, later recalled the euphoric mood of "democrats" at this moment: "Society woke up from its sleep and began to impose new rules on the bureaucracy." It was obvious to them that the center of politics from now on should move from the central Soviet Assembly to the Russian one. Speaking at an international conference, Sheinis said that the end of the unitary state was "inevitable." He even suggested "that soon the Union institutions would be left with nothing to govern."[67]

In Gorbachev's entourage the outcome of the Russian elections evoked a sense of gloomy fatalism. The main question was: who could defeat Yeltsin in the struggle for leadership in the Russian parliament? Gorbachev procrastinated and kept asking: "Whom should we choose?" At the last moment the Politburo chose a candidate: Alexander Vlasov, a pliant apparatchik without any political ambitions, who had chaired the RSFSR Supreme Soviet before the elections.[68] One witness recalled that Gorbachev and Lukyanov sat in clear view of all deputies of the Russian Congress and conspired "like the two owls." Vlasov, however, wilted under the barrage of questions and criticism from the deputies of Democratic Russia. Still, the struggle was long and hard: Yeltsin could not get a majority at the Congress. Even on the liberal flank, some intellectuals mistrusted him and considered him an ambitious authoritarian populist. Conservatives rooted for Ivan Polozkov, the Party boss of a southern Russian region and the leading proponent of "the Russian Communist Party" within the CPSU. Gorbachev agreed, and Vlasov withdrew his candidacy. Polozkov and Yeltsin tied; nobody could gain the majority. Then Gorbachev asked Vlasov to advance his candidacy again. He also personally attacked Yeltsin as an erratic and unreliable man, someone he would never be able to work with. The speech backfired, predictably. Some conservatives, who were allergic to the Soviet leader, switched their support to Yeltsin. After making his disastrous intervention, Gorbachev left Moscow and flew to Washington for a Soviet-American summit. Even figures from Democratic Russia, already critical of Gorbachev, were puzzled by his erratic conduct at this crucial juncture. And the conservatives felt abandoned and betrayed by the Party leader. Vorotnikov fulminated: "What did Gorbachev want? Everyone can see what would become [of the USSR] if Yeltsin is the head of Russia." On 29 May, amid increasing frustration and weariness at the Russian Congress, Yeltsin was elected with a margin of four votes.[69]

Gorbachev learned the news when his presidential plane was above the Atlantic. Just as for his previous visit to the United States, in December 1988, the Soviet leader was accompanied by a huge number of advisors and staffers, dozens of officers from the KGB 9th Directorate protecting him, a big pool of journalists, intellectuals, writers, artists, and academics. The situation, however, changed dramatically. No longer an enlightened potentate with absolute power, Gorbachev was now a hapless reformer, whose domestic power hung on a thread. The Western media wondered whether he would survive the Party Congress. Teimuraz Stepanov, who was on the plane, pondered the news from Moscow: Yeltsin was the political product of Gorbachev's errors and hubris, and his gamble to make the Union a pawn in his grandiose ambitions. "If he now declares Russia's secession from the Union—then what union would Gorbachev represent when he comes back home? And if Gorbachev decides to curb the heretic, then what kind of a traditional Russian rebellion would follow?" Some advised Gorbachev to send his congratulations to the Russian leader. "At least, this can mollify millions of embittered hearts," Stepanov thought. "After speaking with Raisa, the Soviet leader refused to do it."[70]

Instead, he had another scheme in mind. On the first day of the summit, 31 May 1990, when Bush asked him about Germany and NATO, Gorbachev suddenly acknowledged that, according to the Helsinki Final Act, Germany should be given the right to choose any alliance it wanted to join. Bush and other American officials could not believe their ears: Gorbachev was giving away something very significant without bargaining or even consulting his advisors. Was it a slip of the tongue? Marshal Akhromeyev and Valentin Falin, a key Soviet expert on Germany, gesticulated and whispered in evident horror. Even Shevardnadze tried to stop Gorbachev. Chernyaev was the only other man in the Soviet delegation who was not surprised. Gorbachev, he reflected, was sacrificing diplomacy, but not to keep himself in power—instead, in the name of his vision. The Kremlin leader wanted the United States and its allies to help the USSR become "stronger but democratic . . . progressive, dynamic, free, and turned towards the outside world and the US."[71]

The rest of the Soviet delegation did not share such lofty aspirations. There was no longer a sense of common purpose animating them, no faith in Gorbachev or the future of the country. Few had illusions that an alliance with the Americans could save Gorbachev's failed reforms. Most of the delegation just took this opportunity to rummage through American stores, using their per diem dollars to buy goods unavailable at home. Stepanov was disgusted and felt a strong moral urge to resign. Sergey Tarasenko, an aide of Shevardnadze, recalled: "We began to realize that we would be able to stay afloat for a while and even preserve the status of a great power only if we leant on the United States. We felt that if we had stepped away from the US, we would have been pushed aside. We had to be as close as possible to the United States."[72]

Gorbachev was bolstered by the American promise to help him reform the Soviet economy. The Americans firmly believed this meant a rapid transition to market capitalism. "One cannot be half-pregnant," Bush observed. Gorbachev picked up the metaphor: "But neither can you have a baby in the first month. We want to avoid an abortion." He told Bush that American advice and money would be crucial to ease the painful transition.[73] As a starter, the Soviet leader asked Bush to approve economic agreements, especially the Trade Act that would grant the Soviets most-favored-nation status. Shevardnadze almost pleaded with James Baker to concede on this issue. The Soviet leader was then delighted and grateful when Bush consented. Gorbachev also asked him whether he could extend loans to the Soviet Union, to which Bush politely declined. He and Baker explained their reasons: opposition in Congress; the continuation of Soviet aid to Cuba and Afghanistan; and the absence of a Soviet law on the free emigration of Jews.[74]

In the Soviet delegation, everyone felt that Gorbachev would return to a much less governable Soviet Union. The Soviet leader, however, seemed unconcerned and genuinely savored every moment in North America. He basked in American admiration for his historic achievements and the respect that ordinary Americans showed him and Raisa—in contrast to increasingly vulgar attacks at home. American cultural stars flocked to meet the Gorbachevs at a gala reception held at the Soviet Embassy. Mikhail and Raisa felt very relaxed in Camp David, in the company of George Bush and his wife Barbara. Gorbachev rode a golf cart, learned to play the American game of throwing horseshoes, and talked for hours, confiding in Bush about his problems and reforms. Bush listened patiently and showed sensitivity. After the Washington summit, Gorbachev flew to Stanford University, where he was accorded a hero's welcome; former Secretary of State George Schultz hailed Gorbachev as "a great man, a great thinker."[75]

In Moscow, on 12 June 1990, Yeltsin scored a second and much bigger victory at the RSFSR Congress—the declaration on Russian sovereignty. There were several versions of this declaration. The Politburo approved an anodyne version according to the principle: "a stronger center means stronger republics."[76] Yeltsin's version was very different. His "Russia" would have total legal, economic, and political sovereignty. The republic, he declared, "must have the right . . . to pass and cancel economic measures on its territory, carry out fundamental reforms." The British ambassador commented on Yeltsin's "bull-headed" remarks at the Supreme Soviet. "Yeltsin is making the same demands as the Balts, though . . . he has not, as far as I know, suggested that Russia should secede from the Union."[77]

And yet this version formed the basis of the final declaration. Only thirteen voted against it, and nine abstained.[78] This was perhaps the most remarkable vote in Russian history. The declaration blended conservative nationalism ("the multi-century Russian sovereignty") with the message of democracy-building ("to create a democratic and lawful state"). It also legalized Russian separatism. When "sovereign rights of the RSFSR" clashed with Soviet laws, the latter could be suspended. The document also claimed all assets on the territory of the republic to be the possession of the republic's people as their "exclusive owner." In practice, this included the Kremlin as well. Later, on Yeltsin's cue, the Assembly adopted a technical but a truly revolutionary decree that enabled the Russian republican ministries, until this point purely decorative institutions, to take over economic assets on the RSFSR's territory. This, in effect, was a declaration of political and economic war against the central state.[79]

Observers in the West were puzzled: Why did the Russians need independence from their own state? The British scholar Archie Brown later mused that Russian "sovereignty" was comparable to the British practice of "home rule" as distinct from separate statehood. In the United Kingdom, the majority in Scotland, Wales, and Northern Ireland had demanded and received "home rule" in the form of their own parliaments and devolution to them of some important state functions from London. The English conservatives also wanted "home rule," but did not get it.[80] What happened in the Soviet Union in June 1990 was that both Russian conservatives and radicals demanded home rule for the constituent republic of the Union, without bothering about how the Soviet equivalent of Scotland (Ukraine) and Wales (Belarus), would react.

The sociologist Galina Starovoitova was one of the MDG leaders elected to the Russian Congress. She explained the huge success of the declaration of sovereignty as "the striving of Russia to find its sovereignty." It was also, in her view, the expression of a Russian inferiority complex towards other republics, who at least had an appearance of national institutions.[81] The desire of provincials to take control of resources "from Moscow" should not be discounted as well. In one fell swoop, Gorbachev's reforms created a rival "Russian" institution with popular legitimacy and constitutional authority, led by a communist maverick who had transformed himself into a Russian separatist. The RSFSR Congress deputies also formed a "Russian" counter-elite with an aggressive rival project. Few understood at the time that the two elites, the central and "the Russian," could not be reconciled; for one to prevail, the other had to go.

"STABILIZING GORBACHEV"

The Russian declaration of sovereignty triggered "the parade of sovereignties" in other republics. Most notable was the declaration of "state sovereignty of Ukraine" on 16 July 1990. There had been two previous declarations in Ukrainian history. The first had been passed by the Ukrainian Rada in Kiev in January 1918, to protect the land against Bolshevik invasion and insurgency. The second had been made in Lvov on 30 June 1941, by the Organization of Ukrainian Nationalists (OUN), murderous ethnic nationalists, who praised "cooperation with the national-socialist Greater Germany, which under the leadership of Adolf Hitler creates a new order in Europe." The new Ukrainian declaration was mostly a copycat version of the Russian one. It claimed that all resources on Ukrainian territory belonged to "the people of Ukraine" and promised to represent all "Ukrainians" outside the republic. Ukraine owned everything on its territory, could have its own State Bank and armed forces. The declaration referred to the Soviet Union only indirectly, by claiming the republic should share in "Union wealth," such as the state's reserves of gold and currency.[82]

None of the Western leaders could understand the new Soviet politics. They just wondered why Gorbachev provoked so much anger and hatred among his countrymen. Yeltsin and many other critics in the opposition trashed Gorbachev on CNN and other Western media channels. At a meeting with Bush on 8 June, Kohl said: "I think we should stabilize Gorbachev." On 19–20 June, the Chancellor's office invited the deputy head of the Soviet government, Stepan Sitaryan, to come to Berlin to negotiate the financial aspects of a future German settlement. On 25 June, the West German government signed a formal agreement on financial assistance to Soviet troops. Soviet officers would exchange their savings for Deutschmarks, one to one; Soviet forces in the GDR after 1 July would be largely funded from the West German budget.[83]

At the summit, Gorbachev privately said that the Soviet economic reforms needed $20 billion per year for three years to succeed. Bush asked his Treasury Secretary, Nicholas Brady, and the head of the Economic Council, Michael Boskin, what the administration could do to help Gorbachev. Both were adamantly opposed to any financial package for the USSR. Brady reasoned that Congress and the Republicans would excoriate the President. Boskin, a descendant of Jews who had fled from Russian pogroms, responded that Gorbachev and his people would probably not succeed in a country like Russia. "Either they'll be gone, or a political backlash will stop the reforms." Bush candidly admitted later: "We could not give them [the Soviets] the 20 billion dollars of financing they wanted unless they made deep economic reforms—and even then we didn't have the money."[84]

In public, the administration continued to dangle the promise of American assistance, as leverage on the Soviet government. Bush, however, decided to entrust the guidance of Soviet reforms to the experts at the International Monetary Fund (IMF) and the World Bank. The benefits of this decision were apparent: Bush would show Gorbachev that he cared about his reforms, and at the same time the administration would not be held responsible for their possible failure. At the summit in Houston on 9 July, the G-7 leaders discussed a formal Soviet request for funds. President Mitterrand and Canada's Brian Mulroney were Gorbachev's advocates, but Margaret Thatcher and Japan's Prime Minister Toshiki Kaifu supported Bush's line. The leaders signed a communiqué that asked the IMF, the World Bank, and their European homologues "to convene a study on the Soviet economy."[85]

Bush recalled the logic of Western policy at that time as follows: "To make progress on the broad US-Soviet agenda and Germany, the Soviets and Gorbachev needed to save face and their standing, although everything around them was falling to pieces—their empire, and their economy, and now their union."[86] At the meetings in Scotland and later in London, the NATO leaders, prodded from Washington, declared that the alliance's strategies were shifting from deterrence of the USSR to cooperation with the former Cold War enemy. In Dublin, foreign ministers of the European Economic Community made a similar symbolic "open door" gesture to the Soviet Union. As two members of the Bush administration later concluded, it was "the best and final offer" the West could make to Gorbachev.[87]

The G-7, NATO, and EEC declarations came just in time for the Soviet leader. The founding conference of the Russian Communist Party, which opened in Moscow on 19 June 1990, was the culmination of a powerful movement inside the Russian conservative Party elites who wanted to stop Gorbachev's liberalization and reverse the Party's political demise. On 22 June, the day on which the Nazi invasion of the Soviet Union began in 1941, General Albert Makashov, commander of the Volga-Ural military district, appealed to the memory of the millions of Soviet victims who had died during the liberation of Eastern Europe. Now, he said, the Soviet army was being chased out of those countries "without a fight." "A rehearsal of dinosaurs ... before [the Party] Congress," wrote Shevardnadze's liberal aide, Teimuraz Stepanov, with horror in his diary. The majority of Russian communists elected Ivan Polozkov, a hard-line, anti-intellectual, provincial apparatchik, to be their Party leader. Then came the Party Plenum, which included more humiliating attacks on Gorbachev's course of action and threats to remove him from the post of General Secretary.[88]

At this moment, the Lithuanian Supreme Soviet bowed to Western pressure. On 29 June, it made a long-expected concession and suspended the independence declaration. This was a bright spot on Gorbachev's stormy horizon. He immediately lifted the embargo on the republic.

The Twenty-Eighth Congress of the CPSU, held between 2 and 13 July, became the most unusual Party gathering since Lenin's death. On the eve of it, Gorbachev convened the Politburo for an informal dinner and asked them to submit their resignation. If he survived the Congress, he said, he wanted to have a free hand to choose another Politburo. Everyone, including the obstreperous Ligachev, complied.[89] At the Congress, angry and confused functionaries believed their leadership had betrayed them. One after another, the Politburo members stood up before the hostile audience to account for their activities. Ryzhkov survived through 500 questions about the economy; Shevardnadze was asked fifty questions about foreign policy. His aide Stepanov was on edge. "One more step and pogrom would start!" he confided to his diary. Fortunately for Gorbachev, Shevardnadze, and other architects of perestroika, the audience had no common ideology or resolute leadership. The usual tactic of letting off steam worked again. Nobody was booed or chased from the podium for "treason." Yakovlev even received applause for his skillful rhetoric. During the elections of the new Central Committee, delegates voted against all members from "A" down the alphabet. When they reached the end of the alphabet, where Shevardnadze and Yakovlev stood, the anger of the audience suddenly abated; people grew tired of pressing the same red button again and again. In the end, Gorbachev, with procedural ruses, managed to retain most of the former Politburo members in the new Central Committee.[90]

At the critical moment, Shevardnadze passed to Gorbachev an advance copy of the NATO declaration of cooperation with the Soviet Union, provided by their American partners, to rebuff the alarmism of Soviet hardliners. In the end, Gorbachev was re-elected as the General Secretary of the CPSU, even though almost a quarter of the delegates voted against him. Shevardnadze, Chernyaev, and others in the liberal-minded minority were stunned by Gorbachev's comeback. Ligachev, whom the Moscow intelligentsia had rumored to be a possible candidate to replace Gorbachev as Party leader, was the loser. The populist anti-corruption attacks had badly wounded him. And many Party apparatchiks disliked his heavy-handed administrative style. He gained very few votes at the Congress and subsequently left the ranks of the leadership.[91]

Boris Yeltsin stole Gorbachev's thunder again. Suddenly, the Russian maverick took the floor with a prepared statement: he had decided to leave the Party, in order to become the leader of Russia. Accompanied by catcalls, Yeltsin then slowly and deliberately walked from the podium up the aisle towards the exit. For the millions who watched his exit on television, it was the most dramatic and memorable news. After this performance, Yeltsin stopped being Gorbachev's struggling twin and became a national leader in his own right. His popularity in public opinion polls soared.[92]

On 14 July, the day after the end of the Party Congress, Gorbachev met with NATO Secretary General Manfred Wörner, who offered cooperation between the Western alliance and the Soviet Union. This meeting paved the way for Gorbachev's secret meeting with Kohl the next day in Moscow. The Soviet President consented to a unified Germany's membership of NATO and withdrawal of Soviet troops in exchange for "compensation" and acceptance of Soviet security requirements. Those requirements were virtually identical to the terms offered to him by Baker, Kohl, and Genscher back in May. Chernyaev, the only other official who knew about the meeting, and who had helped to prepare it, warned Gorbachev that the deal had to be made on the spot. He worried in vain: Kohl, elated and grateful, accepted the conditions. He just asked Gorbachev to keep the financial assistance to Soviet troops a secret from the German public.[93]

This was the first time since Stalin that a Soviet leader had acted single-handedly. Shevardnadze was not invited to the meeting and only learned about what happened after the event. On 16 July, Gorbachev invited Kohl to a resort in Arkhyz, Northern Caucasus. This was where, many years previously, Gorbachev had entertained Yuri Andropov. Now the Kremlin leader was relying on a powerful Western friend and sponsor to help pull the ailing Soviet Union "into Europe." After strolls and one-on-one conversations, the two politicians were joined by Shevardnadze, Genscher, and a few Soviet and German experts. They haggled over the details of "the big deal." Gorbachev wanted to extend the Soviet troops' length of stay in East Germany, but in the end he agreed that they would leave by 1994.[94] This Blitz-diplomacy by the Soviet leader did not improve the final deal, but it impressed those in Gorbachev's entourage who had criticized him for his concessions.

During the first half of 1990, Gorbachev continued to devolve power to the republican elites; he ended up with increasingly feisty Russian counter-elites in Moscow; one led by Yeltsin in the RSFSR Supreme Soviet, another in the "Russian Communist Party." Those counter-elites represented the contradictory forces of the Russian liberal intelligentsia, populism, and conservative nationalism. As a result, Gorbachev's authority plummeted, and his political base remained shaky at best. His only position of strength, aside from his control of state powers, was as a unique world statesman. With the help of his Western partners, Gorbachev reaffirmed his statesmanship: he became a founding father of German unification and the new European order. With his allies and friends in the West, primarily Bush and Kohl, the Soviet leader hoped to reassert his authority at home. However, Gorbachev lacked a fundamental tool with which to demonstrate success: the Soviet economy was continuing to deteriorate and there was no credible strategy to deal with it.

CHAPTER 5

CROSSROADS

Thus conscience does make cowards of us all . . .
And enterprises of great pith and moment
With this regard their currents turn awry,
And lose the name of action.
William Shakespeare, *Hamlet*

THE TIME OF ECONOMISTS

In February 1989, on a visit to Moscow, the British economist Alec Nove said about the Soviet economy: "Not only can't I see the light at the end of the tunnel. I can't even see the tunnel." Nove was born as Alexander Novakovsky in St Petersburg in 1915, emigrated to the United Kingdom with his family after the Revolution, and taught Soviet economic history in Glasgow. In November 1989, Nove visited Moscow again, and was struck by how much the situation had deteriorated still further. Soviet economists told him that a catastrophe was looming. Nobody could adequately explain the nature of this crisis.[1] The Soviet Prime Minister Nikolai Ryzhkov and his top economist Leonid Abalkin could not explain the crisis either. In their memoirs they complained that politics had intervened and disrupted their plans. They never recognized that the reforms of 1987–88 had created new actors—autonomous state enterprises, cooperatives, and commercial banks—which, instead of generating more consumer goods, cannibalized the existing state economy and hemorrhaged state finances.[2]

Some government officials recognized this threat. The Minister of Finance, Valentin Pavlov, and his experts informed the government that industrial state enterprises were retaining 60 percent of their profits, while passing on only 30 percent toward the state budget. In doing so they "earned" 100 billion rubles, yet spent them on salaries that only added to the inflation-driving cash in the economy. The volume of investments in productivity and modernization kept falling. As a result, the experts concluded, the economy was underfunded, while the state budget deficit was about to soar. The experts at the Ministry of Finance proposed that all state enterprises and cooperatives must pay 50 percent of their profits to the state budget. In response, the lobbyists in the Supreme Soviet launched a fierce counter-attack. They painted the government as a reactionary force that threatened to block economic perestroika. Ryzhkov and Abalkin caved in, suffering from the same syndrome of "no stepping back on reforms."[3] In December 1989, the Ryzhkov government submitted to the Congress of People's Deputies a new program that merely perpetuated the structural and functional errors of previous reforms. The Congress instructed Ryzhkov to revise and resubmit his program with modifications.[4] This work would take most of 1990, which became the year of endless economic debates and decisions not taken.

The Ryzhkov government wanted a state-regulated market; its ministers argued that regulatory institutions—fiscal, monetary, and others—would take five to seven years to create. Leonid Abalkin, a product of Soviet economics, believed that market reforms had to be carried out under state controls and with considerable preparations: the government had first to accumulate a stockpile of goods and create regulatory mechanisms and market institutions, and only then cautiously deregulate the economy. The government, however, confronted immediate and severe challenges: Western banks suspended their lines of credit. An increasing amount of Soviet oil, the main source of hard currency, was sold abroad at market prices by Soviet "cooperative" ventures, which found ways to pocket the profits. The Soviet Union still had gold, but its reserves sank to 784 tons; it was less than half of what Stalin had hoarded by the time of his death. The government began to negotiate with De Beers to sell up to $1 billion of uncut diamonds a year for five years. Simultaneously, the Supreme Soviet increased state expenses to support low-income groups. The Ministry of Finance was forced to print more and more rubles.[5]

In March 1990, the government was shaken by a scandal from which Ryzhkov could never recover. On an abandoned railroad platform near the southern port of Novorossiisk, KGB officials discovered twelve T-72 tanks, registered as "pulling trucks." The paperwork indicated that the tanks came from the Ural Wagon Plant, a huge tank factory, and were commissioned by the cooperative "ANT" for shipping abroad. The export of Soviet arms had always been a state monopoly. What, then, did a commercial entity have to do with it? The cooperative ANT (a Soviet acronym for Automatics—Science—Technology) had been created in 1987 by Vladimir Ryashentsev, a former officer of the KGB's

Ninth Directorate. The cooperative worked under the auspices of an R&D department in Ryzhkov's Council of Ministers, staffed by KGB officers. The idea was to "swap" the products of the Soviet military-industrial complex for foreign goods in high demand, such as personal computers or medicine.[6] Ryzhkov approved of its activities, but failed to take account of the unwanted publicity. The newspaper of Russian communists, *Soviet Russia*, scooped this story. The KGB's Kryuchkov and Ligachev denounced the export of arms on television.[7]

During a televised session of the Congress of People's Deputies, Anatoly Sobchak called ANT a plot of nomenklatura officials to enrich themselves, while thwarting real market reforms. He accused Ryzhkov of a cover-up. Gorbachev, meanwhile, maintained a safe distance from the affair. This episode demonstrated the power of populism. TV viewers forgot Ryzhkov's energy and heroism in Chernobyl, Armenia, and other hotspots, and applauded Sobchak's unmasking of corruption in high places. The investigation of "the ANT affair" lasted for months, without ending in a trial. Ryashentsev later fled to Hungary; a few years later he was found dead.[8]

While the Soviet government suffered from a dual crisis of solvency and confidence, the Polish post-communist government launched a blitz to create a market economy. The press dubbed it "the Balcerowicz Plan," after Leszek Balcerowicz, the Polish economist who designed it. Polish reforms closely followed the recipes of macroeconomic stabilization developed by the IMF and World Bank. The Polish government deregulated prices, liberalized trade and private entrepreneurship, and capped the growth of wages and salaries for state employees. This was a bitter pill to swallow: prices and unemployment soared. Very soon, however, Polish peasants began to deliver food to the cities, money no longer chased scarce goods, and the spike of inflation subsided.[9]

The Polish reforms inspired Soviet economists to think creatively. Gorbachev's newly appointed economic advisor, Nikolai Petrakov, was the first to write a coherent program of rapid market transition. Intellectually, he was rooted to Soviet "mathematical economics" of the 1960s; its adepts hoped to use computers to calculate supply, demand, and investment needs—thus replacing the Party-State bureaucracy.[10] Petrakov's political sympathies lay with the Moscow-based democratic opposition, and he viewed the Ryzhkov government as inept and incompetent.[11]

On 10 March 1990, Petrakov put on Gorbachev's desk an outline of radical economic reform based on the logic of deregulation. The Soviet state, Petrakov argued, should stop distributing resources to the economy. Prices of raw materials and consumer products should be deregulated. Petrakov also proposed to curb *beznal* crediting of state enterprises (*kreditnaia emissia*), which he correctly recognized as the main source of Soviet inflation. In early 1990, not only the State Bank, but also the republican banks, goaded by "sovereign" republican parliaments, began to increase such credits. With the help of private "cooperatives" and commercial banks, the tight partition between the two kinds of Soviet currency, cash and cashless, fell apart. The State Bank had to print ever-growing amounts of money. Petrakov proposed that by Gorbachev's decree the State Bank would become the master of credit and monetary policies, while the Council of Ministers would regain control over the budget. The Supreme Soviet would not have the power to launch new inflationary state programs. The dualism of the Soviet financial system would be gradually dismantled. The circulation of "free" cash, ruinous in an economy of deficit consumer goods, would be sharply reduced. State enterprises should be transformed into joint-stock companies and stop acting like scavengers of state resources. The government would create a stock exchange and cap the budget and credits. Meanwhile, the state would authorize the deregulation of real estate and possibly land, to allow people to invest their surplus cash into long-term projects. The program had a timeline: in March–April, the main decrees, laws, and acts were to be prepared; in May–June, an institutional overhaul would begin; and on 1 July, the privatization of state enterprises would begin.[12]

The Petrakov program was realistic and original. It owed a lot to Chinese experience, and was also quite different from the IMF's "one size fits all" shock therapy implemented in Poland. Had Petrakov's ideas been carried out in 1990, with the state levers and financial system still intact, the fate of the Soviet economy could have been very different. The ruinous "mixed economy" of 1987–88 would have been retracked towards a successful market economy. Unfortunately, Petrakov's brilliant insights went completely over Gorbachev's head. The Soviet leader did like a political point: that in the longer term, market forces would provide a powerful glue to bind the republics together. But he feared the political risks that transition to a market economy would bring. In a conversation with Poland's President Jaruzelski in April, Gorbachev commented on the Polish liberation of prices: "If you or we had done a similar thing, people would have overthrown us." Petrakov responded to this concern by proposing to secure a big Western loan to import large amounts of consumer goods to satisfy demand and alleviate tensions at the crucial moment of structural reforms. He also offered an original solution to protect people's savings: interest on savings accounts would be paid in US dollars.[13]

Gorbachev hesitated. He remembered the miners' strikes from the previous summer. And he had no political will to send Ryzhkov's government into retirement. On 14 April, at the joint meeting of the Presidential Council and the Council of Federation, the government proposed a transition to a market economy and deregulation to start in January 1991. That was the limit of Ryzhkov's radicalism. One economist after another agreed with the government outline, yet they warned about the social and political fallout. After the Soviet collapse, Gorbachev would say that the economists failed him and hedged their bets. They, however, said the most important thing: the transition to a market economy was inevitable and the political risks were high. Temporizing would only make this dilemma worse. The economist Stanislav Shatalin said another important thing: self-accounting by the republics was "the greatest stupidity of all"; it would only encourage republican separatism. The market economy would reconsolidate the Union. This is what Petrakov had said before.[14]

Gorbachev was the only one at the meeting who feigned surprise at the "sudden" eruption and depth of the economic crisis. Instead of promoting Petrakov's reforms, he waited for Ryzhkov to "update" the government program. Gorbachev also delegated the discussion of economic strategy to the parliamentary assembly.[15] Both were exercises in futility. In the atmosphere of polarization, radical populism, and a search for scapegoats, only the President could launch a new policy. The Supreme Soviet's deputies voted for higher minimum wages and other costly state programs of social protection. They were not concerned that such programs could only be paid for by printing more money, thereby increasing inflation. The Ryzhkov government finally proposed a 55 percent tax on the profits of state enterprises, but the populist Supreme Soviet vetoed it. In the republican Supreme Soviets, nationalism magnified this trend.[16]

Gorbachev resumed the discussion of reforms on 22 May at the Kremlin. Primed by economists, he acknowledged that inflationary manipulations of state enterprises and cooperatives "unbalanced the market."[17] Government officials spoke of obstacles, not solutions. They spoke of a Polish-style reform as the only alternative and warned that in that case unemployment would soar to between 15 and 40 million. The KGB chief spoke about possible strikes. The discussion focused on the poorest in society and digressed into specifics. When to raise the price of bread? How to compensate the most needy? The Russian writer Valentin Rasputin urged those in attendance "to seek the advice of the people." Remarkably, none of Petrakov's innovative solutions were brought up.[18] Valentin Pavlov from the Ministry of Finance was among the very few who pushed for action. He proposed raising wholesale prices on energy and bread. He explained that the remaining partition between the two currencies—*beznal* for wholesale prices and cash for retail prices—gave the Soviet government unique leverage to stimulate the oil industry and agriculture, while avoiding an immediate rise in the prices of consumer goods. Gorbachev did not understand what Pavlov was talking about. Ryzhkov suspected that Gorbachev had left him with the bleak business of dealing with retail prices, the Supreme Soviet, and a furious public calling for the government's resignation. Already wounded by the ANT affair, Ryzhkov acted irrationally. He proposed a national discussion on price reform—the worst idea imaginable!

A few days after the Kremlin meeting, he went on television to discuss economic problems and said that prices would have to go up. Those words triggered panic-buying and hoarding across the country. Even Ryzhkov's closest aides were surprised. Gorbachev recalled: "Perhaps Nikolai Ivanovich had a nervous breakdown."[19] Whatever the reason, the planned economic reform from above was again rejected. The furious parliamentarians sent the government program back to the drawing board yet again, with a deadline of September. The Ryzhkov government was doomed, yet it did not want to resign.[20]

THE BATTLE OF PROGRAMS

The declaration of Russian sovereignty and the election of Yeltsin as the head of the RSFSR Assembly closed the window of opportunity that Gorbachev had after becoming President of the USSR.[21] He could not abolish Russian sovereignty; he now had to negotiate with the Russian parliament. The Supreme Soviet of the RSFSR was located in a big white marble building up the river from the Kremlin. For years the building had been rather a quiet place; now it turned into a beehive of activity. Whereas the Soviet leadership consisted of people who were turning sixty, the Russian Assembly attracted younger members in their thirties and forties disillusioned with Gorbachev's leadership. And the deputies from Democratic Russia felt like commissars whom people had elected to clean the Augean Stables. One of them recalled: "We expected that Gorbachev would make a blood transfusion and part ways with [the conservatives]. He had plenty of people inside the Party on whom he could have relied." Instead, Gorbachev "surrounded himself with the same old men, the same speech-writers. For us, they were the men of the past." By default, the RSFSR parliament had to become a focus for opposition to Gorbachev and the old Soviet elites.[22]

Ruslan Khasbulatov, a forty-eight-year-old Chechen economist, became a principal mover and shaker behind the drive for Russian sovereignty. At the age of two, Khasbulatov had been deported from Chechnya to Central Asia. De-Stalinization then allowed him and other Chechens to return home; he studied law and economics in Moscow, and became a professor at the Moscow School of Political Economy. In the summer of 1990, Khasbulatov channeled his ambitions into the battle for sovereignty. On 13 July, on his initiative, the Supreme Soviet of the RSFSR adopted a law that transformed the branch of the

State Bank for the Russian Federation into a "Bank of Russia," subordinate to the Russian parliament. This institution was authorized to perform all monetary functions. The law did not even mention the State Bank of the USSR.[23] The head of the State Bank, Viktor Gerashchenko, viewed this law as the end of the Soviet financial system. How could there be two competing centers of money supply in one economy? Khasbulatov disingenuously denied he meant harm. The group of Moscow banking experts, who helped to create the Russian bank, knew better. They joked darkly that they deserved to be shot. Indeed, they recalled that the first act of the Bolsheviks in 1917 was to seize the imperial bank. Revolutions failed when they could not take control of the money.[24]

The Russian parliament launched the spectacular career of economist Grigory Yavlinsky. Born in Lvov, Western Ukraine, he graduated in economics from Moscow (at the same school where Khasbulatov and Abalkin taught), and worked as a researcher in the Soviet ministerial apparatus. In 1989, Abalkin invited him to join his team of experts in the Council of Ministers.[25] In January 1990, Yavlinsky, then thirty-eight, traveled to Poland as a government expert to observe the Balcerowicz reform. He was deeply impressed and decided that the same had to be done in the Soviet Union.[26] With two other economists, Yavlinsky wrote a program for Gorbachev to deregulate and privatize the Soviet economy within a year. The title of the program was "400 Days of Confidence." It was similar to Petrakov's program, although less coherent and clothed in populist garb for the consumption of ignorant parliamentarians. The key element of success, Yavlinsky argued, was people's trust and savings. Instead of wiping out those savings by freeing up prices, the reformers should help people invest them into privatizing small shops, real estate, trucks, buses, and so on. The Soviet intelligentsia and professionals would thereby become a propertied middle class.[27]

The "400 Days" found admirers in the Russian parliament. Mikhail Bocharov, a talented politician and member of Democratic Russia, was vying for the post of Prime Minister of the RSFSR. He decided to boost his economic credentials: he appropriated Yavlinsky's program, changed the title to "500 Days," and presented it as his own economic "program for Russia." He still lost the election, yet he became head of the Supreme Economic Council, a brain trust of economic reforms. When Yavlinsky discovered what had happened, he met with Bocharov and Yeltsin. The young economist explained that 500 Days could not be just "a Russian program": the Soviet economy was one integrated body, its industries spread across the republics like veins and arteries. One had to treat the whole patient, not just its limbs and parts. Yeltsin, impressed by Yavlinsky's arguments, offered him the post of deputy Prime Minister in the Russian government.[28]

Yavlinsky accepted the offer, but decided that his program needed two sponsors: Yeltsin and Gorbachev. On 21 July, he contacted Petrakov, who immediately recognized the political potential of this idea and informed Gorbachev. The President of the USSR replied: "Where is this fellow? Get him here right away."[29] At Gorbachev's request, Yavlinsky flew to Jurmala, a resort in Latvia where Yeltsin vacationed. The first reaction of the Russian leader was negative: his ego rebelled against an alliance with Gorbachev. In his speeches all over the country Yeltsin had preached "a sovereign Russia" with its own banking system, foreign policy, and foreign trade; it would also withhold "Russian taxes" from the Union's budget. The remaining "center" would only deal with defense, communications, and energy.[30] Still, Yeltsin guessed he could benefit from a tactical alliance with Gorbachev. For the first time, the Kremlin leader was ready to establish an equal partnership with the Politburo maverick. Gorbachev confirmed this by calling Yeltsin himself on the telephone. Yeltsin agreed to a joint reform effort.[31]

Gorbachev, as his biographer William Taubman writes, supported the 500 Days more out of desperation than rational calculation.[32] Indeed, the Soviet leader was searching for a credible response to the Russian declaration of sovereignty, as well as the Lithuanian crisis. Yavlinsky's proposal was a godsend. An economic agreement signed by Yeltsin and leaders of other republics, Gorbachev hoped, would pave the way to a new Union Treaty. The successful deal with Kohl on German reunification had also boosted Gorbachev's self-confidence. He wanted to achieve in domestic politics what he had accomplished in foreign affairs. At the meeting of the Presidential Council on 20 July, Gorbachev enthused about his recent meeting with Jacques Delors, "the father" of the European Union. If European states, with their history of nationalism and wars, had succeeded in integrating, he argued, then the Soviet republics had much better reasons to stay together, despite their troubled history.[33]

Petrakov and Yavlinsky relished a unique opportunity to put their ideas into practice. They drafted a directive tasking an "independent" group of experts to produce "a concept of the Union program for transition to a market economy as the basis of a Union Treaty." They selected several economists who shared their ideas. Stanislav Shatalin, the only economist in the Presidential Council, would lead the group. Within one month, on 1 September, the concept would be presented to the Supreme Soviets of the Union and the RSFSR for discussion and approval.[34] The economists expected that Gorbachev and Yeltsin would sign the directive and get the ball rolling. On 27 July, Gorbachev signed the draft directive without even changing a word; Yeltsin did so as well. Gorbachev, however, insisted that Ryzhkov must also sign. The hapless Prime Minister was the last to have learnt about the directive and felt ambushed. Gorbachev was tossing his program, which had cost Ryzhkov so much effort, into a dustbin and had turned to a rival team of economists! So Ryzhkov refused to sign the document. Gorbachev was annoyed: he and Raisa were preparing to go to Crimea for a summer vacation. The Soviet leader flew to the Black Sea on 30 July. Two days later, after consulting with Abalkin and other deputies, Ryzhkov gave in and signed. He lacked the energy to become once again "an enemy of reforms" and a scapegoat for public opinion.[35]

The outcome was a rivalry between the two teams. Petrakov, Yavlinsky, and the economists they selected moved to Dacha no. 6 in Arkhangelskoye, west of Moscow, a fully equipped state complex of cottages, where they could live and work in comfort. The group worked with a high sense of mission: they believed they knew a way out of the economic crisis. Yeltsin met with the economists two times. Gorbachev called Petrakov every day, to enquire about their progress. He also received drafts and sent them back with his markings.[36] Ryzhkov's team of experts, led by Abalkin, worked at another resort near Moscow. They focused on amending the government program, which had to be submitted to the Supreme Soviet in September. When Gorbachev called from Crimea to express his concern about the lack of cooperation between the two groups, Abalkin replied that nobody had instructed him to suspend work on the government program. Would the President authorize it? Gorbachev did not take this responsibility. The Soviet leader still wanted to keep Ryzhkov in his job, although he barely talked to him anymore.[37]

The rivalry grew into political antagonism. Petrakov and Yavlinsky took the first step: they decided that they should involve the republics' representatives. All of them, including the Balts, came to Arkhangelskoye and discussed the 500 Days. Petrakov recalled: "I believed that if economic stability could be achieved, then the acute ethno-nationalist conflicts would abate. The frustration of the people caused by shortages is automatically translated into the language of nationalism . . . Moscow is the capital of Russia, therefore all economic troubles are blamed on the Russians." This quotation may explain why the economist sacrificed the coherence of his program to ethno-nationalist demands. The economists in Arkhangelskoye, all of them Russians, suddenly acknowledged that the republics must have absolute legal supremacy over the Union authorities; all resources and economic assets within a given republic were declared to be the "property of its people." This was not economics, but pseudo-democratic populism. Naturally, Yeltsin and his emissaries embraced those "principles" with alacrity. They refused to accept the principal condition of a possible future Union—a federal tax. And they insisted that a future Union government must be a committee of republican representatives. That was an invitation to separatism and economic disaster.[38]

Gorbachev hesitated to accept this logic, and the economists turned to journalists for support. Yavlinsky was a talented propagandist and gave numerous interviews to the media. Moscow-based periodicals with an enormous circulation extolled the 500 Days as the last hope for the country; the economists were lauded as the new prophets and saviors. A complicated issue became a matter of binaries. The pro-Yavlinsky media presented the Abalkin team as agents of the military-industrial complex, the inefficient agrarian lobby, and the nomenklatura bureaucracy. In response, the other team counter-attacked by claiming that the 500 Days was a plan to sell the country downriver to foreign capitalists.[39]

In late July 1990, public opinion polls in Moscow demonstrated that about 70 percent of respondents favored transition to a market economy, but only 15 percent wanted to start the transition immediately.[40] The media campaign about the 500 Days filled the pro-market mood with a new sense of urgency. Even some leaders of Soviet trade unions embraced an immediate transition to a market economy and denounced the government for dragging its feet. This was a publicity stunt for the Petrakov-Yavlinsky group, but also for Yeltsin.

On his first day of vacation in Crimea, Gorbachev told Chernyaev he had a new theoretical project: "socialism and the market." He dictated his thoughts, but when his speechwriter produced a draft, Gorbachev rejected it with a grimace. Two more attempts also ended in failure. The Soviet leader stretched his neo-Leninist framework to the limit, yet he could not match market capitalism with Soviet "socialism": one had to go. Gorbachev also worked on theoretical aspects of the Union Treaty, but he stumbled there too. The Soviet leader wanted to create a voluntary federation that would replace the Soviet Union, yet he still counted on the Party as a political instrument to hold the republics together. Gorbachev, educated in constitutional law, acted like an over-zealous editor: he played around with words and paragraphs to reach a satisfactory conclusion. The conclusion pointed, however, to a weak confederation, without a federal center. When Shakhnazarov brought this to Gorbachev's attention, the Soviet leader angrily dismissed him. He continued to read Lenin in search of clues.[41]

While Gorbachev theorized in Crimea, Yeltsin met twice with the Arkhangelskoye economists and approved what they had done. He also campaigned all over the Russian Federation. The 500 Days became his key slogan: this "Russian program," he promised, would change people's lives for the better after two years of transition. On the future Union Treaty, Yeltsin repeated his ultra-democratic mantra of sovereignty that had to emanate from the grassroots upwards; a Russian Federation must be rebuilt as a pyramid in reverse. During his visits to Tatarstan, Bashkiria, and Komi, autonomous regions within the Russian Federation, Yeltsin urged people "to take as much sovereignty as they could digest."[42] Gennady Burbulis would later defend this blatantly populist slogan as "an honest, principled approach," as opposed to the political manipulations of Gorbachev. In reality, Yeltsin was providing another huge boost to the centrifuge of political separatism.[43]

In mid-August, Gorbachev invited Chernyaev and Yevgeny Primakov, his new favorite, to a dinner at his villa. Both advisors urged him to reach an alliance with Yeltsin, fully embrace the 500 Days, and dump the Ryzhkov government. Otherwise, they argued, Yeltsin could strike an alliance with the Russian communists and mobilize forces under the banners of "Russia" against Gorbachev. Gorbachev dismissed the danger. He felt he could control the Russian Communist Party. He vented his fury at Yeltsin, "a scoundrel, with no rules, without morals, no culture." He agreed that he had to deal with him, "because nothing can be done without Russia." Yet if he dumped Ryzhkov, he would be exposed to "another hostile front." Gorbachev assured his advisors that Ryzhkov, the Council of Ministers, and the whole communist apparatus would become "natural victims of an unfolding market system. This will happen already this year."[44] The last phrase indicated that the Soviet President wanted to adopt 500 Days and understood its consequences for the old statehood.

On 21 August, at Gorbachev's request, Ryzhkov, Abalkin, and other members of the Soviet government arrived in Arkhangelskoye, ostensibly to find common ground with the rival team. The meeting turned into a showdown. Yeltsin's emissary Burbulis later suspected a personal motive: deep, half-conscious jealousy of Ryzhkov toward another "man from the Urals"—Yeltsin. The causes of their disagreements, however, were principled and serious. For Ryzhkov and Abalkin, the main actors of a future market economy were central ministries and state corporations. For Petrakov and Yavlinsky, the main beneficiaries of an economic union would be the sovereign republics. The middle ground between the two approaches was gone. Abalkin asked Petrakov what he understood by "the Union." "Is this a state or not?" He did not receive a clear answer. Petrakov recalled the meeting differently, but he admitted that the point about the future of the statehood was central. For Abalkin, he recalled, the collapse of the Soviet Union and a transition from socialism to capitalism "was something awful and unacceptable." Apparently, Petrakov at some point began to take it for granted. In conclusion, Ryzhkov said emotionally that he would "not bury the state with my own hands" and vowed to fight to the end against "the grave-diggers" of the Soviet Union.[45]

This standoff forced Gorbachev to cut his vacation short. On 23 August his plane landed at Vnukovo-2 Airport. Following the Soviet tradition, the members of the Politburo, the Presidential Council, and aides came to greet the President. When the sun-tanned Gorbachev appeared, Ryzhkov, Lukyanov, and Masliukov accosted him and demanded an urgent meeting with the government. After

Gorbachev left, Ryzhkov turned to Petrakov, his face pale with hatred: "You will go down in history!" Lukyanov added: "If you keep it up, in September the Supreme Soviet will oust the government. In November the Congress of People's Deputies and the Supreme Soviet will be disbanded. There will be new elections, and in December the president will be toppled—and you too!"[46]

Gorbachev met with Petrakov and his team next morning. The excited economists, who worked in summer shirts at the state dacha, did not even have time to go home to fetch their jackets and ties. The meeting lasted for five hours, and Gorbachev charmed everyone. He found time to read the draft program, treated young economists as intellectual partners, and posed good questions. Shatalin, who missed most of the work of his team because of sickness, came to the meeting and recalled that "our guys felt as if they had wings." Gorbachev said he would discuss the 500 Days at the Presidential Council and with Yeltsin as soon as he returned to Moscow. He invited Shatalin and Petrakov to attend his meeting next day with the Ryzhkov government. At that meeting, members of the government vociferously warned Gorbachev against an alliance with Yeltsin. At one point the head of Gosplan, Yuri Masliukov, declared: "We must get rid of Yeltsin ... at any price!" The President cut him off: "Stop talking nonsense." Gorbachev had resorted to his method of letting off steam.[47]

Gorbachev met with Yeltsin on 29 August. It was their first one-on-one meeting since 1987. There had been bad blood between them for years. The Russian leader began the meeting with grievances. Why had Gorbachev tried so hard to prevent his election as the RSFSR chairman? There was a chance for a frank talk, yet Gorbachev shrugged him off: "Come on, Boris. Look how you lambasted me in America, in your books, in your interviews."[48] Political differences were even more profound. Gorbachev asked if Yeltsin wanted his job. Yeltsin responded he did not. "I have enough business to do in Russia." In fact, Yeltsin wanted to eliminate the Soviet Union altogether as a strong federated state. He was ready to accept only a confederation of sovereign states, such as Russia, without a strong central government above them. Yeltsin's specific demands were equally radical. He demanded that the Ryzhkov government should go, along with the heads of the Ministry of Finance, the State Bank, and the External Trade Bank. The Ministry of Finance had to be supervised by trustees from all the republics. The Russian Federation must have its own KGB and police, control of Moscow as its capital, its own customs, continental shelves, forests, fisheries, and manage numerous installations and "closed cities" of the military-industrial complex on its territory. The Russian government had to get its share of the gold reserves, diamonds, oil and other resources. The Russian Academy of Sciences, television, and an airline company would be established. And, like the cherry on top of a cake, Yeltsin declared that "the Kremlin is the property of Russia."[49] Yesterday's outcast, elected only by a tiny majority of the republican parliament, spoke the language of ultimatums.

The President of the USSR patiently negotiated with Yeltsin, which only added to the growing perception of Gorbachev's weak position. Chernyaev recorded in his diary: "Telegrams are arriving for Gorbachev from everywhere . . . Screaming about the impotence of the authorities and the President . . . The conditions for dictatorship are ready. Where will it come from? Gorbachev is incapable of this."[50] Gorbachev's appeasement of Yeltsin was the product of his personality, but also an expression of his disdain for his rival. Before their meeting, Gorbachev had received from Boldin information about Yeltsin's medical history which claimed that, from 1986 onwards, Yeltsin suffered from psychological "instability" that affected his political behavior.[51] Similar "diagnoses" for political dissidents had been produced under Andropov. It is likely, however, that those allegations influenced Gorbachev. In his mind, only a sick man could make such demands of him.

Yeltsin challenged Gorbachev from the pedestal of his popularity. According to the data from an independent survey, Yeltsin's approval rating had soared from 27 percent in May 1990 to 61 percent in July. Gorbachev's popularity had sunk from 52 percent in December 1989 to 23 percent in August 1990. In Moscow, only 26 percent of people wanted Gorbachev to remain as President of the USSR; 34 percent preferred Yeltsin.[52] On the eve of his meeting with Gorbachev, Yeltsin said: "I have long stopped fearing him . . . Now we are equals." In a close circle of his entourage, he called the Soviet President a pampered prince, who had reached his supreme post by entertaining his superiors, including Andropov and Brezhnev, at the spa. While Gorbachev viewed himself as a new Lenin, Yeltsin treated him as Kerensky, the vacillating head of Russia's provisional government in 1917.[53]

Yeltsin later asserted that Gorbachev promised to arrange a "voluntary" resignation of Ryzhkov and retirement of other government officials on Yeltsin's list. They also allegedly agreed to put the 500 Days into action within the next two weeks. The tentative plan was that Gorbachev would circumvent the conservative Supreme Soviet of the USSR and approve the 500 Days by presidential decree; then he would send its text to the republican assemblies, including the RSFSR parliament, for discussion. Yeltsin promised that the Russian parliament would approve the program first, setting the trend for the other republics.[54] This agreement, if it ever really existed, was never implemented.

The day after their discussion, Gorbachev convened a huge meeting of the Presidential Council and the Council of Federation, to discuss the economic agreement and the Union Treaty. He invited 170 government officials, ministers, the leadership from eleven republics, except for the Baltics and Georgia, and officials from fifteen autonomous regions within the RSFSR. He even brought a delegation of workers who were on a visit to the capital.[55] Shatalin presented the 500 Days, praising privatization and private ownership as the only long-term solution to nationalist conflicts. "When Estonian money comes to Russia, and Russian investments are made in Ukraine, then normal economic life will begin." He also mentioned the need for preliminary financial stabilization. Otherwise, he said, "the market will simply destroy us." Then Masliukov presented the government program and complained that Western banks had stopped giving credits to the Soviet Union until the central and republican authorities got their act together. Without foreign credits, he warned, the Soviet economy would shrink by one-fifth in 1991. The authors of both programs vowed to keep in place enormous social programs and entitlement payments, which constituted 65 percent of the Soviet budget.[56]

Yeltsin then spoke and admitted that the RSFSR could not take the leap to a market economy alone. This would necessitate borders and customs controls with other republics, and a separate currency. If the Russian government took this road, it "would become an initiator of the Union's collapse." The Russian leader urged Gorbachev again to get rid of the Ryzhkov government. "The center must change . . . It must be a genuinely strong presidential power . . . [It must] exercise firmness . . . without calling it a dictatorship, without a transition to dictatorship . . . People will understand and approve it."[57] The leaders of other republics and autonomous regions struggled to understand the purpose of the meeting. They had come to Moscow to bargain for more rights and resources. Instead, they only heard about the two economic programs. Which one would be implemented? Gorbachev remained the supreme moderator. He proposed to put members of the rival camps on a joint panel, to work out a compromise. Yavlinsky and other young economists protested, and Shatalin threatened to resign. Gorbachev was taken aback. "You are letting me down," he said to Shatalin, and "you should not be part of the group." The economist immediately apologized but also complained that it would be very hard to find a consensus. Gorbachev reacted like a Komsomol cheerleader: "No, you will find it! Comrades, do not give up . . . Just wait, we will have to act when people are out on the streets. Mobilize your creative strengths. Keep on searching!! We will find it!!!"[58]

The presidential conference continued the next day and produced an emotional outbreak from Ryzhkov. The Prime Minister took the microphone several times, in a state of extreme agitation. Without the strong central government and his program, he said, the country would disintegrate immediately. The Supreme Soviet of the USSR, Ryzhkov demanded, should "make a decision" and choose between the two programs. Then, in plain contradiction with this, he described the current parliamentary system as the main reason why the country and the economy had become ungovernable. "We must end this instability [when] the country became topsy-turvy [*khodit khodunom*]." At one point he turned to Gorbachev: "Mikhail Sergeyevich, we are comrades, friends. Act as a President, bring order to the country. Use the capacities and rights you received . . . We will help you."[59] The meeting erupted in a cacophony of competing voices, and Gorbachev hastened to close the session. The two-day gabfest had only added to everyone's sense of political paralysis.[60]

Gorbachev asked the academician Abel Aganbegyan, one of the economic architects of the 1983–87 reforms, to reconcile the two programs. The Soviet leader insisted that the 500 Days should be combined with the existence of the federal government and a federal tax.[61] Many condemned Gorbachev for this position, and some historians even consider it as the point where the Soviet leader lost his last opportunity to relaunch reforms under his auspices. Yet Gorbachev's hesitation had its political logic: without the central government, the President would be left alone to deal with fifteen republics and the huge Congress of People's Deputies. There would be widespread chaos in the Soviet economy where all main industries had been constructed as centrally controlled conglomerates. Without Ryzhkov, or at least without his experienced deputies, the entire class of Soviet economic managers would become an unruly herd. And the second-tier apparatchiks in the republics and autonomous regions had no expertise with which to grapple with corporations located on their territories, but always governed from Moscow.[62]

BLACK SEPTEMBER

Even in times of relative stability, it would have been hard to square this circle. The fall of 1990, however, was marked by political neurosis, polarization, and a dwindling middle ground. Emotions and irrationality flooded and drowned out political and economic calculations. David Remnick, a young *Washington Post* journalist in Moscow, remembered "Black September" of 1990 as a turning point in the drama of the Soviet collapse. It started with a horrendous crime: on 9 September, an Orthodox priest called Alexander Men was brutally murdered in a village near Moscow. The killer was never found. Father Alexander Men was born a Jew, but he had dedicated his life to the Russian Orthodox faith. Remnick's friends, Muscovite and liberal intellectuals, were also of Jewish descent: they and their children had been baptized by Father Men. As people working in media, culture, and the humanities, they had initially backed Gorbachev's perestroika, but they now rooted for Yeltsin and Democratic Russia. They were scared. Father Men's violent death, they believed, was part of a wider conspiracy, which included the anti-Semitic elements of the Russian

Orthodox Church, the KGB, and other "dark forces" inside the Party and the military-industrial complex.[63]

On the day following Father Men's murder, the Soviet military began suspicious exercises around Moscow. For Remnick and his Moscow friends this was reminiscent of Poland in 1980–81, which ended with martial law. The American journalist concluded that "in a totalitarian world," paranoia was the most realistic way of looking at things. "A creeping coup was under way," he wrote in his book. "As we would soon find out in the coming months, first in Vilnius and Riga, then in Moscow, there was indeed a conspiracy under way, and it was the most open, unguarded conspiracy imaginable." Later, Remnick wrote a book about these events. Many other Russian and Western analysts repeated modifications of the same story. It was included in the BBC series "The Second Russian Revolution" that was filmed at the time.[64]

What was going on in September 1990? Was there any conspiracy afoot? Russian historians never discovered any concrete evidence. According to their findings, on 8 September, Colonel-General Vladislav Achalov, commander of the Airborne Troops in the Soviet Army, ordered five divisions to advance towards Moscow "in a state of higher readiness." The next day, the Ryazan airborne division was dispatched to Moscow in full gear with all its weaponry. Two days later, the Pskov airborne division was ordered to do the same. One Russian historian concluded: "Only the President of the USSR Mikhail Gorbachev and the Minister of Defense Dmitry Yazov could put those forces in motion." Achalov later claimed that those orders were part of preparations for a regular military parade in Moscow to commemorate the anniversary of Lenin's October Revolution on 7 November.[65]

It is hard to imagine Gorbachev secretly rehearsing the implementation of martial law just a week after his meeting with Yeltsin The Soviet commander-in-chief was also preparing for his summit with Bush (see p. 143). Still, the story of "Black September" matters. Rumors and fears of violence often go hand in hand with state paralysis and anarchy. The "Great Fear" of July–August 1789 had fueled a peasant uprising and contributed to the French Revolution. The myth of a "creeping coup" fed the Soviet imagination and contributed to fears of a future dictatorship in Moscow in September–December 1990. The Moscow-based journalist Viktor Yaroshenko wrote about this phenomenon in *Novy Mir*. He recognized that the Soviet power structures were crumbling, but he also knew that Russian democracy had no roots—such as private property or political and social traditions. He called the political polarization "the energy of collapse." "We don't have a struggle between democrats and totalitarians," he wrote, "but rather warfare between the two teams of totalitarians, only the new people have put on democratic shirts." Individuals he knew or observed had the most fantastic transformations. The top Party leaders abhorred the use of force. The leaders of Democratic Russia wanted to destroy the state by any means possible.[66] Alexis de Tocqueville, a perceptive commentator on the French Revolution, would have nodded in agreement.

Anatoly Adamishin, the Soviet ambassador to Italy, visited Moscow in September to find that the country "was falling into a precipice." His friends, the economists Petrakov, Aganbegyan and Shmelyov, agreed that only an "emergency" and dictatorship could hold society together. Adamishin's classmate Leonid Shebarshin, head of the KGB's foreign intelligence service, told him: "The next week should be decisive." In what sense? Who would be a dictator? "Gorbachev and his men," Adamishin wrote in his diary, "lacked guts for decisive steps." Still, he returned to Rome with the conviction that something was afoot: "If everything points to dictatorship, one should choose the most appropriate form of it, including face-saving for the outside world."[67] Years later in his memoirs, Pavlov, the Minister of Finance, revealed his own September plot. He and Ryzhkov's deputies, Masliukov and Vladimir Shcherbakov, agreed to pose an ultimatum to Gorbachev to adopt an emergency economic course. If he turned it down, the entire government would submit its resignation. Ryzhkov equivocated. Pavlov recalled him saying: "No, it is too late. They will blame us for fearing difficulties, for provoking a crisis. We will carry our cross to the end." Pavlov recognized that the head of the government was unable to take any independent action. The plot fizzled out.[68]

William Taubman writes about Gorbachev at this time: "There was no good way out—none that Gorbachev could see and perhaps none at all."[69] The old saying, however, goes: "Where there's a will, there's a way." Instead of attending congresses, convening councils, and tinkering with texts, Gorbachev could have replaced the unpopular Ryzhkov and appointed a ruling economic junta with emergency rights. He could have implemented the Petrakov program, without the morass of parliamentary debates or hopeless talks with ethnonationalists. This could have led to chaos, but at least it would be a chaos that Gorbachev, had he acted instead of talking, had the powers to control.

While the revolution in the Soviet economy stalled, Gorbachev and Shevardnadze managed to carry out a quasi-revolution in foreign policy, the next one after the talks on German unification. On 2 August 1990, the megalomaniacal Iraqi dictator Saddam Hussein dispatched his army to annex neighboring Kuwait. Soviet foreign policy was at a crossroads. Iraq was a leading Soviet ally in the Middle East and the biggest buyer of Soviet armaments: the total amount of these purchases over three decades came to 18.3 billion rubles and included 41 warships, 1,093 MIG aircraft, 348 combat and transport helicopters, 4,630 tanks, 5,530 armored personnel carriers (APCs), 3,279 artillery and mortar pieces, and 84 tactical missile systems.[70] Unlike other Soviet allies, Iraq had paid for all this in US dollars. Also, Soviet experts serviced the Iraqi oil industry, while the KGB had trained Saddam Hussein's security. About 8,000 Soviet citizens lived and worked in Iraq. On that day, by chance, Shevardnadze and James Baker were meeting in Irkutsk, near Lake Baikal, for arms control talks. Shevardnadze immediately decided that the USSR must join the United States against the Iraqi aggression. What happened next was kaleidoscopic. While Baker flew off to Mongolia for a pre-planned visit, the Soviet Foreign Minister flew to Moscow with Baker's aides Dennis Ross and Robert Zoellick. In mid-air, they drafted a joint US-Soviet declaration that put embargoes on the sale of weapons to Baghdad. In the Foreign Ministry, after a shouting match with his Arabists, Shevardnadze got his way. Gorbachev, at that point in Crimea, immediately backed Shevardnadze's decision. It was a stunning contrast to the domestic gabfest: there were no Politburo meetings or sessions of the Supreme Soviet. The KGB's Kryuchkov and Minister of Defense Yazov were simply informed about the decision.[71] Baker, who returned to Moscow on 3 August, was amazed and elated: he and Shevardnadze made a joint declaration of intent in the presence of CNN and the world's media. The Secretary of State considered it "the day the Cold War ended" and later would begin his political memoirs with this epochal event. In the White House, the normally skeptical Scowcroft shared this feeling. In Eastern Europe in 1989, and on German reunification, the Soviet leadership had reacted to the needs of the time, at least from an American viewpoint. This time, over Kuwait, Gorbachev and Shevardnadze had made a strategic choice that nobody forced them to do.[72] Bush was immensely impressed too: he called Gorbachev and proposed a summit in Helsinki to discuss cooperation on the Gulf.[73]

Gorbachev and Bush met in Helsinki on 9 September. Scowcroft and CIA analysts had briefed Bush that Gorbachev's authority "was in precipitous decline" and the Communist Party "irreparably weakened." Yet, as Chernyaev observed, it was Bush at the start of the summit who was "very nervous, fearing a failure." The US President desperately needed Gorbachev's support in the United Nations to legitimize his war against Iraq. He told Gorbachev: "Mr. President, I appeal to you as a respected friend, an equal, an important partner and participant in the events whose role is quite significant." Bush offered his Soviet partner the prospect of building a new world order together. American policy, which had sought to exclude the Soviet Union from Middle Eastern affairs, now wanted to include it. And Bush suggested that the two men should be on a first-name basis.[74]

Yevgeny Primakov, a leading Soviet Arabist, proposed brokering a withdrawal of Iraqi forces from Kuwait, in exchange for a promise to Saddam to hold a peace conference on the Middle East. This plan, however, clashed with the American strategy of punishing the Iraqi regime, destroying its military strength, and establishing US hegemony in the Persian Gulf. Shevardnadze was furious at Primakov's interference. His aide Sergey Tarasenko later explained: "We were sinking as a state, the status of a great power was only in our memory. The only way for us to hold on as a great power was to hitch ourselves to the American locomotive." There was also a strong personal motive: like Shevardnadze, Primakov was also from Georgia and his political rival. Shevardnadze and Tarasenko signaled to Baker and Ross that they should undermine Primakov's plan. In Helsinki, Chernyaev sided with Shevardnadze: "We must put America before the Arabs. This is our future and our salvation."[75]

Gorbachev liked Primakov's scheme, yet when Bush offered him the prospect of building a new order, he changed his mind. He agreed to drop Primakov's linkage between Iraq and a peace conference in a public statement. This satisfied Bush and Baker. The Soviet leader then changed the subject: he asked the Americans to help with his economic reforms. The idea, he said, was to free up prices and saturate the market with products, so people could see the positive results. For this, Gorbachev concluded, he needed Western money. "The numbers are not great," he specified, "and we are not asking for grants, just loans that we will pay back with interest." American and Soviet participants set aside the main agenda and began to talk about joint ventures and economic cooperation. Bush promised to release the technology of horizontal drilling for oil, previously denied to the USSR. Gorbachev brought up the negotiations with Chevron to explore the Tengiz oil fields in Kazakhstan. Primakov and even Marshal Akhromeyev joined in this conversation with great interest.[76]

The next day, Baker flew from Helsinki to Moscow to join the US Secretary of Commerce Robert Mosbacher, who brought a delegation of American businessmen to discuss joint ventures. The head of Gosplan, Masliukov, was an official host, but Gorbachev took the leading role. He invited the American businessmen to the Kremlin and promised them his political support. Chernyaev noticed that the Americans kept raising the same question: should they deal with the center or the republics? They hesitated to invest their money, fearing that the parliaments of Russia or Kazakhstan would renege on Soviet commitments. Gorbachev waved aside those doubts. He pressed Baker for more assistance with Soviet reforms and asked him for $1.5 billion of credit. In Helsinki, he had been too proud to ask Bush about it. The Secretary of State praised the Soviet leader to the skies for his international leadership, but explained that a line of credit for the Soviet Union remained blocked due to problems from the past, going back to "the Kerensky debt" of 1917. This was the debt that the Russian provisional government had incurred and the Bolsheviks had refused to honor. Baker joked about this: by the time the US Congress acted to remove these obstacles, the Soviets would have finished with perestroika twice over. He proposed to approach Saudi Arabia, the wealthiest Arab country in the Middle East and a key American ally. In the following days, with American mediation, Gorbachev turned to King Fahd with a request for money.[77]

"He has been begging everyone for money, for credits," Chernyaev wrote about Gorbachev at that time. On 7 September, before the Helsinki summit, the Soviet leader had also spoken with Kohl. They mentioned the signing of the German Treaty in Moscow on 12 September and the celebration in Berlin on 3 October. Above all, however, they had discussed Gorbachev's precarious position at home and his request for money. Kohl had offered 8 billion Deutschmarks to cover the cost of Soviet troops in East Germany and the reset-tlement of officers and their families back in the USSR. That was the most, his ministers told him, that the German budget could bear. Gorbachev, however, wanted twice as much. Kohl called again on 10 September, and offered 11–12 billion DM. Gorbachev said: "The transition to a market economy must begin on 1 October. I am in a bind and cannot haggle." Kohl responded that German companies were eager to support the Soviet transition to a market economy. "In the fall, we will talk about a big credit. I gave you my word and I will keep it." As a form of stop-gap assistance, the Chancellor offered an interest-free line of credit of 3 billion DM over five years. Gorbachev accepted the offer.[78]

The Soviet leader also made a pitch for funds to Israel. The Israelis, he told Chernyaev, would raise $10 billion to support the Soviet reforms. In return, Gorbachev promised to restore Soviet-Israeli diplomatic relations—broken in June 1967 because of the Six-Day War between the Arabs and Israelis—and legalize Jewish emigration. Beyond the Middle East, Gorbachev also turned to EU leaders for financial aid. The Italian Foreign Minister Gianni De Michelis came to Moscow with a preliminary agreement to provide a line of credit. The final amounts were significant: 3 billion DM from Kohl, $1.5 billion from Mitterrand, slightly more from Spain's Prime Minister González, the same from Italy, and $4 billion promised by King Fahd. The Israelis offered nothing.[79]

By the time this fund-raising campaign ended, however, its policy objective had disappeared: the Soviet program of economic reforms was in tatters. In early September, members of the Supreme Soviets of the USSR and RSFSR returned from their vacations. The two assemblies, products of Gorbachev's reforms, both had their seats in Moscow, separated only by a few miles. Instead of collaboration, they created a bipolar disorder in the Soviet capital. In the Russian parliament, which opened its session on 3 September, Yeltsin and Khasbulatov distributed copies of the 500 Days to the deputies, who approved it on 11 September. In the all-Union parliament, Ryzhkov boycotted the program;

Lukyanov told the deputies to wait for a compromise document. The war of laws between the two parliaments flared up. Ryzhkov publicly proposed to raise wholesale prices on meat. On this bombshell, all meat disappeared from stores. The Russian parliament reacted by raising the purchase price of meat on the RSFSR's territory without waiting for the Soviet government. The deputies also increased fivefold the price of "Russian" oil for domestic consumption. They also voted to raise pensions and social assistance to compensate for inflation. Petrakov and Yavlinsky looked on in horror, as the two parliaments were racing to undermine the financial foundations of economic reforms.[80]

Political emotions focused, naturally, on the question of power. On 21 October, after three weeks of delays, Gorbachev asked the Soviet legislature to give him additional presidential authority, to negotiate with the republics and implement market reforms. When the Russian parliamentarians learned this, they passed a law that made the President's decrees void on the territory of the RSFSR. That was a turning point for those in the Union parliament who were elected from Russian districts. They began to feel that their days in politics were numbered. The pressure grew on Gorbachev to build up the executive power and declare an emergency. On 24 September, the assembly voted to grant the President of the USSR power to declare an emergency in some areas of the country. The journalist Yaroshenko, who watched the proceedings from a press gallery, thought again about a creeping coup: Gorbachev had become a legal dictator of the Soviet Union. He was stunned that millions of Russians around the country simply did not notice or care.[81]

The suspense of "Black September" ended in farce. In the Russian parliament, three dozen deputies issued a manifesto with slogans: "The Fatherland is in danger!" "Organize civil disobedience!" "The Army, do not turn your arms against people!" The proclamation proposed to seize power and property, and to form self-defense squads. The faction espoused an extreme form of Russian nationalism; the author of the manifesto was a Party member who was also a crackpot theoretician of Russian neo-fascism. Two days later, *Pravda*, still the newspaper with a multi-million circulation, published a scathing comment on "protest activities" in the Russian legislature.[82] In the Party apparatus where democrats suspected there lurked dark conspiracies, functionaries were scared. They expected democrats to topple the communist authorities at any time, as in the Eastern European scenarios of 1989. The Moscow Party Secretary Yuri Prokofiev said about the manifesto of 24 September: "I have studied [it] with a pencil in my hand. This is a direct call for the overthrow of the existing powers, for anti-constitutional actions."[83]

On 29 September, Gorbachev met with hundreds of representatives of the "creative" Soviet intelligentsia. The majority were from Moscow, members of the guilds of writers and artists with an elaborate system of privileges, paid out of the state budget and endowments. Gorbachev's reforms emancipated them from the Party controls, censorship, and the KGB's informers. At the meeting, however, nobody celebrated those new freedoms and praised Gorbachev. Everyone spoke of a new 1917, fearing anarchy and civil war. The composer Georgy Sviridov and the actor Kirill Lavrov spoke about the flight of scientific and cultural elites, many of Jewish origin, to Israel and the West. Mikhail Shatrov, a playwright with Jewish roots, feared pogroms. "The intelligentsia is capable of capsizing the ship," he said. "Now the intelligentsia should ask itself if it can help to steady the ship, at a time of awful turbulence." The editor of *Novy Mir*, Sergey Zalygin, bemoaned the excesses of glasnost: "In our country everyone has become a critic. And we set the example . . . We instigated the people to take this chattering path." The theater director Mark Zakharov said: "I am for strong presidential power with unlimited functions for some time." The Minister of Culture, Nikolai Gubenko, a well-known actor, grabbed the bull by the horns: "We are drunk with unfamiliar freedoms and destroy our cultural and historical tradition that brought many nations together [and formed the state that] is now named the Union of Soviet Socialist Republics."[84] The same people who wanted to bury Lenin and the Party dictatorship now called for a new dictatorship. It was up to Gorbachev to accept or reject this appeal.

A HOUSE DIVIDED

The date of 1 October came round, but the 500 Days program was dead, torpedoed from all sides: by the Soviet government and by the Russian parliament's populism. Yavlinsky was the first to abandon the sinking vessel of reform. At the end of September, at the peak of the euphoria, he and other fellow economists flew to the United States, paid for by the American billionaire George Soros, to present 500 Days at an international forum organized by the IMF and World Bank. A small army of translators, also paid for by the Soros Foundation, produced a thick English version of the 500 Days overnight.[85] After returning to Moscow, however, Yavlinsky discovered that the program was in ruins and complained about it to Yeltsin. The Russian leader was at home, recovering after a car accident. On 21 September, in downtown Moscow, a compact "Zhiguli" car had hit Yeltsin's chauffeured sedan. Everyone in Yeltsin's entourage and millions of Russians believed it was a failed KGB assassination attempt. Yeltsin told the young economist not to get upset: "We will roll everything back later on, after Gorbachev is out." Yavlinsky later claimed he was appalled by such cynicism. He resigned from the RSFSR government. Yeltsin offered him the post of economic advisor, but Yavlinsky politely declined.[86]

Petrakov continued to serve as Gorbachev's economic assistant until the end of the year. He decided, however, to appeal to public opinion again. On 4 November, *Komsomolskaia Pravda* published a manifesto signed by Petrakov, Shatalin, Yavlinsky, and other economists who had produced the 500 Days. They attacked a compromise program prepared by Aganbegyan—the one that Gorbachev had approved. This document, the manifesto declared, would not solve any problems and only doom the country to misery.[87]

On 15 October 1990, Mikhail Gorbachev was awarded the Nobel Peace Prize. The Norwegian Nobel Committee in Oslo recognized his unique contribution to the end of the Cold War. It was another gift from the grateful West. Raisa collected hundreds of congratulatory and laudatory articles and letters, mostly from abroad. Domestic correspondence, however, denounced Gorbachev for his role in destroying the Soviet state and the stable economy. Gorbachev showed some of the letters to Chernyaev, who wondered why his boss spent his precious time reading this rubbish. Gorbachev's aide believed that the best option for his boss would be to take his Nobel prize and retire. Instead, Gorbachev continued acting as a busybody who "inserts himself everywhere" without any idea what to do.[88]

Boris Yeltsin responded to Gorbachev's Nobel prize in his unique way. On 16 October, in a speech to the Russian Assembly, he blamed Gorbachev for his failure to keep to his side of the bargain. He called Gorbachev's attempt to produce a hybrid program of economic reform "a catastrophe." He blamed economic disaster and inflationary spending on the Ryzhkov government. And he laid out three options for the Russian Federation. First, to implement the 500 Days in "Russia" alone; take full control of RSFSR customs and foreign trade; have its own banks and currency; get its share of Soviet military forces. Second, to form a coalition government between Gorbachev and "the advocates of radical reforms." Third, to wait about half a year, until Gorbachev's plans crumbled.[89]

At the Presidential Council, Kryuchkov and Lukyanov urged Gorbachev to respond to Yeltsin's "declaration of war" by an appeal to the people on television and by going ahead with economic reforms without asking the republican authorities for consent. Ryzhkov feared the opposition would seize power imminently and lynch him as well as other government officials. Medvedev and Shevardnadze opted for a compromise. Boldin cut in: "We must abandon our illusions about Yeltsin. He will never work with us. His state of health drives him to confrontation." His choice was to affirm the central power. Gorbachev exploded: "It is not about Yeltsin. He reflects social trends. People sense the approach of chaos, collapse. They want order and are even ready for emergency measures." Then, however, he agreed with Boldin: "This paranoiac seeks to grab the Presidency [of the USSR]. He is sick. His entourage keeps inciting him. We must deal him a good one in the mug." In a huff, Gorbachev asked Shevardnadze to cancel all his foreign trips for the weeks ahead. Horrified, Chernyaev, Petrakov, Shatalin, and other advisors pleaded with Gorbachev after the meeting. They feared nationwide strikes and civil disobedience. Chernyaev told his boss that he should ignore Yeltsin's bluff and build up his international stature. This was a winning argument. Gorbachev relented and decided to proceed with his foreign trips.[90]

Yeltsin's speech revealed his priorities once again. The Soviet Union, he said at a meeting with the British Foreign Secretary Douglas Hurd, would be replaced by "a pyramid in reverse"—a voluntary union of sovereign republics. "Russia was now in a position to sign treaties with foreign countries, not only on economic matters but, for example, on a nuclear test moratorium." He assured the surprised Hurd that "Gorbachev would not object" to this. The British ambassador Rodric Braithwaite, who was present at this meeting, felt that Yeltsin was "interested in power, and his current tactic is to destroy Ryzhkov, emasculate and discredit the Union government," and later "eliminate Gorbachev as well." For Braithwaite, those objectives were "hopelessly unattainable," and he made a striking comparison between the Russian leader and Hitler: "He evidently believes in the Triumph of the Will, in his ability to achieve what more ordinary people say is impossible."[91]

The Russian people's support was all that Yeltsin had. The Russian Federation was a ghost state without a functional bureaucracy, expertise, money, or resources. For seventy years, this giant republic had followed the orders of the central all-Union ministries and the central Party apparatus. Many in the regional KGB and police branches, ethnic Russians, supported Russian sovereignty and Yeltsin personally, yet there was no "Russian KGB."[92] Yeltsin even lacked a proper security detail: only "Sasha" Korzhakov, a former KGB officer, protected him. Gorbachev promised that some administrative-bureaucratic resources would be transferred from the central government to the Russian state. Yeltsin's October speech seemed to end the opportunity for such generosity. Yeltsin realized it. After making a grand gesture, the Russian leader telephoned Gorbachev to offer his lame excuses. He did not, however, give up on his objectives.

In the fall of 1990, Gennady Burbulis assumed a particularly prominent role next to Yeltsin. The views and activities of this man would have a growing influence on his master. Burbulis, like Gorbachev and Raisa, had studied philosophy and had a penchant for theory and intellectual debates. When perestroika started, he was teaching Marxism-Leninism at the Ural University; in 1987 he launched a discussion club that attracted huge crowds of professionals and the intelligentsia. In March 1989 he was elected to the Congress of People's Deputies and joined a group of Moscow intellectuals around Andrei Sakharov. In 1990, Burbulis concluded that a new democratic Russia should destroy the USSR, an awful totalitarian empire, liberate other nations, and join the West in building a global liberal order. He began to collaborate with Americans from the Republican Right, who provided money for "democracy seminars" in various Russian cities.[93]

In September 1990, Burbulis convinced Yeltsin to set up "a supreme consultative-coordinating council" and invite leading Moscow intellectuals and "intelligent" provincials to discuss political strategy. Yeltsin, who had always envied Gorbachev's intellectual entourage, immediately agreed. The project was an instant success: Moscow's intellectual elite, already disillusioned with Gorbachev, flocked to "the council." At the first sessions in October 1990, Yeltsin sat in awe listening to the best and brightest of the country. "He absorbed new ideas like a sponge," Burbulis recalled.[94] The discussions focused on how to prevail against Gorbachev's center. The theater director Mark Zakharov expressed the common view: "Russia . . . needs to take Napoleonic steps," and therefore "needs its own KGB and police force." Otherwise, "Russian transition and democratic transformation will not be carried out."[95]

Further influential advice for Yeltsin came on 18 September from the famous nationalist writer and dissident Alexander Solzhenitsyn: the newspaper *Komsomolskaia Pravda* published 18 million copies of his pamphlet "How to Rebuild Russia?" The famous émigré writer wrote that Russians for centuries had made up the empire. The Soviet experiment had exhausted Russians; they could no longer carry the imperial burden. Solzhenitsyn proposed to dissolve the Soviet Union, and preserve its Slavic core: the RSFSR, Ukraine, and Belarus, populated by "three fraternal peoples." Solzhenitsyn proposed retaining the northern parts of Kazakhstan, developed and populated by "Russians."[96] The pamphlet had a big impact on Yeltsin. Burbulis reinterpreted Solzhenitsyn's idea: he proposed to form a political union of the three Slavic republics against the Kremlin.[97]

On 21–22 October, Democratic Russia convened its conference in Moscow. Some 1,600 delegates from seventy-three regions of the Russian Federation gathered in a giant movie complex, appropriately called "Russia." About 300 journalists, Russian and Western, and 200 foreign guests attended. Arkady Murashov, the top organizer and a friend of Burbulis, announced to the press the main goals of the movement: "to put an end to the Soviet socialist period of Russian history" and to elect a president of the Russian Republic, who would "neutralize the destructive activity of the communist imperial center."[98] The meeting was a bazaar of liberal anti-communist rhetoric and intelligentsia sectarianism. Gorbachev became a focus of critical attacks, because of his failure to implement the 500 Days. The popular magazine *Ogonyok* quoted the rant of one delegate: "Had we gone to market . . . like the Poles, our stores would have been stuffed with goods; pineapples would have been sold in the streets; rubles would have been exchanged for dollars and pounds at every corner." Never mind that the 500 Days aimed *to avoid* the Polish-style reforms! Other delegates demanded that they get rid of all Soviet state structures at once, including the Party and the President. Only Andrei Sakharov's widow Yelena Bonner called for collaboration with Gorbachev.[99]

After his trip to Madrid and Paris, Gorbachev returned to Moscow to attend another Presidential Council on 31 October. Some in his entourage believed that Democratic Russia and Yeltsin were acting according to the Bolshevik scenario of 1917. "The country has become ungovernable!" Even Shevardnadze and Yakovlev called for a strong executive power. The head of the KGB said: "I assert that even today the Party remains the only force in the country that can make things happen." Yazov fulminated against young popular TV journalists, who mocked the armed forces, and suggested that they "throw this scum out." Lukyanov summed up an authoritarian vision of implementing economic reforms. The Party power should be resurrected. The Party organizations in the Army, the KGB, the police, and courts must be preserved. The Supreme Soviet of the USSR was the last political redoubt on which Gorbachev could rely. People had grown tired of anarchy and crime, and would back the President's strong-armed policies. The intelligentsia, aside from the democratic extremists, would support him as well, out of fear of a civil war. Lukyanov rejected any coalition with Yeltsin. The opposition, he said, only wanted to seize economic resources and was not ready to govern. Contradicting himself, Lukyanov compared the Russian "democrats" to Solidarity in Poland. First, they would make Gorbachev a figurehead president like General Jaruzelski; then they would get rid of him. Gorbachev agreed: "We immediately saw through their scheme." Encouraged by Gorbachev's support, Lukyanov came up with an idea: to set up "a small staff with dictatorial powers." It would "coordinate all processes." Its analytical center would outdo the opposition, "by thinking five–six steps ahead."[100] Everyone waited for Gorbachev's reaction. He pretended not to understand the essence of this proposal. A few minutes later, he said: "Comrades, do not wait for instructions. I am tired of hearing from you 'do this, do that.' Act. You have your powers, the laws." He turned to the KGB chief: "Kryuchkov, who is preventing you from acting? . . . I will correct you if necessary. But do go ahead." This was a startling remark: the President had instructed the KGB chief to improvise as he saw fit.[101]

At the meeting of the Presidential Council on 5 November, Shevardnadze proposed considering an option to bring the opposition to power. It was a bizarre idea, and Gorbachev dismissed it.[102] Then Lukyanov reported about preparations for Revolution Day on 7 November. This was the most important state celebration, including a military parade and people's rally on Red Square. Everybody remembered the disastrous experience on May Day. This time it could be much worse. Moscow newspapers and journals lambasted the Bolshevik "October coup" and ridiculed Gorbachev's rhetoric of "the socialist choice." Radical groups threatened to build barricades, to block the column of tanks from coming to Red Square. The CNN images of Beijing in June 1989, when an unknown man halted the armored column of tanks, could happen on the streets of Moscow. The commanders of the Moscow military district and the KGB officials told Lukyanov that there was no way to prevent anti-Soviet, anti-communist rallies. Lukyanov reported that the officials in Moscow's city council, elected from Democratic Russia, refused to take any responsibility for possible disorder and advised that the festivities be canceled. Gorbachev listened and then exploded: "There must be no demonstrations against the October Revolution, against the power of the Soviets!" He accused Lukyanov of pandering to the democrats. Lukyanov replied that the danger of violent confrontation was real. A movement of "soldiers' mothers" was planning a rally to demand the recall of their sons from the zones of ethnic conflict in South Caucasus and Central Asia. The populist demagogues Telman Gdlyan and Nikolai Ivanov planned a rally on Red Square.[103]

Gorbachev also vented his anger at the Minister of the Interior, Vadim Bakatin. Two years ago, Gorbachev had selected this Party official from Kuzbass to run the notoriously corrupt police forces. Bakatin had become a darling of the Moscow media: he spoke against corruption, improved conditions in prisons, and fired police informants. Now Gorbachev asked him to use the police to guarantee order in Moscow's streets. Bakatin refused: "You may be sorry on the day after. There will be a melee and some corpses. Remember May Day."[104] The Soviet leader accused Bakatin of cowardice and disobedience, but did nothing.[105] Shevardnadze was despondent about these exchanges. He saw Gorbachev drifting towards the use of force and a dictatorial regime.[106]

On 7 November 1990, the celebrations of the Bolshevik Revolution came and went without the much-feared confrontation. At the last moment, Gorbachev suggested that Yeltsin join him atop Lenin's Mausoleum for the festivities, and Yeltsin agreed. The Soviet leader spoke again about "the ideals of October," berated "extremist forces," and referred to the "unique role of the Russians" in achieving political stability and the success of perestroika. The military parade went ahead without accidents. Then Gorbachev and Yeltsin walked across Red Square to join the popular rally. Smiling affably, they led the people's procession. In front of the Mausoleum, Gorbachev, Yeltsin, and others laid wreaths to commemorate the founder of the Soviet state and returned to the viewing podium. For a moment, the protagonists had buried their hatchets.[107]

CROSSROADS

Only one glitch marred the choreographed event. A locksmith from Leningrad, inflamed by radical propaganda, came to Red Square with a gun. He wanted to assassinate Gorbachev, to clear the road for national elections of a new democratic leader of the USSR. The man joined the people's procession and, at a distance of fifty meters from the Mausoleum, aimed the gun at Gorbachev's head. A police sergeant, who happened to be nearby, managed to pull the gun down, averting what could have been the assassination of the Soviet leader. The hapless assassin was arrested by the KGB and ended up in a psychiatric ward. The sergeant was awarded a medal and a ticket to a concert.[108] After this, counter-demonstrations went on peacefully. The rally of Democratic Russia was held next to the Party headquarters. The British ambassador saw the rally as "the usual intellectuals . . . all saying the usual worthy things and doing nothing." In the second half of the day, when everybody had left the Mausoleum and the stalls for guests, a big opposition procession entered and passed through Red Square. Yeltsin joined in, and the crowd welcomed him enthusiastically: "Yeltsin! Yeltsin!"[109] The Russians were divided, as they had never been since the time of the Revolution and civil war. Yet nobody wanted violence.

The next day, Gorbachev met with James Baker and assured him that the celebration of the Leninist Revolution had demonstrated the support of the "silent majority" for law and order.[110] He was being naïve. Separatist processes in the Soviet Union continued. In Kiev, a group of demonstrators with blue-yellow flags, symbolizing the independent Ukraine of 1918, and anti-communist slogans, stood out from the official proceedings. In Minsk, the National Front of Belorussia clashed with the police. In Moldova, the national front decided to secede from the USSR and join Romania, which led to the revolt of the Russian minority in the republic. Georgia, the Baltic republics, and Armenia canceled their celebrations altogether. In Azerbaijan and Tajikistan, there was a regime of martial law. In Lithuania and Estonia, the Soviet military marched in the republican capitals, Vilnius and Tallinn; the republican parliaments denounced this as "a show of intimidation" and "violation of sovereignty."[111]

During 1990, Gorbachev repeatedly secured and squandered chances to regain momentum for himself and the central state. There seemed to exist a window of opportunity, however fleeting, to launch systemic market reform, while still retaining state controls and developing new regulators. This, however, required extraordinary vision, will, and even luck that the Soviet leadership lacked. The ignorance of Soviet (and Russian) elites about the dire economic state of affairs, populist chaos, and lack of any tangible Western support made the window shut soon after it had opened. This had fateful consequences for the future of the common statehood, as a sense of economic doom became the main driver of separatism.

CHAPTER 6

LEVIATHAN

If the essential rights of Sovereignty be taken away . . . the
Commonwealth is thereby dissolved, and every man returneth
into the condition, and calamity of warre with every other man.
Thomas Hobbes, *Leviathan*, 1651

As the winter of 1990 approached, people around Gorbachev became desperate about the looming catastrophe. Shatalin, Petrakov, and other liberal-minded participants insisted that it was impossible to carry out any economic reforms over the resistance of the Russian parliament. Ryzhkov and Lukyanov called for a presidential rule to cancel "anti-constitutional" decrees of the Russian and other republican parliaments. Ryzhkov was simply hysterical: "We all studied it. Chaos breeds dictatorship! If we do nothing, it will come!"[1] The Soviet premier must have been referring to Thomas Hobbes, who had written about this in his treatise *Leviathan*, during the English Civil War of the seventeenth century. The Hobbesian idea, however, cut both ways: anarchy could lead to a dictatorship or to a social contract between warring groups. Gorbachev strongly preferred the latter.

At the end of 1990, the Western media was filled with headlines about Gorbachev's "turn to the right" to consolidate his alliance with entrenched elites: the state apparatus, the military-industrial complex, the military, the KGB, and the Party hardliners. The evidence for what was taking place at the time, however, was specious and mostly based on hearsay. Nobody investigated in detail the views and attitudes of the key groups that formed the foundations of the old Soviet statehood. This chapter will explore "the right turn." Did the Soviet leader really fear a backlash from the main stakeholders of the collapsing state? And did the key elites really put a gun to Gorbachev's head?

THE LAME-DUCK PARTY

At the end of 1990, the Party still collected dues from 16 million Party members, yet 3 million had left the Party, and this was only the start of a bigger political hemorrhage. A visitor to the Party headquarters on Moscow's Old Square would hardly have detected any visible changes. The KGB guards continued to stand at every entrance to the giant building; the cafeteria remained well stocked with delicacies (in contrast to empty grocery stores outside); and many of the same officials sat in the same spacious offices behind tall wood-paneled doors. Behind those same doors, however, the structure of power had changed. Most members of the Politburo and Secretariat after July 1990 were new, relatively unknown individuals. When the delegates of the Party Congress had considered voting for some of them, they would turn to others and ask: "Who are they?"[2] Gorbachev's new Party deputy, Vladimir Ivashko, was a bureaucrat and sought to explain to others and himself what he was supposed to do. With fifteen independent communist parties in all Soviet republics, he was thinking aloud, the CPSU was no longer a concrete monolith. "Our task is to be a brain trust, a coordinating center."[3] A center for what? The new members of the Politburo and Secretariat struggled with the acute crisis of identity. Ivashko, who had previously been head of the Ukrainian Communist Party, agreed that the CPSU had to change. After the Party Congress of July 1990, the Party had become a structure without power and strategy. The only course Gorbachev and Ivashko proposed was "further democratization." "What is this about?" Ivashko asked his colleagues. "We should read the encyclopedia for a definition."[4]

Anatoly Chernyaev stopped attending Politburo meetings. Before the Party Congress, he and other liberal advisors urged Gorbachev to split the Party and become the leader of a liberal wing. In this way, they believed, he would outflank Yeltsin and cancel the forthcoming Congress of the CPSU, which could dismiss him as the General Secretary. Some Moscow apparatchiks formed the Democratic Platform in the CPSU. They wanted to transform the authoritarian hierarchical organization into a social-democratic movement and supported market reforms. In Gorbachev's entourage, Yakovlev, Chernyaev, and some others urged him to lead this movement and perhaps launch a new political party, separate from the CPSU. Gorbachev explained to Chernyaev: "I can't let this lousy, rabid dog [of the Party apparatus] off the leash. If I do that, all of this huge structure will be turned against me." A remarkably candid admission! Years after the Soviet collapse, the Russian historian Rudolf Pikhoia was mystified: why did Gorbachev, who had reached the top of the Party apparatus from within, keep destroying the communist nomenklatura's power? He was a leader who had undermined his old power base, without creating a new one.[5] And there was even more drama in this story than Gorbachev could acknowledge. The architect of reforms did not know how to use his powerful political instrument to implement change, yet he also never learned how to rule without the Party.[6]

In the fall of 1990, "the rabid dogs" in the Party apparatus were consolidating. They included Polozkov and many conservative provincial leaders, who had advanced during perestroika but hated it. Polozkov led the "Russian Communist Party" within the CPSU, a giant structure with 9 million due-paying members.[7] He and his friends cried about "betrayal" of their ideological principles as well as the loss of Soviet imperial domains. It was hard to predict how the KGB and the military might respond to those appeals during the acute political crisis. It was this group that terrified the Moscow friends of journalist David Remnick, who spoke about "Russian fascism." Polozkov and his friends, however, suffered from a major problem: a complete lack of charisma. In the October–November polls, Polozkov received the approval of just 6 percent of respondents, whereas Yeltsin got over 50 percent.[8]

One "rabid dog" whom Gorbachev mistakenly brought into the new Politburo was Oleg Shenin. Gorbachev considered him a neo-Leninist. In reality, Shenin was an admirer of Andropov who wanted to return to strong-hand authoritarian reforms from above. On 16 November 1990, Shenin spoke at the Politburo against the idea of a new Union Treaty and any bargaining with Yeltsin and other republican potentates. "Only emergency measures would help," Shenin argued, based on preservation of the old Soviet Constitution on the territory of the Soviet Union. Gorbachev accused Shenin of a "martial law mentality."[9]

The "Russian communists" still lacked a new language applicable to the mass politics unleashed by Gorbachev's perestroika. Party documents from late 1990 were stilted instead of fiery; stodgy formulaic language instead of pithy appeals and slogans. Next to populist demagogues of that time, the Party apparatchiks were tongue-tied, shy and reactive. Polozkov bemoaned the absence of good Party spokesmen on television and the shortage of skillful writers in the Party's service in newspapers. *Sovetskaia Rossiia*, the newspaper that had published Nina Andreyeva's infamous manifesto in 1988, experimented with a new language of Russian conservative nationalism. The time for it would come, however, only after the Soviet Union collapsed.

Under the old system, Party apparatchiks had lived on fixed salaries and could not officially amass private wealth and property. They clung to the state-provided privileges, including supplies of quality food and gated vacation sites. In contrast, people from the new political elite could accumulate personal wealth. Gorbachev's reforms allowed for the creation of a new banking industry, offshore schemes, and various "cooperative" enterprises. This provided unprecedented opportunities for personal gain.[10] At first, the Party elites were rather slow to realize these opportunities. In August 1989, the minister responsible for the Soviet gas industry, Viktor Chernomyrdin, and his deputies decided to create a state consortium, Gazprom, to take advantage of new liberties. The members of the Politburo were genuinely surprised. They asked Chernomyrdin: "Why do you need such a headache?" The Party potentates still could not imagine why somebody would want to leave the Soviet nomenklatura and take full initiative and responsibility for a huge enterprise, including its possible losses.[11] After the fall of Eastern European communist regimes, however, this psychology began to change. Party officials, including the top ones in Moscow and Leningrad, began to join the process of corporation-building. The list of new Soviet joint-stock conglomerates, formed by the entrepreneurial local Party bosses together with state managers, and entrepreneurs, began to lengthen.[12]

Nikolai Kruchina, the chief Party administrator for economic affairs, saw the future coming. He managed all Party property whose value was estimated at 300 million rubles or more. Gorbachev recalled Kruchina as "a man of integrity, quite intelligent, cautious yet capable of initiative. He could be fully trusted . . ." During 1990, Kruchina realized that to pay the salaries of Party apparatchiks, particularly republican, regional, and local, he had to practice capitalism. He channeled Party money, including the dues of 16 million Party members, into the emerging new corporations, associations, commercial banks, and other enterprises. He also began to commercialize Party assets including office buildings, educational institutions, hospitals, posh resort facilities, publishing companies, thousands of automobiles, construction companies, and so on. With the help of the KGB and Soviet embassies, Kruchina established joint ventures with Western businessmen and politicians. Inside the country, "the Party Inc" that Kruchina headed funded and assisted the first crop of millionaire entrepreneurs and commercial bankers, who came from the ranks of the Komsomol apparatchiks. All this was done in order to transform the receding power of the Party into money.[13]

In the fall of 1990, in the Soviet independent media, scholars and journalists began discussing "nomenklatura privatization." Viktor Yaroshenko in his essay in *Novyi Mir* wrote about "the Party of Cats," probably meaning "Fat Cats." Those were officials from the Party apparatus, as well as their junior associates from the Komsomol and Soviet trade unions, who used the crisis as an opportunity for privatizing property. The media wrote about new commercial banks, joint enterprises, and consortiums that mushroomed and used the initial capital borrowed liberally from the Party budget. The Party owned most publishing houses. Suddenly, there was an association formed by those enterprises and paper manufacturers: it began to export paper to Western countries at a price of

$800–$1,000 per ton. The Party of Cats, concluded Yaroshenko, was not interested in violent conflict. Instead, "they demand from the democratic camp a tacit social contract: you will allow us to retreat safely and with full pockets, and we will . . . not jail you and shoot at you." Ten years later this "contract" metaphor would be picked up by Western scholars.[14]

Leon Onikov, who worked in the Party central apparatus, wrote in his memoirs: "Every professional understood, that the failure to revamp the CPSU inevitably led to the disintegration of the USSR, because [the Party] was the rod in the system." Onikov, like Gorbachev, Yakovlev, and Chernyaev, was a typical "man of the Sixties"; for him the only way to revamp the Party was to make it an association of enlightened bureaucrats and intelligentsia, a force for social democracy. He was not cynical enough to imagine that a communist nomenklatura could be transformed into the ruling class and the main stakeholder of state capitalism, something that was afoot in China at the time.[15] Yet the liberal Party apparatchik made a good point about the Soviet state. Most of the Party nomenklatura could never understand why Gorbachev kept devolving power, especially material power, to other actors, in the name of "socialist democracy." Already under Leonid Brezhnev, the Party had been transformed into the hierarchy of republican and regional clans and managerial elites. They remained loyal to the General Secretary as long they felt they were part of the system that could punish their insubordination, but also protect their clan interests. The reforms of 1989, and particularly the rise of competing republican structures, began to question this loyalty.

During 1990, the Party elites and clans realized that the old nomenklatura with the center in Moscow could disappear, as it had done in Eastern Europe. The power of the purse and authority over state budget had shifted to the Supreme Soviets, their committees. All this made smart Party officials think about how to survive *after the Party*. In the republics and the national autonomies, this rethinking went faster. There it was "natural" for the old nomenklatura leaders to distance themselves from the center and drape themselves in the flag of national sovereignty. At least this gave them new leverage to bargain with Moscow for the control of economic assets. In the republics, such as Ukraine and Belorussia, the Party apparatchiks, together with economic managers, formed ruling majorities in the Supreme Soviets. In Kazakhstan, Uzbekistan, and other republics of Central Asia, the Party Secretaries acted as leaders of ethnic-based clans. This was a rational political and economic choice in a situation of rising uncertainty.[16]

Once a mighty political force capable of mobilizing people and the economy in extreme conditions, the Party had become a huge conglomerate of clans and people acting in their own interests. Many of them would have liked to remove

Gorbachev from power and proceed, without any democratic experiments, towards state capitalism. Yet, as the Party Plenums and the Party Congress had demonstrated many times, Gorbachev had no reason to fear a coup from the nomenklatura. Despite their anger and frustration, nobody dared move against the General Secretary. They realized that, even if they voted Gorbachev out, he would constitutionally remain the commander-in-chief of the Army and in control of the KGB. Those institutions were key to Gorbachev's power.

GREAT RETREAT

At the end of 1990, the Soviet Army was still the largest in the world. Its ground forces were supposed to have at least 4 million soldiers in uniform, filled up by the fall draft. The Army had up to 64,000 tanks, 76,500 armored personnel carriers (APCs), 12,200 military aircraft and helicopters—far more than the NATO forces.[17] At the same time, the revolutions in Eastern Europe and the unification of Germany had destroyed the legal and political grounds for deployment of the Soviet military outside Soviet borders. And this meant the biggest retreat of the Army since 1941–42. Some 650,000 Soviet troops, including 50,000 officers, tens of thousands of tanks, APCs, artillery pieces, aircraft and helicopters, hundreds of thousands of items of materiel and equipment had to be withdrawn from Central and Eastern Europe across thousands of miles back to the homeland. This withdrawal essentially meant the structural and logistical end of the Soviet Army as it had existed for decades. The enormity and chaos of those withdrawals are still to be fully assessed by historians.[18] On top of those huge blows, the Army had to deal with the severe and expensive reductions—that is destruction—of its armaments, proposed in the Treaty on Conventional Armed Forces in Europe (CFE) between NATO and the Warsaw Pact. Gorbachev and Shevardnadze planned to sign this treaty in November 1990 as one of the pillars in the construction of the "Common European Home."

The great Soviet retreat from Europe elicited a range of feelings in Moscow. The journalist Yaroshenko wrote: "We have agreed . . . to destroy the gigantic Soviet military machine—free of charge . . .Yet nobody, including in the Supreme Soviet, had explained what we would get in return . . . Trust? Credits? Assistance? The end of the COCOM sanctions? . . . The harsh reality is: tanks, missiles, and atomic submarines are all we have." Yaroshenko overheard a conversation in a Moscow bus: "Let the West purchase all these goodies from us," one commuter said to another, "and then they can destroy them."[19] As for the top Soviet military commanders, they were outraged and horrified by the retreat. This particularly concerned those who were directly in charge of it: Gorbachev's military advisor Sergey Akhromeyev, Minister of Defense Dmitry

Yazov, and the head of the General Staff, Mikhail Moiseyev. The first two had fought in World War II as soldiers; Yazov could not forget thirty-four of his brothers, cousins, and relatives that perished; Moiseyev had lost his brothers in war. Their entire career had played out during the Cold War. Yazov had been deployed in Cuba with Soviet troops during the Cuban Missile Crisis of 1962. None of them doubted that economic reforms in the Soviet Union were necessary. Akhromeyev, for instance, acknowledged that the Soviet Union had become over-extended and he supported the withdrawal from Afghanistan.[20] Yet psychologically, the Soviet military were incapable of accepting the rapid dismantling of the Soviet war machine, particularly given NATO's economic and technological superiority. According to someone who worked with him, Akhromeyev took the destruction of Soviet medium-range missiles, as stipulated by the US-Soviet treaty of 1987, "as a personal tragedy." The generals could not understand Gorbachev's missionary rhetoric of a new world order. They served Gorbachev out of a sense of duty and discipline, yet their heart was against the great retreat.[21]

Instead of questioning Gorbachev, the top military had since 1987 begun to vent their discontent against Shevardnadze and his Foreign Ministry as the scapegoats. Shevardnadze, in self-defense, proposed to involve Akhromeyev, Yazov, and Moiseyev in negotiations with the West. He hoped this would mitigate their suspicions and educate them in the realities of international affairs. In July 1989, Akhromeyev made an official visit to Washington DC and even traveled to California, as a personal guest of former Secretary of State George Schultz. Akhromeyev was overwhelmed by what he saw in the United States; the contrast between American opulence and Soviet realities depressed him.[22] Gorbachev's military advisor became a bit more flexible and argued for concessions in the arms control talks. Yet the prospect of a unified Germany in NATO became the last straw for him. He revealed his real mood in April 1990, after he had taken part in a round of talks with the Americans, together with Shevardnadze and Soviet diplomats. On the way home, on the plane, the Marshal sat there silently with a dark face. Then he grumbled: "For seventy years the Americans have been trying to destroy our Union, and finally they have reached their goal." Shevardnadze's deputy objected: "They did not destroy it; we did it ourselves." Akhromeyev retorted: "They did it, and we too." In another episode, Defense Minister Yazov barked at Shevardnadze: "Give me a written guarantee, that there will be no war in ten years, and that the Germans will not return to the borders of the Third Reich." Shevardnadze's aide, Teimuraz Stepanov, who was a witness, commented in his diary: "I finally realized that perestroika has no chance; Gorbachev, Shevardnadze, all of us, we have no chance."[23]

LEVIATHAN

During the summer of 1990, Yazov and his Chief of the General Staff acted behind Shevardnadze's back. Yazov ordered the shipment of 21,000 of the USSR's newest tanks and APCs, as well as 20,000 artillery pieces, from East Germany and Eastern Europe to Central Asia—outside the CFE treaty's geographical scope. Rows of tanks, with expensive electronics and optical devices, were left in the desert, surrounded by barbed wire with a few guards protecting them. The leaders of Central Asian republics were not even consulted. This was an act of despair, rather than a well-calculated move.[24] US space intelligence spotted the redeployments, and James Baker complained to Shevardnadze. The Soviet Foreign Minister's word and honor were at stake.[25] On 20 October 1990, Shevardnadze sent Gorbachev a bitter letter about what had happened. The Soviet Union, he wrote, "still stood on both feet and avoided bankruptcy" only thanks to the financial assistance and credits from Germany and "our partners who are interested in seeing in the Soviet Union a stable partner, a unitary state. In our situation we can be toppled not by tanks or aircraft, but rather by the simple refusal to finance us."[26] Gorbachev refused to confront the military, so Shevardnadze did so himself. "You can write down anything you want" in the draft treaty, he said emotionally to Moiseyev, but then there would be the failure of the CFE, Soviet diplomacy, and the European peace process. Would Soviet security win out as a result? "The Pentagon hawks," Shevardnadze concluded, "would applaud comrade Moiseyev."[27]

Yazov and Moiseyev held their ground. Military intelligence reported that in June 1990 the President of Czechoslovakia, Václav Havel, and the post-communist leadership of Hungary wanted to join NATO. The Soviet negotiating positions would have been better off if the Warsaw Pact had disbanded itself before signing the CFE, thereby excluding former Soviet allies from the European balance of forces. At the meeting of the Commission on arms control, the Minister of Defense asked the top Soviet negotiator in Vienna: how come Soviet forces in southern parts of the Soviet Union, from Moldova to South Caucasus, had to be equal in numbers to the armed forces of Turkey and Greece? "We did not give license to do this," Yazov fulminated. He, like his American counterparts, did not believe the Cold War was truly over.[28]

Indeed, the worries of the top Soviet military about the retreat from Eastern Europe can only be understood in the context of the rapidly growing internal instability. The military top brass knew that "the loss" of East Germany and Eastern Europe was only half the drama of the Soviet Army. Most of its remaining combat forces and bases were located on the western arc, from the Baltic republics across Belorussia and Western Ukraine down to Moldova. The group of southern forces were located in South Caucasus and Central Asia. Those troops faced rising instability and the rage of local nationalists, first in

161

South Caucasus and the Baltics, then even in Ukraine. The Army had become a target of public criticism after its bloody crackdown in Tbilisi in April 1989, followed by Baku in January 1990. William Odom, a top American expert on the Soviet army, wrote with empathy later about what the Soviet military had gone through at the time. "Suppose, for example, that a regiment of U.S. troops had come straight back from heavy fighting in Vietnam [in 1968] to an army post in the United States without adequate housing and support facilities, and then imagine that it was dispatched to deal with anti-war demonstrators on a university campus. To say that the potential for violence would have been high is a grim understatement."[29]

Finally, "the parade of sovereignties" after the Russian Declaration for the first time raised the issue of the integrity of the Soviet military machine and armed forces. If the Baltic republics and South Caucasus decided to leave the Union, Yazov warned on 28 September 1990, the military-industrial complex would lose over a hundred enterprises critical for the production of Soviet fighters, "air-ground" missiles, the systems of teleguidance for the air force, automatic systems of surveillance, and so on.[30] In July–September 1990, the Ukrainian Supreme Soviet passed laws and resolutions blocking the conscription of young men from their territory or banning their deployment outside their "national" territories. In the RSFSR Supreme Soviet, Yeltsin declared the same for the Russian draftees. This meant the partition of the Army along republican lines. It also undermined the Soviet military draft system. By October 1990, 400,000 draftees did not show up. The draft completely failed in the Baltic republics, South Caucasus, and Moldova, but the numbers also fell significantly in Ukraine and the Russian Federation.[31]

At the end of October, Gorbachev held a series of meetings with the top military brass. Everyone who spoke there concluded that the Soviet Army was in crisis, and its root was the failure of a central authority. Participants complained loudly about the "impotence" of Gorbachev and Ryzhkov. Colonel-General Vladislav Achalov, commander of Soviet airborne forces and the youngest general in the army, spoke for many: "Nobody carries out the decrees of the president." He also referred to use of the military in ethnic conflicts: "We have to pay with the lives of soldiers for the ambitions of the *führers.*" In January 1990, Achalov had led his airborne divisions to clear Baku from the ragtag Popular Front militants and demonstrations. He was disgusted to see that the political leadership, including Gorbachev, were distancing themselves from the troops at a time when the Moscow media and opposition were accusing them of excessive violence against unarmed civilians. In the Caucasus, the Baltics, Moldova, and West Ukraine, Achalov continued, people treated the army as "Russian occupants." If the President did not act, Achalov concluded, the mili-

tary "will be forced to introduce martial rule" on their own, to protect serv-
icemen and military warehouses. This was a remarkable provocation that was
bound to catch Gorbachev's attention.[32]

The military parade on 7 November 1990 did not improve the morale of the
Soviet military. The officers who commanded tank formations felt for the first
time they were not welcome in the Soviet capital. "After the parade was over,"
one of its participants recalled, "there was only one feeling: great fatigue, as if we
did not celebrate, but accomplished some big, dirty, and disgraceful work."[33] On
13 November, Gorbachev met with a group of over 1,000 Soviet military officers,
elected to the Supreme Soviets and other public positions. The discussion was
so fraught that its complete record was not published. The military obeyed their
commander-in-chief, yet he was clearly losing their respect.[34] One week later,
Yazov was in Paris accompanying Gorbachev at the Conference on Security and
Cooperation in Europe. The Soviet leader was among thirty-five leaders who
signed the Paris Charter for a New Europe, and also the CFE Treaty. During the
ceremony the Soviet diplomat who had negotiated the treaty overheard the
Marshal, who stood close by, muttering to himself: "This Treaty means we have
lost World War III without a shot being fired."[35]

THE WATCHDOG

At the end of 1990, the KGB was a formidable organization: with 480,000
officers, a secrecy-clad vertical structure, and strict military discipline, the KGB
had functioned for decades as "the Party's arm with a sword." Like the Party, the
KGB penetrated all structures of the Soviet state, society, and economy. In
Moscow alone, the KGB had between 65,000 and 89,000 officers. There were
also secret agents and informants on the KGB payroll whose names and positions remained classified. The Committee had its own troops, was in control of
borders and customs, provided secure communications and controls for the
Party and the state, ensured the safety of strategic nuclear weapons, and more.[36]

In February 1990, the US Deputy National Security Advisor, Robert Gates,
accompanied James Baker to Moscow and met with the head of the KGB, Vladimir
Kryuchkov, in his Lubyanka office. Gates was struck by Kryuchkov's comments
on the end of the Party's monopoly on political power. Perhaps, Kryuchkov joked,
"we should divide the [Communist] Party into two parties with identical plat-
forms," as in the United States. Gates asked: "Could one of these parties be capitalist?" The KGB chief did not reply. Privately, Kryuchkov considered Gorbachev's
reform of the Party a huge mistake. Kryuchkov also told Gates that the Soviet
leadership was imposing too many changes on people. "Change should be applied
gradually, like oxygen. Too much too quickly could make one dizzy."[37]

They spoke about the future of the Soviet Union. Gates remarked that many regions had not joined the USSR voluntarily, but rather through force of arms. Now these regions were demanding independence. Kryuchkov responded that during the American Civil War the Confederacy had been forced back into the Union. Besides, all of the Soviet republics belonged to one economic space: "No republic can leave tomorrow without feeling the [negative] effect." This was exactly what Gorbachev had argued.[38] Kryuchkov agreed with Gates that political changes had outrun economic developments. In any case, he affirmed, the Soviet Union had no choice but to undergo fundamental changes. He warned Gates: "If the US tries to corner us, to exploit our current difficulties, or put us in awkward situations," this would influence the attitude not only of the Party, but also of the people.[39] Gates concluded that the KGB chief was no longer a supporter of perestroika. When he returned to the US ambassador's residence, Gates said to Baker that Gorbachev had better watch out. Back in Washington, he shared his concerns with the top Soviet expert in the National Security Council, Condoleezza Rice.[40]

Leonid Shebarshin, head of KGB foreign intelligence, recalled that his organization was afraid "to look at the unvarnished truth about the mood of the people." After inspecting the KGB's offices in the Baltic republics in 1990, Shebarshin compared his colleagues there with decapitated hens: they ran around flapping their wings without any understanding of the problems they faced.[41] Furthermore, in the fall of 1990, the KGB itself was no longer uniform politically. All officers were, as before, Party members; yet some of them wanted to distance themselves from the communist past.[42] In March 1990, 2,756 KGB officers, with the permission of their superiors, ran in the open elections to the RSFSR Congress, as well as regional and local Soviets, and many were elected.[43] A large group of KGB officers from the Sverdlovsk region sent a collective letter to the Russian parliament, arguing that the KGB should serve state interests, not the interests of local communist officials. The KGB collegium in Lubyanka considered it a breach of corporate discipline, yet nobody was punished.[44] In the summer of 1990, the retired KGB General Oleg Kalugin began to speak out as a critic of the Soviet secret police and the intelligence service. Along with Gdlyan and Ivanov, Kalugin attracted tens of thousands of people at the opposition rallies. Gorbachev signed the decree to strip Kalugin of his rank and pension. This only added to Kalugin's huge popularity: he was elected a people's deputy from Democratic Russia and in October was a star at the conference of this movement.[45]

Could the KGB have run a creeping coup in September 1990? Those who knew Kryuchkov replied emphatically 'No.' The KGB chief seemed unable to move a finger without Gorbachev's approval. Shebarshin said in an interview in April 1990: "The KGB and its intelligence service have no independent political interests. This is an instrument, an organ of the state, that helps the state to carry out its policies."[46] In his memoirs some years later, Shebarshin reflected: "Over many years all of us were drilled in the spirit of strict discipline, subordination, and faith in the bureaucratic and state wisdom of our superiors."[47]

Kryuchkov's preferred tool of influence on Gorbachev was feeding information to him. The KGB chief sowed suspicions in the Soviet leader's mind about his entourage and their intentions. As Chernyaev commented ruefully in his diary in February and March 1991: "M.S. [Gorbachev] has a weakness" for the secrets the KGB reports to him, in particular when it concerned his main rival Yeltsin and his American partners.[48] Gorbachev liked to receive KGB intercepts of Western reports and intelligence. He also read "eyes-only" transcripts of tapped telephone conversations between his political rivals and associates. There were also numerous listening devices that the KGB had installed everywhere. Kryuchkov worked in cahoots with Gorbachev's chief of staff, Valery Boldin. The more Gorbachev feared the rising power of Yeltsin and Democratic Russia, the more he relied on the warped "exclusive" information that Boldin and the KGB supplied him. This information was gained through *proslushka*, the clandestine wiretapping of offices and possibly even personal conversations between the opposition leaders.

At the end of 1990, the KGB reports to Gorbachev continued to be written through the specific prism of the secret police mentality and Cold War optics, as if little had changed since Brezhnev's time.[49] Kryuchkov became obsessed with the Soviet "fifth column" and the role of the CIA and Western NGOs in acquiring numerous willing collaborators in the Soviet elites. According to the KGB chief, "certain circles in the United States and the US special services" targeted the people in Moscow who called themselves "democrats" and grouped themselves around Yeltsin, as well as the broader intellectual elite in the Soviet capital. Kryuchkov became convinced that Shevardnadze, Chernyaev, and particularly Alexander Yakovlev were American agents of influence. He also wrote that the IMF, located in Washington, actively promoted in the Soviet Union its views of economic reforms.[50] The KGB was quick to spot ardent Westernization and pro-Americanization that was sweeping through the Soviet elites, particularly as a result of the "post-Wall shock" of 1989. At the same time, in the new political atmosphere, the KGB could do nothing to those "agents of influence" and their purported American sponsors. In the fall of 1990, Gennady Burbulis, Yeltsin's advisor, met Kryuchkov and requested special permission to bring his American guests to Sverdlovsk, which was still "a closed city." Kryuchkov signed the paperwork without any objections.[51]

On 11 December 1990, Kryuchkov appeared on state television to announce that unnamed destructive forces, which were "amply fed morally and materially from abroad," were active and determined to "undermine our society and state, and liquidate Soviet power." The KGB chief ascribed consumer shortages to the activities of the opposition, as well as organized crime. "Many of the difficulties we experience in improving our economy," he added, "have also been created by the activities of a number of our foreign partners, which in essence are close to economic sabotage." He quickly denied that the KGB wanted to return to the "old times" of police surveillance, informants, and a crackdown on freedoms. This speech sent shivers down the spines of many, including Western diplomats, but it was apparently approved by Gorbachev.[52]

The KGB still evoked visceral fear in Soviet society, but not so for Gorbachev. The Soviet leader regarded the KGB as an essential and even natural part of his office and lifestyle. The KGB provided his personal security, information, communications, and even his household staff. The KGB Ninth Directorate officials accompanied Gorbachev, along with his armored limousine, on all his trips around the country and especially abroad, at great cost to the state budget. One could say that the Soviet President worked in a bubble created and maintained by the KGB for his exclusive needs and comfort. And this seemed to suit him well.

THE COMPLEX UNDER STRESS

In the demonology of Democratic Russia, anti-Soviet nationalists, and others who denounced "the totalitarian state," considered the military-industrial complex (MIC)—like the Party apparatus and the KGB—to be a reactionary, secret, and sinister force. In parliamentary debates, radical democrats and populists publicized fantastic, exaggerated numbers of MIC budgets. They could not believe that with such low expenditures the Soviet Union could compete with the United States, whose defense budget was $300 billion. In a political paradox of late Soviet history, hundreds of thousands of MIC engineers, technicians, and scientists took part in rallies, demanding the dismantling of the military-industrial complex that employed them. Eventually, about 300,000 young and highly qualified MIC employees started working for cooperatives, in lucrative operations such as exporting subsidized materials and importing personal computers.[53]

The MIC was facing a sharp decline in state investments and sales. In 1989, the Soviet Union's defense budget was cut from 77.3 billion to 71 billion rubles; and the estimate for 1991 was a further decline to 66.5 billion rubles. Taking into account inflation, this was a sharp cut. The R&D expenditures shrank to 31 billion rubles in 1990, with a projected 22 billion rubles for 1991. The program of the 500 Days demanded reductions in defense expenditure. The leaders of the MIC did not know where to obtain the money for conversion and transition. Who would build the new production capacities? What to do with the old industrial parts that kept churning out weaponry that was no longer needed? And what to do with the stockpiles of unusable but lethal weapons, above all nuclear weapons? The costs of maintaining those stockpiles were immense; the costs of their destruction would be even bigger. There were programs of biological weapons that even Gorbachev did not know about, including stocks of deadly viruses, from smallpox to anthrax; also an array of binary chemical weapons with the code name "Novichok."[54]

Many captains of MIC corporations genuinely wanted to leave the Cold War behind and start joint ventures with their Western partners. Until the summer of 1990, however, none of them were able to travel to the West; any "Western partnership" could be considered state treason. Gorbachev's romance with the market economy broke this taboo. In August, with his authorization, a group of high-level MIC leaders and directors were allowed to fly to Boston, the first trip to the West in their life, to talk to American businessmen about potential projects for cooperation. In September, some of them met with the delegation of American businessmen in Moscow. The US Secretary of Commerce Robert Mosbacher reported to Bush that "[the Soviets] talked about our coming in to convert some military plants and even talked about specific opportunities. If this is pursued, I should think it would make their movement towards peacefully joining the family of Western nations close to irreversible."[55] With the assistance of the Academy of Sciences, some defense industrialists reached out to foreign investors.

On 28 September 1990, Gorbachev convened a special conference of top people from the MIC, to discuss a program for its "conversion" to new market conditions. All had years of experience in running huge state conglomerates employing tens of thousands, often hundreds of thousands of people. They all belonged to the Party supreme nomenklatura. For years the main coordinating bodies for those officials were the Defense Sector of the CC CPSU and the Military-Industrial Commission in the Council of Ministers. Now they came to lay out their problems and grievances. They wanted to learn what the Party and the state could do to help them survive the traumatic transition to a market economy. None of them knew what to expect in the near future. The five-year plan, proposed by Ryzhkov's government, envisaged the production of 2.5 times fewer tanks, and half the amount of missiles and military aircraft than before. Instead, the government wanted the MIC to increase its production of equipment for agriculture by 2.4 times as much, for medicine by 2.5 times as much, and by 1.8 for consumer-oriented state industries; and twice the amount for electronics.[56]

The discussion in Gorbachev's Kremlin office predictably revealed a sharp division between liberals and conservatives. The young economist Yuri Yaremenko, a specialist in Chinese economic reforms, urged the MIC leaders to accelerate "conversion" to the production of civilian goods; its cadres and resources should reinvent the Soviet economy. This was what Gorbachev wanted.[57] The solution looked promising, yet it could hardly be implemented anytime soon. Yevgeny Velikhov, vice-president of the Academy of Sciences, advocated partnerships between MIC enterprises and American corporations. He urged Gorbachev to remove the secrecy rules requiring the highest authorization for senior officials from the MIC to travel abroad and reach business deals.[58] This solution was based on the premise that the Americans would agree to such a revolutionary cooperation with their former enemy and rival.

Some directors of MIC corporations reported to Gorbachev on the market ventures and Western partnerships they had already begun to explore. The director of a big plant of military electronics said he was preparing to begin the mass production of video-recorders. Another manager planned to use military satellites to provide telephone connectivity to the entire country. The minister responsible for the shipbuilding industry established business ties with "a certain Rappaport," a Swiss-based investment banker who was promising to find money for the renovation of naval shipyards on the Black Sea. More striking ventures began to take place. Officials from a Soviet radio-isotope plant, obviously with clearance from above, had approached the US Ministry of Energy with an offer to sell five kilograms of Soviet-made Plutonium-238, the fuel for atomic weapons, at a cost of $1,200 per gram. The offer was for a spot sale, with ten kilograms to be delivered later in the year, and twenty more kilograms in 1991. The Soviet plutonium cost significantly less than the type manufactured in the United States. The surprised Americans deliberated whether they should agree to this unprecedented bargain.[59]

On the conservative flank at the September conference stood Oleg Baklanov, head of the Military-Industrial Commission, and the KGB's Kryuchkov. Baklanov doubted that rapid conversion of the MIC was possible, and voiced his concern that, without state funds, the most valuable sectors of the Soviet economy would simply fall apart, and the most skilled workers would end up selling and buying in cooperatives. The real solution, Baklanov believed, would be to restore financial stability in the country. That was a thinly disguised call for a dictatorship.[60] Kryuchkov dismissed cooperation with the United States. He warned that Americans wanted to destroy the Soviet MIC and use financial incentives to siphon off Soviet secrets. The Soviet Union would remain a superpower only as long as it had its independent R&D base that would allow it to retain its competitive edge.[61] Yevgeny Primakov, a world-savvy academician and Gorbachev's favorite aide, proposed another solution to the MIC problems.[62] Primakov also did not trust the seemingly good intentions of the United States, yet he urged MIC leaders to learn from their Cold War counterparts and expand the global export of arms. Instead of cutting the production of armaments, Soviet arms manufacturers should find markets for them. "Why have we become so scared of the ANT? . . . Others will fill the [arms] market, if we leave. We cannot work with white gloves."[63] Primakov was referring to the spring scandal with the cooperative ANT, the target of populist politics and media attacks.

At a conference with Gorbachev in September, the top MIC managers agreed that Western investors could not replace the budgetary allocations. Western markets remained closed for the products of Soviet military labs and industries. The speakers, one after another, asked Gorbachev to suspend the budget cuts on R&D and other arms-related programs. Furthermore, the industries needed a clear long-term perspective. Gorbachev, however, closed the conference by telling leaders of the MIC to search for their own solutions. Many in the audience left the Kremlin confused and disappointed.

On 12 November 1990, a US delegation came to Leningrad and Moscow to meet with MIC leaders. The event was organized by IMEMO, the leading think tank of the Academy of Sciences, and the non-governmental Council on Economic Priorities (CEP) in the United States. There were no big names from the US arms corporations; the group consisted mostly of university economists, political scientists, and a few business executives. The most visible figures were the governor of Ohio, Richard Celeste, and former CIA director, William Colby. In contrast, the Soviet side was high-profile: Alexander Yakovlev, Velikhov, Baklanov, and a number of directors and managers of MIC enterprises. The economists Shatalin and Yaremenko also attended. Baklanov played the good host and said to the Americans: "We are open to letting your specialists study our military industry."[64]

The Soviet hosts showed the Americans their most advanced and top-secret MIC facilities. In Leningrad, they made a tour of LOMO, the largest manufacturer of optics for the military and civilian economy. This company impressed their American guests as being "in a league with only five other companies in the world, including Bausch & Lomb." In Moscow, the Americans visited "Almaz," a conglomerate with 73,000 workers and 7,000 engineers, which built advanced air-defense systems. Its director, the academic Boris Bounkin, wanted to specialize in radios and television, tape recorders, and other civilian electronic products. They also paid a visit to the Energia Machine-Building Plant, which produced Proton rockets that orbited space satellites. Its director wanted to produce ecological and robotic equipment for radioactive clean-up and cancer treatment, water purification, lasers, and radiology. Meanwhile, the director complained that the government's program of conversion made them produce bikes, sleds, and frying pans instead.[65]

The Soviet directors were remarkably candid with their American guests. They admitted that they had little expertise in international trade, joint ventures, and marketing, but were desperate to get credits and earn hard currency. They asked the Americans for advice on how to do it. The director of LOMO complained that Gorbachev's policies left his enterprise to its own devices. Without American assistance, he said, the defense industries would fall apart, and this would be "dangerous given that we have nuclear weapons."[66] American academics were shocked to find directors of Soviet military plants to be more enthusiastic about market forces than they were. One American economist told his Soviet hosts that only the state could compensate for losses during the transition to a market economy, help make intelligent and profitable choices, and prevent military enterprises from price-gouging and other sorts of attempts to take unfair advantage of the chaos. Another American economist said: "It is amazing to see how many Soviet people are willing to give up their safe government jobs in favor of a chance to be involved in entrepreneurship." The American report on the trip summed up the situation: "Some people consider defense enterprise managers in the Soviet Union the enemy of reform." The conversations in Moscow and Leningrad, however, "made it clear that many of the defense enterprise managers think that they could survive in a market economy."[67]

Velikhov in his memoirs recalls that he brought a Swiss-based investment banker, Bruce Rappaport, to a meeting with Gorbachev. He was the "certain Rappaport" mentioned at the September 1990 meeting. Gorbachev, as always, spoke about the great potential and future of the USSR. Rappaport listened with growing impatience, then interrupted. "Mr President, let me tell you a Jewish joke. A Jew buried his wife. He came to the Rabbi to ask what to do. The Rabbi said: 'You should let a year or two go by. You will adjust and find consolation.' The Jew responds: "A year, two years . . . And what I am supposed to do tonight?"[68] The last sentence summed up the plight of the MIC and the nature of Gorbachev's reforms. The best Soviet industries and their managers embraced the market and reforms, but needed time, expertise, and state support to survive in the global marketplace. The lack of all these, however, left them in the lurch.

LEVIATHAN CONTESTED

Through the fall of 1990, Gorbachev continued to tinker with the Union Treaty, which his consultants had been drafting since June. He was aiming for a strong federation, with the President elected by direct national vote. A powerful

Cabinet of Ministers would include the heads of the republics. The President would remain the sole guarantor of the constitutional order, control borders, set economic, defense, and foreign policies, define the financial credit system, form a common budget, and resolve disputes among the republics. The center would retain control of the entire military-industrial complex and other "all-Union" industries on the territory of the Russian Federation and other republics.[69]

On 11 November, Gorbachev met with Yeltsin, but the Russian rebel rejected Gorbachev's scheme and repeated his own demands.[70] The next day, the Supreme Soviet of the USSR reconvened after a two-week holiday break. The mood of deputies reflected the anger of their voters. In a public survey, when people answered the question about who wielded power in the country, the most common reply was: "Nobody." The main source of discontent was, as before, the crisis of food supplies. Even the parliamentarians began to receive food packages: two packs of groats, a chicken, one pack of sugar, one 250-gram pack of butter, and a box of candies.[71]

Especially vocal in the parliament was the group called "Soyuz," which held Gorbachev and his government responsible for the economic crisis, national separatism, and the retreat from Eastern Europe. The group was created in February 1990 from hard-core communists and those who represented Russian minorities in non-Russian republics. The main speaker of the group was Colonel Viktor Alksnis, elected by the military and Russian speakers in Latvia. A grandson of Stalin's Marshal, killed in Stalin's purges, Alksnis was a diehard Soviet patriot. His solution to the Soviet crisis was martial law, the suspension of parliaments, and the arrest of all troublemakers, "Landsbergis, Yeltsin, whatever it takes." His hero was General Jaruzelski, whose actions in the 1980s "allowed a peaceful transition to reform" in Poland. The Soyuz deputies demanded that Gorbachev deliver a report to the nation.[72]

On 16 November, the President delivered a hastily drafted speech, a smorgasbord of platitudes and an enumeration of his achievements with perestroika. The speech, concluded Gorbachev's biographer, "bombed." Alksnis rose from his seat to warn Gorbachev that he had only thirty days to correct his course; otherwise, the Congress would revoke his presidential rights.[73] Later that day, the Politburo pressured Gorbachev as well. Shenin, Baklanov, Polozkov, and the heads of the Moscow and Leningrad Party organizations demanded an immediate introduction of presidential rule and the purge of liberals in the media.[74] Gorbachev confessed to Shakhnazarov that for him the last word came in the form of a plea by a deputy, an elderly lady, at the Supreme Soviet: "We are praying for you . . . Please give birth to a decision on what needs to be done."[75]

The Soviet President worked through the night to draft another address to the Soviet parliament, this time concise and consisting of eight points. On this occasion he did not consult anyone, neither his aides nor Ryzhkov. The next morning, the President announced to the deputies he would disband the Presidential Council and create new government structures: a cabinet of ministers answerable to the President and a Security Council consisting of "power" ministries. The speech defused the tension. The Soyuz faction, and even the supporters of radical economic reforms, applauded the leader who seemed finally to have decided to address the crisis.[76]

There was another motive in Gorbachev's mind: the fate of his partnership with the West. The enraged Supreme Soviet could kill ratification of the treaties that Gorbachev and Shevardnadze had negotiated.[77] On 18 November, with a new sense of confidence, Gorbachev arrived in Italy to receive a prestigious Fiuggi prize, and then proceeded to Paris to attend the Conference on Security and Cooperation in Europe and append his signature to the "Charter of Paris for a New Europe" and the CFE Treaty. He was a central figure at the conference; Bush, Mitterrand, Kohl, Thatcher, and other Western leaders deferred to him.

It was a perfect moment for Gorbachev to reach an understanding with Bush on the necessity of a crackdown against Yeltsin's unilateral separatism. The American President badly needed Soviet support for a resolution in the United Nations Security Council permitting the use of force in Iraq. Bush explicitly said he would back Gorbachev's steps to restore the constitutional order. "We understand what you want to achieve: preserve the order and unity, which are necessary for the republics." Bush openly dismissed Yeltsin's pretensions. The only exception, Bush added, was the use of force against the Baltic republics: on this issue, American public opinion would not allow him to support Gorbachev.[78]

Instead, Gorbachev took a defensive stand. He probably feared that the Bush administration would proceed to act unilaterally, without the USSR, against Iraq, and Gorbachev would lose a key ally for his scheme of Soviet integration into a new Europe. Meeting with Bush, one on one, Gorbachev invoked the image of the New Deal to explain his domestic predicament. Just like Franklin Roosevelt, he had to respond to people's fears to avoid chaos and violence. Therefore, "to some extent, sometimes, we have to use measures *resembling* [author's italics] harsh administrative measures, so that we do not allow unfolding processes to turn to chaos." The new Union Treaty, he told Bush, was the only means of solving the crisis.[79]

Chernyaev was struck once again by the phenomenon of the "two Gorbachevs": one was a world figure with a striking vision, the other was a lame-duck domestic politician, "out of ammunition" and unable to use his enormous executive powers.[80] When Gorbachev returned to Moscow, he vowed to Shakhnazarov that he would never rule by decree. Nobody, including the Supreme Soviet, and the forthcoming Congress of People's Deputies, he declared, "can force me into dictatorship. I would rather resign . . . This is a firm conviction, a life-long principle."[81] Still, he decided not to travel to the West again for a while. He even canceled his trip to Oslo on 10 December, to receive the Nobel Prize. Instead, a senior Soviet diplomat accepted the honor on his behalf.[82]

While Gorbachev was building a "Common European Home," Yeltsin and Burbulis worked to build an alliance of the Russian Federation with other republics against the Kremlin. On 19 November, the Russian leader arrived in Kiev, to sign the treaty of mutual recognition and cooperation between the Russian Federation and the Ukrainian SSR. This was a cornerstone of the strategy, advocated by Yeltsin, to build a new Union "from below," on the basis of "horizontal" economic and political ties between the three Slavic republics and Kazakhstan. Gorbachev knew about Yeltsin's mission, but he did not intervene.

The Ukrainian republic was still firmly under the control of the Party nomenklatura, and the calls for full independence came only from Western Ukraine and some members of the Rukh.[83] Yeltsin came to tell them that, after the 300-year attachment of Ukraine to the Russian Empire and "the totalitarian regime" in Moscow, Ukraine was now free to choose its own path. Speaking in the Ukrainian Supreme Soviet on 19 November, Yeltsin sounded like the best ally of the Rukh nationalists. Then he signed the prepared text of the treaty and a joint declaration with the head of the Ukrainian parliament, Leonid Kravchuk. In front of journalists, Yeltsin blamed Gorbachev for concentrating "absolute" power in his hands. Russia, he said, would not sign a Union Treaty—a scheme imposed by the "totalitarian" center. Instead, there should be only a Union of Sovereign States, such as the Russian Federation, Ukraine, and others.[84]

Burbulis recalled that Yeltsin, when he went on his trip to Kiev, was under the influence of Solzhenitsyn's pamphlet "How to Rebuild Russia?" Solzhenitsyn wrote about Russians, Ukrainians, and Belorussians as one nation divided by geopolitical calamities and foreign conquest. He appealed to Ukrainians: "Brothers! We do not need a brutal divide! This is the dark delusion of communist days. We suffered the Soviet times together, and ended up in this huge pit. We will get out of it together."[85] Yeltsin used similar rhetoric. At the same time, the Russian leader left no doubt that the road to such a union should be built over the complete destruction of the old state and full recognition of Ukrainian sovereignty.

Not everyone in Yeltsin's entourage agreed. Vladimir Lukin, a top expert on foreign policy in the Russian parliament, argued that the RSFSR "had been artificially created by the Bolsheviks and cannot be identified with Russia either ethnically or historically." The Soviet Union, on the contrary, "was without doubt and remains today the successor state to the Russian monarchy and the Russian Republic (1917), and for seventy years represented Russia's interests in

HOPE AND HUBRIS

foreign policy." If the political elites that controlled the RSFSR "take the course of creating an independent state," Lukin warned, "we should expect a long and creeping ethno-civil war." Lukin believed that instead of destroying the old Union state, the Russian authorities had to help Gorbachev rebuild it. Boosting Ukrainian sovereignty was certainly not in Russia's interests.[86]

Yeltsin, however, was impressed by another of Solzhenitsyn's arguments: that the Russians had exhausted themselves while serving as human clay for "the totalitarian empire." Speaking to the Ukrainian Supreme Soviet, Yeltsin said that Russia "does not want any special role," and "does not seek to become a center of any future empire . . ." And he refused even to raise the issue of "Russian territories" inside Ukraine. He specifically elaborated on the question of Crimea. He said that the "people of Crimea should be given the right to determine their future through a referendum. We should not interfere." In Kiev, Yeltsin reaffirmed that the problem of Crimea "is the [internal] affair of the peoples of Crimea and the parliament of Ukraine."[87]

The Ukrainian parliament ratified the treaty almost immediately, and the Ukrainian nationalists welcomed Yeltsin's message. A few months later, Kravchuk told the British ambassador to the USSR, Rodric Braithwaite, that he embraced Yeltsin's idea of keeping all local taxes, capital assets, and natural resources under Ukraine's control. He was concerned, however, about the potential inequality in Russian-Ukrainian relations, because the Russian Federation was too big. For this reason, Kravchuk explained, some kind of a weaker Union could be in Ukraine's interest.[88] This was the paradox: the Russian leadership in Moscow pushed for Ukrainian independence that the Ukrainian leaders did not actually want.

In the Russian parliament, the Russian-Ukrainian treaty evoked consternation. Article Six stated that the signatories "recognize and respect the territorial integrity of the Ukrainian Soviet Socialist Republic and the Russian Soviet Federative Socialist Republic within their presently existing borders within the USSR [v ramkakh SSSR]."[89] The ratification of the treaty took some time and effort. Still, Lukin and other parliamentarians signed off on the official copy of it. They interpreted the treaty's article as recognition of Ukraine's territory *as long as the USSR was in existence*. No one could imagine that this choice of words would become so heavily contested a year later.

GORBACHEV'S BAD CHOICES

By the end of November 1990, Gorbachev had wasted any political momentum that his "dictatorial presidency" had briefly generated. All his advisors concluded that he was burnt out and had lost his bearings.[90] The most logical step for him

174

would have been to pick a Vice-President as his future successor, a fresh ener-getic leader. One good candidate was Nursultan Nazarbayev, leader of the Party and President of Kazakhstan. The Kazakh was intelligent, prudent and cautious.[91] Instead, Gorbachev's choice was Gennady Yanayev, who, like Gorbachev himself, was of peasant stock and had made his career in the Komsomol. Under Brezhnev, Yanayev led the Committee of Youth Organizations of the USSR, and later had worked for the Union of Soviet Societies for Friendship and Cultural Ties with Foreign Countries. Both jobs entailed endless trips abroad, schmoozing, heavy drinking, and partying with foreign guests. A Party man in every sense of the word, Yanayev was a bizarre choice for Gorbachev.

Gorbachev's other cadre choices also signaled the rise of people who were capable of using force. He appointed Boris Pugo to replace Bakatin in the Ministry of the Interior. Pugo's father, an ethnic Latvian, had served in Stalin's law enforce-ment agency, the NKVD, during the Terror and helped to crush resistance to Soviet power in Latvia after 1945. Pugo had led the Latvian KGB under Brezhnev. As Pugo's deputy, Gorbachev selected General Boris Gromov, a Russian military man who had led the last column of Soviet tanks out of Afghanistan in 1989.

The only exception to the downgrading of Gorbachev's entourage seemed to be the Minister of Finance, Valentin Pavlov, fifty-three years old, well educated and energetic. Pavlov regarded himself as "a pure financial expert," unlike the demagogues and careerists from the Party and Komsomol apparatus. He was one of the few who knew how the Soviet monetary system worked and what the real causes of its crisis were.[92] Pavlov rejected the 500 Days as a disastrous scheme for the Soviet economy. He strongly believed in a transition to a market economy under authoritarian state control, as had happened in Singapore, South Korea, Taiwan, and was occurring under the Party leadership in China. Pavlov favored Soviet membership of the IMF and World Bank, but he believed it would require a special set of state policies to attract foreign capital. On 6 December 1990, Pavlov, the head of Gosplan, Masliukov, and the committee heads of the Soviet parliament presented to Gorbachev an "Agreement to ensure stabilization of the social-economic situation in the country." Pavlov had worked out a detailed new fiscal system between the federal state and the repub-lics, to replenish the state budget. With this in mind, he proposed a 20 percent mandatory tax on all state enterprises: this money would go to a federal stabili-zation fund. This was a new position for negotiating with Yeltsin. The docu-ment warned the President that, if he made excessive concessions to the republics, especially to the Russian Federation, he "will in effect liquidate the economic base for the functioning of the Union of SSR as a federal state."[93]

The Fourth Congress of People's Deputies, extraordinary and plenipoten-tiary, opened in the Kremlin on 17 December 1990. It was a very different assembly from the one a year before. Most pro-democracy deputies identified with "their" republics. The largest faction was from the Russian Federation, including the skeptical and confident Yeltsin, Burbulis, and radical members of Democratic Russia. Nazarbayev led the pack of Central Asian deputies and demanded more autonomy. The Baltic deputies boycotted the Congress, just like the representatives from Georgia, Armenia, Azerbaijan, and Moldova. Many intellectuals were absent: abroad on lecturing tours and multi-month-long fellowships provided by Western foundations and universities.[94] The majority of deputies openly flouted Gorbachev's authority and overruled his proposals. According to Rodric Braithwaite, who observed the session, "no one has any idea how to replace [Gorbachev] if he leaves."[95]

Lukyanov chaired the Congress and seemed to be more in control and in charge. Unexpectedly, he gave the floor for a procedural question to the deputy from Chechnya, Sazhi Umalatova, a hard-line Leninist and bleeding-heart Soviet patriot. Umalatova proposed a vote of no confidence in the President. Gorbachev had wasted his mandate, she explained, and ruined the country. She turned to Gorbachev: "Excuse me, but one should know how to use power for the benefit of the people."[96] Lukyanov put Umalatova's motion to the vote, adding that the Congress could not remove the President, as long as he acted constitutionally. A total of 1,288 deputies voted against the motion. Over 400, however, voted for Gorbachev's removal. What did this episode mean? Umalatova vowed that the speech was her own heartfelt cry. After her motion failed, she ran to a bathroom and wept hysterically.[97]

Gorbachev had to sustain more blows. One came from Ryzhkov. The Prime Minister took the floor to explain why perestroika had been such a failure. He blamed hostile forces who turned on the government program of "genuine, humane socialism." Soon after his speech Ryzhkov suffered a heart attack and left the political scene. At last, Gorbachev was free to choose a new government.[98] A much bigger stab in Gorbachev's back came from Shevardnadze. Pride, a sense of loyalty, jealousy, and frustration collided in this emotional, ambitious man. Shevardnadze became convinced that the Soviet leader was holding him as a scapegoat, while elevating his rival Primakov, to run Soviet diplomacy. He had also become convinced that the Soviet "empire" was doomed to fall apart, and he would have to shift his loyalty from Moscow to Georgia.[99] On the morning of 20 December, Shevardnadze told his two aides about his decision to resign. He did not inform Gorbachev, fearing his "usual tricks." A few hours later, Shevardnadze was at the podium in Congress. He began to speak calmly, then he raised the issue of attacks on his personal dignity, and his emotion waxed. "Dictatorship is coming! I do not know which kind, who will be a dictator . . . I am resigning . . . Do not react now, do not curse me! Let it be my contribution, my protest against the advancing dictatorship." He ended with a declaration that "the future belongs to democracy and freedom." Then he exited the hall, leaving the audience in suspense. Western observers and journalists rushed out to report the sensational news. Alksnis and his associates gloated. Pro-democracy deputies spoke about the danger of dictatorship and urged Shevardnadze to reconsider.[100]

Gorbachev sat with a poker face. When he finally spoke, he said that he had planned to appoint Shevardnadze as Vice-President, and that the unexpected resignation offended him. Shevardnadze, who watched this on television from his office in the Foreign Ministry, cupped his face with both hands, red from anger: Gorbachev prevaricated again. Next morning, Gorbachev invited Shevardnadze to his office in the Kremlin: he was there with Raisa; both tried to talk Shevardnadze out of his decision. "If you resign," Gorbachev said, "I will do so as well." Back in his office, Shevardnadze told his aides that Gorbachev refused to acknowledge the obvious: he was sandwiched between the separatists who wanted to destroy the Union, and the hardliners who wanted to use emergency rule to stop the meltdown. He would have no other option but to use force and spill blood. "Then our entire cause will lose its meaning."[101]

The sense of suspense after Shevardnadze's departure grew even more when two days later Kryuchkov addressed the Congress with his report. The KGB chief, as earlier, spoke about foreign interference in Soviet affairs. The West, he said, was ready to take advantage of the opening of the Soviet economy. It encouraged a "brain-drain" of the skilled scientific and technical workers from Soviet enterprises. He also spoke, continuing Andropov's line of 1983, about the currency war that the West was allegedly waging against the Soviet Union. "There are," he said, "12 billion rubles in Swiss banks alone, which at any moment could find their way onto the Soviet market" and trigger massive inflation. Many of the activities "of our foreign partners," he summed up, "are close to economic sabotage."[102]

When Gorbachev proposed Yanayev for Vice-President, the Congress turned his candidacy down. It was not clear who felt more humiliated: Gorbachev or the deputies who thought Yanayev was an inept buffoon. During the break, a group of intellectuals tried to dissuade the President. Yanayev, they said, was not a good man for reforms. Gorbachev asked: "What are your facts?"[103] Yanayev was elected by a tiny margin in the second round. Chernyaev recorded in his diary: "The Congress is turning into a mob . . . This institution should be disbanded as soon as possible." Gorbachev's closest aide decided to postpone his own decision to resign. He pitied Gorbachev.[104]

The huge question that Congress could not properly discuss, even less agree upon, was the Union Treaty. After resisting it for over a year, Gorbachev finally put this pivotal issue on the table. Many believed it was too late. Gorbachev also pulled another rabbit out of his hat. In his address, he called for a nationwide referendum on the question of whether a reformed Union should be preserved. The Congress voted in favor, leaving the question of timing to the leadership. For the Soviet Union the year ended with the specter of discord between the different parties of the fading and crumbling state. The Western diplomats and journalists, who took their cues from their liberal friends in Moscow, were almost certain that blood would soon be spilt, and that the Soviet military would be involved. Would there be a new commonwealth? Or only growing chaos and possibly bloodshed? No one knew the answer. Yet even at this point very few expected that the Soviet Union would not survive 1991.

PART II

DECLINE AND
DOWNFALL
1991

CHAPTER 7

STANDOFF

But what save foulest defeat can await that man, who wills, and yet wills not?
Thomas Carlyle about Louis XVI in 1789[1]

*Yeltsin and Gorbachev will not be reconciled until they
meet each other in prison.*
A Soviet joke

BLOOD IN THE BALTICS

On the morning of 20 December 1990, Condoleezza Rice, special advisor to George Bush, was still in bed when a call from the Situation Room in the White House woke her up. Rice was part of a small contingency group at the NSC that discussed the future of Gorbachev and the Soviet Union. Brent Scowcroft had set up this group in the fall of 1989, because he became convinced: "either Gorbachev was going to stop this [perestroika] or somebody would stop him." The leader of the group was Robert Gates, a veteran analyst at the CIA. The biggest contingency on the group's agenda was the prospect of a violent collapse of the Soviet Union. The committee examined other dangers: what if Soviet nuclear weapons fell into dangerous hands; what if the US government learned of plans for a coup against Gorbachev; what if Soviet troops in Germany refused to go home? Now Rice was asked to explain Shevardnadze's resignation. "That was the scariest moment," she recalled. "I was surprised, I was very worried." Rice called Scowcroft and warned him: something "really awful" was about to happen in the Soviet Union.[2]

Two days before Shevardnadze resigned, Rice and CIA experts concurred that "a creeping crackdown" was taking place in the Soviet Union. The problem between Gorbachev's government and the separatist republics was "likely to get much worse in the coming weeks." What should the US government do? Until then the White House had discouraged meetings with republican leaders. But how should the US government respond if some separatist leaders demanded recognition by the United Nations or other international organizations? The republics in question were not only the Baltics, but the Russian Federation and Ukraine.[3]

Bush, Scowcroft, and Baker were genuinely puzzled by the Russians' support of Yeltsin. Gates, the CIA's Fritz Ermarth, and the US ambassador in Moscow, Jack Matlock, had been telling them: Yeltsin stood a great chance of becoming the future president of Russia.[4] In the 1950s, Scowcroft had studied at West Point and read books about Soviet and Russian history. They had taught him that Russia, because of its insecurity, geography, and economic backwardness, was destined to be ruled by an authoritarian regime. The emergence of Yeltsin and a bunch of Russian intellectuals, calling for democracy, human rights, and the dissolution of the Union, did not fit this matrix. Scowcroft wrote to Bush: "The absurdity of the situation in the Soviet Union is perhaps best captured by the prospect of Russia—once thought to be synonymous with the Soviet state— seeking autonomy from the Kremlin under Yeltsin's leadership." Scowcroft viewed Yeltsin as a creature of chaos produced by Gorbachev's style of governance, "an ambitious opportunist of the first order and his credentials as a democrat are suspect at best." Jim Baker agreed: Shevardnadze had told him that Yeltsin was a demagogue and possibly a dangerous nationalist.[5]

Rice spent 20 December in the Situation Room of the White House, reading cables and periodically briefing the leadership. Nobody knew what to expect. "It was a black day for us," Baker recalled.[6] Yet nothing happened the next day, nor the day after. And a week later the Soviet ambassador in Washington, Alexander Bessmertnykh, arrived with Gorbachev's letter to Bush. The Soviet leader explained that Shevardnadze's resignation was the result of a nervous breakdown. "You can be absolutely firmly assured," the letter went, "our policy course . . . will remain unchanged in terms of substance, as in form . . . This goes for the European process. This goes for all arms control and security issues. This goes for the Persian Gulf." Gorbachev wanted Bush to confirm the date for the next summit in Moscow, scheduled for 11–13 February 1991. Bessmertnykh would soon become the next Foreign Minister. The American leaders, who called him "Sasha" and knew he was loyal to Shevardnadze's way of thinking, were reassured.[7]

Vytautas Landsbergis, the Lithuanian pro-independence leader, was one of the first to understand the potential of the Russian chaos and split. Suddenly, he saw the possibility that the Soviet Union might collapse from within.[8] The Lithuanian exit could become a fuse for such an implosion. This fuse blew unexpectedly, in early January 1991. The Lithuanian government of moderate nationalists decided to raise prices on basic food commodities. An angry mob, mostly Russian speakers, protested in the streets and even tried to storm the Lithuanian parliament. The government resigned. In the political vacuum, the pro-Moscow communists and the Russian minority leaders decided to invite the Soviet Army to introduce "presidential rule" in Lithuania. The two camps were set for a confrontation. On 10 January, Marshal Yazov ordered General Varennikov to return to Vilnius. And Kryuchkov instructed the KGB Colonel Mikhail Golovatov to fly to Vilnius with "Alfa," a small well-trained group of KGB commandos. The next day, the Lithuanian communists proclaimed "the committee of national salvation" and appealed to the Soviet military for support.[9]

The "Alfa" commander later asserted that initially his KGB superiors had ordered him to take control of the Lithuanian Television Center and announce the appeal of the national salvation committee to establish presidential rule. Then, however, a different order came: to control the television center in order to prevent the broadcasting of any news harmful to the USSR. This made little sense. Golovatov later called this "a stupendous act of betrayal . . . by the country's leadership." He meant not only Gorbachev, but his KGB bosses as well. "Alfa" acted in coordination with the military and the riot police (OMON) from the Ministry of the Interior. At night, the Pskov Airborne Division, supported by tanks and APCs, tried to move towards the television tower, surrounded by a hostile crowd of young Lithuanians. In the skirmish fourteen Lithuanians lost their lives. Inside the television center an "Alfa" officer was shot dead, almost certainly by friendly fire.[10]

The question of Gorbachev's complicity came up immediately and never went away. Many Lithuanians held the Soviet leader responsible for the bloodshed. If so, what had the Soviet leader wanted to achieve? This was the period when the United States and its allies were preparing to launch a war in the Gulf. Had Moscow wanted to crush the Baltic independence movements, this was the perfect time to do so. Those accusing Gorbachev denied that local forces could have acted independently, and ignored the chaos of the night-time confrontations. Few in Lithuania—including the former Prime Minister, Kazimira Prunskienė—claimed that Gorbachev was not fully in control of the military at the time.[11]

Oleg Shenin in the CPSU Secretariat openly pushed for presidential rule in Lithuania and later asserted that Gorbachev had "let people down." The Soviet leader refused to sign the prepared documents that recognized the "national salvation committee." Kryuchkov later claimed that Gorbachev had instructed him, Yazov, and Boris Pugo to prepare for the use of force, but he then reconsidered. Chernyaev, when he learned about the fatalities in Vilnius, thought the same. Shevardnadze was convinced that the Soviet leader had contributed to what happened by his prevarications.[12] At a later date, Shevardnadze told his aides about "a secret meeting" in late October 1990 when Gorbachev, responding to frantic appeals by the communist leaders in Lithuania to protect them from the nationalists, had not excluded the use of force. On 3 January 1991, Gorbachev met Shevardnadze in the Kremlin, during which he asked him one last time to return to the government following his earlier resignation. The Soviet leader looked depressed, on the brink of resignation himself. "I am also ready to leave," he suddenly said. "I even envy you, believe me." Perhaps he was referring to the pressures on him to resort to force in the Baltics.[13]

In his memoirs Gorbachev asserted he had authorized Kryuchkov, Yazov, and Pugo to act only "if the situation in Vilnius should get out of control and there are direct clashes between *Sajudis* supporters and the communists." Had things gone the way the Soviet leader claimed, the Soviet military could have reacted to local resistance with lethal firepower, just as they had done in Baku in January 1990. *Sajudis* leaders feared this scenario and therefore urged their followers to adhere to non-violence. On 11 January 1991, one day before the military assault in Vilnius, Gorbachev called Bush on a secure line to tell him that he would do anything to reach a peaceful settlement with the Lithuanian nationalist government. "People are demanding I introduce presidential rule," Gorbachev said to Bush. "You know what my style is in such matters. It is much like your style. I will do all I can ... to reach a political solution." Gorbachev added that in Lithuania not everything is "within our control."[14]

The Soviet leader found himself in the worst possible situation. He had broken the pledge he gave to Bush. Landsbergis and *Sajudis* activists enjoyed world attention and sympathy. The Western media seemed to have forgotten how they had lionized Gorbachev. Journalists came out with the same old Cold War images: Lithuania was compared to Hungary of 1956 and Czechoslovakia of 1968. The Chinese tanks of Tiananmen Square in 1989 also loomed in the background. Gorbachev's perestroika was declared kaput. His procrastinations over constitutional issues became part of a sinister plan. One liberal observer from *The Washington Post* bemoaned how Gorbachev "could tarnish his Nobel Peace Prize, lose the respect and trust of the West by sending tanks against unarmed people."[15] The leaders of Democratic Russia brought out tens of thousands of Muscovites to protest the violence in Lithuania. The largest rally on Manezh Square near the Kremlin consisted of between 100,000 and 200,000 people. Chernyaev wrote down what he heard on the radio: "Gorbachev is the greatest liar of our times"; "Gorbachev and his clique"; "Gorbachev is worse than Hitler." Galina Starovoitova in her interview with the BBC said: "Gorbachev has become a dictator. He still has not let a big bloodshed occur. Yet he is the person who is profoundly alien to an idea of democracy."[16] The editor of *Moscow News*, Yegor Yakovlev, published an issue of his newspaper in a funereal frame with a screeching title: "Bloody Sunday!" *Arguments and Facts* published a collective protest signed by eighty celebrities and luminaries, the cream of the Russian intellectual, literary, and artistic elites.[17]

This barrage could not help but wound Gorbachev's ego. And still the Soviet leader did not succumb to this ferocious pressure. He even continued to defend Yazov, Kryuchkov, and Pugo from accusations in the Soviet parliament. This only made him appear even more like a culprit. Even Gorbachev's advisors felt the urge to join the protest. Yakovlev was so distressed that he was hospitalized. Chernyaev dictated an emotional letter to Gorbachev, in which he announced his immediate resignation. His secretary (and mistress) typed up the letter, but then refused to finish the job and tore the draft to pieces. Chernyaev, however, went on to reproduce it in his diary for posterity.[18]

A week after the bloodshed in Lithuania, another tragedy struck in Riga: the Latvian OMON clashed with the Latvian armed police. Five civilians died, including a cameraman from Soviet television. Gorbachev refused to take any responsibility for this event either. He blamed the local Latvian militia and even suspected Anatolijs Gorbunovs, head of the Latvian Supreme Soviet, of the insurrection. After all, he mused, who gained most "from this provocation?" The Soviet leader also accused "Russian separatists." Without the expected support from Yeltsin and Democratic Russia in Moscow, Gorbachev claimed, radical separatists in the Baltics would not have acted so provocatively.[19] Two days after the events in Riga, however, Gorbachev issued a statement in which he distanced himself from the violence, regretted the casualties, and once again denounced the use of force against civilians. Chernyaev commented with a mixture of relief and regret: "Gorbachev is in his element: he is always late." The Western ambassadors in Moscow were also relieved: they had been convinced that Gorbachev would introduce presidential rule in the Baltics and use force.[20]

Dictators and some historians are familiar with the effects of an indecisive use of force: better not to use force at all than to use it and recoil. The Baltic affair left the Soviet conservatives demoralized and the military let down. The emergency Party Plenum at the end of January 1991 reflected this spirit. It was all talk, smoke and mirrors, but no action was taken.[21] The Party Secretariat, led by Ivashko, sent a letter to all Party organizations in the Army, KGB, and police forces. "In the new situation," the letter summarized, "we must act exclusively by political means."[22]

On the eve of the Lithuanian tragedy, Yeltsin in Moscow received the head of the Estonian parliament, Arnold Rüütel. Yeltsin appreciated that Rüütel had publicly expressed his sympathy for him when Yeltsin was still a Party outcast. The two leaders met to sign the treaty of mutual recognition between the RSFSR and Estonia. Next morning, after the bloodshed in Vilnius, they flew to Tallinn together. The Latvian leader Gorbunovs arrived from Riga to join them and to sign an RSFSR-Latvian treaty. Landsbergis, who had stayed in Lithuania, joined them by phone.[23] Yeltsin and the three Baltic leaders issued a joint appeal to the United Nations "and other international organizations" to denounce "acts of armed violence against sovereign states." The Russian leader also urged the Russian officers, sergeants, and soldiers who served in the Soviet army in the Baltic states to avoid being "tools and pawns" in the hands of "the reaction." At the same time, Yeltsin appealed to the Russians who lived in the Baltics: their rights would be protected no matter what their citizenship in the future would be. None of these documents and appeals even mentioned the Soviet Union and the Soviet constitution. Yeltsin's support delighted the Balts. His advisor Gennady Burbulis, who accompanied him, believed this to be a milestone in the construction of a new Russia. The appeal to the UN, Burbulis recalled, was "the first time Russia acted as a subject of international affairs."[24]

Yeltsin's dash to the Baltics was prefaced by weeks of deliberations and preparations inside his circle. On 26 December 1990, Yeltsin and his advisory council discussed Gorbachev's "turn to the right." Burbulis, who chaired the meeting, insisted that an alliance of "Russia" with the Balts and other republics would be the only option to fend off a totalitarian backslide. Other advisors argued that the Russian Federation should begin to form a "shadow" Russian army consisting of retired officers and war veterans, which should appeal to the pro-Russian elements in the KGB and the police.[25] Georgy Arbatov, director of the US and Canada Institute, warned Yeltsin. The KGB and the military, he said, after their retreat from Eastern Europe realized they could lose everything and might rally again around the center; there could be a bloody crackdown on separatists. In the Baltics, Arbatov argued, Yeltsin would do best to mediate between the Lithuanian nationalists, the Russian speakers, and the Soviet military. "Russia must think not only about itself," Arbatov concluded, "but must become a consolidating center for the entire country."[26]

Yeltsin wanted to become a leader of all Russians across political divides. He even appealed to Russian émigrés outside the Soviet Union with a call of solidarity.[27] At the same time, he was dead set against reconciliation with Gorbachev. The KGB, he was certain, was after him, perhaps even trying to eliminate him. Yeltsin doggedly pursued his idea of a bottom-up pyramid, with three "Slavic" republics and Kazakhstan uniting against the central government. The Baltic republics, he said, would also join the league, as well as Moldova and Georgia. This was Yeltsin's delusionary scheme that competed with Gorbachev's delusion about a new Union Treaty.[28]

Gorbachev's Baltic calamity seemed to validate Yeltsin's political instincts. The actions of the Russian leader in the Baltics no longer looked reckless and divisive. On the contrary, the entire Moscow liberal-minded elite supported and admired him. Yeltsin took full advantage of Gorbachev's predicament. On 21 January, he addressed the Russian parliament with a crisp analysis of the situation. He denounced Gorbachev's "six years" of vacillation between democracy and authoritarianism. He laid out again his idea of a Union pyramid in reverse. In a word, the leader of the largest republic in the USSR was in open sedition, and most of the educated Russians were backing him.[29]

On 7 February 1991, Kryuchkov sent a grim memo to Gorbachev on the political situation in the country. "The policy of appeasing the aggressive flank of 'democratic movements,'" the memo read, "allows the pseudo-democrats to realize without hindrance their plans to seize power." The subversive forces, led by Yeltsin, had intercepted perestroika's agenda. Instead of renovating socialism, they wanted to destroy the socialist order. Kryuchkov admitted that after the bloodshed in the Baltics, Gorbachev had lost the support of the "scientific and humanitarian intelligentsia." Still, he concluded, there was room for political action. The Supreme Soviet and the Congress of the USSR did not support Yeltsin. The KGB chief spoke very cautiously about "the option of . . . temporary structures within the framework of emergency powers the President received from the Supreme Soviet."[30] He couched this message in the formulaic language taken directly from Gorbachev's orations.

A NEW STRONGMAN

There was a new man of action in Gorbachev's entourage: Valentin Pavlov, who replaced Ryzhkov as Prime Minister of the Soviet government. The Supreme Soviet approved his nomination by Gorbachev on 14 January 1991. Pavlov's memoirs are a minefield for historians, with numerous factual errors and bizarre claims. The author veered between his contempt for Gorbachev and a desire to set his record straight. Still, the book is a valuable source of information on Pavlov himself. He posed as a professional who did not interfere in the politics or foreign affairs of Gorbachev. His domain was economics and finance, the spheres of activity that the Soviet President delegated to him.[31]

In his memoirs, Pavlov wrote that there were two kinds of people in the Soviet elites and the Russian government, who worked to destroy the Soviet Union. Some, such as Gorbachev and Ryzhkov, undermined the state and its economy out of ignorance and because of their short-term interests. Others were determined gravediggers of the USSR, such as Yeltsin, Popov, Sobchak, and many in Democratic Russia. "The demo-Russians and the forces that stood behind them wanted great upheavals," Pavlov concluded. This was a quote from the speech of Prime Minister Pyotr Stolypin in the State Duma in June 1907, when he had announced to the radical deputies: "You want great upheavals, but we want a great Russia!" Stolypin had acted on behalf of the weak Tsar Nicholas II, to introduce conservative reforms by authoritarian means, in order to save the Russian state. Pavlov recalled: "When I became Prime Minister, I still considered and hoped to prevent the collapse of a great power. The state still existed and it could have been saved by legal means."[32] Chernyaev decided that Pavlov could potentially overtake Gorbachev. "He is smart and professional. All those parliamentarians are like puppies in front of him. He despises them and fends off their arguments easily. And he couldn't care less what 'all this intelligentsia' thinks of him. He will do what he thinks is right."[33]

Pavlov believed in what many others in the Soviet leadership ignored: that real power depended on state control over money. As long as its central fiscal and monetary system existed, the Soviet Union could survive.[34] Pavlov had realized already in the fall of 1989 that the central government was delegating control over money to irresponsible political forces. This control had to be reclaimed. When the Russian parliament decided to set up the Bank of Russia in July 1990, Pavlov and Viktor Gerashchenko, head of the State Bank, were horrified. Their dismay grew after Gorbachev failed to use his power to kill the Russian decree. He even chided Pavlov and Gerashchenko for their "imperial ambitions."[35] Pavlov fought against the 500 Days as well. The radical economists proposed to destroy "the super-monopoly" of the State Bank and replace it with a confederation of republican banks. In Pavlov's view, the Soviet Union could not copy the Federal Reserve System in the United States. The State Bank had existed under the Tsars and the Bolsheviks. By questioning its monopoly, ignorant politicians and radical economists were undermining the Soviet finances and the Soviet state.[36]

At the end of 1990, Pavlov's nightmare became a reality. On 2 December, the Russian parliament boosted the status of the Bank of Russia and decreed that it should take over all branches of the State Bank of the USSR on the republican territory. Gerashchenko in the State Bank ignored the decree, yet the Russian separatists began to give out licenses to commercial banks under Russian jurisdiction, which enabled them to execute credit and currency functions. It was a quick way to destroy central controls over the financial system.[37] Even worse, the leaders of the Russian Federation insisted on collecting taxes from state enterprises and cooperatives, and keeping the money for their budget. In December 1990, Pavlov offered Yeltsin a scheme of sharing the income between the RSFSR and the central budget. Yeltsin rejected the deal.[38]

While Gorbachev grappled with the Baltic fallout and the Gulf crisis, Pavlov enacted painful financial reforms. His plan was to triple all state-regulated wholesale prices used in *beznal* transactions between state enterprises, as well as basic items for consumers. The populist contest between the all-Union and Russian parliaments had wrecked common standards and made transactions between state enterprises in different republics almost impossible. Pavlov knew that fixed prices would have to be replaced by market-driven ones. Yet he also believed in maintaining state controls. This time Gorbachev agreed with the price reforms, yet he postponed them until early April.

Another reform that Pavlov enacted in January 1991 was a 20 percent tax on state enterprises to create the federal amortization and investment fund. This was a big correction to the Law on State Enterprises and a nasty surprise for profiteers from "cooperatives" and directors who pocketed huge profits while paying only minimal taxes. They attacked the Soviet and Russian parliaments with protests, pleaded for exemptions, and threated to stop their production lines. The reform, had it been implemented, would have begun to replenish the central budget. The implementation, however, required strong administrative leverage, above all undisrupted tax collection on the territories of the republics, especially the Russian Federation.[39]

The last of Pavlov's reforms caused the most uproar. On the evening of 22 January 1991, Soviet people learned from a television announcement that 50-ruble and 100-ruble bills, the largest in circulation, were no longer valid. Those bills had to be exchanged within three days in the branches of the State Bank with new banknotes of the same value, up to a maximum of 10,000 rubles. Pavlov had been preparing this reform since 1989, but Gorbachev and Ryzhkov had delayed it.[40] This time, Pavlov took full responsibility for the unpopular step. He asserted that the reform could have soaked up 30 billion rubles from the shadow entrepreneurs and currency speculators. Western and domestic critics called Pavlov's reform "crude and ineffective." It did, however, help the government win some time by reducing the cash supply and delaying the financial meltdown.[41]

Like Kryuchkov in the KGB, Pavlov saw a great danger for the Soviet state coming from a collusion between Russian government officials and foreign interests. In his memoir, Pavlov paid special attention to two cases. In the first, Gennady Filshin, deputy Prime Minister of the Russian Federation and a key ally of Yeltsin, worked out a scheme that could, he claimed, fill the shelves in Russian stores. He struck a deal with a couple of British "businessmen": they would get "a loan" of $7.7 billion from the Russian government via the State Bank. This money, Filshin's partners promised, would be used to purchase "deficit consumer goods" on Western markets. The KGB leaked the scam out; it caused a scandal and hearings in the Russian parliament. Filshin had to resign, but he refused to admit he was part of a speculative scheme. Democratic Russia, as well as Yeltsin's entourage, sided with Filshin.[42]

In the second case, on 13 February 1991, Pavlov publicly accused Western banks of a conspiracy to flood the Soviet Union with rubles, thus inducing the collapse of Gorbachev and his government. The exchange of the banknotes, he claimed, helped foil this plot in the nick of time. He also warned Soviet enterprises not to deal with foreign businessmen who used joint ventures with naïve and inexperienced Soviet partners for the purpose of profiteering and shady dealings. Western diplomats and media were aghast. For the British ambassador, this was "a remarkable display of ignorance, fatuity, irresponsibility and xenophobia by the Prime Minister of the second most powerful country in the world." Had the Soviet Union been run normally, he concluded, Gorbachev would have sacked Pavlov.[43]

Pavlov apparently acted on the information he received from Kryuchkov. He was by no means alone in putting conspiratorial spin on the demise of Soviet finances and politics. On the opposite side of the political divide, Yeltsin and some of his advisors competed with Pavlov in conspiratorial thinking. In December 1990, at Yeltsin's advisory council, the economist Nikolai Shmelyov reported that Gorbachev had ordered the KGB to sell 20 billion rubles in new banknotes to Western banks at a market rate. Some had suggested, he added, that the amount was in fact 60 billion rubles. Yeltsin apparently believed this fable.[44]

In his memoirs, Pavlov defended his actions. His main fear was not the profiteering activities of foreign actors. Rather, he concluded that the greatest danger came from unscrupulous or inexperienced people in the Russian government, eager to open up to the global market, hungry for quick bucks, and capable of wrecking the existing financial system in a matter of months. Pavlov wrote his memoirs several years after the Soviet financial system had collapsed, and after the most horrendous and blatant financial schemes had been carried out with total impunity, filling the pockets of a few Russians and foreign investors.

REFERENDUMS

At the end of January, Gorbachev and Lukyanov decided that the all-national referendum on the need for a Union Treaty would take place on 17 March 1991. The referendum question designed by them was incredibly convoluted: "Do you consider necessary the existence of the Union of Soviet Socialist Republics as a renewed federation of equal sovereign republics in which the rights and freedoms of all persons of all nationalities will be fully guaranteed?" Provided the majority would vote "yes," the next step would be to sign the Union Treaty and change the constitution.

In his memoirs, Gorbachev recalled that the referendum formula had emerged from "long discussions with my aides."[45] Shakhnazarov and Chernyaev had long thought that Gorbachev's Union Treaty was a quixotic project, and a referendum would change nothing. At best, there could be something similar to the European Economic Community or the British Commonwealth. Chernyaev also knew, even without the polls, that the majority of Muscovites were becoming livid with Gorbachev and the Soviet government. "The referendum ... can become a detonator" for a catastrophic explosion.[46] Many conservatives were also deeply skeptical about the referendum. At a Politburo meeting on 30 January, Islam Karimov, the Party boss and President of Uzbekistan, said "Preparation for the referendum will help to stoke up passions." An Uzbek proverb said: "Do not step on the tail of the sleeping lion."[47] Kryuchkov did not like the idea for the same reason. In his memoirs, the KGB chief argued that the March referendum was a provocation that could only benefit the enemies of the USSR. "There was no need to do it," Kryuchkov recalled. "For the masses this was not an issue."[48]

In Yeltsin's camp, Gorbachev's referendum was viewed as a conspiracy against a young Russian democratic state. Yeltsin and Burbulis resented that Gorbachev was treating numerous autonomous regions within the RSFSR as sovereign and equal subjects of a future Union. This meant that he wanted to play off the leaders of those regions against Yeltsin and the RSFSR legislature. Instead of having to deal with one "Russia" that threatened his power, the Soviet leader wanted to be able to bargain with sixteen units of the Russian Federation.[49] As the referendum approached, Yeltsin and his entourage noticed that the leaders of Ukraine and Belorussia were in no hurry to sign "a pact" with him against the center. As the future would reveal, the Ukrainians liked the prospect of an unequal alliance with Yeltsin's Russia even less than the idea of a center presided over by Gorbachev.[50]

Yeltsin's main project was, as before, the Russian presidency. There was, however, a legal obstacle: there was no post of president in the RSFSR constitution and only its Congress of People's Deputies could amend it. Yeltsin and his supporters consistently fell short of the two-thirds required majority. Many deputies, Party stalwarts and others, were worried by the danger of having two presidents in the one country. Burbulis and Starovoitova thought of another option: to have a referendum and obtain a "yes" from the Russian people. But such an enterprise across many time zones could cost up to 300 million rubles. Gorbachev's referendum solved this problem: a Russian referendum could be a rider and so cost nothing. The Russian Supreme Soviet approved this scheme by a simple majority.[51] The question of the Russian referendum was succinct: "Do you consider it necessary to introduce the post of the President of the RSFSR, elected by popular ballot?" There was a second question in the Russian referendum: whether to retain the territorial integrity of the Russian Federation, that is to recognize the supremacy of the Russian president over national autonomous regions. Burbulis recalled that the Russian referendum turned out to be a stroke of luck and genius. "Gorbachev unwittingly provided a golden opportunity for us."[52]

DECLINE AND DOWNFALL

Boris Yeltsin turned sixty on 1 February 1991. The most popular politician in Russia decided to arrange his birthday party on the vacated premises of a youth summer camp near Moscow. Yeltsin's wife Naina and their daughters Yelena and Tatiana were told to prepare for a big party; among the guests would be Yeltsin's classmates from the Ural Technical Institute, who flew to Moscow for the occasion. About eighty people were present; Lev Sukhanov, one of his aides, brought a guitar: Yeltsin loved Russian songs and used to sing along. After many toasts, Yeltsin's friends from the Urals unveiled a special gift for him: a half-meter wooden figure that had Yeltsin's features. One of the guests positioned himself in front of Yeltsin's effigy and said: "And now Boris, let me smack you in the jaw . . . let's see how you will take it." Yet after each blow, to everyone's delight, the "wooden Yeltsin" returned to its upright position. It was a Russian *nevaliashka*, a roly-poly toy, symbolizing for his admirers Yeltsin's unflagging spirit.[53]

On 19 February, after months of trying to gain access to national television, Yeltsin finally gave a televised interview to a group of journalists. His advisors prepared him well, and he responded carefully to the probing questions. At the very end of the interview, however, he pulled off a major surprise. His electorate wanted him to cooperate with Gorbachev, he said. "As the Lord is my witness, I have tried many times." Hours of meetings with the President, however, had led to nothing. After six years of failures, Gorbachev had refused to change. Yeltsin then called for the immediate resignation of the Soviet President. Power in the Soviet Union, he said, should be handed to "a collective body—a Council of Federation of republics."[54] Yeltsin did not make this demand emotionally, like Sazhi Umalatova. He wanted to mobilize his supporters for his presidential campaign. An independent poll, conducted among 900 Muscovites, showed that three-quarters of them supported Yeltsin. When asked about the future of the Soviet Union, fewer than 20 percent backed it, and almost 49 percent were in favor of Yeltsin's "Union of sovereign republics." Even more shockingly, almost 28 percent agreed with the option in the questionnaire that said: "the USSR should not exist."[55]

Gorbachev watched Yeltsin on television and convinced himself that his nemesis was drunk. "[Yeltsin's] hands were trembling," Gorbachev recalled years later. "I could see that he did not control himself and could [only] read the prepared text with difficulty." The Soviet leader thought the referendum would be a crushing blow to Yeltsin's plans for separatism. At the end of February, Gorbachev left for Minsk, his first domestic trip in several months. There the Soviet leader unleashed an attack on the "democrats," whom he blamed for destructive "neo-Bolshevism."[56] Upon returning to Moscow, he told the Politburo and the Secretariat "to mobilize the entire Party" for the referendum.

"If the Party sustains this battle, [the victory] will help it to get back on its feet." The head of the Russian Communist Party, Ivan Polozkov, said: "Finally, Mikhail Sergeyevich, you have merged with the conservatives." The time had come for presidential rule, to take over the USSR's ineffective parliamentary structures.[57]

On 2 March, Gorbachev celebrated his sixtieth birthday. He received greetings from the leading functionaries in a Party Secretariat room in the Old Square and gave a brief speech on the role of the Communist Party in his life and in perestroika. His chief of staff Valery Boldin recalled that the atmosphere was almost morose: "Not even the most virtuoso sycophant would have proposed a toast to him as a great, wise man."[58] Then the Soviet leader dashed to the Kremlin, to receive birthday greetings from members of the former Presidential Council, the cabinet, and personal advisors. Lukyanov made a moving speech. Yazov presented Gorbachev with a saber. The Minister of the Interior, Boris Pugo, gave him a handgun in a leather case with an inscription, accompanied by an ammunition clip. The KGB's Kryuchkov also gave Gorbachev a present, but nobody could remember what exactly it was. Chernyaev and Shakhnazarov read their "address" to the leader. History, they said, would remember Gorbachev as a great leader, who did what nobody else dared: "to tear this continent [the Soviet Union] off its rivets, which seemed to lock it forever." Gorbachev did it for "the honor and benefit of the country, driven by conscience and a sense of shame." The text of greetings included a quote from Abraham Lincoln: "If the end brings me out all right, what's said against me won't amount to anything. If the end brings me out wrong, ten angels swearing I was right would make no difference."[59]

Yeltsin's call for Gorbachev's resignation on national television split the Russian Assembly. The majority sharply disagreed with the radical democrats who wanted to use "Russia" as a battering ram to destroy the Soviet government. On 21 February, the top six officials there, including the leaders of both chambers, turned against Yeltsin. They expected an extraordinary session of the RSFSR Congress, to be convened in a few weeks, to bring Yeltsin down. Khasbulatov, the only one of Yeltsin's deputies who remained loyal to him, concluded: "Bad business. The majority is upset with Yeltsin. There will be a tough struggle ahead."[60]

A big groundswell of support for Yeltsin came from Russian industrial cities and provinces. The most resonant was a strike declared by the miners' committees of Kuzbass. A member of Yeltsin's advisory council, Vyacheslav Golikov, triggered this strike. Journalists called him the "Soviet Wałęsa," after the leader of Polish Solidarity, and he acted accordingly. This time the miners, however, did not demand soap, detergents, and better living conditions. They wanted to get rid of Gorbachev. Golikov and the other organizers were surprised by what happened next: 200,000 miners joined the strike, refusing to return to work. It was the second major industrial action that had rocked the economy of the USSR and it would last for a month.[61]

In Democratic Russia, fears of a creeping coup ran strong. Intellectual leaders of the movements debated: should intellectuals follow the Polish example of 1980 and lead the workers to a political revolution? Or would that be too dangerous? Yeltsin was inclined to take the risk. On 9 March, at a big rally of Democratic Russia in the House of Cinema in Moscow, he called again for Gorbachev's resignation and concluded it was time to save democracy and create a powerful organized party. Millions of people heard this speech on the radio.[62] Five days later, the Russian leader met with his advisory council. Popov, the head of Moscow's City Council, took the floor. He did not believe that Russian Solidarity was a good option: 1991 would be the year of "catastrophe equal to a war or the Great Depression." Soviet national income would fall by 10 or 20 percent, he said. Angry and unemployed masses would yearn for an authoritarian leader, he claimed: in America they had found Roosevelt, in Germany—Hitler.

Popov agreed with Yeltsin that Gorbachev was tricky and unreliable. At the same time, calling for his resignation would only push him into the arms of Party hardliners. Those people hated Gorbachev, but they would use him, the Army, and the KGB to set up a dictatorship. Then they would get rid of him. The Soviet junta would not last long, Popov continued, perhaps a year and a half. They would not be able to obtain Western credits or solve any economic problems. Yet, in the short term, the crackdown would also be a huge blow to Russian democracy. Yeltsin and other opposition leaders would be arrested and perhaps eliminated. "All of us may perish," Popov prophesied. "Who are the supporters of perestroika? A small circle: 200, 300, 400 people maximum. When they are gone, what would happen to the country?" The best tactic, Popov concluded, would be to offer Gorbachev a partnership.[63]

Yavlinsky, who returned to Yeltsin's entourage, backed Popov's grim economic and social forecast. The economic realities of the Soviet Union were such, he said, that sovereign republics remained just "decorations." They would perish if they seceded, including the Russian Federation. Yavlinsky regretted that in 1990 everybody had gotten carried away by "democratic games"; now everyone became "prisoners of decorative structures," such as republican parliaments. The Soviet Union, he said, was an airplane, in which Yeltsin and his allies in other republics remained passengers; the central government still sat in the cockpit, ran the economy, and controlled money and credit. The only prudent course now, he concluded, would be to help the people in the cockpit to stay in control. Otherwise, the Russian Federation would explode, just like the Soviet Union. A collapsing economy, ethno-nationalism, and "Russian fascism" would tear the country to pieces.[64] Yeltsin listened with a grim expression. He said that he had received "signals" from Gorbachev's people about possible cooperation, but he dismissed them as "another trick." "Three times [Gorbachev] looked me in the eye and said: 'I guarantee it.' Then nothing!" If the conservatives tried to oust him at the Russian Congress, Yeltsin said, he would not surrender, but would disband the Congress instead.[65]

Two days before the March referendums, Yeltsin met with a group of American economists from Stanford University, who had come to Moscow to help with Russian economic reforms. To clarify his vision to the Americans, Yeltsin said: "We will have here something like the early United States." Cooperation between Russia and other republics, Yeltsin concluded, would be useful in creating a future confederation without a central authority. Economic reforms, he continued, "will be in Russia" and not in the USSR, since Gorbachev was clearly incapable and unwilling to part with the communist legacy. "We are destroying the entire communist totalitarian system," he continued confidently. Russia would take over all Soviet property, including its defense industries. The Union center would only retain the defense complex, roads, and atomic energy. "The big structures of the Union," such as the sixty all-Union ministries, Yeltsin said, "are no longer needed. *The President of the USSR is no longer needed* [author's italics]."[66] This time, Yeltsin had spoken with utmost sincerity and from the heart. When the chance came his way, he would act, as he told the Americans.

UNEQUAL PARTNERS

President Bush was worried by the bloodshed in the Baltics, but he trusted Gorbachev's assurances. And he continued to depend on his "friend Mikhail" to provide international assistance for the "Desert Storm" against Iraq. In January, Bush called Gorbachev after the Lithuanian tragedy, yet he talked exclusively about the Gulf War. He addressed the Baltic crisis only after the first week of the aerial bombardment of Iraqi forces had gone well. Still, he did send a letter to Gorbachev with a strong warning: In case of more violence against the Balts, Bush would have to cancel all economic assistance and impose sanctions on the USSR. To drive this point home, Bush postponed the summit in Moscow. On 24 January, the American ambassador Jack Matlock delivered this letter in person to Gorbachev.[67]

The Soviet leader read the letter and asked Matlock: "Tell me, Jack. How do you read the situation here?" Taken by surprise, the US ambassador said that he personally believed Gorbachev did not want violence, but neither did the Balts. Those who exerted pressure on Gorbachev to use force were working against him and his reforms. Gorbachev listened without interrupting. "Try to help your president understand," he then continued, "that we are on the brink of a civil war. As president, my main task is to prevent it." He said emphatically that he was "not hostage to anyone" and assured Matlock that he would abide by all previous understandings, *even despite American sanctions.* "Tell my friend George Bush: whatever pressure is put on me regarding the Persian Gulf War, the German question, or the ratification of the conventional arms treaty, I'll keep to our agreements." The American ambassador was impressed by Gorbachev's resolve and reported the good news to his superiors in Washington.[68]

The Soviet leader continued hoping that bloodshed in the Gulf could be averted. For him it would be a blow to the vision of a peaceful global order that he and Bush had vowed to build together. Yevgeny Primakov flew to Baghdad in a last-minute attempt to convince Saddam Hussein to withdraw his forces from Kuwait, before the US-led coalition began the war on the ground. On 22 February, shortly before the launch of US ground troops, Bush dismissed Gorbachev's peace initiative. The administration wanted a full military victory and political reconstruction of the Middle East. While the US President argued why the war was needed, the Soviet leader attempted to interrupt him. He shouted: "George! George! George!" But Bush did not listen.[69]

On 23 February, Primakov signaled from Baghdad that he had reached a tentative deal with the Iraqi dictator. Gorbachev spent all day making calls to G-7 and Middle Eastern leaders: John Major, Giulio Andreotti, Mitterrand, Kohl, Kaifu, Egypt's Hosni Mubarak, Syria's Assad, Iran's Rafsanjani. He then called Bush, who was greatly irritated by Gorbachev's peace-making at America's expense, but patiently argued back that Saddam was just trying to drive a wedge between the US and the Soviet Union. The relationship between the two leaders "is too important and it is not going to fall apart over Iraq." Unable to change the American course, Gorbachev recalled Primakov from Baghdad.[70]

The war turned out to be a huge success for Bush. The massive air campaign in January–February destroyed much of Iraq's Soviet-made weaponry. Then 250,000 US troops, assisted by the British and French military, swept through Kuwait. CNN beamed across the world scenes of "turkey-shooting" of Iraqi military and administrative objects.[71] On 28 February, Bush declared victory. The BBC reported that the Western allies had lost 148 soldiers in battle, and 145 more from other causes. The number of Iraqi soldiers killed by aerial bombardment and the ground war was estimated at between 60,000 and 200,000. The American media at the time, mindful of the Vietnam syndrome, downplayed human casualties and focused on destroyed Iraqi equipment and burning oil wells. "Nobody knows," the BBC wrote, "how many civilians died in the war, but estimates for civilian deaths as a direct result of the war range from 100,000 to 200,000."[72] In contrast to the fourteen civilians in Lithuania, the West largely ignored these huge numbers of casualties.

The outcome of the Gulf War left Gorbachev humiliated and diminished. Chernyaev recorded his boss's complaints: "In Washington, nostalgia has grown for the old times and old methods. Apparently, they have a plan to end the euphoria about Gorbachev." The US preparations for war in the Gulf and the bloody clash with nationalists in Lithuania and Latvia were part of the same American plot. The American advisors, he said, "swarm around the opposition, above all Yeltsin."[73] Apparently, Gorbachev relied on KGB reports, yet even Chernyaev concluded that the war had buried the new world order of Gorbachev's dreams. When he spoke with his boss, both agreed that the Soviet Union had to accept the position of junior partner of the United States or perish.[74] Unbeknownst to the Kremlin, Western European leaders at the same time were imploring Bush to treat Gorbachev with respect. Bush promised to do so. After the war was over, he said, "we would work together for a peaceful Middle East … and a constructive and cooperative relationship with the Soviet Union."[75]

In the White House, the taste of victory replaced the tension. Condoleezza Rice informed Brent Scowcroft of her decision to resign from the NSC and return to teaching at Stanford University. "I told him: 'We unified Germany, Eastern Europe is liberated, the Soviet Union is about to collapse, and I don't have the energy for it.' "[76] Before leaving, Rice helped Scowcroft write another piece of Soviet analysis for Bush. It concluded that neither Gorbachev nor Yeltsin nor anyone "have [sic] satisfactory answers to any one of the problems that have befallen the Soviet Union, let alone a coherent program that addresses all of them." The developments in Moscow, the memo continued, revealed "the immaturity of the Soviet Union's political culture" demonstrated by the destabilizing and irresponsible behavior of parliamentary institutions, as well as mutual attacks between Yeltsin and Gorbachev. The memo struck a decidedly pessimist note regarding the chances of Moscow-based "democrats" and "liberal forces." Those who posed as such were a scattered crowd unable to seize or hold onto power. They were similar to members of the liberal Provisional Government that had lost to Lenin and the Bolsheviks in 1917.[77]

Scowcroft liked the memo. Even if things went terribly wrong in the Soviet Union, he thought, the United States could not do much about it. "History will not blame us if the Soviet Union does not find a path to democracy but we will most assuredly be held to account if democracy fails to take root in East-Central Europe." A coup against Gorbachev was not an immediate danger. The current mess would produce only "sporadic and inconclusive acts of violence." Bush read the memo and sent it back to Scowcroft with the note: "Finished. Burn or file."[78] From that moment on, the main debate in the White House was on how fast the Soviet Union's dissolution would proceed and what the American leadership could do to minimize the risks.

On 10 March, the Soviet leader received a belated birthday greeting from the White House. Bush sent a warm personal letter. The US leader reminisced about the relaxed time he and Gorbachev had had at Camp David in June 1990. "I often think about the problems you face at home, and I hope you will tell Jim [Baker] if there's anything you'd like me to know on a private basis." And he added: "As you know I consider myself lucky to be your friend."[79] This letter indicated the end of the hiatus in US-Soviet relations, caused by the Gulf War and the Baltic bloodshed. On 14 March, Baker flew to Moscow to lobby for Soviet ratification of arms control treaties. The Secretary of State decided to stage a dinner at the ambassador's residence in Spaso House for Gorbachev's entourage, but also for all republican and parliamentary leaders. It was a way to get around the thorny problem of meeting Yeltsin separately, which Baker did not want to do. He and Matlock also planned a separate meeting in Spaso House with the leaders of the three Baltic states.[80]

This was an awkward gesture and came at a very sensitive moment on the eve of the March referendum. When Gorbachev learned about the American plans from the KGB report, he was furious. He ordered all members of his entourage to boycott the dinner. Chernyaev was appalled by the American "impudence" of inviting all members of the opposition to the US residency. He wrote in his diary: "Perhaps we have two different mentalities and ethics, and this is normal for Americans. Or this is deliberate crudeness by the victors over Hussein, when they no longer need Gorbachev or participation of the Soviet Union in the European process."[81]

The Americans were surprised by Gorbachev's "childish" behavior. Fortunately, Yeltsin brushed off the invitation; he wanted a "real" meeting with Baker. At the dinner, some republican leaders openly snubbed Gorbachev. The Georgian leader Zviad Gamsakhurdia announced that his republic would boycott the referendum. The leaders of Armenia stated they would hold their own referendum in September to declare full independence. The economist Shatalin ridiculed the idea of a new Union Treaty and prophesied a catastrophe. Baker felt embarrassed; he rose to defend Gorbachev. A dinner like this in the US residence, he said, would have been unthinkable without the perestroika that the Soviet leader had initiated.[82]

Next morning, Baker delivered to Gorbachev a text prepared for him in the White House: in it Bush expressed his belief that Gorbachev had not become a hostage to the forces of the past, and his recent moves to the right were only tactical, to ensure the course of democratic reforms. Baker then said: "Your place in history is secured, as long as you stay your course . . . This is one of the main causes why we believe that there will be no such reversal." Acting on instructions, Baker refrained from any explicit criticism of Yeltsin.[83] The conversation became cordial, and Gorbachev began to confide in Baker about his problems with Yeltsin. Baker in turn resumed his role of American advisor on Soviet politics and economic reforms. "When you win the referendum next Sunday," he said, "you should announce this victory, and then show more flexibility, to make a step towards the republics. You may even say: Now, tell the Center what you want. There are a few things that we cannot discuss with you: defense, currency, perhaps foreign policy. The rest is discussable." This tactical move, Baker said, would change the situation, placing the ball in the republics' court. Baker assured the Soviet leader that the Bush administration would not unilaterally recognize Baltic independence, yet he advised Gorbachev to allow the Baltic republics to go free. "We told you repeatedly that perhaps it would be better for you to have three little Finlands in the Baltics, instead of what you have now. They will not be able to separate from you economically. They will be forced to create an association with you, economic, political, and social."[84]

Gorbachev wanted to talk more about how to pair off economic and political reforms. Baker advised him on this problem as well. "Why not settle the Center-Republic issues first?" After fixing political issues, Baker reasoned, this would be easier than reshaping an economy grounded in seventy years of the traditions and psychology of a command system. If Gorbachev succeeded in signing a Union Treaty with the republics, he would have more time to deal with economic problems.[85] Gorbachev, despite his cordiality, continued to have doubts about American good faith. "One of Yeltsin's associates," he said to Baker, had informed him about a conversation between Yeltsin and Matlock. Yeltsin had allegedly asked how the US government would react if he were to come to power in a "not quite constitutional way." Baker did not know how to respond. Matlock later told him that the story was a canard—a KGB falsification meant to deceive Gorbachev. Matlock called on Chernyaev the next day: Gorbachev's aide arranged for him to meet with Gorbachev. When the Soviet leader listened to the ambassador's explanations he cheered up. Then he restated his strategic choice to be "next to Bush, as long as Bush would be close to him." He dismissed KGB fears of Americans swarming around the seats of power in Moscow. Let the Americans have as much intelligence on the Soviet Union as they could get, he concluded half-jokingly.[86]

The Moscow trip convinced Baker that it was possible for the White House to balance between Gorbachev and Yeltsin without alienating either of them. "Both always valued their relationship with George Bush and the United States, not only in terms of their standing in the world but also their standing at home." He stopped short of saying that the US leadership had already become a key external actor in Soviet politics—a party that all sides in the Soviet drama would turn to for advice and assistance. Bush did not like this double-game. "My view is, you dance with who is on the dance floor," the US President dictated into his personal tape-recorder on the day of the Soviet referendum. "You especially don't do something that would [encourage] destabilization."[87]

SHOWDOWN IN MOSCOW

The national referendum on 17 March was conducted in a transparent manner and without apparent falsifications. The all-Union referendum granted Gorbachev a coveted result. The official statistics recorded that 148,574,606 people participated; 113.5 million (76.4 percent) voted "Yes" in favor of preserving a reformed Union. Still, a sizable 32.3 million (21.7 percent) voted against it. The outcome of the referendum bolstered the conservatives. Kryuchkov, despite his misgivings, recalled that the outcome "exceeded any optimistic forecast." The KGB chief believed it was a perfect moment to introduce emergency rule.[88] In the Party Secretariat, Oleg Shenin addressed senior Party officials with a message: at the approaching Congress of the RSFSR the majority should defeat Yeltsin. Shenin hoped that this time Gorbachev would lead the fight.[89]

In reality, the national referendum did not negate separatist claims in the republics. Six republics, the three in the Baltic together with Armenia, Georgia, and Moldova, had boycotted the referendum. Latvia and Estonia had decided to hold their own referendums two weeks earlier, which gave overwhelming support for independent and democratic states. In Latvia, for instance, 73.7 percent of people voted for independence, with a clear majority of the Russian-speaking population joining ethnic Latvians. This was a surprising and clear verdict. Russians in Latvia and Estonia might be alienated by Baltic nationalism, but they felt even more anger and alienation towards the Soviet leadership and its failed reforms. The nationalist-minded among them rooted for Yeltsin's "Russia," not for Gorbachev's reformed Union. And many shared the aspirations of the Poles and the Balts "to return to Europe."[90]

Almost all the participating republics conducted the referendum in their own way. In Kazakhstan and Ukraine, the very question was altered and was even more ambiguous than the one proposed by Gorbachev. The majority in those two republics voted "Yes" in favor of their sovereign republics joining "a union of sovereign states." In other words, they could proceed with full independence, but then join some kind of a commonwealth without a federal government. Ukraine's Supreme Soviet added another question to the national question, asking the population to vote on its July 1990 declaration of sovereignty. The majority of Ukraine's voters approved the declaration; they supported the "anti-constitutional" move that Gorbachev's referendum was supposed to counter. And three Western regions in Ukraine held their own local referendum, in which people voted for secession from the USSR. The Ukrainian leadership, wrote the British ambassador during an official visit to Kiev on 20 March, was boosted by the referendum results; the majority in the republic had voted for the republic's "sovereignty." Kravchuk and others "radiate the feeling of confidence" in themselves and in their ideas of a future Ukraine.[91]

This avalanche of referendums buried Gorbachev's grand design almost entirely. Most crucially, Yeltsin and his supporters got what they wanted. The idea of the Russian Presidency received the support of 56,860,344 out of 79.7 million voters, three-quarters of the total. Some 21 million voted against the proposal. In Moscow and Leningrad, the support was 77.85 percent and 78.53 percent respectively—while only 50 percent of the same voters supported Gorbachev's Union Treaty. In eighty-four autonomous regions of the Russian Federation, Yeltsin's project won by a solid majority. This outcome affirmed his policy of preventing national separatism within the Russian Federation. Only three autonomous regions, among them the Tatar autonomous republic (renamed "Tatarstan"), held their own referendums and did not participate in the Russian one.[92] For Yeltsin and Democratic Russia, as one retrospective assessment went, "the referendum campaign was a rehearsal for the presidential campaign."[93] The thrust of this campaign was against Gorbachev. Voting down "Gorbachev's Union," as Democratic Russia leaflets read, would mean support "for our Fatherland, the toil and blood of our ancestors, our Nation, Faith, and for our future."[94]

Gorbachev did not introduce emergency measures after the referendum, as Moscow intellectuals had feared. Instead, he talked to economists. He wanted to check once again if there was a chance to launch a program of coherent economic reform. The economists issued all kinds of warnings, but they were nothing new. This discussion reminded Gorbachev of what Baker had said two days before. "President Reagan used to say that we need an economist without one arm. Too many economists like to use two arms to say: on one hand, on the other hand."[95]

Yeltsin's reaction to the results of the referendum was to step up the confrontation. On 22 March, he visited the Kirov Machinery-Building Plant in Leningrad and gave an address reminiscent of those given by Poland's Solidarity. The Russian leader complained that the Union authorities had "robbed Russia" by taking half of its annual taxes, about 56 billion rubles, and using the money to subsidize the non-Russian republics of Central Asia. "Enough feeding the other republics!" Yeltsin exclaimed. He presented himself as the only person who could compensate workers for inflation. Hundreds of industrial workers, angry at empty store shelves and fired up by Yeltsin's inflammatory rhetoric, began to chant: "Gorbachev, resign!"[96]

In Moscow, Democratic Russia's Yuri Afanasyev took the lead. The referendums boosted his optimism. "The process of fundamental change is now inexorably under way," he said to the British ambassador. He had just received a major grant from the National Endowment for Democracy, an influential American think tank in Washington DC, and used this cash to pay for political advertising. Even the Party publishing houses, he said, took dollars to print the opposition's leaflets. Some of the electoral propaganda was flown to Russian provinces by sympathetic Aeroflot crews.[97] Afanasyev overcame the reluctance of Popov and obtained from the City Council of Moscow permission to hold a giant rally in support of Yeltsin.

Yeltsin's rally at the Kirov Plant infuriated Gorbachev. He proposed broadcasting it on state television, so that everyone could see what "this demagogue" was saying. People would realize that Yeltsin was destroying the country. Gorbachev's advisors objected. After this broadcast, they argued, Gorbachev's authority would be reduced to zero; everybody would begin to "wipe their feet on the President." Chernyaev registered an "unbridled and irrational hatred" of Gorbachev by the masses of common Russians—a phenomenon he had trouble understanding. Gorbachev's aides also noticed that in Moscow and Leningrad respectively, 46 percent and 43 percent of those voting in the referendum voiced their opposition to Gorbachev's new Union. Shakhnazarov feared that Yeltsin might lead a national strike, which would finish off the economy and the state. Gradually, Gorbachev calmed down. He also decided not to go to the Congress of the Russian Federation to confront Yeltsin. He admitted that this would only help his rival.[98]

While Gorbachev fumed and dawdled, a new wave of panic spread among the Party leaders of Moscow: Yuri Prokofiev and other apparatchiks feared that "radicals" would lead a huge crowd to storm the Party headquarters, perhaps even the Kremlin itself. Gorbachev turned to his Prime Minister for a solution. Pavlov was already handling the Kuzbass strikes. The KGB informed him that Lane Kirkland, the leader of the American Federation of Labor and Congress of Industrial Organizations (AFL-CIO), was visiting Moscow and had promised assistance to the Russian miners. Pavlov decided that any concessions at this moment would only encourage those who wanted a Russian form of Solidarity. He refused to sit at a negotiating table with the miners' representatives until they resumed work. He also turned down Gorbachev's proposals "to find money" and mollify the strikers with higher wages.[99] On 25 March, Pavlov, with Gorbachev's approval, announced a moratorium on all rallies and demonstrations in Moscow between 26 March and 15 April. Speaking on state television, the Prime Minister offered protection to those Russian deputies who were in opposition to Yeltsin. Gorbachev signed a decree transferring authority over the Moscow police force from Popov's City Council to the Minister of the Interior, Boris Pugo.

Yeltsin's supporters were convinced that Gorbachev and his entourage were planning to remove Yeltsin.[100] The moderates in Democratic Russia, mostly Moscow intellectuals, proposed avoiding the expected showdown.[101] Nobody can say what Yeltsin would have done, but on the evening of 26 March, Gorbachev appeared on national television and, in a stumbling, emotional, and habitually long speech he accused the opposition of setting up a provocation, but he also admitted his own mistakes. He almost pleaded: "If further violence takes place, this would amount to my political death." Gorbachev did not cancel Pavlov's measures, yet his appeal undercut their effect. Emboldened radicals from Democratic Russia demanded the immediate resignation of both Gorbachev and Pavlov. On 28 March, Moscow newspapers appeared with huge headlines: a mass rally in defiance of Pavlov's decree would take place that evening.[102]

On the morning of the same day, Chernyaev received a phone call from Alexander Yakovlev. He urged Gorbachev's aide to see his boss immediately and convince him to prevent an inevitable clash. Yakovlev publicly criticized Gorbachev's introduction of troops into Moscow. Chernyaev was of a different view: he was now convinced that Gorbachev would never become a dictator. Instead, the main danger was the irresponsibility of Democratic Russia. The opposition, Chernyaev said to Yakovlev, had got everything it needed to form a legitimate government and pursue constructive policies. Instead, the opposition leaders were continuing to pursue extremist demands and incite the masses. To give them what they wanted, Chernyaev continued, would mean destroying the state. And without the state, any reforms would become impossible.[103]

Yakovlev insisted that Gorbachev should lean not on the Army, but instead "on democracy." At this point Chernyaev exploded: "What does democracy consist of? . . . Democracy is a form of organized society: parties, institutions, the rule of law, respect for legality. Democracy means leaders who compete for a place in government, not against the state." The polemics between Yakovlev and Chernyaev reflected the perennial Russian dilemma between the intelligentsia's insistence on immediate freedom from state coercion and the need to prevent a state collapse.[104] Shevardnadze, for all his fears of "dark forces," agreed with Chernyaev's logic. The same people who followed radical democrats now could, in his view, follow an authoritarian demagogue tomorrow. That was at least what had happened in Georgia.[105]

An extraordinary session of the RSFSR Congress of People's Deputies opened on the morning of 28 March 1991, in a historic palace inside the Kremlin. Hundreds of delegates to the Congress arrived, passing through the cordons of internal security troops. There were 40,000 armed soldiers outside the Kremlin. When Yeltsin delivered the opening address to the Congress, he was almost defensive. He acknowledged that "there could be no winners in this contest." He proposed a "round table" of all political forces from all the republics to replace the central government. With this, he said, "we would be able to come to a renewed Union." "I am against Gorbachev's course," Yeltsin concluded, "but I am ready to work with him."[106]

The majority at the Congress, however, were incensed by the show of force outside the Kremlin's walls. Deputies lined up in the aisles in front of microphones to demand that the Soviet leadership remove troops from Moscow. The Congress voted 532 to 286 to declare the actions of the Soviet government and Gorbachev "unconstitutional." Khasbulatov was empowered to negotiate with Gorbachev. He returned with Gorbachev's refusal to lift the emergency—but with a promise to remove the troops the next day. A group of enraged deputies suggested relocating the Congress to Leningrad, the cradle of the Russian Revolution. Cooler heads prevailed, however, and the Congress recessed.[107]

The huge Manezh Square next to the Kremlin, the site of previous opposition gatherings, was occupied by troops and hundreds of military trucks. The opposition chose to rally its supporters at the squares of Arbat and Gorky streets, two modest-size intersections on Moscow's Boulevard Ring.[108] CNN broadcast live from the sites of the rallies; all Western journalists joined them. The American journalist David Remnick came with his liberal-thinking Russian friends. He felt jittery, his thoughts racing back to recent memories of the Tiananmen massacre in Beijing. The troops were within a five-minute walk from the protesters. The crowd consisted of employees from academic institutions and military-scientific laboratories, museums, and libraries. There were also pro-independence activists from non-Russian republics, young fans of Western music, some young entrepreneurs, and many foreigners. Remnick bumped into US Senator David Boren, a Democrat from Oklahoma, who had also been attracted by the event. Democratic Russia claimed that 700,000 came to the rallies; the real number was more likely 120,000–150,000. Had the authorities chosen to enforce their moratorium, casualties would have been inevitable. Gorbachev, however, told Pavlov and the military to proceed with extreme caution. The forces of law and order behaved calmly, the opposition rallies became "blissfully boring," and the mood of the crowd changed. Remnick recorded "that the crowd was full of itself. They were celebrating a great victory."[109]

Gorbachev had had enough: he ordered the troops and riot police to pull out from Moscow the following morning. Rodric Braithwaite wrote in his diary about Gorbachev's defeat: "The crowd itself now hates and despises him. His position looks fatally damaged."[110] In his memoirs, Gorbachev wrote that the spring standoff between the government and the Russian opposition had "exhausted" the central government, wasted time that could have been used for solving urgent problems, and made the Union brittle from within. The hard-liners inside the Soviet government and the Party considered the extra-legal actions taken by Yeltsin and his allies and reasoned: "If they dare to do it, by God's will we should do it too."[111]

The news about the withdrawal of troops produced a radical change in the mood of the RSFSR Congress. The radicals were triumphant that Gorbachev had blinked.[112] The communist deputies broke ranks, while those who had hoped to unseat Yeltsin lost their head of steam. One of them, Boris Isakov, continued to blame Yeltsin for dictatorial tendencies, but for balance he urged Gorbachev to cede the presidency "to someone else." A Soviet Air Force veteran, Alexander Rutskoy, who had fought in Afghanistan, announced he was quitting the RSFSR Communist Party. Communists, he said, should form a new faction "in support of democracy" and back Yeltsin. Even Polozkov had to vow that the Russian communists had never plotted against Yeltsin. In the audience, the former Politburo member Vitaly Vorotnikov watched what was happening in utter disgust. He tendered his resignation from the Russian parliament, unwilling to participate in such a travesty.[113]

As the Russian communist opposition melted away, the Congress accorded to Yeltsin additional powers to fix the Russian economy. Nobody understood how he would do this, but the program written by Yeltsin's advisors appeared to be coherent. Most crucially, over two-thirds of the Congress's deputies, including many Russian communists, voted to change the Constitution of the RSFSR to institute the post of President. The date of presidential elections was set for 12 June 1991.[114] This was almost a political miracle. Yeltsin, only a few weeks before a possible casualty of conservatives, was now empowered by the Russian supreme constitutional assembly and had a unique opportunity to become an executive leader, elected by the popular vote of the Russian people. This meant that Gorbachev, his Cabinet of Ministers, the Congress of People's Deputies of the USSR, and Lukyanov's Supreme Soviet found themselves in the position of the King and the National Assembly in France in 1789: outdated and supplanted. In contrast to France, however, this revolutionary development would mean the dissolution of the state and the break-up of the country. Such was the effect of the 17 March referendums and Gorbachev's zigzags.

CHAPTER 8

DEVOLUTION

. . . the surrender of powers to local authorities by a central government.
The definition of "devolution" in the Merriam-Webster Dictionary

NINE PLUS ONE

After a month of indecision after the referendum, Gorbachev finally made up his mind and instructed Shakhnazarov to prepare materials for a meeting on 23 April 1991 behind closed doors, with the leaders of nine republics, to discuss "the key questions of crisis management." The President sent a laconic personal invitation to Yeltsin, "to discuss urgent issues of political, economic, and social nature in a narrow circle." The meeting was planned outside the bustle of Moscow, at "the dacha" in Novo-Ogaryovo.[1]

Novo-Ogaryovo was a luxurious complex, about twenty-five miles west of Moscow, in a bucolic area on the bend of the Moscow river, and very close to Gorbachev's residence. Brezhnev had held talks here with Nixon, and Gorbachev had received Reagan there. On 23 April, Novo-Ogaryovo became synonymous with the devolution of power in the Soviet Union from the central government to the republics. The talks came to be known as "Nine Plus One." "One" was the President, who was the host. The nine were the leaders of those republics who took part in the March referendum. In addition, Gorbachev invited the heads of fifteen autonomous republics and regions located within the Russian Federation.[2]

The economic crisis was the background to the invitation. Pavlov and the State Bank informed Gorbachev that since the start of the year the state budget had not received two-thirds of the expected revenues.[3] The Russian government, followed by other republics, was defunding the Soviet state. The miners' strike had brought many industries to the verge of shutdown. The Central Asian republics had begun to export their cotton abroad, to cover their budget deficit. Ukraine had started limiting food supplies to other republics. Even regions had erected barriers to outgoing goods and imposed excises on incoming ones. This protectionism only created more panic-buying and shortages. On 10 April, Pavlov had presented Gorbachev with an anti-crisis program, an update of Ryzhkov's outline.[4] Gorbachev realized he could not muddle through any longer. He had to move against separatism or try to reach a political agreement. As usual, he chose to negotiate.

During the next two months in Novo-Ogaryovo, the Soviet leader went nine-tenths of the way towards the formula Yeltsin had proposed since the summer of 1990: "a Union of Sovereign States." In effect, Vadim Medvedev commented: " 'a round table' has taken place."[5] In return, Gorbachev expected the Russian leader to make some concessions to nail down a compromise. Yet he could not clearly explain, even to himself, what kind of state would emerge after the devolution of power. Quite possibly, no one at Novo-Ogaryovo knew either. Gorbachev and his aides knew that Yeltsin would fight tooth and nail against a Union with a strong President. Most likely, Shakhnazarov warned his boss, signing the Union Treaty would mean that Gorbachev would have to resign.[6] Gorbachev would not hear of it. He was convinced he would be able to bend and mold the republican leaders. In his memoirs, Gorbachev wrote that his tactics were "to bind the Russian leadership to commitments which it would find hard to break."[7]

Some people around Yeltsin realized that the feud at the top was ruining the country. On 28 March, the day of the Moscow standoff, Vladimir Lukin came to see Chernyaev, whom he had known since the 1960s. Back then they had shared dreams of reform; now they were in rival camps. The meeting apparently went well. Chernyaev sent a note to Gorbachev that Lukin had "a plan of 'removing Yeltsin as an obstacle' [*vyvesti ego za skobki*]." The moderates in the Russian parliament around Lukin, Chernyaev continued, "aspire very much to the speedy conclusion of the Union treaty." Georgy Arbatov, another man from this circle, appealed once again to Yeltsin to end the feud with Gorbachev and align with reform-minded Party members.[8]

"Yeltsin was preparing to be elected the President of Russia," Gorbachev recalled, "and was concerned that the Union and myself, the President of the USSR, should behave loyally."[9] The Russian maverick also learned a bitter lesson abroad, when he traveled to Strasbourg to address the parliamentary assembly of the Council of Europe. Many European deputies, especially on the left, disliked Yeltsin's newly learned rhetoric. And they saw him as a demagogue, Gorbachev's detractor and a dangerous separatist. Confronted with a hostile reception, Yeltsin cut his appearance short and left in huff. In Paris, Mitterrand added to the disgrace: he even refused to invite the Russian leader to the Elysée Palace. "It was a heavy blow," Yeltsin recalled years later. His embarrassment in France contrasted with the news of Gorbachev's state visit to Japan and the enthusiastic welcome accorded to him in South Korea.[10]

On his return to Moscow, Yeltsin decided to suspend the feud with Gorbachev and negotiate. Yet his mistrust of the Soviet leader remained absolute. Yeltsin's entourage fed him with "information" that Gorbachev was plotting to introduce presidential rule after signing the Union Treaty. "Inside sources" assured Yeltsin that all republican parliaments would be disbanded and executive branches subordinated to the center. Those allegations were not entirely groundless, as they reflected the fervent wishes of the Party and KGB conservatives.[11]

Yeltsin was also annoyed by what he viewed as Gorbachev's continuing attempts to play the leaders of national autonomous regions inside the RSFSR off against him. The opportunities for this were legion: in the Caucasus, Chechnya and Dagestan there were ethnic enclaves with a strong secessionist potential. Another major enclave, deep in the Russian heartland on the Volga, was Tatarstan. In early 1991, Mintimer Shaimiev, the communist head of the Tatar autonomous region, vigorously played an ethno-national card. On 16 March, in a special election, Shaimiev was elected President of Tatarstan, promising to take from Moscow control over the oil refineries and huge automobile plants located in his territory. Only a few months before, Yeltsin had promised the autonomists in Tatarstan, Bashkiria, and other ethnic enclaves inside the Russian Federation as much sovereignty as they could digest. Now, the ambitions of Tatarstan's leader threatened the very integrity of his "Russia."[12]

On the morning of 23 April, Gorbachev was very tense. "We knew about Yeltsin's explosive character," recalled Shakhnazarov, "and did not know with certainty if his 'team' had agreed to a rapprochement. We had to be prepared for any eventualities." When the car with the Russian leader appeared at the gates of Novo-Ogaryovo, the tension eased. The meeting of the leaders began behind closed doors, without any advisors. When a break came, Gorbachev appeared with a bright face. He told his aides to type up the text of a joint statement that had been agreed at the meeting. The document decried "attempts to reach political goals by inciting civil disobedience, strikes, and appeals to overthrow the existing legally elected bodies of state power." Shakhnazarov, who prepared the draft statement, noticed that Gorbachev had made fundamental concessions. Instead of the Soviet Union, the document curtly referred to "a Union." The news agency TASS and state television broke the news to the country and the world. Over lunch, Yeltsin and Gorbachev raised their champagne glasses and toasted each other's health.[13]

DEVOLUTION

Yeltsin was the first to realize how much Gorbachev had conceded. "The system of the Union Treaty ... has been shifted upside down." Yet he remained suspicious: why had Gorbachev made such dramatic concessions so easily? Was it a devious scheme to prolong the agony of the "totalitarian center?"[14] A historian from Yeltsin's camp later wrote that the Novo-Ogaryovo agreement "proved to be a very strong political choice for Gorbachev." The Soviet leader, he claimed, was protecting himself against Party hardliners at the CPSU Plenum that opened the following day.[15] Was there a real need for such concessions and at such a political cost? The Party conservatives had nowhere to go. The most energetic among them, Oleg Shenin and Leningrad's Party Secretary Boris Gidaspov, looked forward to the next Party Plenum to read their General Secretary the riot act (yet again!). But they had neither a program nor a language to stage a full-blown mutiny.[16] And the Joint Declaration at Novo-Ogaryovo caught them completely by surprise. One of the Politburo members said to Shakhnazarov at the Plenum: "What have you done, pals? You gave up on power, and along with it, the Union."[17]

Gorbachev opened the Plenum with a warning: he wanted to avoid an open conflict between the hardliners and the democratic extremists. Such a clash would mean the end of a peaceful constitutional process, descent into anarchy and rebellion, and ultimately "a true dictatorship." The conservative critics unleashed the expected verbal barrage. The Party Secretaries, all Gorbachev's protégés, sat impassively while one speaker after another hurled insults at him. Then it was Gorbachev's turn to surprise everyone. He announced that he was ready to resign as General Secretary. This was a Tsar-like gesture that disarmed the hardliners. As if by magic, the angry Party stalwarts turned into pliant and loyal subjects. Kazakhstan's Nazarbayev, a Politburo member as well a participant in the Nogo-Ogaryovo talks, played a crucial intermediary role: Gorbachev agreed to stay on.[18]

A few days after the Novo-Ogaryovo statement, Shakhnazarov told the British ambassador Rodric Braithwaite that everything now depended on Yeltsin's behavior: he could still drive Gorbachev into a corner. The conservatives, Shakhnazarov warned, were still not finished. It would have been better if Gorbachev had split the Party. Braithwaite wrote: "Surprisingly, Shakhnazarov does not at all rule out an army takeover: the first person in such a position that I have heard talk this way." A few hours later, the British ambassador met with the leader of the Russian Communist Party, Ivan Polozkov, who was both defensive and bragging. He boasted that Yeltsin would not win the presidential elections. "Even if Yeltsin is elected, he has no program, and will be out in a year or so." Braithwaite informed London about an unsteady truce in Moscow. He decided to postpone writing Gorbachev's epitaph.[19]

With the Novo-Ogaryovo meeting Gorbachev had scored a tactical success, but the new format of talks only encouraged republican separatism. Ruslan

Khasbulatov recalled that Gorbachev made a psychological mistake: his concessions had confirmed to his republican partners that he was a weak and indecisive leader. "The urge to gain power is the strongest factor that drives political elites," Khasbulatov concluded. Gorbachev was a bizarre political animal, who misunderstood power.[20] Studies and observations by leading scholars have confirmed Khasbulatov's judgement. In the end, Novo-Ogaryovo became a forum where republican potentates could meet and reach an understanding behind Gorbachev's back.[21]

At the end of May, Lukin conveyed Gorbachev's proposal to Yeltsin: "The partners want a speedy conclusion" of the Union Treaty. Gorbachev, he wrote, accepted that not all national autonomous regions, such as Tatarstan, would sign the document, and that only the Russian Federation would. Yeltsin and the Russian parliament would have veto power on all crucial decisions made at the Union level; the Russian Federation would have full control over taxation on its territory. What Gorbachev really wanted in return, however, was a federal tax whose revenues would go directly to the Center, to fund the central ministries and the Soviet Army. Lukin urged the Russian President to agree to this. Yeltsin rejected this deal. He wanted everything.[22]

RUSSIAN DEMOCRATS AND THEIR FRIENDS

In the winter and spring of 1991, the BBC filmed a multi-part documentary in Moscow called "The Second Russian Revolution." For many intellectuals in the Soviet capital, the title captured the moment. The American political scientist Marc Garcelon wrote that the core of the Russian democratic movement consisted primarily of people who worked in the institutes and laboratories of the military-industrial complex and the Academy of Sciences of the USSR. He called this phenomenon "the rebellion of specialists."[23] This was the time when a scholar of the French Revolution managed to get hundreds of thousands of people to protest at a rally, an academic sociologist became the leader of a small nation, a historian of the Italian Renaissance was advising the leader of Russia, and a physicist from a research lab was an envoy from the Russian democratic movement to the US Congress. Even the most rational of minds swelled with revolutionary hubris and a sense of historic mission. One democratic activist of the time later recalled that he and his colleagues wanted freedom of information and travel and intellectual property rights. "This intelligentsia linked all its hopes for justice . . . to Western models." As for the issues of inflation and economic development, as well as state-building, those "were as incomprehensible as quantum mechanics."[24]

On 13 April 1991, the organizers of Democratic Russia (DR) gathered in Moscow for a meeting on the eve of a big conference of the movement. They claimed that the movement had 300,000–400,000 activists and about a million followers. This was a sizable force, but it was fractured and disorganized. The only factor that united the activists was their passionate desire to get rid of Gorbachev and the Soviet state apparatus. The historian and DR leader Yuri Afanasyev gave a report on the political situation. He spoke about the inevitability of an economic crisis and more discontent that would push workers to strike. The democrats should consolidate their ties with the striking miners of Kuzbass and reach out to the workers of Belorussia: this would create a power base from which to dictate terms and conditions to Gorbachev. "We would either ameliorate socialism with Gorbachev and Pavlov," he said with sarcasm, "or we would overcome socialism." Afanasyev wanted the entire Soviet economic and political system to be reinvented. Some in the movement, he continued, considered such a course too radical, a new form of Bolshevism. Nothing was further from the truth. The movement would come to power without using any force, and would build a liberal order in Russia. Garry Kasparov, the world chess champion, ridiculed those who "want to save Gorbachev." Yelena Bonner, widow of Andrei Sakharov, agreed that Gorbachev was finished politically. She declared that "the intelligentsia of Russia should stop trailing behind events."[25]

At the same gathering, Mikhail Shneider, a forty-two-year-old physicist, was inspired by the Polish round-table discussions of 1989. He announced a schedule for the transfer of power from Gorbachev to the democratic forces. In April 1991, he stated, Gorbachev would have to launch round-table talks between all the political forces and resign from the Party leadership; abolish the state monopoly on television; disband Party organizations in the government, the KGB, the Army, and the police. By the end of May, Gorbachev should have disbanded the Cabinet of Ministers, and dissolved the Supreme Soviet of the USSR. While the old state was being dismantled, republican leaders would form a provisional government. On 1 October, the constituent assemblies of the republics would sign a new Union treaty. And at the end of October, an all-Union Constituent Assembly would be elected. If Gorbachev refused to cooperate, Shneider argued, Democratic Russia should declare a national political strike.[26]

Another radical political strategist of the DR movement was thirty-seven-year-old Vladimir Boxer, formerly a pediatrician. In his speech at the conference of DR the next day, Boxer divided the Russian people into three groups. Only a third were "democratic-minded," because they supported Yeltsin and rejected Gorbachev's Union. Another third were "reactionary and conservative forces": they supported the preservation of the Union and rejected the idea of a Russian presidency. The third in between were "a swamp." With energetic propaganda and mobilization, this swamp could be conquered, and Russian democracy would triumph.[27]

DECLINE AND DOWNFALL

By now the leading Russian democrats assumed that all republics of the Soviet Union would become separate states. Russian democracy, in order to win, had to support every movement for independence, recognize every single ethnic autonomous region, even inside the Russian Federation. All ethnic clashes in the Soviet Union, Yelena Bonner claimed, were the product of the communist nomenklatura, its agents, and its corrupt commercial structures. "If democrats in other republics refuse to support you," Bonner told the gathering, "you are finished!"[28] Lev Ponomarev, a human rights defender, acknowledged that the Baltic movements, Rukh in Ukraine, and nationalist movements in other republics rejected a federated state, "even in the post-communist society." A federation or confederation of democratic states, he concluded, should become "a legal successor to the USSR" in order to ensure a peaceful transition.[29]

The Novo-Ogaryovo statement shocked the leaders of Democratic Russia. They felt ambushed and abandoned by Yeltsin. The miners' strike, to their dismay, rapidly came to an end. Afanasyev and Bonner considered the statement a surrender to the central authorities. What about a national political strike? What about the miners and a Russian Solidarity? Why lose the chance to force Gorbachev and his government out of power and hold a real round-table discussion with true democrats and the republican leaders?[30] Yeltsin's advisor Gennady Burbulis had to reassure the confused radicals that there was no backstage deal. Yeltsin's decision to team up with Gorbachev, he explained, was "the only available state-based foundation for reforms." He continued: "Some people believe that Gorbachev has won, but I believe that the situation is in our hands." Everyone should now focus on Yeltsin's presidential campaign. Burbulis was its coordinator and even wanted to become Yeltsin's running mate. After hours of debates, the anger of the democratic stalwarts subsided. The gathering nominated Yeltsin as the candidate of the movement. Only one delegate objected while seven abstained.[31]

In the spring of 1991, both the Republican Right and liberal Democrats in the United States admired the great tenacity of the Russian democratic movement. Instead of being intimidated, Yeltsin and the Democratic Russia activists increased their mass appeal and popular outreach. Particularly impressive was the strong support the Russian democrats gave to the cause of Baltic independence. At the National Endowment for Democracy (NED), funded by Congress, Zbigniew Brzezinski, Richard Pipes, Nadia Diuk, and the Russian dissident Vladimir Bukovsky urged people to back Yeltsin as the strongest ally of the Balts.[32] Democratic Russia had already received $2 million from the Krieble Institute, funded by a friend and sponsor of Ronald Reagan. With this money, Burbulis and his friends funded 120 workshops and training seminars in Moscow, "trainings for democracy" in the Russian provinces, as well as transnational conferences and "schools" in Tallinn, Estonia. They also bought Xerox machines and computers for the DR political campaigning during the March referendum. They would use them for Yeltsin's presidential campaign as well. The KGB was informed but could do nothing: the recipients of American grants had immunity as people's deputies. There was no law banning Soviet parliamentarians from receiving foreign assistance.[33]

Another "friend of Russian democracy" was the National Democratic Institute (NDI), the organization affiliated with the Democratic Party, but acting as its non-partisan and non-governmental arm. A young Fulbright scholar from Stanford University, Michael McFaul, was in Moscow at the time to conduct interviews for a book about the Russian democratic movement. He had volunteered to work for the NDI. McFaul attended the founding congress of Democratic Russia in October 1990, and also its conference of April 1991. He befriended Vladimir Boxer and Mikhail Shneider, as well as Oleg Rumyantsev, a brilliant young Russian parliamentarian who was involved in writing a democratic constitution for the RSFSR. McFaul described his friends and himself at the time as "democratic idealists." He believed that if "these people took power, a new era of partnership in US-Russia relations seemed not only possible but probable."[34]

In early April 1991, Richard Nixon arrived in the Soviet Union to measure the depth of the Soviet crisis. He became the first former US President to visit the Baltic states; he also went to Georgia and Ukraine. In Moscow, Nixon met with Shevardnadze, Primakov, and Kryuchkov. He could not, however, secure appointments with Gorbachev and Yeltsin, because both were too busy.[35] Nixon's Dimitri K. Simes, a Soviet émigré, came up with a ruse: in the lobby of the President Hotel in Moscow, where he and Nixon were staying, they began to talk loudly about a future meeting with Yeltsin. Simes correctly expected the KGB to be eavesdropping on this chat and report it back to Gorbachev. Indeed, within a few hours, Gorbachev's secretary had called and invited Nixon for a meeting. Simes then called Lukin and said that Nixon would be having a meeting with Gorbachev. Yeltsin then also immediately found time for Nixon in his busy schedule.[36]

Nixon reported on both meetings to the Western media and in a highly biased way. He presented Gorbachev as defensive and drained, the man of the past. And he praised Yeltsin for his willingness to conduct swift and decisive reforms. "Gorbachev is Wall Street, Yeltsin is Main Street," Nixon told *The New York Times*. "Yeltsin could be a revolutionary leader ... He has the animal magnetism, he has the ruthlessness."[37] A few days later *Time* had Nixon praising Yeltsin who "totally repudiates communist philosophy," supports private property, would give immediate independence to the Baltics, and would "cut all

Soviet aid to Cuba, Afghanistan, Angola, and other Third World losers." The US government, Nixon concluded, should shift its support from Gorbachev to Yeltsin and his able advisors. This change could cause Gorbachev's displeasure, Nixon admitted. "But we must remember that he needs us far more than we need him," and it was both morally right and in America's national interest. Nixon also learned something else from Yeltsin. "He knows that there's no future for the Soviet Union. None . . . If Russia has any future, Yeltsin is it."[38]

Even before the public message from Nixon, Bush and Scowcroft had been under great pressure to shift US support to Yeltsin and "Russian democrats." President Bush, in a telephone conversation with Italian Prime Minister Giulio Andreotti, complained: "Here, in some quarters, especially in the extreme left and right, Yeltsin is a hero." If only Gorbachev could let the Baltics leave immediately, Bush said wistfully, then he would gain enormous support in Europe and in the US. Andreotti replied that this was politically dangerous for Gorbachev. The Pope, Andreotti added, also held the same view; the Vatican was not pressing for Baltic independence. The path to take was gradual political and economic reforms managed from the Union's center. The US President concurred. "Yeltsin says the right things," but every leader Bush spoke to believed that he was a demagogue, and would become a dictator if he came to power.[39]

On 29 March, Bush received at the White House the Chair of the Supreme Soviet of Estonia, Arnold Rüütel, and his Foreign Minister, Lennart Meri. Rüütel thanked the US President for the role he had played in stopping violence in the Baltics in January. He wanted Bush to exert more pressure, however, to force Gorbachev to begin talks on the Baltic exit from the Soviet Union. Despite all the warnings of his aides, Bush could not conceal from his guests that he cared much more about Gorbachev's delicate position than the Balts. Suddenly, he asked: "But will Gorbachev survive? If you had to bet $10, would you bet he'll survive?" The best way to help Gorbachev survive, answered Rüütel, would be if the West pressed him to let the Baltics go: this would strengthen Russian democracy and would help Gorbachev reassert his power. Meri explained that Gorbachev had become the hostage of "7,000 generals who want to become marshals," and also of the KGB that "always was in full command of the country, and was the main power behind Gorbachev even under Andropov." By acting jointly, the West, the Baltics, and the Russian democrats could free Gorbachev from the yoke of the KGB and the military. This seemed to be a novel idea for Bush. Upon more reflection, however, the US President kept to his former course: gradual change managed from the Union's center was the only path for the USSR. Instead of pushing Gorbachev and risking a right-wing coup, Bush would still prefer to have the Balts slow down their march toward independence.[40]

DEVOLUTION

On the eve of the Novo-Ogaryovo meeting, Scowcroft had asked the CIA and other experts for an update: What could trigger Gorbachev's departure or removal? What were the possible scenarios of succession? Fritz Ermarth, the top CIA Soviet hand, decided this was a good moment to share with the White House everything that was on his mind. In a memo entitled "The Soviet Cauldron" he wrote: "Economic crisis, independence aspirations, and anti-Communist forces are breaking down the Soviet empire and system of governance." The centrally planned Soviet economy "has broken down irretrievably," and no longer represents "a coherent system." The Party was breaking up as well. Gorbachev's credibility, "because of his political meandering and policy failures . . . has sunk to near zero." Ermarth envisaged a violent Romanian scenario, in which both Gorbachev and Yeltsin might be assassinated. Another probable scenario was "a putsch" of hardliners that would target Yeltsin and the democratic forces. The memo mentioned Kryuchkov, Yazov, Marshal Akhromeyev, and the Ground Forces commander Valentin Varennikov as probable executors of this scenario. In any case, Ermarth concluded, the USSR would either disintegrate or would be unable to restore its former superpower capacities and global influence. Privately, Ermarth believed that Yeltsin's plan to build a new confederation "from below" was ultimately a more durable solution than Gorbachev's "center-dominated Union."[41]

The memo was so controversial that for several days the CIA leadership could not decide if it could be sent to Scowcroft. Finally, on 29 April, the Director of Intelligence sent to Scowcroft a paper that incorporated some of the analysis from "The Soviet Cauldron". "The Gorbachev era is effectively over," the paper read. "Even if Gorbachev remains in office a year from now, real power is likely to be in the hands of either the hardliners or the republics. If Gorbachev is forced out in the near term, it most likely would be by hardliners who would rule through a weak front man or some sort of National Salvation Committee."[42]

Scowcroft found the document excessively pessimistic. He still refused to admit that the Russians could destroy their own state so irrationally. Moreover, the Gorbachev-Yeltsin agreement, Gorbachev's victory at the CPSU Plenum, and the end of the workers' strikes made the bleak scenarios less plausible. The CIA experts must have underestimated Gorbachev's ability to muddle through, just like he had done before. Bush agreed with this view.[43]

YELTSIN'S PRESIDENCY

The Russian presidential campaign was a remarkably hasty affair. It officially started in mid-May, when the candidates were registered, and it lasted for less than a month. On 21 May, yet another extraordinary RSFSR Congress of People's Deputies convened at considerable cost in the Kremlin. During four days of sessions, the Russian deputies approved the election's rules and limited the tenure of the presidency to two five-year terms. The Congress also approved Yeltsin and five other candidates for the presidential race.[44]

The most prominent of Yeltsin's rivals was Nikolai Ryzhkov, the former head of the Soviet government. The media dubbed him "a weeping Bolshevik," playing on his emotional nature. His decision to join the race after a recent heart attack, however, evoked respect. His running mate, General Boris Gromov, had led the last Soviet troops out of Afghanistan and later became a deputy Minister of the Interior. Another contender in the election was General Albert Makashov, commander of the Ural military district, who was fiercely critical of Gorbachev's withdrawal from Eastern Europe. He was the embodiment of everything Moscow liberals feared and hated: an undisguised anti-Semite and admirer of Stalin, he rejected the 500 Days program and opposed privatization of land and real estate. The former Minister of the Interior Vadim Bakatin appealed to reform-minded communists. Finally, Aman Tuleyev ran as a spokesman for the workers and miners of Kuzbass.

None of these candidates could compete with Yeltsin in celebrity status and breadth of appeal. Each, however, chipped away at the potential majority he could receive. Ryzhkov and Bakatin posed as the centrists who wanted change, but also stability; they spoke about transition to a market economy, but they appealed to those who feared shock therapy, land speculation, and other market changes. On the populist fringes, Makashov and Tuleyev spoke to the disgruntled military and deeply discontented workers, as well as the lower classes. Finally, all of them rooted for the preservation of the Soviet Union, albeit with changes and reforms. This was a challenge to Yeltsin's emphasis on Russia's separatism.

A nasty surprise for Yeltsin's camp was the appearance in the race of forty-five-year-old Vladimir Zhirinovsky. Running on an anti-communist platform, he was a ball of energy and the best-educated candidate, with a degree in Oriental languages and law from Moscow State University. Although his father was an ethnic Jew, Zhirinovsky was a strident Russian chauvinist. Rumors circulated, although they were never corroborated, that the KGB had recruited Zhirinovsky and encouraged him to enter politics in 1989. He could certainly cost Yeltsin some support among those Russians who hated the Party bosses and intelligentsia, were xenophobic and nationalist.[45]

Gennady Burbulis, who managed Yeltsin's campaign, believed that Yeltsin's rivals had been "carefully chosen" to appeal to every major niche in Soviet society. In provinces and ethnic autonomous regions of the RSFSR, Yeltsin's electoral base was much weaker than in Moscow: only a third of people supported his candidacy. The economic crisis had hit the regions especially hard: stores were empty, salaries were delayed or unpaid. Yeltsin's rivals argued, with some justification, that all this had happened because of "Russia's sovereignty" and Yeltsin's feud with Gorbachev. Burbulis feared there would be a second round of elections. On 14 May, he and other organizers from Democratic Russia met to discuss how to ensure Yeltsin's victory in the first round. Burbulis suggested that the best way would be for Yeltsin to run as an incumbent, the leader so preoccupied with the economic situation that he stays out of the campaign to concentrate on practical issues. His election team and emissaries of Democratic Russia to the regions would instead fight against other presidential candidates on Yeltsin's behalf.[46]

Democratic Russia's activists did an impressive amount of work. They turned the blitz nature of the campaign to Yeltsin's advantage. Theirs was the first presidential campaign in Russian history to import some Western electoral techniques, such as public polls, advertising, and communications. Fortunately, there was no need for fundraising: the Russian Congress voted to fund the campaign from the state budget, with funds divided equally among all qualified contenders. The electoral law also allowed each presidential candidate the state funds to hire a staff of up to 100 people. Some of them had been trained in workshops funded by the Krieble Institute. Yeltsin also enjoyed the support of many Soviet celebrities: nationally known journalists, scientists, scholars, artists, and movie actors. The celebrated filmmaker Alexander Sokurov even shot a film about Yeltsin. The Center for the Study of Public Opinion, the Russian analogue of Gallup, which was led by the sociologists Tatiana Zaslavskaya and Yuri Levada, supplied Yeltsin's team with targeted sociological data. Galina Starovoitova advised Yeltsin on national autonomous regions and minorities.[47]

Democratic Russia supplied thousands of volunteers for Yeltsin's grassroots campaign. Most of them were from the rebellious "scientific-technical intelligentsia" described earlier. The tail end of Yeltsin's campaign consisted of hundreds of thousands of individuals who were his groupies, the followers of his revolutionary charisma. For them, Yeltsin filled the painful vacuum of authority that had been created by Gorbachev's style of governance and the collapse of the old order. He also instilled in them new hope, quasi-religious veneration and trust. The DR's polls revealed that 20 percent of voters supported Yeltsin even if they disagreed with his specific program. Western observers concluded that many Russians simply supported Yeltsin because he was one of them: he drank, liked Russian steam baths, and jumped into icy water. This mass unreflecting support for Yeltsin came in myriad forms and ways. Aeroflot crews flew bundles of Yeltsin's campaign leaflets gratis to cities across the

Russian Federation. Unpaid volunteers and pensioners dropped these leaflets into people's mailboxes and agitated among potential voters. Provincial librarians and teachers, as well as industrial workers, cheered at local pro-Yeltsin electoral rallies.[48]

For a long time, Yeltsin could not decide whom to choose as his running mate. Burbulis, who wanted to become the Russian Vice-President, looked and spoke like an out-of-touch intellectual. Yeltsin's speechwriters from Sverdlovsk suggested instead the military pilot and general Alexander Rutskoy, who had recently given Yeltsin a majority at the Russian Congress. Forty-two-year-old Rutskoy had fought in Afghanistan; his plane was shot down, but he survived. Yeltsin agreed on the spot. A handsome officer with a dramatic mustache, Rutskoy looked excellent on electoral posters. He would also help split the ranks of the Russian conservatives.[49]

Yeltsin ran as an incumbent, but also as a populist. He did not talk about painful and inevitable reforms. Instead, he declared tax breaks for state enterprises, plants, and mines. His decree abolished an unpopular sales tax established by the much-hated Pavlov. And he promised to give even more freedom to national autonomous regions. During his trip to Tyumen, the center of the Soviet oil industry, he promised the oil workers that he would sell oil to other republics at world prices and give them a share of the profits. Before going to Kuzbass, he asked the head of the Bank of Russia to prepare a bag of money, which he could spend there, to encourage his enthusiastic audiences.[50]

The Russian leader also remained deliberately vague on Gorbachev's Union Treaty. At the meetings of Nine Plus One in Novo-Ogaryovo, Yeltsin was mostly passive and silent. None of his brief remarks generated headlines. At a session of the Russian parliament, when the Union Treaty was discussed, Yeltsin let Khasbulatov explain and answer questions. At the same time, at the electoral rallies in Kuzbass, at steel plants and oil enterprises he urged workers to vote on the spot to transfer the jurisdiction of their enterprises from the center to the Russian Federation. Tempted by the promise of higher salaries, workers at some rallies did so.[51]

On 6 June, Yeltsin showed up on the hour-long television program "Who Is Who." It was his first appearance on national television since February. State television was still funded and controlled by the central government, but each presidential candidate was invited onto the program for a live interview. Yeltsin arrived at the studio five minutes before filming began, apparently delayed by a traffic jam. The anchorman Igor Fisunenko used Western techniques to grill every presidential candidate. This approach backfired with Yeltsin and especially his TV supporters. They apparently considered their hero to be a victim of biased interrogation. Many viewers called in to the program, demanding that

Fisunenko stop his "outrageous behavior." Three big sacks of hate mail were eventually delivered to the TV station. Fisunenko later commented that the behavior of Yeltsin and his supporters revealed their political intolerance. They were not ready for dialogue and compromise.[52]

Yeltsin skipped a round-table discussion with other candidates aired on primetime TV on 10 June. He wanted to stay above the pack. Zhirinovsky took advantage of this: he made Yeltsin the main target of his attacks. He compared the Russian leader to Lenin: Yeltsin was not the builder but destroyer of the Russian state. Zhirinovsky also embraced the unabashed language of Russian chauvinism: Russia for him was "the whole country within the boundaries of the USSR," from Western Ukraine to Kamchatka, from Murmansk on the White Sea to the border with Afghanistan. Soviet sovereign republics, such as Ukraine, Belorussia and Kazakhstan, should be liquidated. Russia would be divided into administrative territories, while all ethnic minorities would be "under the protection of the president."[53] Zhirinovsky targeted the tail end of the Yeltsin phenomenon: less educated people who were susceptible to the appeal of strong leadership, reacted to radical populism, and yet identified with the collapsing superpower.

Election day on 12 June proceeded quietly. All observers, Russian and Western, considered the elections free and fair. The enormous state apparatus, the resources of the KGB, and local authorities did not—and perhaps could not—interfere with and control the election results. Gorbachev certainly kept his part of the agreement with Yeltsin. Yeltsin won the first round with 57.3 percent of the votes. He received most votes in Moscow, Leningrad, and other major cities, in industrialized areas, and among better-educated and younger voters. Ryzhkov trailed far behind with 16.85 percent of the votes. The third place unexpectedly went to the demagogic Zhirinovsky, who received 7.81 percent.

There were other elections that day as well. Voters in Leningrad and Moscow elected mayors of their cities, officials who had more executive power than the heads of the City Councils (Soviets). Moscow elected Gavriil Popov, and Leningrad voters chose Anatoly Sobchak, both prominent figures from Democratic Russia. Two years earlier, Andrei Sakharov had recommended that the Russian Federation should move its capital to another city, while Moscow should remain the capital of all the Union's republics. The reason for this was obvious: Moscow was a common capital for all Soviet citizens. Now, however, Moscow was under the control of Russian democrats, and Yeltsin wanted Moscow to be the capital of Russia, with the Kremlin as his residence.

Yeltsin's victory brought him international recognition. He received congratulations from Britain's John Major, Canada's Brian Mulroney, François Mitterrand, Margaret Thatcher, and the President of Czechoslovakia Václav Havel. The

Russian leader waited for recognition from George Bush. He still remembered his first disastrous experience in Washington in 1989, when he was snubbed. Now, he wanted to return to Washington in triumph. For months Yeltsin's people had been trying to arrange an invitation from Bush. The White House, however, instructed the American ambassador not to promise such a meeting to Yeltsin.[54]

In May, Burbulis hosted friends and donors from the American Right, the head of the Moral Majority, Paul Weyrich, and billionaire Bob Krieble. The Russians told them that democracy would triumph in Russia soon. The Americans were startled: "You are utopians. The [Soviet] Empire is very robust and very cruel." They suggested, however, that the time had come for the American political elite and public to meet with Yeltsin again. They could get him invited to Washington as a guest of Congress. At first, Yeltsin rejected the idea: he would go to the United States as a guest of the President or not at all. The Americans replied that perhaps Yeltsin did not know that Congress was equal to the President; Bush would not be able to ignore Yeltsin if Congress invited him. Back in Washington, the "friends of Russian democracy" mobilized their networks. The Republican legislators, including the Senate Majority Leader George Mitchell along with Bob Dole, Strom Thurmond, and Jesse Helms, invited Yeltsin to speak to Congress. Andrei Kozyrev, the young Foreign Minister of the Russian Federation and Yeltsin's trusted man, arranged a meeting with the AFL-CIO leader Lane Kirkland, Dick Cheney from the Pentagon, and the Secretary of Commerce, Robert Mosbacher. Allen Weinstein, a friend of Richard Nixon and the founder of a center for the promotion of democracy abroad, invited Yeltsin to a ceremony to award him a prize for spreading democracy in Russia.[55] Even before the election results were officially released in Moscow, the White House announced that Bush would receive Yeltsin during his official visit to the United States. Burbulis then told Krieble: "Well, Bob, you did it."[56]

Vladimir Lukin, who was also involved in the preparations for Yeltsin's visit, was concerned by this heavy leaning on the American Right. During his visit to Washington in May, Lukin met with Henry Kissinger. A strong democratic Russia, Lukin argued, would help stabilize—and not destroy—the Soviet Union, and this would also be good for the United States and the West. The guru of American Realpolitik seemed to agree. Lukin also contacted Solzhenitsyn, who was living in Cavendish, Vermont: could the famous writer, notoriously critical of American liberalism, meet with Yeltsin and talk him out of his excessively enthusiastic "Americanism?" Burbulis, however, used his influence to veto this idea. In the end, Yeltsin was "too busy" to see either Kissinger or Solzhenitsyn.[57]

On 19 June, Yeltsin's plane landed at Andrews Air Force Base in Maryland. Khrushchev, Brezhnev, and Gorbachev had all started their official visits to the

United States there. Next morning, the Russian President-elect, accompanied by Burbulis, Kozyrev, and Lukin, met with Cheney at the Pentagon and said that Russia was ready to dismantle the Soviet defense industries. Then Yeltsin met with Robert Mosbacher and businessmen at the Ministry of Commerce: he said that Russia's economy and resources were "open" for private investment. That afternoon, Yeltsin met with Bush at the White House. In advance, Bush had read Scowcroft's memo that the White House should cultivate parallel relations with Gorbachev and Yeltsin. It was easy to do so, because each needed American approval and validation even more than before.[58]

Addressing the media in the Rose Garden, the US President greeted his guest as "the first democratically elected leader in the ... one-thousand years long history of Russia." He immediately balanced this statement with a declaration that President Gorbachev's "courageous policy" was the pivotal factor "enabling us to end the Cold War and make Europe whole and free." The party then moved to the Oval Office. In the presence of the Soviet ambassador, Bush told Yeltsin: "I am the US President and Gorbachev is the USSR President and so we will deal with each other. But that does not mean that we cannot do business with you." Yeltsin was delighted to hear that Bush had finally accepted him as an international partner. The Union Treaty, he said, would probably be signed in July. Some republics, however, including Georgia and the three Baltic republics, would leave the Union.[59]

Yeltsin also spoke about another scenario: Russia had bilateral economic arrangements between republics, and if the Union Treaty failed, "we will maintain economic arrangements." In any case, all defense industries, oil and gas and all other resources on the RSFSR territory, would be under Russian control, so Western oil companies should now deal directly with the Russian government. "We no longer need services from the center," Yeltsin explained. "We do not want the command system. We want to destroy it ... All business will be free."[60]

While at the White House, Yeltsin unexpectedly became involved in a bizarre episode involving the fate of his rival. Early on 20 June, Moscow's mayor-elect Popov had asked the American ambassador, Jack Matlock, to meet with him in Spaso House, where he passed him a note: "There is a coup in preparation to oust Gorbachev. Inform Boris [Yeltsin]." On the next piece of paper Popov named the plotters: the head of the Soviet government Pavlov, the KGB's Kryuchkov, Minister of Defense Yazov, and the Speaker of the Supreme Soviet Lukyanov. Matlock immediately sent a secret message to Washington, meant only for the eyes of Bush, Scowcroft, and Baker. Because of the time difference, they received it right on the eve of Yeltsin's arrival at the White House. This entirely changed the tone and content of the conversation in the Oval Office. The Americans informed Yeltsin about Popov's warning. The Russian guest

221

discounted the danger, but suggested that he and Bush call Gorbachev on the hot line from the Oval Office immediately. The KGB had run this line on the Soviet side since the Cuban Missile Crisis. It would be nice to let Kryuchkov know that the leaders of the United States and Russia were supportive of Gorbachev! Strangely, the call did not (or could not) go through. Continuing the conversation, Yeltsin explained to Bush that the Russian elections had demonstrated minimal popular support for the communist conservatives. Some 40 percent of the military had voted for Yeltsin, and "the army as a whole would not come out against the people." Even the middle-rank officials of the KGB were in favor of change. He confidently concluded: "Russia is firmly on the side of Gorbachev."[61]

Bush and Scowcroft were surprised and relieved. The Russian leader apparently had matured significantly since his previous visit to the White House. Also, his suit was well tailored and pressed.[62] The next morning, Gorbachev (who was told that the White House had tried to contact him) returned the call. He laughed at the possibility of a coup against him. Bush told him that Yeltsin had behaved well and added: "I made it very clear that you are our man . . . The Yeltsin visit has done nothing to embarrass the Center . . . I want to do nothing to undermine you there."[63]

Yeltsin was ecstatic. He had succeeded in his goal to return to Washington as a winner. He had even managed to pose as Gorbachev's protector against "dark forces." Other meetings in Washington were also of political and symbolic significance: Yeltsin was treated to an enthusiastic reception on Capitol Hill. Senators and congressmen applauded Yeltsin's pledge to free the Baltics and open Russia "for business."[64] The Russian leader then proceeded to New York, to meet with business leaders in America's financial capital. TASS journalists, who only a few years earlier had labeled Wall Street the center of "American imperialism," reported admiringly that Yeltsin held talks with the leaders of the Federal Reserve System, as well as the heads of Salomon Brothers, Chase Manhattan Bank, J. P. Morgan, and others. Many years later, Burbulis recalled his impressions of that meeting. The Soviet UN office helped Yeltsin to set up a reception including a menu of typical Russian dishes such as caviar and piro-zhki. His American guests gobbled all of this up enthusiastically. Burbulis was overwhelmed. The richest men in the world liked Russian food so much! Yeltsin, Kozyrev, and Burbulis himself felt those Americans would help to rebuild Russia. "We thought there would be a long and fruitful partnership between us." Departing from JFK airport back to Moscow, Yeltsin told journal-ists that he had invited experts from the Federal Reserve System to come and "work with our experts on reforming our credit, financial, and banking system in the Russian Federation."[65]

DEVOLUTION

Journalists in Moscow spoke about "the second recognition of Russia." One television channel even featured a documentary on "the triangle" of Bush-Gorbachev-Yeltsin. The Russian outcast, who earlier had shocked the West and left many of his better-educated compatriots feeling ashamed of his behavior, had finally arrived. He was a national leader, backed by millions of Russian people, and the West had recognized his legitimacy. In the Nine Plus One talks, he would now be the one calling the shots, not Gorbachev.

THE BEAR AND THE FOX

On 10 July, after weeks of preparations, Yeltsin was sworn in as President of the Russian Federation. The ceremony, carefully staged, took place in the Kremlin's Palace of Congresses where all 2,000 delegates of the Russian super-assembly met yet again, invited from all over the country at considerable expense.[66] While Yeltsin had considered enacting a Russian version of the American presidential inauguration, involving swearing an oath on the Bible and an artillery salute, in the end his ceremony was a mix of Russian tradition and Soviet pomp. Yeltsin, his right hand placed over his heart, took his oath on the Soviet constitution of the Russian Soviet Federative Socialist Republic, with the Soviet red flag's hammer and sickle hanging in the background. A moment later, the curtain behind him lifted to reveal the Red Army Band performing music from Mikhail Glinka's nineteenth-century opera *A Life for the Tsar*. In Yeltsin's inaugural speech, he spoke about "one thousand years of Russian history," with the Soviet period figuring as a time of "great tribulations." He promised that Russia, along with the other republics, would persevere "in the complex endeavor to have a fundamentally reformed Union." He did not even mention Gorbachev. And in conclusion he declared: "Great Russia will rise from its knees."[67]

The only truly original element in the ceremony was the speech given by Patriarch Alexyi II. He gave Yeltsin a blessing on behalf of the Russian Orthodox Church and other religious communities of the country, including Catholicism, Protestantism, Islam and Judaism. The President-elect, the Patriarch said, "receives the supreme political power in Russia by popular choice and divine dispensation." This power, however, came with heavy responsibility for a country that was profoundly sick following decades of communist rule. Patriarch Alexyi asked Yeltsin to practice "anthropological realism" in his governance. He explained that it meant understanding and forgiveness of all people in Russia, including political opponents. The communists, after seizing power, had banished the past, expecting to create "a new human material and a beautiful society." This had only led to great tragedy. It was naïve to expect now, Alexyi continued, that after "evil in our country is removed from the political arena, everything would fall into place." The people of Russia "cannot change overnight."[68]

Gorbachev, present at the ceremony, said in his public remarks that the appearance of another president in the Kremlin was "a logical result" of his perestroika.[69] In reality, Gorbachev felt outperformed by his rival. "How ambitious he is," he complained to an aide, "and what a naïve desire for the scepter!" Perhaps, Gorbachev mused, this was how a Russian Tsar should behave—"But I cannot behave like that."[70] Gorbachev provided Yeltsin with an office inside the Kremlin, just across the square from his own presidential office. Yeltsin, however, did not like to be a tenant in the ancient Russian fortress, while Gorbachev was in command of the Kremlin's special regiment and decided who could enter and exit the walled premises. For that reason, Yeltsin used a new office inside the Kremlin only for ceremonial purposes, but he preferred to work in the Russian Parliament a mile and a half away.

Gorbachev's aides agreed that the situation, with two Presidents inside the Kremlin, was extremely abnormal and destabilizing. Anatoly Chernyaev saw in Yeltsin's enthronement a systemic shift: a Russian tide was flooding the structures of the communist regime. The majority of Russians scorned Gorbachev's leadership and his "socialist choice," a synonym for the failed reforms and growing economic hardships. The Politburo and the Secretariat had become redundant; "they have no power even over Party members." Gorbachev could put a good face on his lost gamble and convince himself that Yeltsin's new prominence could help him better balance the stalwarts in the government and in the Supreme Soviet. Yet if Yeltsin were to let Gorbachev down, Chernyaev speculated, the Soviet leader would fall over a cliff. Shakhnazarov was even more pessimistic: if Gorbachev stumbled and fell, the anti-communist hurricane would destroy not only the last vestiges of totalitarianism, but also the structures of the state itself.[71]

Gorbachev, the biggest loser in this shift, continued to delegate the business of running the country and its economy to Pavlov and his Cabinet of Ministers. And he was busy with the Party. Despite its deep unpopularity, the CPSU was the only organized force across the whole Soviet Union. The Party's hierarchical organization of 15 million members included cells in every unit of the armed forces, the police, economic ministries, educational institutions, and cultural organizations. In many republics and outlying Russian regions, local Party committees remained intimately connected with the bureaucracy and economic management. Predictably, many of these officials, removed from formal power, had nothing but scorn and hatred for Gorbachev's leadership. An internal Party memo, commissioned by the head of the Moscow Party organization, Yuri Prokofiev, about the Russian presidential elections expressed this feeling. The document concluded: "People voted against M. S. Gorbachev, the Center, and the CPSU; they voted for B. N. Yeltsin, for a free, wealthy, and prosperous Russia. They voted for a leader with a strong will . . . against the paralysis of will, failures, slyness and fraud, the confusion of mind and inconsistency of action." Prokofiev was one of those who wanted to remove Gorbachev from the Party leadership. The biggest problem for the Party nomenklatura was that the alternative to Gorbachev was nowhere to be seen. And the most visible man "with a strong will" was Yeltsin, an ardent populist who was promising a leap toward an American-style democracy.[72]

Alexander Yakovlev and Eduard Shevardnadze concluded that reforming the Party was a futile task. Shevardnadze had made a public exit from the Party's ranks in June, while Yakovlev was still waging a rearguard fight against neo-Stalinists. On 1 July, Yakovlev and Shevardnadze launched the "Movement for Democracy and Reforms": the idea was to create a new political platform for reform-minded members of the CPSU and more moderate activists from Democratic Russia. Among early sympathizers of this project were the Moscow mayor Popov and Leningrad's mayor Sobchak, Gorbachev's former economic advisor Nikolai Petrakov, Vice-President Alexander Rutskoy, and Yegor Yakovlev, the editor of the influential newspaper *Moscow News*. The organizers turned for support to a growing class of Russian entrepreneurs and pro-market industrial managers. Shevardnadze and Yakovlev claimed that they wanted to help Gorbachev by constructing a new political base for him, in case he stepped down from his post as leader of the Party.[73]

Gorbachev scrambled to paper over the yawning divides between the conservative and liberal flanks of the Party. As in a chess move, he replaced the leadership of the Russian Communist Party: Polozkov stepped down, and his successor was an unknown provincial apparatchik. Gorbachev also instructed that a new reformist program for the Party be drafted, which took many weeks. Shakhnazarov quipped that, after many drafts, the text still looked like a new edition of the Communist Manifesto. Finally, Chernyaev, who was asked to help, deleted most of the language about "socialist choice."[74] On 8 July, Gorbachev confided to Felipe González, the Spanish Prime Minister: if the conservatives refused to adopt his new program, he would split the CPSU and launch a new party.[75]

Yeltsin was frustrated that his fresh-minted presidency was not supported by state levers. In the year following the declaration of Russian sovereignty, the Russian authorities managed to significantly disrupt the functioning of the central government and economic system. At the same time, they had utterly failed to create new effective institutions that could replace the Center. Yeltsin remained an outsider to the state bureaucracy. The Democratic Russia activists lacked any experience of state administration and governance. The Russian Federation remained a "ghost" republic, even compared with the Baltics, Ukraine, Belorussia, and Kazakhstan.

The Russian government was an unruly assembly of entrepreneurial adventurers and ambitious provincial managers. Ivan Silayev, the elected chairman of the RSFSR Council of Ministers, was completely unfit to run it. Pavlov recalled that Silayev never believed that his job would last for long; he even discreetly asked Pavlov to help him get a dacha for his personal use from the reserve of state-owned real estate.[76] The resourceful head of the Bank of Russia, Grigory Matiukhin, reached the limit of the possible. His project to create an all-Russian network of ATMs fizzled out due to lack of funds. When Yeltsin, during his presidential campaign, asked Matiukhin for cash for "giveaways" to workers' collectives, the Russian banker said he had no money. The Russian President asked angrily: "Who is the master in the house?" Matiukhin replied: "You, but there is no cash."[77] For all its pretensions, the Bank of Russia could not print money; only the Soviet government could. Finally, for all the international recognition of Yeltsin, the Russian Foreign Ministry, headed by Andrei Kozyrev, remained a skeletal institution. It totally depended on the premises and services of the Soviet Foreign Ministry, which controlled embassies, consulates, and trade missions across the world.

After months of promises from Gorbachev and several meetings with Kryuchkov, the project of a "Russian KGB" also remained something only on paper. Kryuchkov treated Yeltsin as an enemy of the state and did not provide any sensitive information to him. The KGB chief appointed his subordinate, Viktor Ivanenko, to liaise with the Russian government. A nominal "Russian KGB" was created inside the Lubyanka headquarters; its staff did not exceed twenty officers. That was all that Yeltsin could get. Ivanenko's original brief was to keep tabs on the Russian separatists, but he gradually began to sympathize with Yeltsin and befriended Burbulis.[78]

In his populist speeches, Yeltsin claimed that the central bureaucracy was outrageously expensive, was a seat of privileges, and should be defunded, so that people would live better lives. Privately, he had a different idea. Yeltsin, Burbulis recalled, had rejected the prospect of an across-the-board purge of the bureaucratic class. Instead, he wanted to woo the best of the Soviet bureaucracy to the new Russian state structures. This included the KGB and police. "We all grew up in a country," Burbulis mused many years later, "where the KGB was the main organization that maintained order, worked around the clock, controlled every part of society for decades." Yeltsin suspected the KGB of attempts on his life, but he did not want to antagonize such a powerful force. Yeltsin and Burbulis also knew that the Russian leader had not won in non-Russian "national" enclaves within the Russian Federation. Without the Communist Party, they had to find other state instruments to consolidate Russian territorial and political sovereignty. The KGB was the only such instrument available.[79]

On 20 July, Yeltsin paid a visit to the KGB headquarters. The KGB had convened a conference that day of the heads of regional and district branches from across the Russian Federation. Yeltsin was invited, and he came, accompanied by Khasbulatov, Burbulis, and his young legal aide Sergey Shakhrai. The conference was filmed by the KGB, but liberal journalists were not invited to the event. The Russian President addressed the KGB conference with a carefully drafted and surprisingly accommodating speech. He called for the creation of a strong executive branch in Russia, in which "an appropriate place must be found for the Committee for State Security." The KGB, he said, should become "an effective institution of the democratic state" and focus on a new set of tasks, such as the "protection of the rights and freedoms" of citizens, assisting economic reforms, fighting organized crime, and "the prevention and neutralization of social and national conflicts within the [Russian] republic." Yeltsin spoke out against any purge of KGB officers. "You have selected the best people: true patriots, resistant to corruption. It would be against the state's interests not to use in full measure your potential for the cause of Russia's rebirth."[80]

For Yeltsin's liberal allies, his speech to the KGB would have sounded like an invitation for a wolf to become guardian of the sheep. Yeltsin's intent, however, was to signal that he would treat the future of the Party and the state organs in Russia very differently. The KGB officers were Party members, but many of them were Russian nationalists as well; they contemplated shifting their loyalties to a post-communist Russian state, provided that this state would be governed by a strong leader. Some senior KGB officers had convinced themselves that a pre-emptive break with the Party was the only way to avoid the recent fate of their colleagues in Romania, Hungary, and other Eastern European countries, who had been fired and persecuted by the post-communist governments. Therefore, many KGB officers, listening to Yeltsin at the conference, nodded in approval. "This is what they wanted to hear from the Russian president," recalled the KGB's Lieutenant-General Leonid Shebarshin, who attended the meeting. "A light murmur . . . passed through the hall when Yeltsin spoke about the difficulties expected to occur at the end of the year, [including] the possibility of mass disturbances, and called on the state security agencies to be ready for such a situation."[81]

That same day, Yeltsin signed a decree prohibiting the existence of Party "cells," in other words groups "in state organs, organizations, corporations, and enterprises located on the territory of the RSFSR." The decree was, de facto, destroying the levers of the CPSU inside the KGB, the army, and other power structures.[82] It also cut the symbiotic relationship between the Party and state apparatus. Yeltsin, of course, had no power to implement his decree. He wanted, however, to impress his own supporters and the world. Publicly, Yeltsin argued that with his decree he wanted to help Gorbachev. "I have opened a second front. Those reactionary forces that wanted to deliver powerful salvos against Gorbachev [at the forthcoming Party Plenum] have redirected much of their efforts against this second front."[83]

Yeltsin had once again upstaged Gorbachev. Now the Soviet leader faced an unexpected and undesirable choice: to contravene Yeltsin's decree and side with the Party stalwarts, or accept the decree and face their rebellion.

CHAPTER 9

CONSENSUS

The economy, stupid.
James Carville, 1992

THE WASHINGTON DOCTRINE

The summer of 1991 began without a consensus on the future of the Soviet Union and how to adapt its economy to the global market. The most natural choice would be a combination of state capitalism and liberalization of small businesses, the road already taken by China. The progress in the Chinese economy, however, got very little attention in the Soviet media. Instead, Democratic Russia and liberal journalists regretted the demise of the 500 Days and turned to the West in search of options for a quick market leap.

There was only one Western option available, "the Washington Consensus." Its critics called this concept the "ten commandments" because of its quasi-religious nature. The doctrine emerged among economists who worked in Washington, in the International Monetary Fund (IMF) and World Bank, as well as in the US Treasury Department and the Federal Reserve System. The main theoretical underpinning of this approach had been created by Milton Friedman and other economists from the University of Chicago. The Washington Consensus became an ideological foundation of "the neoliberal revolution" of Thatcher and Reagan. During the 1980s, the IMF applied the Consensus policies in Latin American countries, to make them attractive on the nascent global financial market. Those policies included: sharp reduction of the state-run economy, privatization, liberalization and deregulation, fiscal discipline and a balanced budget. The Harvard University economist Larry Summers, who in 1991 became Chief Economist of the World Bank, said about the Washington

Consensus: "Spread the truth—the laws of economics are like the laws of engineering. One set of laws works everywhere."[1]

The policies of the Washington Consensus deregulated the economy and weakened, often fatally, the existing state institutions. Its cornerstone notion, macroeconomic stability, was usually achieved at the expense of social programs and popular consumption. The fall of communist regimes in Eastern Europe opened up a vast space for practitioners of neoliberal economics. For anti-communists in Warsaw, Prague, and Budapest, the Washington Consensus fitted with their slogans: replacement of the state monopoly by liberalization and deregulation, privatization of state enterprises and free trade. The radical reduction of state funding corresponded with the agenda of anti-communist revolutions. Nobody cared that neoliberal policies created huge social inequality and political tension.[2]

Grigory Yavlinsky, the author of the 500 Days, discovered the Consensus in September 1990, when he presented his program at the IMF-World Bank forum in Washington. The top economists told him that the program was a promising start, yet it did not match the "ten commandments." Above all, it left intact too many state controls and social programs, and did not crush the power of the military-industrial complex. George Soros, who paid for the translation of the 500 Days into English, advised Yavlinsky to end the power of "working collectives" and local Soviets. Yavlinsky considered the Washington Consensus too destabilizing and destructive for the Soviet economy. He continued to argue that radical privatization and deregulation should be done with an eye to avoiding social instability.[3]

However, some Russian economists and social scientists from Moscow and Leningrad did embrace the Washington Consensus. In April 1991, this group traveled to Chile—the only Latin American country that had experienced economic growth in the 1980s. Their leader was Vitaly Naishul, a forty-one-year-old economist with a mathematical background, who had worked in Gosplan. Naishul and his friends agreed that the Soviet bureaucratic system would never work and must be destroyed; the Soviet workforce had been degraded and corrupted by decades of communist totalitarianism; and only a brutal market shock could restore work ethics. In a word, the road to a "normal" economy, they argued, lay through the inevitability of complete collapse, suffering, and survival. In Santiago, they met Hernán Büchi and Sergio de la Cuadra, former ministers of finance in the government of Augusto Pinochet. They even met with the retired dictator. One of them recalled that "Pinochet looked like Stalin in those old films, benign and austere." Pinochet's crimes did not bother them; they were impressed by the Chilean economic success. "Our country," explained Naishul, "lost tens of millions of lives—and mostly in vain—

at the time of the Bolshevik Revolution of 1917 and the ensuing turmoil. Chile lost 3,000 lives and became a highly developed society."[4] In the following months and years, Naishul and his fellow travelers would become influential participants in the discussions of Soviet economic reforms. And one of them, Alexei Golovkov, became an advisor in Yeltsin's entourage, close to Gennady Burbulis. In August 1991, this would be instrumental in changing history.

The economist and journalist Yegor Gaidar was among the first to embrace the Washington Consensus. He came from a family of Moscow high intelligentsia and Soviet nomenklatura; his father worked as a *Pravda* foreign correspondent. When perestroika began, Gaidar, still in his early thirties, organized a seminar of young economists to study economic reforms in the Soviet Union.[5] In July 1990, the Gaidar group took part in an international seminar in Sopron, Hungary, where they met with world-renowned economists: Rudiger Dornbusch from MIT and William D. Nordhaus from Yale University. At this seminar, Gaidar and his associates underwent a radical conversion: they concluded that there was no alternative to radical and immediate marketization and privatization of the Soviet economy. The old economic system could not be reformed. It had to be destroyed.[6] After Hungary, Gaidar flew to Stanford University, and stayed for six months as a fellow at the Hoover Institution, a home for economists from the Reagan administration. His hosts were surprised: Gaidar was the first Soviet economist who demonstrated a clear idea of macroeconomic theory.[7] From Stanford, Gaidar followed the demise of the 500 Days and wrote an article for *Pravda*. He wrote that radical reforms, in order to work, must cut state social programs, and many people would suffer. Indexing, higher pensions, and other well-intentioned projects, Gaidar argued, would only lead to hyperinflation and economic meltdown. He concluded: "When central heating stops, it will be impossible to warm your house by starting a fire from paper money."[8] When Gaidar returned to Moscow, he founded an Institute of Economic Reforms. His ambition was to bring the Washington Consensus to Moscow.

In December 1990, the IMF and World Bank in Washington delivered "A Study of the Soviet Economy" that the leaders of the G-7 countries had requested. In February 1991, the full version was published in three volumes. Leading Western economists knew nothing of the Soviet Union and its economy, so the work was done by a task force of younger experts from the IMF, some of them with an Eastern European background. The task force used open sources. A participant recalled that "the overall picture was crystal clear: the Soviet economy was facing dangerous domestic and external imbalances."[9] The only way Western economists knew how to rebalance this economy was by deploying the policies of the Washington Consensus. The economists on the task force felt conflicted. The Study was drawn up on the assumption that radical reforms would leave the Soviet Union intact. The task force, however, concluded that radical economic reforms ran into resistance from powerful interest groups, including the agrarian lobby and the military-industrial complex. Those groups, along with new lobbies that emerged from incomplete socialist reforms, opposed the end of state subsidies. The only way to break the deadlock of those groups on reforms would be through radical liberalization and deregulation. This also meant a political loosening of the Soviet Union, which would lead to its break-up. Such reforms, the economists argued, would create powerful centrifugal forces that "may spin off the republics, first the Baltic states and then the rest." This argument upset the British economist John Odling-Smee, head of the IMF European Department and supervisor of the task force. The G-7 leaders in Houston had declared their intention to help Gorbachev stay in power and retain central political and military controls. The economists were told to refrain from any explicit conclusions. The Study proposed some cautious reforms "within the system".[10]

In Moscow, most Soviet economists appreciated the moderate nature of the IMF advice. Gaidar was the only exception. He published an article in the liberal *Moscow News*, "The Time of Unpleasant Truths." The Soviet government and the Russian politicians, Gaidar wrote, should heed the conclusions of the IMF report "backed by tens of billions of dollars." He regretted that the Washington economists did not dictate to Moscow decision-makers, as they would have done to Latin American countries. "Somebody should tell the society and the powers-that-be," Gaidar explained, that the Soviet "economy will not bear the burden of state subsidies" that amounted to one-fifth of GNP. The struggle between Gorbachev and Yeltsin, the young economist was convinced, was turning the Soviet Union into a Latin American country, a weak state swaying from crisis to crisis. The idea of compensating everyone for inflation, promoted by Gorbachev, as well as Yeltsin, was folly. No parliamentary laws could ensure that pensions would be paid, while the budget was in crisis. "One can replace party-crats with demo-crats, and then in reverse. This will not change the severe logic of macroeconomics." Gaidar decided to translate the IMF Study on the Soviet economy into Russian, as a basic guidance for future reforms.[11]

In March 1991, a group of American economists from Stanford University, theorists and practitioners of neoliberal economics, arrived in Moscow at the invitation of Mikhail Bocharov, head of the Higher Economic Council at the RSFSR parliament. For the leader of the group, fifty-year-old Mikhail Bernstam, it was a return to his homeland after many years. The KGB had forced him to emigrate to the United States in 1976 due to his activities in the human rights movement and his collaboration with Sakharov and Solzhenitsyn. Having graduated from the University of Chicago, he had served in the Reagan administration and had many friends on the Republican Right.[12] In the spring of 1991, Bernstam no longer wished to bring the Soviet Union down. He wanted to help Gorbachev and Yeltsin save the collapsing economy. The IMF Study upset Bernstam. Before the trip he consulted Milton Friedman and other colleagues at the University of Chicago. He realized that what had worked in Chile would not work in the Soviet Union. Instead of a macroeconomic stabilization and global investments, there would be chaos and destruction. Perhaps, Bernstam thought, the universal rules of neoliberal economics could be bent creatively, to help a new democratic Russia emerge.[13]

On 15 March 1991, the Americans met with Yeltsin. The Russian leader said: "I want you to help me as you helped Reagan." Yeltsin knew nothing about the neoliberal policies, but wanted to adopt them lock, stock, and barrel.[14] The Stanford economists set down to work out a new reform program "for Russia."

AN INVITATION TO LONDON

For several months, President Bush had failed to realize how much anguish the postponement of the US-Soviet summit was causing in the Kremlin. On 7 May, he received a cable from Jack Matlock that brought this issue to light: the American ambassador had just met Gorbachev in confidence, and the Soviet leader had vented his frustration: he had helped the United States on Iraq, but the US did not want to help in return; it only made new demands. His personal appeal for credits to purchase American grain had come to naught; the Americans had not provided computers for Soviet nuclear power plants; a joint project to build civilian aircraft had met with further obstacles. The American media was also predicting his failure, which "hurt him a lot" among his people at home. Gorbachev learned that Matlock would be retiring as ambassador and asked him: "Why should you leave now? Maybe you think this ship will sink?" Gorbachev also asked why the Americans dawdled on joint economic ventures with Soviet enterprises, especially in the military-industrial complex, which now had leeway to pursue business and trade deals independently of the state authorities. The Cold War laws still blocked transfers of Western advanced technology to the USSR and thwarted US-Soviet trade. Could their American friends do more to dismantle those obstacles? Gorbachev suddenly asked Matlock: "Do you want us to hand you the tiller?" "Heaven forbid!" the American ambassador responded.[15]

On Saturday, 11 May 1991, George Bush was resting in Camp David after a week of trouble. He had been diagnosed with a rare thyroid disease. New medical methods had saved him from dangerous surgery, but he was exhausted.

While recovering, he called his friend Gorbachev.[16] He did not know what he could offer specifically. Soviet-American relations seemed to be logjammed by the situation in the Baltics. The best the US President could offer was to place the Soviet Union on the fast track for special associate status at the IMF and World Bank.[17] Gorbachev, however, did not want to be at the end of a long line of Third World countries seeking IMF financial assistance. He told Bush that he wanted to be invited to the upcoming G-7 summit in London. As a way to prepare for this occasion, Gorbachev said, could he send Primakov and Yavlinsky to Washington? Bush, taken by surprise, replied: "I will instruct our people . . . in a positive frame of mind." He even added he would "try . . . not to find problems but find reasons to help."[18]

Gorbachev was under strong pressure from his government to decide on an economic course and find money for it. In early April 1991, Pavlov finally convinced him that without raising prices, nothing would work. The government then raised purchase prices, part of the *beznal* finances, threefold. The same happened to retail prices. The political fallout was predictably huge and negative. The liberal Moscow press, Democratic Russia, and Yeltsin's advisors immediately attacked Pavlov for plunging "100 million Russians" into poverty. Pavlov's reform was a blow to republican populists. The republican parliaments, he argued, could vote for greater compensation to their constituencies, like before, but it would be their political responsibility. And this would unmask populism as a big lie: "There is nothing to give out."[19] Pavlov argued in favor of a radical opening of the Soviet economy to foreign investment, including foreign ownership. He conceded that, to reduce current social tensions, the Soviet government needed $25 billion of Western credits and investments. About one-third of this money would be used to import consumer goods in high demand and sell them to consumers. The accumulated funds would be invested in "conversion" of the military-industrial complex. Another third would be invested in equipment for food processing, packaging, and other consumer-oriented industries. The rest would be spent directly on maintaining the old industries. In his memoirs, Pavlov wrote that his Cabinet was ready to provide collateral guarantees to Western governments and banks: to allow Western companies to buy shares in Soviet enterprises and participate in their restructuring.[20]

Gorbachev feared Pavlov's anti-crisis course would complicate his political bargaining at Novo-Ogaryovo. He desperately needed another magic wand, something similar to the 500 Days of the previous year. This was the moment when Yavlinsky resurfaced again, with a grandiose and well-packaged program. Yavlinsky shared Pavlov's main goal of arresting inflation, but he sharply disagreed with the Prime Minister on the strategy. His solution was not the state capitalism of big corporations, but step-by-step privatization of small enter-prises and services. This privatization, he argued, could no longer be paid from the savings of Soviet citizens. Pavlov's reforms, he argued, completely ruined the trust between the people and the Soviet state. Instead, privatization would be paid for by credits to people from a stabilization fund, and this fund would be formed by Western countries. His reform, Yavlinsky assured, would jump-start the economy and contain hyperinflation. Privately, he called this scheme "a Marshall plan" for the Soviet Union.

Yavlinsky tapped into an influential network in the United States to back his idea. Stanley Fischer, deputy head of the IMF, argued that $20–$30 billion in annual foreign credits for five years would preserve the Soviet Union's macro-economic stability. The former dean of the Kennedy School of Government, Graham Allison, invited Yavlinsky to Harvard University to transform his idea into a policy initiative. Allison was fascinated by the magnitude of the Soviet economic challenge, but he also worried about the catastrophic consequences of Gorbachev's failure. He participated in a US-Soviet initiative on nuclear disarmament and was keenly aware of the potential danger if Moscow lost control over tens of thousands of nuclear weapons. For only a fraction of the Cold War's expenses, Allison argued, the West could transform a former enemy into a partner: this would be a real bargain for both America and the world. Allison's name for the initiative, "Grand Bargain," reflected his approach.[21]

In Moscow, Yavlinsky approached Yevgeny Primakov, who immediately backed the initiative and arranged a meeting with Gorbachev. Allison immedi-ately traveled to Moscow as well.[22] The meeting took place on 16 May 1991. Another American participant was Jeffrey Sachs, the Harvard economist who had advised Balcerowicz on Polish "shock therapy" reforms. Sachs was specific: $150 billion in Western credits to the Soviet Union over a period of five years would ensure successful reforms.[23] Chernyaev recorded in his diary: "M.S. [Gorbachev] agreed that, together with the Americans, [Yavlinsky] would make an 'advance project' for G-7 and for M.S." With this project, the World Bank and IMF "would give us 15, 30, or even 150 billion dollars." Overnight, the theoret-ical calculations of Stanley Fischer and Jeffrey Sachs were transformed into the probability of huge financial assistance.[24] Two days later, Gorbachev convened his Security Council, a new structure that replaced his previous circle of advi-sors. He forcefully argued that the Soviet Union should join the IMF and World Bank. The West would then open its purse. The figure of $150 billion, he said, was "hardly realistic," but half that amount might become available. Primakov, Pavlov, Sitaryan and the head of the Central Bank, Viktor Gerashchenko, spoke in favor. The KGB chief Kryuchkov, usually in agreement with Gorbachev, suddenly contradicted him. The West would not give any money, he said. He also feared the "high political costs" if Soviet reforms became linked to the prospect of Western aid. Gorbachev dismissed Kryuchkov's concerns. The KGB chief, he said to his aide, was acting like a mothballed Soviet patriot.[25]

Yavlinsky flew to the United States with his associates to work on the details of the Grand Bargain. Robert Blackwill, a former CIA and former NSC staff member now at Harvard University, helped him and Allison meet with Ross and Zoellick at the State Department. "My view," recalled Zoellick later, "was that the West could offer a multi-billion-dollar package once, but not twice." Soviet privatization, Zoellick said to Yavlinsky, should come first, framed in patriotic terms; then Western assistance could follow, in a sequenced, targeted manner. Yavlinsky assured the American officials that he also did not want Western money to be on the table. "You have to use *the promise* of money *in the future* to make us do what we must do now."[26]

Pavlov did not like Yavlinsky's intrusion. He sent his deputy Vladimir Shcherbakov to Washington as an official head of the Soviet delegation for economic talks with Bush. Forty-one-year-old Shcherbakov was an experienced apparatchik, shrewd and prudent. Yet, like all Soviet industrial managers, he did not understand macroeconomics or the causes of Soviet economic woes.[27] Shcherbakov and Primakov arrived in Washington on 27 May. They met with James Baker and then Michael Boskin, head of the Council of Economic Advisors. The Soviet officials claimed, quite falsely, that they represented a consensus at home: all of the Soviet republics, except two, had allegedly approved Pavlov's program. In Boskin's recollection, Primakov "wanted to open up his trench coat and show us the list of things he could sell us." Boskin asked what had happened to the money that West Germany had given the Soviets to build housing for the returning Soviet troops. Primakov could not answer this question. Boskin briefed Bush that the Soviet delegation had come to fish around for the prospect of big Western money. The answer should be "no."[28]

On 31 May, Bush received the Soviet delegation in the Oval Office. He deliberately turned to Yavlinsky, who had come from Harvard to join the talks, and asked him to explain his approach. Acting on Zoellick's advice, the economist said that the Soviets had not come as beggars, and that there was no need for vast foreign loans for now. Instead, he called for a radical relaxation of price controls and privatization. At a private luncheon with Bush, Primakov defended Pavlov's course. For economic reforms to work, he said, administrative levers were just as necessary as foreign loans. "Our people won't take the initiative— they wait to be told." Bush said that the US government would not bring any money to the table at the forthcoming summit in London. Unfortunately, he explained, "we are broke right now, more or less. I have to be able to go to our

Treasury and the IMF and present something which is economically feasible." Primakov assured Bush that Gorbachev "will not come to London and ask for $100 billion." The Soviet emissary probably expected the US President to offer a smaller amount, but he did not say so. The meeting left Bush baffled about the real purpose of the Soviet mission. Do they want money or not? He said to Scowcroft: "These guys really don't have their ducks in a row, do they?"[29] At their private luncheon, Bush proudly demonstrated to Primakov his new desktop computer and tried to print something. An older lady, Bush's secretary, instructed the US President as to what button to press. When the Soviet delegation returned to Moscow, Primakov brought Gorbachev a printed note from Bush: "Dear Michael: I just finished a very good lunch with your able representative Mr. Primakov. I want you to have this first message that I have ever sent to a foreign leader on my new computer. Good Luck and Warmest Personal Regards, George Bush." It was clear that the talks had failed.[30]

A few days later, Pavlov obtained Gorbachev's approval of an internal credit of 68 billion rubles to the Ministry of Finance, to plug a hole in the budget caused by unpaid taxes from state enterprises and republics. This was the largest case of ruble-printing in Soviet history. The State Bank also borrowed from people's savings. This measure was taken in complete secrecy, and came to light only during the last days of the Soviet Union.[31] In this situation, the issue of Western credits and investments became a matter of life and death for the Soviet budget and economy.

On 5 June, after a six-month delay, Gorbachev flew to Oslo to give his Nobel Peace Prize acceptance speech. Chernyaev prepared a draft of Gorbachev's speech with the main thesis: perestroika benefited the world more than it did the Soviet Union, so could the West please pay back in kind now when the country was in such a crisis, and prevent a calamity for everyone? Gorbachev told his aide to drop the issue of money. The Nobel laureate wanted to frame his address in terms of a grand strategy: without a reformed Soviet Union, Western powers would not be able to build a lasting and peaceful world order. Still, in his Oslo speech Gorbachev decided to appeal to Western leaders and the Western public to start a serious "conversation" at the G-7 meeting about how to help Soviet reforms at a "critical juncture."[32] On the eve of his departure for Oslo, Gorbachev received an informal message from Washington. Chernyaev recorded that Bush had "finally decided to invite M.S." to London. Perhaps, Chernyaev mused, the London summit would be where the Soviet leader would part ways with the dying Soviet system and receive a proper invitation, for himself and his country, to join the Western liberal order.[33] On 15 June, the British ambassador Rodric Braithwaite passed Gorbachev a formal invitation from John Major to the London summit.

"TURN THEM INTO A THIRD-RATE POWER"

While Gorbachev worried about the lack of funds and the Soviet place in the global Western order, Bush and Scowcroft worried about the treaty on conventional arms reductions in Europe (CFE) and the US-Soviet treaty to reduce offensive strategic missiles (START). Those treaties were Bush's main priority with regard to the Soviet Union. The head of the Soviet General Staff, Marshal Moiseyev, told a meeting with British and American diplomats and military experts that the Supreme Soviet would refuse to ratify the CFE Treaty unless the Soviet Army received the quotas of military equipment that had been assigned to former Soviet allies in the Warsaw Pact.[34] Tipped off by Foreign Minister Alexander Bessmertnykh, the Americans decided to negotiate directly with Moiseyev and press the Marshal for concessions. This approach worked. The two sides agreed a compromise. In the Soviet parliament on 23 May 1991, Akhromeyev declared his personal "moral responsibility" for the CFE Treaty and called for its ratification. On 14 June, an extraordinary conference of ambassadors convened in Vienna and ratified the amendments to the treaty. One major obstacle to the Moscow summit was removed.[35] The talks on START, however, continued to run into resistance on the Soviet side. Moiseyev complained that the draft treaty was unfair: it gave the United States a 1.7:1 superiority over the USSR in missiles and warheads. The Americans expected the Soviet side to make all the concessions, and they refused to reciprocate. This time, Gorbachev sided with his General Staff.[36]

Bush and Scowcroft did not like Grand Bargain from the start. The American media trashed the scheme. William Safire in *The New York Times* referred to Allison and Yavlinsky as well-intentioned dupes, who had come up with a ludicrous scheme of "capitalist-paid crutches for a bailout of the Communist system." If the Soviets wanted to avoid national bankruptcy, Safire wrote, they should reduce the size of the Red Army, stop bankrolling Fidel Castro in Cuba and the regime in Afghanistan, sell houses, apartments, land and factories to the people, and unleash the profit motive. The author concluded: "The political climate required for this is called freedom."[37] Behind the scenes, people from Yeltsin's camp pleaded with the Americans not to give any money to the Cabinet of the "reactionary" Pavlov. Andrei Kozyrev told Baker's aides: "Any money you give to the center will not only be wasted but worse than that, it will keep afloat a system that should be allowed to sink."[38]

Still, the Yavlinsky-Allison project gained some political momentum. Margaret Thatcher, no longer in power, urged Bush to lead on aid to the Soviet Union, as he had led with Kuwait in the Gulf War. After a meeting with the Iron Lady, US Ambassador Matlock wrote in his journal that Thatcher was right.

"Our leaders will simply be bereft of wisdom or courage, or both, if they fail to respond to the challenge."[39]

In the White House, Bush did not know how safe it was to apply more pressure on Gorbachev on arms reductions, without offering him any financial rewards. After Primakov and Shcherbakov had departed from Washington, the President told Scowcroft to convene a special Cabinet meeting to discuss what kinds of "gifts" Bush could bring to the London summit for Gorbachev. In his introductory letter, Scowcroft asked the Cabinet members to think about all elements of the big picture. He added important caveats: any approach to the Soviet side should be developed in harmony with Germany and other Western allies, and should also not detract from the priority of helping the Central and Eastern European countries.[40]

On 3 June, leading members of the administration conferred on the Soviet Union in the Situation Room of the White House. Baker's team in the State Department stood for "respect [for] and engagement" with Gorbachev. They argued that preservation of a reformed and federated Union with a common economic space would not clash with American security interests. Baker was skeptical about the Grand Bargain, but he told Zoellick to keep working with Yavlinsky to see what ideas might come up. Dick Cheney and his Pentagon aides welcomed the break-up of the Soviet "empire" and argued that Gorbachev should be pressed to abandon the Soviet client states in Cuba and Afghanistan, reduce the USSR's nuclear armaments, and start dismantling the military-industrial complex. A third party was the Secretary of the Treasury, Nicholas Brady, and his special aide for international affairs, David C. Mulford. They firmly objected to any large-scale assistance for the Soviet Union on financial grounds. Brady, a close friend of Bush, had enormous influence on the President's decisions. He usually deferred to Baker on international affairs, but this time it was different. At a time of record budget deficits, Bush had broken his electoral promise not to raise taxes. It would be a political folly in such a situation to waste any money by helping Gorbachev.

At the meeting in the White House, Brady raised a question: What was the Grand Bargain? Was it $250 billion? Repeating the central argument from Safire's article, Brady said that it would be "an absolute disaster" to give the Soviets "any money to stay as they are. No one in the room wants to do that." In actuality, the Secretary of the Treasury was describing not Yavlinsky's idea, but rather its caricature, as presented by its critics. At the same time, Brady with rare candor articulated the American strategic priority: "What is involved is changing Soviet society so that it can't afford a defense system. If the Soviets go to a market system, then they can't afford a large defense establishment. A real reform program would turn them into a third-rate power, which is what we want."[41]

Richard Darman, Director of the Office of Management and Budget (OMB), and a veteran of the Reagan administration, spoke next. He dismissed the analogy between the Grand Bargain and the Marshall Plan. "The Primakov or Yavlinsky plans cannot change Soviet history. I don't believe there is any affirmative threat to the U.S. from the Soviet Union's decomposition. The problem is an opportunity cost, not a threat." The American strategy towards the USSR needed to be "somewhat Machiavellian," Darman continued. "What is the minimum amount necessary from us to mollify a regime with which we wish to work on other matters?"[42]

Baker reminded the group of the importance of guiding the Soviet leadership along the path of peaceful reforms. Gorbachev and his people did not understand economics, but they had delivered on political pluralism in Eastern Europe, and on the Gulf War. "We should keep the process going." Darman, wearing his Machiavellian cap, suggested that the administration should not reject Yavlinsky's program outright: "Mikhail Gorbachev is a showman. He will pressure us no matter what. We may need something else later." Brady even suggested inviting the Czechoslovak leader, Václav Havel, and the Polish leader, Lech Wałęsa, to London, "just to screw up Gorbachev's effort."[43]

For many in the US administration the Cold War had continued, and some were happy to see the Soviet Union collapsing. The outcome of the meeting left Bush with only two carrots for Gorbachev. One was an invitation to Gorbachev to attend the London G-7 meeting, which had already been promised. Another was for Bush to fly to Moscow for a summit if the Soviets made additional concessions.[44] Bush felt he had to add something to this proposal. On 10 June, he provided $1.5 billion in credits to the Soviet Union to purchase American grain.

By this point, it should have been crystal clear to Gorbachev and his advisors that the United States had rejected "a Marshall plan" for the Soviet Union.[45] Yet a strange game continued in Moscow: both Gorbachev and many of his advisors continued to speak—and act—as though large-scale US aid was still a real possibility. Jack Matlock later called this "a blindman's bluff." Not only Gorbachev, but other sides played a game of political poker. The Soviet President was confident that his world celebrity would make Western leaders open their wallets. Most immediately, he wanted to use the specter of a massive Western assistance program as a lever in Novo-Ogaryovo, to convince Yeltsin and other republican leaders to join a reformed Union.

Yavlinsky recalled: "We understood that the Administration did not want to rescue the Soviet Union. Graham [Allison] was upset by it, as if he were a Russian. He complained: 'They do not want to do anything!'"[46] Allison and Yavlinsky decided to turn to public opinion and make the Bush administration reconsider. In June, *Foreign Affairs* published a piece by Allison and Robert Blackwill, another supporter of the Grand Bargain. It was possible, they wrote, to envisage the Soviet Union as a great power, and yet at the same time "a normal society" that was integrated into the global economy. "For Russians," they explained, "status as a great power is as much an element of national identity as it is for Americans." Of course, a Western assistance program could fail in economic terms, as there was no formula for Soviet economic transition. Still, "a bargain of the Marshall plan proportions" would provide a huge incentive for the Soviet center, as well as the republics, to collaborate on constructing a "normal" federated Union with a market economy.[47]

On 13 June, Yavlinsky and Allison sent both Bush and Gorbachev a draft of their initiative. Now it was named "Joint Program for Western Cooperation in the Soviet Transformation to Democracy and the Market Economy." They wrote in the cover letter that they "have had informal conversations with representatives of the G-7 governments. We are under pressure to complete this part of the study and to deliver copies to the leaders of the other members of the G-7 no later than next week." On 15 June, the two faxed the text of their program to Yeltsin.[48] Then Yavlinsky flew to Moscow to prepare the home front. He met with Yeltsin and handed another copy of the program to Gorbachev, as well as to the Kazakh leader Nursultan Nazarbayev. Just as in July 1990, the Russian economist used the economic initiative as a vehicle of coalition-building among the most important political players. Gorbachev reacted with alacrity. On 17 June, he invited Yavlinsky to Novo-Ogaryovo, where for an hour and a half the economist explained the program's details to the leaders of the republics and the autonomous regions. They were "very interested and very supportive," wrote Yavlinsky to Allison, and the following discussion lasted for another hour. Gorbachev then introduced Yavlinsky to the assembled journalists and told them that Yavlinsky's report represented a "historic turning point." A few days later, Gorbachev's spokesman announced that Yavlinsky would accompany Gorbachev to London for the summit. Gorbachev said to Yavlinsky and Allison that he was ready to accept "90 percent" of their plan.[49]

On the morning of 18 June, Zoellick and other US officials received a private fax from Allison, informing them about new developments in Moscow. "The plot thickens," the letter concluded. A few weeks before the London summit, Allison and Yavlinsky rushed around European capitals meeting with Sherpas— economic experts and financial ministers of G-7 governments—to lobby for their program. They had used a plane provided by Ann Getty, Allison's friend and the wife of billionaire Paul Getty.

Just as Yavlinsky praised the Grand Bargain in Novo-Ogaryovo, Prime Minister Pavlov and his allies attacked the scheme in the Supreme Soviet. On the morning of 17 June, Pavlov presented to the surprised deputies a report on the need for emergency rule. The Soviet sovereign debt amounted to 240 billion rubles, while Soviet foreign debt had reached $75 billion. The invoices from commercial banks, enterprises, and republican authorities had multiplied out of control. The amount of unspent cash in people's hands had grown exponentially: the net growth was 41.3 percent in April; 61.3 percent in May; and 79.1 percent in June. The State Bank was running out of the technical means to print the new billions of rubles; Gerashchenko warned that soon there would be insufficient amounts of cash to pay salaries. In his speech, Pavlov engaged in polemics with Yavlinsky and his "Harvard sponsors." He was against making economic and financial reforms dependent on Western munificence and political will. Pavlov proposed thinking about domestic sources of investment, such as the massive privatization of economic assets, to plow into the conversion of the most sophisticated sectors of the defense industry. He also proposed that enterprises and cooperatives should purchase foreign currency at a free-floating rate. And he wanted to force the republics to pay taxes to the central budget and restore financial discipline. In order to carry out those measures, Pavlov asked the Supreme Soviet to provide him with extraordinary powers. Gorbachev, Pavlov said, was too busy to deal with such matters; he even expressed concern for his health.[50]

After his report, Pavlov asked Speaker Lukyanov to arrange a special closed session, without television coverage or journalists. At this closed session, the head of the Soviet police forces, Boris Pugo, said that the country was awash with organized crime and torn apart by ethnic conflict. Minister of Defense Yazov spoke about the rapid decline of the Soviet armed forces.[51] Kryuchkov returned to Yavlinsky's scheme. In his view this plan would not save the country. The current crisis, he explained, was the work of the CIA "agents of influence," the radical forces that had destabilized the country in order to come to power. The KGB head said that the talk of "credits in the amount of 250 billion, 150, or 100 billion are fairy tales and illusions." The West, the KGB chief explained, was pragmatic and exclusively pursued its own interests. In the United States "they believe that the collapse of the Soviet Union is a foregone conclusion." Taking advantage of Soviet weakness, Western politicians and diplomats had now begun to "persistently urge, even demand in ultimatum-like ways that the USSR fulfill some specific conditions now in return for the West's vague promises and economic favors tomorrow." Among these conditions, Kryuchkov continued, was the "implementation of fundamental economic reforms in the country not in our way, but in a way conceived across the ocean." Washington wanted military cuts "below an admissible level," a rollback of Soviet "relations with friendly states," and "concessions to the West on the so-called Baltic question." Although couched in a conspiratorial mentality, this was still a correct estimate of American official intentions. Kryuchkov said he had constantly informed Gorbachev about this, but to no avail. In 1941, he said, Soviet intelligence had warned Stalin in vain about the impending Nazi attack. Future historians of 1991, he concluded, "will be struck by how we failed to pay proper attention to very serious things."[52]

Kryuchkov's speech was the main event of the session. As if on cue, "patriots" from the Soyuz faction and supporters of dictatorship rushed to the microphone and demanded Gorbachev's resignation. The news was leaked immediately to Moscow's liberal media. The *Independent Gazette* came out with a headline: "Joint forces of the Union legislature and the government can destroy the President, Novo-Ogaryovo, and perhaps our future." Journalists noticed that many conservative legislators, angry and fearful that the Union Treaty would abolish the Union assembly, were eager to support Pavlov's request. Liberals wondered if this was a conspiracy conducted behind Gorbachev's back and wondered why the Soviet President had allowed it to happen. For the deputies from Democratic Russia, all this was a real coup in the making. The mayor of Moscow, Gavriil Popov, rushed to Matlock to warn the US leadership and—through American channels—to alert Gorbachev. Shevardnadze sent an urgent appeal to his friend James Baker: the Americans' insistence on linking aid to Soviet concessions was provoking the hardliners. The United States must provide financial assistance to Gorbachev, Shevardnadze warned, or "you will find yourselves dealing with some beastly dictator, and you'll end up spending a lot more on defense than what Gorbachev is asking you for now."[53]

Gorbachev showed up at the Supreme Soviet only on the following day and with remarkable self-confidence faced down the rebellious deputies. At the same time, to the dismay of the DR liberals, he chose not to fire Pavlov or Kryuchkov. When Primakov discreetly wondered in Gorbachev's presence if he had entrusted too much of his security to the KGB, the Soviet leader laughed him off. Gorbachev, with his boundless ego, simply could not imagine that his appointees might challenge him.[54]

The political crisis in Moscow, as described in the previous chapter, became the subject of important conversations between Bush and Yeltsin in the Oval Office, during the visit of the Russian President-elect to the United States. Bush asked about Yavlinsky's plan. The Russian leader lied: "I received a copy on the steps of the plane, so I have no opinion yet." In fact, Yavlinsky had spent several hours with the Russian President in Moscow, discussing the program. "Yeltsin was very receptive and supportive," Yavlinsky reported to Allison. The economist misread Yeltsin's mind again. For the Russian President, Yavlinsky's initiative was a betrayal: the Grand Bargain was a rescue anchor for Gorbachev and the central government. Yeltsin wanted the Americans to invest in his "Russia," not in Gorbachev's Soviet Union.[55]

Bush made one more effort to discuss the implications of the Great Bargain. At the suggestion of the NSC's Ed Hewett he invited to his home residence at Kennebunkport a select group of American scholars who were Soviet experts. Bush asked many questions. He was especially concerned as to how the Soviet Union would be governed given Yeltsin's challenge to Gorbachev. Timothy Colton from Harvard recalls giving the following reply: "It would be like the President of the United States having control over only the states west of the Mississippi, while his rival would control the eastern half, as in the RSFSR." That was imaginative, but hardly a conceivable scenario. Arnold Horelick from RAND formulated a crucial Western interest: "What matters is that the economy of the USSR, and especially the Russian economy, should evolve in ways that do not make its viability dependent on authoritarian political structures or leave its assets and outputs too freely at the disposal of authoritarian rulers." In the end, the common verdict of the experts was: nothing would work in the Soviet economy until the Union Treaty was signed, and tax and investment policy were sorted out.[56]

Bush and Scowcroft were concerned about the mounting political momentum in the West in favor of Gorbachev. Boskin recalled later: "Mitterrand and John Major, but especially Helmut Kohl, were bugging President Bush because Kohl was trying to get the Russian troops out of East Germany."[57] Kohl was impressed by Shevardnadze's message, that it was vital "to somehow bring Yeltsin and Gorbachev together." The German Chancellor urged Bush to rally Western leaders in London around helping Gorbachev, and to tell him frankly "what we think he should do."[58] Bush, Baker, and Scowcroft discussed the options. The administration knew that, despite all their kind words, Western European leaders were not eager to open their wallets. The Germans, the primary potential donors to Gorbachev, no longer wanted to be left "holding the money bag alone." The Secretary of State advised the President to strike a fine balance between killing Grand Bargain and not being too "negative to Gorby." James Baker's notes prepared by his speechwriters read: "We cannot look like we are trying to humiliate the Soviets or treat them like Uganda." Baker advocated a "step by step" gradual approach as "an alternative to the Grand Bargain." This was the approach of goading Gorbachev to move swiftly toward "serious economic reforms" while Western governments would avoid any particular commitments. "Let nature take its course," Baker advised. The onus of decisions should be on the Soviets, "while we sound positive." He predicted that the appearance of political support from the G-7 would be sufficient to keep Gorbachev in power.[59]

Bush acted on this advice. He sent letters to John Major, Kohl, and other G-7 leaders, in which he made it absolutely clear that the US government would oppose large-scale financial assistance to Gorbachev *at any point*, without reference to what kind of reforms Gorbachev might agree to. If there were any credits, he wrote, they should be provided to Eastern Europeans, not to the USSR.[60]

"THE USSR IS NOT COSTA RICA!"

Robert Gates recalled that the CIA had learned much about Soviet secrets. The American intelligence agents, however, could not find out what kind of proposals Gorbachev would bring to London, because Gorbachev did not know himself.[61] Part of the problem was growing institutional chaos. In Rodric Braithwaite's estimate, the Soviet government had by that time "become a tribal, or at best a medieval, system in which everyone competes almost on equal terms for the ear of the chief."[62] Above all, Gorbachev still could not make up his mind about economic reforms. The US Embassy learned from its highly placed sources in Moscow that nobody in the Soviet government doubted any more that rapid transition to a market economy was necessary. The main source of hesitation was the political costs of such a transition. One expert from Nazarbayev's entourage informed the Americans that Gorbachev remained uncomfortable with the concept of private property: he kept asking whether there was some way to achieve the same level of economic efficiency through collective ownership. He was concerned that "the mafia would buy up all the enterprises that went on sale" and disenfranchise workers' collectives. According to another informant, Gorbachev half-jokingly remarked that he would not know what his economic package for the G-7 looked like "until he gets on the airplane for London."[63]

Gorbachev delegated preparations of his proposals for the G-7 meeting to the former Politburo member and economist Vadim Medvedev. Medvedev's group of experts met in Volynskoe near Moscow; two weeks before the London summit they produced a polemical text, which was not suitable for discussions with world leaders. Gorbachev asked Chernyaev to correct it. A week later Chernyaev learned that another group, this one appointed by Pavlov, had also prepared a text for London. This text would ultimately be sent to Western leaders in the guise of a personal letter from Gorbachev.[64] The prospect of Western financial assistance remained the most sensitive issue and the greatest source of uncertainty in discussions within Gorbachev's circle of advisors. One Soviet economist involved in the discussions confidentially informed the US Embassy in Moscow that "practically everything is tied to the amount of

Western support." He also said: "The greater the Western support, the further and faster the Soviets would be prepared to go toward the market, i.e. price liberalization, reducing budget deficits, etc."[65] Even the Pavlov Cabinet shared this mood, despite the dark musings of the Prime Minister and Kryuchkov. In the higher economic bureaucracy, the expectation of large amounts of Western money took on a momentum of its own. Every Soviet ministry, from defense to agriculture to heavy industry, wrote to Pavlov and his deputies about their need for foreign currency: to cover the cost of Soviet troops in Germany, to import grain, or simply to purchase the equipment and materials essential for Soviet industries. At Pavlov's request, ministers and the leaders of state enterprises prepared their lists of grandiose projects that required the "participation of foreign capital"—from the modernization of the oil and gas industries to the construction of a "railroad bridge" across Eurasia.[66]

At a brainstorming meeting before the London summit, Vadim Medvedev and economist Abalkin proposed showing their hand and revealing the depth of the Soviet budgetary and financial crisis. Pavlov, his deputy Shcherbakov, and the finance Minister Vladimir Orlov objected. They argued that such openness would have the opposite effect: Western banks would stop giving even short-term credits to the Soviet Union. In the end, Gorbachev waffled. He went to London without even a template of the Soviet Union's financial problems and needs. All the requests prepared by Soviet ministries and corporations remained at home, gathering dust.[67]

Before coming to London, Gorbachev attended a summit with Helmut Kohl in Kiev on 5 July. A lot had changed since their last meeting in Arkhyz. The Kremlin leader no longer held the keys to Germany's future. On 25 February 1991, in Budapest, Yazov and Bessmertnykh had signed the papers on behalf of the USSR to disband the military organization of the Warsaw Pact alliance. On 1 July, at the last meeting of the Warsaw Treaty Organization in Prague, Havel and other leaders of Eastern Europe declared an end to their political alliance. From the Soviet Union, Vice-President Yanayev was present. Also, as proposed by Ryzhkov, all fixed-price commitments within the Council for Mutual Economic Assistance (CMEA) had been replaced by fluctuating world prices. Since January 1991, the State Bank of the USSR had stopped receiving payments in "convertible rubles," a common trade currency within the bloc. The trade within CMEA collapsed. On 28 June 1991, at a meeting in Budapest, the emissaries of the Soviet Union and eight of its former satellites disbanded the economic community. Constructed fifty years earlier by Stalin's iron will, it now went up in smoke.

Since the summer of 1990, the Soviet leadership had good reason to suspect that Eastern European countries would try to join NATO. Václav Havel in

Prague, Árpád Göncz in Budapest, and since December 1990 the new Polish president Lech Wałęsa, did not want to place the security of the region in the hands of the OSCE. The breakdown of trade with the Soviet Union had given additional urgency to the common cry of the new Eastern European political elites: "to return to Europe" and distance themselves from Moscow. In the fall of 1990, Soviet intelligence reported that the governments of Czechoslovakia, Poland, and Hungary had begun approaching Western governments with requests to join NATO. The General Staff forced Shevardnadze's Foreign Ministry to offer Eastern European countries a set of bilateral treaties, with a special clause prohibiting both sides from joining any hostile alliances or making available their territories and infrastructures to forces of third countries. This was a plan for the "Finlandization" of Eastern Europe and a measure to prevent the expansion of NATO to the East. The Eastern European governments rejected these proposals. The liberal media in Moscow indignantly wrote about the "Kvitsinsky doctrine," named for Shevardnadze's deputy, Yuly Kvitsinsky—a reference to Brezhnev's doctrine of limited sovereignty.[68]

In a conversation with Kohl, the Soviet leader dismissed the rift between the USSR and its Eastern European allies as a temporary phenomenon. "They are fed up with us! But we're also fed up with them!" "We noticed," he said, that Eastern European countries "wanted a loophole to join other blocs." "NATO?" asked Kohl. Gorbachev avoided a direct answer and spoke darkly about "some kind of game." Chernyaev viewed this exchange as a probe on Gorbachev's part to have a Soviet-German agreement on the future of Eastern Europe. Kohl called Gorbachev's worries "exaggerated." There were "no hostile alliances" in Europe anymore, the Chancellor said.[69]

Kohl promised Gorbachev that the reformed Soviet Union would become part of a new Europe, and that its economy would be integrated into the liberal economic order. The German Chancellor urged Gorbachev not to ambush the London summit by requesting a big financial package. He warned Gorbachev that this might leave both sides embarrassed: the West would not be able to provide the money, and Gorbachev would end up looking like a bidder whose bid had been refused. Kohl's economic aide at the G-7 told Gorbachev that Pavlov's anti-crisis program should be aligned with the IMF's demands. Gorbachev snapped back: "The USSR is not Costa Rica!"[70] This emotional remark revealed the Soviet leader's pride. He desperately needed Western money, yet he did not want to appear in London as a leader in financial distress. He continued to view himself as a global statesman.

And yet all participants of the Kiev meeting could see that the Soviet edifice was falling apart. On the road from the airport to Kiev, a demonstration of

Ukrainian nationalists carried signs reading: "Kohl yes! Gorbachev no!" On Kiev's main street, Kohl and Gorbachev exited the limousine to meet the local people but found themselves in the midst of a crowd demanding an "independent Ukraine" and waving blue-yellow flags of the Ukrainian state of 1918. The German guests felt awkward. After the meeting was over, the official cortege took a detour around Kiev to avoid further encounters with protesters. On his flight back to Moscow, Gorbachev indulged in geopolitical reflections. Kohl, he said to his aides, had "set his sights on Ukraine," but German ambitions could be checked. "Kohl understands that he cannot digest the USSR. Moreover, without us, he cannot digest Europe and cannot get rid of the Americans. Thus, he would do anything to help our resurrection and to make us stand up next to him."[71] Gorbachev's musings did not match reality. The German Chancellor, for all his affection for Gorbachev, had his sights set on a special partnership with the United States and the construction of a stable NATO and prosperous European Union. After the Kiev summit, Kohl called Bush to reassure him that Gorbachev "would not spring any surprises" at the G-7. This was a clear reference to the Grand Bargain. Bush replied curtly: "I am very comfortable with that agenda if it works out that way."[72]

Shortly before going to London, Gorbachev had a long and emotional meeting with Yavlinsky. He told him that he would not present the Grand Bargain at the G-7 summit. Yavlinsky then refused to accompany Gorbachev to London, went to his dacha near Moscow, and disconnected his phone.[73] A few days later, Gorbachev received a personal letter from Bush, with a polite but firm verdict: "If you still feel that a rapid transition to the market is too risky . . . then we will find it harder to help you."[74] Gorbachev's first impulse was to ignore the American diktat. On the evening before he traveled to London, the Soviet leader signed and sent application letters to the IMF, EBRD, and other economic financial organizations requesting that full membership be offered to the Soviet Union. And he sent another appeal to G-7 leaders.[75]

THE LONDON TALKS

When Graham Allison learned that Yavlinsky was not coming with Gorbachev to London, he faxed a frantic letter to President Bush. The US administration, he wrote, should choose a path of "deep engagement" with the Soviets. In 1989–90, he argued, Bush and Baker had guided Gorbachev and Shevardnadze to act according to an American "framework of ideas and ideals." The Soviet leadership had embraced these ideas as their own, and "this process brought the Cold War to an end." Now, Allison insisted, Bush and Baker should lead Gorbachev and his ministers towards the economic transformation of the Soviet Union and its integration into the world economy. Allison called this program "post-war transformation without occupation."[76]

Bush was determined to lead, but not in the way Allison proposed. The White House continued to pursue the short-term vision of locking in the Cold War gains. In a conversation with his friend Manfred Wörner, Bush said: "I do not want [Gorbachev] to use the G-7 as a springboard to go to the NATO summit." This summit was scheduled for November in Rome, but the American President was already worried that the Soviet leader, still hugely popular in the West, could muddy the waters of the trans-Atlantic alliance with his rhetoric of a "Common European Home." Wörner agreed: "If we can avoid it, we should."[77]

On 14 July, the US President and members of his administration landed in Paris to meet with President Mitterrand on France's national holiday. The next morning, the Americans arrived in London and held preliminary talks with John Major and other G-7 participants. The purpose of these meetings was, as Scowcroft put it, to patch up any "quiet division in our ranks" over the question of financial support to the USSR. Mitterrand and Andreotti expressed sympathy for the Soviet program "of mixed economy and socialist goals." Andreotti reminded Bush that Italy, after the end of World War II, had not deregulated prices overnight. It would be politically dangerous to quickly impose neoliberal conditions on Soviet society after the collapse of communism. Kohl and Major suggested that a special commission should be set up with the brief of helping the Soviet Union. The President of the European Commission, Jacques Delors, and the Dutch Prime Minister, Ruud Lubbers, both spoke favorably about restructuring Soviet foreign debts to enable trade between the Soviet Union and its former allies.[78]

The Americans killed off all of these proposals outright. Bush, helped by Brady, opposed the idea of providing the Soviets with "maneuvering room" on the payment of their debts. Like Latin American countries in debt, the Soviets should bow to the IMF. Gorbachev should just accept the neoliberal Washington Consensus: radical deregulation and privatization, and then competition for private foreign investment. The European Bank for Reconstruction and Development (EBRD) should not credit the Soviet economy: any "special deal" for Gorbachev would send Poland and Czechoslovakia "the wrong message" that they were being neglected.[79]

Bush and his team did not conceal that they had geopolitical priorities on their minds. The idea of Germany, France, and Italy acting as benefactors towards the Soviet Union contradicted the idea of a US-led Europe, as well as the pivotal role of NATO. At a meeting with the German delegation in London, Bush disliked French agnosticism about NATO's future mission. "Let's be sure we don't reopen things," he said. "As long as Soviet missiles are aimed at the

United States, I know who the enemy is." Bush also supported Japan's Prime Minister Toshiki Kaifu, who wanted to link foreign assistance to a territorial issue: the return by the Soviet Union of the four islands that Stalin had annexed in 1945. Aside from the Germans, the Japanese were the only large-scale source of cash.[80]

At the opening session of the G-7, which took place in Gorbachev's absence, Bush shared the advice he had received from the scholars gathered at Kennebunkport. He also raised other points against the "Grand Bargain": the Soviet state continued to spend a lot of money on its military needs, including modernization of strategic missiles, and Gorbachev was still unwilling to set the Baltic republics free. The US President also pitched the priority of helping the Eastern European states, rather than the Soviet Union.[81] Some Western leaders in London felt embarrassed. The American team was finding every possible reason not to help Gorbachev. The Prime Minister of Canada, Brian Mulroney, made a moving speech. In 1985, he said, then Vice-President Bush had attended Chernenko's funeral in Moscow. What would Bush have done then if, meeting him after the funeral, Gorbachev had said: *I will free Eastern Europe, I will dismantle the Warsaw Pact, a united Germany will join NATO, a UN force will start a war against Iraq, the USSR will sign the CFE and START agreements, there will be elections and democracy, I will develop personal ties with America, and economic ties with the West will grow*. "If Gorbachev had said these things in 1985," Mulroney concluded, "I would have hurried in with a check." Andreotti reminded the group of what Reagan had said in 1985: "I don't know if Gorbachev will succeed, but none of us should have on our conscience the responsibility of not helping."[82] Yet nobody at the G-7 wanted to question American leadership. And nobody wanted to hold out the money bag.

A final summary of the G-7 discussions on the USSR included five "main tests of Soviet good intentions" based on the US approach. Those tests constituted: achieving a balance between the Soviet Center and the republics; no less radical economic reform than in Central and Eastern Europe; a tight macroeconomic policy in the near future; a commitment to drastic reductions in military expenditures; and adequate conditions for foreign investment.[83] During lunch that day, Mulroney turned to Kohl and asked him: what if a month from now Gorbachev is overthrown and people are complaining that we have not done enough? Would the German Chancellor still stick to the agreed policy? Kohl allegedly replied that, after all, Gorbachev said himself that he did not expect any massive Western assistance. "What we're proposing is what he needs and what he wants."[84]

On 16 July, Gorbachev arrived in London with his large Soviet team. Ambassador Rodric Braithwaite formally welcomed the Gorbachevs at Heathrow

Airport. He had already read Gorbachev's message to the G-7 leaders and found it "flatulent in the Russian way: words, not action, again." The Soviet leader, he noticed, was "full of beans," but Raisa looked gray and badly run down: "She has obviously been acting as the emotional shock absorber during this very difficult time." Primakov, who was Gorbachev's fixer for the G-7, had already been in London for several days. Ignoring tips from Western colleagues, in the Western media he doggedly tried to drum up support for financial aid. But after each conversation with his Western colleagues he became gloomier. Gorbachev's interpreter, Pavel Palazhchenko, noticed that the Western media lionized Yavlinsky, but privately Western interlocutors "were letting us know that they did not take his program seriously."[85] American leadership was effective in blocking any Western European temptations to offer Gorbachev assistance.

Bush's primary concern remained START: it was not clear until the last moment whether the treaty would be signed. The leaders of Soviet military industries, the General Staff, and arms control experts complained about unequal and even humiliating terms coming from the American side. The director and chief designer of "Yuzhmash," the giant missile plant in Dnepropetrovsk, Ukraine, argued against heavy cuts of the "Topol" (SS-18) missiles that his plant manufactured. This was the only remaining factor, he argued, that made the Americans sit down and negotiate with the Soviet Union. There was also the issue of money: the destruction of heavy missiles, monitoring, and inspections would cost the Soviet budget several billion rubles. And what would then happen to huge Soviet enterprises and tens of thousands of skilled engineers and workers?[86] Gorbachev, however, did not want to argue with the General Staff and arms control experts. As the London summit approached, their resistance melted. The absence of an agreement on START would mean that Gorbachev and Bush would have no summit in Moscow, and perhaps would not cooperate in London. And the leaders of the military-industrial complex, like the other heads of large Soviet industrial enterprises, yearned to receive Western financial assistance. One day before the G-7 summit, Yazov, the head of the military-industrial complex Oleg Baklanov, and other members of the inter-agency committee reluctantly signed off on a draft treaty that the Americans could accept. When Alexander Bessmertnykh received this news from Moscow, he rushed to the US residence in London at Winfield House and jubilantly announced to Bush: "This is the end of a ten-year-long journey, Mr. President."[87]

In the early morning of 17 July, Gorbachev began by meeting with President Mitterrand and the President of the EBRD, Jacques Attali. Mitterrand encouraged him to engage the West in some large-scale projects that the Pavlov plan envisaged. The French President assured Gorbachev that the Italian, German, and French leaderships supported him. Attali went further: he identified Bush as the main opponent of a massive assistance program. He called the American preference for Eastern Europe "absurd," because the emergence of a big Soviet market would help Eastern European countries as well. Attali was catering to Gorbachev's illusions at the expense of the Americans.[88]

Then the Soviet motorcade brought Gorbachev, accompanied by Shcherbakov, Primakov, and Chernyaev, to the American residence in London for a late informal breakfast. Bush was in an excellent mood, and asked Gorbachev cheerfully: "What's up between you and Yeltsin now? Does he support you? Do you support him?" Gorbachev, however, had prepared a statement for Bush. "On the basis of my information," he began pensively, "I know that the US president . . . has not yet made up his mind on the main question: What kind of Soviet Union does the United States need?" Some of his advisors doubted American intentions, though Gorbachev believed in Bush's good faith. But he needed confirmation. The West had found $100 billion to conduct a regional war in the Persian Gulf, but it could not find the money to help the Soviet Union embark on a new economic system. "So, what is my friend George Bush going to do? What does he want? And when we meet with other colleagues, will they say: Way to go, Gorbachev! Keep on going, good luck to you! This is your soup to cook, not ours."[89]

Chernyaev noticed that Bush had interrupted his breakfast and his face had darkened. His gaze shifted from Gorbachev to Baker and Scowcroft. For the US President, the Gulf War, which Gorbachev had dismissively called a "regional war," was the crowning achievement of his presidency. Gorbachev had also bluntly, if correctly, identified American "non-entanglement" with Soviet economic reforms. After a brief pause, Bush responded calmly, but coldly, as if swallowing an insult. "We seek a democratic, market-oriented Soviet Union, integrated into the world economy, having found a resolution of the problems between the center and the republics." The latter, he added, would be "essential for capital flows." Bush was also forced to address the issue: was the Soviet Union still the enemy for the United States? He personally did not believe it. However, the Soviet Union continued to modernize its missiles, and Congress was urging the White House to retaliate.[90] If the USSR was no longer the enemy of the US, Bush seemed to say, Gorbachev should take even more drastic steps to help allay American suspicions and fears.

"I want that unprecedented kind of cooperation to continue," Bush said. "We don't seek economic catastrophe in the Soviet Union, and we know that the demise of the Soviet Union is not in our interests . . . If I have projected something different, I apologize."[91] The President's apology removed the cloud hanging over the conversation. The two leaders began to talk about the outcome of the London summit. The West, said Bush, could only promise the offer of technical advice to the Soviet Union. In the Soviet account of the meeting, Gorbachev said: "You also can raise the question of dollars." However, the American record omits this comment.[92]

The two sides ended the meeting with contrasting impressions. The Americans interpreted Gorbachev's "mini-offensive" as the need for a psychological boost following his failure to get more Western help in London. After lunch, Bush took Gorbachev aside for a confidential talk about START; soon Baker and Scowcroft joined the huddle and then flashed their thumbs up: the experts in Washington had approved the Soviet proposals. Bush recalled: "It was a momentous and exhilarating moment: we had just reached a historic agreement to reduce our arsenals by several thousand of the deadliest of our nuclear weapons." On the Soviet side, Chernyaev believed his boss had spoken tactlessly and revealed his weak hand. Perhaps this was Gorbachev's reaction to reports from Kryuchkov and the GRU. "The Americans, straightforward and trustful by nature," wrote Chernyaev in his diary, "simply could not understand why 'Michael' needed that sort of game." Within his narrow circle of advisors, Gorbachev returned to his "interrogation" of Bush several times; yet he did not mention the episode in his memoirs. The Soviet leader had invited Bush to come to Moscow, and the President had accepted. That was Gorbachev's only achievement in London.[93]

Gorbachev's appearance at Lancaster House for a special session of the G-7 was a rehearsed performance. The Soviet leader kept his word that he would not depart from the prepared script. In his speech, even longer than his usual monologues, he defended his choice of a "mixed economy." He was committed to economic freedom, but he did not want to move faster than the people could bear. He digressed into Russian history to explain why most Russians, former peasants, preferred collective forms of property. Mitterrand and Andreotti backed him. At the end of the meeting the Soviet leader pocketed the modest pledge from Western leaders to continue consultations between the USSR and the rotating President of the G-7, as well as with Western finance ministers.[94]

Bush and Scowcroft still feared that Gorbachev would nevertheless pull the "rabbit" of Yavlinsky-Allison's program out of his hat at the last moment. They were relieved, therefore, when he failed to do so. After the G-7 meeting, Scowcroft said to Bush: "Gorbachev came to collect what he obviously felt was his due, but he never really made his case." Bush responded: "The guy kind of bombed, didn't he? It's funny. He's always been his own best salesman, but not this time. I wonder if he isn't kind of out of touch."[95] Gorbachev seemed to believe that he had played the long game. Margaret Thatcher had urged him in London: "Don't let go of them! You should demand that they act on what they have said, that they put their money where their mouth is." This conversation with the retired Iron Lady, Gorbachev's interpreter noticed, gave the Soviet leader "a good shot in the arm."[96]

On 19 July, Gorbachev flew back to Moscow. As always, the members of his Security Council, the top Party leadership, and the entire Cabinet were waiting for him at Vnukovo-2 Airport in Moscow. As Gorbachev descended from the plane and began to talk to the government officials, one member of his delegation recalled that many of them "had long faces." Kryuchkov's expression was inscrutable, as always.[97] The high-level government officials, despite all the negative warnings, still counted on Gorbachev's magic charisma to yield results. On previous occasions, the Soviet leader had repeatedly managed to extract billions of dollars from his meetings with his Western friends and partners. This time, though, he had brought nothing. On this occasion the magician had failed; his bold-faced attempts to obtain Western assistance had run up against the wall of the Washington Consensus and American skepticism. The salesman of perestroika was facing bankruptcy.

CHAPTER 10

CONSPIRACY

A renewed federation is the legal successor to the Union of Soviet Socialist Republics. The Soviet Union will continue to act as a great world power.
Mikhail Gorbachev, 2 August 1991[1]

TROIKA

In Moscow, Gorbachev's return from London was universally received as a failure. The hordes of critics saw his world statesmanship not as an asset, but as a search for self-promotion. And his Party comrades were openly seeking another leader. On 26 July 1991, the Party Plenum voted for Gorbachev's program of "democratic socialism": instead of heated debates, which he expected, there was indifference and ennui. Nobody cared about Gorbachev's words and programs anymore. The Plenum enthusiastically greeted Anatoly Lukyanov, who projected the image of a confident leader. The majority applauded when Lukyanov urged placing the Party again at the helm of the reforms from above, "against the populist forces of *demokratura*." The latter, he explained, wanted to impose an anti-communist dictatorship in the guise of democracy. He concluded to a standing ovation: "the Party must not lose the President, as much as the President cannot afford to lose his Party." [2] One participant recalled Lukyanov's message as follows: I am the leader that you need.[3] It was agreed to convene an emergency Party Congress in November; everyone thought that this would finally change the person at the top.

Gorbachev returned to his main goal: the Union Treaty. The Soviet leader refused to see that its signing could not solve the underlying problems of the economy and governance. Gorbachev's obsession with legal issues only invited Yeltsin, Kravchuk, and other republican leaders to press the Center for more concessions. Yeltsin refused to agree with a federal tax that would sustain the Soviet government. Georgy Shakhnazarov urged his boss to stop appeasing Yeltsin. Instead, Shakhnazarov argued, Gorbachev should focus on his work with Western leaders and financial institutions on some form of assistance to the Soviet Union.[4]

Shakhnazarov also urged his boss to pay more attention to Ukraine. Each of Gorbachev's concessions to Yeltsin only increased separatist trends in the second largest Slavic republic. On 11 May, the Ukrainian Supreme Soviet supported the idea of a national currency, the *hryvna*. On 7 June, following Yeltsin's example, the Ukrainian Supreme Soviet passed a law placing all Union economic assets on the territory of the republics under its jurisdiction. After Yeltsin became the Russian president, the Ukrainian legislature had decided that the Union Treaty needed additional "expertise" before the republic would join it. Leonid Kravchuk, leader of the Ukrainian Supreme Soviet, decided to emulate Yeltsin's success and become president of the Ukrainian republic. With an eye towards a future presidential campaign, Kravchuk stopped attending the meetings at Novo-Ogaryovo.[5]

On 23 July, after three months of talks, delegations from nine republics and their autonomous regions gathered to sanction the fragile consensus. The Supreme Soviet of the USSR, after weeks of fierce resistance from many anxious deputies, authorized the President to sign the Union Treaty with a vague formula: "after making certain modifications." Gorbachev arrived at Novo-Ogaryovo, accompanied by Lukyanov, Pavlov, and government ministers. Gorbachev's aides had prepared a draft package, the outcome of laborious negotiations and quid pro quo agreements, for the final vote. Gorbachev opened the session and announced: "I already feel dangerous tendencies. We should finish with the Treaty quickly. Very quickly!" And yet the meeting passed without an agreement or a specific deadline.[6]

Gorbachev, as it turned out, had planned another, more restricted meeting. On 29 July, he invited Yeltsin and the Kazakh leader Nursultan Nazarbayev to Novo-Ogaryovo. Nazarbayev was supposed to play a mediator's role between the two rivals. The troika sat and talked into the night behind closed doors; even aides were not invited. In the early morning they came to a provisional agreement. Its essence was the following: Gorbachev fully accepted that Yeltsin would be the only one to sign the treaty on behalf of the Russian Federation and its fifteen autonomous regions. The Soviet President also agreed that the Congress of People's Deputies of the USSR would be allowed to lapse, and the Supreme Soviet of the USSR would be put out of political existence as well, without waiting for a new constitution. Furthermore, Gorbachev complied with Yeltsin's demand to dismiss Yanayev, Pavlov, Kryuchkov, Yazov, and Pugo.

Instead of Pavlov, Gorbachev suggested, Nazarbayev should become the prime minister of the largely ceremonial Union government. In return for all these concessions, Yeltsin pledged to support Gorbachev as the president of a new confederate Union. He also provisionally agreed that the Russian Federation would pay a federal tax to finance the central Union government "at fixed rates, per agreements with republics on the basis of expense items presented by the Union." This was a remarkably vague formula, subject to interpretation. Gorbachev later claimed it was his major achievement.[7]

In his memoirs Gorbachev presented this all-night meeting as a preliminary conversation. It was, in reality, a secret deal between the three leaders that would destroy the central powers and empower Yeltsin and other republics. The troika decided to have the signing ceremony on 20 August, at a time when the Supreme Soviet of the USSR and the parliaments of all republics would be on vacation: sunbathing, swimming, and picking mushrooms in the woods. The leaders agreed that their deal, especially personal changes of leadership, would remain a secret. Yeltsin was especially nervous as if he feared the meeting could have been tapped and leaked. Gorbachev agreed with him: "One did not need witnesses for this occasion."[8]

Gorbachev apparently thought that the end, the Union Treaty, justified the secretive means. He consulted the leaders of four Central Asian republics as to the ceremony date, but without sharing other details. The Central Asian leaders had been consistently in favor of the treaty, eager to maintain the flow of money and subsidies. President Islam Karimov of Uzbekistan said he would add his signature. But what about Ukraine, which was overlooked in this arrangement? Gorbachev's aides, Shakhnazarov and Grigory Revenko, an ethnic Ukrainian and former head of Kiev's Party organization, warned him not to hold the ceremony without Ukraine as it would justify Ukrainian separatism.[9] Gorbachev hoped for a snowball effect, which would induce that second Slavic republic to join as well.

In the morning, after a short nap, Gorbachev showed up in his office on the Old Square in an ebullient mood. He told Shakhnazarov and Revenko to start working on the logistics for a signing ceremony in the Kremlin's sumptuous St George Hall. Gorbachev would be the first to sign the document. Each signatory would receive a copy of the treaty, written in Russian only, and in morocco binding; the pages would be sewn together with silk cord. The signing ceremony would be televised and marked with special coins, stamps, and commemorative pamphlets.[10] Revenko shared the news with Chernyaev, who was pleasantly surprised: "I really wondered if he would pull it off," he said about Gorbachev's agreement with Yeltsin. "It's now a totally different situation." Gorbachev's interpreter, Pavel Palazhchenko, was also pleased: Gorbachev's position would be stronger with two treaties under his belt: START and the Union Treaty. And the Americans would now perhaps encourage Yeltsin to keep his promises to Gorbachev.[11]

Other observers were much more skeptical. British Ambassador Braithwaite had long considered the Union Treaty "a meaningless document which will serve as the starting point, not the conclusion, of the fundamental constitutional and political debate."[12] James Baker, who had come to Moscow to prepare for the US-Soviet summit, had a dinner with his friend Shevardnadze, who said that the treaty "would not discharge the situation." Gorbachev, the Georgian said, had made a mistake by not supporting Yeltsin's decree against the Party. If he had, Shevardnadze argued, he "would have received support from the whole nation."[13]

THE LAST SUMMIT

The Soviet leader planned to get his agreement with Yeltsin in time for his summit with President Bush. The American delegation landed at Moscow's Sheremetyevo Airport late on 29 July, while Gorbachev was conducting his secret talks in Novo-Ogaryovo. Vice-President Yanayev greeted the US President at the airport. Sitting with Bush in the limousine on the way to the American ambassador's residence in Moscow, Yanayev never stopped joking. Yanayev's roots traced back to a peasant family on the Volga: like others, his family had suffered the privations of Stalinist-era collectivization, famine, and the terrible losses of World War II. His Party career had given Yanayev a powerful social lift. He became a "party" man in a different sense of the word: he was in charge of meeting foreign youth delegations, which involved endless schmoozing and drinking. Now he tested his social skills on Bush. The US President found Yanayev "engaging and pleasant, with a good sense of humor," and different from what he had read about him in the CIA dossier.[14]

George Bush came to Moscow with one thing on his mind: to sign the strategic arms control treaty. The talks on this document had long turned into a drag on the US-Soviet relationship. Brent Scowcroft and other American officials had continued to squeeze as much American advantage as possible from the embattled Gorbachev and his crisis-ridden military.[15] On the plane, Bush worried whether the Soviet top military brass would continue to obey their commander-in-chief. The Chairman of the Joint Chiefs of Staff, Colin Powell, who had recently traveled to Moscow, reported that marshals and generals still supported Gorbachev, but assumed that the military would push back to protect their institutions against the hated "democrats" and political chaos. Powell dismissed, however, the possibility of a military coup: "I don't see any guys on horseback taking over." Bush was not persuaded by this complacency. CIA experts had warned him that hardline Party leaders might act against Gorbachev, and that the military would support them if they did. The US President was determined to tread very carefully in Moscow.[16]

The Moscow summit opened with a long conversation between Gorbachev and Bush in the Kremlin's St Catherine Hall. Gorbachev looked surprisingly fresh and upbeat. He told Bush about the secret agreement with Yeltsin and Nazarbayev. Gorbachev explained in detail what would happen after the Union Treaty was signed: "The process will continue until Ukraine decides to sign." In Ukraine, Gorbachev argued confidently, two-thirds of the people, "if not three-quarters," were in favor of preserving the Union. Then Gorbachev asked Bush again for "real support" in order "to win the decisive battle for reform." Bush repeated the old line: the American capacity to provide assistance to the Soviet economy was limited. The US President was relieved when the Soviet leader did not push this further.[17]

When the other members of the delegations joined the conversation, Gorbachev urged the Americans to invest in the Soviet economy. Nazarbayev, whom Gorbachev invited to take part in the talks, wanted to cement a major business deal between Kazakhstan and the multi-national oil company Chevron to develop the enormous Tengiz oil field along the Caspian Sea. There was a lot of red tape on the Soviet side, but also many obstacles on the American side. The Jackson-Vanik amendment to the US-Soviet Trade Act of 1974 had linked American credits and investments in Soviet projects to changes in citizens' freedom of emigration from the USSR. On the eve of the summit a new Soviet law had provided for free emigration rights. In reponse, Bush sent to Congress a proposal to suspend the Jackson-Vanik sanctions. He also promised to help Nazarbayev on the Tengiz deal.[18]

Bush rejected, however, full Soviet membership of the IMF. "The Soviet economy is so potentially enormous," he explained, "it could dominate other countries."[19] In 1944, when Stalin was in the Kremlin, the Americans had offered the Soviet Union the option of being a third founding member of the IMF and the World Bank, in an effort to include the Soviet Union in a future liberal economic order. Stalin had instead chosen economic autarky.[20] In July 1991, Gorbachev was paying for Stalin's decision. It was impossible to erase four decades of confrontation in just a couple of years, no matter how many concessions and how much charm the Soviet leader displayed.

Yeltsin was invited to join the meeting, but he refused to play second fiddle at Gorbachev's summit. He invited Bush to come to his new Kremlin office for separate talks. Scowcroft advised Bush against going: he believed Yeltsin was capable of anything—even possibly claiming a separate seat for the Russian republic at the United Nations. The Americans agreed to come on condition that the meeting would be brief, unofficial, and without media participation. The Russian President arrived ten minutes late, forcing Bush to wait. He then boasted that Gorbachev had finally agreed to recognize Russia's sovereignty and proposed that the Americans "formalize the relationship." Bush feigned surprise: "Which relationship? Do you mean the US and Russia or yours with the Center?" Secretary of State Baker intervened: "President Yeltsin, the answer will depend on what the Union treaty says about the authority of the republics to enter into agreements with other countries. We will have to see this new Union treaty." Yeltsin insisted that the treaty "recognized Russia and the other republics as sovereign states" that "could pursue their own independent foreign policy, including foreign economic policy." He was citing from the text that he, Gorbachev, and Nazarbayev had agreed to sign.[21] When Bush finally managed to leave Yeltsin's office, he noticed journalists waiting for a press conference. Yeltsin began to talk to the media, but the American President ran out of patience: "We've got to go. I am late," Bush said, and went with his entourage to his limousine. He complained to Scowcroft that Yeltsin had "ambushed" him.[22] Yeltsin continued his bombastic self-assertion at the reception to honor Bush, at the Palace of the Facets in the Kremlin. He violated the protocol repeatedly and even made a crude attempt to escort Barbara Bush to dinner. The Americans were appalled.[23]

On the morning of 31 July, Gorbachev hosted the American delegation at his presidential dacha in Novo-Ogaryovo. The Soviet leader was eager to have some quality time with the Americans, away from the media, the pomp, and Yeltsin's pranks. Finally, after a pause of nine months, Gorbachev and Bush were able to speak face to face. They strolled for a quarter of a mile in the woods surrounding the complex, and then sat, together with their teams, on a sunny veranda overlooking the Moscow river. Gorbachev finally had an opportunity to explain to Bush in private, one on one, what he had been through since September 1990. His "turn to the right" had been required to buy time for perestroika—to fend off the conservative reaction. Now he was free to move forward at full speed, to reconstruct the Soviet Union, and build, together with Bush, a new and peaceful world order. "Totalitarian, authoritarian regimes are leaving the scene," Gorbachev said. "We engendered this change." At the same time, he warned, the United States should not fall into the temptation of pressing its advantage and assuming world dominance. The coming world would be multipolar: a reformed Soviet Union would help the Americans promote democracy and stem instability and chaos. Moscow could contribute to the peace processes in the Middle East and South Africa, and mediate in the India-Pakistan conflict. Palazhchenko, who interpreted, recalled Gorbachev speaking about "a kind of axis, which our two countries could provide."[24]

Bush did not interrupt the flow of Gorbachev's thinking. Scowcroft, who was responsible for taking notes, was jet-lagged and dozed through most of Gorbachev's perorations. When Bush finally spoke, he said: "In this changing world, we feel comfortable with a strong, economically powerful, changed Soviet Union." He said that the United States would not play China off against the USSR. Baker chimed in to speak about the Middle East: "This is an area you can point to as a partnership—not just cooperation." The Americans welcomed the establishment of Soviet-Israeli diplomatic relations. The Soviet Foreign Minister, Aleksandr Bessmertnykh, who was also present, suggested that an Israeli-Palestinian peace conference could be held in a neutral place and moderated by Bush and Gorbachev together. "Maybe in Oslo," Baker offered.[25]

After some time, Baker left and returned to the meeting with somber face. "It has just been reported by the AP," he said, "that a Lithuanian customs post on the border with Belorussia has been attacked by armed men, who killed a number of customs officials." This was a humiliating reminder to the Soviet leader, who had just been theorizing about a new world order, that he could not stem the chaos in his own country. Flustered, Gorbachev asked Chernyaev to call the KGB chief, Kryuchkov, to find out what happened. Chernyaev's first thought was that somebody must have staged a provocation to embarrass Gorbachev in front of the Americans. Many years later the truth remains unknown. The Lithuanians blamed the tragic accident on Soviet riot police, the OMON, but it could easily have been a criminal conflict over illegal trade across the republican borders.[26]

Gorbachev and Bush also discussed the collapse of Yugoslavia. Fighting had rapidly escalated in that country between the Serb-dominated Yugoslav Army and the republics of Slovenia and Croatia, which had recently proclaimed their independence. Bush and Gorbachev knew that Germany's Chancellor Kohl wanted to recognize Slovenia and Croatia. But Gorbachev was against this: Yugoslavia's disintegration seemed to mirror the separatism of republics in the Soviet Union. For instance, he said, Belorussia wanted to reacquire territory that had been given to Lithuania when the latter republic became incorporated into the Soviet Union after World War II. In addition, the eastern part of Estonia was settled mainly by Russians and Ukrainians, who might rebel if the Baltic states fully seceded from the USSR. Bush decided to show empathy: "We see your problems in the way Yeltsin conducted himself at dinner last night. We want . . . to be more helpful."[27]

Back at the Kremlin in late afternoon, Gorbachev and Bush signed the START agreement with its voluminous protocols. The treaty reduced the Soviet strategic arsenal by 35 percent, and US strategic forces by 25 percent. Bush achieved what he had long wanted, but he was overwhelmed by the ceremony.

"Idealism is not dead," he wrote in his diary, "and these significant reductions in these damn intercontinental ballistic missiles is a good thing."[28] For the Soviet side, the internal crisis eclipsed the celebrations. During the signing ceremony, Palazhchenko leaned over to Dennis Ross, Baker's aide, and whispered: "If only the conflicts and tensions we've got in our own country could be tidied up as neatly as the ones we've had with the outside world."[29] The Soviet military watched the ceremony with blank faces, yet with clear disapproval. Marshal Yazov called the treaty "balanced," yet he did not believe in what he officially said.[30] Everyone was aware of the profound inequality of the two sides: Bush presided over a military hegemony with unrivaled financial power and global alliances, whereas Gorbachev was a hapless hostage to economic chaos, the leader of a bankrupt state. The world was already unipolar, and Gorbachev's political future depended on Bush's support.

On 1 August, after the meetings in Moscow, the American delegation departed for Kiev. This trip was dictated by protocol, geography, and American domestic politics. Bush knew that Ukrainian-American communities in the United States were pushing for complete independence of the Ukrainian republic from Moscow, which they viewed as a seat of "colonial tyranny." Gorbachev recalled in his memoirs that the US president promised not to do anything that could generate support for separatist tendencies in Ukraine. Actually, in Moscow, Bush was moved by Gorbachev's friendship. He made a decision to be an advocate of Gorbachev's treaty in Ukraine.[31] On board Air Force One, Bush once more enjoyed the company of Yanayev, whom Gorbachev had sent to accompany the American delegation. Bush in particular liked Yanayev's stories about fishing and even promised to send him colorful American fishing lures—unavailable in Soviet stores. The US President also found time to amend the draft speech that his staff had prepared for him to deliver in Kiev. The main idea in the speech was that democracy and freedom could be more successfully built in a Ukraine that remained in a reformed Soviet Union led by Gorbachev. Bush was also thinking of the ongoing violence in Yugoslavia, which was already being replicated in Soviet republics of the Caucasus and in Moldova. He dictated two new sentences for his Kiev speech: "Americans will not support those who seek independence in order to replace a far-off tyranny with a local despotism. They will not aid those who promote a suicidal nationalism based upon ethnic hatred." A few minutes later Ambassador Matlock, sitting in another section of the plane, saw the draft and considered those two sentences an awkward interference in Ukrainian politics. The presidential speechwriter, however, told him that it was too late to change anything.[32]

The official visit to Kiev started with a meeting between Bush and top Ukrainian officials in the beautiful Mariinsky Palace, built by Bartolomeo

Rastrelli for the Russian Empress Elizabeth in the 1740s. Three weeks earlier Ukrainian officials had told Chancellor Kohl in this very palace that they did not want to leave the central Soviet state. Irredentist groups of nationalists, they argued, were very small, and "the number of Russians in the Ukraine was 10 million, especially in the [Donbass] area." As a result, full independence "might lead to violence or upheaval."[33] Now, Bush read in the CIA background papers that the Ukrainian leader Leonid Kravchuk tended to support the idea of a voluntary federated union. Kravchuk, however, did not want Ukraine's interests and his own political future to be "overwhelmed by those of Russia and Yeltsin."[34]

The last point was crucial. The Ukrainian communist leadership was concerned by Yeltsin's growing assertiveness and anti-communism. In July, a group of scholars from the Ukrainian Academy of Sciences argued that the existing draft of the Union Treaty contradicted the Ukrainian declaration of sovereignty. "Ukraine should join the Treaty only as an internationally recognized state," the document concluded, "with its own constitution."[35] Bush's visit to Kiev was the perfect occasion on which to present Ukraine as a subject of international affairs and law. The Ukrainian hosts snubbed Yanayev: the discussions were conducted in English and Ukrainian; nobody bothered to translate for the Vice-President of the USSR. During the talks, Kravchuk and the Ukrainian Prime Minister, Vitold Fokin, asked the Americans to recognize Ukraine's sovereignty and send financial assistance directly to Kiev, not to Moscow. Ukraine, they said, was ready to cooperate with the United States in the UN. Bush flatly dismissed the Ukrainian requests. The United States would deal with Ukraine only as far as the conditions of the Union Treaty would permit it. "I want to deal respectfully with the center," the US President concluded.[36]

After the talks, Bush proceeded to the Ukrainian Supreme Soviet where he delivered his speech. Nationalist deputies were upset, even dismayed by the fact that the US President refused to support their "war of independence" from "the empire." Jack Matlock, who sympathized with Ukraine's national aspirations (and also spoke Ukrainian), believed that the Rukh leaders, most of them intellectuals, wanted too much and too fast. He marveled at how quickly the Ukrainian dissidents from Rukh had forgotten that it was Gorbachev who had given them freedom and a vehicle for political action. Only two years earlier, Gorbachev had forced the Ukrainian Party leadership to allow registration of the People's Movement of Ukraine for Perestroika; now the leaders of this movement were treating the Soviet leader with hatred and slandering him.[37]

In Moscow, Gorbachev's advisors interpreted Bush's performance in Kiev as a decisive shift in favor of Gorbachev and the center. This was highly welcome news, since Gorbachev suddenly was no longer so confident about his deal with

DECLINE AND DOWNFALL

Yeltsin and Nazarbayev. He was drained of energy. In a rare fit of pessimism, he complained to Chernyaev: "Oh, what petty, low-class, provincial people they are, the one and the other. I looked at them and thought: whom I am doing this with and for whom?"[38] Nevertheless, on 2 August, Gorbachev appeared on state television and announced that the Union Treaty would be signed on 20 August at a state ceremony in the Kremlin. The future federation, he explained, would be a legal successor (*pravopreiemnik*) of the Soviet Union. Then Gorbachev added: "The Soviet Union will continue to act as a great world power." Chernyaev immediately spotted contradictions in Gorbachev's speech. He wrote in his diary that the President spoke of federation, but "in effect, he agreed to a . . . confederation." He reflected on the significance of Gorbachev's monumental concession of power. "M.S. used Yeltsin as a bulldozer to clear the road for his ideas," he wrote, but the bulldozer kept moving, turning against Gorbachev.[39]

The loyal aide obfuscated about what was soon to happen: it was not just the end of Gorbachev's power. It was the end of the superpower. The treaty gave each republic in the Union full sovereignty, including the right to establish diplomatic relations with other states. From the viewpoint of international law this was utter nonsense. And only Gorbachev, with his boundless self-confidence, could seriously expect to resurrect a new functional Union from the ruins of the old one.

CRIMEAN VACATION

On 4 August, Gorbachev left Moscow and flew to Crimea for a long-overdue vacation. Mikhail and Raisa Gorbachev had a weakness for luxury. This was apparently their compensation for their early years of poverty and squalor. The presidential recreational villa built near Foros, Crimea, in 1988 satisfied all dreams of comfort. "Zaria" (Dawn), as it was known in classified KGB documents, was a sumptuous mansion surrounded by an exquisite park. The costs of construction and landscaping, concealed among the expenditures of the Ministry of Defense, amounted, by some estimates, to one billion rubles.[40] The entire Soviet defense budget at that time was 77 billion rubles. The KGB supervised every detail of the construction. Gorbachev later asserted that he had nothing to do with the luxuries of the place, but the ideas for its design and decoration originated with Raisa. "Zaria" was decorated with Carrara marble and furnished with expensive furniture made from Karelian birch wood. Majestic mountain cliffs of Jurassic-era limestone guarded the villa from northern winds. An elevator encased in an air-conditioned glass tube brought the occupants down to a private pebbled beach surrounded on three sides by rock formations. The mountains behind and the seafront ahead created a magical balmy effect. The mild and dry sub-tropical climate rivaled the French Riviera.[41]

Mikhail Gorbachev was not sure if he would be able to go on vacation this time. The state of affairs seemed too volatile for him leave the Kremlin. Raisa, however, insisted. The entire family, including Gorbachev's daughter Irina, her husband Anatoly, and Mikhail's two little granddaughters, could not wait to see the Crimean paradise. And Gorbachev could not stay in Moscow alone without Raisa. Their daily strolls and conversations provided essential sustenance for him. Before the flight, the Soviet government and other dignitaries gathered in the usual ceremony on the airfield to see off the First Couple. Valery Boldin, Gorbachev's chief of staff, asked what should be done about Yeltsin's decree, in which he banned Party "cells" in the Army, police, and the KGB. Gorbachev had no answer. His parting words were directed to Vice-President Yanayev: "You stay in charge." Raisa and their daughter Irina noticed that Yanayev's hands had spots from eczema, a skin disease sometimes caused by stress. They decided that when they returned to Moscow, they would suggest a simple treatment they had learned from a relative.[42]

Three hours later the presidential plane landed at Belbek, a military airfield located north-east of the Crimean city of Sevastopol. A delegation of the Ukrainian leadership, including Kravchuk, and the Crimean leadership greeted the Soviet leader there. The atmosphere was tense: at a lunch Kravchuk, instead of the usual words of welcome, began to tell Gorbachev not to lord himself over the sovereign republics, whose leaders were now equal to his leadership. There was an awkward pause after he finished. Stanislav Hurenko, the First Secretary of the Ukrainian Communist Party, sat with a gloomy face.[43]

The beauty of Crimea's nature quickly eclipsed those unpleasant impressions for the Gorbachevs. It was 30 degrees Celsius outdoors, and the sea temperature was 25 degrees; the staff of "Zaria," including a cook, a doctor, nurses, and maids, dozens of men and women, served Gorbachev and his family and met their every need. Active vacationers, Mikhail and Raisa started every day with calisthenics, a swim, and medical checks. Then Gorbachev made phone calls. Later in the morning, the couple took their customary hour-long stroll, and then a longer swim. Athletic KGB bodyguards followed Mikhail and Raisa into the surrounding mountains for their strolls, with machine guns in their backpacks. They also accompanied the couple in a circle when they swam in the sea. The dacha was surrounded by a triple perimeter of protection, manned by the KGB's Ninth Directorate. There was even a detachment of scuba divers who secured the underwater perimeter around the villa and beach. During their siesta after lunch, the First Soviet Family read and relaxed. Time after dinner was for cultural activities: watching TV or movies in the home theater. Irina Gorbacheva and her husband Anatoly had a less organized style of vacation, managing their two children, eleven-year-old Xenia and three-year-old Nastya. When Gorbachev was not busy with his official duties, he read the non-fiction books he had brought from Moscow. One of them was a historical account of the fate of Pyotr Stolypin. The Russian Prime Minister, who had tamed the first Russian revolution in 1907 with unpopular reforms, was ultimately assassinated in 1911. Another book was the Russian translation of Stalin's biography by the American scholar Robert C. Tucker.[44]

Gorbachev could not imagine a vacation without deep thinking and writing. After a few days in "Zaria," Gorbachev told his wife that he wanted to write an article about what he had done as leader. "Was perestroika needed? Are we moving towards a catastrophe? Did I sell the store to American imperialism?" As usual, he dictated his thoughts to Chernyaev. The draft painted an "unprecedented and unique" integrated country, which was to replace the formerly totalitarian Soviet Union. Voluntary and democratic agreements between the republics would grant the future federation "unprecedented stability." Gorbachev confided to Raisa, however, that he did not know how to accelerate reforms further. The anti-crisis program had stalled, and state mechanisms were paralyzed.[45]

Gorbachev continued to call republican leaders by phone, canvassing their support for the Union Treaty. Nikolai Dementey, head of the Belorussian Supreme Soviet, agreed to participate in the signing ceremony. On 10 August, the Gorbachevs played host to Ukrainian leader Kravchuk and his wife Antonina, who were vacationing in a nearby resort. This meeting was informal and cordial. At the dinner, Raisa dominated the conversation and asked all the questions. When the two couples went out for a stroll, Gorbachev and Kravchuk stayed behind their wives and, according to Kravchuk, had a substantive talk. Gorbachev asked: "Why don't you want to sign the Treaty?" Kravchuk said that it should be a treaty of confederation. Back in 1922, when the USSR had been established, Ukraine had the right to have its own armed forces and all other attributes of a real state. Then Stalin took it all away. Why should Ukraine now accept a deal that would be much worse than Lenin's offer decades earlier? Kravchuk also opposed a federal tax: Ukraine should decide how much it would pay to the central budget. Gorbachev asked: What about the Union's president? Kravchuk recalled he proposed to Gorbachev to rotate the presidency among the republics. Gorbachev shook his head: "No, no, no . . . The President must be elected by all the people." Kravchuk said that Ukraine would no longer vote for Gorbachev. The Soviet leader stared at him incredulously. Kravchuk insisted. Gorbachev does not mention this conversation in his memoirs.[46]

On 18 August, Raisa Gorbacheva perused the Moscow newspapers, and then wrote in her notebook: "What is happening around the Union Treaty?!

Some people cry that the bureaucratic unified state is being regenerated. Others say that the country is falling apart and being ripped to pieces—that the foundations of the Treaty are vague and undefined. Why do we need such a Union Treaty?"[47] Raisa's description was perceptive. Liberal anti-communists from Democratic Russia were among the most vocal critics of the Union Treaty. On 8 August, the liberal *Independent Gazette* published "an appeal to the President of Russia, B. N. Yeltsin," signed by Yuri Afanasyev, Yelena Bonner, and other leading figures from Democratic Russia. They urged Yeltsin to reject the treaty with Gorbachev. They pointed to the absurdity of having dual sovereignty in one country: it should belong either to the center or to the republics. The new Union "would be doomed to constant and perhaps bloody conflicts." The authors proposed continuing the discussion and perhaps holding another national referendum.[48] The status of these critics as intellectual celebrities forced Yeltsin to respond in the same newspaper. He called for realism. Without the treaty, he argued, "Russia will remain a hostage to the central structures." Only a legal and constitutional process could make the Union ministries relinquish their power. The abrogation of the treaty, not to mention yet another national referendum, would be "the best possible gift to the Union bureaucracy."[49]

Another attack came earlier from *Sovetskaia Rossiia*, a newspaper of Russian conservative nationalists, in an article entitled "A Word to the People." This was a manifesto, signed by a group of nationalist writers, but also senior members of the military: the commander of Soviet ground forces, General Valentin Varennikov, and the Deputy Interior Minister, General Boris Gromov. The article was styled after medieval Russian chronicles, proclaimed "Motherland in danger," and called people to rise up and fight to end the Time of Troubles. It blamed "the perfidious and voluble rulers, cunning apostates, and avid profiteers" for the current crisis, and appealed to the army, the military industries, the Orthodox Church, and to all Russians, from liberals to nationalists.[50] The author of the manifesto was Alexander Prokhanov, a fifty-three-year-old journalist with notoriously imperialist and nationalist views. In effect, he called for a rebellion against Gorbachev. In a contemporaneous interview with David Remnick, he explained: "We live in a democracy, don't we?" At the Party Plenum one of Gorbachev's aides, Andrei Grachev, proposed censuring Gromov and Varennikov for signing "A Word to the People." The conservative audience booed him. A few days later somebody set fire to Grachev's dacha near Moscow.[51]

Gorbachev wanted to keep the official text of the treaty confidential until the ceremony. Yet on 14 August, the English-language edition of the weekly *Moscow News* published the full text. Moscow's major newspapers printed the original Russian version the next day.[52] The leak was inevitable: numerous copies of the draft circulated in the Soviet government, the Russian, Ukrainian, and other republican Supreme Soviets.[53] Yet Gorbachev was upset. He was especially concerned that this publication would generate more tension and controversy. He also saw that Yeltsin, in response to criticism, began to waver. The Russian leader said publicly that "Russia" would have only a one-channel tax system, without the federal one. This undermined Gorbachev's plans for devolving power.[54]

Kryuchkov informed Gorbachev that Yeltsin had held a separate meeting with the five leaders of the Central Asian republics that opened in Alma-Ata. Indeed, Yeltsin wanted to talk to Nazarbayev before the ceremony. The Russian President had his own concerns: that Gorbachev would renege on his promises at the last moment. In that event, Yeltsin wanted to return to the idea of a quadripartite agreement of four republics, including Kazakhstan. Boldin recalled that Gorbachev called him from Crimea and shouted on the phone: "This is separatism! They ignore the opinion of the President of the USSR. The provincial chieftains decide the issues of statehood. This is a conspiracy. I will not let it go. One must act immediately . . ."[55]

On 15 August, Gorbachev called Yeltsin. The Russian President admitted that he was under pressure to renege on the deal. Gorbachev responded that there was pressure on him as well. Both leaders, according to Gorbachev's recollections, agreed to stay the course and meet at the signing ceremony. Yeltsin asked about the layout of the participants: he and the Russian delegation had to be in the center. "We ended on a good note," Gorbachev recalled. "Still, I had the feeling that Yeltsin had not been completely frank with me."[56]

Observers discussed what would happen after the signing of the Union Treaty. In Leningrad, the mayor Anatoly Sobchak was sanguine: "the Right can be discounted now."[57] Vadim Zagladin, an aide to Gorbachev and an experienced apparatchik, believed that there was real danger of a political blowback. Alexander Yakovlev feared that the treaty-signing ceremony could force the hardliners to act pre-emptively. He told the Western officials that neo-Stalinist leaders of the Russian Communist Party, backed by the military, would form a "national salvation committee." On 16 August, Yakovlev issued a public letter in which he warned about an imminent coup by a "shadow" alliance of neo-Stalinists, army generals, the KGB, and the military-industrial complex.[58]

Gorbachev remained an optimist. He approved a schedule for the signing of the treaty and circulated it to the republican leaders and the republican Party organizations. The document listed five republics slated to sign on 20 August: the Russian Federation, Kazakhstan, Uzbekistan, Belorussia, Tajikistan. Turkmen and Kirgiz leaders promised to join in September. The date of 10 October was when Gorbachev expected Ukraine, Azerbaijan, and "other republics" to sign the treaty.[59] There was no other road to take, he confided to Chernyaev. He noted that by the summer of 1991 both Party hardliners and some anti-communists had called for a strong hand and the use of force. Both sides thought it was necessary for market transition and stability. "Introducing emergency rule," Gorbachev concluded, "is the road to perdition—to a civil war."[60]

UNWANTED VISITORS

Gorbachev completely denied the possibility that people from his government or entourage were capable of acting on their own and against him. In this, he was fatally mistaken. Stalin had always suspected his inner circle and continuously purged it. Gorbachev, who modeled himself on Lenin, spurned Stalinist recipes of power. At the same time, he continued to behave like any Party apparatchik who assumed the KGB was part of the natural environment. Kryuchkov never gave him any reason to be suspicious. The head of the KGB called his boss every day, sometimes several times a day, reporting on developments. This routine did not change during Gorbachev's vacation time.

On the day Gorbachev left for Crimea, as a later investigation revealed, "all documents pertaining to the decision to establish the Emergency Committee and declare a state of emergency were prepared." This paperwork had been in preparation since the sanctions against Lithuania in the spring of 1990. And Gorbachev had been aware of it.[61] Some people later claimed that the KGB chief implemented those contingency plans out of self-interest. Perhaps, they said, Kryuchkov knew from KGB wiretapping that he would be fired after the Union treaty was signed. Kryuchkov always denied it. Indeed, fighting for power at any cost could hardly have been his motive. He was a loyal bureaucrat, not a power-hungry adventurer. The KGB chief simply could not see how Gorbachev's hybrid Union could become the basis for a stable state and economy. Everything he knew indicated the opposite: Yeltsin's Russia was on the way to gobbling up most of what was the Soviet Union. Kryuchkov could be paranoid about "foreign interference," yet he was right about the chaotic decomposition of the centrally planned economy. All this convinced him that signing the Union Treaty meant the end of the Soviet state. And it had to be stopped.[62]

Gorbachev's twists and turns during the previous months, his vague language ("you should act, and I will correct you later"), made the KGB leader think that the Soviet President would yield to a *fait accompli*. Kryuchkov knew how deeply unpopular Gorbachev had become in military, parliamentary, and Party circles, as well as among the general public. The KGB sources abroad also reported that Western leaders had already begun to treat Gorbachev as a lame-duck leader. In one anonymous report, a Soviet agent informed Kryuchkov: "The close circle around President Bush has come to the conclusion that Gorbachev has exhausted his potential as a leader . . ." The same agent reported: "President Bush and his close circle categorically refuse to consider B. N. Yeltsin as a possible figure to replace Gorbachev." In his memoirs, Kryuchkov referred to a report from another source, who warned him that the leaders of the major capitalist countries expected "termination of the existence of our state." The agent wondered why the Soviet leadership could not do anything to prevent this "tragic development."[63]

Two other men agreed with Kryuchkov on the need to act. Valery Boldin, greatly trusted by Raisa Gorbacheva, said later to a sympathetic interviewer: "Our task was to delay the Union Treaty." He also claimed that the conspirators did not want to seize power: "We already had enough power." Instead, Boldin claimed, they wanted to convene the Supreme Soviet of the USSR and the Party Plenum and make them elect a new leader to replace Gorbachev. The plotters wanted to abide by the constitution, at least in appearance.[64] Oleg Baklanov, head of the military-industrial complex, had special reasons to approve such a move. Baklanov saw that Gorbachev was doing nothing to save the MIC from market forces; he also feared that Ukrainian separatism, among other factors, could ruin the Soviet military industries. As early as April 1991, Baklanov had already spoken at a Party Plenum in favor of emergency rule, "including the introduction of martial law." Baklanov later claimed in an interview that in August 1991 he did not want to remove Gorbachev; he still believed that his twists and turns had been the product of circumstances and misunderstanding. He wanted to convene the Supreme Soviet as quickly as possible to cancel Gorbachev's unilateral decision on the Union Treaty.[65] Kryuchkov later recalled that Baklanov was one of "only two or three men" in the leadership who was "ready for decisive action to save the country." The troika of Kryuchkov, Boldin, and Baklanov had come together by pure chance: all three belonged to a "dacha cooperative" near Moscow—a community of country houses, where they had each bought plots of land. Their plan emerged from their informal conversations.[66]

Another recruit to the conspiracy was Party Secretary Oleg Shenin, who during Gorbachev's absence was in command of the CPSU apparatus. An ethnic Russian from Siberia, Shenin had been an ardent supporter of Gorbachev in the earlier years of perestroika, but he became a bitter critic of political liberalization, which he thought was destabilizing and disastrous. In January 1991, Shenin had openly advocated the use of force in the Baltics; in April he worked unsuccessfully to have Gorbachev dismissed as General Secretary. Yakovlev had considered Shenin to be the most likely leader of a national committee of salvation: "ambitious and decisive, his brains had been cooked in Stalinist stew." Recalling his motives to join the plot, Shenin said that the Union Treaty of 20 August would have turned the Soviet Union into "a federation of hundreds of states." "This was an utter collapse." Like Baklanov, Shenin did not believe that Gorbachev fully realized what he was doing.[67]

The day after the Gorbachevs had left for Crimea, Kryuchkov's personal bodyguard called one of Yasov's chauffeurs with an unusual request: the Minister of Defense was invited to come to "object ABC," a KGB safe house on the outskirts of Moscow. This unusual method of arranging an encounter between two key officials ensured plausible deniability. The conspirators took precautions to stay below the radar of any intelligence surveillance, including American electronic espionage. The meeting was inconclusive and produced only a modest agreement: to analyse possible public reactions to the introduction of emergency rule. This was, however, also a crucial step: the meeting happened behind Gorbachev's back, and he was not informed.[68]

The KGB leader was the only man in the Soviet leadership who could arrange such a meeting: after all, since Stalin's time it was the duty of the secret police to ensure that members of the top political class would not congregate, unless specifically commanded by their supreme leader. At the same time, it was not so easy for Kryuchkov to involve the KGB apparatus and facilities. He could not rely on the absolute loyalty of his senior staff. And he knew that some KGB officials sympathized with Yeltsin. As a result, Kryuchkov turned only to those few deputies and aides whom he personally trusted. Following the meeting with Yazov, Kryuchkov ordered two KGB analysts from his close circle to provide "a strategic forecast" of what could happen if emergency rule was declared. The analysts used the materials prepared in December 1990.[69] In their report they presented arguments *against* emergency rule, at least against introducing it before the Union Treaty was signed. The KGB experts warned that emergency rule would lead to destabilization and a power struggle, possibly including massive civil disobedience. One of their longer-term scenarios was the possibility of a counter-coup "from the left," with consequences similar to Hungary in 1956 or Romania in 1989. In any case, the KGB analysts concluded, an agreement with republican leaders would be necessary to restore stability in the country.[70]

On 14 August, Kryuchkov acted against his analysts' recommendations. He told them: "The leadership of the country has made the decision to introduce an emergency regime. After the signing of the Union Treaty this measure will be too late to implement." It is not clear what was the trigger for Kryuchkov's new resolve. On 17 August, the KGB chief arranged another secret meeting at the ABC safe house. This time, the gang of four decided to create the State Committee for the State of Emergency; its Russian acronym was GKChP. Nobody was able to come up with a less awkward-sounding name. Yazov was present and brought his two subordinates, the commander of the ground forces General Valentin

Varennikov and General Vladislav Achalov, the long-time commander of the airborne troops and now Deputy Minister of Defense. Both had commanded Soviet military operations in Afghanistan and were scathing critics of Gorbachev's leadership. Varennikov had been a participant of the victory parade in Moscow in June 1945, a true soldier of the superpower. After reading the text of the Union Treaty in the newspapers, he allegedly exclaimed: "This is not a treaty, but a death sentence!"[71]

Another crucial participant at the meeting was Valentin Pavlov. He recalled that on that day he had been invited to a birthday party at a dacha outside Moscow. He was already on his way in his official limousine when he received a call from Kryuchkov on a secure government line, asking him to change his plans and attend a discussion that would take "one hour, no more" of his time. He arrived at the ABC safe house and stayed there for the rest of the evening. Later Pavlov confided to his deputy Shcherbakov that he was appalled by what Kryuchkov told him. The KGB chief informed him that "democrats" had plans to topple the government and only emergency rule could stop them. It is quite implausible that Pavlov had not already been informed of the conspiracy. Why did the shrewd Prime Minister choose to believe in the improbable charade that Kryuchkov concocted? Most likely, it was because of the lack of another credible reason to introduce emergency rule at the time, when everything was quiet and people were on their summer vacations. Pavlov wanted to abort the Union Treaty, because he believed it would destroy the central government's ability to control and manage the Soviet economic and financial system. In his memoirs, however, he argued that the Emergency Committee was not planning to remove Gorbachev by force. The main reason for it was Soviet bankruptcy. "The Western world would have declared a real blockade on the Soviet Union," he reasoned. "The forceful removal of President Gorbachev at the time would have meant complete international isolation. Everybody understood that very well!" These conflicting beliefs would determine Pavlov's strange behavior two days later.[72]

The plotters discussed how to make their actions appear constitutional. They assumed that Anatoly Lukyanov, the Speaker of the Supreme Soviet of the USSR, would join them and convene the Congress of People's Deputies, which would elect a new President of the Soviet Union in place of Gorbachev. Lukyanov was the most likely candidate for this position. At the time of the meeting, he was on vacation at the resort of Valdai, 400 kilometers away from Moscow. Yazov proposed sending a military helicopter to bring Lukyanov to Moscow from the resort and convince him to cooperate. No one, however, knew exactly how Lukyanov would react; this politician was wily and close to the Gorbachevs.[73]

It was Kryuchkov who proposed sending a delegation to Foros, to speak with Gorbachev. To what purpose? Boldin summed it up in his recollections: to make Gorbachev approve emergency rule or isolate him.[74] The KGB chief knew that Baklanov, Pavlov, and Yazov were not ready to act against the Soviet leader. A trip to Crimea had to give the whole enterprise a semblance of legitimacy, a hope that Gorbachev would give in to peer pressure. After a long discussion, the plotters decided that Kryuchkov and Yazov would stay in Moscow for preparations, while Baklanov, Boldin, and Shenin, accompanied by General Varennikov, would go to meet Gorbachev. Everyone knew that it would be a nasty surprise. Looking at Boldin, Marshal Yazov quipped: "Et tu, Brute?!" At 13:02 on 18 August a military TU-154 aircraft took off from Moscow, carrying the group to Crimea. General Varennikov gave orders to the pilots: the aircraft was his "command center." After meeting Gorbachev, Varennikov planned to fly to Kiev to ensure that Ukraine would stay under control.[75]

On the plane ride to Crimea, Shenin showed Varennikov a document he was carrying for Gorbachev's signature: the Soviet President was to temporarily transfer his powers to Vice-President Yanayev "for reasons of illness." Another man on the plane was KGB General Yuri Plekhanov, the man in charge of the Ninth Directorate that ensured the security of the political leadership. When the aircraft approached Crimea, Plekhanov called the KGB officers in charge of government communications at the presidential villa. He ordered that at 4.30 p.m. all means of communications at Gorbachev's disposal be disconnected. The plane with the plotters landed at Belbek Airport and, after a brief lunch, a motorcade with armed KGB officers drove at top speed to Foros. The plan was to arrive at "Zaria" at exactly 4.30.[76]

Inside the villa, Gorbachev was at work, revising the speech he had prepared for the treaty's signing ceremony. He ordered his staff to get him and Raisa ready for a flight to Moscow next morning. Then he called Shakhnazarov, who, like Chernyaev, was staying at a resort nearby. "Are you ready to fly with me to Moscow? We will come back in two–three days, and there will be more time to swim." Shakhnazarov confirmed that he was ready to go and asked after Gorbachev's health: the President had suffered an attack of lumbago three days earlier during a mountain stroll with Raisa. "It is all right," Gorbachev responded. "I am back in shape." Gorbachev hung up the phone. A few minutes later, the head of his personal security service, Major-General Vladimir Medvedev, came to see him. Medvedev looked confused: the KGB guards on the perimeter had just let a group of visitors into the villa without Gorbachev's authorization.[77]

Gorbachev's first reaction was to call Kryuchkov, but the secure phone line was dead. In the KGB communications center at Mukhalatka, eighteen kilometers from the villa, the resident officers cut off all eight cables of communications running to

Gorbachev's dacha. The five phones on Gorbachev's desk had all gone dead, from his local landline telephone to the "red" satellite phone used to reach the Ministry of Defense. The most powerful man in the country, the commander-in-chief of Soviet armed forces in control of the nuclear "button," had been made incommunicado by order of Kryuchkov. Gorbachev rushed to his wife and and found her alone, reading newspapers. "Something bad—perhaps terrible—has happened," Gorbachev said. "They demand a meeting with me . . . All the telephones are disconnected. Do you understand? This is isolation! It means conspiracy? Arrest?" Gorbachev led the shocked Raisa to a bedroom. Perhaps he thought it was the best place for a confidential talk, secure from eavesdropping. He said: "I will not agree to any schemes or bargains. No threats or blackmail will work." He fell silent, and then added: "But it may cost us all dearly, the entire family . . ." Raisa responded: "It is your decision to take. I will stand by you whatever happens."[78]

When Gorbachev came to see the group, he asked: "Whom do you represent? On whose behalf are you speaking?" From their confused replies, the Soviet leader quickly realized that the conspirators were not planning to get rid of him. On the contrary, they needed him to cancel the Union Treaty and convene the Supreme Soviet—in a word, to avoid the impression of starting a coup. Gorbachev later claimed that his position was crystal clear: outright rejection of any emergency rule. His mistake, however, was to speak to the delegation for too long: almost one hour of back-and-forth discussions. Later, he explained that he wanted to force his subordinates into submission—to make them back down, "as I did many times before." His ability to hypnotize them with words, however, did not work this time, but it left room for conspiracy theories that would haunt Gorbachev for many years to come. In the end, the Soviet leader refused to sign anything. Varennikov expressed everyone's feelings: "Then it's time for you to resign!" In Boldin's recollection, Gorbachev replied with a crude Russian profanity. At the end, however, he saw the group off with the words: "Damn you, go ahead!" This phrase could be interpreted in any number of ways. After the plotters had left, Gorbachev felt relieved; the worst had not happened. Raisa and the rest of his family were still safe. Chernyaev, who met Gorbachev an hour after this meeting, found him smiling.[79]

The plotters left Gorbachev without any lines of communication. On Kryuchkov's orders, the 500 KGB officers and marines protecting the presidential dacha complex ensured that the President would stay under de facto house arrest during the coup. Only five KGB officers from Gorbachev's personal security detail disobeyed these instructions and pledged to defend the President and his family to the end. Their decision would not in fact have mattered had the plotters really decided to get rid of Gorbachev. In the villa at the time—and therefore unable to leave—were Gorbachev's aide and speechwriter Anatoly

Chernyaev, the stenographer Olga Lanina, maids, cooks, gardeners, swimming-pool staff, chauffeurs, and even KGB couriers who happened to be inside "Zaria" at the moment the place was shut down.

With time, the significance of what had happened began to dawn on Gorbachev. In conversation with Raisa, Chernyaev, and others he called the initiators of the coup "suicidal" and "murderous." "The country is in a grave position," he reasoned. The world would turn away from the USSR, there would be an economic and political blockade, and there would be a tragic outcome to everything that perestroika had achieved.[80] The Gorbachev family gathered around a portable Sony transistor radio that they had brought with them to Crimea. In the Soviet Union, however, everything was calm. The country still did not know what had happened.[81]

The Gorbachevs' long-awaited vacation had been rudely interrupted. And something much more important snapped on that day. It was the end of Gorbachev as a political magician who could walk the tightrope, balancing in the middle without falling off. He did not know it, but it was also the end of all his global agreements with the Americans and his fantasy of a great and demo-cratic European Home.

Boldin, Baklanov, Shenin, Varennikov, and Plekhanov returned to Belbek Airport in a somber mood. Varennikov boarded a military plane for Kiev. The rest of the group flew back to Moscow in Gorbachev's presidential IL-62. They also took with them two KGB officers in charge of the "nuclear briefcase." From this moment on for the next three days, command and control of Soviet strategic nuclear forces would be in the hands of Kryuchkov and Yazov. Plekhanov called the KGB chief from the plane to report: Gorbachev would not support emergency rule.[82] The conspirators were in a quandary: how to demonstrate the legitimacy of the new regime in the absence of the President. The only remaining option was to declare Gorbachev "sick." In his absence, the Vice-President of the USSR became a provisional constitutional leader of the country. The new ruler of the Soviet Union, Gennady Yanayev, learned about his role at the last moment. While the delegation was in Crimea, Kryuchkov began to search for Gorbachev's replacement. He finally tracked down Yanayev at a friend's dacha near Moscow. They were partying with lots of alcohol.[83]

On the evening of 18 August, the plotters met for a final planning session in Pavlov's office in the Kremlin. Kryuchkov gathered under one roof all the main figures of the Soviet leadership, including Lukyanov who was brought by a military helicopter from his Valdai resort. When Lukyanov learned about the plot, the man whom the Party elite had recently applauded as a resolute leader suddenly transformed into an indecisive, pedantic lawyer. Lukyanov rejected on constitutional grounds the offer to become an acting President and removed his name from documents produced by the Emergency Committee. Another half-hearted participant was Gennady Yanayev. He was clearly taken by surprise and not at all ready to become temporary leader of the Soviet Union, replacing Gorbachev.[84]

The last addition to the meeting, Soviet Foreign Minister Bessmertnykh, arrived at the Kremlin shortly before midnight. Kryuchkov had summoned him from a resort in Belorussia, and the diplomat did not even have time to change into a formal suit. Kryuchkov wanted him to be added to the Emergency Committee, apparently to reassure the West that the junta would observe the international commitments made by Gorbachev. Bessmertnykh was appalled. He argued that it would be easier for him to talk to his Western counterparts if he were not formally implicated. He took out a blue pen and deleted his name from the committee's list.[85]

The return of the delegation from Crimea that evening had sealed the psychological trap for the reluctant and surprised participants. Boldin told them: "You should not think that you can get away scot-free. Gorbachev knows all your names. The bridges are burned ... We are now in the same boat." Kryuchkov then said softly to Yanayev: "Don't you see? If we do not save the harvest, famine will occur, in a few months people will go out into the streets, and civil war will start." Yanayev finally crumbled under pressure and agreed to become acting leader "for no more than two weeks." The shared assumption was that during this time the Supreme Soviet and the Congress of People's Deputies would elect a new leader. Yanayev, and then other officials, signed two documents: "The Declaration of the Soviet Leadership" and "An Appeal to the Soviet People." Lukyanov went to his office and quickly penned another "Declaration" which argued that the Union Treaty betrayed the spirit of the national referendum in March, undermined the USSR's shared economic space, shattered its banking system, and failed to establish "property rights that would allow the Union to function as a federal state." The conspirators decided that state radio and television would broadcast all three texts at 6 a.m. the next morning.[86]

It was decided that every region and major city of the Russian Federation would be ruled by local "emergency committees," consisting of the heads of the Soviet authorities and municipal administration, and the commander of the military district. Some Party officials, among them Shenin and the head of the Moscow Party organization, Yuri Prokofiev, supported the plot enthusiastically, and began to use the Party communication lines to dispatch secret instructions to their colleagues in the republican, regional, and district organizations. The plotters wanted to make use of the Party infrastructure, yet they decided that Shenin's name should not appear on the committee's list. "The CPSU had at the time the black mark of a reactionary force," Baklanov recalled. The Emergency Committee "had to symbolize the birth of something new."[87]

Finally, Yanayev signed the appeal to heads of states and governments of the world, as well as the UN Secretary-General, Javier Pérez de Cuéllar. Yanayev also signed the prepared letters to Bush, Mitterrand, Kohl, the Prime Minister of Great Britain, John Major, and other Western leaders. The appeal and the letters explained that the economic crisis, "a situation of uncontrollability with too many centers of power," and "the threat of the country's disintegration," necessitated "a state of emergency in some areas of the USSR for a period of six months." This did not constitute an abandonment of Gorbachev's policies, the texts continued. "The reforms shall be continued." Yanayev pledged allegiance to democracy and glasnost, civil rights and freedoms. He assured the leaders that all treaties and agreements with the West would remain in force, and he vowed to govern constitutionally, "within the framework of existing laws." The letters assured Western leaders that "Mikhail Sergeyevich [Gorbachev] is in complete safety, and nothing is threatening him." Bessmertnykh sent the letters through diplomatic channels to the heads of Western governments.[88]

The organizational meeting of the Emergency Committee broke up at 2:30 a.m. on 19 August. Some members went home and succumbed to various illnesses. Boldin was already suffering from high blood pressure; he went to a hospital. Pavlov was another casualty. He tried to control his emotions and stress with a disastrous mixture of sedatives and alcohol. At daybreak, his bodyguard summoned medical help, as Pavlov was incapable of functioning. Of the remaining members, Yazov proved to be the most decisive. He convened his subordinates at the Defense Ministry, informed them about Gorbachev's "sickness," and ordered them to bring the armed forces to a heightened level of combat readiness. Other measures included the safeguarding of strategic rocket bases and storage facilities for nuclear and conventional munitions. The Army, Yazov said, was to coordinate its actions with "all healthy forces," including republican and local authorities, the Party, the KGB, and all other public and political structures that "support the Constitution." The language in which Yazov couched his orders to his military subordinates was remarkably vague, as if the very existence of the country were not at stake. He did not stipulate what to do in case of conflicts with civilians. Yazov merely mentioned that he did not want any blood to be spilled.[89]

The most far-reaching of Yazov's orders was the one to move troops into Moscow. Several airborne regiments were placed in strategic areas across the capital. The Second Taman motorized rifle division and the Fourth Kantemirov tank division received orders to move into the city. In total, the military force that entered the Soviet capital amounted to 350 tanks, 140 BMPs, and 150 APCs.

Orders to the troops also cautioned against possible "death and mutilation of personnel": a double warning that the troops could be attacked, but also that they should refrain from the use of lethal force as much as possible. The commander of the Soviet Air Force, Yevgeny Shaposhnikov, later recalled that Yazov instructed his subordinates to do everything to avoid "excesses," especially bloodshed. It is not even clear whether the troops received live ammunition.[90] What mattered more was the massive display of military force. For the first time in their lives, Muscovites witnessed lines of tanks in the city as a means of intimidation. This was bound to produce a shock.

CHAPTER 11

JUNTA

C'est pire qu'un crime, c'est une faute.
Antoine Boulay de la Meurthe, 1809

People can forgive [authorities] everything except weakness.
D. Volkogonov to Boris Yeltsin, December 1994[1]

SHOCK AND FEAR

On Saturday, 17 August 1991 the Soviet Minister of Culture, Nikolai Gubenko, celebrated his birthday at his dacha in Nikolino Polye near Moscow. Members of the Soviet government and artistic elite mingled and gossiped at the party. The Soviet ambassador to Italy, Anatoly Adamishin, who was an old friend of Gubenko, attended. The prevalent mood was conservative. Nobody believed that the Union Treaty would help to solve the Soviet crisis. Deputy Prime Minister Vladimir Shcherbakov bemoaned that Gorbachev had no resolve for the unpopular but necessary economic measures. He could not explain what should be done, but was confident that in a time of economic crisis, people would sooner or later turn to the Kremlin for help. Yet nobody expected that anything drastic would happen. Valery Boldin, Gorbachev's chief of staff, called Gubenko from the Kremlin to wish him a happy birthday. Gubenko also expected Prime Minister Valentin Pavlov to come. He never showed up. The guests drank a lot of alcohol, many stayed at Gubenko's dacha overnight, and the party continued through the next day. Many guests returned to Moscow only on Sunday evening.[2]

On Monday, Adamishin awoke to one of the greatest surprises of his life. On television, a female presenter was solemnly announcing that Gorbachev was sick and unable to act in his capacity as President. Vice-President Gennady Yanayev had taken over the levers of power. A State Committee for the Emergency Situation had been formed to govern the country for six months. Outside, Adamishin saw columns of tanks moving through the streets, crushing asphalt under their tracks. His first thought was: Whatever happens, this is the end of the Union Treaty. He did not regret this outcome. At the same time, the diplomat doubted that those in charge of emergency rule would be able to stay in power. Adamishin wrote in his diary that it would be hard to tame the rebellious republics and control the vast country through brute force. And what about the economy? How to get people to work?[3]

It was a brutal morning for the leaders and activists of Democratic Russia. Yelena Bonner, the widow of Andrei Sakharov, usually never watched Soviet television. This time, however, her daughter told her to turn it on. Bonner's first reaction was shock and fear: the long-anticipated dictatorship was coming; the forces of reaction had finally struck back. She had a flashback to 1941 and the German attack on the Soviet Union, when she had volunteered as a young nurse. Stalin had said then on the radio: "Our cause is just. The enemy will be crushed. The victory will be ours!" When American journalists began to call her, this was what Bonner said to them. Then she paused: "What am I saying?!" Still, there was no time for reflection. This was a war of extermination to the end.[4]

Shevardnadze, who woke up on Monday in his apartment in Moscow, said to his aides: "This is fascism." He called Alexander Yakovlev and was relieved to find he was at home and had not been arrested. Then he called Yeltsin: the Russian leader was also at liberty and picked up the phone. Shevardnadze was convinced, however, that arrests would come very soon. He invited Western journalists to a press conference. The only way to survive, he thought, was to turn to Western public opinion for political and moral support: "We must speak about human rights." When his colleagues from the democratic movement learned about this idea, some of them got scared. Any appeal to the West would be considered a state crime. "None of us would survive until Tuesday," one of them suggested.[5]

Many people in the Soviet Union, the children and grandchildren of Stalin's victims, thought of the mass killings of Stalin's time, the KGB's mental asylums, and the persecution of dissidents. All of a sudden, the few years of Gorbachev's liberalization and new freedoms appeared to have been just a dream. Would they now be doomed to life under the tyranny of lies, hypocrisy, and oppression?[6] The majority heeded their instincts and decided to hunker down. Some of Shevardnadze's associates from the movement for democratic reforms stopped responding to phone calls. The fear was contagious: it gripped foreigners in Moscow as well. The American scholar Victoria Bonnell, who was on a research trip to Moscow, recalled: "Our emotions—a mixture of caution and daring, hope and despair, exhilaration at being there and fear for our personal safety and that of our family—were too contradictory to guide us to a decisive action."[7]

A small number of people began to channel their fear into action. Yelena Bonner's daughter Tatiana and her friends had grown up as the sons and daughters of heroic dissidents under Brezhnev's rule. She rushed to the Russian parliament, to join her young friends. In their eyes, this institution was the only seat of opposition to the junta.[8] Some people from Yeltsin's entourage went there as well. Vladimir Lukin was a child of the Great Terror: both his parents, who were Party members, had been arrested soon after his birth. He was not afraid, because he knew Yanayev and the other leaders of the emergency committee personally. He did not believe them to be capable of ruthless actions. In the still empty building of the Russian parliament, Lukin gathered together those parliamentary members he had managed to reach by phone. His plan of action was to convene the Russian Congress to delegitimize the coup.[9]

Yeltsin returned to Moscow very late on Sunday, 18 August, after his meeting with the Kazakh leader Nursultan Nazarbayev in Alma-Ata. His ghostwritten memoirs said little about their meeting. Other sources report that Nazarbayev feted his Russian guest non-stop, with vodka galore, and at some point Yeltsin decided to take a dip in an icy rapid river that flowed down from the mountains. In the end, Yeltsin had to take a nap and his plane back to Moscow was delayed by five hours and landed at night. For reasons that are unclear, it was re-routed to a reserve military airport. Yeltsin slept through the entire flight, and then his bodyguards delivered him by car to his house in Arkhangelskoye-2, a gated community for state officials in a north-western suburb of Moscow. He immediately went to bed.[10] Next morning, his daughter Tatiana woke him up at 6 a.m. to announce the bad news. For the next thirty minutes Yeltsin sat in front of the television in his underwear, utterly bewildered. Meanwhile his wife Naina and Tatiana tested the landline phone; improbably it worked. They began to call other members of the Russian leadership who lived in the same gated community. Soon Yeltsin was joined by Khasbulatov, Burbulis, Silayev, and Yuri Luzhkov, the deputy mayor of Moscow. The mayor of Leningrad, Anatoly Sobchak, also happened to be at the gathering. Everyone was shell-shocked and expected KGB commandos to arrive any minute.[11]

Yeltsin called General Pavel Grachev, commander of the Soviet Airborne Troops, whom he knew personally, and asked for protection. He did not know that Marshal Yazov had put the general in charge of logistics of the military emergency. After a moment's silence, Grachev promised to send a platoon to Yeltsin's dacha. He never did. Sobchak left in haste to take a flight to Leningrad.

Somebody suggested that Yeltsin should call Yanayev, but the Russian leader was having his Churchillian moment: no talks with the enemy! Yeltsin and his aides decided to issue "an appeal to the citizens of Russia": they would denounce what had happened as an anti-constitutional coup. There was a brief discussion about Gorbachev. Burbulis suggested that Gorbachev was letting his subordinates do the "dirty work," in order to return later and take the reins of power back from the plotters. Khasbulatov disagreed: it would be wrong to associate Gorbachev with the conspiracy. They should demand Gorbachev's return to Moscow as the only legitimate leader. Burbulis admitted later that this was the best tactic. The Russian people no longer cared for Gorbachev, but Yeltsin would fulfill his pledge to President Bush to support the Soviet leader against reactionaries. The text of the appeal was drafted to demand Gorbachev's return. It stated that "the coup . . . discredits the USSR before the entire world, undermines our prestige in the world community, returns us to the era of the cold war and isolation." Yeltsin's daughter Tatiana typed the appeal up with one finger on an old typewriter. Then she sent the text from the home fax machine to Western journalists, embassies, and international organizations. All the messages reached their destination without a hitch.[12]

The next step was to try to get to the Russian parliament. Around 9:30 a.m. a car carrying Yeltsin left Arkhangelskoye and headed for Moscow. The Russian leader, protected only by his bullet-proof vest, Korzhakov and a few bodyguards, expected an ambush. His wife and daughter, who stayed behind, were in danger of becoming hostages of the KGB. Yet nothing happened. Yeltsin reached the Russian parliament without any obstruction. Bizarrely, there were still no police or troops around the parliament building. Only a few of Yeltsin's supporters were milling about in front of it. A handful of the parliamentarians gathered in the building. Foreign diplomats and journalists also arrived, eager for the news. Fifteen minutes later, Khasbulatov opened an extraordinary meeting of the rump Supreme Soviet of the Russian Federation.[13] Meanwhile, a few tanks from the Second Taman Division arrived outside the building. From his office on the sixth floor of the parliament building, the Russian leader could see that the tank-drivers had opened their hatches; some civilians had also begun talking with them. Then Yeltsin had his second great moment. Overruling the warnings of Burbulis and others to stay in safety, he got out of his car onto the square in front of the parliament building, flanked only by Korzhakov and other bodyguards. He spoke with the commander of the unit and then climbed onto one of the tanks. From this pedestal, the Russian President read out his appeal to the people of Russia. He also called for a general strike against "a right-wing, reactionary, anti-constitutional coup d'état." Someone in the crowd asked him if there would be a civil war. Yeltsin replied: "The Army will not go against the people!"[14]

It was an extraordinary act of posturing. Yeltsin's call for a general strike did not work. His claim about the Army was mere bluster as well. The crews of the motorized divisions in Moscow included officers who had voted for Yeltsin and sympathized with him. Many of them welcomed Gorbachev's removal from the political scene. Yet the elite troops, especially the KGB's "Alfa" commandos and the airborne regiments, were following orders from Kryuchkov and Yazov. Even worse, the republican leaders and parliaments failed to join Yeltsin in taking a stand against the Emergency Committee. The Russian President called Kravchuk and Nazarbayev and "was shocked" by their restraint. In Georgia, the nationalist leader Zviad Gamsakhurdia immediately complied with the demands of the junta and disbanded the Georgian republican militia. In the Baltic republics, Vytautas Landsbergis was the only one calling for a campaign of disobedience in support of Yeltsin. Some republican elites and the leaders of the RSFSR ethnic autonomous regions were prepared to reach a bargain with the junta. The only real hotbed of unrest was in Moldova.[15]

In Moscow, the odds also seemed stacked against Yeltsin. Few were excited about the prospect of a struggle to return Gorbachev to power: polls gave the Soviet leader a 17 percent approval rating; 45 percent of people mistrusted him. Patriarch Alexyi did not respond to Yeltsin's appeal for support and "was taken sick."[16] Later that day, Andrei Kozyrev confided to the American chargé d'affaires Jim Collins that Yeltsin's strategy of resistance did not count on mass popular support. On the contrary, the idea was to urge Russian citizens to stay in their homes to avoid any confrontation with the security forces that could lead to bloodshed.[17] The American Embassy summed up the situation: "The vast body of the population went about its business more or less as usual," ready "to acquiesce with whatever the power struggle would have yielded."[18]

Nobody seemed to notice that Yeltsin had flip-flopped: from being a major destroyer of the Soviet constitutional order he had transformed into its main defender. Radio Liberty placed a correspondent inside the Russian parliament and broadcast Yeltsin's words across the Soviet Union. A CNN cameraman captured him standing on the tank for the whole world to see. This coverage had immense significance in the unfolding events, placing Yeltsin at the center of "the struggle for democracy in Russia."

Because of the eight-hour time difference, George Bush was in bed at his family estate of Kennebunkport, Maine, oblivious to the events in Moscow. It was almost midnight on Sunday when CNN began to report on Gorbachev's "illness" and the emergency rule in Moscow. Brent Scowcroft watched the news on television in his hotel, not far from the Bush family estate. He called Robert Gates, who was in charge of the Situation Room in the White House, and enquired about a coup in Moscow. Gates asked, "What are you talking about?"

Scowcroft woke up Bush and James Baker, who was vacationing at his ranch in Wyoming. Bush went back to sleep, as he would need all his energy next morning. Baker spent a sleepless night wondering about the fate of his friend Shevardnadze. Scowcroft continued to monitor the situation, liaising with Gates and CIA officials. They did not learn much.[19]

When Bush woke up at 5:30 a.m. on the Monday, he decided to dictate his thoughts to his tape-recorder for posterity. His first thoughts were about Yanayev: "He was the guy that congratulated me after our speech in Ukraine about the respect for the Union and the people choosing. I liked the guy. I sent him fishing lures. And, he was rather pleasant. Now it appears from these early reports that he's but a figurehead, which we knew all along . . . There's little we can do—in fact, nothing I'd say . . ." Then Bush's thoughts focused on Gorbachev. He never suspected his friend Mikhail might have been involved in the conspiracy. "I think of his sense of humor, his courage . . . I'm proud we have supported you and there will be a lot of talking heads on television telling us what's been wrong, but you have done what's right and strong and good for your country." This sounded like a goodbye.[20]

Scowcroft came to Kennebunkport and urged the President to focus on America's strategic interests. The administration's paramount goals were to ensure that Soviet troops completed their withdrawal from Central Eastern Europe, and that the Kremlin should honor its commitments to reduce Soviet nuclear and conventional forces. At a press conference held at Kennebunkport, Bush decided to avoid any gestures that might provoke Soviet hardliners into further recklessness, for instance in East Germany or the Baltics. On the phone from Bonn, Chancellor Kohl had told Bush earlier that he did not want to provoke the Soviet military, still stationed on his country's territory. The main issue was that the junta should observe all international treaties and obligations. Meanwhile President Mitterrand had told Bush: "Let's not create a perception that all is lost. The coup could fail in a few days or months. It's hard to impose by force a regime on a changing nation. It won't work. Soviet republics now have elected officials."[21] Bush took Mitterrand's advice at the press conference. "Coups do fail," he said, and people in Russia already "tasted freedom." He called the emergency rule "extra-constitutional." Still, he did not mention any sanctions and did not burn any bridges with the leaders in Moscow. Privately, he hoped Yanayev would honor the existing treaties.[22] Bush also called the Prime Minister of the Netherlands, Ruud Lubbers, and asked him to help block possible calls for an emergency session of NATO in Brussels. "I am very concerned that inadvertently our position in NATO would look like commitments that would be a repeat of Hungary in 1956 or, on the other hand, send a signal of total impotence." Lubbers agreed with the President.[23]

JUNTA

Brian Mulroney, on the phone from Ottawa, had reminded Bush of the G-7 meeting: "Some may say if you people had been more generous in London, maybe this wouldn't have happened." The Canadian Prime Minister asked Bush: "Any doubt in your mind that he was overthrown because he was too close to us?" Bush replied: "I don't think there is any doubt." He decided after the press conference to interrupt his vacation at Kennebunkport to fly back to Washington, so as to demonstrate he was in command of the situation.[24]

KRYUCHKOV'S BLUNDER

The Emergency Committee, or GKChP, could have gained popular legitimacy if only it had showed overwhelming power. This was a clear lesson to be learned from many coups around the world—and a lesson from Russian history. Vladimir Kryuchkov, head of the KGB, was no stranger to violence. In Budapest in 1956, he had watched Soviet tanks crush the anti-communist revolution. In 1979, KGB commandos had assassinated the leader of Afghanistan in a prelude to the Soviet occupation. In 1981, Kryuchkov had advised General Jaruzelski on his introduction of martial law in Poland: the entire opposition leadership and thousands of activists were then arrested overnight. This experience, however, had made Kryuchkov aware of the high political and economic costs associated with brute force. The Soviet intervention in Afghanistan and the crackdown in Poland had triggered Western sanctions.[25]

Kryuchkov considered his current dilemma. Arresting Yeltsin and other elected Russian officials could lead to a storm of indignation in the West, even a return to the Cold War. The Soviet economy and budget could not afford to endure Western sanctions. Kryuchkov also knew that Yazov, Yanayev, and Lukyanov were not ready for violence. They could only be convinced of the need for emergency rule by gradual step-by-step tactics, capitalizing on their common responsibility. When Defense Minister Yazov decided to send hundreds of tanks into Moscow's streets as a show of force, Kryuchkov did not object. He faked an "intelligence report" claiming that an armed opposition allegedly wanted to seize control of Moscow. The KGB leader counted on the instincts of Soviet citizens to welcome a strong hand at a time of rising disorder and economic crisis. Two years later, Yeltsin would say: "The cunning apparatchik from the intelligence services reasoned with good sense."[26]

In the small hours of Monday, 19 August, Kryuchkov convened the KGB Collegium. General Shebarshin jotted down instructions: "The task is to preserve an integrated financial and currency system . . . We will move to the market, but not a wild market. Foreign interference must not be allowed. There will be no signing of the Union Treaty: we cannot leap from one state to another immediately." Kryuchkov telephoned the leaders of Soviet republics and some autonomous regions, telling them to abort their trips to Moscow, since the treaty ceremony had been canceled.[27]

He also called Kravchuk. Ukraine was the key republic to keep under Soviet control. The Ukrainian leader received the call in his office, where he was sitting with Stanislav Hurenko, the First Secretary of the Ukrainian Communist Party, and General Varennikov. The general had just told the Ukrainian officials that "power at last is in the hands of resolute and brave people." He demanded that the Ukrainian parliament introduce martial law in Kiev, Lvov, Odessa, and in Western regions of Ukraine "where the Soviet power has collapsed." Kravchuk felt shocked and defenseless, but he objected to martial law as needlessly provocative. When Kryuchkov called, Kravchuk timidly asked if the state of emergency was constitutional. One hour later Varennikov informed Kryuchkov: "Kravchuk and other comrades agreed with the proposals." Later in the evening, Kravchuk appeared on the *Vremia* news program broadcast across the USSR. His well-crafted remarks cut both ways: he expressed his concern for democracy and the constitution without saying exactly who was threatening them. He also called on Ukrainians to work and stay calm, just as the junta in Moscow demanded. Kravchuk said nothing about the state of Gorbachev's health, although he had dined with him a few days earlier.[28]

The Emergency Committee squabbled about what to do with Yeltsin. Baklanov recalled that a day earlier, on 18 August, Kryuchkov, Pavlov, Yazov, and himself planned to meet with Yeltsin at the airport, upon his return from Kazakhstan. "The meeting did not take place, because it was not logistically arranged by those who were told to do it." Nazarbayev's hospitality and Yeltsin's bout of drinking, which delayed the latter's return to Moscow, and to another airport, might have disrupted the plotters' plans.[29] Kryuchkov's calculations, however, were also significant: he wanted to avoid Yeltsin's arrest. Instead, he expected to browbeat him with an impressive demonstration of force, and perhaps even cut a deal with the Russian separatist at Gorbachev's expense. The KGB chief believed that the Russian Federation and the Soviet Union could not exist one without the other. Shebarshin recalled his phrase: "Russia is the bulwark of the USSR. The USSR is the bulwark of Russia." Kryuchkov knew that Yeltsin was an enemy of the Union, yet he somehow believed it would be possible "to strike a deal with Yeltsin on the basis of his fundamental antipathy to Gorbachev." In the end, Kryuchkov ordered that Yeltsin's dacha be kept under close observation, "with the aim of securing him for negotiations with the Soviet leadership." This absurd formula camouflaged the absence of a clear answer to the political problem at hand.[30]

Yeltsin's resolve, and his declaration on top of the tank, created a new political situation. Kryuchkov continued to believe, however, that his gradualist scenario would work. With the support of Lukyanov and the Supreme Soviet, the Emergency Committee would soon be legitimated, and Yeltsin would be isolated as a troublemaker.[31] In Crimea, Gorbachev had a better instinct. He said to Chernyaev: "You know, in this situation I count on Yeltsin. He will not give up, and he will not yield to them. This means there will be bloodshed."[32]

Leaving Yeltsin at large proved to be Kryuchkov's great blunder. Other errors compounded this one. The plotters did not know how best to deploy television, the most formidable weapon they possessed. Instead of using TV to spread massive and aggressive propaganda about the emergency rule, the junta aired only pre-recorded censored news, beginning with clips from the *Swan Lake* ballet. This epitomized the political and ideological impotence of the Emergency Commitee. The KGB did not deploy its vast arsenal of psychological warfare, accumulated during decades of the Cold War. There were Russian nationalists with a big following, who supported emergency rule, such as the television journalist Alexander Nevzorov, journalist Alexander Prokhanov, and politician Vladimir Zhirinovsky. However, they were not even invited to the TV studios and stayed on the sidelines of the unfolding drama.[33]

In the early afternoon, members of the Emergency Committee gathered again in the Kremlin. Frayed nerves and a lack of sleep made some of the plotters feel "almost euphoric." Initial reports contributed to a feeling of success. The military and KGB findings indicated compliance with the new rule. Reactions from Western leaders were also reassuring. While Bush still slept in Washington, Helmut Kohl met with the Soviet ambassador and listed five conditions that the Committee would need to meet for Germany to continue its economic assistance. The Chancellor also asked for a guarantee as to the "personal safety of Mikhail Gorbachev." Mitterrand talked to journalists about Yanayev's "amazing letter" and also asked the new leadership in Moscow to provide "guarantees for the life of Mikhail Gorbachev and Boris Yeltsin."[34] Those were signs that Western leaders would recognize the junta, in the absence of any major violence.

Kryuchkov felt justified. In order to emphasize business as usual, the Committee decided to hold a press conference and invite foreign journalists. This event began at 5 p.m. on 19 August at APN (Agency for Press News) and turned into a public-relations disaster for the junta: Yanayev could not calm his nerves and was an awful performer; the Prime Minister, Pavlov, was unavailable; Kryuchkov and Yazov decided not to show up. The bland Boris Pugo was the only individual representing the security agencies at the press conference. The audience, instead of exhibiting signs of fear, was contemptuous and defiant. When Western journalists asked Yanayev about Gorbachev's health, he responded: "Gorbachev is entirely safe. I hope that my friend, the President, will be back in shape soon, and we will work together." An Italian journalist asked

Yanayev—amid smirks and laughter—whether the interim President had consulted the Chilean dictator Augusto Pinochet. The twenty-four-year-old journalist Tatiana Malkina from the *Independent Gazette* asked: "Do you realize that last night you instigated a coup d'état?" Yanayev's reply was deadpan: "We are reliant upon constitutional norms." Instead of using television to suit their purposes, the conspirators unwittingly turned its power against themselves. The TV cameras zeroed in on Yanayev's trembling hands. This, recalled Yegor Gaidar a few days later, did more to doom the plot than all the tanks around Moscow. Instead of a ruthless junta, the Soviet people were witnessing a line of colorless bureaucrats who lacked the will to hold onto power.[35]

Many Soviet citizens, in the absence of reliable news on television and radio, turned their short-wave radios to catch Western radio broadcasts. The KGB's General Shebarshin, who had personally witnessed the Iranian revolution, watched CNN. "The situation was unbelievable," he recalled later. The KGB analysts were learning "about the situation in the capital of our Motherland from American sources." Western media outlets owed much of their excellent coverage to many Russian collaborators and friends, above all in Moscow and Leningrad. The independent Russian news agency "Interfax" continued to channel raw news straight to CNN and other Western media. Those Moscow journalists who worked for state-run newspapers and magazines that had been shut down organized "Common Newspaper" and pooled information to share with Western colleagues by phone and fax. Most importantly, at the Ostankino television center, pro-Yeltsin news editors managed to cheat the censors and aired a few seconds from CNN's footage of Yeltsin's speech during prime-time news on the First Channel of Soviet television.[36]

General Varennikov, who watched the news from Kiev, was very angry. "It was a sordid scene. Creatures alien to Soviet society mounted the tank!" He cabled to his comrades-in-arms in Moscow: "The lack of action with regard to the destructive forces is inexplicable, since we had agreed on everything in advance." Varennikov urged the Committee "to take immediate measures to liquidate the group of the adventurist Yeltsin," cordon off the seat of the Russian government, and cut off the water, electricity, telephones, and other communication lines to the Russian parliament. If members of the Emergency Committee continued to abide by "democracy" and "legality" in their actions, Varennikov wrote, they would doom themselves and Soviet statehood. Varennikov had pointed his finger at the plot's cardinal paradox. Yeltsin later noted: "The plotters were afraid of violating the Constitution."[37]

Yeltsin called Kryuchkov on a secure government line to warn him that people might try to block the tanks and there could then be "innumerable casualties." Kryuchkov responded calmly: "No, there will be no victims. First, this is an entirely peaceful operation, and the tanks have no live ammunition . . . All the trouble comes from you, the Russian leadership. Our information shows that the people are quiet and life is going on normally." The KGB chief conducted a personal reconnaissance tour of Moscow by car: Muscovites were getting on with their normal lives; the weather turned bleak and it began to drizzle; tanks and trolley-buses stood next to each other in the street traffic; there was a huge line in front of the first and only McDonald's on Gorky Street. Kryuchkov returned to KGB headquarters reassured: there was no need to react to Varennikov's alarmist cable from Kiev.[38]

It was exactly at this moment when events in Moscow began to develop in a way that no one envisaged. The awareness that Yeltsin was alive, free, and defiant mobilized tens of thousands of people in Moscow and elsewhere to resist emergency rule. The spell of fear was broken. That night they began to gather spontaneously, of their own free will, outside the Russian parliament, now popularly called "The White House" because of its color. The crowd grew from several hundred to several thousand. People chanted slogans in support of Yeltsin and called on the military to leave the city. They began to build the first barricades. Yelena Bonner's daughter Tatiana came home and asked her mother for the keys to her car. "Do you want to use my car for a barricade?" Bonner asked anxiously. "No," Tatiana answered, "we need it to bring gas masks." Her friends feared that the military could use tear gas to break into the building.[39]

The British ambassador, Rodric Braithwaite, was on holiday in the Russian provincial town of Vologda. When he learned what happened, he boarded the first plane back to Moscow. In his first cable to the Foreign and Commonwealth Office he wrote that the coup had "an oddly tentative, even gentlemanly air." The "barons" who seized power, he said, certainly did not want to restore "communism" as the Western press and Russian democrats claimed. Instead of arresting Yeltsin, the coup leaders talked about him like "a parent trying to chide a wayward child."[40] The American chargé d'affaires Jim Collins and the entire US Embassy were caught by complete surprise. The diplomats had been hearing rumors of a coup for so long that they became a "crying wolf story." Collins summed up the observations of his staff, who canvassed many contacts and common Muscovites. The coup, Collins wrote, was strange: the hardliners had permitted Yeltsin to act as a focus of opposition. Collins also reported that Yeltsin called Yanayev and complained that he could not get to his Kremlin office. Yanayev reportedly assured Yeltsin that his car would be allowed to enter the Kremlin. Collins recommended the US government to "keep its distance from the perpetrators of the coup in both words and deeds."[41]

The American Embassy also reported on the amazing activism of Anatoly Sobchak in Leningrad. The mayor rallied the City Council officials under his leadership. He negotiated with the commander of the military district and convinced him to keep the troops away from the city. He appealed to the workers of the Kirov plant to come out en masse next day to a rally against "the criminals" who had staged "the coup."[42] In fact, the situation in the second major Russian city was even messier than Western diplomats could imagine. The Leningrad Party organization, the local KGB, and the commander of the Leningrad military district, Viktor Samsonov, waited for instructions from Moscow. Instead, they received confusing and garbled signals.[43] In Leningrad's KGB, officers were among the first to recognize that the junta did not know what it was doing. A KGB colonel called Vladimir Putin worked at the time as Sobchak's personal aide. A year and a half earlier, Putin had witnessed the crumbling of the GDR. On 19 August, Putin told his boss that he could not work simultaneously for both sides in the conflict. He had made his choice: "I will work with you." Putin said he wanted to submit a formal request to the KGB to discharge him. Sobchak replied: "OK, do this and I will call Kryuchkov." Putin was surprised: "I thought Kryuchkov would send him to hell." Instead Kryuchkov not only listened to Sobchak, but also agreed to Putin's request.[44]

"STAND BY US!"

Galina Starovoitova, Yeltsin's advisor on nationalities, was in London on 19 August. She had come to the United Kingdom at the invitation of a British publisher, to write a book about the "Russian revolution." She decided, instead of returning to Moscow and risking probable arrest, to use Radio Liberty, the BBC's Russian Service, and Voice of America to reach her compatriots and to call for resistance against the junta. Many of Galina's friends, émigré dissidents, worked at these radio stations. On air, Starovoitova said that the plotters would fail, just as the hardliners had failed in January 1991 in Lithuania.[45] Before the junta took power, Starovoitova had argued that Gorbachev should resign. Now her message was different. In Starovoitova's rhetoric, Gorbachev was transformed from a failed leader into a potent symbol of legitimacy and constitutionality. It was the moral duty of Western leaders, she said, to help Gorbachev return to Moscow. Starovoitova compared the initial reactions of Western leaders to the appeasement of Hitler and Stalin.[46]

In Moscow, Andrei Kozyrev met with Jim Collins in order to pass a letter from Yeltsin to Bush. The US administration must avoid any appearance of "business as usual" with the junta. This would grant legitimacy to its actions.[47] Next morning, Kozyrev flew from Moscow's Sheremetyevo Airport to Paris. No one tried to detain him. His brief from Yeltsin was to fly to the United States, meet with Bush, and appeal to the United Nations. If need be, Kozyrev was tasked to set up a Russian government-in-exile. Once in Paris, Kozyrev was on camera for the BBC, calling the Emergency Committee a bunch of thugs who were trying to "restore the totalitarian regime." "No appeasement of those bandits who claim to be the leaders of the Soviet Union," he declared. He also chided those in the West who were arguing that "this regime will be a partner in the new world order." The BBC's correspondent asked him: "What can we in the West do?" Kozyrev replied: "It will be appropriate to recognize the independence of Estonia and the Baltic States. It will show the criminals that they are breaking the empire by their use of force . . ." Galina Starovoitova, on the same program from the BBC studio in London, intoned: "I agree with my colleague and friend Mr Kozyrev. Recognize immediately the independence of the Baltic countries. It will be the sign that you will not recognize the legitimacy of state criminals."[48]

There was no time for the Russian democrats to consider the consequences of the radical break-up of the Soviet Union. Like all revolutionaries, they believed that history was on their side. Gennady Burbulis said to a trusted journalist on 18 August: "We are dealing with the historical collapse of the totalitarian system of power." This process, he continued, "was necessary and inevitable, like an unstoppable force of nature."[49]

On the morning of 20 August, Starovoitova asked her friend Lord Nicholas Bethell, a leading Tory expert on Russia, to put her in contact with Margaret Thatcher. Russian dissidents and anti-communists had long admired the Iron Lady for her policies, rhetoric, clarity, and firmness. Thatcher immediately invited Starovoitova and Bethell to her private office for a briefing. Starovoitova shared her concerns: the British Foreign Office was being soft on the junta in Moscow. She suggested that Thatcher might speak with Yeltsin and express solidarity with him. After a minute of searching in her handbag, Starovoitova found a number for the direct line to Yeltsin's office in the Russian parliament. "To my astonishment," Thatcher later recalled, "I was put through." She and Yeltsin spoke for half an hour, with Bethell and Starovoitova translating. This was the moral and political boost that Yeltsin badly needed at that precarious moment.[50]

From Paris, Kozyrev called Allen Weinstein, the head of the Washington-based Center for Democracy, who had feted Yeltsin on his trip to the United States in June. The Center was a pivot of the pro-Yeltsin lobby in Washington, along with the National Endowment for Democracy and the Krieble Institute. During the first two days of emergency rule, Weinstein and his staff served as a de facto embassy for the Russian President. They received by fax Yeltsin's decrees and eyewitness accounts from their friends inside the Russian parliament, translated them and passed them to American government officials, Congress, and the media. The Center also maintained constant telephone contact with Yeltsin's circle, updating them on American news. Now Kozyrev called Weinstein to dictate to him over the phone an appeal to the American public. It was entitled "Stand by Us!" and concluded with the words: "We are certain that the response from Americans and their government to the present crisis, which threatens not only democracy in my country but peace everywhere, will be one of wholehearted support. Free people understand each other." Weinstein immediately called *The Washington Post*. Kozyrev's appeal was published the next morning, 21 August.[51]

Bush and Scowcroft were still on Air Force One, on their way from Maine to Washington DC, when they received an intelligence briefing from Robert Gates: the situation in the Soviet Union remained murky and the long-term prospects looked dire. The first CIA analytical cable concluded that Gorbachev was most likely isolated or had even been killed, although a "genuine health crisis" could not be totally ruled out. "The 60-year-old Soviet leader suffers from several serious health problems—including hypertension, diabetes, high cholesterol, and chronic stress—all factors that place him at increased risk for a heart attack or a stroke."[52] Nevertheless, Yeltsin's call for Gorbachev's restoration to power had a big effect on Bush. The US President was stung by the media's criticism of him for having swallowed Chinese propaganda around the Tiananmen Square crackdown in 1989. Now he was doing the same in the case of the Soviet Union. For the first time, Gates and other pro-Yeltsin experts found a receptive audience in Bush. The CIA's analysis of the situation on the ground began to change. One analyst argued: "You can't pull off a coup in phases." "We began to think," Gates recalled, "that the coup leaders did not have their act together and that maybe, just maybe, this action could be reversed." James Baker was not the only person in the administration who wondered why Yeltsin, Yakovlev, and Shevardnadze had not been arrested. He thought: "I would certainly have arrested them if I were leading a coup."[53] Kryuchkov's gradualist scenario proved to have the opposite effect in Washington, as well as in Moscow: the Americans interpreted restraint as weakness. At about 3 p.m. on 19 August, the Soviet ambassador Viktor Komplektov showed up at the White House, bringing Yanayev's personal letter to Bush. The administration, however, no longer wanted to talk to the junta.[54]

On the morning of 20 August, Bush placed a telephone call to Yeltsin. It went through at 8:18 a.m. EST. Bush said: "Just checking to know how things are going at your end." Yeltsin responded calmly, as if he were not in extreme danger. He even called Yanayev "President." Yeltsin was remarkably well informed about Gorbachev's circumstances. The Soviet leader, Yeltsin said, was in Foros, Crimea, surrounded "by three circles of armed guards and the KGB." The Russian leader then said what Galina Starovoitova in London had advised him: "Mr President, it would be good if you yourself could demand to speak on the phone with

Gorbachev and to rally world leaders to the fact that the situation here is critical." Bush asked if it would help to speak with Yanayev and restrain him. "No, absolutely, you should not do it," responded Yeltsin in apparent horror. "An official call from you would legitimize them." Yeltsin's chutzpah overwhelmed Bush. "You have our full support for the return of Gorbachev and the legitimate government," he said. "We sympathize and pray with you. All the American people support you. What you're doing is absolutely right."[55]

The British Prime Minister, John Major, also called Yeltsin soon after Bush. Germany's Foreign Minister, Hans-Dietrich Genscher, sent a message of support to Yeltsin and the Russian government. Each of these calls was announced to the crowd in front of the Russian parliament and cheered by thousands. It was also likely that the moment Bush hung up, the content of their conversation would have been reported to Kryuchkov. It was now obvious that international legitimacy went to Yeltsin and was denied to the junta.[56]

In their Crimean captivity, Mikhail Gorbachev and his family avidly listened to the news on the BBC, Voice of America, and Radio Liberty. The news that Yeltsin had not been arrested and had offered resistance made Gorbachev muse that the coup would lead to bloodshed. And the remarks of Yanayev at the press conference in Moscow made Gorbachev and Raisa fear for their lives. It was logical for the junta to blackmail the Soviet leader, to obtain from him consent under duress to their actions. In case he refused, the KGB had ways to "make him sick," even terminally. Gorbachev recorded a video appeal to the Supreme Soviet of the USSR and the nation, in which he called the junta's actions "an anti-constitutional act," "rude lie," and "state crime." He and Raisa discussed with Chernyaev how to smuggle this video out of the villa, but they concluded it was impossible. Raisa decided that the family would stop eating any food delivered since the day of their captivity. The only glimmer of hope for the Gorbachevs was the rejection of the junta by Western governments and the appeals to return the Soviet President to Moscow. Chernyaev recorded Gorbachev's comments: "All [Western] credit lines will be terminated, all 'faucets' will be turned off at once. Our banks will go bankrupt immediately . . . Everything would grind to a halt. The plotters have the mind of mice, they could not understand elementary equations."[57]

A TIPPING POINT

In 1931, the Italian author Curzio Malaparte wrote a book, *The Technique of Revolution*, in which he described the essential ingredients of a successful coup. He analyzed Lenin and Trotsky's coup in 1917. Malaparte's main thesis was that a passionate minority, with a determined leadership, could succeed only if they acted resolutely at a tipping point, when everything hangs in the balance—without worrying about the consequences. Kryuchkov was well aware of the requirements for a successful coup, but he simply lacked the guts to implement them.[58] Had the KGB chief been a resolute counter-revolutionary or a fanatical Stalinist, history would have turned out differently. Instead, the Emergency Committee was rapidly nearing the tipping point—of losing power.

Many in the Soviet bureaucratic class, according to one public-opinion expert, at first thought: "All of this is not entirely legal, but something would have to be done; the country is in a critical situation." On 19 August, an independent poll service in Moscow surveyed 300 "elite representatives," including parliamentary deputies, government officials, leaders of the media, and opinion-makers. The survey began four hours after emergency rule was announced, reaching people on the telephone: 60 percent of respondents did not support the junta and backed Yeltsin; 40 percent strongly supported the Emergency Committee or were unwilling to side with the RSFSR government. The pollsters found, to their surprise, that a large number of people were taking a wait-and-see attitude. Many had either refused to talk to pollsters or had not clarified their position.[59]

Money preoccupied the supreme bureaucratic elite. How could deploying tanks in Moscow help in the search for hard currency and investment in declining industrial output? The use of force could only result in Western sanctions and Soviet bankruptcy.[60] The junta had demonstrated an extraordinary lack of economic strategy. Its appeal to the people pledged a "solution to food and housing problems," to end crime and ethnic violence, and to defend the interests of people with lower incomes. Yet the text of this appeal did not explain how this would be achieved and left readers with the strong impression that the junta was returning to the economic policies of Brezhnev, Andropov, and Chernenko. Yet even this option was impossible, because the Soviet economy was already in the "Polish situation" and critically dependent on Western credits. The only thing the junta members talked about was the supply and availability of goods. The Army and security services could not yield the harvest and put food on the tables of Soviet citizens. The only idea that Yanayev could think of was to take food supplies from state reserves and sell them to consumers at affordable prices.[61]

In the late afternoon of 19 August, the Cabinet of Ministers of the Soviet Union was in emergency session. Pavlov had apparently recovered and attended. He started by defending emergency rule and soon went off on a tangent. The junta, he said, had prevented the imminent arrest of the entire government by the militants who had infiltrated Moscow with American weapons. The ministers listened to their boss with dismay. Shcherbakov thought Pavlov was either hallucinating or drunk. He spoke next and said that Western assistance, "on which we had counted, will not come." Without Western money and supplies of food, medicine, and vital industrial parts, "a chain reaction might bring the whole economy to a halt." Since early that morning Shcherbakov had been preparing the country for Western sanctions and a probable freeze on all Soviet assets abroad. He had issued Soviet foreign trade representatives and banks abroad instructions to execute the immediate transfers of Soviet money from accounts in the United States and Europe to "neutral countries." "I am in favor of discipline," Shcherbakov concluded, "but ... without a return to 1929." He was referring to Stalin's resort to terror against the peasants and entrepreneurs.[62]

Pavlov's other deputies, Vitaly Doguzhiev and Yuri Masliukov, shared Shcherbakov's verdict. The Union Treaty ("after serious revision") would be an essential political foundation for keeping the economy going. With his own arguments turned against him, Pavlov changed tack. He assured his deputies that he was also in favor of a future Union Treaty that would clearly define the rights and responsibilities of the center. "We are professionals," he concluded, "and we have our own understanding of what an integrated economic space should be." The meeting was adjourned without any decisions having been taken.[63]

Outside the Cabinet, economists knew better than anyone that the junta had doomed itself. Yegor Gaidar was at his dacha, finishing his book about Latin American economies, when his wife Masha called, in tears, and yelled about the tanks in the streets and Gorbachev's removal from power. Gaidar's initial reaction was that the junta would stay in power for five to seven years, perhaps decades, defying Western sanctions. After all, the Soviet Union had huge resources at its disposal. But after hearing Yanayev's appeal on the radio, Gaidar changed his prediction. No one among the new rulers was a Pinochet or a Deng Xiaoping with political will or an economic vision. In Moscow, together with his colleagues, Gaidar penned a manifesto and faxed it to all the foreign news agencies in Moscow. The junta, the text went, was killing the economy and Yeltsin's victory was the only hope for the country. That same evening, Gaidar and his associates tore up their Party membership cards.[64]

The Speaker of the Supreme Soviet of the USSR, Anatoly Lukyanov, was an opportunist. On the morning of 20 August, Ruslan Khasbulatov, Alexander Rutskoy, and Ivan Silayev, the RSFSR Prime Minister, came to Lukyanov with a comprehensive proposal: he should convene the Presidium of the Soviet parliament and disavow the junta's decrees as anti-constitutional. He should also arrange a meeting between Gorbachev and the Russian leadership "with the involvement of Yanayev." Lukyanov refused to act. He repeated the false story about Gorbachev's incapacity and even insisted that he had medical evidence to support it.[65] "One word from you would have been enough to stop all this funny business," Gorbachev would later tell his former friend. The opposite was true as well: one word from Lukyanov could have legitimized the junta. Lukyanov, however, sat on the fence. Years later, when asked what he had expected, Lukyanov replied: an emergency Party Congress in September that would have replaced General Secretary Gorbachev.[66] Meanwhile, he did not want to take any risk.

The day of 20 August was a crucial one for both the junta and the Russian democratic opposition. In Leningrad, Anatoly Sobchak, tall and charismatic, opened a 10 a.m. rally of 200,000 people in front of the famous Winter Palace. In a massive release of quasi-revolutionary fervor, people chanted: "Down with the junta! Fascism will not pass!" Eminent intellectuals and artists claimed that only Yeltsin held "the supreme legitimate power in the Russian state." Radio Liberty, the BBC, and a Leningrad radio station under Sobchak's control broadcast the voices of resistance. Veterans of the war in Afghanistan offered protection to the crowd; many industrial workers joined. The Party apparatus headed by Boris Gidaspov was not even in evidence.[67] That afternoon, Sobchak told the American consul Jack Gosnell that he hoped the coup would end without bloodshed, and "with the simple arrest of those responsible, like the attempted coup in Spain." Sobchak was referring to 1981, when King Juan Carlos denounced a military coup on television, calling for the continuation of democratic rule. "We have no Juan Carlos," Sobchak said smiling, "but we do have a Yeltsin."[68]

That same morning in Moscow, tens of thousands of people flocked to the square in front of the Russian "White House." At 3 p.m., Shevardnadze gave a speech to the crowd and recalled to rapturous applause that he had been right about the coming coup back in December. When he spoke about Gorbachev, the crowd jeered at the absent Soviet leader. Shevardnadze ended with the slogan "Long live freedom!" He told his aides later that this was the most sublime experience of his life. Alexander Prokhanov, an enthusiastic supporter of the junta, came to the square to assess the situation. He saw "a large quantity of women and young girls" on the barricades. Russian women kept appealing to the tank drivers: "Don't kill! Stop! God preserve you!" Veterans of the Afghan war, who had arrived from different cities and regions, were organizing the defense of parliament. There were young intellectuals and academic scholars from the elite Moscow think tanks who had connections in the top echelons of the Soviet bureaucracy. There were also many foreigners in the crowd, even a few American students. A journalist from the *Independent Gazette* wrote that "business and commercial circles backed the Russian government with stunning energy." The Moscow Stock Exchange and Russian commercial banks shut down, and many young brokers marched in protest across Moscow against emergency rule. Young businessmen supplied food, tents, tools, and construction materials to the crowd in front of "The White House."[69]

A report from the Ministry of the Interior on 20 August said there were mass rallies in twenty-seven Russian cities, with a total of 250,000 participants. Summoned by the city's Soviet, 5,000 people protested in Volgograd, Kryuchkov's home town. Across the Urals, and in most important cities throughout Siberia and the Far East, local governments backed the Russian leadership, transmitted Yeltsin's speech on local television and radio, and demanded that the junta be disbanded. Although a general strike campaign failed, some academic institutions in Moscow and Leningrad and the coalminers' unions in Vorkuta and Kuzbass went on strike.[70]

Kryuchkov's gradualist scenario was in a shambles. At this point he ordered his deputy General Ageyev to prepare "Operation Thunder," an assault on "The White House," and the arrest of the Russian opposition. Yet the KGB leader still did not want to take full responsibility by signing the order for decisive action. Yazov found himself in an awkward position: he had brought massive military force onto the streets of downtown Moscow, yet he did not want to use it. According to "Operation Thunder," the military would have to clear a corridor for the KGB commandos. Yazov's subordinates in the General Staff convened a planning meeting; the minister did not attend it. General Varennikov, who had returned from Kiev, and General Vladislav Achalov found themselves in charge of all preparations. Achalov sent his subordinate, General Alexander Lebed, to visit the Russian parliament and to carry out a reconnaissance. Lebed returned to the Ministry of Defense and reported that the crowd around the "The White House" numbered around 50,000 people. It would be impossible to avoid civilian casualties.[71]

Yevgeny Primakov, Gorbachev's pragmatic advisor, had managed to return to Moscow from a resort in Crimea, and quickly canvassed the opinions of his friends and colleagues about the Emergency Committee. All of them agreed that the junta was "the conspiracy of the doomed." Some gave the Committee two to three days to survive. Senior diplomats in the Foreign Ministry began to contact officials in the American Embassy privately, to inform them that they would not serve the junta. In his testimony to the later investigation, Primakov recalled that he saw Yanayev, his old friend, in his Kremlin office and urged him "to meet with Yazov immediately and withdraw troops. The nominal head of the junta was in a cloud of denial and fear. Yanayev moaned that he was 'a hostage' and that 'they twisted his arm.'" When Primakov asked about Gorbachev, Yanayev replied: "Zhenya, believe me, everything will be fine. Mikhail Sergeyevich will return, and we will work together." In his later interviews, Yanayev claimed that the democrats had plans to execute him. He seemed to believe in what he said.[72]

Defections from the ranks of the junta were only a matter of time. The first big defector was Pavlov. He took some medicine during the session of the Cabinet of Ministers to control his nerves, and later had a second breakdown that incapacitated him for days. Yanayev was next. At the evening session of the Emergency Committee on 20 August, the acting President of the USSR opened the session by reading a draft of his TV declaration: he was prepared to say that the rumors of an imminent assault on "The White House" were groundless. Leonid Kravchenko, head of the state television company, was also present at the meeting and later testified that Pugo, Kryuchkov, Shenin, Baklanov, and Yazov were surprised by Yanayev's declaration. Interrupting one another, they argued vociferously that such an announcement would be a bad idea. Yanayev asked the group: "Is there indeed anyone among us who wants to attack 'the White House'?" There was an awkward silence. In the end, Yanayev, feeling once again that he was in a bind, signed a decree introducing a curfew in Moscow in the hope of dispelling the crowd in front of the Russian parliament. Still, it became clear that the acting President did not want to take responsibility for any bloodshed. The burden of this decision was firmly on Kryuchkov and Yazov.[73]

In public and in front of CNN's cameras, Yeltsin and his spokesmen repeatedly stated that the Russian military would not engage in violence against the Russian people.[74] Some Afgantsy, veterans of the war in Afghanistan, volunteered to defend Yeltsin in Moscow and Sobchak in Leningrad.[75] Documents from the General Staff, however, show no evidence of any disobedience or defections by the military. The officers on duty, however, followed the orders of their superiors. They acted on their oath of allegiance to the Soviet constitution, and took it seriously. Only a few of them, however, including Varennikov, were ready to use any means "to restore order." On too many occasions in the recent past the political leaders had made the military scapegoats for the use of lethal force against civilians. Soviet officers remembered the lessons of Tbilisi, Baku, and Vilnius. General Alexander Lebed was one of them. At first, he received an order from Pavel Grachev, head of the airborne troops, to "organize the defense" of the Russian parliament. Lebed met with Yeltsin, who gave his consent for the deployment of a tank batallion. Neither could quite understand what was happening. Next day, Grachev rebuked Lebed for "a stupid act" of deploying tanks and ordered him to withdraw them. Lebed realized that his boss was using him in some kind of game. Democratic-minded journalists reported on Western radios that Lebed had defected to Yeltsin's side. Then there was a rumor that Lebed had committed suicide. Lebed's superiors believed in this misinformation; Yazov was surprised to see him alive and well in his office on 20 August.

All this made Lebed behave with extreme caution, and refrain from any violence in the absence of clear written orders from his superiors.[76]

The "Alfa" commandos thought likewise. Led by a KGB officer, Viktor Karpukhin, this elite detachment was in readiness for an assault on the Russian parliament. One of the group's veterans recalled that Alfa had the back-up of GRU commandos, a squadron of helicopters, and some airborne units. Everyone realized it would be impossible to carry out the mission without inflicting many casualties. "None of us wanted to have the blood of Russian people on our hands." When this became clear to everyone, the veteran explained, "the problems with back-up forces began. The helicopter pilots told us that they could not carry out a missile attack on the Russian parliament, because they might mistakenly hit the US Embassy. Everyone else sought to pass the buck on starting this combat operation to others. The guys from the airborne troops complained they could not advance to their bases, because they were out of fuel. The GRU guys also sought to opt out."[77]

Inside the Russian parliament, however, nobody knew how the military and the KGB would act under orders. Yeltsin and his entourage had come to believe that an assault was imminent. From various sources in the KGB, as well as from the Afghan veterans, they were receiving warnings about lethal preparations. The RSFSR nominal Minister of Defense, General Konstantin Kobets, together with Vice-President Rutskoy, frantically called the commanders of the military units deployed in Moscow, some of them being close friends from their service in Afghanistan. The office of Gennady Burbulis in "The White House" was another center for reconnaissance and action. From there, Viktor Ivanenko, head of "the Russian KGB," called his colleagues and friends. Burbulis admiringly recalled that Ivanenko worked the phone "for three days without eating or sleeping. I heard him saying: 'Kolya, remember that hunting expedition we did together? Please, use restraint. This is a foolish affair, nothing good will come of it, and we'd better stay friends.'" Ivanenko even called the head of the Alfa group and warned him not to carry out anti-constitutional orders. An Alfa officer confirmed: "The most unpleasant thing for us was that the defenders of the White House and those who prepared to attack knew each other. We had all worked together in the KGB for years, and it was impossible to conceal any secrets from one another." The majority of regional KGB officials in the Russian Federation sat on the fence from day one of the junta, waiting to see which side would win.[78]

Fearing the worst, some people quietly left the parliament building. One of them was the RSFSR Prime Minister, Ivan Silayev. Yeltsin could read in his eyes: "Defeat is inevitable. I am an old man." The mayor of Moscow, Gavriil Popov, who had just returned from vacation, huddled in a fortified basement of the building, fearful for his life and totally drunk.[79] Tens of thousands of people outside the Russian parliament—standing in a cold drizzle—felt completely unprotected, but they stayed. They were resolved to act as a human shield to protect the parliament building in the event of an attack, to defend their democratically elected government. Among the defenders was Jill Braithwaite, wife of the British ambassador. A courageous woman, she had convinced her Russian friends to go to the barricades "to stand up for Gorbachev, and all the liberal values." From time to time, a high-profile person would turn up and boost the defenders' morale. The world-famous cellist Mstislav Rostropovich arrived from the United States to defend the Russian "White House." The deputy mayor of Moscow, Yuri Luzhkov, came to stay in the parliamentary building overnight, together with his pregnant wife. Eduard Shevardnadze also arrived that evening, without telling his wife Nanuli, and showed his face to the crowd in front of the building. The appearance of such celebrities gave the crowd some hope that violence could be avoided.[80]

Around 11 p.m., Yegor Gaidar arrived at the Russian parliament and came to Burbulis's office, where he found many eminent intellectual figures who were prepared to die in the name of democracy. "The informational vacuum contributed to fear," he recalled two days later. Everyone expected the assault would begin sometime between 2 and 3 a.m. on 21 August. This was what the Alfa commandos had in fact planned. Gaidar, like many others, was thinking about Chile's democratically elected President, Salvador Allende, and his last stand in La Moneda Palace after Pinochet had launched the military coup in 1973. He forgot the rational conclusions that he had come to just two days before.[81] The Americans in the US Embassy across the street were also convinced that the junta would strike. They evacuated everybody from the vulnerable side of the Embassy residence to an underground gymnasium for safety. James Baker, who was on a plane heading to Brussels to attend a NATO meeting, expected officials from the Situation Room in the American White House to call him at any minute and announce that the KGB and the black berets "had attacked and overrun the barricades, killing Yeltsin in the process."[82]

Around 2:30 a.m., shots were heard from the Garden Ring, near the wide Kalinin Avenue that leads to "The White House." Most of the defenders decided that the long-expected assault had finally begun. The head of Yeltsin's personal security detail, Alexander Korzhakov, had several options to spirit Yeltsin out of the building. Korzhakov procured a wig, a beard, and a moustache to disguise the Russian President. The easiest option was to cross the street in a car and find refuge in the US Embassy. Korzhakov woke up Yeltsin, who had dozed off with his clothes on, and led him to a car for his evacuation. Yeltsin, when he came to his senses, refused to claim American asylum. This was another example of

Yeltsin's panache, but also his sense of predestination. "Through the coup," he recalled, "I had the feeling that some sort of miraculous force was helping us."[83]

Marshal Yazov was Kryuchkov's best asset. His concern for the future of the Soviet Army in the event of the state's collapse had made him join the Emergency Committee. Yazov had personal concerns as well. A month before the coup, his wife Emma had suffered a serious car accident; miraculously she survived, but both her legs had been broken. The Marshal told her nothing about the plot. When Emma learned about it on 19 August, she called her husband several times from their dacha, where she was recovering, but he refused to speak to her. Then she asked a female friend to drive her to Moscow to see him, taking her wheelchair. Yazov was waiting for her in the lobby of the Ministry of Defense. When Emma was wheeled by her friend into his office, she began to cry. It was clear that her tears affected Yazov. She told him that a civil war was starting and urged him to stop the nightmare and call Gorbachev. "Emma, you have to understand; there is no communication," Yazov responded. On a television screen in Yazov's office Emma saw the junta's press conference starting. She said sobbing: "Dima, what company you have got yourself into! You always ridiculed them. Call Gorbachev . . ."[84]

The lack of any action increased Yazov's frustration. After several hours, the tanks and armed transports seemed less a symbol of power than an embarassment for the junta: there were no facilities to provide hot food for the troops; officers and soldiers could not change their clothes and had to sleep inside their vehicles through the cold and rainy nights; there were not even any toilets for them to use. Muscovites brought them food and water and tried to convince the officers to violate their orders and withdraw from the city. After Kryuchkov started planning "Operation Thunder," Marshal Yazov had slowly begun to realize that the use of lethal force might put the Army at even greater risk than inaction. In the presence of the commander of the Soviet Air Force, Yevgeny Shaposhnikov, Yazov wondered aloud what he should do. Shaposhnikov allegedly recommended that he pull the troops out of Moscow: "With dignity, to preserve the prestige of the Armed Forces." Yazov never acknowledged or denied this conversation.[85] His deputy, Vladislav Achalov, also had the sense that Yazov was trying to distance himself from the operation. Even Varennikov, despite all his resolve to use force, was against the military doing the dirty work for the KGB and the riot police.[86]

At the evening's session of the Emergency Committee, disagreements among the junta broke out. Baklanov and Kryuchkov argued that the situation was still favorable, while Yanayev referred to unfavorable information. Kryuchkov replied: "One should receive useful information, not truthful information." The head of the KGB argued that they needed to liquidate "the seat of resistance" and arrest Yeltsin. Nobody objected, but no decision was made either. Baklanov was so upset by this foot-dragging that he even sat down to write his formal resignation from the Committee. Yazov observed the acrimony in the room with a gloomy face.[87]

Then came the report from the Cabinet of Ministers. The ministers knew that the Soviet government was running a huge budget deficit. Pavlov's deputy, Doguzhiev, informed him that essential supplies would run out in a few days, while the Soviet Union no longer had any lines of credit to purchase the necessary imports. Someone mentioned the strategic reserves of food stored in the event of war. At this point Yazov exploded. He recalled during his interrogation: "I knew that the army reserves could only feed the army itself for a few days. The [Soviet] population of three hundred million would consume all of it in one day. This was not a solution." Everyone in the room was considering the hopelessness of the situation.[88]

After the meeting of the Emergency Committee broke up around 10:30 p.m., Kryuchkov returned to the Lubyanka to make the final preparations for an assault on the Russian parliament. The time for the attack was set for 3 a.m. by the KGB and the military. This was when the crowd in front of "The White House" would be at its smallest size. Kryuchkov's deputy Genyi Ageyev conducted a personal reconnaissance around "The White House" and returned with the conclusion that any attempt to occupy it would result in a bloodbath. Kryuchkov never issued the order to begin the assault.[89]

Yazov returned to his office in the General Staff building, his nerves on edge. He was waiting for bad news, and it came soon. A column of armored personnel carriers from the Taman Division had been carrying out its orders to impose a curfew, when it was ambushed by a crowd of young men, some of them veterans of the Afghan war. They used a barricade built from trolley-buses to trap the military column inside an underpass. The young men threw Molotov cocktails at the APCs and covered the vehicles' observation ports with pieces of fabric. The young soldiers, scared and disoriented, opened fire. In the melee, three young Muscovites died. Twelve people, including some soldiers, were wounded.[90]

Vladislav Achalov reported on the incident to Yazov and added that the riot police had entirely disappeared from the streets, leaving the army without protection. For Yazov, this was the breaking point. He took off his tie, unbuttoned his shirt, and said to Achalov: "Issue the order 'Stop'!" This meant that the troops must freeze in their positions and stop following any other orders. Yazov proceeded to call Moscow City Hall: he wanted the Moscow authorities to help remove the barricades, to clear the way for withdrawal of the tanks and APCs. Yazov then instructed Achalov and Varennikov to go to KGB headquarters and tell Kryuchkov that the army was out of the plot.[91]

JUNTA

Those in "The White House" continued to expect the worst. Around 3 a.m., Burbulis dialled Kryuchkov's number, using the secure government line. The KGB chief told him: "You can sleep safely." Gaidar, who heard this conversation, was stunned: one person was preparing to kill the other, and yet they chatted over the phone like two government officials.[92] Two hours later, on Yazov's orders, the military commander of Moscow called off the curfew. Then Yazov opened the collegium of the General Staff and the Ministry of Defense and ordered them to remove the troops from Moscow. He refused to meet with other members of the junta. Kryuchkov, Baklanov, and Shenin rushed to Yazov's office in an attempt to change his mind. "Kryuchkov urged me to continue to act," Yazov testified under interrogation. "He said that not everything was lost: one should wage 'a tenacious struggle' (*vyazkuiu bor'bu*). I could never understand what he meant by that." When one member of the delegation accused Yazov of betrayal, he replied: "We did not start all of this to open fire and kill people."[93]

Later, when Yeltsin no longer needed to embellish the August events for his own political goals, he called the junta members "average, ordinary Soviet people," not ruthless cynics and totalitarian despots. He even admitted that they had respect for human life and legality—and that was why they had surrendered and lost power.[94] In October 1993, during the constitutional crisis in Moscow, Yeltsin acted very differently: he ordered his tank commanders to fire at the building of the Russian parliament when it resisted him, arrested all of his political rivals, and stayed in power for another six years.

Kryuchkov and other fathers of the junta had launched emergency rule without any clear plan or a viable economic program, and, most importantly, without the determination to crush resistance by any means. Emergency rule would end in a farce of repentance and moral breakdown. Yazov, determined to save the Army, came up with the idea of going to Gorbachev to seek his forgiveness. The Minister of the Interior, Boris Pugo, was the only full member of the junta who played by the rules: he and his wife were found dead, with a gun next to them, having left a note for their children and relatives: "I have committed an absolutely unexpected blunder, equal to a crime."[95] This was a paraphrase of the famous words, "This is worse than a crime—this is a blunder," delivered by a French politician in 1809 when commenting on Napoleon's assassination of an aristocratic enemy: the act was criminal yet the Emperor had blundered, for it only made him more enemies.

Some witnesses in the state apparatus characterized what happened on 21 August as a "political meltdown." The conspirators had achieved something that no one could have predicted: the complete surrender of the executive branch of central government. The botched emergency rule provided Yeltsin

and his democratic followers and allies with an historic opportunity to seize the
levers of executive power on behalf of Gorbachev and the constitutional order.
The unimaginable became inevitable. And this meant the political death of the
Soviet Union.

SAVING GORBY

Rumors about the retreat of the Emergency Committee spread down the grape-
vine of the Soviet bureaucracy and elites. The earliest reaction came from
Primakov and members of the centrist movement for "democratic reforms."
They gave a press conference and publicly announced that they were joining
forces with the "democratic opposition." Those who sat on the fence began to
join the winning side. On the Old Square, members of the CPSU Secretariat
and the Politburo did their best to separate themselves from Oleg Shenin. The
acting General Secretary, Vladimir Ivashko, who had emerged on 19 August
from hospital after surgery, proposed sending an appeal to the Emergency
Committee and arranging a meeting with Gorbachev. Shenin, when he learned
about it, considered this idea to be a complete capitulation.[96]

In the Cabinet of Ministers, two of Pavlov's senior deputies, Shcherbakov
and Doguzhiev, met with senior officials from the State Bank and drafted a plea
to the leaders of the G-7 countries not to cancel their economic and financial
transactions with the Soviet Union, "since the constitutional process would
soon be restored."[97] Lukyanov, in his Kremlin office, cursed himself for betting
on the wrong horse. He called Yeltsin and, in a rare display of emotion, said he
had decided to go to Crimea alone and free Gorbachev. His deputies in the
Supreme Soviet of the USSR hastily gathered to pass a resolution: the legitimate
President of the USSR must be brought back to Moscow.[98]

On the drizzly cold morning of 21 August, the Russian parliament was still
surrounded by barricades; 50,000 people milled around in front of the building.
A few tanks stranded between the barricades reminded them of the night of
fear. At 11:15 a.m., the Speaker, Khasbulatov, opened an extraordinary session
of the Russian parliament. Only half of the deputies attended. A few Western
ambassadors and journalists came along to observe.[99] As the news about the
meltdown of executive power began to trickle in, the mood of the parliamentarians began to change from caution to triumphalism. In his opening speech,
Khasbulatov spoke about a ruthless junta that had "carried out its goals firmly,
cynically and on a grand scale." After liquidating "The White House as the last
bulwark of freedom," the junta "would have been in a position to achieve a
complete victory all over the country and unleash bloody terror against the
people, who have chosen the path of liberty and rejuvenation of the Fatherland."

The people of Moscow, continued Khasbulatov to thunderous applause, had stopped those reactionary forces and saved the honor of Russia. The speaker also emphasized the support of the West as a crucial factor of legitimacy for the Russian revolution. "The leaders of Western countries, including President Bush, the Prime Minister of Great Britain, Eastern European leaders . . . absolutely, unequivocally said that the only guarantor of the free development of the USSR at this moment . . . was the stand taken by the Russian Federation, its President, and its Supreme Soviet."[100]

Yeltsin spoke next. He had been awake since 5 a.m. He called Kryuchkov with a proposal: they should fly to Crimea together to check on Gorbachev's well-being. Much to Yeltsin's surprise, the KGB chief agreed. He was desperate to find a legitimate way out of the standoff. Then the Russian President called his family. It was his daughter Yelena's birthday, and she hollered into the phone: "Papa, you have given me the best present there ever was. You gave us freedom!"[101] Facing the deputies, Yeltsin was sharp and confident. The coup, he said, had occurred after two earlier botched attempts: the bloodshed in the Baltics in January and the closed session of the Supreme Soviet of the USSR in June. The forces of the Right had been stopped by a coalition of democratic forces. Yeltsin thanked the people of Moscow, who had helped bring the tanks and Spetsnaz forces to a standstill. The military had not turned against the people: the Tula division of General Lebed, instead of taking the parliament building by storm, had assumed the duty of defending the Russian parliament, "and for a day stood firmly in its defense." Adding to a revolutionary narrative that Khasbulatov had begun to build, Yeltsin also mentioned "His Holiness," the Russian Orthodox Patriarch Alexyi II, who allegedly had "expressed full support for the Russian leadership."[102] Western support was mentioned prominently in Yeltsin's speech as well: "I should say right away that both Bush and Mitterrand and others declared firmly that they denounced the anti-constitutional coup and the actions of the group that declared emergency rule, [and] did not back any of its actions."[103]

Democratic triumphalism was the mood of the day. Russia had finally joined the countries of Eastern Europe and the Baltic republics in the sequence of peaceful democratic revolutions. Above all, Yeltsin wanted to legitimize his takeover of the Soviet Army, KGB, and police as now part of the "Russian state." He also told the deputies that "there was an agreement with" Gorbachev to place all the enterprises and property on the territory of the Russian Federation under the jurisdiction of the Russian authorities. Gorbachev had linked that promise to the signing of the Union Treaty and creation of a new federal government. Yeltsin conveniently "forgot" about this linkage. Democratic Russia had won, and its elected leader began to claim the spoils.

After speaking for an hour to the RSFSR deputies, Yelsin dropped a bomb-shell. He announced that Kryuchkov "agreed with my proposal to fly together with me to Foros and return President Gorbachev." The deputies erupted in disbelief and rejection. No deals with the KGB! Khasbulatov looked over at Yeltsin as if to say: "I told you so." Theatrically, Yeltsin pivoted and proposed arresting Kryuchkov and other members of the junta. He would not go to Crimea for reasons of security. Instead, a delegation headed by Prime Minister Silayev and Vice-President Rutskoy would go there and bring Gorbachev back. The parliament approved the proposal.[104]

Outside the walls of parliament, however, the situation was changing more rapidly than anybody had expected or planned. A few minutes later, Yeltsin told Vadim Bakatin, who had arrived at "The White House" to speak at the session, that Kryuchkov had just "cheated" him: instead of coming to "The White House," the KGB chairman had left for Crimea to meet with Gorbachev. It was in fact unclear who had cheated whom.[105] Minutes later Yeltsin again took the floor of the Supreme Soviet to announce: "All these adventurists, the members of the so-called Committee, have left for Vnukovo [Airport] . . . Their inten-tions are unknown: maybe they want to escape . . ." The unspoken danger was that the hapless conspirators would strike a bargain with the zig zagging Soviet leader. Amid great commotion, the deputies voted to send a delegation to Crimea immediately, to apprehend and arrest the conspirators. Riding on the wave of fear and uncertainty, Yeltsin immediately called for a mandate to act. The deputies approved Yeltsin's emergency decrees, giving him authority and control over economic assets on Russian territory—in clear breach of the Soviet constitution. The Russian President was also authorized to replace any regional and local authorities who had collaborated with the junta with provisional commissars. It was the mandate for a political revolution.[106]

At 2.30 in the afternoon on 21 August, Marshal Yazov kissed his wife Emma goodbye at Vnukovo Airport and boarded the presidential IL-62 plane, together with Kryuchkov, Baklanov, and Yuri Plekhanov, the head of the KGB's Ninth Directorate. Baklanov later called this trip "a senseless act from the start," yet he went all the same. The plotters were also not even the first delegation to leave for Crimea that afternoon. Apart from the junta, two other men boarded the plane: Anatoly Lukyanov and the acting Party head, Vladimir Ivashko.[107] And about two hours later, a TU-134 took off with the team sent by the Russian Parliament, accompanied by some journalists. The Russian authorities had invited Western statesmen and diplomats, as well as international medical experts and a CNN crew, to join them, but because of traffic jams, caused by the retreating columns of tanks, only two foreigners made it to the plane on time.[108]

This race of the two planes was deadly serious; the sense of drama was absorbing for each participant. When Bush called Yeltsin at 3:30 p.m. Moscow time, the Russian leader told him that the conspirators wanted to intercept Gorbachev and either force him to sign a document of resignation or take him to points unknown. Yeltsin also told Bush that he had called Kravchuk and the head of the Soviet Air Force, General Shaposhnikov, asking them to intercept the IL-62. This turned out to be impossible. The Russian President then said that "through Gorbachev's guards" the opposition had learned that Gorbachev was in good health and determined not to sign "any documents that would give his power to anyone." The plan, Yeltsin continued, was to arrest the junta either in Crimea or upon their return to Moscow. Understandably, he could not share any details with Bush over the phone. "I will do everything I can to save democracy in Russia and throughout the USSR," Yeltsin concluded.[109]

The presidential plane landed at the Belbek airfield in Crimea without any problems. ZIL limousines took the passengers at top speed to "Zaria." The local KGB and military commanders continued to follow orders from Yazov and Kryuchkov: they blocked the airfield with trucks to prevent the third incoming "Russian" plane from landing. The limousines arrived at the presidential villa shortly before 5 p.m., entered the gates, and headed for the main house. At this point, armed bodyguards loyal to Gorbachev stopped them. General Plekhanov and Kryuchkov went to speak with the guards—officially their subordinates—but the guards warned them that they would shoot to kill if the limousines moved any closer. "And they will," Plekhanov muttered, as he retreated back to the vehicles. Kryuchkov, Baklanov, and Yazov had no plan for this eventuality. They went to a nearby guest house, unsure of what to do. Lukyanov and Ivashko sent a personal note to Gorbachev, begging him to receive them.[110]

The historian Serhii Plokhy wrote: "Those who managed to 'save' Gorbachev first would determine the success or failure of the coup and the political— perhaps even physical—survival of the main players on the Soviet political stage." This sentence captures the mood on the two planes, but the reality was entirely different. Gorbachev was not in a position "to pick winners and losers."[111] Yeltsin and the Muscovites had created a new political narrative in the country and around the world, and the Soviet President could only join this narrative. And the most crucial factor for Gorbachev was Raisa. When the BBC began to report on the race of the two planes to Crimea, Raisa convinced herself that the plotters were coming to get rid of witnesses, including her whole family. She collapsed into the arms of her daughter Irina and son-in-law Anatoly. It was a massive hypertension attack. Unfortunately for Gorbachev, he would lose his beloved wife eight years later; her terminal illness was caused by the shock of 21 August. The Soviet President was determined to get rid of the plotters.[112]

After assisting his wife into bed and calling for the doctor, Gorbachev sent a request to Kryuchkov: his telephone lines must be restored immediately. The KGB chief complied, and at 5:35 p.m. the operators in Mukhalatka reconnected Gorbachev's phones. The President's first call was to Yeltsin. Then Gorbachev telephoned Nazarbayev and Kravchuk. After that, he called the Ministry of Defense, the KGB, and the commander of the Kremlin regiment, telling the latter to follow only his orders. They complied. Gorbachev also ordered the Belbek authorities to open the airfield for the arrival of the Russian delegation and prepare his presidential plane for departure to Moscow.[113] Then there came a call from George Bush, who by that time had returned to Kennebunkport to continue his interrupted vacation. "Oh my God, it's wonderful, Mikhail!" Bush exclaimed, when he heard Gorbachev's voice. The Soviet President got straight down to business. He needed all the assistance that Bush could provide to resume the course of events that had been interrupted by the coup: the Union Treaty, international aid to the Soviet Union, and reconstruction of the Soviet state and economy. The failure of the coup, Gorbachev said, had vindicated his cooperation with the republics, since all the republican leaders "have taken positions of principle . . . against illegal acts." He also added that the coup "was prevented by democracy. This is a guarantee for us." Bush was delighted by the phone call: "Sounds like the same old Mikhail Gorbachev, one full of life and confidence," he said.[114]

Gorbachev returned to his wife, who remained in bed, to tell her about his actions: "I will not receive Kryuchkov, Baklanov, and Yazov at all. There is nothing to talk with them about now." He had made up his mind. He would embrace the Russian government and try to outperform Yeltsin on his own territory. Meanwhile, the "Russian" plane landed at Belbek after circling for an hour over Crimea. Those on board discussed what to do. Rutskoy, who had brought a group of officers with him, was ready to storm "Zaria" if the KGB guards offered resistance. Bakatin and Primakov, who had also joined the expedition, talked him out of this idea. In Belbek the local KGB and military division, after some disagreement, provided the Russian delegation with cars, trucks, and a bus with which to reach Foros. When the delegation arrived at the villa, it was already dark. The officials got out of their cars and, flanked by Rutskoy's armed men, walked towards the gates. They were open and no one stopped them. In the light of a nearby lamp, they saw Yazov, Kryuchkov, and Baklanov, who were discussing something. Rutskoy nodded to them reflectively; Kryuchkov made a gesture of greeting. Gorbachev's loyal bodyguards immediately let the delegation into the main house, where Gorbachev was waiting in the lobby, dressed in a beige sweater. Silayev was amazed at how well the President looked. Raisa, by contrast, was trembling, her face wet with tears. Both sides expressed genuine relief and happiness. Rutskoy told an investigation a few weeks later: "When we entered the main house and saw Gorbachev and Raisa Maksimovna, it became clear that nothing had been staged. They really were isolated and prepared for any developments."[115]

Chernyaev wrote in his diary: "Politics seemed to evaporate at this moment, not to mention past disagreements, offenses, and quarrels."[116] Gorbachev's aide later admitted he was naïve and emotional. Instead, this was the beginning of Gorbachev's political demise: having rejected emergency rule and its perpetrators, he had lost the executive levers of power as well. Gorbachev did allow Lukyanov and Ivashko to visit him in the presence of the Russian officials. He hectored Lukyanov: Why did you fail to convene the Supreme Soviet? Why did you not stand next to Yeltsin? Lukyanov attempted to interrupt his monologue, but Gorbachev shut him up: "Cut the bullshit. Stop pulling wool over my eyes." Then he chased Lukyanov and Ivashko out of the room as if they were two delinquent kids. Gorbachev's outrage was genuine, yet it was a remarkably demonstrative way of dismissing his closest political partner. Gorbachev never saw Lukyanov again; nor did he want to hear his explanations.[117]

Rutskoy continued to fear that the KGB might ambush them in Crimea and insisted on their immediate departure for Moscow. Gorbachev, concerned about Raisa's health, wanted to stay overnight, but ultimately conceded. After some hasty packing, the First Couple departed for Belbek in the armored presidential ZIL, accompanied by Rutskoy's armed officers and the rest of the Russian company. Once on the presidential plane, Gorbachev invited all the Russian officials to his section and spent the entire flight sitting around one table with them, chatting and toasting. Raisa stayed huddled silently in a seat with their youngest granddaughter Nastya on her lap, while the older Xenia slept on the floor. Kryuchkov was held in the rear section of the presidential plane, where Gorbachev had ordered he be put as a possible precaution against a KGB ambush. The head of the KGB Ninth Directorate, Plekhanov, was on another plane, together with Yazov and others. He muttered to himself: "What a bunch of good-for-nothing old cowards! And I fell in with them like a chicken ready to be plucked." The Soviet Air Force sent MIG fighter jets to provide air protection. At Vnukovo Airport everything was quiet: a crowd of journalists, television cameras, and a small group of Soviet officials, including Marshal Moiseyev and Alexander Bessmertnykh, awaited Gorbachev's arrival. Kryuchkov and Yazov were arrested at the airport. Other junta members had parliamentary immunity and were allowed to go home.[118]

Gorbachev emerged from his plane in a light sweater and windbreaker, dazed and feeling disoriented. Addressing the media, he thanked Yeltsin and the defenders of democracy. "Our society and people have changed . . . And that is the greatest victory of perestroika." Yet he had nothing new and dramatic to say. He repeated his old slogans about "socialist choice," and attempted to exonerate the Party from its participation in emergency rule. Gorbachev was emotionally drained. Once off the plane, Raisa had collapsed again, and even Gorbachev's daughter, normally stoic, had broken into uncontrollable sobbing. He escorted them straight home.[119]

Some observers, including Gorbachev's biographer, believed that the Soviet leader should have gone instead to "The White House" to be greeted by the euphoric crowd. Galina Starovoitova believed it would have afforded him popular legitimacy. Most likely, however, such an opportunity wasn't in the offing. Gorbachev would have been the odd man out at the exuberant show of Russian triumphalism that day. At "The White House," the Russian officials divided everyone into heroes and villains. The general mood among them was that Gorbachev had failed and should go. Rutskoy announced to a roar of approval: "All the scoundrels will be arrested!" Silayev intoned: "You overthrew the fascists, the cruel fanatics that raised their arms against freedom . . . Thank you! God let Russia flourish and pursue its happiness." Mayor Popov spoke to the crowd the next morning and he said that Gorbachev should learn his lesson and leave the Communist Party. The crowd roared: "He must resign!"[120]

Gorbachev's popular authority had been utterly ruined over the previous years, so this one moment of triumphant reception could hardly have changed that reality. The Soviet leader still formally commanded the Army and the KGB. He could not, however, regain the support of the Russian people—that now belonged, irrevocably, to Boris Yeltsin.

CHAPTER 12

DEMISE

Things fall apart; the center cannot hold
W. B. Yeats, "The Second Coming," 1919

THE PARTY IS OVER

On the morning of 22 August 1991, Yeltsin called President Bush to report that Gorbachev had been returned safely to his residence in Moscow; Yazov, Pavlov, and Kryuchkov had been arrested, and "a great victory of democracy" could be celebrated in Russia. Bush was surprised and moved. "Your stock is sky-high over here," Bush said. "You displayed respect for law and stood for democratic principles . . . You were the ones on the front-line, who stood on the barricades . . . You brought Gorbachev back intact. You restored him to power. You have won a lot of friends around the world . . . If you will now accept some advice from a friend—get some rest, get some sleep."[1] Bush himself was back at Kennebunkport, fishing and golfing.

Yeltsin, despite his promise to Bush "to save Gorby," was convinced that the Soviet President had been behind the junta as well. Analysts at the American Embassy in Moscow reported to Washington that Russian democrats "defended Gorbachev—despite themselves."[2] Yeltsin's decrees, announced during the days of emergency rule, had been "extra-constitutional" just like the decrees of the Emergency Committees. In essence, the head of the Russian republic had seized constitutional powers from Gorbachev. For Yeltsin, it would have been ideal if Gorbachev had come back to Moscow and resigned. Khasbulatov and Burbulis realized, however, that it would be impossible to get rid of Gorbachev immediately.

The last thing Yeltsin wanted was to restore Gorbachev to power. Since early 1990, the Russian leader had been on a mission to destroy "the totalitarian empire" and "restore Russia" as a free, democratic state. Gorbachev was the main obstacle to this goal. On 22 August, the Russian President appeared before the Russian parliament to deliver a message that the forces of totalitarianism, represented by the Party and the KGB, had only paused for the time being; they would soon strike back. The hydra of the old order had been decapitated, but it should now be crushed.[3]

Gorbachev was woken at 7 a.m. on 22 August, after only a few hours of sleep, because a courier had delivered a thick envelope to his residence. It contained a bundle of decrees signed by Yeltsin and approved by the Russian parliament. During the three days of junta rule, Yeltsin had proclaimed himself commander-in-chief of the Soviet Army, seized all executive powers on Russian territory, and appropriated the central television and news agencies, as well as all Soviet centrally managed industries, on behalf of "Russia," not the Union. Now he wanted the President of the USSR to approve this coup. The indignant Gorbachev refused to sign anything, sent the courier away, and went back to sleep.[4] He arrived at his Kremlin office at noon, ready to chair an emergency meeting of the presidential Security Council—the first such meeting in weeks. In the famous Chestnut Room where the General Secretary had made sensitive decisions with select Politburo members, Gorbachev signed a document canceling every decree passed by the junta. Then he began to form a new Soviet government. He fired Foreign Minister Bessmertnykh, appointed Marshal Moiseyev to replace Yazov as Defense Minister, and made Leonid Shebarshin the new head of the KGB. He also appointed Grigory Revenko to be his new chief of staff, replacing Valery Boldin.[5] At a secret troika meeting back in July, Gorbachev had promised to make such high-profile appointments only with the consent of Yeltsin and the Kazakh leader Nursultan Nazarbayev—but this was conditional upon their signing the Union Treaty. He expected to meet with the two leaders the next morning, at an urgent session of the Nine Plus One group. Perhaps he hoped that the leaders of the other republics would back him against Yeltsin's grandstanding.

The Soviet leader was still in denial about the new political reality. He was also engrossed in his personal drama of having just spent three days captive in Crimea. At a press conference that he held that day, he spent most of the time denying any involvement in the junta's conspiracy, yet the media, apart from Western journalists, was hostile. Yuri Karyakin, Yeltsin's advisor and a radical democrat, asked Gorbachev why he had appointed such "apparent scoundrels" to vital positions in his government? Gorbachev lamely admitted that he had "trusted" Kryuchkov and Yazov. He also unwisely added, with a wide grin on his face, "I will never tell you everything." This remark would feed conspiracy theories for years to come. Gorbachev defended the Party apparatus; some of

1. General Secretary of the Communist Party Mikhail Gorbachev at the funeral of Konstantin Chernenko, 11 March 1985. The new Soviet leader told his wife: "We just can't go on living like this."

2. Gorbachev in November 1985 at the unveiling of Lenin's monument in Moscow. The Kremlin reformer admired Lenin as a revolutionary leader and emulated him in launching "socialist democracy" in the USSR.

3. Nationalists in Estonia, fall 1988. Mass movements in the Baltic republics, empowered by Gorbachev's perestroika, quickly became vehicles for separatism across the Soviet Union, including the Russian Federation.

4. Nobel Peace Prize winner and dissident Andrei Sakharov became a parliamentarian, thanks to Gorbachev's reforms. He proposed a complete democratic overhaul of the Soviet Union, with an emphasis on national minorities. Galina Starovoitova (to his right) was even more radical than him.

5. An ex-Politburo maverick, Boris Yeltsin became the "people's Tsar" in the Russian imagination in early 1989. Nine out of ten Muscovites voted for him in the first contested elections since 1917. Later Yeltsin channeled his popularity into the struggle for power in the Russian Federation, the core part of the USSR.

6. Gorbachev and George Bush at the summit in Malta after the fall of the Berlin Wall. The Soviet leader accepted the collapse of communism in Eastern Europe and pledged not to use force in the Baltics. He said that the USSR no longer treated the United States as an enemy. The US President wondered how long Soviet "good behavior" would last.

7. Gorbachev takes the oath to become the President of the USSR. He wanted to replace the Soviet communist system with "socialist democracy," but growing chaos caused him to hold dictatorial powers in the post. In fact, he never even tried to use those powers.

8. Gorbachev, Marshal Dmitry Yazov and Prime Minister Nikolai Ryzhkov salute the victory parade on Red Square, 9 May 1990. Sandwiched between conservatives and radicals, the Soviet leader was desperate for a way out.

9. Night rehearsal of the military parade in May 1990. Meanwhile the Soviet Army was in hasty retreat from Eastern Europe, and Lithuania announced secession from the USSR. Growing disorder fed fears of a civil war and military dictatorship.

10. Young Soviet economist Grigory Yavlinsky offered "500 Days" of comprehensive market reform to Gorbachev as a magic wand. The Soviet leader took the wand, but then dropped it.

11. Boris Yeltsin filled the political vacuum that Gorbachev's style of governance had created. On 12 June 1990, Yeltsin led the Russian Federation to declare "sovereignty" from the Soviet Union; in July he resigned from the Party. Those acts divided the people and the country.

12. Yeltsin and Leonid Kravchuk, leaders of the newly elected parliaments of the RSFSR and Ukraine, met in Kiev in November 1990 to recognize mutual sovereignty and territorial integrity. This act had no legal power, but inspired Ukraine's pro-independence forces.

13. "Democratic Russia" in action. Yuri Afanasyev (to the speaker's right) mobilized Moscow's middle classes against the Soviet Union, in support of Yeltsin's idea of sovereign "Russia."

14. Vladimir Zhirinovsky challenged Yeltsin as an anti-liberal candidate for Russia's presidential election in June 1991.

15. Fearful of a civil war, Gorbachev devolved powers to the leaders of nine republics of the USSR in the hope of creating a voluntary Union. In this photo, he gathered republican leaders in Novo-Ogaryovo, near Moscow, for a conference. His concessions, however, only played into Yeltsin's ambitions and separatism.

16. Gennady Burbulis, a self-made strategist of Yeltsin's, wanted to destroy the Soviet Union as "the worst totalitarian empire" in history. By doing this, he thought, "Russia" would liberate itself and the world.

17. A month after his victory in the RSFSR elections, Yeltsin was inaugurated in the Kremlin as the first democratic President of Russia. The Orthodox Patriarch Alexyi II attended and blessed the ceremony.

18. Gorbachev invited himself to the G-7 summit in London in July 1991. He knew the US leadership had decided not to give him financial support. Deeply unpopular at home, however, he leaned on the West as his greatest source of authority.

19. The last US-Soviet summit took place on 30–31 July 1991. At the Kremlin reception after the signing of the historic arms reduction treaty, Yeltsin vied with Gorbachev for the attention of George Bush and his wife, Barbara.

20. Gennady Yanayev, Vice-President of the USSR and Gorbachev's appointee, became a hapless figurehead of the junta on 19 August 1991. He was one of many factors that doomed "the coup."

21. Russian liberal parliamentarian Galina Starovoitova, who happened to be in London, connected Yeltsin with Margaret Thatcher. Thatcher was the first world-class Western politician to denounce the Soviet junta.

22. The junta, organized by KGB chief Vladimir Kryuchkov, expected that Russians would not fight for Gorbachev and back the stronger hand. This was an epic blunder. Here Muscovites are photographed on 20 August 1991 building a barricade against tanks to defend Russian democracy.

23. A human shield before "the Russian White House" (the headquarters of the RSFSR parliament), a symbol of resistance to the junta. The junta lacked an appetite for bloodshed and collapsed.

24. On 22 August 1991, Russians celebrate the triumph of democracy in front of the Russian parliament. Yeltsin addressed the people. The crowd demanded that Gorbachev should resign.

25. Gorbachev came to the Russian parliament on 23 August seeking civil unity. Instead, Yeltsin forced him to disband the Soviet government and ban the Party. At this moment, it became clear to everyone who was the boss in Moscow.

26. Yeltsin in a Latvian resort town in July 1991, with the leaders of the three Baltic republics. On 24 August, with the Union's authority smashed, the Russian leader decreed unconditional independence to Estonia and Latvia. The US leaders waited in vain for Gorbachev to do the same.

27. After August 1991, Gorbachev tapped into his global celebrity status to raise Western money for his Union and to regain his domestic centrality. He failed on both counts. Here Gorbachev is flanked by Anatoly Chernyaev (right) and interpreter Pavel Palazhchenko (left).

28. In October–November 1991, young Russian economist Yegor Gaidar convinced Yeltsin that, in order to build "a great Russia," he should dismantle the Soviet Union. Yeltsin agreed on condition that the Russian Federation would succeed the USSR as a world power.

29. On 3 November 1991, Stanford economist Mikhail Bernstam (right) told Gaidar (left) that his plan to immediately lift economic controls in the RSFSR alone could lead to the specter of "nuclear Armageddon" between Russia and Ukraine.

30. After the failure of the Soviet junta, Leonid Kravchuk, once the top Ukrainian communist propagandist, led Ukraine to full independence. The Ukrainian nationalists viewed Ukraine as "a colony of Moscow." Kravchuk instead posed as a pragmatic leader who could reach deals with Yeltsin's Russia.

31. Rome was the first Western destination Yeltsin visited after he, Kravchuk, and the Belarusian leader Stanislav Shushkevich dissolved the USSR. In Italy, Yeltsin was relieved to see that the West was ready to accept the Russian Federation as a legal successor to the Soviet Union.

32. On 21 December 1991, Yeltsin and eight other leaders of ex-Soviet republics met in Alma-Ata, Kazakhstan, to confirm that the Soviet Union was null and void.

them had behaved like "real democrats" during the coup. The British ambassador Rodric Braithwaite compared the Soviet President to the Bourbons after the French Revolution: he had "learned nothing, forgot nothing." Gorbachev's admirers explained his out-of-touch conduct as the result of post-traumatic shock and misinformation. Gorbachev's health and energy, however, belied his descriptions of his Crimean ordeal.[6]

While Gorbachev was being grilled by journalists and Russian democrats, Yeltsin met with a huge jubilant crowd on the panoramic balcony of the Russian parliament. Khasbulatov, Rutskoy, and Burbulis flanked the victorious leader; other deputies and officials huddled around them. The Russian tricolor was hoisted on top of the building. Yeltsin declared that the arrested junta members were in "Russian" custody and would soon be put on trial. He accused Lukyanov of being the coup's chief ideologue. He also stated that the KGB, police, and other forces on Russian territory were now under "Russian" jurisdiction. Khasbulatov followed him by proposing to "nationalize" the Party headquarters on Old Square and shut down any newspapers that had supported the coup. The mayor of Moscow, Gavriil Popov, proposed bestowing upon Yeltsin the medal of the "Hero of the Soviet Union." Yeltsin smirked at this absurd proposal as if to say: who needs the Soviet Union anymore? The crowd in front of "The White House" chanted, "Yeltsin! Yeltsin! Ros-si-ya! Ros-si-ya!"[7]

Another crowd had gathered four kilometers away, in front of the Party headquarters on Old Square, ready to break into the building. Riot police were nowhere to be seen; only a few armed KGB officers protected the Party complex. Gorbachev telephoned Mayor Popov and asked for his help. Lacking clear leadership, however, the crowd then relocated to the nearby Lubyanka Square and refocused its fury on the KGB's main offices, which flanked the square on two sides, as well as on the statue of Felix Dzerzhinsky, founder of the Bolshevik secret police, at the center of the square. There were calls in the crowd to storm the KGB, to save its archives from destruction, and to free the political prisoners in its headquarters.[8]

When news of the crowd's intentions reached the Russian parliament, it sent a new wave of fear among the deputies. One witness recalls there was an acute sense of danger. "If KGB officers opened fire, then our entire victory would have evaporated in a second." The deputies suspended the session and rushed to Lubyanka Square, where they formed a human cordon around Dzerzhinsky's statue, in lieu of the absent police.[9] Vladimir Lukin from Yeltsin's entourage called the new head of the KGB, Shebarshin, whom he knew personally, and urged him to allow two parliamentarians to inspect the KGB building. The request was granted, and this calmed the crowd a bit. Its attention then shifted to Dzerzhinsky's statue. Deputy Sergey Stankevich managed to convince the crowd to remove the statue from its pedestal carefully and safely. The statue's weight was eleven tons: if toppled, it would have damaged underground communications, including the metro station. The Moscow authorities sent in two huge Krupp construction cranes, which hooked the statue by the neck and raised it from its pedestal. The huge piece of bronze hovered in the air, only to be landed on a military truck and carted away.[10]

Shebarshin observed the scene from his office, which had once belonged to Yuri Andropov. Evening came, but the KGB buildings were dark; all their lights were turned off. Shebarshin thought about the cunning of the crowd's leaders and the naïveté of those who followed them. He ordered KGB guards not to open fire under any circumstances, then he slipped out of the building unobserved, through a back door into an empty street. With the removal of the statue, the threat of civilian violence had passed. The KGB complex was not seized and looted—a great relief for some people, an eternal regret for many others.[11]

Yeltsin, who had slept through the afternoon, watched the *Vremia* news program in the evening and learned about Gorbachev's new appointments. He was furious: the captive of Crimea was restoring his control over the KGB, the Army, and the police, behind his back! He called Gorbachev: "What are you doing? Moiseyev was one of the organizers of the coup and Shebarshin is a man close to Kryuchkov, the chief coordinator of the coup."[12] In the morning of 23 August, Yeltsin came to Gorbachev's office in the Kremlin, with the copies of Yazov's orders that Marshal Moiseyev had signed and transmitted for the Emergency Committee. The copies had been saved from a shredder by an officer sympathetic to Russian democracy. Nothing could be found against Shebarshin, who had not been involved in the plot.[13] Yeltsin demanded the appointment of his candidates: Marshal Shaposhnikov as Minister of Defense and Vadim Bakatin to be the KGB chief. Both had joined the resistance to the junta before the leaders of the coup were arrested. Gorbachev's thinking at this moment may be reconstructed as follows: *If I resist, Yeltsin could brush me aside and declare me to be a part of the failed conspiracy. People would believe him, there would be civil war and blood in the streets. If I consent, there's still hope of taming the irascible winner; Western leaders would side with me.* Gorbachev might also have had a more idealistic way of thinking. He had claimed many times that he never sought power for power's sake. He wanted to retain his constitutional powers, but he also wanted to rule together with "Russian democracy," not against it.

Whatever he was thinking, Gorbachev surrendered yet again; he agreed to Yeltsin's demands. From this point on, the Soviet President became a nominal commander-in-chief. He lost control of the military and the KGB. There is indirect evidence that Yeltsin obtained Gorbachev's consent to share the nuclear weapons' codes with him.[14] The transfer of power from Gorbachev to Yeltsin continued at the Nine Plus One meeting that began one hour later. The Soviet President, under Yeltsin's gaze, invited his recent appointees to appear before him, one after another, only to fire them. When Moiseyev's turn came, Gorbachev told the Marshal he was ousted and added: "And please, no funny business." Moiseyev turned pale and responded: "I have not wronged you . . . And I will not engage in any funny business—and also will never leave the Party." When Shebarshin's turn came, he smiled: "Thank you! I will finally sleep well tonight." Gorbachev raised his eyebrows: "It is still early to sleep well." Kravchuk, Nazarbayev, Belorussia's leader Nikolai Dementei, and the leaders of four Central Asian republics watched this performance in silence.[15]

During the meeting, Yeltsin's bodyguard Korzhakov brought in a handwritten note from Burbulis. The note said: "Intense destruction of documents is taking place at the Central Committee of the CPSU. It is urgently necessary to temporarily suspend all activities in the building." Yeltsin asked Gorbachev: "Will you sign this?" Gorbachev obediently scribbled on the note: "Agreed."[16] He probably did not anticipate what would follow. Popov and his deputy Luzhkov ordered all Party committees in the Soviet capital to be shut down. Moscow city officials, zealots from Democratic Russia, immediately acted on this command. Using Gorbachev's approval, Popov issued an executive order to close the Party headquarters "temporarily, until the end of the investigation on the complicity of the CPSU" and the Russian Communist Party "in the organization of the state coup . . ."[17] This was certainly not what Gorbachev had in mind when he signed off. The rest was pure improvisation. Nikolai Kruchina, the chief Party administrator, was shocked to see Gorbachev's signature on Burbulis's note, but complied. A large crowd of angry Muscovites had gathered outside the building, ready to storm it at any moment. The emissaries from Democratic Russia used the internal radio system, set up for war and other emergencies, to order all staff at the CPSU headquarters to leave the building by 15:00. Those who stayed, they announced, would be arrested. Party officials and staff who began to leave the building then faced a mob outside. People abused them and searched their bags. The head of the Moscow Party organization, Yuri Prokofiev, was kicked in the face. People howled with rage when they found food from the Party's closed cafeterias and stores; many of these items had long vanished from general food stores. The Moscow city officials were now in control of a complex that had been the Soviet center of power for decades. Just a few days earlier, they expected to be arrested. One of them, a physicist from the Institute for Atomic Energy, recalled: "I could not deny myself the pleasure of telephoning Mayor Popov: 'Your order has been fulfilled. I am calling you from Gorbachev's office.'" The anti-totalitarian revolution that Russian "liberals" dreamed about had finally triumphed.[18]

Anatoly Chernyaev was furious when he heard the order to leave the Party headquarters. He continued to work, ignoring the threat of arrest. Two hours later, KGB officers ushered him and other members of Gorbachev's staff to the basement, where they were surprised to discover a secret underground metro station. A train brought them from Old Square directly to the Kremlin. Gorbachev, when he heard about what happened, only smirked. "He really had no time to spare for me," Chernyaev later wrote.[19] The writer Daniil Granin visited the Party headquarters a couple of days later. The once sacral seat of power was now an abandoned, poorly ventilated office building, with scattered scraps of paper everywhere and rows of silent telephones. The Party had been a giant corporation: no one had been able to leave it with impunity. Suddenly, it had vanished like a mirage. Instead of feeling the joy of liberation, Granin was worried about a power vacuum and the vast horizon of uncertainty that lay ahead.[20]

Later that day, Gorbachev was forced to disband all the power structures that he led. This happened in a most humiliating way at an emergency session of the Russian parliament. Gorbachev went there apparently to seek some common ground. Instead, he encountered feelings of revenge and hatred. The session was broadcast to the entire country. Minutes before Gorbachev entered the hall, Yeltsin's aide claimed from the podium: "We do not need the President of the Union . . . We should remove this odious figure . . . who is clearly not our friend." Gorbachev began by praising the parliamentarians for their heroism, but all he subsequently heard was: "We don't need you, but you need us." Gorbachev tried to reason with his critics: "We need each other."[21] Then Yeltsin took the stage and accused the principal Soviet institutions of collective complicity in the totalitarian coup. He began with the Cabinet of Ministers.

The newspaper *Izvestia* had published informal, and apparently heavily redacted and changed, minutes from the Cabinet's session on 19 August. This version conveyed the clear but false impression that almost all the ministers had backed the conspiracy. Gorbachev had received a different, more accurate account from Pavlov's deputy Shcherbakov. Yet he avoided any confrontation with Yeltsin at the emergency session of the Russian parliament. He said he would study the report. Yeltsin shoved a paper at him: "Then read it! Read!" Gorbachev began to read aloud, and then announced: "The whole [Soviet government] must resign." Yeltsin triumphantly declared that the next Prime Minister of the Soviet Union must be nominated by the Russian Federation. Gorbachev did not resist.[22] Yeltsin demanded that Gorbachev agree to transfer control of the gas and oil industries, the military-industrial complex, and other major Soviet industrial assets into the hands of the Russian Federation. This time Gorbachev balked. "It's a very major task, and we have got to solve it in such a way that it does not worsen the functioning of the economy."[23]

DEMISE

The Russian leader's last surprise was the most dramatic. Yeltsin declared with a mischievous grin: "And, on a lighter note, shall we now sign a decree suspending the activities of the Russian Communist Party?" He proceeded to push a piece of paper towards the stunned Gorbachev. "What are you doing . . .," he stammered. "I . . . haven't we . . . I haven't read this . . ." Yeltsin, he argued, had no constitutional authority to ban the Party. In the end, however, Gorbachev countersigned Yeltsin's decree. Many in the Soviet Union felt transported with joy. Yet many more felt revulsion at this scene of Gorbachev's humiliation. Shevardnadze's aide wrote in his diary: "Yeltsin played with him like a puppet."[24] Why did Gorbachev do it? His aides later explained this was the moment of profound change in his political philosophy: Gorbachev had finally broken with the Party and was now focused on "saving the state."[25] The so-called change of philosophy looked more like a political rout.

Gennady Burbulis, who had helped Yeltsin to prepare documents for this meeting, recalled: "A cruel, malicious, wicked scene. Yeltsin acted like a predator, like a killer." Burbulis felt nevertheless that he was justified: for him, personalities were mere vehicles of larger historical forces. He thought that Gorbachev was a "chatter-box," a master of palaver, about-turns, and procrastinations. And Yeltsin had executed a mission of global importance: he had ended the East-West divide and helped to dismantle the totalitarian "empire" peacefully. Yeltsin's actions were probably his revenge for past humiliations. After demonstrating his capacity for sadistic malice, Yeltsin now changed his tone. He took the humiliated Gorbachev to his office and said: "Mikhail Sergeyevich! You've just been through so much recently." Both their families, he continued, were at risk. "Let's have a family get-together." Burbulis was stunned by how much compassion, warmth, and naïveté Yeltsin demonstrated. Gorbachev stared at him in silence and declined the awkward offer. Yeltsin then closed down again—his extraordinary display of compassion was gone once and for all.[26]

On Saturday, 24 August, the Russian government and Moscow's City Hall held the funeral of three young men killed in a confrontation with the military. This was staged on Manezh Square, where all the big rallies of Democratic Russia had taken place. The Russian colors of white, blue, and red were everywhere. The atmosphere was reminiscent of the Russian Easter, and bearded Orthodox priests in black frocks were everywhere. Russian Cossacks materialized out of nowhere to maintain order. Liberal-minded intellectuals came to the square to revel in their new-found freedom and Russian identity. Russian émigrés also hailed Yeltsin's victory. The Russian President dominated the proceedings, whereas Gorbachev, sporting a red armband, seemed like a ghost from the past. Everyone agreed that his perestroika had failed and was finally over.[27] Only a few Russian nationalists regarded the days of August as a crushing defeat; they remained in a state of shock at the historic collapse of the state.[28] Alexander Nevzorov, a television journalist with extreme nationalist views, railed against "an imitation of a coup" staged by unnamed puppeteers. The failure to demonstrate brute force, he said, had discredited the "patriotic forces." "Now anybody who speaks about the indivisibility" of the Soviet Union, he concluded, "will be called a fascist, a coup-maker, and a supporter of the junta."[29]

After the funeral ceremony, Mikhail Gorbachev returned to his Kremlin office. By presidential decree he ended the existence of Party organizations in the armed forces, police, and other state organizations. He also approved the transfer of the Party's property to the Russian government and the governments of the other republics. Finally, he resigned as General Secretary of the Party. Gorbachev convinced himself that now his main task was to ensure the legality of transition from the Soviet Union to a "democratic Russia" and a future voluntary Union. He still hoped to have a new Union Treaty, the project that only he now seemed to believe in.

When the arrested members of the junta heard the news, they regarded it as an act of treason. Yet only one believer in the old order decided he could not live through this ignominy. Marshal Sergey Akhromeyev was on holiday in August, yet he had rushed back to Moscow to support the Emergency Committee. Now, Akhromeyev sent a letter to Gorbachev, explaining why he had broken his military oath to serve the Soviet President: "From 1990 on I was convinced, as I am convinced today, that our country is marching towards its death. Soon it will be dismembered." He added: "I cannot live when my Fatherland is dying, when everything I considered to be the cause of my life is being destroyed." On 24 August, the Marshal of the Soviet Union hanged himself in his office.[30]

THE CHAIN REACTION

On 21–22 August, the governments of Estonia, Latvia, and Lithuania glimpsed an incredible opportunity to leave the USSR without any legal preconditions. Soviet troops and riot police in the Baltic national capitals were leaving, heading back to their bases. On 20 August, the Estonian parliament had declared that the coup in Moscow made talks with the USSR impossible; the republic proceeded to declare its independence unilaterally. The Latvian parliament did the same the next day. Western governments, however, withheld recognition of Baltic sovereignty, until Gorbachev and Yeltsin could find a legal way to let the Baltic republics go.[31]

The head of the Estonian government, Arnold Rüütel, decided to use his friendship with Boris Yeltsin to cut ties with the USSR. He knew that Yeltsin's support had been crucial for the Baltic journey toward independence. The previous month, on 29 July, Yeltsin had met with the leaders of the three Baltic republics in Jurmala, Latvia, where he agreed to recognize full Lithuanian independence; the legal foundation was Russia's agreement that the Baltic annexation of 1940 was null and void. Yeltsin planned to unveil the document after the signing of the Union Treaty, but events had since taken another turn.[32] On 22 August, Rüütel called Yeltsin to congratulate him on his victory and flew to Moscow, accompanied by legal experts. The next day was the anniversary of the infamous Molotov-Ribbentrop pact, and Rüütel expected Yeltsin to recognize Estonian independence. The Latvian leader Anatolijs Gorbunovs flew to Moscow to join him.[33] In his talks with Western diplomats in Moscow, Rüütel said that the Balts needed Yeltsin's support to immobilize the extremists in the Russian minority population, the Army, and the KGB. The Balts were aiming higher: they wanted to use Yeltsin's acceptance as a tool to open the gateway for recognition by the West.[34]

Yeltsin met the Estonians only on 24 August, after the funeral ceremony on Manezh Square. After Rüütel made his request, Yeltsin asked what kind of document he should sign. Andrei Kozyrev, the Russian Foreign Minister, advised the Estonians to draft what they wanted, which their legal experts did on the spot. The decree acknowledged the Estonian declaration of independence with no strings attached and urged Gorbachev to reach a settlement between the USSR and the Estonian republic. It also encouraged the "international community to recognize the state independence of the Estonian republic."[35] Yeltsin signed the paper and declared with a broad smile: "I wish the Estonian republic all the best." As the satisfied Estonians were leaving Yeltsin's office, they ran into the Latvian delegation, who were waiting their turn. After a brief conversation, Yeltsin handed Gorbunovs a signed paper with the same text copied from the Estonian draft.[36]

The Estonian legal expert Rein Müllerson, who drafted the decree for Yeltsin, later admitted that "legally this recognition was nonsense. Russia was not sovereign, and its act of recognition had no legal force." In the eyes of the world, the USSR was still the only legitimate subject of international law. Politically, however, Yeltsin's decree was crucial. "At that moment," recalled Müllerson, "Yeltsin dictated to Gorbachev what to do and where to add his signature." After meeting with Yeltsin, the Baltic leaders paid visits to the US ambassador in Moscow and other Western embassies. Their message was: Yeltsin has recognized our independence, what are you waiting for?[37] The next day, Norway and Finland, previously hesitant, recognized the state sovereignty of the Baltic republics. In Bonn, Foreign Minister Hans-Dietrich Genscher convinced a skeptical Chancellor Kohl that the international norms of the Helsinki Act of 1975 dictated the supremacy of national sovereignty over status quo borders.

Meanwhile, President Mitterrand gave the green light to his Foreign Minister, Roland Dumas, to announce France's recognition of the Baltic states as well.[38] The Balts, armed with Russian leverage, had accomplished their goal.

Another leap toward independence was taking place in Ukraine. After Gorbachev accepted the Nine Plus One format, Leonid Kravchuk and the Ukrainian communist apparatchiks became absolute masters of the Ukrainian Supreme Soviet, the seat of authority on the republic's territory. The talks with President Bush in Kiev and Kravchuk's meetings with Gorbachev in Crimea demonstrated how far the ambitions of the Ukrainian politicians had progressed. Still, until August 1991, there was no solid pro-independence majority in the second largest Slavic republic of the USSR; only the regions of Western Ukraine annexed by Stalin after the dismemberment of Poland in 1939 were determined to break away from the USSR.

When the junta declared emergency rule, many people in Russian-speaking regions of the republic greeted the removal of Gorbachev as a chance to bring an end to economic and social disorder. A similar mood prevailed in the Ukrainian capital. If the strongmen of Moscow "had used force and did not fear to hurt people," recalled one senior Ukrainian KGB official, "they would have become masters."[39] In this environment, even the most resolute Ukrainian nationalists decided to play the long game. The Rukh leaders decided against the actions in support of Yeltsin, for fear of civil war. The only exception was the Ukrainian Republican Party, led by a member of the Ukrainian Helsinki group, Levko Lukianenko, who had spent twenty years in Soviet jail and camps. He equated the Soviet Union with the Russian Empire and urged open resistance to the Moscow junta. The resulting casualties "would be a lancet that opens an abscess," causing the empire's quick collapse. In his recollections, Lukianenko called the power struggle between Gorbachev and Yeltsin "a gift from God." While it lasted, he said, "the Russian Empire was unable to direct all its strength against Ukraine."[40]

The grotesque failure of "the putsch" had a boomerang effect: millions in Ukraine no longer expected Moscow to call the shots. In the absence of a central power, people turned to the republican parliament and government for solutions.[41] And the breakdown of the Soviet center was forcing the Ukrainian communist leadership and their nationalist rivals to think quickly. Kravchuk, who had stayed in Moscow on 22–23 August, witnessed Yeltsin's takeover of the Soviet statehood and Party resources, the levers of the Soviet economy, and his control over the Soviet Army and the KGB. It was no longer possible for Ukraine to strike a balance between a weak Gorbachev and an assertive Yeltsin.[42] Kravchuk's leadership was in danger, because of his lukewarm support for emergency rule on 19 August. He and his comrades were having to face radical nationalists, but also a democratic movement of the Russified intelligentsia from Kiev and the cities of Central, Southern, and Eastern Ukraine. Their leader was the deputy speaker of the Ukrainian parliament, Vladimir Grinev, who had many friends in Democratic Russia. He had publicly opposed the coup and wanted to unseat communist potentates in Ukraine. "For the communists [in Ukraine]," Grinev recalled, "Yeltsin with his democratic ideas and the movement in Russia was a much bigger threat than the homegrown Rukh," which was unable to take power. Crowds of demonstrators proceeded to gather in front of the Ukrainian Supreme Soviet chanting: "Yeltsin! Yeltsin! Down with Kravchuk! Shame on Kravchuk!"[43]

One observer described what happened in the Ukrainian Supreme Soviet. "I saw on television how, over a couple of hours . . . all of the communists transformed into the most principled Ukrainian nationalists. This happened in one fell swoop." Some of them alluded to the Russian democrats: "They grabbed [the Soviet institutions of power] for themselves. We should do the same now. Tomorrow it may be too late." The Party stalwarts in Kiev had colossal economic assets in mind. Over half of the plants, factories, mines, shipyards, Black Sea fleet, and other assets in the republic were under the control and de facto ownership of the Moscow-based central ministries and conglomerates. Ukrainian sovereignty would allow the republican and regional Party potentates to claim those assets as "national."[44]

Kravchuk took charge. He proposed that all structures of the KGB, police, and Soviet Army on Ukrainian territory should be subordinated to the *Rada* (the Ukrainian name for the Supreme Soviet of the republic), ergo himself as head of the republic. He also emulated Yeltsin's decree in Moscow, to dissolve the Party organizations in all structures of the Ukrainian state. These laws, Kravchuk claimed, would help to protect the republic's sovereignty against any future coups. But Levko Lukianenko understood the real motive: the Ukrainian communist elite wanted to erect a barrier of state sovereignty against Yeltsin.[45] For pro-independence figures, this was a golden opportunity. They drafted "The Act of Declaration of Independence" that stated: "In view of the mortal danger that almost befell Ukraine with regard to a state coup in the USSR," the Rada proposed to "continue the thousand-year long tradition of state-building" and declared the creation of an independent state of Ukraine, with "indivisible and inviolable" territory. In Rukh, many intellectuals wavered: would it not be better to remain in one country with a democratic Russia rather than end up in a national state with the disguised communist nomenklatura in full control? Finally, they decided to support the Act.[46]

The writer Vladimir Yavorivsky read the Act to the Rada and proposed that they vote. The communist faction took time out. During the break, Kravchuk called Yeltsin and Gorbachev and informed them that under pressure the Party faction could vote for full independence. Yeltsin responded: "This is normal." The Russian leader, Kravchuk recalled, totally supported Ukrainian independence. Gorbachev was dismayed, but then consoled himself by saying that the March referendum would always take constitutional precedence over the Rada vote. The session resumed and Kravchuk spoke out in favor of the Act. Grinev rebelled against the unholy alliance between the Ukrainian democrats and the Party bosses. He proposed that the Act should be linked to a ban on the Communist Party and the nationalization of its property. Only a few backed him. The Rada voted for the Act of Independence with 346 deputies in favor, two opposed, and five abstaining.[47]

When the results of the vote were announced, the Party apparatchiks joined their enemies in an outpouring of national joy. Those who had prosecuted and jailed Ukrainian nationalists embraced their former victims and sang Ukrainian songs with tears in their eyes.[48] Kravchuk, however, was not overwhelmed by emotion. Gorbachev's mention of the March referendum gave him a new idea. He proposed to the Rada to conduct a Ukrainian referendum on the same day as the elections of the President of the Republic, on 1 December. Many nationalists were opposed: Why another referendum? The Act was enough. Kravchuk insisted: "If we do not do it, the world will not recognize us." The Ukrainian parliament approved the proposal. The deputies also voted to create a Ministry of Defense and pledged to "nationalize" all Soviet military units on the territory of the republic.[49] This move would generate serious tensions between Kiev and Moscow in the months to come.

A WAR OF SLAVS?

The state that Gorbachev led had, de facto, disappeared. In this situation he decided to rule together with the leaders of the post-communist republics. Always a legalist, he convened the Supreme Soviet of the USSR, another relic of the past, to take a decision: to convene one last time the emergency Congress of People's Deputies. The supreme assembly of the collapsing Union would change the Soviet constitution, to make room for a provisional government, with Gorbachev at the top.

The Supreme Soviet of the USSR, which returned from vacation on 26 August, was leaderless: Speaker Lukyanov was under investigation for his role in the junta. The majority of deputies realized that their assembly was doomed and were desperate to find new bearings. The most radical of them proposed disbanding the Supreme Soviet immediately. Everyone understood that Gorbachev was a hostage to Yeltsin. Khasbulatov came, on Yeltsin's behalf, to announce Russia's conditions for a future Union. First, the Russian Federation was "united and indivisible"—there was no possibility of exit for its autonomous regions: they should negotiate with Yeltsin only, not with Gorbachev. The leaders of these regions, such as President Mintimer Shaimiev of Tatarstan, listened in silence. They had tacitly supported the junta and were now among the losers of "the August revolution." Second, all Soviet property, economic assets, and resources on Russian territory must belong to "Russia." Always a shrewd political player, Nazarbayev echoed the Russian demands: he claimed Soviet assets, including the giant Baikonur space complex, and also announced that Kazakhstan would have its own army and its own foreign policy and international treaties. At the same time, with an eye on Yeltsin's grandstanding, Nazarbayev remarked: "Kazakhstan will never become 'the underbelly' of any region and will never be a 'junior brother' to anyone. We will enter a union only with equal rights and opportunities."[50]

Kravchuk did not attend the Assembly. Yuri Shcherbak, a Ukrainian writer, ecologist, and republican parliamentarian, acted as a self-appointed ambassador who spoke on behalf of independent Ukraine. Shcherbak had grown up as a Soviet patriot, then he became a liberal democrat, and eventually a late convert to Ukrainian nationalism. He admitted that Ukrainian democrats had remained passive during the days of the junta, but he then read out the Act of Ukrainian Independence, which he had translated into Russian on his way to Moscow. The coup, he said, had triggered "a political Chernobyl" that made any idea of a Union moot. The only good option left for all democrats was to accept Ukrainian independence without any strings attached, just as Yeltsin had accepted independence for the Baltics.[51]

Anatoly Sobchak took the floor for a rebuff. The mayor of Leningrad, now renamed St Petersburg, believed that a new democratic Russia should play a dominant role in creating a federation of democratic states around it. He was upset by Yeltsin's decision to let the Baltic republics go without negotiations. Russia had too many commercial and other interests there.[52] There were ten times as many in Ukraine. In Kiev, Sobchak said, the Party nomenklatura had sought to create a "preserve" under its control against democratic forces. He called the decision to create Ukrainian armed forces "political insanity." The Soviet Army could not be partitioned, he said. "We are a nuclear power."[53]

Yeltsin seemed to be having second thoughts as well. On 26 August, his press secretary Pavel Voshchanov issued at Yeltsin's request a declaration to the media: "The Russian Federation casts no doubt on the constitutional right of every state and people to self-determination. There exists, however, the problem of borders, the non-settlement of which is possible and admissible only on condition of allied relations secured by an appropriate treaty. In the event of their termination, the RSFSR reserves the right to raise the question of the revision of boundaries. This refers to all neighboring republics, with the exception of the three Baltic republics."[54]

The declaration was aimed above all at the Ukrainians. It reflected the strong influence of Alexander Solzhenitsyn: the nationalist writer had decried the decisions of the Bolshevik dictatorship to transfer "historic Russian lands" to the Ukrainian Soviet republic as a divide-and-conquer ploy.[55] Vladimir Lukin in Yeltsin's entourage strongly believed that the borders of the Russian Federation, Ukraine, and Kazakhstan "were the products of the Bolsheviks' cynical manipulation of nationalism in order to construct their totalitarian empire." Internationally monitored referendums, Lukin argued, should be called to allow these areas to decide whether they wanted to become part of a new democratic Russia or stay as they were. The territories in question were Crimea and the Donbass region.[56]

At a round-table discussion in Moscow, Alexander Tsypko, a political scientist with Ukrainian roots, argued that this declaration could lead to a war with the two Slavic republics. It would be, he warned, worse than the conflict between Serbia and Croatia in the collapsing Yugoslavia. The only way to keep the peace would be to recognize the current borders of Ukraine. Lukin objected: "And what would remain [of Russia] after everybody took what they considered necessary?" He rejected the analogy with Yugoslavia. The Soviet Army was still under Moscow's control. Yeltsin should quietly, but firmly, use economic pressure to force Ukraine to return Crimea, where the majority of the population were ethnic Russians. The Ukrainian leaders, he concluded, "would have enough brains to understand that they cannot operate without Russia."[57]

Gennady Burbulis continued to claim even many years later that the declaration to the Ukrainians was the work of Yeltsin's press secretary, Voshchanov. Burbulis's mother came from Luhansk, Donbass, and his son was born in Kiev. He could not imagine Ukraine and Russia as being separate, but he rejected Solzhenitsyn's ethno-nationalism.[58] Voshchanov later recalled the motivation of his boss: "Yeltsin of course did not have any political desire to hold onto the Union at any cost." At the same time, Yeltsin was offended by the Ukrainian Act. He had been supporting Ukrainian independence all along, yet he convinced himself that this would assist a rapprochement between Russians and Ukrainians. Instead, Kravchuk and the Ukrainian communists had tricked him, and decided to separate themselves from a democratic Russia, while taking Russian-speaking Crimea as well. Yeltsin decided to send a strong signal to Kiev. When Voshchanov finished his draft, he called Yeltsin, who was on his way to the Latvian resort of Jurmala, and read the text over the phone. "Fine," Yeltsin said. "Send it to the press."[59]

Vice-President Rutskoy as well as the mayor of Leningrad, Anatoly Sobchak, and Gavriil Popov, mayor of Moscow, welcomed the declaration. In a televised interview, Popov mentioned not only Crimea but also some areas on the left side of the Dnieper and Odessa as disputed territories. Voshchanov did the same, when he held a press conference. A Ukrainian journalist accused Yeltsin and the Russian leadership of clinging to communist-imperialist legacy. Voshchanov replied that Ukrainian nationalists regarded this "legacy" highly selectively: "You don't want to live with Russia in a union? This is a communist legacy for you? Then go, but return Crimea and Donbass to us! Because they became part of Ukraine due to the 'communist legacy'! You received them from Nikita Khrushchev with the approval of the CC CPSU Presidium."[60]

The next day, Kravchuk called Yeltsin to protest. Hadn't they both agreed in November 1990 on the territorial integrity of the two republics? Yeltsin prevaricated. He denied he had authorized the declaration, arguing only that there could be a problem with having borders between Russia and Ukraine in the future, should the Union fall apart. Kravchuk agreed, but urged Yeltsin to solve this problem when it arose, "in a civilized manner."[61] Yeltsin's waffling was a reaction to the political storm that the declaration triggered in the West and among Russian democrats. Western ambassadors were telephoning him to express their concerns. Journalists besieged Yeltsin's office with enquiries: Had Yeltsin changed his colors? Would Russia go to war with Ukraine over Crimea? In Moscow, the *Independent Gazette* published an op-ed piece whose author compared Yeltsin's territorial revisionism to Hitler's claims on the Sudetenland in 1938.[62]

Yeltsin was stunned. On 27 August, he asked Rutskoy to fly to Kazakhstan in order to reassure Nazarbayev. The Kazakh President feared for the northern regions of Kazakhstan, populated mostly by ethnic Russians. Rutskoy declared in Alma-Ata that Voshchanov had made this declaration without Yeltsin's consent and promised to punish the wayward press secretary. The next morning, Yeltsin sent Rutskoy, Sergey Stankevich and others to Kiev as troubleshooters. Sobchak, Lukin, and Shcherbak joined this mission on behalf of the Supreme Soviet of the USSR.

The delegation from Moscow landed at Borispol Airport that afternoon. The group met with Kravchuk and other Ukrainian parliamentarians in the Rada. The Russian-Ukrainian talks lasted through most of the night. With emotions running high, Kravchuk and Rutskoy signed a Russian-Ukrainian agreement. They confirmed that the Ukrainian-Russian treaty of November 1990 remained the basis for all present and future negotiations. Journalists noticed that both sides spoke about the "former Union." The Ukrainians promised to suspend the formation of a separate army "during transition"—a pledge they did not mean to keep. Kravchuk agreed that Ukraine would return to the Novo-Ogaryovo talks, but with a caveat: the Ukrainian people would decide on the republic's membership in a future Union on 1 December, the day of the Ukrainian referendum and presidential elections.[63]

The first standoff between the Slavic republics ended in Ukraine's favor. The Ukrainian leader could now start his presidential campaign without alienating Russian speakers in Eastern, Southern, and Central Ukraine. Russian participants at the talks knew, however, that they did not resolve basic disagreements. Crimea remained the bone of contention. Russia had already ceded Soviet ports and bases on the Baltic Sea to the Balts; Ukrainian secession would mean that the Russian state would lose nineteen out of twenty-two ports on the Black Sea. The feeling that the Russian-Ukrainian accord was unfair would become the main source of conflict for years to come.[64]

"A RUN ON THE BANK"

August was the last month in the life of Nikolai Kruchina. As the chief Party administrator, he was in charge of all Party assets, money, and investments. As a young man, Kruchina had entered rebellious Budapest with Soviet tanks in November 1956. On 23 August 1991, after Soviet tanks had left Moscow, the democratic emissaries from the Moscow government forced him to shut the Party headquarters; Kruchina felt broken and betrayed. Then Gorbachev called him to announce the Party's dissolution: he ordered Kruchina to pay severance packages to the Party members. The emissaries from Democratic Russia came to interrogate Kruchina about Party funds and investments. This was the last straw. In the early morning of 26 August, Kruchina fell to his death from his balcony in a guarded apartment building in which he resided. In his last note he wrote: "I am a coward." The autopsy and trial did not find any signs of foul play.[65]

Kruchina's fall symbolized the dramatic end of the Soviet Union's state capitalism under the aegis of the central nomenklatura. The terms for appropriation of state property accumulated by the Soviet state over many decades had dramatically changed. A young American scholar who was in Moscow at that time, doing research on the Soviet economy, came up with a metaphor: "a run on the bank." The Soviet nomenklatura, he argued, was rushing to grab state assets like customers of a bank on the eve of bankruptcy. Kruchina's death may have been suicide, yet it was very convenient for many people in power. And Just over a month later, on 6 October, Kruchina's predecessor, eighty-one-year-old Georgy Pavlov, also fell to his death from his balcony. Ten days after that another Party official, in charge of finances sent to foreign communist parties, fell to his death from the windows of his apartment building. These mysterious falls would continue to nourish rumors about "disappeared" Party funds. Several investigations were launched, none of them successful. The enormous transfer of wealth from the collapsing Soviet state to private accounts in London, New York, Switzerland, and various offshore accounts continued.[66]

Mikhail Bocharov, head of the Supreme Economic Council of the RSFSR, was among the losers. In the months before the junta, Bocharov was planning to create a state conglomerate to sell Soviet military assets in the Baltic republics and Eastern Europe. The items for sale included military bases, infrastructure, warehouses, and heavy equipment. Bocharov believed that his conglomerate could earn up to $100 billion in the Baltic republics alone. He negotiated with Yazov, Kryuchkov, and Pugo, whose troops protected military bases in the Baltics. Lukyanov allegedly told him: "When Gorbachev comes back, we will sign all your documents!" The junta's fiasco ruined Bocharov's plans. During the days of emergency rule, he was on a business trip in Vienna and did not rush back. He then lost Yeltsin's trust; his rivals Burbulis and Khasbulatov eased him out of the Russian power structures.[67] Kruchina and Bocharov relied on the central bureaucratic apparatus as a hub for new corporate chains and investments. The self-annihilation of the Soviet state had left them flat-footed.

Viktor Chernomyrdin, the head of Gazprom, suddenly discovered that he was on his own; his corporation was left without state credits and subsidies. Hundreds of "red directors" like him were in a similar situation. The state budget managed by the Minister of Finance virtually stopped receiving taxes from the republics; only 11 percent of taxes were submitted. Meanwhile, pensions, wages, and salaries remained indexed against inflation and nominally doubled in comparison with the previous fall. Directors of state conglomerates did not have money to pay the salaries of their employees, even those in charge of nuclear weapons.[68]

The sudden collapse of the central state set in motion anarchical processes in the Soviet economy. In the classic film *Zorba the Greek* (1964), Greek villagers ransack the household of a deceased well-to-do lady; the house is stripped from top to bottom in a matter of minutes, reduced to an empty carcass. There were obvious winners in the Zorba-like environment in the USSR: young entrepreneurs, who had got a head-start during Gorbachev's reforms, yet whose real goal was to make money by any means possible. Many of them had roots in the Komsomol: the Soviet authorities granted Komsomol activists unique privileges to launch "socialist cooperatives," including the first commercial banks. The British journalist Paul Khlebnikov, who knew many of these activists-cum-businessmen, later wrote: the KGB and the Party "made the same mistake that the czarist secret police had made a century earlier," namely by sponsoring agents of revolution in order to control them. Eight decades later,

Nikolai Kruchina and the KGB spawned "the gangsters and capitalists who went on to destroy the Soviet Union."[69]

Whatever role the new capitalists played in the Soviet drama, after the junta's failure they felt free as never before. *Kommersant*, "a newspaper of business," was published on 21 August with the headline: "Thank God, perestroika is over!" The newspaper's editor, thirty-two-year-old Vladimir Yakovlev, was the son of Yegor Yakovlev, the editor-in-chief of *Moscow News*, a leading glasnost newspaper. In contrast to his father, a believer in "humane socialism," the younger Yakovlev declared his indifference to any ideals or ideologies. He wanted to build a "normal society," by which he meant laissez-faire capitalism. This was a generational shift. In a fascinating conversation with his father, published in *Moscow News*, Vladimir explained that all Gorbachev's decrees had long stopped working because they ceased to reflect realities on the ground. The local authorities, he argued, had become vitally dependent on young entrepreneurs, who provided them "not only with the luxury items they coveted, but also whatever food their fridges could store."[70]

Other Gorbachev-era entrepreneurs shared this chutzpah. "Business is thriving," Konstantin Borovoy, one of *Kommersant*'s sponsors, told the Soviet ambassador Anatoly Adamishin when he visited Rome, "but political power stands in the way." In November 1990, Borovoy had been authorized by Yeltsin's government to set up a Moscow Stock Exchange. The stockbrokers helped giant corporations and plants to trade their products for the materials and goods they needed, making huge and largely untaxed profits. On 20 August, young brokers defied the junta and carried a giant Russian national flag across Moscow.[71] Borovoy boasted to Adamishin that he and his business partners knew "everything that the coupmakers were doing" due to their high-placed sources, including some KGB officials. "My brokers have already become billionaires," he explained. "They must invest their money, but they are not permitted to do so." The removal of the state, he hoped, would allow young Russian capitalists to use their accumulated liquidity to buy cash-strapped state enterprises and other assets.[72]

Mikhail Khodorkovsky was another entrepreneur who capitalized on the new horizons. As the young chief executive of the Menatep Group, which owned eighteen commercial banks, two insurance companies, and one trading house, Khodorkovsky was also an advisor to the RSFSR government.[73] By offering high salaries, Menatep lured the best experts from the State Bank and Soviet ministries. When he learned about the emergency rule, Khodorkovsky's first thought was that the junta would unleash a populist assault on young millionaires like himself. This did not happen. For the three dangerous days of 19–21 August, Khodorkovsky stayed in the Russian parliament, but he also continued to lead Menatep, located in the building next door, which had once housed the operations of the defunct economic bloc of socialist countries. At the end of August, young bankers celebrated victory and demanded new freedoms of financial transactions and privatization from the RSFSR government.[74]

When his vacation ended, Ambassador Anatoly Adamishin returned to the Soviet Embassy in Rome. Many prominent officials traveled from Moscow to Italy to propose lucrative business opportunities to the Italian business elite and government officials—in exchange for Italian medicine, food products, and other goods. Adamishin met with Sobchak, Popov, Rutskoy, and many others. Their lack of business skills shocked the ambassador. Those officials in his view were acting like carpetbaggers; one sought to undercut the other. Ministers and mayors used their official posts to promote their personal businesses. Yet the same people grumbled that an unregulated market economy was dragging the country into a state of complete chaos. Even Borovoy confessed that Russia needed a strong statesman with a vision, perhaps someone like Lenin, only on the side of capitalism.[75]

Adamishin was surprised to hear the same doubts expressed by his Italian friends and colleagues: statesmen, financiers, and politicians. It would be tragic, they argued, if the Soviet state should suddenly disappear. Much of the Soviet Union's wealth would then end up in the pockets of "mafia."[76] The Italians knew what they were talking about. And in Moscow, St Petersburg, many provinces of the Russian Federation, in Ukraine, and in South Caucasus, criminal elements were already mingling with the mid-ranking nomenklatura officials and populating the networks of patronage for an emerging "free" market. This process would define and shape the future of post-Soviet economies in Russia, Ukraine, the Baltic states, and other republics of the Soviet Union.[77]

PROVISIONAL OLIGARCHY

On 27 August, Gorbachev told Georgy Shakhnazarov to start working with the leaders of Russia, Ukraine, and other republics on a new Union Treaty. The seasoned advisor shook his head in disbelief: did Gorbachev really hope to convince Yeltsin and the republican barons to return the power they had grabbed earlier in the month back to the central government? Gorbachev said: "We should explain to them that none of their republics would survive without the Union. Even Russia." Shakhnazarov proceeded to contact Yeltsin's headquarters.[78]

It was a weird moment of anarchy in Moscow. The Soviet central state and Party structures that had previously managed the economy and finances had been dissolved. Those who remained in their jobs were in limbo, without political backing. One example of the anarchy was the uncertainty surrounding the status of the State Bank of the USSR during the last days of August. On 25 August,

Yeltsin signed an order for the Russian government to take over the State Bank of the USSR and the Ministry of Finance. His government also tried to take into its control Soviet gold and diamond reserves, as well as the facility for printing rubles.[79] On 26 August, Viktor Gerashchenko, head of the State Bank, learned he had been dismissed because of his collaboration with the junta. During emergency rule, he had issued instructions to the branches of the Bank to collect tax arrears from the Russian Federation. He had also cracked down on the commercial banks, registered under the Russian jurisdiction. Now, the emissaries from the Russian government came to Gerashchenko and demanded "the keys" from the vaults—a poor parody of what the Bolsheviks had done in 1917. Instead of acceding to their request, Gerashchenko picked up the telephone and called all the numbers of influential people in Moscow, in other republics, and abroad. Under growing pressure, especially from Kravchuk and Nazarbayev, Yeltsin had to suspend the operation. The Russian emissaries quietly left the Bank, and Gerashchenko resumed his job. The Bank continued to function as if it belonged to all the republics, not only the RSFSR.[80]

The new uncertainty also cast a cloud over the future of Soviet energy production and distribution. On 31 August, the Russian President signed a decree to "nationalize" Soviet oil and gas industries on RSFSR territory. It covered the entire Soviet fuel complex, including the state corporation Gazprom and a state pipeline-building corporation.[81] In the past, the Council of Ministers of the USSR and its committees had decided how oil and gas were distributed and delivered from the fields of Western Siberia to the republics and abroad. Suddenly, this mechanism had now disappeared, while new market-based agreements and networks were still not available. In Ukraine, petrochemical industries "came to a screeching halt." An energy catastrophe was looming. To prevent the disaster, the last Soviet minister of the petrochemical industry, Salambek Hadjiev, an ethnic Chechen, had to return to his abandoned office, to make phone calls and contract deals to resume the flow of oil.[82]

The economist Abel Aganbegyan told Adamishin, when he was visiting Rome, that the republican economies simply could not exist separately from each other, nor without Moscow's coordinating authorities. The centralized distribution of credit, products, and supplies had stopped, according to Aganbegyan. The export of wood, minerals, and metals had also shrunk dramatically, by one-third and sometimes two-thirds. The miners of Donbass were left without wood to construct their shafts; the Ukrainian-Russian separation, argued the leaders of their trade union, was causing their mines to shut down and leading to massive unemployment. The euphoria about independence would end soon, Aganbegyan confidently predicted, "and the republics would crawl on their knees back to the center."[83]

This was the moment that Gorbachev used to his advantage. While Yeltsin was in Latvia on vacation, playing tennis, Gorbachev created an "operational committee" to act as a stop-gap replacement for the disbanded Cabinet of Ministers. He asked the RSFSR Prime Minister, Ivan Silayev, to head this enterprise. Surprisingly, Yeltsin gave his consent to both steps. Grigory Yavlinsky, author of the 500 Days program, also joined the economic "operational committee" as deputy chairman. All republics immediately sent their representatives to the committee; even the Baltic states dispatched "observers." Gorbachev seemed to have emerged yet again as an essential mediating figure capable of compensating for Yeltsin's destructive actions.[84] The "operational committee" acted without any constitutional authority, solely on the basis of inertia. Yavlinsky recalled that he had been on the telephone all the time, cajoling and cursing directors of enterprises, redirecting trains with coal or wheat from one region to another, and liaising between one industry corporation and another. He did not even know if any of his calls produced the intended results on the ground.[85]

Gorbachev's scheme was to turn this provisional committee into a post-Soviet government—a bridge to the creation of a new Union on the ruins of the old one. On 31 August he met with Yeltsin and Nazarbayev and offered them a political deal. The troika would convene the Congress of People's Deputies and make this body legitimize a provisional government. Gorbachev had three new institutions in mind. First, a joint economic committee of the participating republics to run the economy. Second, a State Council consisting of republican leaders and chaired by Gorbachev, which would deal with political affairs. Third, a new Supreme Soviet of the USSR, whose conservative majority would be replaced by delegated deputies from the republican legislatures. After approving those institutions, the Congress would disband itself and would never be convened again. Yeltsin accepted the deal. He, Burbulis, and others in his entourage believed that Gorbachev's scheme of rebuilding the Union was an exercise in futility. Yet Gorbachev had made an offer that the Russian leadership could not refuse.

On 1 September, Gorbachev invited leaders of the republics to his office in the Kremlin. Nazarbayev came; Yeltsin sent Vice-President Rutskoy. From Central Asia, Karimov and other leaders attended. The head of Georgia's parliament arrived as an observer. The leadership of the three Baltic republics and Moldova declined to participate. The leadership of Ukraine was absent: Kravchuk was "sick" while the Ukrainian Prime Minister, Vitold Fokin, was "on vacation." Vladimir Grinev represented the republic without any formal authority.[86] Gorbachev opened the meeting with a statement: the people were demanding a new legal order and Western leaders "are simply in panic." Otherwise, there might be a war, as in Yugoslavia, "some kind of Armageddon . . ." He unveiled, on behalf of the troika, his plan for a constitutional transfer of power to the republics. Then he proposed signing the Union Treaty "within the next week."[87]

The republican potentates approved the joint statement to the Congress that Gorbachev had prepared. Their feelings, however, were confused. Even those who opted for independence suddenly realized they were responsible for the developing chaos, and were dismayed by the new obligations and huge uncertainties they faced. After the meeting, they went to talk to the delegates from their respective republics, who had already begun to arrive in Moscow for the Soviet mega-assembly. Nobody could predict, however, how the majority of the Congress, elected in 1989, would react. Yevgeny Primakov, a savvy insider and Gorbachev's aide, predicted that the deputies would unseat the Soviet President rather than eliminate the Congress. The three Baltic prime ministers, who happened to be in Moscow at the time, were very nervous. If the Congress took the wrong decision, their acts of independence would be in danger.[88]

The Congress opened on 2 September, at 10 a.m. in the Kremlin Palace; 1,900 delegates registered to attend. Gorbachev and republican leaders used all available administrative and political resources to pack out and stage the event. Sobchak "worked" on the "Russian" delegates elected in the precincts of the Russian Federation. Nazarbayev provided extra transportation for the Kazakh delegates to arrive in Moscow in time; other Central Asian republics did the same. As the session opened, Nazarbayev delivered a shock-and-awe statement from the republican leaders. Despite all the preparations, it took many delegates by complete surprise. Many expected Gorbachev to elect a new Soviet Cabinet of Ministers and a new Supreme Soviet, and were ready to approve it. Instead, they were asked to consent to an anti-constitutional coup. The joint statement proclaimed the republics' right to join the United Nations as "subjects of international law." Immediately after Nazarbayev had finished, the Congress was adjourned for almost three hours without any discussion.[89] Bamboozled and leaderless, delegates wandered into the lobbies. Vadim Medvedev, Gorbachev's aide, later claimed that "a pre-emptive shock" worked well.[90]

After the Congress resumed its work, Yuri Shcherbak said on behalf of the deputies from Ukraine that the republic supported an immediate economic agreement, but did not want to be "a slave" of any Soviet institutions. He suggested holding a conference "about the geopolitical space of the former USSR," modeled after the Helsinki Conference of 1975. Ukraine did not want to participate in a common monetary system, because "the only real way to defend Ukraine's interests was to create its own currency system." The Ukrainians also claimed their share of the Soviet gold and currency reserves among the republics. They were not so eager to inherit their share of Soviet debts. The new head of Belorussia's

Supreme Soviet, Stanislav Shushkevich, backed the Ukrainian proposals.[91] The followers of Solzhenitsyn, if they were at the Congress, must have shuddered: their project of a common Slavic statehood had gone up in smoke.

Delegates from Democratic Russia supported the creation of an oligarchy of republican leaders. Alexander Obolensky was the only exception. He denounced what he called a conspiracy of the nomenklatura against the idea of a "common democratic space." He compared the joint statement of Gorbachev and eleven republican leaders to Lenin's dissolution of the democratic Constitutional Assembly in January 1918. Pointing his finger both at Yeltsin and Gorbachev, Obolensky declared: "Perhaps it is time we stopped treating the Constitution like a harlot, accommodating it to the pleasure of the new Tsar's courtier!" Gorbachev, he continued, had failed on two counts: he had created the conditions for a coup, and he had now betrayed the constitution he had pledged to defend. Such a leader should be removed immediately, and a new President of the Union had to be elected on the spot.[92]

The rebellion fizzled out. The majority of deputies chose loyalty to their republican leaders, rather than to the constitutional principles. The Russian communists and nationalists kept a low profile. Obolensky's proposal to remove Gorbachev was idealistic, but for many it only added to the specter of anarchy and civil war. The post-Soviet oligarchy of republican leaders would at least offer some semblance of orderly rule. The academician Dmitri Likhachev, the scientist Yevgeny Velikhov, and other major public figures implored the Congress to keep Gorbachev as the leader. The Russian democrats used the commotion to propose a "Resolution on the Rights and Freedoms," a lofty declaration of social-economic and human rights for the entire former Soviet territory. It was adopted almost unanimously.[93]

Yeltsin was not present during the Congress's first session. When he finally appeared, he said he trusted Gorbachev "much more than even three weeks ago, before the coup." Gorbachev, when he took the floor, sounded like a converted democrat; he fully adopted the narrative of the winners. He regretted he had not broken with "the totalitarian system" and not relied on "all democratic forces" a year earlier. He rejected Obolensky's accusations: by staying together, the republics would overcome economic crisis. "The West will support us as well ..." During the break, Gorbachev met with select groups of delegates and reassured them: the Supreme Soviet of the USSR would still be around as a guarantor of the common statehood.[94]

Gorbachev was tireless at the Congress. He found legalist tricks to avoid explosive debates; he worked backstage with the confused delegates and buried divisive proposals. When the republican leaders failed to marshal the constitutional majority of two-thirds required to cancel the Soviet constitution and dissolve the

Congress, Gorbachev, who chaired, presented the deputies with a sudden ultimatum: they should either go home or vote on the end of the constitution by a simple majority! Later Gorbachev would admit to the British ambassador: "I had to fiddle with the laws a bit to get the result they [the republican leaders] needed." The deputies surrendered. On 5 September, the Congress and the constitution went quietly into the dustbin of history. The 1,900 delegates packed up and headed home; in their suitcases they carried sausages and other scarce food items available in the Kremlin buffets.

Gorbachev's aide Vadim Medvedev argued that the Soviet President had acted correctly: the dismissal of old unitary structures was dictated by "the nature of the situation." Shakhnazarov and Chernyaev also agreed. In retirement, Ryzhkov called the dissolution of the Congress and the end of the Soviet constitution an act of "stupidity": the President of the USSR had helped Yeltsin to destroy the legal framework, without gaining anything tangible in return.[95]

On 6 September, the President of the USSR convened in his Kremlin office the first meeting of the State Council. The new ruling oligarchy of republican potentates still could not believe their political good luck. Yeltsin let Gorbachev occupy center stage again, at least for a while.[96] The first question on the agenda was Baltic independence. There was no time to discuss it at the Congress. Gorbachev did his best to build a legal firewall between the Baltic "restoration" of statehood, destroyed in 1940, and the sovereignty of other republics of the USSR. Two years previously, this would have been a revolutionary move. Now it appeared to be a specious legal trick. The Balts did not attend, but the Estonian Prime Minister, Edgar Savisaar, happened to be at the meeting "by accident." In reality, he was worried that "an interregnum" in Moscow would abruptly end at any moment: Yeltsin and Gorbachev would reach an agreement, and then the Russians would question Baltic independence. At the meeting, Savisaar addressed other republican leaders as "comrades" and did everything to send a conciliatory message. "We should not dramatize our divorce," he said. "We are in the same geographic space. We will not fly to the moon."[97]

The republican leaders voted to form a delegation, which would conduct negotiations with the three Baltic states "on the entire complex of issues connected to the rights of individuals and the interests of these republics in the USSR." This meant long settlement talks on a divorce contract, with many terms and conditions: Gorbachev asked Yakovlev, Shevardnadze, and Sobchak to lead these negotiations, one for every republic. The next day, *Izvestia* published the recognition declaration in small print, next to news about the bloody skirmishes between the Croatian military and the Serbian army.[98]

Gorbachev's gamble of a provisional government was his last and most desperate move. The only assets he still had were his constitutional status as

President of the USSR, international fame, and the republics' fear of total economic collapse. In just two months, however, the specter of a new Union would fade away like Moscow's Indian Summer. Yeltsin wanted "Russia" to become a natural leader in the post-Soviet space without any power being exercised above him. Gorbachev deluded himself by thinking that the threat of economic collapse and his support by Western leaders would be sufficient to herd the republican potentates into a common political project. In reality, he was shouldering a political burden for Yeltsin and the republican barons. Or, as his press secretary Andrei Grachev later said, the President of the USSR had placed himself in the position of King Lear—giving away tangible assets in exchange for promises of good faith.[99]

CHAPTER 13

CACOPHONY

*All the king's horses and all the king's men
Couldn't put Humpty together again.*
English nursery rhyme

What fell from the cart is lost.
Russian proverb

THE END OF CREDIT

The Soviet Ministry of Foreign Affairs, known as the MID, was in trouble after the August crisis, because most of its diplomats had followed the orders of the junta. "If I had been a senior Soviet official," the British ambassador Rodric Braithwaite wrote in his diary, "I would probably have gone the way of Bessmertnykh and other collaborators." The Russian Foreign Minister, Andrei Kozyrev, sent a group of investigators to MID headquarters to purge the top echelon of Soviet diplomats. After Gorbachev fired Bessmertnykh, it was the turn of his first deputy, Yuli Kvitsinsky, to be sacked: he had signed cables to Soviet embassies and consulates, telling them to comply with emergency rule. Anatoly Adamishin, the Soviet ambassador in Rome, realized he was lucky to have been on vacation in Moscow during the coup. That gave him an alibi.[1]

On 28 August 1991, a delegation of senior MID officials came to Shevardnadze with a plea to return and save Soviet diplomacy from the revolutionary pogrom. Sergey Lavrov, one of the group, said: "We feel a collective guilt and came to you as prodigal sons to a wise father ... It is not only about foreign policy," Lavrov continued. "Your return would prevent a massive exit of other republics ... We may be expelled from the United Nations. We may cease to be a great power even in legal terms." Shevardnadze agreed that Kozyrev's assault on the Foreign Ministry was "madness." He did not decline the offer to lead Soviet foreign policy again, but expressed grave doubts about Gorbachev. The real culprit of the current situation, Shevardnadze said, was the Soviet President, who had encouraged the emergency plans and ignored all warnings of the impending coup.[2]

Gorbachev did not call Shevardnadze. Instead, Boris Pankin, the ambassador to Czechoslovakia, would become the next Foreign Minister of the Soviet Union. He was the only Soviet ambassador to have publicly denounced "the coup." Gorbachev and Yeltsin also chose him because neither wanted Shevardnadze. Foreign policy became an instrument of power that the two presidents had reserved for themselves.[3] In the late afternoon of 28 August, Pankin arrived at the Kremlin to meet with Gorbachev. The presidential office, once a quiet haven of supreme power, was like a beehive: doors opened and closed constantly, letting visitors in and out. Gorbachev was forming his provisional government.[4] Following a brief talk with Pankin, Gorbachev signed his letter of appointment. After a few hours of waiting in Gorbachev's lobby, Pankin learned from television news that the Supreme Soviet had approved him without any hearings. That evening, Gorbachev invited the new minister for a heart-to-heart talk. The President put his arm around Pankin's shoulder, as if they were old classmates and friends. He said that the world had rallied around him and the Soviet Union during the days of August. "Time to change directions, to get rid of prejudices . . . Enough of double standards." Pankin, who had had many discussions with President Václav Havel in Prague, said that Eastern Europeans felt that everyone in Moscow had forgotten about them. Gorbachev, however, was not interested in that subject. His priorities were partnership with the West and fundraising. He showed Pankin his desk, where one of many telephones was marked "Foreign Minister." "You pick up a receiver there, and I pick it up over here. No intermediaries." Pankin left the meeting charmed, but without any idea what to do and which tasks to focus on.[5]

The next morning, instead of briefing Pankin in some depth on his new role, Gorbachev sent his new chief of staff, Grigory Revenko, to introduce Pankin to the Foreign Ministry Collegium. One month earlier, this snobbish body of senior Soviet diplomats might have treated Pankin as an upstart. Now, however, they received him without a murmur. Improvising desperately, Pankin told them that the Soviet Union needed the "foreign policy of a victorious democracy." Then he retired to the enormous office vacated by his predecessor, to collect his thoughts. Two portraits hung in the office: those of Lenin and Gorbachev. Neither could offer Pankin any advice.[6]

Gorbachev acted as if he was the only senior offical in the Soviet Union who could ask the West for financial assistance in order to save his country. On

1 September, during his meeting with eleven leaders of the republics, Gorbachev suddenly excused himself: he had to step out to receive Prime Minister John Major and Foreign Secretary Douglas Hurd of Great Britain, the first Western statesmen to visit Moscow after the "coup." Major chaired the G-7 group of wealthy nations and he had brought with him Nigel Wicks, a senior Treasury official who would soon attend a meeting to discuss Soviet debts and Western financial assistance. Gorbachev wanted to remind the republican potentates of his unique standing in world affairs. Meeting with Major and Hurd in the Kremlin's golden St George Hall, the President told them he had just saved the Soviet Union from disintegration. To consolidate his success, he needed Western assistance. The British Prime Minister and Foreign Secretary were impressed by Gorbachev's renewed confidence.[7] After returning to the leaders of the republics, Gorbachev said the British visitors had promised to help. Wicks would stay in Moscow, to work with Yavlinsky on a plan of economic reforms and aid from the International Monetary Fund, the World Bank, and Western governments. This plan could result in much-needed Western financial assistance.[8]

The discussion of "money for reforms" continued at the State Council on 6 September, the second formal meeting of Gorbachev's provisional government. The RSFSR Prime Minister, Ivan Silayev, informed leaders of the republics that the foreign debts of the Soviet Union stood at $52.2 billion; $20.9 billion were due in 1991. The Pavlov government had paid most of this, but $3.9 billion were still in arrears, and "so far we have nothing to pay with." The Soviet gold reserves had been exhausted. "In practical terms," Silayev concluded, "we are on the brink of all-Union bankruptcy." Where to find the money? Should one declare a default? Silayev turned to Gorbachev: "Only you can do it."[9] Gorbachev, who was at the helm again, said he would send his emissaries to raise funds: Yevgeny Primakov would go to Saudi Arabia and the Emirates, Yakovlev would travel to Germany, somebody else would go to South Korea.[10] Nazarbayev took the cue. He pleaded with Yeltsin: "Let's demonstrate to the country that we are united ... We should stop clobbering each other." The Russian President sat with a sullen face, saying nothing. Vadim Bakatin, head of the KGB, recalled that Gorbachev dominated the meeting: he juggled budget numbers easily and always had the last word.[11]

On 9 September, a conference held by the Organization for Security and Co-operation in Europe (OSCE) "on the humanitarian dimension" opened in Moscow. The idea of this conference dated back to the early days of perestroika, when the Politburo had considered human rights a Western instrument of Soviet foreign policy. In September 1988, after much diplomatic traffic, the meeting was set. Three years later, it appeared to many to be totally incongruous. In the MID, which was responsible for the event, everyone advised

Pankin to delay it. Western diplomats agreed.[12] Pankin, however, had an inspiration. The OSCE conference was a great opportunity to tell the world that Moscow was not the center of a collapsing totalitarian empire, but rather a capital of democratic revolution.[13] Gorbachev, after some hesitation, gave the green light. In just a few days, thirty-five foreign ministers and other dignitaries received official Soviet invitations to attend. The conference opened in the Hall of Columns in the House of the Soviets, where Lenin's associates had been tried and condemned to death in the period 1936–38, and where Stalin's coffin was displayed in March 1953. Quite a location to discuss "humanitarian issues"!

Thirty-eight flags of the OSCE members decorated the Hall of Columns, among them flags of the independent Baltic states. Pankin had also invited "foreign ministers" from Ukraine, Belarus, and other Soviet republics to attend as observers. In his opening speech, Gorbachev spoke about "a Great Eurasian Democracy." No one dared mention the Soviet Union anymore. Next day, Yeltsin hosted the foreign ministers in the Russian parliament. Gorbachev and Yeltsin also hosted two separate galas inside the Kremlin. Black limos, sequestered from the stockpile at the Party headquarters, drove dignitaries around Moscow. The hosts spoke about the victory of freedom and democracy, new partnerships, and ideology in international relations giving way to human rights. The Soviet delegation, chaired by Sergey Kovalev, a former political prisoner and friend of the late Andrei Sakharov, presented a package of breathtaking proposals, including the supremacy of international law over national sovereignty. This was more than the Americans and other Western governments were ready to accept.[14]

The leaders and followers of Democratic Russia were seized by a fever of admiration for the West, which represented a new mythology, a substitute for the collapsing Soviet world. The democratic-minded Russians expected to enter "the family of a civilized international community" tomorrow, if not today. For Moscow's cultural elites, the social events at the conference satisfied their desire to belong to, and be accepted by, the West. Some Western guests were stunned by the spirit of optimism. The country was going to the dogs. What was there to celebrate? Some asked their hosts: Why had the Soviet economy sunk so low? Were there fears of a new dictatorship?[15]

Gorbachev used the Moscow forum to confirm his status as a world celebrity and to request Western ministers for financial assistance. He asked Hans-Dietrich Genscher for one billion DM of credit. By that point the government of Chancellor Kohl had already given Gorbachev over 25 billion DM. Remarkably, Gorbachev could not even explain what the money had been used for. He did say to the US Secretary of State, James Baker, with stunning nonchalance: "Things disappear around here." Genscher, however, promised to talk to

Helmut Kohl immediately. Gorbachev commended German generosity and contrasted it with the American reaction: "Some people want to call the tune without even paying the piper." That same day, Gorbachev invited Yeltsin, Silayev, and Yavlinsky to listen in on his telephone conversation with Kohl. In it, the German Chancellor promised him the one billion DM. Kohl also offered to justify his assistance to the Soviet Union at the upcoming G-7 meeting in Dresden, where Sherpas (representatives of heads of the leading industrial powers) would be gathering.[16]

Gorbachev also spoke to France's Minister of Economy and Finances, Pierre Bérégovoy, and the Foreign Minister, Roland Dumas. He counted on France as a leader of the European Community. President Mitterrand's former advisor, Jacques Attali, was the director of the European Bank for Reconstruction and Development (EBRD) which gave credits to Eastern Europeans. "Let President Mitterrand know," Gorbachev said to his French guests, "that we need your help very much . . . This is our last chance." He urged Western powers to create a stabilization fund of $10 billion to save the Soviet economy. He also asked the Paris Club, an informal association of Western banks that handled difficult problems of international finances, to help restructure Soviet debts. Unfortunately, Gorbachev would not receive any financial aid from France. French foreign policy priorities began to shift from the OSCE to Maastricht, the negotiating process to create the European Union—a project that excluded the USSR.[17]

Foreign ministers of Western European countries still lionized Gorbachev. Thorvald Stoltenberg, from Norway's Foreign Ministry, met with the Soviet leader along with colleagues from Denmark, Sweden, Finland, and Iceland. He said: "Why not use the experience of post-war Western Europe and implement some kind of Marshall Plan?" If the West failed to assist change in the Soviet Union, he concluded, "we may destroy everything that we had created after the war."[18] In reality, the Nordic countries had been scrambling to assist the Balts. The rest of the Soviet Union was outside their remit.

Czechoslovakia's Foreign Minister and former dissident Jiří Dienstbier warned Gorbachev: "[The Western leaders] are afraid that this money will be gone with the wind, just like it was with Poland in the 1970s."[19] By the end of his fundraising marathon, Gorbachev had received only two pledges of financial aid. The Germans promised to deposit their 1 billion DM in the State Bank by 15 October. Another pledge came from Italy: a state credit of $1 billion. When Gorbachev asked the German Sherpa Horst Köhler for an additional low-interest credit, the Germans stalled. Any further money, Köhler said, required a joint decision by the G-7 leaders.[20] Gorbachev had reached the limit of his personal credit.

CACOPHONY

"CHICKEN KIEV"

President Bush and Brent Scowcroft were baffled by the rapid changes in Moscow. They understood that the old Soviet center was gone. Yet they did not know how Yeltsin's "democratic revolution" would turn out. Bush feared that hardliners could still regroup and strike back.[21] Yeltsin's hasty decrees on Latvia and Estonia and the Ukrainian Act of Independence put the American President in a bind. The US Congress urged Bush to accept the sovereignty of the Baltic states, but also grant recognition to Ukraine. On 26 August, Prime Minister Brian Mulroney, on a visit to Bush at Kennebunkport, told his friend that Canada was about to recognize Baltic sovereignties. Then Helmut Kohl called the American President the next day: the assembly of EEC foreign ministers in The Hague had also decided to recognize the Baltic states. Bush reacted pensively: "I wish we knew a little more on the effect this would have on other republics." In his memoirs, Bush explained that he wanted to give Gorbachev the opportunity to recognize the Baltic states first, "before we in the West act."[22]

Bush's primary concern and interest was Ukraine, not the Baltic republics. On 29 August, *The New York Times* published an op-ed piece by William Safire entitled "After the Fall." "The Soviet empire is breaking up," wrote the popular conservative columnist. "This is a glorious moment for human freedom. We should savor that moment, thanking God, NATO, the heroic dissidents in Russia and the internal empire, and the two-generation sacrifice of the American people to protect themselves and the world from despotic domination." The columnist attacked Bush for his timidity: "Why isn't the President of the United States on the air, welcoming the Russians, Ukrainians and all to the free world, urging the dissolution of the police and cutbacks in the army, showing the path to prosperity?" Instead, Bush was "foolishly placing Washington on the side of Moscow centralism and against the tide of history." The columnist singled out Bush's address to the Ukrainian parliament on 1 August and dubbed it the "Chicken Kiev speech."[23] This was a resounding claim for immediate recognition of Ukraine's independence.

President Bush was furious and deeply wounded. Safire's "Chicken Kiev" could not be easily forgotten and it appeared at an exceptionally sensitive moment. Bush and Baker were considering the implications of Ukraine's secession for the Soviet nuclear arsenal. The strategic implications of its exit from the Union were of special concern. A total of 176 intercontinental ballistic missiles (ICBMs) in silos and forty-two strategic bombers on airbases were deployed on Ukrainian territory, with an estimated 1,800 nuclear warheads stored in special bunkers. The biggest missile plant in the Soviet Union, which produced SS-18 missiles, was located in Ukraine's Dnepropetrovsk.[24] Who would be in charge of this enormous nuclear capability if Ukraine were to become independent?

DECLINE AND DOWNFALL

The US President decided to ignore Safire and other critics. The White House decoupled the Baltic Question from Ukrainian independence; the latter had to be delayed until the nuclear issues were clarified. The next day, 30 August, Bush informed Gorbachev that he could wait no longer on the issue of Baltic recognition. The Soviet leader pleaded for him to be patient until the opening of the Soviet Congress. The new American ambassador to the Soviet Union, Robert Strauss, and other sources backed Gorbachev's plea: the Congress could dismiss the Soviet leader. Bush said he would give Gorbachev a few more days. Then he telephoned Vytautas Landsbergis of Lithuania. Bush told him to wait for "an important announcement on Monday." He concluded reassuringly: "I want you to know that we are with you."[25]

On the morning 2 September, Bush met the press and announced the restoration of diplomatic relations with the Baltic states. Shortly before, he called the presidents of Estonia and Latvia and explained that he had waited this long because he had been trying "to get the Soviets to permit independence." The US President believed he had just performed a delicate diplomatic maneuver. Bush spent his lunchtime pondering the special meaning of this day in his life. On 2 September 1944, a military aircraft that Bush piloted was shot down over the Bonin islands in the Pacific Ocean, south of Japan. His crewmates perished, and he was the only survivor. It was a moment to think about life, his good fortune, and service to one's country.

In their recollections, Bush and Scowcroft continued to insist they had acted wisely. The National Security Advisor commented that they "were striving for a permanent solution" to the Baltic issue. "That could best be achieved by voluntary Soviet recognition of Baltic independence." Otherwise, should the nationalist Right come to power in Moscow, they could easily reverse the situation "claiming the USSR only acted under duress in a weakened condition." Neither man mentioned Safire's article.[26]

With the Baltic issue resolved and Ukraine's recognition postponed, the White House focused on other aspects of the Soviet conundrum. On 4 September, Bush and his Cabinet debated whether a weak Soviet Union or its break-up would best serve American interests. "We were split, badly split," Scowcroft recalled. The Pentagon's chief, Dick Cheney, publicly advocated abandoning Gorbachev for Yeltsin, who was a real democrat and embraced Western values. Cheney supported the appeal from the Ukrainian-American organizations and the National Endowment for Democracy (NED) to recognize Ukrainian independence.[27]

James Baker argued that a weak Union under Gorbachev would be more in US interests than an unpredictable cacophony of independent republics. He took inspiration from his aides, Andrew Carpendale and John Hannah.

Carpendale had written a memo "What Is to Be Done," after Lenin's famous dictum, in which he rooted for Moscow's liberal intellectuals and backed their idea of "a common democratic space" across the Soviet Union. Yeltsin's ambitions, Carpendale argued, could lead to a Yugoslavia-like confrontation between the republics. Hannah proposed a framework of five principles derived from the OSCE legal framework, within which the process of Soviet dissolution could "occur peacefully and orderly." This framework consisted of peaceful self-determination consistent with democratic values and principles, in the spirit of the Helsinki Final Act; respect for existing borders, both internal and external, when any changes occurred peacefully and consensually; respect for democracy and the rule of law, especially elections; human rights, particularly equal treatment of minorities; and respect for international law and obligations.[28] Shevardnadze also urged Baker to affirm those principles. He hoped the US administration would convince Gorbachev and Yeltsin to forge a partnership.[29]

Baker, like his aides, was thinking about Yugoslavia, the country that was irrevocably sliding towards a state of violent chaos. On 4 September, the Secretary of State announced the five principles at a press briefing in the State Department. He emphasized that the Baltic states "have always been and indeed remain a special and separate case for the United States." The future of the Union, Baker continued, "is for the Soviet peoples to determine themselves," according to the "internationally accepted" principles. When a reporter asked Baker about the parallels between the Soviet Union and Yugoslavia, he responded: "[The Yugoslavs] did not follow five principles and look what happened!"[30]

Two wild cards lay on the horizon of US diplomacy. One was the idea of a massive Western financial package to stabilize the Soviet economy in its transition to capitalism. On 27 August, Graham Allison and Robert Blackwill in an op-ed piece in *The Washington Post* urged the Bush administration to take the lead on this initiative.[31] John Major, one of the G-7 leaders, warned Bush: some Western leaders wanted to expedite Soviet membership of the IMF, so that Moscow could draw on its funds. Bush, advised by his Secretary of the Treasury, Nicholas Brady, was firmly against this idea. He responded: "We have just had a momentous triumph for our values and for our vital interests. I think we are in a strong position not to be rushed into hasty decisions. We should be able to resist pressures for large-scale cash assistance."[32] At the Cabinet meeting on 4 September, Baker had to agree with him. The President could not propose spending taxpayers' money on the USSR while the US economy was ailing.[33]

Ukrainian independence remained the second wild card. Ed Hewett, the top Soviet expert on the National Security Council, wrote to Bush and Scowcroft: "Both Yeltsin and Gorbachev feel that Ukraine must stay in the Union." Ukraine's secession could provoke huge economic dislocation and a nationalist backlash in Russia. "It is likely in the end," speculated Hewett, "that Kravchuk will not win the key December elections, but that Ukraine will stay in the union, primarily as a way to try to control Russia."[34] The Ukrainian controversy was discussed in the White House on 5 September. Bush opened the meeting by admitting that the declaration of independence by other republics "was a complex issue." There were smaller autonomous regions inside the Russian Federation and other republics, and all of them were threatening to secede. The President's uncertainty prompted Cheney to argue again for an "aggressive" approach. The United States, he said, must use its enormous leverage in the Soviet space to break it apart. "We could get an authoritarian regime [in Russia] still," he said. "I am concerned that a year or so from now, if it all goes sour, how we can answer that we did not do more . . ." The full record of the discussion remains classified, but the meaning of Cheney's words was clear. Russia had never existed as a democratic country, and most likely it would not become one. The recognition of an independent Ukraine would be a good policy in any case. "If democracy fails, we're better off, if they [the Russians] are small."[35] Baker reminded Cheney of the other horn of the dilemma: what if the break-up led to violence? "We don't want another Yugoslavia." Scowcroft recalled: "Baker thought it was important that we try to keep the Soviet Union together, principally because of command and control over the nuclear forces . . . I thought we were better off with a broken-up Soviet Union, because it would fractionate the Soviet nuclear forces—and a large part of them, we could stop worrying about." Scowcroft, however, disagreed with Cheney. If the US openly backed Soviet disintegration, Scowcroft reasoned, it "would almost guarantee long-term hostility on the part of most Russians, who constituted the majority of the Soviet Union." "In the end," he recalled, "we took no position at all. We simply let things happen."[36]

For Baker, the OSCE forum in Moscow was an opportunity to deliver his five principles to the intended audience and determine how American diplomacy could benefit from a Soviet break-up. His log included the ratification of START and CFE (the Treaty on Conventional Armed Forces in Europe), which meant cuts to the Soviet strategic arsenal and the removal of Soviet troops from Central Europe. He also wanted to end Soviet aid to two key clients: Cuba and Afghanistan.[37] Baker arrived in Moscow on the morning of 11 September. His first meeting was with Foreign Minister Pankin. Astonishingly, Pankin handed Baker a list of ten proposals, some of which pre-empted the American requests. The list included the termination of Soviet assistance to Cuba and Afghanistan, talks on the Northern Territories claimed by Japan, the opening of previously restricted areas of the Soviet Union to American tourism and business, and the recognition of the right of Eastern European countries to enter into any alliances they wished. These proposals, Pankin concluded, were not Soviet concessions, but reflected a new philosophy on the part of those who "run our foreign policy today."[38]

After that, Baker met with Gorbachev. The Soviet leader confirmed that Soviet assistance to Cuba and Afghanistan would be terminated, but gradually and subject to negotiations. Gorbachev still hoped to avoid the appearance of unconditional retreat. But he desperately needed Western assistance, including food and medicine. He also asked (with Yavlinsky present) if the West could set up a stabilization dollar fund to maintain the Soviet balance of payments. Baker gave a noncommittal response: an IMF-approved program of economic reform, supported by Yeltsin, "would enable the West to provide rather substantial aid." In contrast, the Secretary of State was specific about Soviet debts to Western banks: they must be paid on time, or the United States "might be forced" to stop humanitarian aid.[39]

Yeltsin waited for Baker to tell him that he was now the boss in Moscow. All Soviet foreign policy was "rubbish," Yeltsin said. The Cuban community in Florida had lobbied Yeltsin to end Soviet subsidies to Castro's dictatorship immediately. Now he presented this as a gift for Baker. The Soviet Union, Yeltsin said, would cut off military and economic assistance to Havana and Kabul by the end of the year. The entire contingent of Soviet troops, 11,000 men in uniform, would leave Cuba by 1 January 1992. Yeltsin promised to get Gorbachev's consent to this—and in a few hours he did. That same evening, Baker and Gorbachev made a joint announcement on this at a news conference.[40] The decorum of "democratic foreign policy" aside, it signaled a hasty dismantling of the Soviet superpower. One historian called this episode a "fire sale of Soviet foreign policy assets." In fact, those "assets" were discarded like garbage. Pankin, who had not even begun consultations with the Cubans and Afghans, was shocked when he heard the Gorbachev-Baker announcement.[41]

The Cuban regime would unexpectedly survive the end of Soviet subsidies, remaining a thorn in the American side. The regime of President Najibullah in Kabul would fall four years later, to be replaced by the ruthless fundamentalists of the Taliban. This did not benefit American interests at all. Had Baker in September 1991 managed to look into a crystal ball, he would have seen the smoke billowing out of New York's Twin Towers and decades of American military occupation of Afghanistan.

In a cable to Bush from Moscow, Baker wrote about the "extraordinary flexibility" of Yeltsin and Gorbachev and linked it to their hopes of American assistance. The United States, Baker argued, should be in "even more of a hurry to 'lock in' gains then and there."[42] Still, the Secretary of State could not fully explain what he had just experienced. The Russians' willingness to please the

American went far beyond what their interests and common sense dictated. All the officials whom Baker met in Moscow behaved like born-again Christians, except their new source of inspiration was Uncle Sam's support and money. Everyone pleaded for Baker to help. Kozyrev needed him to convince Yeltsin to act even more resolutely to throw out the "rubbish" of Soviet foreign policy: the Russian President would listen only to the Americans![43] The Minister of Defense, Yevgeny Shaposhnikov, wanted Baker to restrain Ukraine and Belarus, where politicians were about to fragment the Soviet Army. The United States, Shaposhnikov pleaded, should "not to rush to recognize" those republics. Baker, struck by such naïveté, assured the Marshal that it was not US policy to do so. The head of the KGB, Bakatin, asked Baker to back him in his talks with the Baltic states: they sought the immediate destruction of secret police networks on their territories. Bakatin also needed American assistance in transforming the KGB into something akin to the CIA. "This is one helluva country," Baker marveled. "A month ago, the head of the KGB is arresting President Gorbachev, and now the head of the KGB is studying American legislation to model the Central Intelligence Agency!"[44]

Bakatin wrote in his memoirs that Baker cared about the future of the Soviet Union more "than some of our prominent politicians." The Secretary of State was appalled by the desire of the former Soviet republics to apply immediately for UN membership. What would then happen to the Security Council where the Soviet Union still had a permanent seat? Baker shared this concern with Kozyrev, who agreed that this "nightmare" should be prevented. At a dinner in Spaso House with the attendees from twelve republics at the OSCE conference, Baker urged them to cooperate and sign an economic treaty. His meetings with Silayev and Yavlinsky, however, convinced him that there was no unity of purpose between the two Russians. They quarreled constantly. Whereas Silayev wanted to ask the IMF and World Bank for money, Yavlinsky said any money would be wasted without a program of reforms, based strictly on his ideas. Mayors Popov and Sobchak sought to convince Baker that it would be better if Western business dealt with Moscow and St Petersburg directly, bypassing Gorbachev's provisional government. Popov urged NATO to ship all its dated army food reserves to Moscow. "Do not give money to the center," Sobchak told Baker.[45]

The emotional peak of Baker's trip was a dinner with Shevardnadze in his Moscow apartment. The former Foreign Minister saw no bright future for democracy in Russia without massive Western involvement. The Union's disintegration would tear the economy to shreds; populists like Vladimir Zhirinovsky would ride a wave of mass discontent.[46] Shevardnadze reminded his American friend: in the past the West had conditioned its assistance on the exit of the

Baltics from the Union. "Now, the Balts are gone, and there is no assistance." Baker remained immune to this reasoning. Perform the "economic revolution" and "our assistance will be provided without delay," he said. Before this "assistance" comes, Shevardnadze objected, Ukraine would be gone, Kazakhstan would go too, and Central Asia would end up in the grip of Islam. "Kravchuk is weak," Baker objected. "He runs for the presidency against nationalists." The West was on the side of the center and against nationalists. In the end, Baker stuck with the official US line of non-involvement, where all responsibility was delegated to post-Soviet actors and the IMF. "Baker's discipline, once again, almost prevented him from being human with the guy," recalled Robert Zoellick, one of Baker's principal aides who was present at the dinner.[47]

Still, Baker left Moscow emotionally engaged with Russian democracy. The failure of democrats in Moscow, he wrote to Bush, "would produce a world far more threatening and dangerous . . ." If, however, against very high odds, the Russian democrats would deliver "economic revolution" that would match their "political revolution," then "the onus will be on us, especially if we hang back."[48] This sense of moral responsibility cooled somewhat, when Baker traveled to the Baltic states, where he received a hero's welcome. Landsbergis and his colleagues wanted Washington to press Moscow into immediately withdrawing Soviet troops, demilitarizing Belarus, and stopping Soviet military traffic from crossing Lithuania into the Kaliningrad region, now a Soviet enclave. When Baker cited Shaposhnikov's arguments that all this was logistically impossible, the Lithuanians were angry. The Balts also refused to honor any Soviet commitments. As for Estonia, said its Foreign Minister Lennart Meri, it was no more of a successor state to the USSR than Namibia. Baker was struck by "a reaction bordering on open hostility" when he spoke about Russian-speaking minorities. Arnold Rüütel, head of the Estonian government, said that most Russians and Ukrainians in Estonia worked in defense and security sectors and should leave the country. Baker did his best to talk him out of this idea.[49]

Baker then flew with his team to Kazakhstan for talks with President Nazarbayev. The Kazakh republic had on its territory an estimated 1,000 strategic ICBMs with multiple nuclear warheads on each, and about 1,800 nuclear weapons in total in storage depots.[50] In Alma-Ata, their host entertained the Americans lavishly: vodka flowed and toasts were raised "to a US-Kazakh strategic alliance." Nazarbayev subscribed to the five principles, confirmed that Kazakhstan would remain nuclear-free, and asked Baker to open a diplomatic "representation" in the capital of the republic. He also shared with the Americans his concerns about a strong streak of Russian nationalism in Yeltsin's entourage. "If you travel around my country," he complained, "you'd see Russian kids beating up Kazakh kids. That's how it was for me. It was not easy to live with them." He clearly had in mind not only his childhood traumas, but also the geopolitical and historical realities. Kazakhstan was established as a Soviet republic by Stalin in 1936; during the Cold War the republic became a playground for the Soviet military-industrial complex. The republic's leadership had no clue as to what happened in "closed cities" on its territory, including the giant space center, biological and chemical laboratories, and so on. Those were funded and controlled by Moscow. "The Kazakhs," Baker summed up later, "surrounded virtually on every side by a great power, wanted to reach out to the United States, the one power in the world that could ensure their peace and stability."[51]

Baker had another thought: what looked like a great idea in Moscow appeared very different on the periphery. The Baltic leaders wanted to quit the Soviet Union—politically, economically, and culturally—disregarding the negative consequences. And Nazarbayev, apparently so cooperative and reasonable in Moscow, had changed his tune radically once on his home turf. Faced with such mercurial attitudes, Baker mused, could Gorbachev actually survive?[52]

"EXERCISE IN EMPTY TALK"

On 5 September, the leaders of Democratic Russia gathered for the first time in Moscow following the dramatic events of August. Arkady Murashov, a leading radical democrat, greeted his colleagues with the words: "Today, at eleven hours thirty minutes in the morning, the USSR ceased to exist." He was referring to the dissolution of the Congress of People's Deputies and the end of the Soviet constitution. The majority in the room, most of them Moscow liberal intellectuals, equated this seismic shift with the end of a totalitarian empire and the start of a new democratic era. They believed that Yeltsin would hold new elections, that they would form the future Russian government, much like in Poland, free of communist apparatchiks.[53] It was unclear, however, what they should do next. The leader of the movement, Yuri Afanasyev, and other Russian democrats felt like a cavalry brigade whose attack had suddenly come to a screeching halt. The Party they had opposed was gone, and there was now no other visible common target. The Russian democratic movement did not quite know how to deal with the economy, state-building, and the stabilization of finances. None of those problems could be solved merely by mobilizing crowds and printing propaganda leaflets.[54]

On 14 September, a conference held by Democratic Russia opened in Moscow. A total of 153 delegates arrived from fifty-five regions. Famous dissidents from the Soviet era, Vladimir Bukovsky and Yuri Orlov, sat in the presidium. Yeltsin, however, remained on vacation and did not show up. The

Russian President already viewed himself as separate and above the movement of intellectuals that had supported him. Yuri Afanasyev, who chaired the conference, reminded the audience that this was a day of special historic significance. Seventy-four years earlier, the provisional government, headed by Alexander Kerensky, had proclaimed Russia to be a republic. Unfortunately, the first Russian republic had lasted only two months, before Lenin and Trotsky destroyed it. For a few seconds, the delegates reflected on this fact. Afanasyev then invited the audience to stand up to salute the tricolor flag of the second Russian republic, born in June 1990 and now finally free from its totalitarian shackles.[55]

Ilya Zaslavsky, another leading figure of the movement, presented the main political report. Three political forces, he said, would decide the future of Russia. The first consisted of the old nomenklatura members who promoted state capitalism. The second force, Democratic Russia, comprised professionals, the intelligentsia, skilled workers, and new business entrepreneurs. And the third force consisted of the "trash" of Soviet society, people "who do not want to work, but would like to divide and share everything." The populist Vladimir Zhirinovsky appealed to this group. Then Zaslavsky spoke about the possible scenarios. In the worst case, a majority, driven by misery and anger, might join Zhirinovsky's mob. Another scenario would be if the democratic leaders joined forces with the pro-capitalist nomenklatura. Zaslavsky opted for the third scenario, in which Democratic Russia would continue its conditional support of Yeltsin and strengthen its position in the Russian parliament.[56] The discussion of the report revealed that many delegates were pessimistic about the future. "Our people are savage, undereducated," warned one delegate from St Petersburg. The former Party bosses had the money to bribe the electorate, and many would vote for those who brought them "a sausage on a plate." One delegate from Yekaterinburg complained that activists in the local municipal councils (Soviets), the mainstay of Democratic Russia a year before, were now unemployed and lacked funds. Democracy would fail, the speaker warned, if democrats remained a chattering class without economic power.[57]

Yevgeny Savostyanov, one of the Moscow officials who had shut down the Party headquarters on 23 August, urged the movement to unite on a practical program of economic reforms.[58] The 500 Days was no longer applicable, he admitted, and he presented his own program of action. The document called for an immediate freeing-up of prices, the end of regulations hampering currency exchange and real estate, and the transfer of state pensions into investment funds. This list of policies was borrowed directly from American economic practices. Murashov proposed privatizing universities and health care, and dismantling Soviet-era public services in favor of private ones. "Liberal ideas," concluded Murashov optimistically, "in conjunction with the indigenous features of Russian history and culture . . . will demonstrate a Russian miracle to the world." He did not elaborate on which "indigenous features" from Russian history and culture he had in mind. Neither did he explain who would implement such a program, nor how.[59] No one asked any questions. This was a time when any number of increasingly radical economic programs, dreamt up by well-intentioned amateurs, continued to circulate in Moscow.

Few at the conference spoke about state-building. The Soviet intelligentsia, from which most of Democratic Russia's activists derived, had an acute sense of their leading status in broader society, yet they despised bureaucracy and shunned paperwork. Murashov was an exception: he accepted an offer from his friends in City Hall to become head of Moscow's police force. He urged his colleagues to follow his example. "If we stay away," he argued, "who will implement reforms?" The majority were not ready to follow this line of thinking. Leonid Batkin, a literary historian, spoke with great passion against any collaboration between democrats and state structures: "We should remain who we are," he said. Democratic Russia, instead of infiltrating the state, should focus on grassroots and parliamentary activities. "We should remind Yeltsin and the Russian authorities," Batkin concluded, "how much they owe us and stop being their 'wagging tail.'"[60]

The majority of delegates hoped that, instead of the "evil empire" of the Soviet Union, there would emerge a commonwealth of independent democracies, loosely based on the British Commonwealth. Some argued that all post-Soviet republics should become legal successors to the USSR. Batkin, never to be outdone in radicalism, urged his colleagues "to bring to the end . . . the destruction" of the KGB and the old Army.[61] And what should be done about the Soviet nuclear arsenal? Batkin, a specialist in the Italian Renaissance, had an answer to this as well: all members of a future Commonwealth would have joint control and command over strategic armed forces. Had James Baker attended this meeting, he would have thought he was among a bunch of raving lunatics. Another observer, a Russian scholar, recalled: "I still cannot understand how people, generally not so courageous in life . . . did not fear that after the breakup of the USSR our space would turn into a terrain in which everyone was fighting everyone else, similar to the former Yugoslavia, but with nuclear weapons. Americans feared this very much, yet our [intellectuals] did not."[62]

Not everyone at the conference celebrated the collapse of the Union. One of the delegates supported Gorbachev's Union Treaty and considered the August events a tragedy. "No matter into how many parts we split our former empire," he argued, "every state that emerges from this would still be multi-ethnic." In Georgia and Moldova, violent ethnic conflicts were already raging. The same could happen elsewhere. Why did Democratic Russia back the Baltic, Ukrainian, and Georgian separatists, but not Russians living in other republics? And what about Russian-speaking Crimea, should it decide to leave Ukraine and join Russia?[63] A speaker from Eastern Ukraine stood up to object. Any call for changing borders, he said, "sounds louder than the click of a gun." He added that the majority of people in Ukraine were ready to leave the Soviet Union for good, and the Russians should mind their own business.[64] Those altercations presaged the end of the noble idea of "a common democratic space."

On 16 September, the State Council gathered in Gorbachev's Kremlin office to discuss a common economic program and the Union Treaty. This was the most important meeting of the short-lived republican oligarchy. Yeltsin attended and he seemed to be in agreement with Gorbachev, which set the tone of the meeting.[65] Yavlinsky proposed giving extraordinary powers to himself and a group of professional economists for the next five years, until the transition to a market economy was secured. If his program were not accepted, he said, then in a few months hordes of hungry and miserable people would sweep away all existing parliaments and councils. Yavlinsky's technocratic utopia put the cart of economics before the horse of politics. His logic only momentarily appeared to be overwhelming. Yeltsin listened with a poker face. Ukraine's chairman of the Rada, Leonid Kravchuk, and Prime Minister, Vitold Fokin, were the first to object: "How then should we understand independence?"[66] Ukraine, Fokin said, had a surplus of food which it planned to export and thereby gain hard currency. The republic could live without a dictatorship in Moscow and distribute its wealth as it wished. Ayaz Mutallibov, the President of Azerbaijan, and Vyacheslav Kebich, the Prime Minister of Belorussia, complained they could not go back to their republican parliaments with Yavlinsky's plan: there would be cries of treason.[67]

Yavlinsky spoke like a teacher whose students had failed to learn his lesson. He singled out the misguided project of the Ukrainian Rada to establish a Ukrainian currency. It was possible, he said, for several state banks to be located in Moscow, Kiev, and other cities of the Soviet Union, resembling the Federal Reserve System in the United States. Yet there could be only one currency and only one central money supply. If Ukraine and other republics issued "national" currencies, Yavlinsky warned, the notes would become worthless bits of paper. His plan, he replied to Kravchuk and Fokin, did not involve distributing existing state assets, but instead creating a viable common market that would increase the standard of living of everyone.[68]

Gorbachev kept pushing for a Union Treaty. He chided Kravchuk: "And why are you [in Ukraine] taking over the armed forces even before the Treaty? And what is your reason for taking over border troops?" Kravchuk answered that this was the republic's reaction to the August coup, the measures with which to protect itself. Stanislav Shushkevich, head of Belorussia's Supreme Soviet, took Kravchuk's side. Everyone looked at Yeltsin. After a long silence, the Russian leader spoke again in favor of a Union Treaty, as well as an economic agreement. "Certain groups started to press me," Yeltsin said, that Russia "should go it alone and resolve its problems independently . . ." He did not finish the sentence.[69] During the rest of the meeting, the Russian President remained silent. In his writing pad he jotted down only a few notes. One of them was: "Rule from the center or separately?"[70] Yeltsin's indecision was palpable. He remembered what Yavlinsky had said before: effective economic reforms could not work in one republic alone; they had to be implemented across the whole of the Soviet Union. Yet uncertainty had paralyzed the Russian leader, the man of radical decisions. He did not know how to answer the question he posed in his writing pad.

President Nazarbayev joined the meeting after some delay, having finished his talks with James Baker in Alma-Ata. Here in Moscow, the Kazakh leader changed his colors yet again: he appeared as a wise man, in favor of the Union. Baker had told him, he said, that the G-7 powers would offer financial assistance to the post-Soviet republics only if they acted together. If the republics approached the West separately, they "would be treated like colonies." Turning to Kravchuk, Nazarbayev said: "Diasporas can help, but this will not cover the needs of any republics . . . Leonid, my dear friend, I worry what might happen to Ukraine." He concluded his intervention on a reassuring note: "Economic matters will unite us. I am certain of this."[71]

Gorbachev jumped at the chance to apply peer pressure on Kravchuk. "The Slavs cannot separate," he said. "Leonid, you should not be afraid to speak more about the Union." Gorbachev assumed that the leader of the Ukrainian Rada was in favor of a confederation, but just feared that his nationalist rivals could outflank him in the presidential race. Kravchuk reacted wanly, with a touch of apology. He expressed concern that the mines of Donbass in Eastern Ukraine were shutting down, because of a lack of wooden pit props that had stopped arriving from the Russian Federation. Gorbachev reassured him: "After the Treaty, the wood will come." Kravchuk replied with unexpected candor: "I wish, Mikhail Sergeyevich, I could say that everything will be fixed tomorrow . . . It will not happen, nothing will happen . . ." Shushkevich, who overheard their dialogue, later admired how cleverly Kravchuk had outfoxed Gorbachev. "Whatever Gorbachev wanted to get from him, he could never get it."[72]

The ruling oligarchy was a product of expediency and uncertainty. No one believed it would last. When Gorbachev and Yeltsin asked Silayev to step down as Prime Minister of the RSFSR, to focus on his new duties in the provisional government's economic committee, the experienced bureaucrat hesitated.

Silayev knew that this position would be like building castles in the sand. Gorbachev, in contrast, behaved as if he had regained the right to lead the Soviet Union.[73] Shushkevich recalled that Gorbachev "did not want to listen to anybody else . . . He thought he was so smart and good, and that everybody would back him." Instead, the republican barons viewed Gorbachev as a windbag whose time in power had long expired. During a break between the long sessions, some of them shook their heads at Gorbachev's performance: "Another exercise in empty talk!"[74]

After digesting James Baker's findings, Bush and Scowcroft signaled to their allies that it would be impractical to offer more than humanitarian assistance to the Soviet Union. David Mulford, Under-Secretary for International Affairs in the Department of the Treasury, flew to the meeting of Sherpas in Dresden, where he killed the German initiative to refinance the Soviet debt. Then he joined Nicholas Brady and the chairman of the Federal Reserve, Alan Greenspan, who had arrived in Moscow to deliver the bad tidings to Gorbachev: the West would not give him any more money, beyond what had already been promised. "This is also the view of the Germans," Brady added, "and our other partners." Gorbachev received the news stoically. "We are realists," he said, "and we fully understand that if the United States does not take a stand, nothing will happen." He commented on the disparity in the Soviet-Western partnership. "The Russians, the Slavs," Gorbachev said, expected to be treated in the West like friends. Americans, however, counted their money. Brady pressed on with the Western demands: in order to receive humanitarian assistance, Moscow should make a full disclosure of its finances, including its gold reserves. This could cause Gorbachev a degree of public embarrassment: in 1990–91, he had been secretly authorizing massive sales of gold to cover trade and budget deficits. Brady, however, stood firm.[75] In his report to Bush, the Secretary of the Treasury concluded: the Soviet economy was contracting more rapidly "than we thought." No measures to stop this freefall would be effective until the relationship between the center and the republics was resolved. And this was highly doubtful.[76]

"RUSSIA'S STRATEGY"

Gennady Burbulis, appointed as Yeltsin's Secretary of State in July 1991, told a friendly journalist in September that he had been reading the poet Osip Mandelstam and Sigmund Freud, as well as Western and Russian philosophers, to clear his head. When the journalist asked Burbulis what was on his mind, he responded that it was "a transition from the totalitarian Soviet empire to fully fledged democratic structures of power and government." After the junta's fall, Burbulis had "curated" for Yeltsin issues to do with foreign policy, police forces, the KGB, and the media. In September 1991, he later recalled, "there was no government in the country." Activists from Democratic Russia urged Yeltsin to carry out "lustration," effectively banning the Party and KGB officials from taking government jobs. Burbulis knew that this would be impossible: there were simply no "democratic cadres" available. In Yeltsin's entourage many came from the Party nomenklatura and the KGB.[77] Burbulis restrained the zeal of his friends, who wanted to get rid of the entire rank of senior Soviet officials. He was against a massive purge of Soviet diplomats and the KGB.[78]

Burbulis also needed someone who could propose a viable set of measures to deal with the economic crisis. He discounted the Silayev committee; he also dismissed Yavlinsky. "Grisha" Yavlinsky, he recalled, was like Gorbachev: good at talking the talk, but not walking the walk. Yeltsin was the only man with the power and the will to act. However, Burbulis feared that Yeltsin's clout would be wasted on Gorbachev's futile schemes; instead, it had to be used for constructing a democratic Russia. For Yeltsin's principal advisor, the creation of the Russian state, appropriation of Soviet economic assets, and the launch of radical market reforms were three essential elements of the one package.[79]

Burbulis had a brief romance with the model of "Swedish socialism," yet he quickly rejected this option in favor of market libertarianism. "You can give a fish to a hungry man," he said to a journalist, "or you can teach him to catch a fish." This Biblical parable originated with Burbulis's friends on the American Right as an argument against state socialism. The Swedish socialist model was too costly and would only perpetuate Russian habits of dependency. The Russians had to learn in a hard way to rely on their own initiative. Burbulis knew that it was hopeless to expect the radicals of Democratic Russia to come up with a viable economic strategy.[80] None of the existing economic programs matched Burbulis's criteria. Yeltsin's economic advisor, Igor Nit, a professor of mathematics, wrote a report that drew on Soviet mathematical econometrics of the 1950s and 1960s. Nit also relied on the experience of the Bolsheviks in the early 1920s: they had successfully introduced a parallel gold-backed currency and set up two economies: state-run and market-oriented. Yet, in September 1991, there was no dictatorship in place; the peasantry and the old commercial classes were also missing. Moreover, there was no gold in the state's vaults.[81]

The second serious effort was a program by Stanford economists, headed by Mikhail Bernstam, who had worked in Moscow under the auspices of the RSFSR's Supreme Economic Council since March 1991. The American team designed a fascinating alternative to the Washington Consensus. Bernstam called this approach "a reform without a shock." Instead of big Western credits, Bernstam and his colleagues proposed to use people's personal savings from their bank accounts as a pool of investment, to refinance state enterprises on market terms. In this way, they reasoned, several birds would be killed with one stone: Soviet enterprises would be weaned off the state budget, millions of Soviet people would become investors, and the need for Western money would be reduced. Bernstam was convinced that such a strategy would be feasible for "a strong decentralized Union."[82] Yet in September the Stanford economists lost their main political support: Mikhail Bocharov, head of the Supreme Economic Council of the RSFSR, was gone. And Burbulis ignored Bernstam and his Stanford team.

Finally, there was a program put forward by Yevgeny Saburov, Minister of the Economy in the Russian Federation. Forty-five-year-old Saburov had graduated in mathematics and belonged to the semi-dissident milieu of the Moscow intelligentsia. He owed his government career to the brief euphoria for democratic liberalism; his real passion was not economics, however, but poetry.[83] Saburov's program was written by a team of his friends at one of the government dachas; *Kommersant* published its draft in early September—a loose mix of market economics and good intentions. Burbulis disliked Saburov's program, just like Yavlinsky's plan, because of its main goal: to preserve the Union.[84]

Burbulis knew that time was running out, and that Boris Yeltsin might support Saburov's program. The Russian President wavered between his new faith in American-style capitalism and his experience in the industrial Urals. He liked to demonstrate to Burbulis his superior knowledge of how the Soviet economy worked: he crunched numbers of distribution, supply, and demand. Yeltsin's buddies from the Sverdlovsk Party nomenklatura believed that Russia was not ready for capitalism. One of them told the British ambassador, Rodric Braithwaite: "At present, there is no real body of entrepreneurs, only swindlers." Yeltsin said almost the same thing to Burbulis: Russian people wanted stability, not shocks, and one had to respect that. After the State Council with Gorbachev on 16 September, Yeltsin canceled all appointments and disappeared again. Western diplomats did not even know where the Russian President was. Burbulis felt that Yeltsin was escaping from a situation of uncertainty and complexity that he had no idea how to fix. "The culture of Boris Nikolaievich," Burbulis recalled, "did not include the option of an agonizing choice." Only one thing could reverse this trend: a new, bold, and simple strategy that Yeltsin would trust, adopt, and act upon.[85]

Burbulis met Yegor Gaidar by chance, on the evening of 20 August, the decisive moment for the Russian government. The person who introduced Gaidar to Burbulis was Alexei Golovkov, one of Yeltsin's advisors: he had traveled to Chile a few months earlier to meet General Pinochet and neoliberal economists.[86] Burbulis quickly realized that Gaidar could offer him everything he wanted. While everyone else, including Yavlinsky, Nit, Bernstam, and Saburov, sought to alleviate or avoid the impending shock to the system, Gaidar considered it inevitable. When Leszek Balcerowicz, the author of Poland's "shock therapy" program, visited Moscow in September, Gaidar and his group welcomed him as a guru. Balcerowicz advised them that only the most radical transformation could force society to change its ways. Also, like a successful surgery, reforms must be carried out as rapidly as possible. Gaidar was absolutely convinced: market forces must be released at full strength; after a traumatic adjustment, everything would fall into place.[87] Gaidar's previous experience in the Soviet government had taught him a lesson: a program of reforms could not walk without "legs." If the program clashed with corporate interests, it would remain just words on a piece of paper. However, if it offered immediate benefits, it would be eagerly implemented. Gaidar translated the tenets of the Washington Consensus and shock therapy into the language of bureaucratic decrees that left no loopholes, and incentivized existing economic actors and government officials to enact changes and benefit from them.[88]

Burbulis asked Gaidar to write a memorandum for Yeltsin, explaining to him what must be done. Gaidar and his team[89] began to work at the state "dacha no. 15" in Arkhangelskoye-2. Saburov's team worked nearby in "dacha no. 6." The competing teams stayed on friendly terms, and even invited each other over to drinks and dinners. Gaidar, however, knew he was in a race.[90] Burbulis, Kozyrev, and Yeltsin's legal advisor Sergey Shakhrai frequented "dacha no. 15" and discussed the work in progress. Burbulis and Gaidar formed an effective team. Gaidar recalled that Burbulis knew "how to calculate options, attract promising people and experts." In turn, Burbulis commended Gaidar for ensuring his policy was "backed by a legal structure, drafts of legal acts."[91]

A scion of the Soviet high elite, Gaidar did not share the ideological zeal of Burbulis and his friends, who wanted to destroy the Soviet Union. Until late August, his scenario had been that Gorbachev would simply appoint Yeltsin as his successor. In this scenario, "Yeltsin legitimately subordinates Union structures to himself and, with absolute authority as the leader of all Russian people, ensures the merger of the two centers of power."[92] Instead, Yeltsin had usurped Gorbachev's powers, but refused to take his job; Ukraine had declared its independence; and Gorbachev had set up his stillborn provisional government. A unique opportunity had been squandered. Gaidar was convinced that Gorbachev's State Council had no future. It was better to destroy such a hybrid than work for it. Western economists, whom Gaidar consulted, agreed with him. One of them, the Stanford economist Rudiger Dornbusch, had researched the collapse of Austria-Hungary in 1918. The key, he advised, was to restore a stable currency.[93]

In his memoirs, Gaidar wrote that he had to act like the pilot of a nose-diving plane. The Soviet system of distribution of resources and goods had collapsed.

There was beggar-thy-neighbor protectionism. The ruble had stopped working, and people had begun to hoard food and stockpile goods. The pilot had to switch on a new engine, the market economy, or the plane would crash. There was no time for deliberations and details. The metaphor was convincing, yet the Soviet economy was not an aircraft. It was part of a state that, as Gaidar and Burbulis were convinced, had already self-destructed. One had to discard the shell of the Soviet Union so that "Russia" could be born and live.[94]

On 23 September, Gaidar's team produced the first draft of a document with the title "Russia's Strategy in the Transition Period." The text began with a brief world history of market reforms during the twentieth century, including Lenin's New Economic Policy and Margaret Thatcher's reforms. The key to success was having a combination of professional economists and a resolute political leader. Yeltsin's authority, the document continued, "is still sufficient for the conduct of a stabilization policy." If his authority was wasted, the situation would evolve in favor of a conservative opposition. "For a charismatic leader it is better to become unpopular at the start of the difficult road of reforms, rather than [after years of] populist games without real progress towards his goal."[95] The message was clear: Yeltsin could spend his political capital in a grandiose act of creating a new Russia or become another failed leader, like Gorbachev. Burbulis did not discuss the document with anyone outside his advisory council. "Russia's Strategy" was written with one reader only in mind: Boris Yeltsin.

Next day, Burbulis flew to Sochi with the document in his briefcase; Yeltsin was resting nearby in the government residence "Bocharov Ruchey." But the Russian leader emphatically rejected the plan. Burbulis recalled that the Russian President wanted to "wait a bit more, until someone else would walk in and bring a more convenient plan, to avoid radical measures."[96] Yeltsin had been courted once again by Gorbachev. Flanked by Rutskoy, Silayev, Saburov, Popov, Sobchak, and Yavlinsky, the Soviet leader had called Yeltsin from the Kremlin and argued that the best way for Russia to defend its economic interests vis-à-vis other republics would be to sign an economic treaty with them. Gorbachev implored Yeltsin "to accept the responsibility and unite everybody around Russia." Just before Burbulis appeared in Sochi, a competitor of Gaidar's, Yevgeny Saburov, had talked to Yeltsin as well. The Russian President agreed that Saburov's program was a good basis for negotiating an economic treaty between the post-Soviet republics.[97]

Burbulis had to undermine the arguments of Gorbachev, Yavlinsky, and Saburov. He read Gaidar's paper aloud and answered Yeltsin's questions. Having established control over property on their territories, the document said, the republics now wanted to use a new Union "to share the property and resources" that were located on the territory of the Russian Federation. This meant, above all, oil and gas. Only full sovereignty could give Russia real control over its resources. The Russian government must set up its own monetary, fiscal, and budgetary policies, the right to print money and set up customs posts. Burbulis and Gaidar proposed "to initiate covert construction of an economic common-wealth ... where Russia, because of its geopolitical situation, its industrial power and raw materials, would assume the position of an informal leader" via a system of bilateral military and political alliances, a trade zone where the ruble would remain the common currency, with shared energy and transporta-tion complexes, as well as scientific-technical cooperation. And what to do with the Soviet Army? The memorandum recommended conducting "confidential talks with the leaders of the Armed Forces that the only way to preserve the army would be to turn it gradually into a Russian army."[98] The authors were essentially proposing what Gorbachev was seeking to achieve—but without Gorbachev and his "Union center."

It took Burbulis three days to convince Yeltsin. "There were just three of us," Burbulis recalled. The third man was Yeltsin's bodyguard Korzhakov, who "would bring food for us to the seashore, and from time to time offered some kind of entertainment ... Tennis, bath-house." The Russian *banya* was a customary place where naked men conducted heart-to-heart talks and made difficult decisions. In the process Burbulis endured searing steam and heat. Nevertheless, he knew it would help Yeltsin make up his mind.[99] Yeltsin, of course, had always wanted to get rid of the Soviet president and his provisional government. Just a week ago, the State Council, chaired by Gorbachev, had commandeered Yeltsin and Nazarbayev to Nagorny Karabagh with a peace-making mission on behalf of the State Council. The trip had been a failure, the hostilities between Armenians and Azeris continued, and Yeltsin had grown frustrated. He had just wasted his political capital on a futile enterprise. This confirmed the main point of Gaidar's argument: every time the Russian President expressed some support for Gorbachev's provisional government, his authority diminished.

The economic part of the memorandum was a dark forest for Yeltsin, yet it promised a way out for the Russian Federation: it would start its own economic reforms and lead other republics. At last, the Russian President agreed: "If nothing else is there, then we should do it. Period." There was a brief discussion about who would be in charge of the economy. Burbulis said that Gaidar and his people should implement what they believed in. The future government of reform would draw on "three forces": professionalism, political will, and popular support. Gaidar would provide the first; the second and third would come from Yeltsin. The Russian leader said he would meet Gaidar in Moscow and make a final decision. Burbulis flew back to Moscow on 28 September. He told a close circle of his friends and associates that the countdown for Gorbachev's provisional government had begun.[100]

UKRAINE AND NUCLEAR WEAPONS

After he had attended the State Council in Moscow on 16 September, Leonid Kravchuk packed his bags again to cross the Atlantic. He went to North America as head of the Ukrainian Supreme Soviet to attend the UN General Assembly. The Ukrainian Soviet Socialist Republic had been one of the founding members of the United Nations. In 1945, Stalin, in his talks with Roosevelt and Churchill, had demanded sixteen seats at the UN for the Soviet Union, one for each of its republics, to balance off the votes of the British Commonwealth. Ultimately, Stalin had to settle for just two: Ukraine and Belorussia. The Russian Federation did not get its own separate membership. The dictator even created foreign ministries in Kiev and Minsk. In 1991, the officials of Ukraine's UN legation in New York helped to prepare and coordinate Kravchuk's trip. He was the first Ukrainian leader to speak at the world forum.

Kravchuk arrived in North America with a new sense of legitimacy and purpose. All polls since August showed three-quarters of Ukraine's population wanted full independence. This meant that Kravchuk could become the first president of an independent Ukraine. The historian Serhii Plokhy has observed: "Kravchuk decided that his best strategy was to campaign not for himself but for Ukrainian independence."[101] The journey to Canada and the United States was an ideal time and the proper venue for such a campaign. During the ten days of his trip, Kravchuk met with the Canadian Prime Minister, Brian Mulroney, then flew to Washington DC, where he met with President Bush and members of Congress. Kravchuk targeted other key audiences as well. The most important was the Ukrainian diaspora. As a Party official in charge of ideology, for many years Kravchuk had treated this diaspora as an enemy. Now, he received an extraordinary welcome and assistance from the influential people of Ukrainian descent, some of whom worked in the US government, Congress, the media, and public organizations. In every American city where Kravchuk toured, he addressed local Ukrainians with a message of reconciliation and asked for support to build an independent and democratic Ukraine. He spoke in Ukrainian and always concluded his speeches with the words "*Slava Ukraiini!*" (Glory to Ukraine). This was a rallying cry of Western Ukrainian nationalists, who had fought against Stalin in 1941–44. Those Ukrainians, émigrés in North America, and their descendants felt an epiphany. In New York, the Ukrainian community held a gala dinner in the Waldorf Astoria. When Kravchuk spoke, the audience interrupted him with cheers and applause.

All newspapers in Ukraine reported on his trip as a triumph, in both Ukrainian and Russian, for millions of Kravchuk's future voters.[102]

Another target of Kravchuk's campaign was the Jewish community. With every instance of turmoil on Ukrainian territory, Jews had been the victims of horrendous violence, administered by both the local population and the invading powers. In 1941, as a village boy in the region of Volynia, Kravchuk had witnessed the German occupying forces and their Ukrainian collaborators executing all the Jewish men, women, and children. He became the first Ukrainian leader to address this terrible legacy. On 30 September, the day Kravchuk spoke to the UN General Assembly, the Ukrainian Supreme Soviet marked a special week to mourn and memorialize the victims of Babi Yar, to whom Kravchuk and Bush had paid tribute during the American visit on 1 August. Most of the victims had been Jews. In his address to the United Nations, Kravchuk did not cite the Holocaust and anti-Semitism explicitly, yet he said that "genocide should never be repeated anywhere." He also mentioned the victims of Stalin's "Holodomor," the mass famine of 1932–33 that the Ukrainian diasporas considered a genocide of the Ukrainian nation. Kravchuk's semantic tightrope-walking was the act of a skillful propagandist who was seeking to appeal to two potentially hostile audiences. Having trod carefully across the minefield of the past, Kravchuk spoke about a better future. He presented Ukraine as a young nation with ancient roots, one that was eager to join the universal quest for national independence, along with the nations of Africa, Asia, and Latin America.[103]

The highlight of Kravchuk's trip was his meeting with President Bush in the Oval Office on 25 September. "The Soviet Union has virtually disintegrated," the Ukrainian politician stated. "It has no national government." The December referendum would certainly confirm the Act of Independence, declared by the Ukrainian Rada. Kravchuk asked the US President for diplomatic recognition of Ukraine. This was the issue that Bush had been trying hard to dodge. He repeated to Kravchuk the official American line: there would be no recognition of unilateral acts of independence, including by Ukraine. Equally, after William Safire's "Chicken Kiev" article and with mounting pressure from the Ukrainian community, Bush had to tread carefully. "Ukrainian-Americans," Scowcroft recalled, "they were ever-present, very vocal . . ." So Bush said to Kravchuk: "The Ukraine has a special standing in the minds of the American people."[104]

Scowcroft believed that a confederation between Russia and Ukraine was not against American interests. "The Ukraine," he reported to the President, "is the only republic that can hope to balance Russia in a new union structure." Without Ukraine, Scowcroft continued, "there may be little to prevent the new government" in Moscow "from being little more than a new Russian empire."[105]

Yet Kravchuk was clearly against such a confederation, and his self-confidence surprised Bush. He asked the Ukrainian leader: "Do you see that there must be an economic union with the center or not? We think that is a necessary step to encourage investment." Kravchuk responded: "The center is incapable of doing anything. We're losing time. The Soviet Union is a huge country. It is impossible to pursue economic reform at a rapid pace in the entire country." Western credits and assistance, therefore, should go directly to Ukraine. Kravchuk extolled Ukrainian economic assets. A few days later, at the Council on Foreign Relations in New York, he would stress that Ukraine had 30 percent of the entire Soviet military-industrial potential and possessed a "favorable geopolitical position in Europe." Kravchuk told Bush that Ukraine gave more of its resources to Russia than it received in return; once independent, it would be a prosperous scientific-industrial powerhouse. He "forgot" to mention that Ukrainian industries received cheap gas and oil from Siberia, as well as enormous investments from the central budget.[106] The meeting lasted much longer than scheduled, and it left Bush skeptical. He recalled that the Ukrainian leader "did not seem to grasp the implications and complexities of what he was proposing." The economic picture that the Ukrainian leader had presented was unrealistic.[107]

There was also uncertainty about the future of nuclear weapons located on Ukrainian territory. On 5 September, the meeting in the White House between senior American officials had addressed this concern. Colin Powell, head of the Joint Chiefs of Staff, said: "We want to see the dissolution of the old Soviet Union." Yet who would ensure the safety of nuclear weapons in Ukraine, Belorussia, and Kazakhstan if the Soviet military "would move back to Russia?" Brent Scowcroft had supported Dick Cheney's idea of fracturing the Soviet nuclear arsenal. "It did not bother me," Scowcroft recalled, "that the Ukraine may have nuclear weapons—or Kazakhstan. Because under no circumstances were they going to be pointed at us." He admitted, however, that there could be problems with tactical nuclear weapons and their safety and control. Bush asked him: could the United States come up with a major initiative to reduce nuclear uncertainty?[108]

Responding to the President's request, Cheney and Powell prepared a proposal for unilateral reductions of US nuclear weapons: tactical, mid-range, and strategic. The Pentagon's scheme included removal of multiple independently targeted warheads (MIRVs) on intercontinental missiles and withdrawal of short-range (tactical) nuclear weapons from Europe. Most dramatically, B-52 bombers armed with nuclear bombs would stop flying along Soviet borders. The proposed cuts also included "Tomahawk" cruise missiles in the Navy, which the US arms-control negotiators had staunchly refused to reduce before.[109]

Bush praised this move as the "broadest and most comprehensive change in US nuclear strategy since the early 1950s." The "disarmament offensive" had multiple targets. Above all, Bush and Scowcroft expected Gorbachev to reciprocate with even more sweeping nuclear cuts on the Soviet side, including the weapons in Ukraine. Scowcroft explained to NATO's Secretary-General, Manfred Wörner, that "if the Soviets reject our proposals, we may have to reconsider."[110] Gorbachev, they expected, would grasp this opportunity to enhance his status as a world statesman. And Baker's talks in Moscow showed that Yeltsin, Shaposhnikov, and the General Staff were also willing to get rid of tactical nuclear weapons while they were still under central control. Scowcroft also hoped that Moscow would agree to destroy "heavy" Soviet ballistic missiles located on Ukrainian and Kazakh territory. The second target of the nuclear initiative was NATO. The tactical and short-range nuclear weapons had transformed from a military asset into a political liability, particularly in Germany and Eastern Europe. After the Soviet military retreat and the dissolution of the Warsaw Pact, American weapons systems that had faced them lost any reasonable purpose.[111] Lastly, the target of Bush's nuclear initiative was American domestic politics. If the Soviets reciprocated with cuts to their nuclear arsenal, the President could tell his voters that he had made America more secure.

Gorbachev indeed was pleased and wanted to reciprocate. Yet the military, the head of the General Staff, Vladimir Lobov, and the START negotiator, Viktor Karpov, resisted more cuts of Soviet MIRVs. In his diary, Anatoly Chernyaev fulminated at the pig-headed military who clung to their obsolete weapons at a time when the fate of the Soviet Union was in the balance.[112] On 27 September, Bush arranged a call to Gorbachev. The Soviet President decided to use the American President as a sounding board and invited Shaposhnikov, Lobov, and Karpov to listen in to his conversation with Bush. He asked 'naïve' questions: Was Bush's initiative unilateral? Should the Soviet Union respond? Would there be cuts in the US Navy and strategic submarines? At the end of the call, prompted by Chernyaev's notes, Gorbachev congratulated Bush: "It is an historic initiative, comparable to Reykjavik." In 1986, at the summit in Iceland, Reagan and Gorbachev had discussed a similar sharp reduction of nuclear weapons. Yet Gorbachev said nothing specific to Bush about the Soviet response, leaving the American President disappointed.[113]

Gorbachev wanted to impress his top brass with his shrewd statesmanship. After his conversation with Bush, he told his military chiefs about the novel *The Ides of March* by Thornton Wilder, which dealt with the last days of the Roman republic; he and Raisa had seen it recently dramatized on stage. Gorbachev especially praised Julius Caesar: the Roman leader was a master of the strategic situation, knowing how to concentrate all his energy and forces in the moment, divide his enemies, and defeat them one by one. Amazingly, Gorbachev did not add that Caesar, despite his strategic genius, fell victim to a plot and was assassinated by his senators. Instead, Gorbachev's thoughts were focused on planning his comeback. He subsequently instructed Yavlinsky to fly to Bonn and London and find more sources of credit for the failed Soviet state.[114]

At the United Nations, Kravchuk spoke of a future Ukraine as a neutral and non-nuclear state. He remained, however, ambivalent as to the fate of ICBMs and nuclear warheads on Ukrainian territory. In some of his talks he spoke against the transfer of nuclear weapons to the Russian Federation and insisted that they should be destroyed on Ukrainian territory. On other occasions, he said that Ukraine accepted central control over the nuclear arsenal, yet insisted on a "dual key" control over those weapons located in Ukraine. The American experts were worried. On 27 September, when Kravchuk gave a talk at Harvard University, Philip Zelikow from Harvard's Kennedy School of Government asked him whether he could clarify what would happen to the nuclear arms in Ukraine. Would they be eliminated or transferred to Russia? If there were political alliances involved, could Kravchuk describe these links and open the way to frank negotiations between the parties involved? Zelikow had worked with Condoleezza Rice under Brent Scowcroft in the National Security Council, after which he had returned to an academic position at Harvard. Kravchuk invited Zelikow to meet the Ukrainian Foreign Minister and come to Kiev. "The nuclear issue," mused Zelikow in a memo to his NSC colleagues, "has a critical technical dimension but is also likely to be linked to broader Ukrainian political concerns," such as Crimea and Donbass.[115]

Kravchuk returned to Kiev in an excellent mood, confirmed in his belief that the United States and Canada would recognize Ukraine's sovereignty. The Ukrainian press wrote in glowing terms that Kravchuk had radically changed the perception of their country abroad. Ukrainian journalists reported that most influential figures in Canada and the United States supported "the strivings of the Ukrainian people to create their own statehood," while big business was eager to invest in the Ukrainian economy. Later, Kravchuk admitted that he had been a bit too optimistic.[116] In reality, he hoped to swap the nuclear arsenal in Ukraine for Western political and financial assistance. In the fall of 1991, Kravchuk probably did not realize that "Ukrainian nukes" were not a political asset, but rather a huge liability. The nuclear warheads and bombs in Ukraine's warehouses had been assembled in two nuclear laboratories on Russian territory; their expiration date was in ten years' time and they required special maintenance. For all its scientific-technical potential, Ukraine needed many years and many billions to acquire the skills and capacity to maintain and use those weapons. Most worrying of all, their malfunction could cause problems that would make Chernobyl appear a small affair! The nuclear arsenal on Ukrainian territory would become the focus for Ukraine's relations with the Russian Federation and the United States for years to come.[117]

From Kiev, Kravchuk formally launched his presidential campaign. He toured the diverse republic, with different messages for Russian speakers in the eastern and southern regions, Ukrainians in western regions, and other communities. At the Babi Yar memorial, he asked the Jewish people for forgiveness on behalf of the Ukrainian nation. He concluded this speech in Yiddish, the language that had died many a death during the Holocaust. Kravchuk did not speak out publicly against a new Union. Like Yeltsin, he did not want to be seen as an out-and-out spoiler of Gorbachev's project. Instead, he just commented, with a note of regret, on the disintegration of the central government. "Everybody knows: the Cabinet of Ministers of the USSR does not exist; the Supreme Soviet of the USSR does not exist. There is nobody to cooperate with on the state level!" Gorbachev's name was conspicuously absent from Kravchuk's speeches and press conferences, both in North America and in Ukraine.[118]

CHAPTER 14

INDEPENDENCE

Unfortunately, we have 1,000 different understandings of "independence."
A. N. Yakovlev to George Bush, 19 November 1991[1]

RUSSIA'S PRIMACY

On 28 September 1991, Gorbachev's aide Georgy Shakhnazarov met with Yeltsin's State Secretary, Gennady Burbulis, to urge him to support a Union Treaty.[2] Burbulis replied that this was now off the table. "We should save Russia, affirm its independence," he said in his stentorian voice, "by creating some distance from others." After Russia had built its statehood and got back on its feet, "everyone would gravitate towards it, and it would be possible to rearrange everything."[3] Shakhnazarov argued that a new union would work better for Russian interests. It would keep the republics of Ukraine, Belorussia, and Kazakhstan within Russia's geopolitical zone of influence. Otherwise, those republics would be "pulled into other blocs and alliances, and it would be unthinkable to bring them back by force." The countries of Eastern Europe, Shakhnazarov said, had already begun to make approaches to NATO. Ukraine might do the same. "If this happens," he continued, then we "would get [NATO] on our borders." And what about Crimea? Would this peninsula, so integral to Russian national identity, become foreign territory?[4] Burbulis replied that all this could be resolved by skillful diplomacy. Perhaps the President of the USSR, he said, instead of pursuing his illusory pursuit of a new union, should dedicate his excellent abilities to this task?[5] The two parties ended their conversation without finding any common ground.

Yeltsin gave his consent to Yegor Gaidar's strategy of reforms on one condition: Russia must be recognized by the West and other republics as a great power and the primary legal successor to the Soviet Union. In other words, the post-Soviet states would receive their sovereignty from Russia, and Russia would inherit the Soviet nuclear arsenal and other global assets. Yeltsin returned to this issue two years later, when he was under fierce attack by Russian nationalists. He defended the idea of Russia as a legal successor to the USSR as "absolutely informed and logical." He also raised a fascinating alternative: "What would have happened if Russia had taken a different route and had restored the legal succession of the other Russia, destroyed by the Bolsheviks in 1917?" He wrote about the Russian Republic, proclaimed by the provisional government in September 1917. That route had its benefits. "We would reject Soviet law ... Most important, we Russians would think of ourselves in a different way; we would feel that we were citizens of a newly reclaimed nation ... The unquestionable advantages of such a step were quite possibly lost back in 1991."[6] These reflections show how significant this issue was for the Russian leader.

Burbulis mentioned the idea of Russia's legal primacy on 1 October, in his speech to the Russian parliament. "Russia is the sole republic," he said, "that could and should be the successor to the Union and all of its structures." Sergey Stankevich, Yeltsin's advisor, explained this did not mean that Russia would take over all functions of the Soviet state immediately, for instance control over nuclear weapons. If, however, the republics failed to reach a deal on this issue, the Russian Federation "appears to be the only natural" heir to the Soviet nuclear arsenal and status. Stankevich hinted that if other republics opted for full independence, then the USSR's permanent seat at the UN Security Council should belong to the Russian state. To compensate for this, Russia was ready to pay all Soviet debts.[7]

The idea of Russia as the sole successor to the USSR triggered a flurry of emotional reactions. Oleg Rumyantsev, head of the constitutional committee of the Russian parliament, argued: "Russia is much larger than the RSFSR appendix ... The Soviet Union was a form of existence of Russia." If Ukraine decided to separate from Russia, then "the issue of Crimea will be raised." Nikolai Travkin, the founder of the Democratic Party, backed the Burbulis declaration with passion. Vice-President Rutskoy, whose nationalist views now matched his interests in the RSFSR oil business, joined the chorus.[8] The political scientist Alexander Tsypko in *Izvestia* wrote about "the drama of Russia's choice." A commonwealth of democratic states, he argued, was the self-delusion of Moscow intellectuals, but the idea of Russia's primacy among the post-Soviet states would generate nothing but conflict, especially with Ukraine. He advised the leaders of the Russian Federation to retreat from their state-building folly and support Gorbachev's center.[9] Vitaly Portnikov in the *Independent Gazette* wrote even more forcefully. If other republics, he wrote, opposed the Russian ambitions to

INDEPENDENCE

become master of the post-Soviet space and the sole possessor of nuclear weapons, then "the Yugoslav scenario would be guaranteed for us." The Russians had already destroyed two "Russian empires"—imperial Russia and the Soviet Union. If they decided to play imperial games again, the Russian Federation would suffer a similar fate.[10]

The "misunderstanding" between Russia and Ukraine was suddenly back and raging. President Kravchuk warned that Russian ambitions could lead to a serious conflict. He excluded "any change of status" of Crimea and declared that Ukraine would demand the two-key controls over Soviet nuclear missiles on its territory.[11] In Moscow, Yeltsin's advisor complained to the British ambassador Rodric Braithwaite that Ukraine planned to field a big army "whose only potential enemy will be Russia." Chernyaev vented his anger at Kravchuk: "He appropriates nuclear missiles, and Donbass, and Crimea . . . What an idiot . . . Does he really believe that Sevastopol also belongs to him!? . . . Even a super-democrat, if he is a Russian democrat, would stand up against this!" The naval base of Sevastopol was widely considered by Russians to be the city of Russian glory since the Crimean War of 1854–55. It happened to be inside the Ukrainian SSR, after Crimea was transferred to the republic under Nikita Khrushchev. The city's population, however, passionately believed in their Russian identity.[12]

Burbulis, who started this polemic, knew that Yeltsin did not want another quarrel with Ukraine. The State Secretary and his aides stepped in to end the discussion. Andrei Kozyrev rejected accusations of Russian imperialism. "Many apparently perceived Russia in an old imperial image," Burbulis explained to journalists. "Who reacts in this way? The surviving communist regimes in the republics. They do not need a truly de-communized Russia."[13]

This was a sensitive moment. In Alma-Ata, Kazakhstan, a conference of republican representatives gathered to prepare a treaty that would regularize their economic and trade relations. Most of the participants wanted a post-Soviet economic zone to remain tariff-free and with a single currency—the ruble. The dominant figures in Alma-Ata were Yavlinsky and the Russian Minister of the Economy, Yevgeny Saburov, who came with a mandate from Yeltsin. They both believed that the Russian Federation would serve as an ice-breaker of radical economic transition across the Soviet space. Russian economic power, especially in the production and supply of oil and gas, was the reality that other republics could not ignore. Indeed, Kazakhstan's President Nazarbayev and other Central Asian leaders were ready to sign the economic treaty. And even the Ukrainian Prime Minister, Vitold Fokin, initialed the draft.[14] It seemed as though Burbulis and his allies had timed his rhetoric of "Russia's primacy" to complicate this endeavor. Kozyrev, then on a visit to Rome, told the Soviet ambassador Anatoly Adamishin that only an immediate dissolution of the

Union and the full sovereignty of Russia would stop the robbery of Russian resources by other republics.[15]

Gorbachev also threw a curve ball. Instead of backing Yavlinsky, Saburov, and their economic treaty, he canceled his trip to Alma-Ata. Now he wanted the republics to sign the Union Treaty first. He pressed Shakhnazarov: "Stop being afraid of [the Russians], Georgy ... Have you fallen under the influence of Burbulis?" It was another miscalculation, when the disunity of the Russian government made the Soviet President believe he could take back the reins.[16] Gorbachev lived in a bubble. The managing director of the IMF, Michel Camdessus, came to Moscow to prepare papers for Soviet associated membership in the Fund. The joint communiqué studiously avoided "the USSR" as a subject of the agreement ("perhaps a unique case when the state remains without a name," Chernyaev commented). Camdessus told Gorbachev that in a few years Western investments and know-how would turn a Union into an economic superpower. In his briefing of G-7 ambassadors in Moscow, however, Camdessus described Gorbachev as a pathetic and lonely figure. The Soviet economy, he said, was beyond resuscitation, because of the "current constitutional and institutional tangle" between the republics, and within Russia itself.[17]

President Bush finally released $1.5 billion of humanitarian assistance to "the USSR." On 6 October, the Soviet leader decided to reciprocate the American goodwill: the military grudgingly agreed to cut all three "legs" of the Soviet strategic triad, including the MIRV-capped heavy missiles. During a telephone conversation with Bush, the Soviet leader spoke again about his political troubles. He asked his American friend to intervene in post-Soviet politics and urge Yeltsin to sign an agreement on the economic union, initialed by the delegations of twelve republics.[18]

Bush was gratified by the success of his nuclear initiative and was ready to show his loyalty and support to Gorbachev. At a discussion of the National Security Council, he said: "The guys in the center *are* reformers. We should not establish the policy of supporting the breakup of the Soviet Union into twelve republics."[19] The American ambassador Robert Strauss reported from Moscow that Yeltsin's government was a wreck. On 8 October, the US President telephoned Yeltsin, who was still vacationing on the Black Sea. Bush enquired after Yeltsin's health and invited him to come to the United States for medical treatment. Then he turned to the main point of his call. "Clearly this is an internal matter, not really any of my business," he began. "But I just wanted to share one thought with you. Some voluntary economic union could be an important step for clarifying who owns what, and who's in charge, thus facilitating humanitarian assistance, and any economic investment which might be forthcoming."[20]

The words of Bush, his invitation and request all flattered Yeltsin enormously. He replied that he still needed time to make up his mind on what to do next. Yeltsin also recalled his pledge to the US President to support Gorbachev. He promised that Russia would sign the Alma-Ata economic treaty. "We understand that we have the least to gain from the economic treaty," he continued. "As a matter of fact, we might even lose something. But we'll sign because of a bigger political goal—to save the Union."[21] After Bush hung up, Yeltsin scribbled with an unsteady hand in his pad: "Mr. Bush: vacation; invitation for medical treatment; economic union on 15th of October; economic assistance is linked to this." Then he wrote and underlined: "I will sign the treaty." This was a demonstration of American soft power. Only hours before, Yeltsin had told Burbulis he would *not* cooperate with Gorbachev.[22] Now he promised Bush the opposite. He realized that both Russia's primacy and his future role as the legal successor of the USSR and a great power would completely depend on American consent.

The State Council met again on 11 October, in Gorbachev's Kremlin office. The Ukrainian leadership came in full force, including Kravchuk and Fokin. Yeltsin's seat remained vacant. Gorbachev was nervous: his attempts to reach Yeltsin had come to naught. At the last moment, he had invited a television crew to the meeting, as a way to appeal to the public. This did not help: Kravchuk immediately tried to veto any discussion of a Union treaty. At this embarrassing moment, Yeltsin showed up. He glared uncomfortably at the television cameras and muttered: "a compromise." With this one word, the balance at the Council changed immediately. Gorbachev's proposal to discuss a draft Union treaty was accepted. Gorbachev sent the television cameras away.[23]

Yavlinsky in his report knocked down one by one the republics' objections to the economic unity. His main thesis was that only a common market and free trade would defeat the beggar-thy-neighbor attitudes that prevailed between the republics and even some regions. His eloquence, however, was lost on the republican leaders. Kravchuk and Fokin repeated that they did not want any supra-national institutions located in Moscow. Yavlinsky felt he was in a losing fight.[24] Finally, Yeltsin said brusquely: "We would like to sign the treaty as soon as possible. Uncertainty has a bad impact on the state of the economy." He meant the economic agreement made in Alma-Ata. Yet, he continued, this depended on specific agreements on finance, budget, property, and trade—still to be negotiated. "Second," Yeltsin's finger jabbed the air, "we consider it is time to stop financing those organs that are not provided for in this economic agreement. And all those organs that Russia does not delegate to the center."[25]

Then he raised a third point. A central bank must not tell republican banks what to do. Instead, Yeltsin proposed a banking union. The republics could, if they wished, introduce their "national currency." There would be joint control of Soviet gold and currency reserves, stored in Moscow. Yeltsin fulfilled his pledge to Bush, but maintained his demands. The result was economic gibberish. The Russian leader diverged from Gaidar's strategy and was assisting the Ukrainians. Kravchuk immediately seconded the Russian terms and conditions. If they were met, he said, Ukraine would also sign the economic treaty.[26]

Yavlinsky made one more effort to save the situation. He explained that if the republics printed their own money, the ruble zone would collapse. "It is a law of nature," he said and spread his arms helplessly. The republican leaders began to squabble about who could deliver what to a common pool to feed major cities. Kravchuk said that Ukraine would not send food to Moscow and St Petersburg. Gorbachev snapped: Would you feed the Army? Fokin replied that Ukraine could feed the armed forces located on its territory. Gorbachev exploded: "You passed all those laws over there . . . On the Army! You may bring the President of the country to such a state . . . I will be forced to cancel your [decrees] . . . I've tolerated them until now." Fokin wanted to interrupt, but Gorbachev did not allow him. "And now you want to have separate finances, separate potatoes . . . You act as if there is no constitution, but the constitution still exists!"[27] Gorbachev had cut a sad figure: this was just another outburst without consequences.

Finally, nine republican leaders agreed to sign the economic agreement, and the ceremony was scheduled for 15 October. At the last moment, however, Yeltsin changed his mind again. He demanded that each republic should have a proportional quota for printing rubles within this zone.[28] The ceremony had to be postponed. Gorbachev was like the bridegroom whose bride fails to show up. He dedicated his time to a lesser goal, a meeting in the Kremlin with Slobodan Milošević of Serbia and Franjo Tudjman of Croatia. This was a poor cover for his domestic embarrassment. Chernyaev commented with sarcasm: "To convince Serbia and Croatia to avoid bloodshed? Laughable! As if we have nobody to pacify, the Chechens, the Ingushis, the Ossetians, the Armenians, etc."[29] Yeltsin and the leaders of seven more republics signed the amended treaty of economic union a few days later. Meanwhile, Russian-Ukrainian disagreements kept growing. The Ukrainian leaders demanded their share of Soviet reserves of gold, diamonds, and other valuables before they would sign the treaty. The Kiev officials complained that Moscow-based joint stock companies sought to seize control of the ports in Odessa and Crimea. And oil producers in Russia blamed Ukrainian officials for appropriating oil and selling it abroad at world prices; the oil flow to Ukraine declined from 55 million down to 40 million tons. "A civilized divorce is not possible between us. Each side attempts to grab what it can," wrote the well-informed Adamishin in his diary.[30]

INDEPENDENCE

THE GOVERNMENT OF REFORMS

The next day after the frustrating meeting of Gorbachev's provisional government, Yeltsin finally met with the leaders of Democratic Russia. Yuri Afanasyev accused Yeltsin of taking a vacation at a time of crisis. He denounced the calls for Russia's primacy as "chauvinism," and demanded immediate economic reforms. He also protested against Yeltsin's collaboration with Gorbachev and even threatened to take his opposition to the streets of Moscow. In response, Yeltsin told his democratic critics that he had made up his mind. He would form a new Russian government of "national trust," whose members would be recommended by the leaders of the democratic movement. In the next few months, he promised, the Russian government would deregulate prices and launch a massive wave of privatization.[31]

This was the promise that Yeltsin intended to keep. He told Burbulis to arrange a meeting with Gaidar. The economist and the Russian leader subsequently met on 16 October. Burbulis recalled that Yeltsin's first reaction was negative: young, short, and plump, Gaidar looked like a nerd. Yet his calm resolve was impressive. Burbulis recalled that Yeltsin had had enough of the "self-confident blabber" of "experts" who in reality knew nothing about the Soviet economy. Gaidar avoided jargon and gave "clear answers to the most complex questions, and in addition a sequence of actions to implement reforms." One member of Gaidar's team recalled: "The Saburov team did not understand what a transitional period was about and how to carry it through. They kept mumbling. Yegor was great and mighty, confident in his theory."[32] Such was the confidence of the newly converted believer in neoliberal doctrine. It swayed Yeltsin as well.

The Russian leader and Gaidar also shared common roots in the Urals. The economist's maternal grandfather was the Russian writer Pavel Bazhov, the author of folkloric stories about the Ural settlers and miners. Gaidar stayed in the region when he was a child. Gaidar's grandfather on his father's side, Arkady, was an iconic literary figure known to every Soviet citizen; his novels of the 1920s and 1930s had extolled the revolutionary regime and social justice. All in all, the powerful symbolism of Gaidar's name could not escape Yeltsin's attention. Grandfather Gaidar had fought for the communist utopia. His grandson has now stepped forward to dismantle totalitarianism and lead Russia toward market prosperity. "He is a giant in economics," Yeltsin told his wife following their meeting. "We shall break through! [*Prorvemsia!*]"[33]

Gaidar had no illusions about the scale of his task: he was asked to steer a sinking ship in the direction of the free market, without any financial reserves and in the absence of basic structures and habits common to a market economy.

He could not refuse such an offer; it was a matter of personal honor.[34] Yet even in his worst nightmares Gaidar could not possibly imagine how much trouble awaited him. Yeltsin himself was a major part of the problem: the Russian President could not grasp the macroeconomic logic and multiple problems involved in such a market leap. He made contradictory and half-coherent public announcements about planned reforms. Burbulis recalled that Yeltsin was able to "make an effort to immerse himself in a matter of concern, but quickly grew tired." Meanwhile, his drink problem continued. It soon became clear that Yeltsin was not available for daily discussion and management of every step and measure of the planned reforms. He delegated it all to Gaidar, while exercising paternalistic trust in him. "Very soon," Burbulis recalled, "Yeltsin would say: 'Forward march, go!'"[35]

The Stanford economist Mikhail Bernstam, an observer of and participant in this historic moment, wrote that the dissolution of the Soviet Union was "a two-track policy merging to one end." The first track was the attempt of the Russian reformers to take over the "rump" USSR and run it without Gorbachev. Their second track was an attempt to find a settlement with other republics and stop the system of subsidies and subventions. The reformers wanted to achieve three goals: distribute Soviet assets fairly, build democracy, and create a multi-ethnic Union. Unfortunately, Bernstam concluded, it was impossible to meet all three goals. One had to go. The resulting conflict "led to the dissolution of the Soviet Union."[36] The American economist overlooked the fourth goal: Yeltsin and Burbulis wanted to rebuild a strong Russian state from the Soviet ruins, which alarmed the leaders of Ukraine, and other republics. This Russian goal, as we shall see below, was one of the major drivers of the Union's dissolution.

Readers may consider this analysis as an intellectual exercise. This approach, however, provides a much better grasp of the dilemmas that faced the Russian leadership in October–November 1991 than familiar narratives of the empire's collapse and nationalism. The logic of economic reform, the struggle for Soviet assets, the realities of power and state-building pushed the Yeltsin government to get rid of Gorbachev. Other factors, above all economic interdependence and the fear of an uncontrollable break-up, and the need for recognition and legitimacy from the United States and Western Europe, forced Yeltsin to keep the Union afloat.

The Russian President was eager to inform Western governments about his new course of action. Braithwaite wrote in his diary on 16 October: "Yeltsin is at last determined to introduce real reform, however unpopular."[37] On 25 October, Yeltsin telephoned President Bush. "I will announce substantial economic plans and programs and say that we are ready to go quickly to free up prices, all at the same time, privatization, financial and land reform . . . It will be a one-time effort." Living standards would drop in Russia, then after "four to five months, maybe six months" the situation would improve. Yeltsin offered to send Andrei Kozyrev to Washington to explain the details. He concluded: "I am full of energy, play tennis, and my heart is good."[38]

On 28 October, Yeltsin convened the extraordinary Congress of People's Deputies of the RSFSR and asked for extraordinary powers to enact reforms. Standing before the giant bust of Lenin, he announced the strategy of quick transition to market capitalism. Reading from Gaidar's script, Yeltsin said that this was the only way for Russia to survive, to restore its currency and economy. Facing the obvious question as to how the Russian Federation could act alone, Yeltsin claimed that his course would be an ice-breaker, clearing the way for other republics to follow. He urged Ukraine to join the economic treaty and assured his audience that the reforms marked Russia's path "towards democracy, not towards an empire." Yeltsin concluded by announcing his fundamental ambition: if the project of a shared community failed to work, "Russia will be able to assume its responsibility as a legal successor to the Union."[39]

Gaidar's faith that price liberalization would restore macroeconomic stability and fix everything was the driver of Yeltsin's text. Still, the Russian President remained ambivalent. He did not clarify what would become of the Soviet Army and how it would be funded. He was also vague on what would happen to vast social programs and commitments. The IMF economists and Gaidar wanted to cut them drastically. Yeltsin, however, promised to protect those in need. The majority of delegates barely understood the logic behind the reforms, but they were enthralled by the magic of a bold new course of action. On 1 November, the Congress granted Yeltsin everything he was demanding: the postponement of elections, the shelving of a new democratic constitution, the power to govern by decree, and a green light to abolish any Soviet laws that stood in the way.[40] Most Russians understood only one thing from Yeltsin's speech: prices would go through the roof. Panic-buying started to sweep across the country. Later, Gaidar admitted to Braithwaite that Yeltsin had hyped himself up to make a resounding speech, and could not be restrained.[41]

Bernstam happened to be a witness to this historic moment. On 19 October, he received a fax from Khasbulatov telling him to return to Moscow as soon as possible. Changing flights in Frankfurt am Main on 21 October, Bernstam read in *The Financial Times*: "Yeltsin may be planning reforms for Russia alone."[42] In Moscow, the American economist learned that Yeltsin had put Gaidar in charge. Bernstam called him, but Gaidar was too busy to talk. On 26 October, Saburov, Bernstam's friend, invited him to his wife's birthday party. A chauffeured government limousine brought Bernstam to Arkhangelskoye-2, where the party was being held. The crowd consisted mostly of economists and their spouses. At some point Gaidar showed up. Yeltsin's new favorite gave Saburov a bear hug and greeted his spouse. Then the two economists left the party for a confidential talk and after half an hour appeared with somber faces. Bernstam guessed that Saburov had probably asked Gaidar for a role in the new Russian government, but his request was turned down. Gaidar planned a dictatorship of professionals drawn only from his team.[43]

Gaidar approached Bernstam and asked him for his expert opinion on a sensitive document he was writing. After the Stanford economist had returned to his hotel, a government courier delivered the document in question. It was a draft of the presidential decree, "On the liberalization of foreign economic activities in the RSFSR." The decree abolished all Soviet laws and controls over exports and imports; dues and taxes on them were also to be canceled. It granted freedom of international trade to all economic actors registered in the Russian Federation. The licenses and quotas on the export of oil, gas, and other raw materials—a hugely profitable business for Soviet government officials and select enterprises—would now be sold at auction. Finally, the decree removed the Soviet state monopoly on the exchange of rubles into foreign currency. Russian citizens, resident aliens, and even foreigners would be able to open currency accounts in Russian commercial banks. This was a revolutionary move: by Soviet law, all foreigners had to exchange dollars and Deutschmarks for rubles at the official rate or they used the black market, risking legal prosecution. The decree was dated to come into force on 10 November 1991. It was typed up on Russian presidential stationery; only Yeltsin's signature was missing.[44]

Bernstam was stunned. "When I looked into it," he recalled, "I saw a nuclear Armageddon lurking behind." The economist was familiar enough with Soviet society and its economy to realize what would happen if such reforms were to be implemented in the Russian Federation alone. People from other republics—"resident aliens" of the decree—would rush to the RSFSR to open bank accounts and exchange rubles for dollars. Governments of non-Russian republics would run out of rubles to pay the salaries and wages of their citizens. They would start borrowing rubles from the State Bank to cover the sudden deficit. The Bank would have to print astronomical amounts of rubles; the exchange rate would collapse, and hyperinflation would set in. This would happen even before price liberalization could take effect. A similar destructive short circuit would affect oil production in Kazakhstan and Azerbaijan and steel industries in Ukraine: they would start to export all their output to Russian companies, who would immediately re-export it abroad. The Russian government would be forced to set up checkpoints on its republican borders to stop the inflow of goods and rubles into Russia. The governments of other republics would do the same to prevent the flight of their resources. Border clashes would flare up between national militias and criminal armies that would seek to cross the new borders. As the conflict escalated, the old chain of command within the armed forces would start to crumble; different segments of the army would take sides. The military located in Ukraine, Belorussia, Kazakhstan, and other republics would side with their republics. What would then happen to all the nuclear weapons, Bernstam wondered, especially tactical weapons scattered around the Soviet Union?[45]

A nuclear dispute between post-Soviet republics was an outlandish idea for anyone living in the Soviet Union. A few days earlier, however, a troubling incident had occurred. Vice-President Rutskoy had used the nuclear argument in his negotiations with Ukrainian government officials. He was acting as an envoy of Gazprom, to bargain on the commercial price of natural gas in pipelines that ran from Siberia to Western Europe across Ukraine. The talks quickly touched on other issues, including the future of Crimea, and grew heated. Rutskoy, no diplomat, said that Ukraine should not behave so stubbornly "with a nuclear power." The Ukrainian negotiators responded that their republic also had nuclear weapons and would defend its borders by all means available. Newspapers wrote about the threat of "a Russian nuclear strike against Ukraine." Yeltsin was forced to provide explanations.[46]

Bernstam decided that the whole matter was too sensitive for a phone call. He requested an appointment with Gaidar, and was eventually received on 3 November. Gaidar had just moved into the former Party complex on the Old Square and now occupied the former office of Leonid Brezhnev. With Lenin watching him from a big portrait on the wall, Bernstam laid out his apocalyptic scenario. If the Russian reformers, he said, wanted to have both reform and peace, they had only three options to choose from. First, abandon immediate liberalization, and instead introduce it only gradually in the future and with distinct limitations. Second, wait until other republics agreed to join these measures and come up with a synchronized liberalization program for the entire post-Soviet space. Third, disengage Russia from the Union and other republics completely, and make the Russian Federation an independent state. Bernstam said that he personally preferred the first two options as being less traumatic for the people of the former Soviet Union.

Gaidar asked the American economist to write down what he had said. Then he compiled a list of officials for an emergency meeting and asked his secretary to summon them to his office immediately. He asked Bernstam to retire to a room located behind the office. It was already late in the evening. Bernstam smoked his pipe and dozed off. After a while, Gaidar woke him up and invited him back to his office, which was now empty. In the presence of the Stanford economist, Gaidar called Yeltsin on the secure telephone line. He repeated what

Bernstam had told him, including the nuclear scenario. Then he passed the phone to Bernstam. Yeltsin thanked Bernstam and expressed his wish to meet with him. The Stanford economist left the enormous building deep at night and after a short walk reached his hotel.[47]

Bernstam did indeed meet with Yeltsin—but he did not have a chance to discuss his alternative vision for Russian reforms. On 6 November, Yeltsin inaugurated his new government. Gaidar became both deputy Prime Minister and Minister of Economy and Finance, a position combining control of two crucial ministries. Burbulis and Gaidar convinced the Russian President to take charge of his own government as Prime Minister himself. It was, they argued, the best option. The Supreme Soviet would not approve Gaidar as Prime Minister. And anyone else in this powerful position could decide to play political games and become an obstacle to implementing reforms. Those from Yeltsin's entourage took non-economic positions in the new administration, such as defense, security, and chief of police. The activists from Democratic Russia were awarded only a few secondary posts.[48]

On 15 November, at their first Cabinet meeting, Yeltsin signed a decree on the liberalization of foreign trade. But it was an entirely different document from the earlier one. This decree was decoupled from price liberalization and became contingent on the ultimate agreements of other republics to join the free-trade zone.[49] Yeltsin and his government continued reforms on the dual track, as if they simultaneously agreed to be part of an economic and political confederation with the other republics, and yet intended to run the post-Soviet space themselves, instead of Gorbachev's provisional government.

The moves on the first track concerned the State Bank and the Ministry of Finance. At the State Council back in October, Gorbachev and Yeltsin had appeared to agree that those institutions should be kept as the nucleus of a future Union, but supervised by representatives from the republics. The logic of Gaidar's neoliberal reforms, however, demanded the very opposite. On 15 November, Gaidar told Yeltsin that all Soviet financial and budgetary institutions and instruments had to be taken under Russia's control, in order to restore macroeconomic stability and ensure the success of their reforms. The State Bank of the USSR would remain, yet the Bank of Russia would, from now on, control currency exchange. Yeltsin also tried to abolish the Ministry of Finance of the USSR by unilateral decree, but after "the battle" with other republican leaders he agreed to keep it provisionally. He told his government that in the near future the ministry would be merged into Russia's Finance Ministry. And Goznak, the special facility for printing currency and minting coins, would be taken over under Russian jurisdiction. Without any fanfare, he said, Russia should also seize all Soviet gold and diamond reserves and mines in Siberia.

INDEPENDENCE

Yeltsin called these decisions "historic"—and indeed they were.[50] And what about Bernstam's warnings and arguments? The Stanford economist commented many years later that Yeltsin and Gaidar had understood him very well. They just decided they needed a bit more time to swallow up the central institutions and turn the Russian Federation into a legal successor to the Soviet Union.[51] That was certainly true of Gaidar. In Yeltsin's mind, however, as we shall see, rational considerations coexisted with other ideas.

On the second track, the Russian government planned to replace Soviet political controls over other republics with economic and financial leverage. Gaidar's initial plans to sell oil at world prices to other republics, if they became fully independent, had to be corrected. "We have to be careful with Ukraine," Yeltsin said. "Too many Russians live there." The Baltic states, with their Russian minorities, would also continue to receive oil and gas subventions. This leverage, as the future would soon reveal, would be limited and costly. Gaidar was unhappy with this policy. He discovered that 126 million tons of Russian oil, over a quarter of the entire output, had already been distributed to corporate structures and state enterprises for licensed export. Oil had replaced the devalued ruble as a much more valid form of currency, to keep the Russian economy going.[52]

Following their historic first meeting, Yeltsin and his new Cabinet met with the press. After explaining their strategy, Gaidar declared that he and other ministers had decided to abjure all official privileges, such as state-funded apartments in Moscow, state-funded dachas, special food packages, and the like. By making this gesture, Gaidar wanted to demonstrate that he and his associates would share with the Russian people all the sacrifices involved in the painful reforms. Boris Yeltsin was pleased by this gesture. At this point, Andrei Kozyrev raised his hand. Yeltsin nodded in expectation that another minister would add to the uplifting spirit of the occasion. "My mother and I," Kozyrev said, with cameras clicking and rolling, "are in the process of converting two separate apartments into a single one . . . a three-room and a two-room into a five-room apartment. Can we do it? Will it contradict what Gaidar has announced?" Yeltsin's jaw dropped. The high moral tone of the occasion had evaporated.[53]

THE FICTION OF A CENTER

Meanwhile, the NSC contingency group in Washington were meeting every ten days to catch up with runaway developments in the Soviet zone. Americans had excellent sources of information in Moscow: they included people in the Soviet Foreign Ministry, Yeltsin's entourage, and even Gorbachev's provisional government. On 24 October, the NSC group's coordinator Nicholas Burns sent Brent

Scowcroft a paper entitled "Gathering Storm," which began with a Leninist phrase: "The Soviet revolution is on the verge of taking another leap forward." Most of the central Soviet ministries, the memo concluded, "have been taken over by the Russian government. Even [the Ministry of Foreign Affairs] and the military are increasingly under Russian sway." Gorbachev and Yeltsin "have sought to maintain the fiction of a 'center' to facilitate formation of an economic union and provide political legitimacy for maintaining the Soviet army." This fiction also allowed Gorbachev to maintain his role "as a useful interlocutor with the West." The immediate forecast was: Gorbachev would resign before the end of the year; there would then be Russia, instead of the Union center, to deal with; the Soviet Army would become the Russian Army; a declaration of Ukrainian independence following the referendum on 1 December would be "a foregone conclusion." The post-Soviet republics would form "a crazy quilt" of potentially dangerous conflicts, such as that surrounding the future of Crimea.[54]

Bush and Scowcroft, who read these forecasts, remained fixated on the worst-case scenarios. The intelligence reported with a great degree of certainty that the General Staff in Moscow had managed to maintain central control over strategic and tactical nuclear weapons. However, it was not clear whether Gorbachev or Yeltsin now controlled the Army, the KGB, and the nuclear "button."[55] Scowcroft considered the CIA's Soviet division to be "pro-Yeltsin" and therefore biased. He accepted, though, that the Soviet Union was disintegrating. "I think I did not realize," he recalled many years later, "the extent to which all of this was happening." Yeltsin, he continued, wanted to get rid of Gorbachev, and an "almost complete" destruction of the Soviet Union was the way to do it. "He really pulled the Soviet Union from under" Gorbachev.[56]

Gorbachev's huge office in the Kremlin became an island, isolated from the world outside. The numerous telephones on his desk were mostly silent. The people who would previously have called him were now imprisoned, fired, or had defected to Yeltsin's side. The KGB experts, demoralized and discredited, stopped sending him analytical reports. The established Soviet intelligentsia, once part of Gorbachev's court, had long decamped to Yeltsin. The Academy of Sciences of the USSR, and "creative" unions of writers, artists, and others, voted to come under the Russian jurisdiction. Raisa Gorbacheva, whose August sickness had led to an ongoing depression, retreated from public life, blaming everyone for betraying her husband.[57] The tiny circle of Gorbachev's advisors included Chernyaev, Shakhnazarov, Yakovlev and Shevardnadze; the latter two returned to help the isolated Soviet leader in his plight.

Gorbachev discussed with them what to do about Yeltsin's new course of action. Yakovlev and Shevardnadze recommended that he maintain his distance, and wait until "the Russians make mistakes" and returned to the idea of a Union.

Gorbachev said he would fully back the Russian government of reforms. "The key issue is to help Yeltsin. If he considers himself deceived, abandoned, he can throw a tantrum." It was "a dangerous academic utopia," he said, to imagine that the RSFSR could survive as a separate state. People of other republics, he explained, "are ready in their majority to acknowledge Russia's leadership, but only in the form of a new Union . . . where Russia would perform this role in practice." Gorbachev still imagined that he would become an elected president in such a Union.[58]

On 21 October, the reformed Supreme Soviet of the USSR reconvened after a long absence. Gorbachev opened the first session, but the procedure only highlighted his isolation. Many parliamentarians had been sent into retirement, their seats replaced by "republican deputies" delegated from the RSFSR and other republican assemblies. Only seven republican flags were displayed behind the podium, next to the flag of the Soviet Union. The Ukrainian Rada, after many weeks of promises, had not sent its delegation. "Ukraine is not represented," recorded Vadim Medvedev, "as well as the Baltics and Georgia . . . In effect, only so-called democratic forces are represented. The [conservative] forces are purged."[59] Gorbachev in his speech compared the occasion with the Constitutional Assembly elected in Russia in November 1917. This was a bizarre analogy: that assembly had been disbanded by Lenin before it could even sit. Major newspapers printed only a summary of what Gorbachev said.[60]

The last spike to Gorbachev's international prestige was the international conference on Middle Eastern affairs held in Madrid between 30 October and 1 November. This was a culmination of many years of Soviet and American diplomatic efforts. Boris Pankin, the Soviet Foreign Minister, and James Baker, the US Secretary of State, had achieved miracles in convincing hostile parties involved in the Arab-Israeli conflict to attend. It was a diplomatic drama of last-minute agreements and extreme emotions, all balanced on a knife edge, and sensational announcements. On 18 October, the Soviet Union had resumed full diplomatic relations with Israel after twenty-four years of hostility and estrangement. Baker met with Yasser Arafat, leader of the Palestinian Liberation Organization (PLO), which Israel and the United States had considered a terrorist organization. US-Soviet cooperation in the Middle East had been an old dream of Leonid Brezhnev. It was a bitter irony that Gorbachev saw this dream fulfilled only when the Soviet Union had shrunk to the size of his Kremlin office.[61]

President Bush dictated in his diary on the eve of his trip from Washington: "The briefing book indicates this might be my last meeting with him of this nature . . . It will be interesting to figure out his mood."[62] On 30 October, Bush and Gorbachev sat as two co-chairmen at the opening of the conference, the US and Soviet flags were prominently displayed, and Pankin struck the ceremonial gavel to start the proceedings. The Soviet leader performed with such natural confidence that Bush and other Westerners wondered whether what they had read about his political demise was true. The conference, however, proved to be the death knell to Gorbachev's statesmanship and Soviet diplomacy. The same day that the Soviet leader flew to Madrid, Andrei Kozyrev announced that the Soviet Foreign Ministry would be reduced to 300 officials, one-tenth of its size, and perform only those functions that Russia and other republics would delegate. In private conversations, Kozyrev explained that the MID and its assets abroad had been owned by the Russian state before 1917 and must belong to a new Russia. In Moscow, many Soviet diplomats quietly negotiated with Kozyrev and his staff to get jobs for themselves in the Russian Foreign Ministry. After all, some of them argued, "we are all Russians."[63]

Pankin expected Gorbachev to call Yeltsin to discuss the issue of the MID, yet apparently in Madrid the Soviet leader was savoring every minute on the world stage and was too busy to do so. Gorbachev expected his friend the American President to back him publicly, but Bush maintained a diplomatic silence. Instead, he asked Gorbachev about the Soviet military, control of nuclear weapons, and Ukrainian independence. The Soviet leader dismissed those concerns.[64] He asked Bush for money again: "$10–$15 billion is not much for us, and repayment is not a serious problem." Bush pledged to give $1.5 billion "for the winter," and quickly added: "If that is insulting to you, I will go back and consult and see what might be done." Baker was more direct: he intimated to Gorbachev's interpreter Pavel Palazhchenko: "Take a billion and a half in ready cash; take it before we reconsider." Gorbachev, too proud for his own good, declined the offer.[65]

On 1 November, Pankin received a cable from his deputy: "Instead of restoring peace in the Middle East, you should come to save your Ministry." The Foreign Minister had to abandon the conference and fly back to Moscow, to prepare for a meeting with Yeltsin and the republican leaders. Before leaving, he explained the reasons for his departure to Baker, who expressed his understanding. He even suggested that Bush should call Yeltsin. "Good Lord, this didn't even occur to me," Pankin recalled in his memoirs. "To this day I don't know if such a call was ever made."[66]

On 4 November, the future of the Foreign Ministry was discussed at a closed meeting of the State Council at Novo-Ogaryovo. Pankin argued that winding down the MID would endanger the legal succession to the Soviet Union. At stake were a permanent seat at the UN Security Council and 15,000 treaties and agreements. He also wondered what would happen to the multi-billion properties and assets of the Ministry: 133 embassies, ninety-three consulates, six offices at international organizations, trade offices, and the like. As it turned out, on the eve of the meeting, Gorbachev had spoken with Yeltsin: "The MID was formed by Russian people over the centuries, why do you want to ruin it? . . . Clearly you would rather take it to Russia. This will happen someday, but now you should take care of it."[67] Yeltsin grudgingly agreed with Gorbachev's compromise proposal: to merge the MID with the Ministry of External Economic Relations. It would now be called the Ministry of External Relations. The crisis seemed to be resolved. A senior diplomat from Kozyrev's ministry would be sent to Washington as a second-ranking official.[68]

At the meeting, Pankin observed Yeltsin, Nazarbayev, and Kravchuk closely, and was horrified by their ignorance of foreign affairs. He left Novo-Ogaryovo with a sense of relief, but also with the uneasy feeling that both he and the MID were "the card in a game with much bigger stakes."[69] In fact, Gorbachev and Yeltsin had already agreed behind Pankin's back to offer the top foreign affairs job to Eduard Shevardnadze. Gorbachev hoped that Yeltsin would have enough respect for the celebrated Georgian statesman and therefore leave the MID alone.[70]

The secret meeting of the State Council also discussed the future of the Soviet Army. Marshal Shaposhnikov reported that the superpower's military force was being under-drafted, defunded, and pulled apart between "national" armies. Ukraine, Georgia, Azerbaijan, and Moldova had announced that their recruits would only serve in "national" units on their territories. Republican parliaments demanded that the military on their territories should take an oath of allegiance not to the Soviet Union, but to the newly independent states. And the Baltic states demanded that all Soviet bases, including strategic anti-missile and anti-aircraft systems on their territory, should be dismantled and withdrawn immediately. Moreover, there was no longer enough money to maintain Soviet troops and material in eastern Germany. Even the withdrawal from Central Europe was costing much more: the Polish government was demanding a high price for the movement of Soviet military across its territory. Finally, there was a danger of corruption and the illegal sales of arms and military equipment under the guise of "business activities."[71]

Gorbachev proposed establishing a new status for the Soviet Army, so that its forces could stay legally in the now-independent republics. No one openly questioned Gorbachev's role as the commander-in-chief. Yet the discussion quickly sank into the quagmire of legal and political details. There was no precedent for an army that would "belong" both to many states and yet to no one state in particular. Time went by, but no consensus emerged. Nazarbayev, Karimov, and other Central Asian leaders wanted a common army, so long as someone else picked up the tab. Ukraine and Belorussia continued to insist that Soviet troops on their territory should become "nationalized."[72]

The future of the KGB was another subject of debate. The formidable institution remained in effect under the dual command of both Yeltsin and Gorbachev. They agreed that the "Alfa" commandos could be used only if both consented.[73] Democrats in Moscow wanted to split the KGB into "a Russian CIA" and a Russian Ministry of the Interior. The head of the "Russian KGB," Viktor Ivanenko, lobbied to appropriate "Alfa" and the Ninth Directorate, along with the central apparatus and territorial branches. He wrote to Yeltsin: "The republic without its security organs would be defenseless before the aggressive demands of its neighbors and the actions of extremists." He cited threats to the Russian Federation: separatism, organized crime, and looting of state property. Burbulis backed Ivanenko.[74] Yeltsin, however, sided with those who wanted to break up the KGB. Therefore, the State Council decided that the leviathan should be broken up into several parts under the equal control of all republics. Gorbachev's aide Yevgeny Primakov became the head of the external intelligence service. The counter-intelligence service was attached to the military. Border guards and railroad troops became part of a separate agency. Amid this huge level of uncertainty, KGB personnel in Moscow "drank vodka, burned their papers, watched TV, and waited for what would happen." Many began to look for jobs in the burgeoning private security sector.[75]

The State Council meeting on 14 November became the final battleground for Gorbachev to obtain his Union Treaty. He pressed Yeltsin and other republican leaders to agree to a "Union of Sovereign States." Yeltsin opposed it.[76] Gorbachev's press secretary recalled that Yeltsin "*valyal Van'ku*"—acted like a village Vanya. (Vanya was a figure from folklore, a lazy drunkard who obstinately refused to join a common project that a village community wanted to accomplish.) Others present at the meeting wondered why, instead of one strong leader, the country had a bizarre couple of rivals who were tearing everything apart. Shakhnazarov rued "the split Russian mentality" that made the Yeltsin phenomenon possible. Pankin had an insight: if only Yeltsin and Gorbachev could trade posts and roles, with Yeltsin as President of the USSR, then the Union would be preserved. At one point Gorbachev's patience ran out. He bristled, began to collect his papers, and prepared to leave. The republican leaders called for a break, in order to allow Yeltsin and Gorbachev to have a private conversation. After the break, Gorbachev returned looking happy. Yeltsin had agreed that a new structure would be called a "democratic confederate state." The Russian "Vanya" had yielded to peer pressure—one last time.[77]

The future "Union state" would have a president elected by direct, equal, and secret ballots for the duration of five years. This president would chair rather than rule. There would be no common constitution, but a common parliament with deputies elected by districts, not just delegated by the republics. All financial and decision-making powers would remain with the republics that would form the Union, yet there would be coordinating structures. After much haggling, Yeltsin also agreed that the central Ministry of Finance and Ministry of Economics would remain in place for two more weeks for the purpose of "transition." This was the final sacrifice that Yeltsin was prepared to make to the idea of a Union.[78]

Gorbachev had to endure yet another humiliation, when he asked the Supreme Soviet of the USSR to authorize his request for 30 billion rubles; there was no money in the central budget to pay salaries to the central ministries. The assembly, now dominated by the Russian Federation, voted down his request. Gorbachev was then forced to ask Yeltsin for authorization.[79] On 22 November, Yeltsin ordered that all branches of the State Bank of the USSR on Russian territory be appropriated. Three days later, he took over the "mobilization reserves" of the Soviet Union, a colossal system of warehouses filled with materials and goods in the event of a major war. At the last minute, however, Yeltsin granted Gorbachev's request for 30 billion rubles in credit.[80] There was one last factor preventing Yeltsin from toppling the fiction of the central state. He wanted, he said to his government, to wait for Ukraine to hold its referendum and decide on its future. On 15 November, at the meeting of the Russian government, the Russian President told an unhappy Gaidar to postpone freeing up prices and currency exchange until 1 January 1992. For Gaidar this was "perhaps the most difficult of all decisions" that his government had to make: every extra day of procrastination meant one day lost for "Russian sovereignty" and macroeconomic stabilization—and more inflation in the near future.[81]

WAITING FOR UKRAINE

The historian Serhii Plokhy wrote about Yeltsin's new course: "The Russian Ark was leaving the Soviet dock." This Biblical metaphor suits Ukraine even more. In October, Kravchuk refused to sign the economic treaty until Ukraine got its severance package—a 16 percent share of all Soviet financial reserves, including gold, diamonds, and foreign currency. The Ukrainian leaders also refused to join Russia and other republics in arranging the repayment of Soviet debts to Western banks. Burbulis recalled that he and his colleagues were completely in favor of Ukraine's independence. Yet "it was inconceivable, for our brains, for our minds, that this would be an irrevocable fact." Burbulis had family connections with Ukraine and knew well that tens of millions of Russians, Ukrainians, and people of mixed origin, like him, could not imagine Ukraine and the Russian Federation as separate entities. For the Russians, Ukraine was like Scotland to the English, only closer. From the Russian perspective, Ukraine was filing for divorce without a settlement. This Russian mindset was bound to clash with Ukrainian nationalism and become a source of great tension and trouble for decades to come.[82]

The seeming impossibility of divorce was reinforced by hard economic facts. The Soviet economy had been constructed as intertwined, and practically indivisible. This unity had pre-dated the Revolution, but became much deeper in Soviet times. The Russian Federation and Ukraine had a common industrial and scientific-technical complex. Most plants and laboratories in Kharkov, Dnepropetrovsk, and other industrial cities of Ukraine had clones and partners in Moscow, St Petersburg, the Urals, and Siberia. Ukraine's businesses and households could not operate without Tyumen oil and gas; Donbass mines could not function without Russian wood; Norilsk aluminum smelters required Ukrainian bauxite. Soviet strategic missiles and most of the high-tech military weaponry were constructed in Ukraine or required "made in Ukraine" parts. For decades this economy had been managed, funded, and innovated from Moscow. The Ukrainian separatists wanted to end this state of affairs at any cost, yet those costs were huge. For decades Soviet bureaucrats and experts had run most of the Ukrainian economy from the center. No one in Moscow could imagine that the Ukrainian Ark would leave the Soviet-Russian dock—and sail without sinking immediately.

Had the two leaders in Moscow, Yeltsin and Gorbachev, made a joint effort, they probably would have succeeded in steering Ukrainian politics away from secession. The republic was not united in what Ukraine's independence would mean. And for the industrial regions of Ukraine, Kiev was not the center of gravity at all. They associated themselves with Moscow, Russian history, and Russian culture.[83] For millions of people in those regions, with mixed ethnic origins and shared identities, Ukrainian "sovereignty" was something vague that could still imply a common country with the Russian Federation. Georgy Shakhnazarov thought those people should be mobilized to oppose Ukrainian separatism and support a common statehood. He wrote to Gorbachev with a proposal to organize a campaign against "Galician nationalism and its collaborationists." Russia, Gorbachev's aide continued, should officially declare that Crimea, Donbass and southern parts of Ukraine "constitute historical parts of Russia, and Russia does not intend to give them up, in case Ukraine leaves the Union." Yet Gorbachev and Yeltsin could never agree on Ukraine.[84]

The internal Russian divide was ideal for Kravchuk's campaign. After a successful debut in North America, he quickly gained support across Ukraine's regions. His ratings in October stood around 30–40 percent in most regions, with a sharp drop in Western Ukraine and a modest majority in southern and eastern regions, as well as in Crimea.[85] While his opponents represented new political parties and movements, Kravchuk ran as an "independent." The old Party elites rallied around him. For many of them, writes Plokhy, "independence became a new religion and Kravchuk its prophet." The Ukrainian Party media and journalists, formerly supervised by Kravchuk, rooted for him as well. *Pravda of Ukraine*, a newspaper with a wide circulation, declared itself for Kravchuk. The Ukrainian KGB also rallied around him. One source even boasted to the Americans that the KGB's republican apparatus, troops, border guards, and railway troops on the republic's territory were "eighty-five percent loyal Ukrainians" responding to Kravchuk's leadership in Kiev.[86]

His campaign rested on several pillars. First, he outflanked his nationalist rivals, above all the candidate of Rukh, Vyacheslav Chernovol, by advocating complete independence and a full share of Soviet assets, including military power for Ukraine. Second, he posed as the best consolidator of the country divided by history. Third, he posed as the candidate most likely to obtain international legitimacy from the West and the best possible economic deal from Russia.

Kravchuk was able to appeal to all major electoral groups of the republics, including the majority of Ukraine's intelligentsia and scientific-technical professionals, both ethnic Ukrainians and Russians, who wanted to distance themselves from the nightmares of the Soviet past and make a fresh start. And he attracted voters in southern and eastern Ukraine who did not identify much with Ukrainian history, but instead felt a strong connection with the common Soviet state, and wanted a return of stability and order. They were worried by Yeltsin's announcement of price liberalization. Kravchuk promised them that an independent Ukraine would remain a haven of stability and cheap food.[87]

One of Kravchuk's early objectives in the campaign was to neutralize Crimea's separatism. The peninsula was as much a threat to Ukraine's integrity as Tatarstan and Chechnya were to Russia's. Shakhnazarov, as part of his anti-separatist campaign, advised "to work in the Crimea in agreement with Comrade Bagrov."[88] Nikolai Bagrov was the head of the Crimean Party leadership, who had organized a local referendum that turned the peninsula into an autonomous republic within Ukraine, with the right to sign the Union Treaty. After the Independence Act, the Crimean pro-Russian activists insisted on another referendum, to return the peninsula to the Russian Federation. Bagrov was sitting on the fence, ready to jump to one side or the other.[89]

Kravchuk went to Crimea on the day its regional assembly gathered to decide on the referendum. He presented himself as a "godfather of Crimean autonomy" and promised to turn the peninsula into "a free economic zone" if it remained within Ukraine. A decision to return to Russia, he said, would violate Ukraine's constitution. Of course, Kiev would not use force to stop this. Yet all enterprises and farms of Crimea would have to pay much higher prices for energy and water that came to the peninsula from Ukraine. A canal brought the Dnieper water to irrigate the arid lands of Crimea. If the people left Ukraine, Kravchuk said, they would have to pay about $3 billion every year for this water.[90] Kravchuk succeeded in using persuasive arguments. The parliament of Crimea canceled the referendum; the separatist momentum fizzled out. Bagrov, after a heart-to-heart talk with Kravchuk, supported his candidacy and advocated the Ukrainian choice for Crimea.[91] Kravchuk worked in a similar way with the regional elites in Dnepropetrovsk, Kharkov, Nikolaev, and Donbass.

On 4 November, Kravchuk went to Moscow to attend the State Council, but his real purpose was to hold economic talks with Yeltsin. The Ukrainian and Russian leaders reached a bilateral agreement on an economic and trade partnership. On the same day, Kravchuk signed the economic treaty he had earlier dismissed. At their joint press conference, Kravchuk and Yeltsin affirmed their friendship, open borders, mutual respect of territorial integrity, and protection for ethnic minorities. When a journalist asked Yeltsin about Crimea, he repeated: "This is the sovereign business of the Ukrainian state."[92] Kravchuk could congratulate himself. He appeared to have squared the circle and consolidated the fragmented Ukrainian electorate. He gave the impression that he had all the answers to Ukraine's problems and knew how to proceed without hurting anyone. This would soon be revealed as a myth, yet Kravchuk remained in the eyes of many the father of the Ukrainian nation. Many Russians, on the contrary, viewed him as a cunning fox who fooled everyone, while sowing the seeds of future conflicts.

On 21 November, Yeltsin met with Galina Starovoitova, his advisor on nationalities. The President of Russia disconnected all telephones and told his secretary not to disturb him until the end of the conversation. He had one question for Starovoitova: how would Ukraine vote? She responded that at least three-quarters of Ukrainian voters would support independence. Yeltsin was incredulous. "It cannot be true! This is our fraternal Slavic republic! There are 30 percent of Russians there. Crimea is Russian! All the people who reside eastward of the Dnieper gravitate to Russia!" For about forty minutes, Starovoitova went through the data she had received from her colleagues, ethnographers and democratic politicians who lived in Ukraine. Finally, Yeltsin was convinced. "In this case," he said, "we will recognize this new political reality." After the referendum, he continued, he would wait for a week, then hold a meeting of the three Slavic republics. The venue for this meeting would not be Moscow, which is "the imperialist center for them," nor Kiev, where Ukrainians would celebrate their triumph, but modest Minsk. "This was Yeltsin's idea," Starovoitova recalled.[93]

INDEPENDENCE

The historical significance of Yeltsin's decision was enormous. It ran against the grain of centuries of Russian history and mindset. The British ambassador Rodric Braithwaite wrote: "Perfectly sensible Russians froth at the mouth if it is suggested that the Ukraine (from which they all trace their history) might go off on its own." Russian-Ukrainian relations "are as combustible as those in Northern Ireland: but the consequences of an explosion would be far more serious."[94] The mayor of St Petersburg, Anatoly Sobchak, in conversation with a British official, accused the West of courting Ukrainian separatism. This encouraged the break-up of the Union, he said, and would kill Russian democracy. The British official argued that the West had no option but to deal with practical realities. Sobchak countered that the West underestimated its capacity to influence events. "It was the West's policy of 'recognizing realities' that allowed Hitler to rise to power."[95]

Yeltsin's new certainty about Ukraine explained what happened on 25 November at the last meeting between Gorbachev and the republican barons. The Soviet leader expected them to approve the draft of a Union of Sovereign States. Instead, Yeltsin said he could not conceive of a union without Ukraine and suggested they wait until 1 December. The treaty without Ukraine, he said, would be useless and provocative: "Then Ukraine will take decisions that destroy the Union. If it makes a decision to have its own national currency— then that would be the end." Gorbachev had another outburst of frustration and left the room. For a while, the barons deliberated without him. Then Yeltsin and Stanislav Shushkevich, head of Belorussia's Supreme Soviet, came to Gorbachev's office to invite him back to the discussion. With a wry expression on his face, Yeltsin said: "We came to kowtow to the Khan." Gorbachev replied: "OK, Tsar Boris, get down to business." Yeltsin had to sit next to Gorbachev and other leaders for hours, and went, point by point, through the final draft of the Union Treaty. At the end of the meeting, however, he did not join Gorbachev to meet the press; the embarrassed Soviet leader had to do it alone.[96]

Why did Yeltsin spend so much time on the Union Treaty project if he already knew it was null and void? Most likely, he was playing the role of the village "Vanya" yet again. At the meeting, Gorbachev and other republican leaders protested Russia's takeover of the State Bank and Goznak. "You cannot do it without the republics, without us," Gorbachev bemoaned. The Bank must belong to a banking union of the republics and Goznak should be returned to the Ministry of Finance of the USSR. "This is piracy," Gorbachev concluded. Yeltsin stubbornly denied that he had done anything wrong. Gaidar told him that Goznak's equipment had to be upgraded, because after the price liberalization it would have to print at least a trillion rubles. At the State Council, the Russian leader simply promised that Goznak would print as much money as would be necessary for all the republics. Karimov asked him how Uzbekistan, for example, would know how many rubles Russia printed? Yeltsin shot back: "And did you know about this amount before?" Other republican leaders voted to return Goznak to the control of the State Bank of the USSR; Yeltsin ignored this decision.[97]

Gorbachev kept his word and backed the Russian reformist course of action. At a special closed meeting of the State Council, Yavlinsky praised Yeltsin as a hero who took risks that the country had not faced since World War II. Ukraine and even the Balts, Yavlinsky said, would be hamstrung by the decisions of Russia, whether they wanted to be or not. Shushkevich asked incredulously why other republics had to follow Russia's leap into the unknown. Perhaps a separate statehood and national currency could save Ukraine or Belorussia from future Russian shocks? Yavlinsky responded that this would not help. As long as Ukraine and other republics were unable to close their borders with Russia and create their own financial system, they would remain in the same boat as Russia in macroeconomic terms. And Ukraine had better refrain, he said, from wrecking this boat or punching holes in it.[98] If Ukraine, however, did begin to print its own currency, Yavlinsky admitted, this would cause "terrible suffering to Russia, with no end in sight." Another currency would be like a transfusion of the wrong blood type. Ukraine could kill the Russian economy, but it would also destroy its own economy.[99]

Gorbachev asked Yeltsin for more money, 90 billion rubles, to lend to the provisional government. Yeltsin refused, then reconsidered.[100] In a telephone conversation with President Bush later, he said that Russia had decided to "save the entire country." He then added: "But all must fully understand that we cannot always be so altruistic. In 1992 all republics must be responsible for their own affairs."[101]

At the end of November, the Russian President and his ministers hurried to take over the most lucrative chunks of the Soviet economic heritage: conglomerates of the oil and energy industries, including Gazprom; the gold and diamond industry; the state storage for gems and gold reserves; the aluminum industry; and the military construction corporations. Yeltsin was completely uninterested, however, in the jewels of the military-industrial complex, such as anti-aircraft and anti-missile defense corporations. He was even indifferent to the future of the nuclear industry (Minsredmash). The Russian state, of course, would be forced to take responsibility for those industries later.[102]

At a meeting of the Russian government on 28 November, Yeltsin was impatient about the last structures of Soviet statehood that remained under the Union's jurisdiction. Kozyrev and other Russian ministers agreed that the central apparatus of the Foreign Ministry, embassies, villas, and other assets abroad, should be placed on the Russian payroll, but not yet claimed as legal property. Yeltsin proposed: "Let's rename [RSFSR] into Russia fast, and we will become legal successors to this property." On 29 November, Yeltsin instructed the MID to be put on the Russian payroll. Nevertheless, he still had to wait for the world to recognize Russia as a worthy substitute for the Soviet superpower.[103]

On 28 November, Burbulis proposed that the Ministry of the Interior with its riot police should be placed immediately under Russia's jurisdiction. With anticipated social unrest after the launch of radical reforms, the Russian state had to maintain order on the streets. Yeltsin began to speak again, for the first time since August, about the takeover of the Soviet Army. He was impressed by Kravchuk's move to convert the Soviet military on Ukraine's territory into a "national" army and to double its salary. "No umming and aahing there," Yeltsin remarked approvingly. "It was a powerful political move."[104] He wondered why the Army, largely paid by Russian taxes, should remain under Gorbachev's command? And why should Russia pay for the military deployments outside its own territory, for instance in Nagorny Karabagh, when its own territorial sovereignty was at risk?[105]

The last point was about the explosive issue of separatism in Chechnya, a strategic part of Russia's borderlands in the Caucasus. The ethnic Chechens who lived there had a tragic history: Imperial Russia had conquered their lands and suppressed their insurrection; during World War II, Stalin ordered them to be deported to Kazakhstan because of their collaboration with the German invaders. After Stalin's death, Khrushchev allowed the Chechens to return to their homeland and restored their autonomous republic within the RSFSR. Their tragic history seemed to be a thing of the past. The implosion of the Soviet state in August 1991, however, turned Chechnya into a zone of anarchy. One sociologist observed that "the mountains reclaimed the valleys" as militant youths and tribal nationalists pushed aside the discredited Soviet elites. General Dzhokhar Dudayev, veteran of the Afghan war and former commander of an air force division in Estonia, led a Chechen "national revolution." He and his armed followers proclaimed the creation of a 750,000-strong "nation," the Republic of Chechnya, independent from the Soviet Union as well as the Russian Federation.[106]

In contrast to Kravchuk, who flew to a separatist Crimea, Yeltsin refused to do the same for Chechnya. He delegated the business of negotiating with separatists to Khasbulatov and Rutskoy. After the talks failed, on 7 November, the Russian President declared a state of emergency in the unrecognized republic. Rutskoy proposed to send in troops and even wanted to deploy the air force as back-up. Gorbachev was notified about it at the last moment and was horrified.

He was convinced that Yeltsin had made this decision in an alcoholic haze. He tried to call Yeltsin, but the Russian leader wasn't available to talk. Gorbachev then called Rutskoy to tell him that, as commander-in-chief, he would block any orders to the military and police that could ignite a war. This gave the military, as well as the Minister of the Interior, Viktor Barannikov, room to drag their feet on Yeltsin's decree. Meanwhile, the Russian parliament voted not to use military force in Chechnya and to withdraw their troops. Yeltsin was humiliated and blamed Rutskoy for what had happened.[107]

Yeltsin was also determined to take command of the military himself. The Army, however, was not just another post-Soviet item for sale. The Americans were keeping an eye on just how responsibly the Russian government would behave with regard to nuclear weapons. The formation of the Russian Army was delayed, to let Ukraine "determine its course" (*opredelitsia*). Yeltsin wanted Kravchuk to take full credit for the dismantling of the most important of the Union's structures.[108]

Yeltsin and his entourage also felt caught in their two-track approach when holding talks with the West on the subject of Soviet foreign debts. By the end of October, the External Economic Bank of the USSR (Vneshekonombank) was bankrupt. Soviet-owned banks in London, Singapore, and other foreign countries had to be refinanced or closed. The Russian Prime Minister, Ivan Silayev, appealed to the Paris Club of creditors for a delay in repayments and agreed to start discussing Soviet debts with the G-7. A team of experts from the G-7 arrived in Moscow in early November and stayed at the Oktyabrskaia Hotel for the rest of that month. They were stunned by the chaos of the Soviet finances. Many oil exports were in the hands of autonomous corporations and shady enterprises, and oil revenues weren't reaching the Ministry of Finance. Other state enterprises had also practically stopped sending to the State Bank the foreign currency they had earned from their export operations. No one, moreover, seemed to know what had happened to the Soviet gold reserves. And the Ministry of Finance had to send vast quantities of diamonds to the Bank of England as deposits to cover trade imbalances. The G-7 team decided to force the post-Soviet actors to reassert control over their finances. There would be no rescheduling and restructuring of Soviet debts, they told them. In the event of non-payment, Western countries would stop sending food and humanitarian assistance. The Western stance was more bluff than blackmail, yet such a firm position came as an ugly surprise to Yeltsin and Gaidar.[109] The US Treasury's David Mulford told the Russians that they would be eligible for IMF membership and Western credits only if they avoided a default. Mulford demanded that Russia provide one hundred tons of gold as collateral, Gaidar recalled. This diktat appalled him, reminding Gaidar of how the

Germans had forced the Bolsheviks at Brest-Litovsk in 1918 to surrender all the Russian gold reserves.[110] The G-7 team were indifferent to the fact that Russia needed its remaining currency and gold as a back-up to finance the urgent reforms.

Mulford recalled that there was "a lot of hostility around the table between . . . Ukraine and some of the others, and Russia." The Ukrainians claimed their right to Soviet assets, such as gold, diamonds, and currency reserves, but refused responsibility for Soviet liabilities. Other republics followed their example. When the Russian delegation proposed paying all Soviet debts in exchange for control over Soviet assets, the republics took this "as another manifestation of Russian imperialism." Gorbachev could feel vindicated, and the Russians had to pay now for all the sins of past imperial regimes.[111]

At a meeting of the Russian government, Pyotr Aven, the young Russian Minister of Foreign Economic Relations, proposed that Russia should suspend the debt talks. Galina Starovoitova, however, argued that Russia should agree to pay all Soviet debts: an easy task given its resources. This would send a signal to the world that Russia was now the sole legal successor to the USSR and the Russian Republic of 1917. Yeltsin balked: the Russian people would not accept this, and there would be no money to pay for food imports to cover the winter! Starovoitova countered: the West would let Russia off half of those debts, as it had done with Poland. And the debts of African countries to the USSR could be sold to foreign banks. The debt of Mozambique would be sufficient to feed St Petersburg through the winter. In the end, it was decided that Russia should remain in the talks to preserve its financial credibility and the network of former Soviet banks abroad. Gaidar issued a public declaration that Russia would not, from now on, honor any credits received by other republics or Gorbachev's provisional government without Russia's consent. The Western partners got the message. From now on Russia, instead of "the USSR," was the subject of international financial transactions.[112]

Gorbachev called Yeltsin on the evening of 3 December and suggested an immediate meeting with Kravchuk and Nazarbayev to conclude the Union Treaty. The Russian leader responded that "nothing would come of it anyway." Instead, he was in favor of a four-way alliance between Russia, Ukraine, Belorussia, and Kazakhstan. Gorbachev thundered: "And what would be my place in it? If that's the deal, then I'm leaving. I'm not going to bobble like a piece of shit in an ice hole." According to Gorbachev, Yeltsin was drunk and played the role of the village "Vanya" once again: "And what will we do without you, Mikhail Sergeyevich!" When Gorbachev again asked what his own role would be, Yeltsin replied in his stupor: "Well, just stay."[113]

DECLINE AND DOWNFALL

THE UKRAINIAN VOTE

In Washington, Bush and Scowcroft continued to worry about the danger of another coup in Moscow and Ukraine's nuclear weapons. On 24 October, the Rada declared that Ukraine wished to be a non-nuclear state. But did those words match their deeds? In early November, the US administration received important signals from Kravchuk's allies that eased their worst fears. The deputy head of the Ukrainian KGB, Yevgeny Marchuk, and the deputy Minister of the Interior, Valery Durdinets, conveyed to an American contact that the Ukrainian leadership was steering a more responsible course than it had demonstrated in public. There was a "plan" to dismantle nuclear weapons on Ukrainian territory under the international controls established before 1996. Marchuk and Durdinets informed the Americans that Kravchuk would allow Moscow to retain control of nuclear weapons. Moreover, he would not object to a removal of Ukrainian tactical and strategic weapons to the Russian Federation. In addition, Ukraine would make no attempt to take over the Black Sea fleet in Sevastopol, a big bone of contention with Russia. After those signals, Kravchuk's credibility in the White House increased significantly.[114]

By mid-November, all US diplomatic and intelligence agencies concurred that the referendum of 1 December would confirm Ukraine's independence. For Bush and Scowcroft, however, the vote posed a problem. Ukraine's voters "almost certainly would vote for sovereignty," recalled Scowcroft, "but not necessarily independent [sic] from the Soviet Union . . . What became clear to me was that Yeltsin was maneuvering so that the Ukraine would be the proximate cause of the break-up of the Soviet Union." Should the United States therefore announce its recognition of Ukraine straightaway and thus set the final break-up of the USSR in motion? Dick Cheney and his deputies in the Pentagon proposed just that. This, they argued, was "an insurance policy" against "a retrograde Russia." Without Ukraine's enormous resources, population, and geography, a Pentagon official recalled, Russia "would never become the threat posed by the Soviet Union."[115] The Secretary of State, James Baker, however, continued to object. An immediate recognition of Ukraine, he argued, would "destroy any chance for confederal and even bilateral arrangements that would make a peaceful transition possible." One had to be certain, he said, that Ukraine's referendum would not trigger "further fragmentation" of a Ukrainian state. Baker heeded Shevardnadze's warning of a possible conflict over Crimea, Donbass, and Eastern Ukraine. Scowcroft sympathized with Cheney's argument, yet he continued to insist that the United States should maintain "total neutrality" on the Ukrainian referendum, to avoid antagonizing Russian nationalists.[116]

INDEPENDENCE

Bush was torn between loyalty to his friend Gorbachev and the need to appeal to his domestic audience. The Republican Right held him responsible for raising taxes and for the economic recession, and they ridiculed his "Chicken Kiev" approach to the Soviet collapse. Many in the US Congress had already forgotten about Gorbachev's Nobel Peace Prize and still considered him and his circle "unreconstructed communists." With the referendum date quickly approaching, Bush and Scowcroft were forced to do something. On 25 November, at a meeting between the principals, the administration agreed that the United States would recognize Ukraine's independence, but only after a few weeks, in order to let Gorbachev and Yeltsin first make up their minds. US politics, however, caught up with Bush. At the suggestion of Cheney and John Sununu, the Chief of Staff, he received representatives of the Ukrainian diaspora and informed them confidentially of his decision. The American-Ukrainians immediately leaked the news to the press. Scowcroft recalled later: "While it didn't make any difference, it turned out it was a humiliation of Gorbachev, and given where we were, we shouldn't have done that."[117]

The announcement made a huge impression on the public mood in Ukraine. During the last week before the vote, Kravchuk redoubled his efforts to present the referendum as an existential choice between Soviet misery and future prosperity. The myth of Ukraine as "an economic superpower and breadbasket of Europe" that was feeding Russia and other republics, writes Serhii Plokhy, was "ingrained in the minds of the country's inhabitants."[118] The recognition of the United States, the most powerful and wealthiest country in the world, meant that a separate Ukraine would flourish, not perish. This myth would soon be painfully dashed. Ukraine's economy would tank, not soar. And US recognition would not be matched by financial generosity or investments.

Gorbachev continued to act as if Ukraine would stay in his Union—by virtue of economic and financial necessity, if not common roots and culture. On 19 November, Alexander Yakovlev met with Bush in the White House to deliver Gorbachev's message: even if Ukraine's referendum result was "yes" for independence, this should not necessarily mean that Ukraine would leave the Union with Russia. In the declassified portion of the conversation, Bush said that much depended on what was meant by independence. Yakovlev seconded: "Unfortunately, we have 1,000 different understandings of 'independence.'" When pressed, however, Yakovlev gave his personal opinion that Yeltsin would recognize Ukrainian independence after 1 December. He also did not think there was any danger of a "civil war" in Ukraine, between ethnic Ukrainians and heavily Russian areas of Donbass. This was not what Gorbachev wanted him to say.[119]

On 25 November, the Soviet leader made an appeal on state television to the people of Ukraine. He repeated his position that the Ukrainian referendum would not cancel the all-Union referendum in March. Like many other speeches by Gorbachev, this one produced the opposite effect. Kravchuk retorted: "Gorbachev has no right to speak on behalf of Ukraine . . . Let him say what he wants, and we will mind our business." In Moscow, television commentators ridiculed Gorbachev, and *Izvestia* blamed him for his awkward meddling in Ukrainian affairs. The liberal-minded *Independent Gazette* came up with the headline: "The empire is finished." One article urged Ukraine to keep its nuclear weapons, to defend itself, to deter aggressive Russian nationalists like Vladimir Zhirinovsky. Another article claimed that the emergence of a powerful, flour-ishing Ukraine next door would force Russia to bury its imperial dreams, in order to stay in Europe. Otherwise, it would have to look for its place in Asia.[120]

The news about American recognition of a future independent Ukraine enraged the Soviet leader. His press secretary Andrei Grachev proposed protesting against American interference in Soviet domestic affairs; Chernyaev penned the draft. Later, in 1992, the former leader Gorbachev would write that US recognition of an independent Ukraine tipped the delicate balance against the Union Treaty. He convinced himself that "the separatist position of Ukraine's leadership was 'a gift' to Yeltsin." Yeltsin, he argued, was unwilling to speak out against the Union publicly, for fear of antagonizing Russian public opinion. He was glad, however, to use Kravchuk's intransigence as an excuse to ruin the treaty.[121]

On 30 November 1991, Bush finally reached Gorbachev by telephone to explain his stance. The United States, he affirmed, would not recognize Ukraine until its leadership fulfilled the conditions on nuclear weapons, implementation of Soviet treaties, and on human rights. Gorbachev said he would refuse to take the vote for Ukraine's independence as the right to secede. Otherwise, he warned, a conflict between Ukraine and Russia could arise that would be worse than Yugoslavia. Yeltsin had "forces" in his camp who wanted to claim Crimea and Donbass for Russia. At this point Baker cut in: "Yes, yes, this is very dangerous." Bush also expressed empathy: "I am under a little pressure at home. I can't understand what you have been through, but people are piling up on me." American "delayed recognition" of Ukraine, he argued unconvincingly, might even help to bring Ukraine back to the idea of a new union by allaying nation-alist concerns.[122]

Five minutes later Bush called Yeltsin. He was prepared for a difficult conver-sation. Earlier he had received a letter from the Russian leader, who urged Bush not to recognize Ukraine immediately, because this would encourage the nationalist radicals. Ambassador Robert Strauss cabled from Moscow about his conversation with Kozyrev. The Russian Foreign Minister was imploring the Americans to help calm Russian fears about Ukrainian independence.[123] This time, however, Yeltsin reversed his own position from a few days earlier. He told Bush that if more than 70 percent of Ukrainians voted for independence—more than had voted for the preservation of the Union in March—then Russia would recognize Ukraine's independence immediately. Bush asked: "Right away?" Yeltsin said: "Yes, we need to do it immediately. Otherwise our position is unclear, since we are approaching . . . a new reform." If recognition of Ukraine's independence was linked to any conditions, Yeltsin said, this would only cause "an uprising of extremist forces" and "would have a very negative effect on democracy." Yeltsin also announced his idea of meeting with Kravchuk after the referendum: "I think the new Ukrainian president will not begin negotiations with Gorbachev, but will begin talks with Russia." He confided to Bush: "Gorbachev does not know it. He still thinks that Ukraine will sign [the Union Treaty]." Russia, he explained, did not want a union with "five Islamic states" in Central Asia, "whom we feed all the time." Yeltsin's intention was clear: after the Ukrainian referendum he wanted to dissolve the Soviet Union and reach an agreement with the Slavic republics.[124]

The vote on 1 December astonished even the most enthusiastic advocates of Ukrainian independence. The referendum bulletin read: "Do you support the Act of declaration of independence by Ukraine?" Some 28.8 million voters, or 84 percent of the registered electorate, came to the polls. Over 90 percent of them voted "yes." In some areas of Western Ukraine 97–99 percent voted in favor. The referendum was monitored by international observers and countless watchers from the diasporas, who had come to witness this historic moment. Astonishingly, 84 percent voted "yes" in the Luhansk and Donetsk regions of Eastern Ukraine. In Crimea, 54 percent voted "yes" and in Sevastopol, "the city of Russian glory," 57 percent did, although many didn't show up to vote. Many voters later claimed they had been fooled and did not expect the referendum would lead to the end of the Soviet Union. Yet the fantasy of future Ukrainian prosperity—against the background of the Soviet economic crisis—clearly worked. Kravchuk won solidly in all regions of Ukraine, except Galicia. He received 19.6 million votes and a huge popular mandate.[125]

On 2 December, Yeltsin called Kravchuk to congratulate him on his victory and tell him that Russia would recognize Ukraine after the full results of the vote were announced. He was looking forward to receiving a Ukrainian ambassador. Poland and Canada immediately declared their formal recognition. Gorbachev agonized over how to respond, but he held his line that the vote changed nothing: independence did not mean divorce from the Union. Bush called Kravchuk on 3 December and congratulated him on a "wonderful display of democracy" in Ukraine. He said he would send a special emissary "to consult on the US-Ukraine relations." The American President, despite the political pressure, stayed the course of delayed recognition. Kravchuk informed him that "this Saturday" he would meet with Yeltsin in Minsk "to discuss all issues of our policy, and the priority considerations in relations with the Russian republic." "Very important," Bush reacted. "It's wonderful."[126]

Galina Starovoitova decided to demonstrate that Russian democrats would welcome Ukraine's independence. She bought a bouquet of roses and went to see the plenipotentiary for the Ukrainian republic, Pyotr Kryzhanovsky. She congratulated him on the first day of Ukrainian independence. "He was thunderstruck," Starovoitova recalled. "He called Kravchuk in my presence and said in Ukrainian that for the first time in his life a lady gave him flowers." Then she added laughing: "They expected tanks more than flowers."[127]

CHAPTER 15

LIQUIDATION

Two Romes have fallen, a third stands, and a fourth there will not be.
Monk Philotheus, Pskov, 1524

We . . . acknowledge that the USSR as a subject
of international law and a geopolitical reality
ceases to exist.
The agreement on a Commonwealth of
Independent States, Minsk, 8 December 1991

Leonid Kravchuk later claimed that Ukraine's referendum became the last push that led to the collapse of the Soviet Empire. "Ukraine should take credit for it."[1] The evidence contradicts this claim. The Ukrainian referendum was a reflection of the Soviet collapse, not its cause. On 2 December 1991, the Soviet Union was already a carcass, destroyed first by Gorbachev's reforms and then by the implacable separatism of Yeltsin's course of action. The financial obituary of the Soviet Union tells the story of its destruction best. In 1986 and 1987, the years of Chernobyl and the vodka deficit, the Ministry of Finance printed only 3.9 and 5.9 billion rubles respectively. By contrast, in 1988–89, when the Laws on Enterprises and Cooperatives punched permanent holes in the financial system, the injections of ruble liquidity increased respectively to 11.7 and 18.3 billion. In 1990 parliamentary populism, the sovereignty of republics and their "war of laws" against the central government made the ministry print 28.4 billion rubles. In 1991, as Gorbachev devolved authority to the republics, the infusion of rubles rose to 93.4 billion. The "savings" of the Soviet population grew exponentially, yet they quickly turned into worthless piles of paper. A state that could not ensure its main function, a stable currency, was bound to fall apart.[2]

What happened in December was the coup de grâce for Gorbachev and his fantasy of a voluntary Union. And it was delivered by Yeltsin's new course. Ukraine's vote did not change the choices of the Yeltsin government. As we have seen, in anticipation of Ukraine's independence, Gaidar and his team had already been preparing to take over the functions of the fictional center. After the Ukrainian vote, the Russian reformers were finally free to liquidate this center.

COUP DE GRÂCE

Yeltsin did not articulate his plans to his own government, riddled as it was with factionalism and intrigues. Later, some members of the Russian government claimed that what happened in a forest in Belarus (now the name for Belorussia) a few days later was at least in part a planned conspiracy. The evidence is more nuanced. Yeltsin did not want to antagonize an independent Ukraine. At the same time, he assumed that Kravchuk would badly need an agreement with the RSFSR for his own international legitimacy. "Both of us," Starovoitova recalled, "had an erroneous impression" that Kravchuk's decision to take "a crucial step outside the norms of international law" would depend on Yeltsin's consent.[3]

Yeltsin flew to Minsk on 7 December with a group of loyal ministers and advisors: Burbulis, Gaidar, Shakhrai, Kozyrev, and his personal aide Viktor Ilyushin. Others, including Rutskoy, Stankevich, Lukin, the parliamentary leaders and ministers, were not even informed of the preparations.[4] Before leaving Moscow, Yeltsin met with Gorbachev and assured him that his mission was to invite Kravchuk back into the talks on the Union Treaty. Burbulis insisted in his recollections that Yeltsin did not cheat the Soviet leader at all. "It was absolutely our goodwill and our conscientious stand." Yeltsin never stated as much.[5]

Gaidar also claimed he did not know what would happen in Minsk.[6] His official actions, however, suggest otherwise. On 1 December, the Russian top economist hastily prepared a slew of decrees. One decree placed under Russian state control all Soviet conglomerates and consortiums that had emerged in 1989–90 and operated on the territory of Ukraine, Kazakhstan, Belarus, and other republics. Another decree liberalized prices in the Russian Federation from 2 January 1992. The document declared that trade with the "former union republics" would be conducted "as a rule at world prices." These documents constituted the act of liquidation for the Soviet Union. Yeltsin signed the decrees on 3 December.[7]

Yeltsin was invited to Minsk by Shushkevich and the Belarus Prime Minister, Vyacheslav Kebich, on 24 November, during a chat on the margins of the State

LIQUIDATION

Council. Belarus was in dire need of oil and gas from Siberia. Shushkevich promised Yeltsin a good rest after talks that they would be holding in a hunting lodge and resort at Viskuli. This complex for the highest Party nomenklatura was located in the middle of Belovezha forest, fifty miles from Brest and only five miles from the Soviet-Polish border. A few days later, Yeltsin called Shushkevich and asked him to invite Kravchuk to Viskuli as well.[8] On the afternoon of 7 December, Shushkevich shuttled between Minsk and its modest airport to greet Yeltsin and take him to the parliament of Belarus and then, in a separate ceremony, to welcome Kravchuk and fly with him to a military air base near Viskuli.

Formerly a student and professor of physics, Shushkevich had already had a brush with history in having tutored Lee Harvey Oswald. President John F. Kennedy's future assassin had defected to the USSR in 1959 and requested Soviet citizenship. Oswald had lived and worked in Minsk with his Russian wife Marina before returning with her and their daughter to the United States in 1962. The KGB had considered young Shushkevich trustworthy and discreet enough to give Russian lessons to the dissolute young American. Shushkevich never thought his pupil capable of killing an American President.[9]

Perestroika had convinced Shushkevich, still a Party member, to become a democratic politician. In March 1989, he was elected from Minsk to the Congress of People's Deputies, and joined the Russian opposition along with Sakharov, Afanasyev, Burbulis, and others. He opposed the junta in August 1991 and was elected head of the republic's Supreme Soviet. By that time, he had come to view Belarus as a colony of the Soviet Empire.[10]

Viskuli was a place where Khrushchev and Brezhnev had hunted. A list of foreign guests included Fidel and Raúl Castro and Erich Honecker. In the evening of Saturday 7 December 1991, the place was guarded by a special KGB force to ensure absolute security and secrecy of the talks among the three Slavic republics. Yeltsin and the Russian team arrived last from Minsk. Kravchuk had already shot a boar while out hunting and had rested. The leaders and their retinues met for an evening chat. The conversation quickly became political: what to do about Gorbachev and the Soviet Union? Kravchuk had come with Prime Minister Vitold Fokin and three nationalist deputies from Rukh who were there to ensure that Kravchuk would not "sell out" to the Muscovites. Yeltsin told Kravchuk that he had a duty to perform: to convey Gorbachev's invitation to join the Union Treaty. The Russian leader theatrically declared he was ready to sign the Union Treaty "here and now" if Kravchuk agreed to do the same. The President-elect of Ukraine listened to this performance with a wry smile. He replied that Ukraine had suffered and now had earned its statehood; the referendum did not give him a mandate to sign an agreement with the center. Pressing his point home, he mockingly asked: Who is Gorbachev?

Where is the Kremlin? The Rukh deputies grumbled that perhaps they should fly back to Kiev. Only Fokin, worried about the state of the Ukrainian economy, quietly lobbied for some kind of economic treaty.[11]

Yeltsin knew that Kravchuk would reject Gorbachev's Union Treaty. He did not expect, however, that the Ukrainians would refuse to sign an agreement with him. Burbulis and Gaidar were surprised as well. This jeopardized the future of the Russian reforms. By contrast, the delegation from Belarus was cooperative and reasonable. The head of Belarus's government, Vyacheslav Kebich, a Soviet-style economic manager, knew that the republic could not survive without cheap Russian energy. He viewed nationalists and democrats in the Belarus parliament as lunatics who were ready to sacrifice their industries in a fit of ideological madness. Kebich sent his deputy to sit with Yeltsin's ministers, to work out a possible draft of an economic agreement between the two republics, which Ukraine could join as well. It was late at night when Yeltsin's legal advisor Sergey Shakhrai came up with a revolutionary idea. The USSR had been formed in December 1922 by four republics; three of them were represented in Viskuli; the fourth, the Trans-Caucasian republic, no longer existed. What if they now decided to dissolve the Soviet Union? Shakhrai was improvising as he spoke. Publicly, Yeltsin, Kravchuk, and even Burbulis had said many times that the Treaty of 1922 was the fig leaf that the Bolsheviks had used to camouflage their totalitarian policies. Now Shakhrai was proposing to use this fig leaf to destroy legally what Lenin had constructed by force. Burbulis recalled it was a stroke of luck that President Nazarbayev had not come to Viskuli. His presence would have ruined the plot, because the Kazakh SSR had joined the Soviet Union only in 1936.[12]

To placate Kravchuk, the Russians and the Belarus officials agreed to drop the word "union" from any future agreement. Instead, they would form a "commonwealth of independent states," borrowing the example of the British Commonwealth that had seen a civilized divorce between the center and its colonies. Gaidar wrote down the draft of an agreement to form the new Commonwealth, but his handwriting was difficult to read. Andrei Kozyrev, the Russian Foreign Minister, was tasked with finding someone to type the documents up. That "someone" was a female typist whom the KGB brought to Viskuli. As it was now 4 a.m., Kozyrev found a room where he believed the typist was sleeping and slid the handwritten draft under the door. He got the wrong door, however. On the next morning it took a while to find the draft and type it up.[13]

On Sunday, 8 December, Burbulis announced Shakhrai's idea to the principals who were seated at the conference table after breakfast. Shushkevich recalled Burbulis proclaiming: "Esteemed Lords! Would you agree to put your signatures under the following proposal: 'The USSR ceases to exist as a subject of international law and a geopolitical reality'?" This seemed to be a way to suspend the Russian-Ukrainian dispute about the legal succession: all three republics would act as equals. In the chorus of voices, Yeltsin declared: "The Commonwealth would be a message that would give hope to people and the world, not to scare them. It would be construction, not destruction. Who needs the USSR, the CPSU and now the Union of Sovereign States any more?" Kebich also recalled the Russian leader saying: "Gorbachev must be removed. Enough! No more playing the tsar."[14]

Kravchuk, to everyone's delight, agreed to sign the proposal. The principals sent their teams, led by Burbulis, Fokin, and Kebich, to a nearby billiard room, to write up the final document. Some points for a Commonwealth agreement were taken directly from the bilateral treaties that Russia, Ukraine, and Belorussia (Belarus) had signed in 1990. Among the potential disagreements was the one about control of nuclear weapons. Kravchuk recalled that this was discussed in great detail. He insisted that the three republics would have equal control, and Yeltsin consented—at least he appeared to.[15]

Before Yeltsin's departure from Moscow, Galina Starovoitova had advised him to offer the Ukrainian leader an option of negotiated changes to the borders after a moratorium of three to five years. She was concerned about Crimea. Reflecting on the Armenian-Azeri dispute in Nagorny-Karabagh, Starovoitova wanted to give time to the people of Crimea to think and decide whether they wanted to stay in Ukraine or return to Russia. This option would have helped to placate Russian public opinion and leave open the possibility of settling the territorial issue according to international law. Yeltsin, however, did not raise this issue in Viskuli. Burbulis explained the reason: Kravchuk had arrived in a triumphalist mood and would not even have given such a proposal a second thought. Starovoitova believed it was a political mistake not to raise this issue at all. Had she been invited to Viskuli, she would have done so. The meeting, however, was a wholly male affair, apart from female typists and waitresses. "In Russian politics," Starovoitova commented, "many things are decided in the steam room of a spa, with drinking, with rough language, and the presence of a woman would have been a purely technical obstacle. This is why they left me out."[16]

The first paragraph of the agreement on the Commonwealth included Shakhrai's formula. When it was agreed, the room rang out with cries of "hurrah"; other points were quickly drafted and agreed. Yeltsin said that he would drink a glass of champagne to each article. There were fourteen, and by the end of the talks the President of Russia was unable to speak coherently. The formal ceremony took place around 2 p.m. Yeltsin, Kravchuk, and Shushkevich signed the documents, as well as Kebich, Fokin, and Burbulis. Some 160 journalists had arrived, intrigued by the proceedings. They spent the night in a nearby village, in miserable conditions and without food. Now they were told that the Soviet Union was no more. All federal structures and agencies on the territories of Russia, Ukraine, and Belarus became invalid. The Commonwealth of Independent States (CIS) would have its headquarters in Minsk. The texts of the foundational documents were not available for distribution.[17]

Yeltsin in his ghostwritten diary recalled a "sudden feeling of freedom and lightness" that overwhelmed him when he realized that "the last hour of the empire" had arrived. He also wrote that "another way" was feasible for him: to take Gorbachev's place, run for the presidency of the USSR, and keep the country together. Why did he not take this road? Yeltsin remained cryptic on this matter: "I could not psychologically take the place of Gorbachev."[18] Psychology alone does not explain the demise of the Soviet Union in Viskuli, but it does shed light on how the new potentates performed then and later. The three Slavic leaders would insist for years that the Soviet Union had already been dead when they met. Yet they behaved at the meeting as if it were an act of ritual killing. Kravchuk recalled that Yeltsin was very tense and released his tension with alcohol. Kozyrev recalls that Yeltsin drank heavily in Viskuli, because "he had no clear vision of the outcome and was not sure he would do the right thing. So, he acted erratically, and only re-established a firm footing when he realized that a peaceful solution to the puzzle of a crumbling Soviet state and the creation of a new commonwealth was at hand."[19]

Kravchuk, for all his post-election bravado, also felt insecure. He recalled that Viskuli was "not for people with weak nerves." He slept very little there and at night read some kind of memo he had written for himself, but which nobody saw. The recollections of the Belarus participants varied from anxiety to panic. The leaders who met to dissolve the Soviet Union in Viskuli couldn't stop thinking about the KGB and military officers who protected them there yet who had sworn an oath of allegiance to the country that was being dissolved. Kebich recalled that the head of Belarus's KGB whispered to him that he had informed his superiors in the central KGB in Moscow about "a coup d'état" in progress. "I am waiting for Gorbachev's command!" he added. Kebich felt shivers down his spine. He asked: "Do you think the command will be given?" "Of course," replied the KGB officer. "The fact of high state treason is clear and unmistakable. You must understand. I could not sit idle. I took the oath." Yevgenia Pateichuk, a professional typist whom the KGB had brought to Viskuli, was an ethnic Ukrainian, yet the text she was asked to type shocked her. Her fingers failed her, and she made an error in the very first word.[20]

In his memoirs, Yeltsin mentioned that Gorbachev, had he not been removed, would have become "a tool of evil forces." Quite the psychological subterfuge! The Russian President could hardly have feared that the Soviet leader would use force. At the same time, Yeltsin must have sensed the colossal uncertainty that his actions had created. His bodyguard Korzhakov, a former KGB officer himself, explained the mood: "Dual power is fraught with danger because in such a period people stop recognizing any authority. Gorbachev was no longer taken seriously; people ridiculed him. But Yeltsin still lacked the levers of power. This situation in effect was worse than anarchy." In his memoirs, Gaidar compared the moment to the Russian anarchy of 1917. The military could not be relied upon. The crisis in Chechnya demonstrated that "the state has no army . . . its behavior was hard to control." As for the police, they had simply disappeared.[21] Yeltsin must have felt an enormous emotional conflict at this historic moment. A former Russian peasant from the village of Butka in the Urals had just disbanded the realm that Peter the Great and Catherine the Great had built, and which Lenin and Stalin had resurrected. It was the Soviet Union that had defeated Hitler's armies, the country with which Yeltsin had identified until only very recently. And how would those tens of millions of people, who had voted for him and for Russia's sovereignty, feel when they learnt that their common home had been taken away from them?

The natural remedy for anxiety, aside from alcohol, was to find new sources of legitimacy. Kravchuk could lean on the overwhelming victory he had earned in the Ukrainian referendum. Yeltsin had no such outlet. His rationale was negative: Gorbachev's government did not work. He even refused to call the Soviet leader. "The USSR does not exist anymore," he said. "Gorbachev is not the president any longer, his decrees are nothing for us." A few hours later, after spending time in a spa, Yeltsin decided that Gorbachev must be informed, but he delegated this unpleasant task to Shushkevich. Yeltsin, instead, wanted to call George Bush. One ironic aspect in this astonishing liquidation drama was that Yeltsin yearned for American approval even more acutely than did Kravchuk.[22]

Shushkevich and other participants said later that they called Bush and Gorbachev simultaneously. Bush answered immediately, Gorbachev did not. Kozyrev in his memoirs recalls that it was his job to connect Yeltsin with Bush, and he was completely unprepared for the task. This was years before mobile phones and instantaneous global connectivity. Kozyrev searched through his pocket notebook and found there the State Department phone number. It was early Sunday in Washington. Kozyrev talked his way up from an incredulous receptionist to someone high enough to arrange a top-level conversation. Kozyrev's estimate was that this operation took him thirty minutes. If this is true, then the story of calls being placed to Bush and Gorbachev simultaneously was a fantasy. In any case, Shushkevich recalled hearing Yeltsin talking to Bush while he waited for Gorbachev to pick up the receiver. Yet all the recollections are remarkably vague timewise—perhaps another indication of the anxiety that had gripped all the participants in this drama.[23]

Only the American record is precise. It was 9:08 p.m. in Viskuli and Moscow, and 1:08 p.m. in Washington, when Bush answered the call. Yeltsin did all the talking. The three leaders, he said, had decided that "the system and the Union Treaty *everyone is pushing us to sign* [author's italics] does not satisfy us." He quoted bits and pieces from the Commonwealth declaration, praising it as "the only way out of the critical situation" and an effort to strengthen international peace and security. Yeltsin hastened to add that its members recognized all Soviet commitments "including foreign debts" and "the unitary control of nuclear weapons and non-proliferation." In a moment of confusion, he told Bush about "sixteen articles" of the agreement, instead of the actual fourteen. He said that he had just spoken with Nazarbayev, who "is fully in accord with all of our actions and he wants to sign the accord." That was wishful thinking at best. The Kazakh leader learned about the accords only after the event, and refused to join. For Yeltsin, however, it was crucial to report to Washington that all four former Soviet nuclear republics were in agreement.[24]

Before Bush could even respond, Yeltsin clarified: "President Gorbachev does not know these results." He begged for "understanding." Bush asked: "What do you think the center's reaction would be?" Yeltsin responded that the Commonwealth was taking Soviet strategic forces and the rest of the Army under its joint control. "As a matter of fact, Shaposhnikov fully agreed and supported our position." The head of the Ministry of Defense was indeed the first person that Yeltsin had called from Viskuli on the secure government phone. In his memoirs, Shaposhnikov confirmed this version of events; he immediately accepted Yeltsin's offer. Thus, he became the first senior officer who reneged on his oath and shifted his loyalties. Shaposhnikov's example would soon be followed by countless others. Bush thanked Yeltsin for his "special courtesy to the United States." He added: "We realize this must be sorted out by participants, not by outside parties like the United States." This sounded very much like a formula of delayed recognition. Yeltsin lapped it up: "We will guarantee it, Mr President."[25]

On Yeltsin's orders, Andrei Kolosovsky, the young head of the Russian mission in Washington, was instructed to meet with US officials and answer their questions on the spot. For some reason, Kozyrev failed to fax the documents signed at Viskuli via his ministry. Perhaps he did not want to. Kolosovsky's mission was located inside the Soviet Embassy, and the documents could have been passed to Gorbachev. Kozyrev turned to his American friend Allen Weinstein, director of the Center for Democracy, who happened to be in Moscow at the time. Weinstein had recently opened a Moscow-based office of the Center, courtesy of Yeltsin, and was glad to help out. On Monday, 9 December, he faxed the documents on the dissolution of the Soviet Union to his deputy in Washington DC with a note: "Please deliver this memo and the accompanying text to Andrei Kolosovsky—PERSONAL HAND DELIVERY ONLY—at the Soviet Embassy ASAP." Weinstein added to the message his greetings to Kolosovsky and "best of luck in his historic meetings" in Washington.[26]

On the substantive side, Burbulis, Kebich, and Fokin signed a two-page document, largely drafted by Gaidar, to coordinate the economic policies of the three republics. The governments of Ukraine, Belarus, and the Russian Federation agreed to "refrain from any actions that could cause economic harm to others." They confirmed they would stay in the ruble zone, and would introduce a new national currency only after a special agreement between them. The troika also pledged to keep money-printing to a minimum, to create a system to control mutual transactions, and to keep their borders open after liberalization of trade and prices. Kravchuk later admitted: "We agreed that borders between Ukraine, Belarus, and the Russian Federation did not exist—only borders of [the Commonwealth]." This was the best Gaidar could get from Ukraine to limit its possible harmful actions. In turn, Yeltsin promised to cover the costs of the never-ending works to keep the destroyed Chernobyl power plant safe. And he made a concession, agreed in advance, that economic liberalization would start on 2 January, to allow the partners to prepare for the shock. Gaidar considered this a big sacrifice. The hoarding of goods in expectation of high prices continued for two more weeks. The spring of inflation would then recoil with even greater force. He did not trust Ukraine to keep to the agreements—and he was right.[27]

Gaidar recalled: "I am proud that we then managed to avoid a full-scale civil war like the Yugoslav scenario, and in a nuclear country." Burbulis agreed that "a bloody partition of the empire" was prevented. He also claimed that the Viskuli meeting "ended the Cold War" and "created miraculous prospects for a new global order." Kravchuk many years later confessed that he also feared a civil war and felt relieved. Ukraine signed up to the agreements because it could not really control its economy. "Russia emphasized that [the Commonwealth] was a form of slow divorce."[28] This last point would define Russian relations with Ukraine and Belarus for years to come.

AMERICAN RECOGNITION

The Viskuli documents came under legal attack in Moscow. The constitutional committee of the USSR, a body of professional experts, declared that the Viskuli accords had "no legal force." The founding republics of the 1922 treaty had no right to dissolve the Union they had once created. In his MID office, Shevardnadze wanted to issue a declaration of protest. "Did you want a civil war?" he asked Burbulis. "Three republics had no right to do it. They cannot remove Gorbachev. It is an anti-constitutional coup." Burbulis's friend Nikolai Travkin tried in vain to mobilize street protests.[29] This storm in a teacup lasted for two days—and then stopped. People did not care for either Gorbachev or the constitution.

A journalist once asked Gaidar why Gorbachev did not use force to stop the liquidation of the USSR. Gaidar answered: "And did he have at least one combat-ready regiment at his disposal?" The Russian reformer argued that Gorbachev "most probably did not want to use force, but what is certain, he also could not use it." William Taubman concedes that Gorbachev "would have been mad not to explore this possibility," but his exploration was "very mild" and "half-hearted." In theory, Gorbachev could have used "Alfa." In practice, the KGB commandos would not have obeyed his orders.[30]

Notorious for his use of Russian profanities, Gorbachev resorted to them liberally on 8–9 December as a fig leaf for his political impotence. When Shushkevich called him to announce the Commonwealth, the Soviet President demanded that all three leaders come to Moscow and present their decision to the State Council. Kravchuk flatly refused, flew back to Kiev and stayed at his dacha, protected by loyal Spetsnaz. The Belarus leaders stayed in Viskuli, protected by the KGB, feeling it was safer than returning to Minsk. Yeltsin was left to conduct the unpleasant task alone. On Monday, 9 December, he arrived at the Kremlin with a fully armed escort organized by Korzhakov. This was the last time Gorbachev treated Yeltsin like a wayward baron. The Russian leader hated swear words, but Gorbachev didn't care. The Soviet leader recalled he spoke Realpolitik to Yeltsin. Nazarbayev, who was present, recalled Gorbachev's line of questioning: What will happen to the strategic forces? Who will man the borders? What will occur in other republics? How could he trust Kravchuk? The Baltic leaders had also promised to fix all problems, yet they reneged on their promises after extracting from Russia what they wanted. Now they declare: "Russians out!" Yeltsin stood up to leave, but Gorbachev said: "Well, sit down. But tell me what we shall tell people tomorrow?" Yeltsin told Kravchuk later: "I never want to have that kind of conversation with anyone ever again."[31]

The effect of Gorbachev's verbal offensive was nil. The State Council never reconvened again, and the Silayev-Yavlinsky economic committee was dead. Gorbachev, however, told his entourage that "he is determined to fight to the end." He would convene the Congress of People's Deputies and demand a new referendum. His advisors tried to dissuade him. He no longer controlled any funds, and could not even pay for convening a Congress without Yeltsin's consent. The best option was to resign. Every day in the Kremlin made the

President of the USSR look ever more pathetic, clinging on to his office. Gorbachev's aides began to move top-secret documents from their safes to their home archives, while the Kremlin guards were still not searching them at the exit. Chernyaev carried piles of cables, memos, and notes of Politburo and other meetings away from his office in his briefcase, to store them at home. Shakhnazarov, Medvedev, and others did the same. Later, those documents would form the archive of the Gorbachev Foundation.[32]

Meanwhile, Burbulis took care of the main structures of power. He called Bakatin, the head of the rump KGB, as well as Primakov, in charge of foreign intelligence. He then sent Ivanenko to negotiate with them both. According to Bakatin, the message was: the Russian government "counted on our good behavior, cautioned against any 'actions,' and asked us to ensure order." Bakatin was surprised: "Neither Primakov nor I have ever thought of creating disorder. We were brought up this way." Two days later, he had a chance to ask Yeltsin what would happen to the KGB apparatus. Would it be relocated to Minsk, the capital of the Commonwealth? Yeltsin replied that one should not ask such naïve questions and take everything at face value. All the main structures of power would remain in Moscow.[33]

Yeltsin consolidated his control of the military. Shaposhnikov greeted his new boss at Vnukovo Airport upon Yeltsin's arrival from Minsk. The Russian democrats, however, continued to fear the former Soviet military. One advisor warned Yeltsin that one "cannot exclude a spontaneous explosion which neo-Stalinist forces might exploit to restore the old system." Yeltsin appointed Pavel Grachev, the man who had not arrested him on 19 August, to be Shaposhnikov's deputy. Two days later, Yeltsin invited the top military command, about fifty men, to a conference at the Russian parliament. Shaposhnikov presided over the tightly scripted meeting. Yeltsin's message was that Russia had taken under its wing a more than three-million-strong Army, preserving the unity of command and control. This would save the military from falling prey to national extremists, gangs, and profiteers. Soviet forces located along non-Russian peripheries of the former USSR, including the Baltics, South Caucasus, and Central Asia, would either be withdrawn or stay legitimately, with the consent of the new states. The Black Sea fleet would not be ceded to Ukraine. No one would ask the military to take another oath. Yeltsin promised the military he would double their salaries—an effective way to ensure their loyalty.[34]

That same day, Gorbachev arrived at the Ministry of Defense. He said many of the same things that Yeltsin had already announced, but nobody was listening. "He had nothing substantive to say," recalled Shaposhnikov. Nor did Gorbachev have any money to pay the salaries of the military. Yeltsin became de facto commander-in-chief. He also replaced the head of the Kremlin regiment with his own man. He was now in control of all government communications, including Gorbachev's own phones.[35] The briefcase with nuclear codes (*chemodanchik*) was still with Gorbachev, yet he could not use it without Yeltsin's consent.

Gorbachev's last ally was Nazarbayev. The Kazakh leader arrived in Moscow at Gorbachev's request on the day the troika dissolved the USSR. Then Shushkevich phoned him from Viskuli and invited him to come and add his signature to the Commonwealth documents. Nazarbayev was offended by his exclusion from the plot and decided to remain with Gorbachev. He recalled that Yeltsin arrived at the Kremlin on Monday, 9 December, showing signs of a strong hangover. "He cut a painful figure." The Kazakh leader was caught in a bind. He knew that his republic would be heavily dependent on Russia's resources and Yeltsin's goodwill. He called the leaders of the other republics in Central Asia and learnt that they thought the same. None of them wanted to side with Gorbachev against Yeltsin. Nazarbayev immediately returned to Alma-Ata.[36]

Yeltsin told Bush that Kazakhstan had joined the Commonwealth, yet the reality was different. The Russian leader recognized that this republic should be part of the Commonwealth, because six million Russians lived there. At the same time, he wanted to keep "the Muslim" republics of Uzbekistan, Tajikistan, Kirgizstan, and Turkmenistan, with their fast-growing populations, out of the Commonwealth. Shevardnadze, who met with Yeltsin on 4 December, told him that Central Asia would become a geopolitical problem, an Islamic hothouse and a playground for other great powers, including communist China. Yeltsin listened attentively. Gaidar and his economists urged him to let go of the heavily subsidized Central Asian republics as they were a net burden for the Russian budget. Inadvertently, however, Yeltsin's actions forced Nazarbayev to create a bloc of the excluded non-Slavic Asian republics.[37] When Yeltsin persuaded him to return from Alma-Ata, the Kazakh leader set out his conditions. He agreed to join only together with the four Central Asian presidents. Moreover, the Commonwealth treaty, he insisted, had to be renegotiated and signed in Alma-Ata. Yeltsin ordered Kozyrev to figure out how to do that without losing face. The Foreign Minister discovered "a Polish precedent." In 1945, Poland was not able to attend the founding conference of the United Nations, but it was later added to the roster of founding nations. It was a specious analogy, but Kozyrev had nothing better up his sleeve.[38]

In Kiev and Minsk, the parliaments had already approved the Viskuli accords. Yeltsin, now backed by the military, addressed the leaders of factions in the Russian Supreme Soviet. He explained that the Commonwealth was the only choice on the table: "The main task was not to have Russia and Ukraine on the opposite sides of the barricades." If Ukraine had its own Army, currency, state borders, "there would be no peace between Russia and Ukraine." He then repeated what Bernstam and Yavlinsky had said earlier: an agreement on the common ruble zone with Ukraine had helped to forestall an economic war: otherwise, a "ruble avalanche" from Ukraine would have flooded the Russian economy. He elaborated on this theme the next day in his speech to the parliament. Had Russia not agreed with Ukraine, "tomorrow our reality could be a trade blockade, closed borders, and economic wars . . . The worst that could have happened would be a war using nuclear weapons." The Commonwealth of Independent States (CIS), Yeltsin confidently concluded, was the only path towards reintegration of the common post-Soviet space. Ukraine and Belarus would not stop the transit of Russian oil and gas to Europe. Even those deputies who had wanted to reconstruct a new union around Russia voted for the ratification; there was no other option in sight. A total of 188 deputies voted to approve the Commonwealth accord, seven abstained, six voted against. The parliamentarians also decided to recall their deputies from the Union's Supreme Soviet, thereby disabling the last constitutional body that could have opposed the Commonwealth accords. Finally, it was decided to remove the words "Soviet" and "Socialist" from the republic's full official name. The RSFSR officially became the Russian Federation or simply "Russia."[39]

Yeltsin and his lieutenants regarded this vote and lack of protest against the Viskuli decisions as de facto legitimation. Sergey Shakhrai became deputy head of the Russian government for "legal support of reforms"; he now supervised the forces of law and order. Shakhnazarov later compared Shakhrai to one of those lawyers on whom Napoleon had relied to justify his conquests.[40] Burbulis recalled that "world history is rich with precedents when legitimacy in law emerges post factum, after an accomplished act . . . I always note with surprise and admiration, that on the 8th, or the 9th, or the 10th of December . . . not a single government body, not a single military unit" protested against the dissolution of the Soviet Union.[41] Many supported the end of dual power; they expected Yeltsin, the man with political will and radical actions, to pull the country out of its economic morass. In Moscow, the polls showed 84 percent of the population in favor of the Commonwealth accord.[42] Popular discontent would arise a few weeks afterwards. Two years later, it would grow into a political tornado that would cause a constitutional crisis in Russia and would almost cost Yeltsin his job.

Gorbachev, regarded mostly with contempt and indifference, lingered on. "Petty minds," was his reaction to the decisions of the Russian parliament. "The era of Gorbachev only begins now." In his long interview with the editor of the *Independent Gazette*, the leader without a country did not admit he had made any mistakes. "I do not know any happy reformers," Gorbachev said. "And I am content with my destiny." What would he do next? "I'm keeping that to myself," he replied. "Who in the world knows what is on Gorbachev's mind?" Gorbachev's calculations no longer mattered. He was about to be history.[43]

On the day the Russian parliament ratified the Commonwealth documents, Burbulis traveled to Paris and Brussels. "We wrote a memorandum and went to all the leading countries," he recalled. Yeltsin wanted the international community to accept what he had done. Only about a month before, President Mitterrand had hosted Mikhail and Raisa Gorbachev in his country house; they spoke about world affairs and a new world order. Now, the French leader sat listening to Yeltsin's strategist. "I told him," Burbulis recalled, "we managed to abolish the most totalitarian empire of the twentieth century with the maximum of legitimacy, within the Soviet constitution," and with a peaceful transfer of nuclear weapons to Russia. Mitterrand could not restrain his emotions and raised his arms in astonishment, Burbulis recalled. The French leader said: "We could not even imagine that this could be done!"[44]

Yeltsin and Burbulis attributed even more significance to meetings with Jacques Delors of the European Commission and Manfred Wörner, the Secretary-General of NATO. After Burbulis repeated to Wörner what he had told Mitterrand, he added that Russian reformers "decisively consider the possibility of joining NATO, as part of our primary mission to remove all conditions for confrontation." Burbulis recalled that his words left Wörner "confused, if not shocked. He was silent for a couple of minutes and then looked into my eyes and said: 'Mr State Secretary. Your confession is very unexpected for me. I think this is a very complicated task.' And almost without searching for arguments, he said: 'You are such an enormous country. I cannot imagine under what configuration this may become reality.' "[45]

Burbulis recalled he was quite perplexed by the Western lack of enthusiasm at the prospect of including a democratic Russia in NATO. He and Yeltsin continued, however, to pin their hopes on the Americans. The Russian leadership believed that, if they adhered to their course of action, the Russian Federation would receive President Bush's full recognition and support.

The news about the end of the Soviet Union was nevertheless a shock to the Bush administration. Francis Fukuyama, who worked as an analyst at the State Department in 1990–91, explained: "When change happens, it always takes bureaucracy by surprise." Nick Burns, coordinator of the contingency group on the Soviet crisis, recalled: "I think it was the first time it became very, very clear that the Soviet Union was going to be disintegrating rather shortly."[46] Bush dictated into his tape-recorder: "Can this get out of hand? Will Gorbachev resign? Will he try to fight back? Will Yeltsin have thought this out properly? It's tough—a very tough situation."[47]

The Secretary of State James Baker's speechwriter Andrew Carpendale wrote to his boss, it was time to release the maximum amount of aid and mobilize American allies to help the democrats in Russia: "Next few months may determine their fate." He referred to a recent speech by Bush on the anniversary of Pearl Harbor: "We crushed totalitarianism, and when that was done, we helped our enemies give birth to democracies. We made our enemies our friends, and we healed their wounds, and in the process we lifted ourselves up." The United States, Carpendale continued, "face the same situation today: we've won the Cold War peacefully; now we have to decide, as Yavlinsky says, what to do with the people we've defeated." If the democrats in Russia, Ukraine, and elsewhere succeed, "we truly can usher in the New World Order." Otherwise, "we face a danger of authoritarian reversal or fascism."[48]

Baker did not believe in stark binaries. He knew that another Marshall Plan for the Russians was not on the cards. The Secretary of the Treasury, Nicholas Brady, as well as Congress, would never support this. The only practical plan was to help dismantle and control Soviet nuclear weapons; Senators Sam Nunn (Democrat) and Richard Lugar (Republican) made Congress approve $400 million annually for this mission. Baker knew, however, that in American politics government initiatives had to be linked to an idealist vision. Carpendale's points resonated powerfully. A call to assist the former Soviet countries would help combat the return of American isolationism.[49]

On 12 December, with Bush and Scowcroft's consent, the Secretary of State arrived at Princeton, his alma mater, to deliver a speech on "the state of post-Union". He praised the wisdom of George Kennan, the father of containment of the Soviet Union, who was in the audience. He urged the West "to take advantage of this new Russian revolution, set in motion with the defeat of the August coup." The theme of nuclear weapons was dressed up in lofty rhetoric. His biographer commented: "Only a magician could turn threadbare cloth into a new major government initiative." Baker's speechwriter ditched the grand analogy with defeated Germany and Japan. Instead, he used an allegory: while during the Cold War the two superpowers remained "two scorpions in a bottle," now the Western nations and the former Soviet republics were "awkward climbers on a steep mountain" towards freedom and democracy. "A fall towards fascism" by any country, say Russia, would mean a fall for everyone. Baker's practical proposals resembled the Berlin airlift of 1948–49, not the Marshall Plan. American military transportation planes would deliver humanitarian assistance, including the US Army's outdated rations, to cities across the Soviet Union throughout the winter.[50]

Next day, Yeltsin called Bush with a progress report. Russia had agreed with Kazakhstan and the four other "stans" to reset the Commonwealth agreements; Moldova had decided to join, as well as Armenia. The document would be signed on 21 December. Yeltsin had met with the Army General Staff and the internal security forces. "They all support our decision . . . All is very calm in

Moscow. I talk to Mikhail Sergeyevich Gorbachev every day to carry through the transition calmly and without disturbances." He stressed that "the all-Union Soviet organs will be moved to Russia ... intelligence, security, and the like."[51]

Baker flew back to Moscow again. When he and his team landed at Sheremetyevo Airport on 15 December, they discovered they had been lucky to land at all. Most Soviet airports and aerial transportation had shut down for lack of jet fuel. In the gray zone of statelessness and anarchy, Soviet oil was being redirected as an export commodity, with or without official licenses. While billions of petrodollars were being siphoned off to offshore accounts, Soviet pilots had no fuel to fly with, and most gas stations around the Soviet Union stood empty. Baker had to call Kozyrev to ensure his aircraft would be refueled for the homebound trip. The Russian Foreign Minister assured him that the fuel crisis "was not so bad," and promised to fix the problem.[52]

After resting for a few hours at the Penta Hotel in the comfortable Arbat district, Baker went to see Kozyrev in his new office inside the former Party building on the Old Square. The Secretary of State and his aides peppered Kozyrev with questions. The Russian Foreign Minister was overworked and tired: he had conducted multilateral talks with Kazakhstan, Uzbekistan, Ukraine, Belarus, and other republics. The original design, he said to the Americans, was for Russia to be in a commonwealth only with the republics which adhered to Baker's five principles (see Chapter 13), above all adherence to democratic values and principles, respect for existing borders, and respect for human rights and the protection of minorities. Four Central Asian states did not qualify. Today, Kozyrev said, this design was gone. "Nazarbayev would bring five others with him" to the CIS. The Americans asked Kozyrev who, instead of Gorbachev and Shevardnadze, would be the US partner in the Middle East peace process, as well as the START, CFE and other talks. Kozyrev had no answers. Kolosovsky intervened: "Many of the republics," he said, "do not have cadres for independent foreign ministries. This is not a problem for Russia, which will take over the Soviet Ministry of Foreign Affairs." Baker and his team also wanted to know who would be in charge of receiving the US humanitarian airlift. The cost of delivering grain assistance was to be paid by the receiving country; who would now pay the $60 million for the freight of ships that had already unloaded this grain? Also, a $1 billion US loan had to have gold as the collateral. How much gold did Russia have? "The disarray is so great," Kozyrev replied. "We are very nervous. This is why we seek to dissolve central organs of government ... We do not know the size of our gold reserves nor any data." What had happened to the Soviet oil and gas revenues? Kozyrev could only say that the Russian treasury had not received most of it. He also revealed that the

External Trade Bank of the USSR was bankrupt. The Americans left the meeting "dejected."[53]

Next morning, Yeltsin received Baker in the Kremlin's majestic St Catherine Hall. It used to be Gorbachev's privilege to welcome foreign dignitaries here. The President of Russia greeted the Americans "in a Russian building on Russian soil." Marshal Shaposhnikov and General Grachev, along with Viktor Barannikov, Minister of Internal Affairs, flanked Yeltsin to demonstrate his control over the levers of power. Burbulis, Kozyrev and Kolosovsky were also present. After a long explanation of what had happened on 8 December, Yeltsin read from his wish-list. He wanted Russia and the two other Slavic republics to be included in NATO's cooperation council (NACC), created for Eastern European states. He urged the Americans to remove Russia "from the list of communist countries." And he wanted "the United States to be the first to recognize the Russian Federation" by a special treaty.[54]

Baker was struck by the urgent need for US recognition expressed by all the former Soviet actors. There was something incongruous, however, in Yeltsin's demands. He spoke about Russia as the country with "one thousand years of history," but he also demanded the Soviet Union's permanent seat in the UN Security Council. He wished to be fair and act equitably with the other republics, yet he also declared all Soviet embassies abroad to be the patrimony of the Russian Empire "prior to 1917." He wanted each republic to join the OSCE (Organization for Security and Co-operation in Europe), yet the former Soviet military "to merge with NATO." Baker proposed that the US could recognize Russia as a successor state to the USSR in "a symbolic act"—yet he linked this to "critical substantive issues," above all control over nuclear weapons. Yeltsin, beaming with pleasure, took Baker to another room, with only Shaposhnikov and an interpreter in attendance. There were two "hot-line nuclear systems," he explained. The first was a conference system, used for consultations only, connecting the leaders of Russia, Ukraine, Belarus, and Kazakhstan. Other republics "have no say," because they had no nuclear weapons on their territory. Among the four nuclear republics only Russia had the capacity to launch nuclear weapons. Ukraine could not do it, and incidentally the withdrawal of tactical weapons from Ukrainian territory to Russia was almost complete. The leaders of Ukraine, Belarus, and Kazakhstan, Yeltsin intimated, "do not know how things work—that's why I tell only you. They'll be satisfied with having telephones." After their nuclear weapons were moved to Russia, their telephones would be removed as well. The second system, to decide on launching the weapons, connected Gorbachev, Yeltsin, and Shaposhnikov. But, Yeltsin revealed, "for now" only he and Shaposhnikov had "the briefcases to press the nuclear button" and "Shaposhnikov can't do it alone." This meant that Gorbachev's nuclear briefcase had already been disconnected. Gorbachev's nuclear phone, Yeltsin concluded, would also be removed "before the end of December."[55] The Russian leader had met the main US condition on the spot. He was convinced that the road to American recognition of Russia had been cleared.

Baker's flowery rhetoric about Russia's democratic revolution produced a spike of expectations among Moscow reformers. Kozyrev recalled his conversation with Baker in August, at the moment of the junta's collapse: "We are waiting, for Bush or you to give a Fulton speech in reverse." Instead of the crusade against communism, the White House should now lead a crusade to help Russian democrats. "Normal people have come to power in Russia, good guys, fools, idiots—does not matter—they simply want to be in the same place where you are . . . You need to support them, to give them another Marshall Plan. You must close your eyes to all other things and give them money." In his Princeton speech, Kozyrev believed, Baker had said "exactly this, word for word." The Russian Foreign Minister told Gaidar that Baker's trip was the moment to cash in on the American pledge. "We spoke once, on the run, about Baker's announcement." Kozyrev assumed that Gaidar would discuss it with Yeltsin.[56]

Kozyrev was poorly informed. On 6 December, Gaidar passed to the Americans a request for "a stabilization fund" to support Russian reforms, to the tune of $4 to $5 billion. He also passed to the US government a detailed outline of those reforms, something that many in the Russian government had not even seen. With empty coffers, without gold and oil revenues, with all credit lines cut off, Gaidar badly needed a cushion. His government, he reasoned, could not wait and decrease the pace of reform, because very soon Yeltsin would lose his mandate as a popular leader. At the same time, few democracies could survive political shocks of the magnitude that the reforms would generate. The message was: we may perish whether we act or not, but with Western money we may beat the odds.[57] On 10 December, David Mulford of the US Treasury tore Gaidar's idea to pieces in his memo to the White House. Macroeconomic stabilization, he argued, would not happen in Russia any time soon. "If Yeltsin frees prices without monetary and fiscal discipline firmly in place, he will certainly have the hyperinflation he fears, with or without any Western assistance." In a world of financial globalization, Mulford wrote, speculators would smash the ruble. Mulford completely ignored Gaidar's political predicament and that of the survival of the reformers in power.[58]

Gaidar was unaware of Mulford's damning verdict. He spent two days before Baker's visit talking to an IMF-sponsored delegation of foreign economists. He invited Rudiger Dornbusch, a world-famous economist, who had written about financial stabilization following the collapse of the Austro-Hungarian Empire. The IMF's John Odling-Smee and Richard Erb were also invited but did not come. The rest of the group consisted of economists who were promoters of the Washington Consensus: Jeffrey Sachs from Harvard University, Anders Åslund from Uppsala in Sweden, and Sergio de la Cuadra from Chile, among others. Mikhail Bernstam remarked that Gaidar did not need the advice of foreigners. He wanted them to confirm to Yeltsin that Gaidar was on the right track. The President of Russia was under huge pressure from other people in his government, including his friends from the industrial Urals: they told him that Gaidar's reforms were sheer madness.[59]

Kozyrev expected to make a pitch for a Marshall Plan in Baker's presence. Nothing came of it. The Secretary of State arrived late from his meeting with Gorbachev, Kozyrev recalled, and Yeltsin was full of swagger and "was talking plain nonsense." At one moment Baker asked how the United States could assist Russia. Yeltsin requested humanitarian assistance in the way of food; he had forgotten about the stabilization fund. When Kozyrev proposed inviting Gaidar to speak, Yeltsin dismissed him with a peremptory gesture. "Nobody could speak, when he spoke," Kozyrev explained. He and Gaidar viewed this episode as a missed opportunity. "With Bush and Baker," Kozyrev commented, "we could do gigantic things." Burbulis concurred. Yeltsin had a "false sense of grandeur," he recalled, and boasted that Russia was rich enough. "This was an absolutely immoral position. He should have never taken this kind of pan-Slavic attitude while ignoring realities, difficulties, and consequences."[60] Was there any opportunity for aid at all? Baker was hamstrung by the Treasury's position, but he was willing to promote some financial assistance for Russian reformers. The State Department began to work on such a program in early 1992.[61]

REPLACING THE SUPERPOWER

In his Princeton speech, Baker singled out Gorbachev and Shevardnadze as two heroes of the end of the Cold War. The US Secretary of State and Shevardnadze met in Moscow for dinner in the residence-studio of the Georgian sculptor Zurab Tsereteli. Both knew it was "the last supper." Shevardnadze confessed to his aides that he felt trapped. It "would be childish" to resign from Gorbachev's government a second time. His attention was split between Moscow and Georgia. With the stormy career of his political nemesis Zviad Gamsakhurdia nearing its end, the Soviet statesman began to think that his next career move would be in his homeland. Shevardnadze shared with Baker the thoughts that tormented him: Why had perestroika failed? He and Gorbachev "did not have timelines or schedules," got the stages and timings of reform wrong, and "should have done more in the economic field." Baker consoled his friend. For him everything that had happened to the Soviet Union was absolutely inevitable. The "evil empire" was bound to fall apart once "the freedom genie is out of the bottle." Gorbachev and Shevardnadze, he said, had shown unparalleled courage to start the process. "That will be the judgment of history," Baker promised. "The other way would have been a violent explosion, and you still could have civil war." Next morning, Sergey Tarasenko told Teimuraz Stepanov: "Baker answered the question that haunts you and me. Everything that is taking place would have happened anyway, but with more terrible consequences. You had the courage to launch the process, and I am convinced that after 50 years everything here will be good and people will remember you." After this heart-to-heart talk, Shevardnadze invited the Americans to the dinner table. The resourceful Tsereteli made a wonderful Georgian meal. Georgian wine flowed, as well as flavored *Tarkhuna* vodka—green as if made by the Wizard of Oz![62]

This was the last time that Baker saw Gorbachev in office. Bush was worried what Yeltsin would do to the Soviet leader after he resigned. Chancellor Kohl urged the Americans to protect Germany's most popular Russian. Bush called Yeltsin on 13 December and "advised" him to avoid ugly scenes during the transition. Yeltsin repeated several times that he and other republican leaders "are treating Mikhail Sergeyevich Gorbachev warmly and with the greatest respect . . . We do not want to force the issue and want him to come to his own decision." Bush politely pressed on, and Yeltsin added: "I do guarantee, I promise you personally, Mr President, that everything will happen in a good and decent way. We will be treating Gorbachev and Shevardnadze with great respect."[63] When Baker arrived in Moscow, however, Strobe Talbott from *Time* magazine passed him a message from an anonymous official in Gorbachev's entourage: Yeltsin's over-zealous investigators wanted to put Gorbachev on trial for his role "in the August coup." Gorbachev's interpreter Pavel Palazhchenko asked Talbott to pass this memo to the American officials.[64]

Baker found Gorbachev in bad shape. He felt pity for the fallen leader and thought he should step down with dignity, for the sake of his historical reputation. Gorbachev instead waited until 21 December, when republican leaders, now representing eleven republics (all but the Baltic states and Georgia), would decide on the Commonwealth accords. No one invited him to Alma-Ata. Gorbachev did not want the United States to recognize Russia and the other republics immediately. It was easy for Baker to promise that. He recalled: "We did have a clear interest in shaping the outlook and behavior of . . . successor states. Recognition was the largest 'carrot' we had available, and I wanted to maximize our leverage by holding it back . . ."[65]

Soon after Baker left, Galina Starovoitova requested an appointment with Gorbachev. She was one of the few democrats from the Russian parliament who did not vote to approve the Viskuli accords; she preferred a negotiated Union to its hasty liquidation, if only to protect ethnic minorities, including Russian

LIQUIDATION

minorities in Central Asia and the Caucasus. She also feared that an independent Russian state would become a home for Russian nationalism and imperialism. Starovoitova felt pity for the man who had launched change, but then squandered so many opportunities. They spoke for three hours, as Gorbachev had nothing else to do. "Everyone abandoned and forgot him," Starovoitova recalled. She knew that Gorbachev was disconnected from all channels of government information, including the KGB. "I already knew that his government communication, the buttons that managed the rocket strategic forces, were already disconnected. He still did not know it." They also reflected on the fate of perestroika. Starovoitova could not understand why Gorbachev had dragged his feet and wasted so much time trying to reform the Party. She asked: "Mikhail Sergeyevich, why you did not lean on us? . . . We had huge support from the people, and you had the power apparatus, the entire state was in your hands. Thatcher, Bush, NATO, and whoever else would help you, if you had only asked them." Starovoitova was disappointed with Gorbachev's answers. The Soviet leader did not admit his mistakes. "He thought within those narrow apparatus boundaries, he never thought in terms of street politics . . ."[66]

What Starovoitova judged narrow and futile in Gorbachev's actions, his biographer Taubman found tragic. Was Gorbachev's leaning on "democracy" a realistic option at any point until August 1991? Starovoitova wanted to smash the Soviet Leviathan, but she grossly overestimated the capacity of liberal-minded intellectuals, even together with Gorbachev, to carry out reforms and maintain social order. And could Gorbachev, even with the full support of Russian liberals, really dispatch the Party and dissolve "the empire" without facing a severe backlash? The dispute between the Soviet liberal ruler and the anti-communist radical politician was brutally aborted: seven years later, Starovoitova would be assassinated in St Petersburg by a hitman hired by a criminal gang. Her family and friends blamed her murder on former KGB elements. Remembering Starovoitova, Gorbachev said: "She demanded from the authorities what we still could not do."[67]

Yeltsin and his ministers were ready for the last act of this drama: replacing the provisional government and appropriating the remains of the Soviet state apparatus. The annexation of the Foreign Ministry, now headed by Shevardnadze, was the most important and symbolic move. The factor of international legitimacy, however, was key to the timing of this action. Kozyrev recommended waiting until eleven republics had signed the new accord in Alma-Ata. Otherwise, he argued, the leaders of Ukraine, Belarus, and Kazakhstan could demand their share of Soviet international assets.[68]

Yeltsin, however, did not wait. A decisive trigger was his visit to Italy, planned by Kozyrev through his own channels before the Viskuli meeting. The Soviet

Embassy had not even been informed; Anatoly Adamishin only learned about Yeltsin's visit two days before his arrival, on 17 December. At a meeting with the media at the airport, before boarding his flight to Rome, Yeltsin also announced that there would be no positions for Gorbachev or Shevardnadze in the Commonwealth structures. The ambassador joined the dots: "The life of my glorious MID will come to an end one of these days." He told Italian officials to prepare for a state visit. They complained they did not even have Russian tricolor flags. Adamishin replied: "We have destroyed our country and created a new one in two days." By the time Yeltsin's plane landed at Fiumicino, the staff had decorated both the airport and the Soviet Embassy with Russian flags brought from Moscow by Yeltsin's protocol officer.[69] The Italians, who had revered Gorbachev, now rushed to please his victorious rival instead. President Francesco Cossiga held a state reception for Yeltsin in the Quirinale Palace and decorated him with the highest Italian order; this required them to rush to a nearby jewelers to find necessary stones for the decoration. Pope John Paul II received the Russian leader in the Vatican. Buoyed by the attention and recognition of the Italians, Yeltsin decided on the spot to sign a decree to merge the MID into the Russian Foreign Ministry. When Kozyrev called Shevardnadze to report the news, the latter responded stoically: "Tomorrow you can come and run the ministry." The proud Georgian concealed his wrath at what he regarded as an illegal raid. A year before, on the same day, Shevardnadze had decided to resign. Now he had been evicted. "You cannot imagine," he said to Teimuraz Stepanov, "how I feel."[70]

Unwilling to face his former boss, Kozyrev sent his deputy Georgy Kunadze to carry out the unpleasant task. An expert on Japan from the Institute of World Economy and International Relations, Kunadze had left the Party in January 1991; a few months later, Kozyrev offered him a job on his skeleton staff. Kunadze called Shevardnadze to set up a transition meeting, but the minister told him he was too busy. Kunadze, who was also Georgian, arrived at the ministry in two cars accompanied by his aides. "I joked: 'Here come the commandos!'" In Shevardnadze's office on the seventh floor of the MID headquarters, Kunadze presented the minister with Yeltsin's decree. "He read, was silent for a long time, and then said: 'Why is he doing this to me!'" Then Shevardnadze took his briefcase and left. That was the only civilized element of the transition.[71]

On the same day, Yeltsin signed another decree to disband the Silayev-Yavlinsky economic committee. Upon his return from Rome, he held a secret meeting with Primakov and the senior staff of Soviet external intelligence. Apparently, he promised the spooks continuity in their practices; Primakov stayed at the helm. Yeltsin also merged the KGB central apparatus into the apparatus of the central ministry of internal security. Bakatin lost his job, as

Yeltsin did not need another ambitious politician in such a sensitive institution. By other decrees Yeltsin appropriated the Kremlin, including Gorbachev's office and presidential facilities. The Soviet Ministry of Defense and the General Staff remained "commonwealth" institutions, because the issue of control over nuclear weapons had still not been formally resolved.[72]

This flurry of annexations became a headache for Kozyrev, who was now in full control of foreign policy. In his view, Yeltsin's personal ambitions overruled state interests. "Yeltsin evidently could not wait," he wrote in his memoirs, "to take the [nuclear] attaché case and the glamorous president's office space in the Kremlin from Gorbachev. He dreamed of it as a symbol of power, almost as a young boy dreams of wearing a necktie as a symbol of being an adult." In fact, Yeltsin already had the nuclear authority, but he wanted the whole world to know about it. Kozyrev worried: Would the international community accept Russia as a substitute for the Soviet superpower? Would Russia get a Soviet seat in the United Nations?[73] He called James Baker, Douglas Hurd, and Roland Dumas for advice. The British doubted the legality of Yeltsin's moves. "The coup continues," Rodric Braithwaite wrote in his diary. Still, the Foreign and Commonwealth Office (FCO) was remarkably cooperative. Braithwaite wrote that London was "keen that Russia should move into the seat with minimum of fuss: controversy will bring into question the right of ourselves and the French to continue to occupy our seats in a world where neither of us can convincingly claim to outrank the Germans, the Japanese and even the Indians any longer." The FCO lawyers constructed an argument that Russia was a continuation state, "only the Soviet Union under another name." The British ambassador communicated this decision to Kunadze, who provisionally occupied Shevardnadze's office. The next day, the Russian ambassador to the United States, Viktor Komplektov, passed Brent Scowcroft a memorandum with Yeltsin's signature drafted along the lines recommended by the British.[74]

Kozyrev worried that Ukraine and Belarus might object to Russia's appropriation of superpower assets. Much to his relief, this did not happen. In his memoirs, he explained that the republican leaders in Alma-Ata were preoccupied with the awful state of their economies. Indeed, the republics were captives of the ruble zone and after 2 January 1992 would suffer the consequences of Russia's economic reform. Azerbaijan's Ayaz Mutallibov, Armenia's Levon Ter-Petrosian, Tajikistan's Rahmon Nabiyev and Moldova's Mircea Snegur were desperate to get Yeltsin's military and financial support: their countries were in a state of anarchy and war. And for every participant, the signing of the Alma-Ata accord was a gateway to international recognition. During his trip to the former Soviet countries, James Baker saw "the intense desire to satisfy the United States ... desire to be accepted, almost 'approved' by us." Baker believed it was the result of American "moral authority."[75] It was, rather, the daughter of necessity: having lost and sometimes rejected the old center, the republican potentates yearned for another way to legitimate their new-born sovereignty. Kravchuk and others closed their eyes to Moscow's ambitions, at least for a while, in order to get US recognition as soon as possible.

The Eleven in Alma-Ata voted unanimously to approve the Protocol prepared by Russia's experts that confirmed the troika declaration and agreement of 8 December. In this propitious environment, Kozyrev asked Yeltsin to raise the issue of a permanent seat at the UN Security Council. The Foreign Ministry prepared a half-page agreement on Russia's "continuation" of Soviet functions. Yeltsin made a pitch: since Russia was not a UN member, it could take over the Soviet seat with the financial burdens and responsibilities that it involved. Other leaders welcomed it. Kozyrev whispered in Yeltsin's ear that it would be better to put the proposal to a vote. This ruse worked. The leaders, Kozyrev recalled, "wanted to end the day with a positive move in the international sphere, especially since their domestic affairs were in such bad shape." They voted immediately and unanimously for the proposal. Later, the Ukrainian Foreign Minister, Anatoly Zlenko, and Belarus's representative, Piotr Kravchenko, tried to revise this decision. "But dinner was being served, and the principals were in the mood to celebrate, not argue."[76]

Two days after the Alma-Ata gathering, the twelve countries of the European Community welcomed Russia as a legal successor to the superpower. The People's Republic of China gave its approval as well. The communist country had performed the same substitute act as Russia, by taking the seat of "The Republic of China" (Taiwan). For the leaders of Beijing, however, it had taken over twenty years to achieve this goal. The nuclear scepter was the last to be passed. In Alma-Ata, Yeltsin proposed to create a Joint Military Command of the CIS and to keep Marshal Shaposhnikov in charge of the strategic nuclear forces. The final decision on this, however, was postponed until the next Commonwealth meeting on 30 December.[77]

Everyone waited for a formal recognition of Russia by the United States, but George Bush delayed this announcement for one simple reason: he was waiting for "his friend Mikhail" to leave. In Alma-Ata, the Russian president pledged to send Gorbachev into retirement "in a civilized manner," and not the demeaning way in which the Politburo had treated Khrushchev after his ouster in 1964. Yeltsin reached an agreement with Gorbachev on the deadline for his resignation at the end of the year, yet another part of him just could not wait anymore. And Gorbachev did not leave in a hurry.[78] With every day that passed, Gorbachev stayed on in the Kremlin office while Yeltsin's behavior became more brazen. Then on 23 December, Yeltsin came without any warning to Gorbachev's office to dictate, not negotiate, terms. Their meeting lasted for eight or nine hours. At first, the leaders spoke one to one but could not agree. One issue was a personal guarantee against prosecution, which Gorbachev requested but Yeltsin refused to grant. Gorbachev invited Alexander Yakovlev to act as a mediator. The leaders agreed that Gorbachev would observe a public silence and would not criticize Yeltsin and his government. In return, he would receive premises in Moscow to establish his presidential foundation, and he would keep his enormous country house on the outskirts of Moscow, with a staff of twenty servants, including cooks, waiters, and a small detail of bodyguards. Gorbachev would also retain two government limousines with chauffeurs, one for himself and another for his wife. During their meeting, the Soviet leader passed Yeltsin the keys to the safes where he kept the most sensitive historical documents, including the secret protocols of the Molotov-Ribbentrop Pact of 1939. They agreed that on 25 December, Yeltsin and Shaposhnikov would come to take from Gorbachev the nuclear briefcase, the symbolic scepter of nuclear power. They also spoke about other sensitive matters, including the secret program of biological weapons, something that the Western powers had long quietly urged Gorbachev to terminate.[79]

Yeltsin later remembered an "enormous" list of material requests from Gorbachev. Otherwise, his account was confused and even misdated. Gorbachev devoted only two lines in his memoirs to this meeting; he obviously wanted to forget it. He did mention, however, his conversation with John Major, whose call interrupted the meeting with Yeltsin. While Gorbachev was answering the call, Yeltsin wooed Yakovlev to abandon Gorbachev and come to work for him.[80]

Toward the end of their long meeting, Gorbachev began to lose his nerve. He drank a few small glasses of cognac, then excused himself, went to another room to rest behind the office that was no longer his. Yakovlev stayed for another hour, chatting with Yeltsin. After haggling with Gorbachev, the Russian leader wanted to show his generosity to someone else. He promised Yakovlev that he would issue a special decree to give him exceptional status and endowment "for special services to the democratic movement"—a promise he later forgot. When Yeltsin left the room, Yakovlev observed to himself: "This was a victor on the march." Then Yakovlev entered the backroom and found Gorbachev reclining on a couch with tears in his eyes. "This is how it happens, Sasha," he said. Yakovlev felt choked up, "as if some kind of injustice had happened." The two men who had together launched enormous changes were now at the end of their journey. Gorbachev asked Yakovlev for some water, then begged him to leave. Reflecting on this scene later, Yakovlev imagined what would have happened if Gorbachev had decided to exit the scene with a bang.

He could have refused to meet with Yeltsin. He still could have demanded that the Congress of People's Deputies of the USSR reconvene, and wait until a new President was elected to replace him. "This was possible! One can only imagine where it would have left the country, and the embarrassment of the governments of foreign states."[81] Apparently, Gorbachev toyed with this idea but then abandoned it.

Instead, he spent all his remaining time in office preparing a speech. No more neo-Leninist theorizing this time; the "socialist choice" and the Party that should represent it were gone. All international ambitions of a "new thinking," including the joint construction of a new Europe, had been scrapped, together with the Soviet Union. Russia, Yakovlev recalled, behaved like a stupid mare that had thrown off a rider who wanted to bring it "into European stables."[82] Millions of Russians thought differently: Gorbachev's perestroika had led to an inflation of promises, followed by real inflation and economic collapse. People had lost their faith in ideological rhetoric and any grand designs—an unintended consequence that even Brezhnev's "stagnation" had not achieved. Had a real Lenin appeared by magic in downtown Moscow in December 1991, nobody would have paid any attention to him. People were overwhelmed by everyday troubles, in search of their daily bread.

Gorbachev tinkered with various drafts of his farewell address for two weeks. He found Shakhnazarov's version anodyne and Yakovlev's text peevish; he chose the one by Chernyaev. In it, Gorbachev did not acknowledge any failures of his leadership, did not respond to any criticisms. Instead, he listed perestroika's achievements, liberalization at home, and the end of the Cold War. With those successes, why then did the country break up and why did he lose power? Gorbachev blamed this failure on others: resistance of the Party and economic bureaucracy, outdated customs and ideological inertia. He also spoke about "intolerance, a low level of political culture, fears of change." This was, he explained, "why we lost so much time." The address did not mention Yeltsin at all, thus denying the legitimacy of his resolve to seize power. The decision to dissolve the Union, Gorbachev said, "ought to have been decided on the basis of a national vote."[83]

The main guarantors of Gorbachev's place in history were Western powers, media, and public opinion. On the day of his resignation, he received telephone calls from Cossiga, Mulroney, and Genscher. Yet not a single leader of the former Soviet republics called him. His last days and minutes in office were filmed by American television companies. The ABC TV network had made an arrangement with Gorbachev to film him after the August events, and preparations took until late December. The crew led by Ted Koppel and Rick Kaplan had barely made it to Moscow before the curtain was drawn on Gorbachev's rule. Another television crew, from CNN, was in Moscow already, waiting to rush to the Kremlin with their equipment. They obtained exclusive rights to broadcast Gorbachev's departure to the world; only they had the satellite technology to do so. The Irish journalist Conor O'Clery, who meticulously chronicled what happened in the Kremlin on 25 December, marveled that at the end of his career Gorbachev was surrounded mostly by Americans. The Soviet television crew, with their antiquated cameras from the 1970s, looked like poor relatives next to the US media operation.[84]

The American hegemony to create a dominant narrative about the end of Soviet history seemed absolute at this moment. The US journalists had no time for nuances. They recorded "the end of communism," although the Party had long been out of power and was now banned. In the American interpretation, the collapse of statehood was just a backdrop to Gorbachev's phenomenal conversion to the last and true faith—liberal democracy. The economic and financial crisis, the standoff between democrats and the central government, Yeltsin's separatism, Gorbachev's "turn to the right," and the August junta—all those ill-understood developments were presented to the world as obstacles to or milestones along Gorbachev's political journey. The rest of the international community, by and large, followed this script.

The Soviet leader's old-fashioned elegance on the day of his resignation reminded Koppel of his Canadian father, an old-world European, who dressed up before making a visit to a notary public. The prospect of a global show gave Gorbachev adrenaline. He said to Koppel that his resignation did not mean his political death. He had enacted a peaceful transition of power "probably for the first time here. Even in this I have turned out to be a pioneer."[85] Yegor Yakovlev, the head of central television, wanted Gorbachev to sign the act of resignation in front of the cameras. Gorbachev refused. Shortly before the broadcast began, Gorbachev tried his own Soviet-made pen that he would use to sign his resignation. The pen did not work. CNN's president Tom Johnson lent him his Mont Blanc. Conor O'Clery, present at the scene, could not help quipping: "Once again a member of the media provides the instrument for the Soviet Union's liquidation." The broadcast started at 7 p.m. and ended twelve minutes later. Yakovlev stepped in again; he did not like some of the visual effects. "Let's retake it," he proposed. Gorbachev looked at him in disbelief: "Yegor, this cannot be retaken, all is signed. This is a historic act."[86]

Gorbachev's advisors viewed the moment as the tragic failure to keep a complex multi-ethnic country together by peaceful evolutionary reforms, as the closure of the thousand-year-long statehood. Even Chernyaev, who focused on Gorbachev's historic achievements, described 1991 as "the year of degeneration of the state, destruction of the economy, social chaos ..."[87] Shakhnazarov commented a few months later: "The country is ruined, the people became poorer, blood flows everywhere." He tried to wax optimistic: "From this chaos a new, transformed Russia should emerge." Shevardnadze's aide Stepanov found Gorbachev's address "boring and bland, as always, without any repentance." Most Soviet people did not even bother to watch it. The country seemed to have frozen, and the only activity was desperate shopping. Even Gaidar's wife and the wives of Yeltsin's close aides had to stand in food-lines. In expectation of price liberalization, all corporate suppliers refused to deliver food to Moscow and St Petersburg. Cargo ships waited for payment, before discharging their loads. Warehouses were controlled by "mafia" dealers who hoarded supplies until price liberalization.[88]

Yeltsin was the most important observer of Gorbachev's address, and he hated it. He refused to come to see Gorbachev for an agreed public ceremony, where the nuclear "button" would be transferred. Instead, he ordered Shaposhnikov to meet the former Soviet leader on "neutral territory," in the Kremlin's enormous St Catherine Hall. Gorbachev refused. Shaposhnikov was confused: he needed the signatures of both leaders on the transfer paperwork. Improvising, the Marshal came to Gorbachev's office with two colonels to have the Soviet leader check the nuclear "briefcase" and sign the papers. He promised he would come back with the document countersigned by Yeltsin. Then he left with four colonels, including the two who had accompanied Gorbachev until that moment. Gorbachev said to Koppel: "Now it is Yeltsin who holds his finger on the nuclear button." Nobody had the heart to tell him that this had been the case for some weeks.[89]

Yeltsin revealed his control in yet another symbolic way. Half an hour after Gorbachev gave his speech, two workmen lowered and removed the enormous flag of the Soviet Union from the illuminated flagpole inside the Kremlin, visible from Red Square. A Russian tricolor replaced it. This was premature. The Russian leader had planned this event not for that day but for midnight on 31 December, with fireworks and a gathering of people. Yet his temper had again proved stronger than all the state pomp and circumstance. Yeltsin's erratic behavior would backfire again later and would complicate many of his endeavors. If he was trying to upstage Gorbachev one last time, he failed. Next to the US-staged departure of the Soviet leader, Yeltsin, with his antics and theatrics, looked like a boorish provincial actor.

President Bush was at Camp David and watched his friend's resignation on CNN. "The finality of it hit me pretty hard," he dictated into his tape-recorder. "It was Christmas time, holiday time." Two hours earlier, he had received a personal letter and a telephone call from the departing Soviet leader. Gorbachev assured him that he would pass the nuclear powers to Yeltsin under strict control and without the slightest hitch. "There will be no disconnection. You can have a very quiet Christmas evening." Gorbachev urged his friend to encourage accord between the former Soviet republics and to give particular support to Russia in its pioneering reforms. Bush responded emotionally: "Our friendship is as strong as ever and will continue to be as events unfold." He assured him again that history would recognize his enormous contribution. After Gorbachev hung up, Bush was sentimental. Something enormous, he felt, had just occurred: the second superpower, the long-time foe of the United States, had ceased to exist. Despite all the CIA's memoranda, despite all assurances by Yeltsin and Russian liberals, despite Ukraine's referendum landslide, the top US leaders believed that the Soviet superpower still existed up to the very last days of December 1991, and was merely abolished "with the stroke of a pen." This was an event that Bush and his administration had never imagined they would see in their lifetime. "It was, it is, an unparalleled situation in history," Scowcroft acknowledged. After ending his phone call with Gorbachev, Bush thought: "God, we're lucky in this country—we have so many blessings."[90]

On Christmas Eve, the NSC staffers Nick Burns and Ed Hewett had been working in the Executive Office next to the White House long after all the other officials had gone home to join their families. They received conflicting signals from Scowcroft: Were they to write a speech about Gorbachev's contribution or simply a statement about it? In the end, the order came to write a special address. It combined the themes of great relief from being spared a nuclear nightmare and the victory of American values in Eastern Europe and the post-Soviet space, which now guaranteed peace on earth. The tribute to Gorbachev transformed into a message of welcome to the Commonwealth of Independent States. Burns recalled that, despite the US administration's friendship with Gorbachev and Shevardnadze, "many of us viewed" the state they represented "as an evil empire, as in Reagan's words."[91]

Indeed, Scowcroft and other members of the administration discounted Gorbachev's vision of a democratic Soviet Union as a Eurasian partner of the United States. Scowcroft believed that Gorbachev's own qualities as a leader had ensured the Soviet collapse. "For all his brilliance, Gorbachev appeared to have a fatal flaw," he reflected. "He seemed unable to make tough decisions and then stick with them. He made a fine art of temporizing and trimming his sails." This flaw "from our perspective . . . was very much of a blessing . . . Had Gorbachev possessed the authoritarian and Stalin-like political will and determination of his predecessors, we might be still facing the Soviet Union."[92]

Bush delivered his address at 9 p.m. on Christmas Day. The US President gave the speech for which Yeltsin and other members of the Alma-Ata meeting had waited so long. The United States, Bush said, "recognizes and welcomes the emergence of a free, independent, and democratic Russia, led by its courageous President, Boris Yeltsin. Our Embassy in Moscow will remain there as our Embassy to Russia. We will support Russia's assumption of the USSR's seat as a permanent member of the United Nations Security Council. I look forward to working closely with President Yeltsin in support of his efforts to bring democratic and market reform to Russia." In the next paragraph of the speech, Bush recognized the international sovereignty of Ukraine, Armenia, Kazakhstan, Belarus, and the republic of Kirgizstan, whose president Askar Akayev impressed Baker as a liberal. The three other Central Asian republics, Azerbaijan, Georgia, and Moldova still had to meet the five-point criteria.[93]

When Yeltsin learned about the US recognition, he invited Burbulis and other members of his entourage to his Kremlin office, vacated by Gorbachev, to celebrate their victory. They finished a bottle of cognac. At least they had the presence of mind not to invite American television to film this scene. On the same day, the Russian Foreign Ministry, in the process of moving to the MID headquarters, wrote a letter to the United Nations Secretary-General, Javier Pérez de Cuéllar, stating that the participation of the USSR in the UN and all its activities would be "continued" by Russia. With this in mind, the name "the Union of Soviet Socialist Republics" should be replaced by "The Russian Federation." On the evening of 27 December, the Soviet ambassador to the UN, Yuli Vorontsov, took his usual seat but now spoke for another country, Russia. All other Soviet ambassadors around the world followed his example.[94]

The Russian Federation became the nuclear successor to the Soviet Union with the advice and consent of the United States and other Western powers. Several years would pass before Yeltsin began to suspect that the West did not really regard Russia as a great power and an equal partner. In his memoirs, Kozyrev distanced himself from this suspicion, yet in many specific ways he acknowledged that this was the case. The admiration for "Russian democracy" in the United States did not last for long; and after Bush lost the presidential election to Bill Clinton in November 1992, any hope of substantial US aid for the Russian economy faded as well. That is, however, another story.

CONCLUSION

As this book has explored, the Soviet Union fell victim to a perfect storm and a hapless captain. In the 1980s, after fifteen years of resisting any reforms, the Soviet leadership under Mikhail Gorbachev launched economic and political changes of great magnitude. The ideas and designs underpinning those reforms were, however, fatally outdated, economically flawed, and led to the destruction of the existing economy and polity from within. The architects of the reforms, above all Mikhail Gorbachev, were unable to recognize their failure and modify their course. At the same time, they enabled new actors to emerge from the rubble of the old system, who were to inherit chaos.

Any leader of the Soviet Union who inherited the old system in 1985 and ruled the people corrupted by it would have faced a Herculean task and opened a Pandora's box of problems. But Mikhail Gorbachev was no ancient hero. He wanted to emancipate Soviet people from the legacy of oppression and conformism, yet did not learn enough from the great reformers of Russia's past, such as Tsar Alexander II, Count Sergey Witte, or Prime Minister Pyotr Stolypin. Instead, his role model was Vladimir Lenin, the great destroyer of Russian statehood. Gorbachev felt his destiny was to embrace change on a revolutionary scale, just like the furious Bolshevik had done in 1917–22. Like Lenin, he wanted to unleash forces of chaos in order to create a society that had never existed—a dangerous exercise in ideological messianism. At the same time, in a major paradox of Soviet history, Gorbachev consistently rejected methods and features that were at the core of Lenin's revolutionary success. He preferred speeches to action, parliamentary consensus to violence, and devolution of power to dictatorship. In a word, his messianic idea of a humane socialist society was increasingly detached from the realities of Soviet power and its economy.

DECLINE AND DOWNFALL

Those who have studied Gorbachev's reforms before contend that he had to walk a tightrope, balancing between making long-overdue changes and offsetting the backlash of hardliners. Otherwise, he would have been ousted as Nikita Khrushchev had been in 1964. It is often said that "the August coup" of 1991 validated this. This book demonstrates questions and qualifies these assumptions. There were still plenty of diehard ideologues in the Party, yet in the 1980s the Soviet bureaucracy was no longer a phalanx of "Stalinists" determined to resist any sort of change. Had that been the case, Gorbachev would have been ousted on one of many possible occasions between 1988 and 1990. Opposition to Gorbachev inside the Party and state always remained diffuse, leaderless, lacking a clear alternative strategy. The junta's three-day rule in August 1991, prompted by a desire to preserve the unitary state, was an act of folly, lacking a clear design and policy options. The Army, security services, and bureaucracy merely sat on the fence, waiting to see who would emerge the winner.

Gorbachev's leadership, character, and beliefs constituted a major factor in the Soviet Union's self-destruction. He combined ideological reformist zeal with political timidity, schematic messianism with practical detachment, visionary and breathtaking foreign policy with an inability to promote crucial domestic reforms. Those features made him unique in Soviet history. His aversion to force and violence, however, was typical of his generation, shared by many, even conservatives. This points to a deeper cultural and social transformation of the Soviet elites during the decades after Stalin. They turned out to be surprisingly feckless when the political and economic storm came. Gorbachev's aide Georgy Shakhnazarov, who observed the Politburo's collective paralysis of will, called it a systemic crisis.[1] No one in the Politburo could stomach enacting painful reforms or, if need be, maintaining order through force. The policies that Gorbachev favored, appeasing the intelligentsia and devolving responsibilities to the republican ruling elites, constituted a road to chaos, not to better reforms. This enabled and legitimized runaway separatism in the Baltics and in South Caucasus, and, ultimately, in the core Slavic republics of the USSR.

Only a hardcore determinist could believe that there were no alternatives to Gorbachev's policies. A much more logical path for the Soviet system would have been the continuation of Andropov-like authoritarianism, which enjoyed mass support, combined with radical market liberalization—just what Lenin had done many decades earlier. Even in 1990–91, the majority of Russians wanted a strong leader, a better economy, and consolidation of the country—not liberal democracy, civil rights, and national self-determination. Gorbachev failed to provide this, so they backed Yeltsin instead.

In late 1988, some of Gorbachev's lieutenants proposed a constitutional affirmation of the unitary state, at least a strong presidential federation, with central control over taxes and finances. Instead, Gorbachev promoted a fatal policy of "stronger republics," despite the glaringly bad example of Yugoslavia. And he empowered institutions, such as the Congress of People's Deputies and Supreme Soviet, representative but unwieldy bodies, incapable of governance. The Party dictatorship at least could launch and control painful and difficult reforms. The system of "socialist democracy" that replaced it meant emancipation and liberalization, but it also opened the gateways to virulent populism and national separatism, above all in the Russian Federation, without providing checks and balances. A parallel disaster happened to the economy. The reforms, prepared by well-meaning but hapless economists and technocrats, enabled new economic actors to make profits by cannibalizing the existing economy and appropriating state taxes and funds, instead of creating a stable new economy with new assets. This resulted in an ever-growing hole in the state budget. The "republican self-financing" reforms only fueled separatist aspirations and killed the chance of creating a new federal system.

In early 1990, Gorbachev had a big opportunity, perhaps his last one, to snatch victory from the jaws of defeat: his economic advisor Nikolai Petrakov designed an excellent program of radical economic reforms. The Soviet leader still had new presidential power and still controlled the Party. Lithuania was in open rebellion, but the Russian core of the Union was still controlled by the center. Gorbachev could have appointed a new government, introduced presidential rule, rolled back the republic's rights, and proceeded with market reform. It would have been a huge gamble, but it was still feasible and could have changed the climate in the whole country. Instead, Gorbachev hesitated and waited, and then the window of opportunity closed: 1990 continued and ended as the year of wasted opportunities, when the impotence of the Union government became clear to everyone. Yeltsin was the main beneficiary of this state of indecision. At the same time, Gorbachev was capable of acting resolutely in foreign policy, on the German Question and in the Middle East. Had he acted in the same way domestically, the future of the Soviet Union could have taken a different turn. Lenin's admirer, however, turned out to be a sorcerer's apprentice; he did not know how to regain control over the forces he had unleashed.

Gorbachev's indecision and decentralization of power alienated and fragmented the Party nomenklatura. The empowerment of republican institutions and nationalist movements left Soviet functionaries with only one choice: to "go nationalist" and identify themselves with ethno-territorial interests, republics, and regions. The fact that the first fully free elections of March 1990 took place in the republics, not nationwide, propelled the decomposition of Soviet elites along nationalist lines. This pushed Soviet politics in the same disastrous direction as in Yugoslavia at the same time. The rapid decomposition of the old ruling class meant the demise of unitary statehood. A huge factor was the awakening of the sleeping Russian giant and the emergence of a "Russian" counter-elite in Moscow, legitimized by a free popular ballot in the largest republic of the Union.

Simultaneously with the demise of the Soviet elite, the alienated and semi-dissident professionals, members of the former Soviet intelligentsia, turned out to be a ready-made base for an anti-systemic revolt, a mass base for the maverick Boris Yeltsin and "Democratic Russia." Those people could not by themselves seize control of the biggest Soviet republic. What enabled them to do so was broad discontent with the Soviet government and Gorbachev's leadership, and fragmentation of the Party nomenklatura and the KGB. Yeltsin ended up posing as the leader of a counter-elite, vying with the central authorities for power and property. This "Russian" counter-elite attracted diverse people, from a few genuine democrats to many status-hungry intellectuals and demagogues. It capitalized on many different grievances: populist revolt against the Party, economic discontent, fear of anarchy and civil war, the genuine liberalism of Moscow intellectuals, and anti-imperial and anti-Moscow sentiments in the provinces.

It was the weakness of the Kremlin leadership, however, not the strength of the "Russian opposition," that remained the principal factor in the systemic crisis that pulled the country apart. In March 1991, about 20 percent of people in the core republics of the Union thought that it would be better to live in separate republics rather than in a common state. This minority became the majority by August, most apparently in Ukraine, but also in the Russian Federation. Overwhelmingly, this was not the result of a sudden national awakening. Rather, it was a choice in favor of law and order, a distancing from the grotesque ineptness of the central authorities and the vacuum of central power. As one young scholar put it, after August 1991, "hierarchical breakdown was not a consequence of some broader 'collapse' of the Soviet system but rather constituted the systemic collapse itself."[2] Translated into plain English, the Soviet system was dismantled and dismembered largely by the internal tug of war.

This tug of war had no consensual resolution: it had to end either in a decisive showdown or in a collapse of statehood. Gorbachev sought to avoid either scenario, yet the Union Treaty deal he negotiated with Yeltsin was a final act of appeasement, which made decomposition of the state inevitable, perhaps only a bit more gradual than what happened in reality. Kryuchkov and a few other members of Gorbachev's entourage realized this inevitability; so they went over his head to stop the signing of the new Union Treaty that made the Soviet constitution and state null and void. Yet they also shied away from the specter of a civil war. Fortunately for Yeltsin and the opposition, there was no Deng-like or Pinochet-like figure in command of the Soviet Army and the KGB. The lack of ideological unity also weakened the junta: its members were not inspired by any particular ideology, communist or anti-communist. The Party was already a carcass of its former self; it no longer shaped the direction of the Soviet state, society, and economy. It was the Party's demise that made the junta's plot possible in August 1991. The junta's leaders—Kryuchkov, Yazov, and Pavlov—were not bound by the Party hierarchy, discipline, and authority; they acted on their own. The Army and security forces followed the orders of their superiors, yet they also lacked unity of command and purpose. A resolute use of force could have cemented and crystallized the state structures, yet the order for this never came.

Ideology and ideological divides loomed large during the last years of Soviet history. After Stalin's death, Khrushchev and his colleagues had been able to offer people a refurbished utopia, a less cruel form of socialism with Sputnik, more food, and individual housing, as well as a bit more openness, to compensate for the trials and Terror of the past. Gorbachev had sought to do the same in 1987–89, but he quickly failed, being unable to support his domestic promises with any tangible achievements. While glasnost tore apart the entire socialist utopia, including Leninist mythology, the gaping vacuum between ideals and realities was filled by cynical profiteering, but also nationalism, anti-communism, and populism. Yeltsin and many from "Democratic Russia" became passionate anti-communist ideologues, with an allegiance to Western liberal democracy. Those who later suspected that Yeltsin and the Russian elites simulated their faith are wrong: they sought to liberate "Russia," other "nations," and the world from the Soviet "totalitarian empire," expecting to create a "normal" state and society from the rubble.[3] Very few of them took into account the huge dangers of this enterprise, including partition of the economy and the arsenal of nuclear weapons, and the resulting ethno-territorial conflicts. Just like the Bolsheviks in 1917, they felt that history was on their side; this combination of ignorance and confidence gave them a big advantage over Gorbachev and his government. With breathtaking naïveté, incredible as it appeared to many people at the time and later, the Russian leaders wanted to be recognized, legitimated, adopted, and incorporated by the West. Without such expectations, amounting to an ideological revolution, one simply cannot understand the story of the Soviet implosion from within.

Like any historical drama of great speed and magnitude, the Soviet collapse consisted of turning points where the main actors faced dilemmas and made or shirked vital choices. Gorbachev was a grandmaster of nomenklatura politics, but a poor decision-maker. His one real gamble was the political reform of 1988–89; before and after that he temporized, searched for an illusory consensus, reacted to pressure, and often passed responsibility to others. Yeltsin's path to power, by contrast, was one long streak of gambling. In 1989, he bet on the future of "Russia" instead of the Soviet Union; in 1991, he upped the ante repeatedly, putting everything on the line. In the fall of that year, when Yegor Gaidar convinced Yeltsin that the choice was between keeping the Union and "saving Russia" by an IMF-style liberalization, the Russian leader did not hesitate to choose the latter. Many people in Yeltsin's entourage, armed with their hatred of the old system and their new faith in a liberal future, acted decisively. The nomenklatura reformers, defenders of the state institutions, disarmed by doubts and lack of strong leadership, hedged their bets or sat on the fence.

The speed and ease with which the Soviet central structures collapsed baffled even the most experienced Western observers. The British ambassador, Rodric Braithwaite, concluded his Annual Review with the phrase: "In 1991 . . . Gorbachev began the year without friends, and ended it without a job. Yeltsin triumphed, to face an economic collapse which could bring his reign, too, to an early end."[4] As much of this book details, the main institutions of Soviet statehood actually proved to be remarkably resilient and lasted until almost the end of the Soviet Union's existence; even the eruption of democratic fury in August 1991 could not destroy them. The state apparatus was simply taken over by "the Russians"; the Russian Federation, instead of designing a new state out of thin air, inherited the bulk of the old central statehood. After a period of chaos, this statehood was recreated and reinvented during the presidency of Vladimir Putin.

The Western factor in the Soviet reforms and collapse, as this book demonstrates, was always central, albeit poorly understood by both sides. Contrary to the old narrative, Ronald Reagan's offensive, Cold War pressures, and the unaffordable costs of defense spending did not push the Soviet leadership toward reforms; the realization of their necessity dated to the early 1960s. Western power grew correspondingly with the stages of the Soviet crisis and demise. As the reforms began to fail, and the Party regime declined, this power increased enormously. By the end of 1988, Gorbachev, Shevardnadze, and their entourage were once again adhering to the old Russian tradition of viewing the West as a partner in a grandiose project—but this time of the Soviet Union's modernization. In 1989, Soviet domestic troubles and the sudden meltdown of the Eastern European communist regimes made Gorbachev combine his role as the architect of a new international order with the need to beg for foreign credits and assistance. At the same time, for many in the Russian opposition, the West became a model of "normality," in the name of which they wanted to smash the Soviet system and state. And by the end of 1990, even the most conservative and secrecy-bound segments of the Soviet elites were beginning to ask Westerners to help them reform and survive. In the summer of 1991, the expectation of a new Marshall Plan among the Soviet elites became almost universal.

Had the US-led West tried to "preserve" the Soviet Union, there was a chance of survival. But the West did not invest in the collapsing Soviet Union, and many in Washington wanted to break it up for security reasons. Western leaders, experts, and opinion-makers could not comprehend how their Soviet adversaries could suddenly transform into eager partners and even supplicants. The Americans, after decades of Cold War rivalry, continued to view the internal Soviet tug of war through binary lenses: "communists" versus "democrats," "reformers" versus "hardliners," and so on. Only a few experts had the knowledge and patience to discern the nuances. Congress, think tanks, and many members of the Bush administration continued to treat the Soviet Union as an "evil empire" that could not be reformed. Eastern European and Baltic diasporas, the Republican Right, and liberal Democrats had their brethren and friends in the Soviet Union to help; they rooted for anti-communism and separatism. The Bush administration, because of its uncertainty, preferred to maintain its distance from Soviet politics and reforms. Yet domestic lobbying, the national security stakes, and the sheer intensity of revolutionary change forced US policy-makers to take sides.

In any case, whether Bush and his people wanted to participate or not, every actor in the Soviet drama, from Baltic nationalists to members of the junta, looked to "America" as a crucial factor shaping their behavior and choices. The most remarkable part of this story was the desire of both Gorbachev and Yeltsin to lean on the United States and follow its guidance and advice, in exchange for recognition and inclusion.

In the West, the collapse of the Soviet Union became conflated with the happy exit from the Cold War, victory over communism, the triumph of liberal values, and expectation of eternal peace and prosperity. Above all, there was great relief that the geopolitical rival and militarized giant had disappeared. The Soviet dissolution, wrote the historian Odd Arne Westad many years later, "removed the last vestige of the Cold War as an international system."[5] So much for Gorbachev's endeavors to change the Soviet Union's image! There was no political will or imagination among Western leaders to seize the unprecedented and historic opportunity to consolidate democracy in Russia. The widespread view was that the post-Soviet space was too huge and unpredictable for integration within the Western orbit. It was more realistic and pragmatic to pick the low-hanging fruits of the Cold War victory, above all in Eastern Europe and the Baltics. Still, the Bush administration made an effort in 1992 to appeal to Congress with a loan of $24 billion to help sustain "Russia's freedom." This promising initiative was quickly lost in Bush's re-election campaign; and in the end, Bush lost to a young Democrat, Bill Clinton. Strobe Talbott, a friend of Clinton's, recalled him saying how lucky he was that the August 1991 coup had failed and the Soviet Union had vanished. Otherwise, Clinton believed, the American public would have continued to think in terms of the Cold War and Bush would have won the election. Clinton praised Bush for assuming "the role of a sympathetic, attentive, highly competent air-traffic controller, guiding Gorbachev as he piloted the Soviet Union in for a soft landing on the ash heap of history." Clinton and Talbott were now determined to guide Yeltsin, until there would be a place for Russia in a US-led new global order. This ill-defined project did not succeed.[6]

On 2 January 1992, the Yeltsin–Gaidar government of Russia launched liberalization and market reforms, and started the privatization of state property at breakneck speed. The historian Kristina Spohr wrote: "The big-bang approach to the post-Soviet economic transition was probably the greatest economic reform ever undertaken." Yet the reformers continued to wait in vain for that massive Western economic and financial assistance package. Western money went to Eastern Europe instead; and very soon huge amounts of money also started pouring into communist China, which was reopened for business by Deng Xiaoping in 1992.[7] The Washington Consensus and global money markets left not only Russia in the lurch, but Ukraine and other former Soviet republics as well, with the exception of the three Baltic states. Russia and Ukraine competed in counting on Western generosity, support of "democracy," and geopolitical far-sightedness. Instead, they were left to compete for greedy investors—a zero-sum game that both countries lost. Global financial structures made a mockery of national sovereignty and pride. The elites and peoples of the former superpower suddenly found themselves near the bottom of the world's food chain.[8]

After the unification of Italy in the mid-nineteenth century, a liberal politician famously said: "Italy is made. The rest is to make the Italians."[9] In December 1991, the leaders of the former Soviet states could have said: "The Soviet Union is unmade. The rest is to make new states and their citizens." There were no fully sovereign, economically viable states on post-Soviet territory. The populations of the former Soviet republics had to learn to absorb their new identities. The common Soviet economy had to be partitioned and privatized: its torn and tattered remains had to be reconnected by profit and the market. That was not a happy process. The former Soviet elites did not live up to the magnitude of the task at hand. They mostly mimicked and simulated economic blueprints coming from the West. And they redistributed state property.

The Yeltsin-Gaidar government, left without a Western stabilization fund, but with a gaping balance-of-payments crisis and an empty budget, was soon

consumed by the enormous domestic backlash and buffeted by illiberal populists and nationalists such as Vladimir Zhirinovsky. The Russian economy was
plunged into the greatest recession it had experienced since 1917–21 and the
Nazi invasion in the summer of 1941. Russia experienced the worst of the Latin
American capitalism of the 1980s and 1990s, including huge social dislocation
and wealth inequality, while experiencing a steep economic decline. Instead of
modernization, there was massive de-industrialization—in part inevitable, but
mostly barbaric and senseless. Privatization failed to produce a burgeoning
middle class; the distribution of state assets was blatantly unfair, and it created
a new clique of so-called "oligarchs" who resembled the Latin American export-
oriented comprador bourgeoisie, indifferent to their own citizens. The privatized stores gradually filled up with food and other goods, but most Russians
did not view this as a miracle. For years after 1991, tens of millions would
struggle to put even basic food on their tables. In the 1980s about 30 percent of
Russians lived in poverty; during the 1990s, 70–80 percent did so. In the Soviet
Union, there was a safety net and basic food items were available at artificially
low fixed prices. In the new Russia, many institutions of social care and welfare
were destroyed; the old safety net was gone—with rampant crime and mafia-
like rule in most towns and regions. The life expectancy of Russians dropped
from 69 years in 1990 to 64.5 years in 1994; for males the plunge was from 64
years down to 58 years. By the end of the 1990s there were 3.7 million fewer
children in Russia than there were in 1990; there were also 3.4 million premature deaths of working-age men. Many young women could not afford to have
and raise children. This was a demographic catastrophe in peacetime, which
Russia has not overcome to this day.[10] While life was not good under the Soviet
Union, for the majority things became much worse once it was gone. In Russia,
people felt they had been cheated twice, by Gorbachev in the recent past, and
now by Yeltsin.

Yeltsin felt cheated, too. In Western eyes, the Russian President did not have
the status his predecessor Gorbachev had. "For all the talk about the new
Russia," Spohr comments, Gorbachev "represented a recognized ideological
system and unquestioned superpower." It was not clear what Yeltsin's Russia
represented, with its collapsing economy, ethnic conflicts in Chechnya and elsewhere, and an impoverished population.[11] Russian elites became sharply
divided. An entrepreneurial educated minority, especially in Moscow, enjoyed
new freedoms and learned to benefit from them materially and spiritually.
Many, however, began to rethink their pro-American and pro-Western stance.
The anti-communist mania of 1991, of destroying the old economic and financial controls, while rushing toward capitalist uncertainty, began to look retro-
spectively like ideological madness. The triumphant West seemed to have left

the struggling Russia and other post-Soviet states out of its zone of comfort. And soon suspicions were raised that Russia would not be included in the dominant Western structures, NATO and the European Union.[12]

Gorbachev and Shakhnazarov, both now out of politics, felt vindicated: the break-up of the Soviet Union failed to bring what Yeltsin, Burbulis, Kozyrev and other Russian leaders had expected and promised. The Commonwealth of Independent States indeed turned out to be just a cover for the dissolution of the Union; the forces of domestic and international markets and geopolitics pushed Russia and Ukraine to compete, not integrate. And the old Roman saying *Vae Victis*, "woe to the vanquished," proved to be as prophetically true as ever. The fate of the weak, poor, and defeated was still to run after the chariot of the powerful, wealthy, and victorious—to be accepted or rejected. The European Union and NATO defined structures of power, wealth, and security. The Balts, with their steady determination "to return to Europe," were the only success story among the post-Soviet states. Ukraine, Belarus, Moldova, and Georgia, not to mention Kazakhstan and the republics of Central Asia, remained outside the coveted Western dreamland.

The tension between Yeltsin's insistence on Russia's primacy and the aspirations of the elites in Ukraine and other republics did not go away, and continued to cause further pressures. Outright war between the new states, aside from the Armenian-Azeri conflict, was avoided, yet the immediate flare-up of a Russian-Ukrainian dispute over Crimea, Russian-Baltic tensions, conflicts in Transnistria, Chechnya, Georgia, and Nagorny Karabagh pointed to lasting trouble, not an eternal peace. Ukrainian and Georgian aspirations to align with NATO in order to contain Russia led to Russian claims of a "zone of influence" or "a liberal empire"; it was a vicious circle of mutual insecurity and recriminations. Yeltsin wanted Russia to join NATO, and he supported the idea of a common structure for all Eastern European and post-Soviet states, in which Russia would not be singled out or left behind. Instead, the Clinton administration chose to expand NATO and offer Russia "a partnership" with this alliance. It was essentially the same idea that Burbulis had heard voiced in Brussels in December 1991: Russia is simply too big to fully belong! Washington offered Yeltsin a place in the club of world leaders and many plaudits, provided the Kremlin did no funny business in its neighborhood or on the international scene in general. Most Western scholars later concluded this was the best option—to keep Russia in, while at the same time containing it.[13]

The history of Russia took another turn in 1999, just eight years after the Soviet collapse, when Yeltsin, his health and authority utterly ruined, chose his successor—Vladimir Putin, a young ex-KGB officer who had helped to defeat the junta in 1991. In just a few years, Putin tapped into the vast and deep disillusionment and discontent that the Soviet collapse had generated. Many, who had watched indifferently or with sympathy how the old Soviet state had been dismantled, now wanted to build a strong Russian state, as a guarantor of economic and social stability. Putin had carried out Yeltsin's promise of 1991: "Russia will rise from its knees"—but in a very different way. Yeltsin warned that NATO's enlargement could lead to a new division in Europe; Putin acted on this warning. In 2008, he used military force against Georgia, and in 2014 he annexed Crimea and waged an undeclared war on Ukraine in Donbass.

After those actions, Putin's Russia was dismissed in the West as a declining yet revisionist and dangerous power. Increasingly, Western commentators began to write about an "eternal Russia," a superficial image of a country that had never been European or experienced "true" democracy, remained forever steeped in despotism, and was always hostile to its neighbors. I hope this book demonstrates the falsity of this view. It is not the fault of many Russians that the transition from communism to capitalism has made them yearn for a stable strong statehood and left them rather skeptical about the slogans of freedom and liberal democracy.

The economic calamity and social traumas of the Soviet collapse do not explain, even less justify, what happened many years later. What they point to, however, is the possibility of great reversals and historic surprises ten or twenty years down the road. The Russians have a saying: "history has no subjunctive mood." They mean that what happened, happened. True, but what would have happened if Peter the Great had not reformed Russia back in the eighteenth century? And what if Lenin and the Bolsheviks had not retained power in 1918–21? Without Gorbachev's reforms, the Soviet Union could have scraped by for another decade and then collapsed much more violently than it did. Yet one can also imagine that the Soviet Union would have been reformed in a more conservative way, the one that Andropov had envisaged. There was significant potential for change inside the Soviet elites, including even the Party nomenklatura and the military-industrial complex. The power of money was central and crucial to the behavior of Soviet elites during the last years of the Soviet Union. Had the Kremlin ruler made different choices, to tap into this power, turning the existing elites into stakeholders of the transition, instead of alienating them, even the KGB officers would have supported state capitalism and privatization, just as they later did under Yeltsin and Putin. The Soviet Union could have gradually made its way into the world economy by a process of trial and error, with a nomenklatura-style state capitalism, and certainly with its institutions of power preserved. This is, of course, a completely distasteful scenario for many, especially non-Russian nationalists and Russian liberals. This was what they feared and fought against back in 1991, but only

Gorbachev's penchant for compromise and antipathy to the use of force helped them succeed.

It is much harder to imagine how Gorbachev's scenario of a voluntary Union could have succeeded. Those who criticized that option back in 1990–91 were on the mark: former communist clans in the republics took advantage of a unique opportunity to become "nations," and quickly allied themselves with external powers, who legitimized and protected them from the perceived or real hand of Moscow. Gorbachev's course towards "socialist democracy," the empowerment of national republics, and his hesitancy with regard to full-scale market reform, opened the gateway to economic and political crisis. At the end of Gorbachev's rule, the Soviet Union was on the brink of bankruptcy, the old ruling class was de-legitimized, and the state was in ruins, just like in 1917. The main beneficiaries of this were the Balts, who became independent, but also the Soviet-made elites of Ukraine, Kazakhstan, and other republics.

The human mind cannot envision long-term changes. Who could imagine in 1991 that China, ruled by the Communist Party and virtually isolated after the violent crackdown on Tiananmen Square, would become the second and potentially first economic power in the world? And yet, instead of billions of investments into the post-Soviet space and more jobs for Americans, as President Bush had proposed in his Russia package of 1992, hundreds of billions went into China, and many American workers lost their jobs. A quarter of a century later, Graham Allison, co-author of the Grand Bargain to rescue Gorbachev in 1991, began writing about a global pivot of power in favor of China and an "inevitable" Sino-American contest.[14] Even the Washington Consensus had to be modified, to acknowledge the undeniable success of the Chinese economy.[15] Who could predict in the early 1990s that commentators three decades later would be discussing a new crisis of the global liberal order, the decline of US power, and pervasive Euroskepticism? Few doubt today, however, that the era of widespread faith in an invincible liberal democracy is over. In the last decade, populism has reared its head again to challenge the old order, this time against liberalism, in the American heartland and in Eastern Europe.[16]

Most would indignantly refute any parallels between the Soviet collapse and recent developments in the West. Yet some former Soviets experienced sudden frissons of recognition. In 2008, Western governments had to bail out corporations using people's taxes and even savings, similar to the destructive Soviet policies in 1988–91. When the Nobel laureate Barack Obama, enveloped in lofty rhetoric, got mired in Afghanistan and the Middle East, he elicited comparisons with Gorbachev. The results of the Brexit referendum in 2016 reminded some observers of Gorbachev's referendum in March 1991, a supposed solution that became a huge problem.[17] And Donald Trump's "Make America Great

CONCLUSION

Again" evoked distant memories of Yeltsin's rhetoric of the victimization of "Russia" by the Soviet "empire." Some older citizens of the former Soviet Union even began to suspect that Western elites, so prudent in the time of the Cold War, no longer knew what they were doing. A reminder of the eras of Brezhnev, Chernenko and late Gorbachev! It may be that the Soviet puzzle is not completely irrelevant after all. History has never been a morality play about the inevitable victory of freedom and democracy. Instead, the world remains what it always was: an arena of struggle between idealism and power, good governance and corruption, the surge of freedom and the need to curb it in times of crisis and emergency.

The ghost of the disappeared Soviet Union does not stalk Europe, Asia, and the world. Yet the puzzle of its sudden disappearance still haunts the imagination of contemporaries, particularly as they see the certainties of the previously triumphant Western liberal order shaking and eroding under their feet. The end of the Soviet Union was a human drama of historic magnitude and epic uncertainty. It cannot be reduced to a footnote in the global narrative of the Cold War's end, decolonization, and liberal capitalism. This amazing story teaches us not to trust in the seeming certainty of continuity and should help us prepare for sudden shocks in the future.

ABBREVIATIONS

AY	Arkhiv Prezidentskogo Tsentra B. N. Yeltsina (Archive of the Presidential Center of B. N. Yeltsin)
BOHP	George H. W. Bush Oral History Project, the Miller Center, University of Virginia
CC CPSU	Central Committee of the Communist Party of the Soviet Union
FBIS	Foreign Broadcast International Service
GARF	Gosudarstvennyi Arkhiv Rossiiskoi Federatsii (State Archive of the Russian Federation)
GBPL	George H. W. Bush Presidential Library
HIA	Hoover Institution Library & Archives
MIC	military-industrial complex
MSG SS	Mikhail Sergeyevich Gorbachev, *Sobraniie Sochinenii* (Collection of Works)
NSC	National Security Council
RFE	Radio Free Europe
RGANI	Rossiiskii Gosudarstvennyi Arkhiv Noveishei Istorii (Russian State Archive of Contemporary History)

NOTES

INTRODUCTION: A PUZZLE

1. See Stephen F. Cohen, "Was the Soviet System Reformable?" *Slavic Review* 63:3 (2004), pp. 459–88; Mark Kramer, "The Reform of the Soviet System and the Demise of the Soviet State," *Slavic Review* 63:3 (2004), pp. 505–12.
2. Putin's address is at http://kremlin.ru/events/president/transcripts/22931; Donald Tusk is at https://www.rferl.org/a/eu-leader-to-putin-soviet-union-s-collapse-was-a-blessing-not-a-catastrophe/30049755.html.
3. James Wilson, *The Triumph of Improvisation: Gorbachev's Adaptability, Reagan's Engagement, and the End of the Cold War* (Ithaca, NY: Cornell University Press, 2015); Robert Service, *The End of the Cold War, 1985–1991* (London: Macmillan, 2015).
4. Kate Geoghegan, "A Policy in Tension: The National Endowment for Democracy and the U.S. Response to the Collapse of the Soviet Union," *Diplomatic History* 42:5 (2018), pp. 771–801.
5. On this parallel universe and imitation see for instance Alexei Yurchak, *Everything Was Forever, Until It Was No More: The Last Soviet Generation* (Princeton, NJ: Princeton University Press, 2006).
6. Aspects of this huge topic were explored in: Michael Ellman and Vladimir Kontorovich (eds.), *The Disintegration of the Soviet Economic System* (New York: Routledge, 1992), and also *The Destruction of the Soviet Economic System: An Insider's History* (London: Routledge, 1998); Philip Hanson, *From Stagnation to Catastroika: Commentaries on the Soviet Economy, 1983–1991* (Westport, CT: Praeger, 1992); David Woodruff, *Money Unmade: Barter and the Fate of Russian Capitalism* (Ithaca, NY: Cornell University Press, 1999); Juliet Johnson, *A Fistful of Rubles: The Rise and Fall of the Russian Banking System* (Ithaca, NY: Cornell University Press, 2000); Yegor Gaidar, *Collapse of an Empire: Lessons for Modern Russia*, trans. Antonina W. Bouis (Washington, DC: Brookings Institution, 2007).
7. Mark R. Beissinger, *Nationalist Mobilization and the Collapse of the Soviet State* (New York: Cambridge University Press, 2002). The role of Ukraine in the demise of the USSR is overstated in Serhii Plokhy, *The Last Empire: The Final Days of the Soviet Union* (New York: Basic Books, 2014).
8. The early and only effort on this was by John Dunlop, *The Rise of Russia and the Fall of the Soviet Empire* (Princeton, NJ: Princeton University Press, 1993); see also Geoffrey Hosking, *Rulers and Victims: Russians in the Soviet Union* (Cambridge, MA: Belknap Press, 2005). Questioning of the "empire" is in Edward W. Walker, *Dissolution: Sovereignty and Breakup of the Soviet Union* (New York: Rowman & Littlefield, 2003).
9. David M. Kotz and Fred Weir, *Revolution from Above: The Demise of the Soviet System* (New York: Routledge, 1997); Steven Solnick, *Stealing the State: Control and Collapse in*

Soviet Institutions (Cambridge, MA: Harvard University Press, 1998); Stephen Kotkin and Jan Tomasz Gross, *Uncivil Society: 1989 and the Implosion of the Communist Establishment* (New York: Modern Library, 2009); Georgi M. Derluguian, *Bourdieu's Secret Admirer in the Caucasus: The World-System Biography* (Chicago, IL: Chicago University Press, 2005).

10. Archie Brown, *The Human Factor: Gorbachev, Reagan, and Thatcher, and the End of the Cold War* (London: Oxford University Press, 2020); see also his "Did Gorbachev as General Secretary Become a Social Democrat?" *Europe-Asia Studies* 65:2 (2013), pp. 198–220.
11. William Taubman, *Gorbachev: His Life and Times* (New York: Simon & Schuster, 2017), p. 688.
12. Odd Arne Westad, *The Cold War: A Global History* (London: Allen Lane, 2017), pp. 613–14.
13. Vladimir Kontorovich, "The Economic Fallacy," *The National Interest* 31 (1993), p. 44.
14. Frank Costigliola, ed., *The Kennan Diaries* (New York: W. W. Norton, 2014), p. 199.
15. See the contributions of Stephen F. Cohen, Archie Brown, Mark Kramer, and Stephen E. Hanson in *Slavic Review* 63:3 (Autumn 2004), pp. 473–4, 483, 486, 493, 500, 503, 506–8, 512, 533.

CHAPTER 1: PERESTROIKA

1. http://liders.rusarchives.ru/andropov/docs/rech-yuv-andropova-na-plenume-tsk-kpss-15-iyunya-1983-g.html.
2. Leonid Mlechin. *Yuri Andropov. Posledniaia nadezhda rezhima* (Moscow: Tsentrpoligraph, 2008), pp. 2–18. This was the first biography of the KGB leader based on documentary evidence from his personal files.
3. Ibid.
4. Interview with Arkady Volsky, "Chetyre genseka," *Kommersant*, no. 169, 12 September 2006, at https://www.kommersant.ru/doc/704123.
5. On this see Moshe Lewin, "Kosygin and Andropov," in his *The Soviet Century* (London: Verso, 2005).
6. Mlechin, *Yuri Andropov*, pp. 87–8.
7. Vladislav Zubok, *Zhivago's Children: The Last Russian Intelligentsia* (Cambridge, MA: Belknap Press, 2009).
8. Georgy Shakhnazarov, *Tsena Svobody* (Moscow: Rossika Zevs, 1993), p. 23.
9. Ibid, pp. 27–30.
10. Ibid, p. 23.
11. Stasi note on a meeting between its chief, Erich Mielke, and KGB chairman Andropov, 11 July 1981, trans. Bernd Schaefer, at http://digitalarchive.wilsoncenter.org/document/115717.
12. Riccardo Cucciolla, "The Crisis of Soviet Power in Central Asia: The Uzbek 'Cotton Affair' (1975–1991)," PhD Dissertation, IMT School for Advanced Studies, Lucca, 2017.
13. Interview with Nikolai Ryzhkov by Michael McFaul, 25 August 1992. The McFaul Collection, Hoover Institution Library & Archives [hereafter HIA].
14. The group included Stepan Sitaryan, Lev Belousov, Nikolai Petrakov, Abel Aganbegyan, Tatiana Zaslavskaya, Georgy Arbatov, Leonid Abalkin, and Valentin Pavlov.
15. Nikolai Ryzhkov, *Perestroika: Istoriia predatelstv* (Moscow: Novosti, 1993), pp. 33–8; Nikolai Ryzhkov, *Desiat' let velikikh potriasenii* (Moscow: Kniga. Prosveshcheniie. Miloserdiie, 1996), p. 45.
16. Shakhnazarov, *Tsena Svobody*, pp. 32–3.
17. Andropov's diary documents his frequent meetings with Ryzhkov, RGANI, f. 82, op. 1, d. 53–4. Recollections of Nikolai Ryzhkov at: https://lenta.ru/articles/2020/04/23/35/?fbclid=IwAR00Uocg8CZYJyrQgxdnZo8jkbqY_t8dBXEAOX7IVM3JbvyuRXJ3VvHs2NQ, accessed on 26 April 2020.
18. Stasi note on meeting between Minister Mielke and KGB chairman Andropov, 11 July 1981, trans. Bernd Schaefer, at http://digitalarchive.wilsoncenter.org/document/115717.

19. Mark Harrison, "Secrets, Lies, and Half Truths: The Decision to Disclose Soviet Defense Outlays," Political Economy Research in Soviet Archives, Working Paper no. 55, September 2008, at https://warwick.ac.uk/fac/soc/economics/staff/mharrison/archive/persa/055.pdf. Harrison draws his conclusions on the unique collection of papers of Vitaly Katayev at HIA. Also on Soviet defense outlays see: Dmitri Steinberg, "The Soviet Defence Burden: Estimating Hidden Defence Costs," *Europe-Asia Studies* 44:2 (1992), pp. 237–63; Iu. D. Masliukov and E. S. Glubokov, "Planirovaniie i finansirovaniie voennoi promyshlennosti v SSSR", in A. V. Minaev, ed., *Sovetskaia voennaia moshch ot Stalina do Gorbacheva* (Moscow: Voennyi parad, 1999), pp. 82–129.

20. Andropov's remarks to the Plenary Meeting of the CC CPSU, 22 November 1982, RGASPI, f. 2, op. 3, d. 614, pp. 32, 33, 34, as cited in Robert Service, *The End of the Cold War, 1985–1991* (London: Macmillan, 2015), pp. 55–6.

21. Vitaly Vorotnikov, *A bylo eto tak . . . Iz dnevnika chlena Politbiuro TsK KPSS* (Moscow: Sovet veteranov knigoizdaniia, 1995), pp. 24–6; Ryzhkov, *Desiat' let*, p. 50.

22. S. A. Sitarian, *Uroki budushchego* (Moscow: Ekonomicheskaia gazeta, 2010), pp. 71–3.

23. M. S. Zotov. *Ia—bankir. Ot Stalina do Putina* (Moscow: Rusaki, 2004), pp. 281–2.

24. Ryzhkov, *Desiat' let*, p. 48.

25. The best source on Gorbachev's background is Taubman, *Gorbachev*, esp. pp. 76, 134.

26. Mikhail Gorbachev, *Zhizn i reformy*, vol. 1 (Moscow: Novosti, 1995), p. 265; Raisa Gorbacheva, *I Hope* (New York: HarperCollins, 1991), pp. 4–5; Taubman, *Gorbachev*, p. 209.

27. A. Ross Johnson, "The Cold War and East-Central Europe, 1945–1989," *Journal of Cold War Studies* 19:2 (Spring 2017), p. 203.

28. Taubman, *Gorbachev*, pp. 1, 5, 693; Nikolai Andreiev, *Zhizn Gorbach*eva (Moscow: Dobroie delo, 2016), p. 691.

29. The first scholar who identified him as such is Stephen E. Hanson, "Gorbachev: The Last True Leninist Believer?" in Daniel Chirot, ed., *The Crisis of Leninism and the Decline of the Left: The Revolutions of 1989* (Seattle, WA: University of Washington Press, 1991).

30. More on this in: Ludmilla Alexeyeva and Paul Goldberg, *The Thaw Generation: Coming of Age in the Post-Stalin Era* (Boston, MA: Little, Brown, 1990); Zubok, *Zhivago's Children*; Benjamin Tromly, *Making the Soviet Intelligentsia: University and Intellectual Life under Stalin and Khrushchev* (Cambridge: Cambridge University Press, 2014); Kathleen S. Smith, *Moscow 1956: The Silenced Spring* (Cambridge, MA: Harvard University Press, 2017).

31. Anatoly Chernyaev, *Sovmestnyi iskhod. Dnevnik dvukh epokh 1972–1991 gody* (Moscow: ROSSPEN, 2008), 23 April 1989, p. 790; Valery Boldin, *Ten Years that Shook the World* (New York: Basic Books, 1994), p. 95; Taubman, *Gorbachev*, pp. 215–16.

32. Vystupleniie A. N. Yakovleva, 29 August 1985, GARF, f. 100063, op. 1, d. 116, https://www.alexanderyakovlev.org/fond/issues-doc/1023305.

33. Ibid; Zapiska Yakovleva Gorbachevu, "Imperativ politicheskogo razvitiia," the end of December 1985, GARF, f. 10063, op. 1, d. 380. https://www.alexanderyakovlev.org/fond/issues-doc/1023329.

34. Taubman, *Gorbachev*, pp. 230–1; *XXXII Sezd Kommunisticheskoi Partii Sovetskogo Soiuza. 25 fevralia–6 marta 1986 goda. Stenograficheskii otchet*, vol. 1 (Moscow: Izdatelstvo politicheskoi literatury, 1986), p. 121.

35. *V Politburo TsK KPSS*, p. 117.

36. Ibid, p. 103.

37. Andreiev, *Zhizn Gorbacheva*, pp. 286–9.

38. Michael Ellman and Vladimir Kontorovich, *The Destruction of the Soviet Economic System: An Insider's History* (London: Routledge, 1998), p. 122.

39. Vorotnikov, *A bylo eto tak*, pp. 83–4. On the successful case of renovation and creation of a new Western-style plant in the late 1960s see: S. V. Zhuravlev, M. R. Zezina, R. G. Pikhoia, and A. K. Sokolov, *Istoriia Volzhskogo Avtomobilnogo Zavoda, 1996–2006* (Moscow: RAGS, 2006), ch. 1; Valentina Fava, "Between Business Interests and Ideological Marketing: The USSR and the Cold War in Fiat Corporate Strategy, 1957–1972," *Journal of Cold War Studies* 20:4 (Fall 2018), pp. 26–64.

40. Rudolph Pikhoia, *Sovetskii Soiuz: istoriia vlasti. 1945-1991* (Moscow: RAGS, 1998), pp. 508-9.
41. Gorbachev at the Politburo, Chernyaev's notes, around late May–early June 1986 (not published); *V Politburo TsK KPSS*, 3 July 1986 and 16 February 1989, pp. 64-5, 445; Ryzhkov, *Perestroika*, pp. 145, 150. Serhii Plokhy, *Chernobyl: The History of a Nuclear Catastrophe* (New York: Basic Books, 2018); Taubman, *Gorbachev*, p. 241.
42. Bill Keller, "Gorbachev, at Chernobyl, Urges Environment Plan," *The New York Times*, 24 February 1989, at https://www.nytimes.com/1989/02/24/world/gorbachev-at-chernobyl-urges-environment-plan.html.
43. Politburo minutes on 3 July 1986, *V Politburo TsK KPSS*, pp. 82-3.
44. The notes of Anatoly Chernyaev in the author's personal archive; the last remark is missing in the published version of the notes in *V Politburo TsK KPSS*.
45. Taubman, *Gorbachev*, p. 242.
46. Vorotnikov, *A bylo eto tak*, pp. 118, 132.
47. Chernyaev's notes at the Politburo, 20 June 1986, Chernyaev Papers, St Antony's College, Oxford.
48. Ibid, 25 September 1986.
49. Ellman and Kontorovich, *The Destruction of the Soviet Economic System*, pp. 142, 144. Among the "lunatic fringe" were the economists Larisa Piyasheva and her husband Boris Pinsker; see L. Popkova [alias of Piyasheva], "Gde pyshneie pirogi?" *Novyi mir* 5 (1987), pp. 239-41.
50. Interview with Nikolai Ryzhkov by Michael McFaul, 25 August 1992. The McFaul Collection, HIA.
51. The Politburo minutes, 22 January 1987, *V Politburo TsK KPSS*, pp. 134-5.
52. The Politburo minutes, 12 February 1987, Chernyaev Papers, St Antony's College, Oxford.
53. The Politburo minutes, 14 May 1987, *V Politburo TsK KPSS*, p. 184. Chernyaev's diary, 5 July 1987, in his *Sovmestnyi iskhod*, p. 313.
54. The Politburo minutes, 21–2 May 1987, Chernyaev Papers, St Antony's College, Oxford. *V Politburo TsK KPSS*, pp. 188-9.
55. Ryzhkov at the Politburo, 16 July 1987, *V Politburo TsK KPSS*, p. 209.
56. The working notes of Anatoly Chernyaev at the Politburo, 11 June 1987, Chernyaev Papers, St Antony's College, Oxford; *V Politburo TsK KPSS*, pp. 196-7.
57. Rudolf Pikhoia, "Pochemu nomenklatura ne stala zashchishchat Sovetskii Soiuz," at http://www.russ.ru/Mirovaya-povestka/Rudol-f-Pihoya-Pochemu-nomenklatura-ne-stala-zaschschat-Sovetskij-Soyuz.
58. The analysis is taken from http://lexandbusiness.ru/view-article.php?id=4716; Bernstam in "Mogilshchiki Sovetskogo Soiuza" at https://www.svoboda.org/a/usa-today-belovezh-skiye-soglasheniya/28167677.html.
59. I. A. Chudnov, *Denezhnaia reforma 1947 goda* (Moscow: ROSSPEN, 2018).
60. The Politburo minutes, 14 April 1988, p. 332; Ryzhkov, interview by McFaul, 30 September 1992. The McFaul Collection, HIA; the Politburo minutes, 14 April 1988, *V Politburo TsK KPSS*, p. 332. According to Ryzhkov's statistics, the state budget did not receive 40 billion rubles of oil sales and 34 billion from the reduction of vodka sales.
61. The Politburo minutes, 30 October and 4 December 1986, *V Politburo TsK KPSS*, pp. 103, 116-17.
62. Valentin Pavlov, *Upushchen li shans? Finansovyi kliuch k rynku* (Moscow: TERRA, 1995), pp. 71-2, 79-80.
63. Yakov Feygin, *Reforming the Cold War State: Economic Thought, Internationalization, and the Politics of Soviet Reform, 1955-1985*, PhD, University of Pennsylvania, 2017, pp. 135, 150.
64. Zotov, *Ia—bankir*, pp. 285-9, 290-1. Interview with Nikolai Ryzhkov by Michael McFaul, 30 September 1992. The McFaul Collection, HIA.
65. Zotov, *Ia—bankir*, p. 296.
66. Taubman, *Gorbachev*, pp. 3, 338.
67. Daniel Thomas, *The Helsinki Effect: International Norms, Human Rights, and the Demise of Communism* (Princeton, NJ: Princeton University Press, 2001); Sarah Snyder, *Human Rights Activism and the End of the Cold War: A Transnational Story of the Helsinki*

Network (Cambridge: Cambridge University Press, 2011); Richard Davy, "Helsinki Myths: Setting the Record Straight on the Final Act of the CSCE, 1975," *Cold War History* 9:1 (2009), pp. 1–22; Michael C. Morgan, *The Final Act: The Helsinki Accords and the Transformation of the Cold War* (Princeton, NJ: Princeton University Press, 2018).

68. Vladimir Pribylovskii, review designated for publication in the journal *Varianty*, dated by RFE as before April 1982, 2, 4, 5. Open Society Archives 300-80-1, Box 880, 3. Cited by Natasha Wilson in her PhD draft.

69. Chernyaev's diary, 31 August 1987, *Sovmestnyi iskhod*, p. 720.

70. Anatoly Chernyaev, "Fenomen Gorbacheva v kontekste liderstva," *Mezhdunarodnaia zhizn* 7 (1993), pp. 52–3.

71. Ibid, p. 53.

72. Vadim Medvedev, *V komande Gorbacheva: vzgliad iznutri* (Moscow: Bylina, 1994), p. 74; Shakhnazarov, *Tsena svobody*, p. 73.

73. Medvedev, *V komande Gorbacheva*, pp. 73–5.

74. Interview with Nikolai Ryzhkov by Michael McFaul, 30 September 1992. The McFaul Collection, HIA. On the constitutional crisis see William E. Pomeranz, *Law and the Russian State: Russia's Legal Evolution from Peter the Great to Vladimir Putin* (London: Bloomsbury, 2018), pp. 108–22.

75. Vorotnikov, *A bylo eto tak*, p. 49.

76. Chernyaev's notes, 5 August 1988, Chernyaev Papers, St Antony's College, Oxford.

77. Medvedev, *V komande Gorbacheva*, p. 78.

78. The author's interview with Eduard Shevardnadze, 20 August 1999, Tbilisi.

79. Chernyaev, *Sovmestnyi iskhod*, pp. 758–9.

80. Timothy J. Colton. *Yeltsin: A Life* (New York: Basic Books, 2011), chs 5 and 6.

81. Taubman, *Gorbachev*, pp. 330–1.

82. Boris Yeltsin, *Against the Grain*, trans. Michael Glenny (New York: Summit Books, 1990), pp. 184–5; Colton, *Yeltsin*, pp. 147–8; Taubman, *Gorbachev*, pp. 322–36, 362–3. The author's conversation with Shakhnazarov in Jachranka, Poland, 9 November 1997.

83. Chernyaev's letter of 13 November 1987, Chernyaev Papers, St Antony's College, Oxford.

84. Taubman, *Gorbachev*, pp. 342–51.

85. Chernyaev, *Sovmestnyi iskhod*, p. 761.

86. Medvedev, *V komande Gorbacheva*, pp. 78–9; Taubman, *Gorbachev*, pp. 371–2; Chernyaev, *Sovmestnyi iskhod*, pp. 761–7; Vorotnikov, *A bylo eto tak*, pp. 259–60.

87. MSG SS, vol. 12, p. 37.

88. Medvedev, *V komande Gorbacheva*, pp. 78–9; Vorotnikov, *A bylo eto tak*, pp. 259–60.

CHAPTER 2: RELEASE

1. *V Politburo TsK KPSS*, pp. 419–20, 422; Chernyaev, *Sovmestnyi iskhod*, 31 December 1988, p. 776.

2. For the generational and ideological sources of Gorbachev's new thinking see Robert English, *Russia and the Idea of the West: Gorbachev, Intellectuals, and the End of the Cold War* (New York: Columbia University Press, 2000); Andrei S. Grachev, *Gorbachev's Gamble: Soviet Foreign Policy and the End of the Cold War* (Cambridge: Polity, 2008); and Taubman, *Gorbachev*, pp. 262–6.

3. Enormous amounts of literature have emerged on the nuclear aspect of Soviet-American relations. See, for instance, David Hoffman, *The Dead Hand: The Untold Story of the Cold War Arms Race and its Dangerous Legacy* (New York: Anchor Books, 2010); Yevgeny P. Velikhov, "Nauka rabotaet na bezyadrnyi mir," *Mezhdunarodnaia zhizn* 10 (1988), pp. 50–1; Roald Sagdeev, *The Making of a Soviet Scientist: My Adventures in Nuclear Fusion and Space from Stalin to Star Wars* (New York: John Wiley, 1994), pp. 261–2, 273.

4. The record of the speech in M. S. Gorbachev, *Gody trudnykh reshenii* (Moscow: Alfa Print, 1993), pp. 48, 50.

5. Zubok, *Failed Empire*, p. 287; for greater detail see Elizabeth C. Charles, "The Game Changer: Reassessing the Impact of SDI on Gorbachev's Foreign Policy, Arms Control, and US-Soviet Relations," PhD Dissertation, Columbia University, 2010.

6. See "On the impact of COCOM and the US oil embargoes of petroleum equipment petrols," at www.cia.gov/library/readingroom/docs/CIA-RDP83B00140R000100080019-7.pdf; also https://www.cia.gov/library/readingroom/docs/CIA-RDP83M00914R000600020038-7.pdf; on the Toshiba scandal, see Sergey Radchenko, *Unwanted Visionaries: The Soviet Failure in Asia at the End of the Cold War* (New York: Oxford University Press, 2014), pp. 79–85.

7. Dmitry Furman, "Fenomen Gorbacheva," *Svobodnaia Mysl'* 11 (Moscow, 1995), pp. 68, 70–1.

8. Vadim Medvedev, *Raspad: Kak on nazreval v "mirovoi sisteme sotsializma"* (Moscow: Mezhdunarodnye otnosheniia, 1994), pp. 141–3; Jacques Lévesque, *The Enigma of 1989: The USSR and the Liberation of Eastern Europe* (Berkeley, CA: University of California Press, 1997), pp. 59–65.

9. The Politburo minutes, 23 October 1986, *V Politburo TsK KPSS*, p. 93; Chernyaev's notes of this meeting, Chernyaev Papers, St Antony's College, Oxford.

10. The Politburo minutes, 8 October 1987, *V Politburo TsK KPSS*, p. 242.

11. The terms of "liability" and "assets" with regard to the Eastern European "empire" appeared in 1985 in the article by American sociologist Valerie Bunce, "The Empire Strikes Back: The Evolution of the Eastern Bloc from a Soviet Asset to a Soviet Liability," *International Organization* 39:1 (Winter 1985), pp. 23, 28.

12. Morgan, *The Final Act*, esp. pp. 237–40; Marie-Pierre Rey, "'Europe is our common home': A Study of Gorbachev's Diplomatic Concept," *Cold War History* 4:2 (2004), p. 39.

13. The discussion on the reduction of Soviet troops in the Foreign Ministry, 26 April 1988, Teimuraz Stepanov-Mamaladze Papers, Box 2, Envelope 7, HIA.

14. https://nsarchive2.gwu.edu//rus/text_files/Masterpiece/1988-10-06.pdf; Chernyaev, diary entry, 21 December 1988, *Sovmestnyi iskhod*, p. 776.

15. https://nsarchive2.gwu.edu//rus/text_files/Masterpiece/1989-02-00.pdf.

16. *V Politburo TsK KPSS*, p. 436.

17. Robert M. Gates, *From the Shadows: The Ultimate Insider's Story of Five Presidents and How They Won the Cold War* (New York: Simon & Schuster, 1996), pp. 265, 266; George P. Schulz, *Turmoil and Triumph: My Years as Secretary of State* (New York: Charles Scribner's/Macmillan, 1993), pp. 760, 765; Don Oberdorfer, *From the Cold War to a New Era: The United States and the Soviet Union, 1983–1991* (Baltimore, MD: Johns Hopkins University Press, 1998), p. 320; Taubman, *Gorbachev*, pp. 422–3.

18. Philip Zelikow and Ernest May, Interview with Brent Scowcroft, 12–13 November 1999, p. 16; Interview with Dick Cheney, 16–17 March 2000, p. 121. George H. W. Bush Oral History Project, the Miller Center, University of Virginia [hereafter BOHP].

19. Taubman, *Gorbachev*, p. 400.

20. Gorbachev, *Zhizn i reformy*, vol. 1, pp. 35, 61; Alexandr N. Yakovlev, *Sumerki* (Moscow: Materik, 2005), pp. 35–66.

21. Geoffrey Hosking, *Rulers and Victims: The Russians in the Soviet Union* (Cambridge, MA: Belknap Press, 2001), pp. 72–3, 80.

22. Ibid.

23. Miroslav Hroch, *Social Preconditions of National Revival in Europe: A Comparative Analysis of the Social Composition of Patriotic Groups among the Smaller European Nations* (Cambridge: Cambridge University Press, 1985).

24. Mark R. Beissinger, *Nationalist Mobilization and the Collapse of the Soviet State*, pp. 54, 55.

25. Interview with Arkady Volsky, "Chetyre genseka," *Kommersant* 169, 12 September 2006, at https://www.kommersant.ru/doc/704123.

26. Ibid.

27. Beissinger, *Nationalist Mobilization*, p. 74; *V Politburo TsK KPSS*, p. 197; Chernyaev's notes at the Politburo, 11 June 1987, Chernyaev Papers, St Antony's College, Oxford.

28. Alfred J. Rieber, "Stalin, Man of the Borderlands," *The American Historical Review* 106:5 (December 2001), pp. 1651–91; also his *Stalin and the Struggle for Supremacy in Eurasia* (Cambridge: Cambridge University Press, 2015); Jamil Hasanli, *The Sovietization of Azerbaijan: The South Caucasus in the Triangle of Russia, Turkey, and Iran, 1920–1922* (Salt Lake City, UT: University of Utah Press, 2018).

NOTES to pp. 54–60

29. On the Nagorno-Karabagh conflict see Thomas de Waal, *Black Garden: Armenia and Azerbaijan through Peace and War* (New York: New York University Press, 2013), pp. 11–55, 83–93.
30. Shakhnazarov, *Tsena svobody*, p. 209.
31. *Soiuz mozhno bylo sokhranit: Belaia kniga: Dokumenty i fakty o politike M. S. Gorbacheva po reformirovaniiu i sokhraneniiu mnogonatsional'nogo gosudarstva* (Moscow: Izdatel'stvo AST, 2007). For an electronic copy at the site of the Gorbachev Foundation, see https://www.gorby.ru/userfiles/union_could_be_saved.pdf.
32. Shakhnazarov, *Tsena svobody*, pp. 206–7; Pavel Palazhchenko, "*Professia i vremia. Zapiski perevodchika-diplomata*," *Znamia* 10 (2020), at https://znamlit.ru/publication.php?id=7755.
33. Shakhnazarov, *Tsena svobody*, p. 210.
34. Politburo, 3 March 1988, in *Soiuz mozhno bylo sokhranit*, p. 26.
35. *V Politburo TsK KPSS*, p. 317; on the crisis of Yugoslavia's federalism see e.g. Sabrina P. Ramet, *Balkan Babel: The Disintegration of Yugoslavia from the Death of Tito to the Fall of Milošević* (Cambridge, MA: Westview Press, 2002), pp. 3–48; and Veljko Vujacic, *Natsionalizm, mif, i gosudarstvo v Rossii i Serbii. Predposylki raspada SSSR i Yugoslavii* (St Petersburg: European University, 2019).
36. *Soiuz mozhno bylo sokhranit*, pp. 38, 39, 43.
37. Chernyaev's notes, 9 October 1988, *Sovmestnyi iskhod*, p. 767.
38. Diary of Teimuraz Stepanov-Mamaladze Papers, 14, 17, and 23 November 1988, Box 5, Folder 4, HIA.
39. Shakhnazarov, *Tsena svobody*, pp. 215–16.
40. De Waal, *Black Garden*, pp. 83–93.
41. Alfred Senn, *Gorbachev's Failure in Lithuania* (New York: St Martin's Press, 1995); Anatol Lieven, *The Baltic Revolution: Estonia, Latvia, Lithuania and the Path to Independence* (New Haven, CT: Yale University Press, 1993); Ronald Grigor Suny, *The Revenge of the Past: Nationalism, Revolution, and the Collapse of the Soviet Union* (Stanford, CA: Stanford University Press, 1993); Nils R. Muiznieks, "The Influence of the Baltic Popular Movements on the Process of Soviet Disintegration," *Europe-Asia Studies* 47:1 (1995), pp. 3–25; Una Bergmane, "French and US Reactions Facing the Disintegration of the USSR: The Case of the Baltic States (1989–1991)," PhD Dissertation, Sciences Po, Paris, 2016.
42. Beissinger, *Nationalist Mobilization*, pp. 170–4.
43. Yakovlev's argumentation for the Politburo is at https://www.alexanderyakovlev.org/fond/issues-doc/1023735. On Yakovlev's appeasement of the Balts see: Yegor Ligachev, *Inside Gorbachev's Kremlin*, introduction by Stephen F. Cohen (New York: Westview Press, 1996), pp. 137–40.
44. Senn, *Gorbachev's Failure in Lithuania*, pp. 25–6; Beissinger, *Nationalist Mobilization*, pp. 174–5.
45. Valery Boldin, *Krushenie piedestala. Shtrikhi k portretu M.S. Gorbacheva* (Moscow: Respublika, 1995), pp. 261–2; Bergmane, "French and US Reactions," p. 118.
46. For more on this see Muiznieks, "The Influence of the Baltic Popular Movements," pp. 3–25.
47. Chernyaev, *Sovmestnyi iskhod*, p. 773.
48. The Politburo on 10 November 1988, Vorotnikov, *A bylo eto tak*, p. 265.
49. Andrei Zubov and Alexei Salmin, "Optimizatsiia natsionalno-gosudarstvennykh otnoshenii v usloviiakh 'natsionalnogo vozrozhdeniia' v SSSR," *Rabochii klass i sovremennyi mir* 3 (1989), pp. 62–84; Zubov's recollections to the author, 13 September 2017, Moscow; "Silnyi tsentr—silnye respubliki," Interview with the head of Gosplan, Yuri Masliukov, *Pravda*, 23 March 1989.
50. Chernyaev, *Sovmestnyi iskhod*, p. 773.
51. The Politburo minutes, 24 November 1988, Chernyaev Papers, St Antony's College, Oxford; the Politburo minutes, 16 February 1989, in *Soiuz mozhno bylo sokhranit*, pp. 58–60.
52. Shakhnazarov, *Tsena svobody*, pp. 400–2; Pomeranz, *Law and the Russian State*, p. 109.
53. Taubman cites Ezra Vogel, *Deng Xiaoping and the Transformation of China* (Cambridge, MA: Harvard University Press, 2011), p. 423.

447

54. Vogel, *Deng Xiaoping and the Transformation of China*, pp. 625-32; Kristina Spohr, *Post Wall, Post Square: Rebuilding the World After 1989* (New York: William Collins, 2019), pp. 55-8.

55. Taubman, *Gorbachev*, p. 480.

56. See more in: Chris Miller, *The Struggle to Save the Soviet Economy: Mikhail Gorbachev and the Collapse of the USSR* (Chapel Hill, NC: University of North Carolina Press, 2016), pp. 52-4, 180-1; Vladislav Zubok, "The Soviet Union and China in the 1980s: Reconciliation and Divorce," *Cold War History* 17:2 (Spring 2017), pp. 131-3.

57. Gorbachev to Chernyaev on 5 August 1988. Chernyaev Papers, cited in Service, *The End of the Cold War*, 385.

58. Roy Medvedev, "Vizit M. S. Gorbacheva v Pekin v 1989 godu," *Novaia i noveishaia istoriia* 3 (2011), pp. 93-101.

59. Gorbachev at a press conference in Beijing, 17 May 1989, Mikhail Sergeyevich Gorbachev, Sobraniie Sochinenii, vol. 14, p. 23.

60. Shakhnazarov, *Tsena svobody*, p. 133.

61. *V Politburo TsK KPSS*, p. 412; William Moskoff, *Perestroika in the Countryside: Agricultural Reform in the Gorbachev Era* (New York: M. E. Sharp, 1990).

62. Ryzhkov at the Politburo, 28 March 1989, MSG SS, vol. 13, p. 481.

63. Leonid Abalkin, *Neispolzovannyi shans. Poltora goda v pravitelstve* (Moscow: Izdatelstvo politicheskoi literatury, 1991), pp. 8-10; also an interview with him, "Lunnyi landshaft," in *Komsomolskaia Pravda*, 8 February 1989, p. 2; the estimate at Abalkin's site, https://web.archive.org/web/20070927185048/; http://www.biograph.comstar.ru/bank/abalkin.htm; *Gosudarstvennyi biudzhet SSSR. 1989. Kratkii statisticheskii sbornik* (Moscow: Finansy i statistika, 1989), p. 5.

64. Abalkin, *Neispolzovannyi shans*, pp. 15-17; Mikhail Bernstam, information to the author on 16 April 2020.

65. Gorbachev on 29 October 1988; Gorbachev to Rajiv Gandhi, 18 November 1988, in MSG SS, vol. 12, pp. 291, 380.

66. Adamishin's notes of a conversation between Ryzhkov and Vranitzky on 18 April 1989, Adamishin Papers, HIA. Most economists, including Abalkin and Aganbegyan, thought the same. A. G. Aganbegyan, "Gde vziat milliardy?", *Izvestia*, 2 August 1989.

67. See Gorbachev at the Politburo, 3 October 1988 in MSG SS, vol. 12, pp. 143-4.

68. Chernyaev, *Sovmestnyi iskhod*, 3 April 1989, pp. 787-8.

69. Vorotnikov, *A bylo eto tak*, 15-16 March 1989, p. 285.

70. The figures on the MIC come from the report of Igor Belousov, the head of the military-industrial commission of the Council of Ministers of the USSR, Stenogramma zasedania prezidentskogo soveta, 28 September 1990. RGANI, f. 121, op. 3, d. 71, ll. 4-5.

71. Clifford G. Gaddy, *The Price of the Past: Russia's Struggle with the Legacy of a Militarized Economy* (Washington, DC: Brookings Institution Press, 1996), pp. 47-8.

72. MSG SS, vol. 12, p. 381; "Kadrovaia otstavliaiushchaia," *Ogonyok* 2 (20 January 2020), p. 16.

73. MSG SS, vol. 13, pp. 172-7; CIA memorandum, "CIS Candidate Cities for Defense Industries Conversion," 5 February 1992. Scowcroft Collection: OA/ID CF01343-009, GBPL.

74. Chernyaev's notes, 21 December 1988. Chernyaev Papers, St Antony's College, Oxford.

75. Chernyaev, *Sovmestnyi iskhod*, 15 and 22 January 1989, pp. 779, 783.

76. On Gorbachev's ideological evolution see Archie Brown, "Did Gorbachev as General Secretary Become a Social Democrat?" *Europe-Asia Studies* 65:2 (March 2013), pp. 198-220.

77. Chernyaev, *Sovmestnyi iskhod*, 19 February 1989, p. 784.

78. Dominic Lieven, "Western Scholarship on the Soviet Regime," *Journal of Contemporary History* 29:2 (1994), p. 217.

79. Tocqueville, *The Ancien Régime and the French Revolution*, trans. Arthur Goldhammer (New York: Cambridge University Press, 2011), p. 157.

NOTES to pp. 70–79

CHAPTER 3: REVOLUTIONS

1. A. V. Berezkin and V. A. Kolosov, i.a., "The Geography of the 1989 Elections of People's Deputies of the USSR (Preliminary Results)," *Soviet Geography* 30:8 (1989), pp. 607–34.

2. At the Politburo on 28 March 1989, Lev Zaikov said that 74 percent of the staff of the Supreme Soviet and the Council of Ministers voted for Yeltsin; the overwhelming majority in the Higher Military Academy and 80 percent in the Higher School of the KGB voted for Yeltsin. MSG SS, vol. 13, pp. 484–6; Shakhnazarov's memo to Gorbachev, 30 March 1989, in Shakhnazarov, *Tsena svobody*, p. 465.

3. MSG SS, vol. 13, p. 486.

4. Ibid, pp. 486–7.

5. The full transcript of the discussion was published in *Pravda*, 27 April 1989.

6. Chernyaev, *Sovmestnyi iskhod*, 30 April 1989, pp. 790–1; MSG SS, vol. 14, pp. 137–41. Vorotnikov, *A bylo eto tak*, p. 294; Matthew Evangelista, "Norms, Heresthetics, and the End of the Cold War," *Journal of Cold War Studies* 3:1 (Winter 2001), p. 12.

7. Roy Medvedev, *Sovetskii Soiuz. Posledniie gody zhizni* (Moscow: AST, 2010), pp. 256–7.

8. Vladimir Lenin's letter to Maxim Gorky, 15 September 1919, Library of Congress, at https://www.loc.gov/exhibits/archives/g2aleks.html.

9. Benjamin Tromly, *Making the Soviet Intelligentsia: Universities and Intellectual Life under Stalin and Khrushchev* (New York: Cambridge University Press, 2013), p. 258.

10. For more see Zubok, *Zhivago's Children*, esp. ch. 7.

11. Chernyaev, *Sovmestnyi iskhod*, 15 January 1989, p. 780.

12. Ibid, 13 May 1989, p. 794; *V Politburo TsK KPSS*, pp. 479–80, 482; Vorotnikov, *A bylo eto tak*, pp. 301–2; Taubman, *Gorbachev*, pp. 435–6.

13. Vladimir Kormer, *Dvoinoe soznanie intelligentsii i psevdokul'tura*, https://readli.net/chitat-online/?b=153810&pg=1.

14. Filipp Bobkov, interview on 22 February 1999 for the project on the end of the Cold War by the Gorbachev Foundation-HIA; Derluguian, *Bourdieu's Secret Admirer*, ch. 5.

15. Recollections of Sergey Stankevich, "25 let MDG. Pochemu pogib SSSR?" https://www.svoboda.org/a/25404259.html.

16. Ibid.

17. Chernyaev, *Sovmestnyi iskhod*, 16 April, 2 May 1989, pp. 789, 792; Ligachev, *Inside Gorbachev's Kremlin*, pp. 146–69.

18. Medvedev, *V komande Gorbacheva*, pp. 91, 95; Taubman, *Gorbachev*, p. 428.

19. Taubman, *Gorbachev*, p. 441; Medvedev, *Sovetskii Soiuz*.

20. "Na S'ezde tsarstvuiet svoboda," *Uchitelskaia gazeta*, 3 June 1989; D. S. Likhachev, "K voprosu o vlasti," *Smena*, 20 June 1989, p. 1.

21. T. Gdlyan and N. Ivanov, *Kremlevskoe Delo* (Moscow: Gramota, 1996); Ligachev, *Inside Gorbachev's Kremlin*, pp. 204–53; Leslie Holmes, *The End of Communist Power: Anti-Corruption Campaigns and the Legitimation Crisis* (Oxford and New York: Oxford University Press, 1993); Cucciolla, "The Crisis of Soviet Power in Central Asia".

22. Shakhnazarov, *Tsena svobody*, pp. 77–8.

23. *Rahvarinne* in Estonia got 29 out of 36 Estonian seats; Latvia's People's Front got 30 out of 41 Latvian deputies; *Sajudis* won 36 out of 42 seats in Lithuania; Bergmane, "French and US Reactions", pp. 115–16. Senn, *Gorbachev's Failure in Lithuania*, p. 58.

24. Medvedev, *V komande Gorbacheva*, p. 98; Vorotnikov, *A bylo eto tak*, pp. 309–11.

25. Medvedev, *Sovetskii Soiuz*, pp. 263–6, 268.

26. Vitaly Korotich, editor-in-chief of "Ogonyok," in *Molodezh Estonii*, 18 February 1989.

27. Anatoly Sobchak, *Khozhdeniie vo vlast. Rasskaz o rozhdenii parlamenta* (Moscow: Novosti, 1991), pp. 43–8.

28. Gorbachev, *Zhizn i reformy*, vol. 1, p. 468.

29. At the Politburo, 31 July 1989, in MSG SS, vol. 16, p. 501.

30. Recollections of Viktor Gerashchenko in Nikolai Krotov, *Ocherki istorii banka Rossii* (Moscow: Ekonomicheskaia letopis, 2011), pp. 162–4.

31. A detailed treatment of the workers' movement is in Medvedev, *Sovetskii Soiuz*, pp. 268–71.

32. Ryzhkov, *Desiat' let*, pp. 407–10; "Obrashcheniie k Sovetskomu narodu," *Izvestia*, 27 July 1989, p. 1; "Zakon o neotlozhnykh merakh po uluchsheniiu pensionnogo obespecheniia i sotsialnogo obsluzhivaniia naselenia," *Izvestia*, 4 August 1989; the figure on the state budget deficit comes from Yuri Masliukov, head of the Gosplan, during his deposition to the Supreme Soviet, *Izvestia*, 6 August 1989, p. 3. Ryzhkov's estimate of the strikes' cost is at the Politburo, 12 October 1989, Chernyaev Papers, St Antony's College, Oxford.

33. Diary of Teimuraz Stepanov, end of July 1989. Stepanov-Mamaladze Papers, Box 5, Folder 7, HIA; Chernyaev, *Sovmestnyi iskhod*, 28 May 1989, pp. 799–800.

34. Gorbachev, *Zhizn i reformy*, vol. 1, pp. 461–2; on the "hanging" of cooperatives' entrepreneurs, see *V Politburo TsK KPSS*, 14 July 1989, p. 496.

35. See Eleonory Gilburd, *To See Paris and Die: The Soviet Lives of Western Culture* (Cambridge, MA: Harvard University Press, 2018); Yurchak, *Everything Was Forever, Until It Was No More*; Sergey I. Zhuk, *Rock and Roll in the Rocket City: The West, Identity, and Ideology in Soviet Dniepropetrovsk, 1960–1985* (Baltimore, MD, and Washington, DC: Woodrow Wilson Center Press and Johns Hopkins University Press, 2010); Maya Plisetskaya, *Ia, Maya Plisetskaia* (Moscow: Novosti, 1994).

36. "Poezdka za granitsu. Novoie v pravilakh vyezda i v'ezda v SSSR," *Izvestia*, 23 August 1989, p. 6.

37. On the "public diplomacy" of the early Gorbachev years and its Soviet participants from elite institutions see David Foglesong, "When the Russians Really Were Coming: Citizen Diplomacy and the End of the Cold War," *Cold War History* 20:4 (2020), pp. 419–40.

38. Taubman, *Gorbachev*, pp. 149–52.

39. Diary of Teimuraz Stepanov, 12 and 15 May 1989. Teimuraz Stepanov-Mamaladze Papers, Box 5, Folder 7, HIA.

40. About "normality" as the greatest yearning of the 1989 revolutions, see Ivan Krastev and Stephen Holmes, *The Light That Failed: Why the West Is losing the Fight for Democracy* (New York: Pegasus, 2020).

41. The author's conversation with Gennady Burbulis, 13 April 2020, by phone.

42. Nikolai Travkin's interview with Andrey Karaulov, 22 June 1991, in Andrey Karaulov, *Vokrug Kremlia* (Moscow: Slovo, 1993), pp. 163–4.

43. Pavel Voshchanov, *Yeltsin kak navazhdenie. Zapiski politicheskogo prokhodimtsa* (Moscow: Algoritm, 2017), pp. 17–38: Lev Sukhanov, *Kak Yeltsin stal prezidentom. Zapiski pervogo pomoshchnika* (Moscow: Eksmo, 2011), pp. 47–52.

44. Jack Matlock, *Autopsy on an Empire* (New York: Random House, 1995), pp. 247–9; Sukhanov, *Kak Yeltsin stal prezidentom*, pp. 52–68.

45. Sukhanov, *Kak Yeltsin stal prezidentom*, p. 71.

46. Voshchanov, *Yeltsin kak navazhdenie*, pp. 39–41; Sukhanov, *Kak Yeltsin stal prezidentom*, pp. 81–4.

47. Leon Aron, *Boris Yeltsin: A Revolutionary Life* (New York: HarperCollins, 2000), pp. 328–9; Colton, *Yeltsin*, pp. 172–3; Sukhanov, *Kak Yeltsin stal prezidentom*, p. 84; Pavel Voshchanov in Sergey Kiselev's film, "Prezident Vseia Rusi," part 1, at https://www. youtube.com/watch?v=UZYMNqkdKzg, accessed 10 November 2015.

48. Matlock, *Autopsy*, pp. 227–32.

49. Senn, *Gorbachev's Failure in Lithuania*, pp. 71–2; Frédéric Bozo, *Mitterrand, the End of the Cold War, and German Unification* (Oxford: Berghahn Books, 2010), p. 85; Bergmane, "French and US Reactions," pp. 131–5.

50. The Politburo notes, 31 July 1989, in *V Politburo TsK KPSS*, pp. 503–4.

51. Senn, *Gorbachev's Failure in Lithuania*, pp. 74–7; Bergmane, "French and US Reactions," pp. 120–1, 128.

52. The Politburo notes, 14 July 1989, in *V Politburo TsK KPSS*, pp. 497–500; for the original notes of the meeting, which vary from the published version, see Chernyaev Papers, St Antony's College, Oxford.

53. Beissinger, *Nationalist Mobilization*, pp. 192–3; Alla Yaroshinskaia, "Narodnyi Rukh na sluzhbe KGB," 9 October 2010, at https://www.rosbalt.ru/ukraina/2010/12/09/798964.

html; for some refutations, see http://khpg.org/index.php?id=1252007024. Braithwaite, diary, 4 November 1989.

54. See https://www.segodnya.ua/lifestyle/fun/20-let-rukhu-shevchenko-konjak-i-ahent-khb-171273.html; the interview with Vladimir Yavoryvsky, head of the organizing committee of the Rukh Congress. http://oralhistory.org.ua/interview-ua/382. Yavoryvsky at the time was the People's Congress deputy from Kiev and the Party member.

55. On Sakharov's project see the materials and discussions in "Remembering A. D. Sakharov's Constitutional Project 15 years," *Ab Imperio* 4 (2004), pp. 341–411; esp. see Kimitaka Matsuzato, "Ethno-Territorial Federalism and A. D. Sakharov's Constitutional Draft," *Ab Imperio* 4 (2004), pp. 387–91.

56. Interview with Galina Starovoitova for the Ukrainian project *Rozpad Radians'koho Soiuzu. Usna istoria nezalezhnoi Ukrainy—1988–1991*, at http://oralhistory.org.ua/category/interview-ua/page/3/; *Sobesednik* 36 (1989).

57. *Izvestia*, 28 August 1989, p. 1. Chernyaev and Shakhnazarov worked on the declaration; Chernyaev, *Sovmestnyi iskhod*, 11 September 1989, p. 800.

58. Chernyaev, *Sovmestnyi iskhod*, 11 and 16 September 1989, pp. 800–1.

59. Chernyaev, ibid, 16 and 17 September, 5 October 1989, pp. 803, 805–6.

60. Chernyaev, ibid, 15 October 1990, pp. 809–11; Vitaly Korotich, *Zal Ozhidaniia* (New York: Liberty Publishing House, 1991).

61. The Politburo, 7 September 1989, MSG SS, vol. 16, p. 482.

62. On Gorbachev and Kryuchkov, see Amy Knight, "The KGB, Perestroika, and the Collapse of the Soviet Union," *Journal of Cold War Studies* 5:1 (2003), pp. 72–4; Taubman, *Gorbachev*, p. 227; Braithwaite, diary, 4 November 1989.

63. *Pravda*, 3 December 1989.

64. Chernyaev notes at the Politburo, 12 October 1989, Chernyaev Papers, St Antony's College, Oxford.

65. Ryzhkov to Vranitzky, 18 April 1989, Adamishin Papers, HIA.

66. Memorandum from Anatoly Chernyaev to Vadim Zagladin, 4 February 1989, in Svetlana Savranskaya, Thomas Blanton, and Vladislav Zubok, eds., *Masterpieces of History: The Peaceful End of the Cold War in Europe, 1989* (Budapest: Central European University Press, 2010), p. 389; Spohr, *Post Wall, Post Square*, pp. 82–3.

67. Gorbachev-Kohl conversation, 12 June 1989, in Alexander Galkin and Anatoly Chernyaev, eds., *Mikhail Gorbachev i Germanskii vopros. Sbornik dokumentov. 1986–1991* (Moscow: Ves Mir, 2006) pp. 161–2; MSG SS, vol. 15, pp. 156–73, 178–81, 252–4; Malcolm Byrne and Vojtech Mastny, eds., *A Cardboard Castle? The Inside Story of the Warsaw Pact* (Budapest: Central European University Press, 2005), pp. 644–54.

68. Conversation on 14 June 1989 in Galkin and Chernyaev, *Mikhail Gorbachev i Germanskii vopros*, pp. 194–5.

69. The thesis of "uncivil society" that accelerated changes from above in Eastern Europe was introduced in Kotkin and Gross, *Uncivil Society*.

70. For the best treatment see Mary Sarotte, *1989: The Struggle to Create Post-Cold War Europe* (Princeton, NJ: Princeton University Press, 2011); Spohr, *Post Wall, Post Square*, ch. 2.

71. Teimuraz Stepanov, diary, 18 and 19 August 1989. Teimuraz Stepanov-Mamaladze Papers, Box 5, Folder 8, HIA.

72. Beissinger, *Nationalist Mobilization*, p. 185; Teimuraz Stepanov, diary, 14–17 August 1989, Teimuraz Stepanov-Mamaladze Papers, Box 5, Folder 8, HIA.

73. Braithwate, diary, 6 October 1989; Chernyaev Papers, St Antony's College, Oxford entry of 5 October 1989, pp. 805–6.

74. George Bush and Brent Scowcroft, *A World Transformed* (New York: Knopf, 1998), p. 130; Russel Riley and Melvyn Leffler, interview with Philip Zelikow, 28 July 2010, BOHP, p. 16. On Scowcroft's views of Russian-Soviet history and expansionism, see an interview with him on 12–13 November 1999, BOHP, p. 8; Gates, *From the Shadows*, pp. 443–8; Jeffrey Engel, *When the World Seemed New: George H. W. Bush and the End of the Cold War* (New York: Houghton, Mifflin, Harcourt, 2017), pp. 137–8; Matlock, *Autopsy*, pp. 182–90, 195–7.

75. See e.g. NSC memo to Brent Scowcroft on an inter-agency discussion on 28 July 1989 in the papers of Condoleezza Rice; Subject Files, OA/ID CF00718-011, GBPL.

76. Bush and Scowcroft, *A World Transformed*, pp. 142–3; Colton, *Yeltsin*, pp. 171–2. From the handwritten notes of the conversation with Yeltsin in Condoleezza Rice Papers: PA/ID CF 00717–021, GBPL.

77. For the memcons see: https://bush41library.tamu.edu/files/memcons-telcons/1989-09-21--Shevardnadze%20[2].pdf; https://bush41library.tamu.edu/files/memcons-telcons/1989-09-21--Shevardnadze%20[1].pdf; Bush and Scowcroft, *A World Transformed*, pp. 144–5.

78. The literature on this episode is too extensive to be listed. For a good English-language account see Mary Sarotte, *The Collapse: The Accidental Opening of the Berlin Wall* (New York: Basic Books, 2014).

79. The best analysis of this process is in Lévesque, *The Enigma of 1989*; Kotkin and Gross, *Uncivil Society*.

80. Sarotte, *1989*, pp. 67–8; Emily S. Rosenberg, "Consumer Capitalism and the End of the Cold War," in Malvyn Leffler and Odd Arne Westad, eds., *The Cambridge History of the Cold War* (New York: Cambridge University Press, 2010), vol. III, p. 489.

81. On the first reactions of scholars see *Daedalus* 119:1 (Winter 1990). For a balanced approach see M. Kramer and V. Smetana, eds., *Imposing, Maintaining, and Tearing Open the Iron Curtain: The Cold War and East-Central Europe* (Lanham, MD: Lexington Books, 2014); Taubman, *Gorbachev*, p. 486.

82. MSG SS, vol. 17, pp. 47, 52, 56. Braithwaite's record does not contain these words, diary, 17 November 1989.

83. Bush and Scowcroft, *A World Transformed*, pp. 154–5.

84. Bergmane, "French and US Reactions," pp. 138–41.

85. Anatoly Chernyaev, "Gorbachev-Bush. Vstrecha na Malte v 1989 godu," 7 June 2001, at https://www.gorby.ru/presscenter/publication/show_152/

86. See the US transcripts of the meeting: https://bush41library.tamu.edu/files/memcons-telcons/1989-12-02--Gorbachev%20Malta%20Luncheon%20Meeting.pdf; https://bush41library.tamu.edu/files/memcons-telcons/1989-12-03--Gorbachev%20Malta%20Second%20Expanded%20Bilateral.pdf. The Soviet record is in Gorbachev, *Zhizn i reformy*, vol. 2, pp. 143–4.

87. The US version is in: https://bush41library.tamu.edu/files/memcons-telcons/1989-12-03--Gorbachev%20Malta%20Second%20Restricted%20Bilateral.pdf. On the key significance of Gorbachev's declaration, see Chernyaev, *Sovmestnyi iskhod*, 2 January 1990, p. 833.

88. Bush and Scowcroft, *A World Transformed*, p. 177.

89. Teimuraz Stepanov, diary, 4 December 1989. Teimuraz Stepanov-Mamaladze Papers, Box 5, Folder 8, HIA.

90. Ibid, 4 December, between 10 and 16 December 1989.

CHAPTER 4: SEPARATISM

1. *Pervyi s'ezd narodnykh deputatov SSSR, May 25–June 9, 1989. Stenograficheskii otchet*, vol. 2 (Moscow: Politizdat 1989), pp. 456–9; "Na S'ezde tsarstvuiet svoboda," *Uchitelskaia gazeta* (3 June 1989).

2. The Politburo, 14 July 1989, published in *V Politburo TsK KPSS*, p. 496–503; see also the unpublished original minutes by Chernyaev in Chernyaev Papers, St Antony's College, Oxford.

3. The Politburo minutes, 14 July 1989, MSG SS, vol. 15, pp. 247–50; also in *V Politburo TsK KPSS*, pp. 500–3.

4. G. V. Myasnikov, "Dusha moia spokoina . . .: Iz dnevnikov raznykh let". Published by M. G. Myasnikov, *Nazhe naslediie*, 59–60 (2001), the entry of 19 April 1980, http://www.nasledie-rus.ru/podshivka/6012.php.

5. Chernyaev's diary, 15 January, 11 September 1989, *Sovmestnyi iskhod*, pp. 779, 800–1; see more in Vladislav Zubok, *The Idea of Russia: The Life and Work of Dmitry Likhachev* (London: I. B. Tauris, 2016), ch. 8.

6. Vorotnikov, *A bylo eto tak*, the entry of 25–27 October 1989, p. 353; Braithwaite's diary, 27 October 1989.

7. Andrei Sakharov, *Trevoga i nadezhda. Vol. 2. Stat'i, pis'ma, vystupleniia, interview, 1986–1989* (Moscow: Vremia, 2006), pp. 591–2; materials of the constitutional project of A. D. Sakharov, *Ab Imperio* 4 (2004), pp. 357–60.

8. Dunlop, *The Rise of Russia*, p. 93; interview with Mikhail Afanasyev in *Literaturnaia Rossiia* 4 (January 1992), p. 2; the text of the platform is reproduced in Viktor Sheinis, *Vzlet i padeniie parlamenta. Perelomnyie gody v rossiiskoi politike (1985–1991)*, vol. 1 (Moscow: Moscow Carnegie Center, Fond INDEM, 2005), p. 261.

9. Yeltsin, *Against the Grain*, pp. 258–61; Voshchanov, *Yeltsin kak navazhdeniie*, pp. 48–52, 74–80; Vorotnikov, *A bylo eto tak*, entry of 16 October 1989, pp. 351–2.

10. B. N. Yeltsin, Tezisnoe soderzhaniie predvybornoi programmy, g. Leningrad, December 1989; Predvybornaia programma B. N. Yeltsina, December 1989, the Archive of B.N.Yeltsin [hereafter AY], f. 6, op. 1, d. 8, ll. 5–12, 13–42, at https://yeltsin.ru/archive/paperwork/8576; https://yeltsin.ru/archive/paperwork/8577.

11. B. N. Yeltsin, Vstrechi s trudiashchimisia g. Sverdlovska, 28 January–2 February 1990, AY, f. 6, op. 1, d. 8, ll. 43–9.

12. The translated version from *The Sunday Times*, 11 February 1990, AY, f. 6, op. 1, d. 212, ll. 1–12; Chernyaev, *Sovmestnyi iskhod*, the entries of 3 and 21 January 1990, pp. 835, 838.

13. On Alexander Zinoviev's views and life see his *Russkaia tragediia* (Moscow: Algoritm, 2007); also his *Catastroika. Povest o Perestroike v Partgrade* (Moscow: EKSMO, Algoritm, 2003); Philip Hanson, "Homo Sovieticus among the Russia-watchers," in *Alexander Zinoviev as Writer and Thinker: An Assessment* (New York: Macmillan Press, 1988), pp. 154–72.

14. Boris Yeltsin's interview on the French channel Antenne-2, 9 March 1990, at http://zinoviev.info/wps/archives/518; https://www.youtube.com/watch?v=4r9e-QzP6Y, accessed 20 March 2020.

15. Chernyaev, *Sovmestnyi iskhod*, 1 January 1990, p. 833.

16. Senn, *Gorbachev's Failure in Lithuania*, p. 84.

17. See this argument in Edward W. Walker, *Dissolution: Sovereignty and the Breakup of the Soviet Union* (New York: Rowman & Littlefield, 2003); also at https://sites.fas.harvard.edu/~hpcws/comment21.htm.

18. David Remnick, *Lenin's Tomb: The Last Days of the Soviet Empire* (New York: Random House, 1993), p. 301; Taubman, *Gorbachev*, pp. 503–4; *Soiuz mozhno bylo sokhranit*, the entry of Gorbachev's January 1990 trip.

19. *Soiuz mozhno bylo sokhranit*, the entries of January 1990.

20. Raisa Gorbacheva, "Ia nadeius," at https://www.gorby.ru/ru/gorbacheva/I_hope.

21. On the television see complaints of the Politburo members, 22 February 1990, *V Politburo TsK KPSS*, pp. 565–6.

22. Gorbachev's meeting with miners, 2 February 1990, MSG SS, vol. 18, p. 221.

23. Vorotnikov, *A bylo eto tak*, p. 408.

24. Chernyaev, *Sovmestnyi iskhod*, the entry of 28 January 1990, p. 839.

25. Ibid, the entries of 21, 28 January, 21 April 1990, pp. 837, 838–9, 851.

26. Vorotnikov, *A bylo eto tak*, pp. 392, 394; *V Politburo TsK KPSS*, pp. 567–8; Chernyaev, *Sovmestnyi iskhod*, p. 841.

27. Vorotnikov, *A bylo eto tak*, p. 402; *V Politburo TsK KPSS*, p. 562.

28. MSG SS, vol. 18, pp. 621, 622.

29. Boldin, *Krushenie piedestala*, pp. 245–8.

30. Sobchak, *Khozhdenie vo vlast*, pp. 167–86.

31. *Vneocherednoi Tretii S'ezd Narodnykh Deputatov SSSR, March 12–15, 1990. Stenograficheskii otchet*, vol. 2 (Moscow: Izdanie Verkhovnogo Soveta SSSR, 1990), pp. 30–1; MSG SS, vol. 18, p. 515.

32. Vorotnikov, *A bylo eto tak*, pp. 406, 409; Chernyaev, *Sovmestnyi iskhod*, pp. 844, 847; Shakhnazarov, *Tsena svobody*, pp. 139–46.

33. Shakhnazarov, *Tsena svobody*, pp. 140–1, 144–5; Taubman, *Gorbachev*, p. 512.

34. Vorotnikov, *A bylo eto tak*, the entry of 30 March 1990, pp. 413–14.

35. Alexander Galkin and Chernyaev, *Mikhail Gorbachev i Germanskii vopros*, pp. 307–1. More on this in Vladislav Zubok, "With His Back Against the Wall: Gorbachev, Soviet Demise, and German Reunification," *Cold War History* 14:4 (2014), pp. 629–30.

36. Interview with Brent Scowcroft, 10–11 August 2000, BOHP, pp. 44, 45.

37. The memo of the meeting is at https://bush41library.tamu.edu/files/memcons-telcons/1989-12-03-Kohl.pdf, accessed 31 March 2020; Bush and Scowcroft, *A World Transformed*, pp. 197–9. Sarotte, *1989*, pp. 78–9; Spohr, *Post Wall*, ch. 4.

38. Galkin and Chernyaev, *Mikhail Gorbachev i Germanskii vopros*, pp. 334, 338.

39. Ibid, p. 354; telephone call from Helmut Kohl to George Bush, 13 February 1990, http://bushlibrary.tamu.edu/research/pdfs/memcons_telcons/1990-02-13-Kohl%20%5B1%5D.pdf.

40. Vneshekonombank to the Council of Ministers of the USSR (by Yuri Moskovsky), 16 June 1990, State Archives of the Russian Federation (GARF), f. 5446, op. 162, d. 1464, at http://gaidar-arc.ru/file/bulletin-1/DEFAULT/org.stretto.plugins.bulletin.core.article/file/2251, retrieved 1 April 2014; Tuomas Forsberg, "Economic Incentives, Ideas, and the End of the Cold War: Gorbachev and German Unification," *Journal of Cold War Studies* 7:2 (Spring 2005), pp. 142–64.

41. Bush and Scowcroft, *A World Transformed*, pp. 221–2; Memorandum of Conversation, Helmut Kohl, Bush, Baker, i.a. Camp David, 24 and 25 February 1990, at http://bushlibrary.tamu.edu/research/pdfs/memcons_telcons/1990-02-24-Kohl.pdf; http://bushlibrary.tamu.edu/research/pdfs/memcons_telcons/1990-02-25-Kohl.pdf. Adamishin to Braithwaite, 22 January 1990; Chernyaev to Braithwaite, 24 February 1990, Braithwaite's diary.

42. Chernyaev's notes at the Politburo, 13 February 1990, Chernyaev Papers, St Antony's College, Oxford; the Politburo notes for 2 March 1990, *Soiuz mozhno bylo sokhranit*; NSC Files 1989–1991, Baltics, from the American Embassy in Moscow to Secretary of State, "Ambassadors Call on Yakovlev," 30 March 1990, GBPL.

43. Senn, *Gorbachev's Failure in Lithuania*, pp. 90–7. Lieven, *The Baltic Revolution*, pp. 230–9. The declaration of the Congress of People's Deputies of the USSR on 15 March 1990, in *Raspad SSSR: Dokumenty i fakty (1986–1992)*, vol. 1 (Moscow: Walters Kluwer, 2009), pp. 296–7.

44. Vorotnikov, *A bylo eto tak*, pp. 408–9; *V Politburo TsK KPSS*, p. 581; Chernyaev, *Sovmestnyi iskhod*, entry of 22 March 1990, p. 846. For Yakovlev's stand see NSC Files 1989–1991, Baltics, from the American Embassy in Moscow to the Secretary of State, "Ambassadors Call on Yakovlev," 30 March 1990, GBPL.

45. *Raspad SSSR*, vol. 1, pp. 172–3.

46. https://ru.wikisource.org/wiki/Закон_СССР_от_03.04.1990_№_1409-I.

47. Stenographic record no. 2 of the Presidential Council of the USSR, RGANI, f. 121, op. 3, d. 48, ll. 4–19, 30, 31–6.

48. "Poslanie Prezidenta SSSR i predsedatelia Soveta Ministrov SSSR," *Raspad SSSR*, vol. 1, pp. 304–5.

49. Senn, *Gorbachev's Failure in Lithuania*, pp. 101–4.

50. https://bush41library.tamu.edu/files/memcons-telcons/1990-04-06-Shevardnadze.pdf. For the Russian records see Stepanov's diary, Teimuraz Stepanov-Mamaladze Papers, Box 5, Folder 8, HIA, pp. 439–40.

51. Meeting with Prime Minister Brian Mulroney of Canada, 10 April 1990, at https://bush-41library.tamu.edu/files/memcons-telcons/1990-04-10-Mulroney.pdf. Compare it with a quite different tone in the joint memoirs, Bush and Scowcroft, *A World Transformed*, pp. 222–7, 228–9, and the interview with Scowcroft no. 2, pp. 41–2, BOHP.

52. Bergmane, "French and US Reactions," pp. 172–6, 179; Bush and Scowcroft, *A World Transformed*, p. 216; interview with Scowcroft no. 2, pp. 42–3, BOHP.

53. Meeting with Foreign Minister Hans-Dietrich Genscher, 4 April 1990 at https://bush-41library.tamu.edu/files/memcons-telcons/1990-04-04-Genscher.pdf.

54. Meeting with President Mitterrand, 19 April 1990, at https://bush41library.tamu.edu/files/memcons-telcons/1990-04-19-Mitterrand%20[1].pdf.

55. Bergmane, "French and US Reactions," pp. 189–91, 202; Braithwaite's diary, 21 March 1990.

56. Shakhnazarov to Gorbachev, 5 May 1990, in his *Tsena svobody*, p. 470.

57. Chernyaev, *Sovmestnyi iskhod*, entry of 7 May 1990, pp. 855–6; Braithwaite's diary, 18 May 1990; Gorbachev's meeting with Baker, 17 May 1990, MSG SS, vol. 19, pp. 584–6; vol. 20, pp. 27–9, 135–44.

58. Remnick, *Lenin's Tomb*, pp. 325–7. Chernyaev, *Sovmestnyi iskhod*, p. 854; Vorotnikov, *A bylo eto tak*, p. 425; Braithwaite's diary, 8 May 1990.

59. Remnick, *Lenin's Tomb*, p. 328; Chernyaev, *Sovmestnyi iskhod*, entry of 5 May 1990, p. 854.

60. Chernyaev, *Sovmestnyi iskhod*, entry of 5 May 1990, p. 854; Vorotnikov, *A bylo eto tak*, p. 426; *V Politburo TsK KPSS*, pp. 494–5. The transcript of the Politburo discussion on this question remains unpublished.

61. The letter of Chernyaev to Gorbachev, 4 May 1990, in Galkin and Chernyaev, *Mikhail Gorbachev i Germanskii vopros*, p. 425.

62. See more on this in ch. 5.

63. "Iz Besedy s Kh. Telchikom," 14 May 1990, MSG SS, vol. 19, pp. 522–46; vol. 20, p. 518, n. 7; Taubman, *Gorbachev*, p. 549.

64. There were 17 police officers and 10 officers of the KGB elected. Sheinis, *Vzlet i padeniie parlamenta*, vol. 1, pp. 273–4.

65. Ibid, pp. 276, 281–2.

66. Yelena Fanailova, "Zakon o pechati," Radio Liberty at http://www.svoboda.org/a/27159049. html, accessed 24 March 2020.

67. Sheinis, *Vzlet i padeniie parlamenta*, vol. 1, pp. 264, 267–72.

68. The Politburo, 20 April 1990, in Vorotnikov, *A bylo eto tak*, pp. 423–4, 428–9.

69. Vorotnikov, *A bylo eto tak*, pp. 432–5; Sheinis, *Vzlet i padeniie parlamenta*, vol. 1, pp. 302–3. On Gorbachev's "amazing nonchalance" see Braithwaite's diary, 29 May 1990. The author's interview with Gennady Burbulis, 21 April 2020, by phone.

70. Diary of Stepanov-Mamaladze, 29 May 1990, Teimuraz Stepanov-Mamaladze Papers, Box 5, Folder 9, HIA, ll. 99–100, 105.

71. Taubman, *Gorbachev*, p. 553; Bush and Scowcroft, A *World Transformed*, pp. 282–83; Philip Zelikow and Condoleezza Rice, *Germany Unified and Europe Transformed: A Study in Statecraft* (Cambridge, MA: Harvard University Press, 1997), p. 278.

72. Diary of Stepanov-Mamaladze, 29 May 1990, Teimuraz Stepanov-Mamaladze Papers, Box 5, Folder 9, HIA, ll. 99–100, 105, 109, 120–1. Interview with Sergey Tarasenko, 19 March 1999, Moscow, courtesy of Oleg Skvortsov, head of the Oral History Project on the End of the Cold War, the Institute for General History, Russian Academy of Sciences.

73. https://bush41library.tamu.edu/files/memcons-telcons/1990-05-31-Gorbachev.pdf.

74. Taubman, *Gorbachev*, pp. 554–5; diary of Stepanov-Mamaladze, 1 June 1990, Teimuraz Stepanov-Mamaladze Papers, Box 5, Folder 9, HIA, ll. 127–8; the first meeting of Gorbachev and Bush, one on one, at https://bush41library.tamu.edu/files/memcons-telcons/1990-05-31-Gorbachev.pdf.

75. Chernyaev echoed Gorbachev, see Chernyaev, *Sovmestnyi iskhod*, entry of 17 June 1990, p. 858.

76. Gorbachev expressed this approach in his interview with the BBC on 8 June 1990, MSG SS, vol. 20, pp. 396–404.

77. Yeltsin's speech on 22 May 1990, Braithwaite's diary, 29 May 1990.

78. Sheinis, *Vzlet i padeniie parlamenta*, vol. 1, pp. 318–19.

79. Deklaratsiia S'ezda narodnykh deputatov RSFSR, 12 June 1990, "O gosudarstvennom suverenitete Rossiiskoi Federativnoi Sotsialisticheskoi Respubliki," in *Raspad SSSR*, vol. 1, pp. 181–3. The author's interview with Yevgeny Kozhokin, in 1990 a deputy from Democratic Russia, 15 September 2017, Moscow.

80. Archie Brown, "The End of the Soviet Union," *Journal of Cold War Studies* 17:4 (2015), p. 163.

81. Starovoitova in *Komsomolskaia Pravda*, 7 June 1991, cited in Dunlop, *The Rise of Russia*, p. 24; interview with Galina Starovoitova for the Ukrainian project *Rozpad Radians'koho Soiuzu*, at http://oralhistory.org.ua/interview-ua/566.

82. For the background see Serhii Plokhy, *The Gates of Europe: A History of Ukraine* (New York: Basic Books, 2015); the text of the Ukrainian declaration is in *Raspad SSSR* vol. 1, pp. 191–5.

83. Memo, Bush-Kohl meeting, the White House, 8 June 1990, at https://bush41library.tamu.edu/files/memcons-telcons/1990-06-08-Kohl.pdf; Zapiska N. I. Ryzhkova v TsK KPSS, 29 June 1990, f. 89, perechen 8, d. 77, 4–10; Vypiska iz protokola no. 178 of the Politburo session on 10 May 1990, RGANI, f. 89, per. 10, dok. 58, HIA, f. 89, Reel 1.990.

84. The author's interviews with Michael Boskin, HIA, 19 April 2013; Michael J. Boskin, *Capitalism and its Discontents: The Adam Smith Address* (Hoover Institution: Stanford University, 1999), pp. 9–11; Brady to Bush, 24 May 1990, Michael Boskin Files, Folder OA/ID CF01113–43, GBPL. Bush and Scowcroft, *A World Transformed*, p. 277.

85. Bush-Gorbachev telcon, 17 July 1990, at https://bush41library.tamu.edu/files/memcons-telcons/1990-07-17-Gorbachev.pdf. On the Houston summit see Svetlana Savranskaya and Thomas Blanton, eds., *The Last Superpower Summits: Reagan, Gorbachev and Bush at the End of the Cold War* (Budapest: Central European University Press, 2016), pp. 584–5.

86. Bush and Scowcroft, *A World Transformed*, pp. 276–7. Meeting with Chancellor Helmut Kohl, 8 June 1990, at https://bush41library.tamu.edu/files/memcons-telcons/1990-06-08-Kohl.pdf. Meeting with Brian Mulroney, 8 July 1990, at https://bush41library.tamu.edu/files/memcons-telcons/1990-07-08-Mulroney.pdf.

87. Zelikow and Rice, *Germany Unified*, pp. 277–8; Bush and Scowcroft, *A World Transformed*, pp. 282–3.

88. Diary of Stepanov-Mamaladze, 11 July 1990, Teimuraz Stepanov-Mamaladze Papers, Box 5, Folder 9, HIA, p. 170.

89. Vorotnikov, *A bylo eto tak*, pp. 440–3; Chernyaev, *Sovmestnyi iskhod*, entries of 24 June, 8 and 9 July 1990, pp. 861–2.

90. Diary of Stepanov-Mamaladze, 3 July 1990, Teimuraz, Stepanov-Mamaladze Papers, Box 5, Folder 10, HIA, ll. 188–91. Yakovlev's speech on 2 July 1990, *Pravda*, 4 July 1990.

91. Grachev, *Gorbachev's Gamble*, pp. 189–90. Diary of Stepanov-Mamaladze, 12 July 1990, Stepanov-Mamaladze Papers, Box 5, Folder 9, HIA, 12 July 1990, ll. 207, 212.

92. Sheinis, *Vzlet i padeniie parlamenta*, pp. 355–6. For Yeltsin's approval rating see the data from VTsIOM (around October 1990) at AY, f. 6, op. 1, d. 59, ll. 117–22.

93. Chernyaev, *Sovmestnyi iskhod*, entries of 11 and 14 July 1990, pp. 863, 864; Galkin and Chernyaev, *Gorbachev i Germanskii vopros*, pp. 492–503. The meeting with Secretary General Manfred Wörner of NATO, 5 July 1990, at https://bush41library.tamu.edu/files/memcons-telcons/1990-06-08-Kohl.pdf.

94. On the details of the talks in Arkhyz see Hanns Jürgen Küsters and Daniel Hoffmann, *Deutsche Einheit: Sonderedition aus den Akten des Bundeskanzleramtes 1989/90* (Munich: De Gruyter Oldenbourg, 1998), pp. 1,357–64; Spohr, *Post Wall, Post Square*, pp. 242–3.

CHAPTER 5: CROSSROADS

1. Braithwaite's diary, 31 March and 23 November 1989.

2. Mikhail Bernstam to the author, communication of 3 September 2020. Compare this with what China did at the same time: Barry Naughton, *Growing out of the Plan: Chinese Economic Reform, 1978–1993* (New York: Cambridge University Press, 1996).

3. Ryzhkov, *Perestroika*, p. 130; Pavlov, *Upushchen li shans?*, pp. 94–7; Gorbachev, *Zhizn i reformy*, vol. 1, p. 566; V. Pavlov to the State Commission on Economic Reform, 2 November 1989. GARF, f. 5446, op. 150, d. 64, ll. 53–62; V. G. Panskov to the Council of Ministers, 11 November 1989. GARF, f. 7733, op. 65. d. 4847, ll. 35–41. Abalkin's interview in *Pravda*, 16 December 1989, p. 1.

4. Gorbachev, *Zhizn i reformy*, vol. 1, p. 567. See the government's economic program and its discussion in *Pravda*, 11 and 14–15 November 1989; Ryzhkov's presentation of the program at the Second Congress of People's Deputies, *Pravda*, 15 December 1989.

5. Ryzhkov, *Perestroika*, pp. 234–5, 254–5. Ryzhkov on "bankruptcy": Shevardnadze's remark to his aides. Stepanov-Mamaladze diary, 16 July 1990, Teimuraz Stepanov-Mamaladze

Papers, Box 5, Folder 7, HIA. On the speculative external trade see RGANI, f. 121, op. 3, d. 13, l. 13. The price of oil is at https://www.eia.gov/dnav/pet/hist/LeafHandler.ashx?n=-pet&s=f000000 3&f=m.

6. "Zanyat 'oboronku,'" Part II. *Novaia gazeta*, 11 February 2008, at https://novayagazeta. ru/articles/2008/02/11/39365-zanyat-oboronku-chast-ii.

7. Ryashentsev's interview to *Kommersant* on 5 March 1990, at https://www.kommersant. ru/doc/265944; Sobchak, *Khozhdeniie vo vlast*, pp. 55–60; Ryzhkov, *Perestroika*, pp. 259–66; the later journalistic investigation in "Zanyat 'oboronku,'" parts I–IV, *Novaia gazeta* 9, 10, 11, 12 February 2008, at https://novayagazeta.ru/articles/2008/02/11/39365-za-nyat-oboronku-chast-ii; https://novayagazeta.ru/articles/2008/02/14/39323-zanyat-obo-ronku-chast-iii.

8. Braithwaite's diary, 14 and 23 March 1990; Sobchak's accusations and Ryzhkov's emotional defense at https://www.youtube.com/watch?v=suFhs9CypMc.

9. On the Polish reform see Henryk Kierzkowski, Marek Okolski, and Stanislaw Wellisz, eds., *Stabilization and Structural Adjustment in Poland* (New York: Routledge, 1993).

10. See Yakov Feygin, "Reforming the Cold War State: Economic Thought, Internationalization, and the Politics of Soviet Reform, 1955–1985," PhD Dissertation, University of Pennsylvania, 2017, p. 91.

11. Nikolai Petrakov, *Russkaia ruletka. Ekonomicheskii eksperiment tsenoiu 150 millionov zhiznei* (Moscow: Economika, 1998), pp. 102, 104–5.

12. Petrakov prepared the program jointly with the economist Boris Fyodorov; Petrakov, *Russkaia ruletka*, pp. 109–16.

13. Gorbachev to Jaruzelski, 13 April 1990, Moscow, in MSG SS, vol. 19, pp. 245, 248.

14. See the discussion at the Presidential Council on 18 April 1990 in Vorotnikov, *A bylo eto tak*, pp. 420–1; Gorbachev, *Zhizn i reformy*, vol. 1, p. 570.

15. Braithwaite's diary, 25 April 1990.

16. Abalkin, *Neispolzovannyi shans*, pp. 167–8.

17. See Gorbachev's answers on 11 May 1990, MSG SS, vol. 19, p. 458; *Pravda*, 14 May 1990.

18. Stenographic report no. 4 of the joint meeting of the Presidential Council and the Council of Federation, 22 May 1990, RGANI, f. 121, op. 3, d. 56, ll. 29, 41–55, 67–70, 84, 96–7, 108–9, 130–1.

19. Abalkin. *Neispolzovannyi shans*, pp. 165–6; Gorbachev, *Zhizn i reformy*, vol. 1, p. 570; Ryzhkov, *Perestroika*, pp. 310–11.

20. Vorotnikov, *A bylo eto tak*, p. 422; Braithwaite's diary, 22 and 23 May 1990; interview with Stanislav Shatalin by Andrey Karaulov, 28 July 1991, published in *Nezavisimaia gazeta*, 24 August 1991, at http://www.yavlinsky.ru/said/documents/index.phtml?id=2422.

21. On the Russian declaration see Shakhnazarov's note to Gorbachev, 13 August 1990, in his *Tsena svobody*, p. 486.

22. The author's interview with Alexander Drozdov, now the head of the Yeltsin Center, 31 March 2020, by phone.

23. GARF, f. 10026, op. 1, d. 270, ll. 58–61; Gerashchenko in Krotov, *Ocherki istorii*, pp. 172–3.

24. Vladimir Rasskazov's recollections in Krotov, *Ocherki istorii*, pp. 246–50.

25. https://bio.yavlinsky.ru/#round-five.

26. Grigory Yavlinsky's interview to PBS, on 9 October 2000, at http://www.pbs.org/wgbh/commandingheights/shared/minitext/int_grigoriiyavlinsky.html, accessed 17 January 2016.

27. G. A. Yavlinsky, A. Yu. Mikhailov, M. M. Zadornov, "400 dnei doveriia," Moscow, 1990, at https://www.yabloko.ru/Publ/500/400-days.pdf, accessed 26 April 2020. Yavlinsky's interview on 4 March 2010, at https://www.forbes.ru/interview/45575-reformatory-prihodyat-k-vlasti-grigorii-yavlinskii, accessed 16 April 2020.

28. Ryzhkov, *Perestroika*, pp. 320–1; Yavlinsky's interview on 4 March 2010.

29. Petrakov, *Russkaia ruletka*, pp. 133–4.

30. Boris Yeltsin to the Austrian newspaper *Kurier*, trans. TASS, 25 July 1990, AY, f. 6, op. 1, d. 36, ll. 22–8, and Yeltsin's press conference on 26 June 1990, AY, d. 37, ll. 125–54, at https://yeltsin.ru/archive/paperwork/9433.

31. Petrakov, *Russkaia ruletka*, p. 135.
32. Taubman, *Gorbachev*, p. 528.
33. https://zakon.rada.gov.ua/cgi-bin/laws/main.cgi?nreg=55-12#Text; RGANI, f. 121, op. 3, d. 59, l. 104; for a different, more economy-centered view, see Taubman, *Gorbachev*, pp. 522–3; *Raspad SSSR*, vol. 1, pp. 191–5. MSG SS, vol. 21, pp. 288–9.
34. Petrakov, *Russkaia ruletka*, pp. 136–8. For the political and legal assumptions of Shatalin, Yavlinsky, Petrakov, and their team, see https://www.yabloko.ru/Publ/500/500-3.html, accessed 20 April 2020.
35. Petrakov, *Russkaia ruletka*, p. 138; Ryzhkov, *Perestroika*, pp. 322–4; Abalkin, *Neispollzovannyi shans*, p. 197.
36. BBC interview with Shatalin for the documentary "The Second Russian Revolution." The Transcript, cited in Taubman, *Gorbachev*, p. 523; Petrakov, *Russkaia ruletka*, p. 139.
37. Abalkin, *Neispolzovannyi shans*, pp. 201–3; Ryzhkov, *Perestroika*, p. 329.
38. Petrakov, *Russkaia ruletka*, pp. 139–42; "500 Days. The Concept of a Program of Transition to a Market Economy as a Foundation of an Economic Union of Sovereign Republics," at https://www.yabloko.ru/Publ/500/500-days.html, accessed 20 April 2020. The version submitted to Gorbachev on 29 August is in RGANI, f. 121, op. 3, d. 60, ll. 97–116.
39. Vasily Seliunin, "Uroki polskogo," *Ogonyok* 33 (11–18 August 1990), pp. 3–5; Igor Klyamkin, "Oktyabrskii vybor prezidenta," *Ogonyok* 47 (11–24 November 1990), pp. 4–5; Petrakov, *Russkaia ruletka*, pp. 150–2.
40. Informatsiia o politicheskikh nastroeniakh moskvichei v avguste 1990, AY, f. 6, op. 1, d. 59, ll. 94–107.
41. Anatoly Chernyaev, *My Six Years with Gorbachev* (Moscow: Progress, 1993), pp. 284–6; Chernyaev, *Sovmestnyi iskhod*, 21 August 1990, p. 866.
42. *Sovetskaia Tatariia*, 12 August 1990; *Sovetskaia Bashkiriia*, 14 August 1990; cited in *Soyuz mozhno bylo sokhranit*, pp. 185–6.
43. The author's interview with Gennady Burbulis, 6 May 2020, by phone.
44. Chernyaev, *Sovmestnyi iskhod*, 21 August 1990, pp. 867–8.
45. Ryzhkov, *Perestroika*, p. 328; Abalkin, *Neispolzovannyi shans*, pp. 200, 206–7; Petrakov, *Russkaia ruletka*, pp. 142–3. The author's interview with Gennady Burbulis, 6 May 2020, by phone.
46. Petrakov, *Russkaia ruletka*, pp. 152–3; Chernyaev, *My Six Years with Gorbachev*, p. 868.
47. Petrakov, *Russkaia ruletka*, pp. 153–4; Shatalin's interview cited in Taubman, *Gorbachev*, p. 527.
48. Petrakov, *Russkaia ruletka*, pp. 155–6.
49. Yeltsin's theses and notes on the results of the meeting with Gorbachev, 29 August 1990. AY, f. 6, op. 1, d. 31, ll. 16–26.
50. Chernyaev, *My Six Years with Gorbachev*, p. 286; Chernyaev, *Sovmestnyi iskhod*, 27 August 1990, p. 870.
51. Medical notes on Yeltsin to V. Boldin, 15 and 29 August 1990, AY, f. 6, op. 1, d. 203, ll. 11–17; also Adamishin's diary, 14 September 1990, Adamishin Papers, HIA.
52. The data from VTsIOM (around October 1990) at AY, f. 6, op. 1, d. 59, ll. 117–22.
53. The author's interview with Gennady Burbulis, 6 May 2020, by phone.
54. Notes on the results of the meeting with Gorbachev, 29 August 1990. AY, f. 6, op. 1, d. 31, ll. 22–6.
55. *Raspad SSSR. Dokumenty i fakty*, vol. 2 (Moscow: Kuchkovo pole, 2016), pp. 366–73.
56. The minutes of the meeting on 30 August 1991, RGANI, f. 121, op. 3, d. 67, ll. 1–5, 24–32, 34–43.
57. RGANI, f. 121, op. 3, d. 67, ll. 147–52.
58. Ibid, ll. 234–5.
59. Ibid, ll. 188–92.
60. RGANI, f. 121, op. 3, d. 68, ll. 110–12.
61. Gorbachev, *Zhizn i reformy*, vol. 1, p. 578; Abalkin, *Neispolzovannyi shans*, p. 216.

62. Adamishin's diary, 7 September 1990, Adamishin Papers, HIA.
63. Remnick, *Lenin's Tomb*, pp. 358–9; also Braithwaite's diary, 15 September 1990.
64. Remnick, *Lenin's Tomb*, pp. 359–67.
65. Pikhoia, *Sovetskii Soiuz* pp. 601–2. Rudolf Pikhoia, "Nikto ne khotel ustupat," *Ogonyok* 37 (2010), published online on 20 September 2010, at https://www.kommersant.ru/doc/1503613, accessed 2 May 2020.
66. Viktor Yaroshenko, "Energiia raspada," *Novyi Mir* (March 1991), p. 171.
67. Adamishin's diary, entries of 9 and 10 September 1990, Adamishin Papers, HIA.
68. Pavlov, *Upushchen li shans?*, pp. 27–8.
69. Taubman, *Gorbachev*, p. 529.
70. The numbers are from the papers of Vitaly Katayev, Box 12, Folder 27, HIA.
71. Savranskaya and Blanton, *The Last Superpower Summits*, pp. 709–10, and Pavel Palazhchenko, *My Years with Gorbachev and Shevardnadze: The Memoir of a Soviet Interpreter* (University Park, PA: Pennsylvania State University Press, 1997), p. 209; diary of Stepanov-Mamaladze, entry of 3 August 1990, Teimuraz Stepanov-Mamaladze Papers, Box 5, Folder 9, HIA, pp. 286–7.
72. James A. Baker, *The Politics of Diplomacy: Revolution, War, and Peace, 1989–1992* (New York: G. P. Putnam's Sons, 1995), p. 1; Bush and Scowcroft, *A World Transformed*, p. 326; the information of Jim Collins to Vladimir Pechatnov (related by Pechatnov to the author), 29 April 2020; Sergey Tarasenko, interview (undated), The Hoover Institution and Gorbachev Foundation Collection, Box 3, Folder 2, HIA, pp. 68–9. On the American perspective and intentions see Baker, *The Politics of Diplomacy*, pp. 10–15, and Dennis Ross, *Statecraft* (New York: Farrar, Straus, Giroux, 2008), ch. 4; interview no. 2 with Brent Scowcroft, 10–11 August 2000, BOHP, pp. 78–84.
73. Bush and Scowcroft, *A World Transformed*, pp. 358–63. Savranskaya and Blanton, *The Last Superpower Summits*, pp. 713, 730; "Soviet Economic Reform at a Crossroads," 3 August 1990, Directorate of Intelligence, Michael Boskin Files, Folder OA/ID CF01113–43, GBPL.
74. Chernyaev, *Sovmestnyi iskhod*, 13 September 1990, p. 872; MSG SS, vol. 22, pp. 45–56; Savranskaya and Blanton, *The Last Superpower Summits*, pp. 714, 734. The American memo does not contain Bush's effusive proclamation; https://bush41library.tamu.edu/files/memcons-telcons/1990-09-09--Gorbachev%20[1].pdf.
75. Sergey Tarasenko recalled this formula repeatedly in his conversations with the author in 1998. The citation is from Savranskaya and Blanton, *The Last Superpower Summits*, p. 716. Also Tarasenko's interview in The Hoover Institution and Gorbachev Foundation Collection, Box 3, Folder 2 HIA, pp. 64–7, esp. p. 66; Scowcroft, BOHP, p. 84.
76. Bush and Scowcroft, *A World Transformed*, p. 368, at https://bush41library.tamu.edu/files/memcons-telcons/1990-09-09--Gorbachev%20[2].pdf.
77. Chernyaev, *Sovmestnyi iskhod*, 13 September 1990, p. 872.
78. Sarotte, *1989*, pp. 192–3; Galkin and Chernyaev, *Gorbachev i Germanskii vopros*, pp. 554–9, 563–6.
79. Chernyaev, *Sovmestnyi iskhod*, 14 and 15 September, 31 October 1990, pp. 872–3, 884.
80. *V Politburo TsK KPSS*, pp. 610–11; Petrakov, *Russkaia ruletka*, pp. 166–7; Braithwaite's diary, 24 September 1990.
81. Yaroshenko, "Energiia raspada," pp. 181–5.
82. *Pravda*, 26 September 1990; Yaroshenko, "Energiia raspada," pp. 180–1.
83. Pikhoia, *Sovetskii Soiuz*, p. 533
84. "Vremia sovmestnykh deistvii. Vstrecha M. S. Gorbacheva s deiateliami sovetskoi kultury," *Pravda*, 3 October 1990, p. 2.
85. Peter Reddaway and Dmitri Glinski, *The Tragedy of Russia's Reforms: Market Bolshevism against Democracy* (Washington, DC: United States Institute of Peace, 2001), p. 176.
86. Yavlinsky's letter to Yeltsin on 5 November 1990, AY, f. 6, op. 1, d. 41, ll. 132–3. The author's interview with Grigory Yavlinsky, 24 December 2016, Moscow.
87. Petrakov, *Russkaia ruletka*, pp. 167–70.

88. Chernyaev, *Sovmestnyi iskhod*, 14 and 23 October 1990, pp. 879, 883-4.

89. *Izvestia*, 16 October 1990.

90. *V Politburo TsK KPSS*, pp. 617-21; Chernyaev, *Sovmestnyi iskhod*, 17 October 1990, pp. 880-1.

91. Braithwaite's diary, entry of 13 September 1990.

92. The notes of Yeltsin on his meeting with Kryuchkov, 18 September 1990. AY, f. 6, op. 1, d. 60, ll. 92-5; Ruslan Khasbulatov, *Poluraspad SSSR. Kak razvalili sverkhderzhavu* (Moscow: Yauza Press, 2011), pp. 187-8.

93. The author's interviews with Gennady Burbulis, 21 and 28 April 2020, by phone; Gennady Burbulis, interview by David C. Speedie, 8 February 2011. The End of the Cold War: The US Global Engagement Interview Series, at: https://www.carnegie-council.org/studio/multimedia/20110208c/index.html, accessed 21 May 2016.

94. The minutes of the council, 18 and 24 October 1990, AY, f. 6, op. 1, d. 22, ll. 1-2, 8-11, at https://yeltsin.ru/archive/paperwork/9315.

95. The minutes of the council, 18 and 24 October 1990, AY, f. 6, op. 1, d. 22, ll. 8-11, at https://yeltsin.ru/archive/paperwork/9315.

96. Alexander Solzhenitsyn, "Kak nam obustroit Rossiiu," *Komsomolskaia Pravda* (18 September 1990).

97. The author's interviews with Gennady Burbulis, 21 and 28 April 2020, by phone.

98. Dunlop, *The Rise of Russia*, pp. 102-3.

99. The report to the CC CPSU on the Congress, 24 October 1990, f. 89 (created from the materials collected for the CPSU trial), op. 12, d. 29, copies at HIA; Yaroshenko, "Energiia raspada," pp. 178-9; *Ogonyok* 44 (October 1990), pp. 2-3.

100. The minutes of the Presidential Council, 31 October 1990, RGANI, f. 121, op. 3, d. 78, ll. 137, 170, 207-9.

101. Ibid, l. 209.

102. Ibid, ll. 93-4, 97, 102-16, 133-4; Gorbachev, *Zhizn i reformy*, vol. 1, pp. 583-4.

103. RGANI, f. 121, op. 3, d. 78, ll. 244-5.

104. Ibid, ll. 246-9.

105. Ibid, ll. 250-7, 268.

106. Shevardnadze discussed it with his aides on 24 August 1991, after the collapse of the coup. Stepanov-Mamaladze Papers, Box 3, Folder 28, HIA.

107. https://ria.ru/20151107/1314380162.html and https://www.youtube.com/watch?v=I0wPT-Ec4NA, accessed 11 May 2020.

108. https://ria.ru/20151107/1314380162.html and https://www.youtube.com/watch?v=I0wPT-Ec4NA, accessed 11 May 2020.

109. https://www.youtube.com/watch?v=711ZgWTIm4g; Braithwaite's diary, 7 November 1990.

110. MSG SS, vol. 23, pp. 43, 52.

111. *Ukrainian Weekly*, 11 November 1990, p. 1; https://www.youtube.com/watch?v=I0wPT-Ec4NA.

CHAPTER 6: LEVIATHAN

1. The minutes of the Presidential Council, 5 November 1990, RGANI, f. 121, op. 3, d. 81, ll. 71, 81.

2. Roy Medvedev, *Boris Yeltsin. Narod i vlast v kontse XX veka. Iz nabliudenii istorika* (Moscow: Vremia, 2011), p. 48; Vorotnikov, *A bylo eto tak*, p. 452.

3. "Stenogramma soveshchaniia sekretarei TsK KPSS," 19 July 1990, RGANI, f. 121, op. 103, d. 178, l. 2.

4. Ibid, ll. 2, 20.

5. Pikhoia, *Sovetskii Soiuz*, p. 544.

6. Chernyaev, *Sovmestnyi iskhod*, entries of 8 and 9 July 1990, pp. 861-2.

7. One, albeit quite biased, source for this is Yuri Prokofiev, *Do i posle zapreta KPSS. Pervyi sekretar MGK KPSS vspominaet* (Moscow: Algoritm, Eksmo, 2005), at http://www.velykoross.ru/1189.

8. The data of VTsIOM (around October 1990) in AY, f. 6, op. 1, d. 59, ll. 123–5.

9. Oleg Shenin, interview by Oleg Skvortsov, 14 December 1998, p. 14. The Oral History Project of the Institute of General History (Moscow) and the National Security Archive (Washington, DC). The transcript in the author's personal files.

10. Rudolf Pikhoia, "Pochemu nomenklatura ne stala zashchishchat Sovetskii Soiuz," a lecture on 24 February 2012, at http://www.russ.ru/Mirovaya-povestka/Rudol-f-Pihoya-Pochemu-nomenklatura-ne-stala-zaschischat-Sovetskij-Soyuz, accessed 13 March 2016.

11. V. S. Chernomyrdin, *Krasnyi director. 1938–1990 (memuary)* (Moscow: Muzei Chernomyrdina, 2013), pp. 195–7.

12. Andrew Barnes, *Owning Russia: The Struggle over Factories, Farms, and Power* (Ithaca, NY: Cornell University Press, 2006), pp. 53–61.

13. On the estimate of the Party property cost see the note of M. Bocharov to R. Khasbulatov, "Ob imushchestve KPSS," around July 1991, GARF, f. 10026, op. 10, d. 3, ll. 209–10. See also the discussion of Party commercial activities at the Party Secretariat on 19 July 1990, RGANI, f. 121, op. 103, d. 178. Paul Khlebnikov, *Godfather of the Kremlin: The Decline of Russia in the Age of Gangster Capitalism* (New York: Harcourt, Inc., 2000), pp. 56–9; David Hoffman, *The Oligarchs: Wealth and Power in the New Russia* (New York: Public Affairs, 2011), p. 125.

14. Yaroshenko, "Energiia raspada," p. 173; Kotkin and Gross, *Uncivil Society.*

15. Leon Onikov, *KPSS: anatomiia raspada* (Moscow: Respublika, 1996), p. 10; a similar view in Roy Medvedev, *Boris Yeltsin*, p. 48.

16. Doug McAdam, Sidney Tarrow, and Charles Tilly, *Dynamics of Contention* (New York: Cambridge University Press, 2004), p. 250; Derluguian, *Bourdieu's Secret Admirer.*

17. Masliukov and Glubokov, "Planirovaniie i finansirovaniie", p. 121; Vitaly Shlykov, "Chto pogubilo Sovetskii Soiuz? Amerikanskaia razvedka o sovetskikh voiennykh raskhodakh," *Voennyi vestnik* 8 (2001), p. 13.

18. Interview with Gen. Eduard Vorobiev, deputy head of the Defense Committee of the Russian Federation in 2000–3, at http://ru-90.ru/content/трудности-становления-российских-вооруженных-сил-интервью-с-эа-воробьевым.

19. Yaroshenko, "Energiia raspada," p. 166.

20. D. T. Yazov, *Udary sud'by. Vospominaniia soldata i marshala* (Moscow: Tsentrpoligraf, 2014). Sergey Akhromeyev and Georgy Kornienko, *Glazami marshala i diplomata. kriticheskii vzgliad na vneshniuu politiku SSSR do i posle 1985 goda* (Moscow: Mezhdunarodniie Otnosheniia, 1992).

21. On the conflict between the military and Shevardnadze, see Savranskaya and Blanton, *The Last Superpower Summits*, pp. 260–1. On Akhromeyev see Vitaly Katayev's recollections, HIA, pp. 196–9.

22. The author's interview with George Schultz, 10 April 2013, Stanford, CA.

23. Braithwaite noticed in Yazov "deep-rooted uneasiness about Germany." Braithwaite's diary, entry of 12 November 1990; Grachev, *Gorbachev's Gamble*, p. 191; interview with Moiseyev in 2011, at https://www.gzt-sv.ru/articles/3252-general-moiseev-detstve-gk-chp-zhurnalistah. Teimuraz Stepanov-Mamaladze Papers, Box 3, Folder 11, HIA, ll.

24. William Odom, *The Collapse of the Soviet Military* (New Haven, CT, and London: Yale University Press, 1998), pp. 272–80; Katayev Papers, Box 3, Folder 1, HIA. For minutes of discussions on the Warsaw Pact, the Vienna talks, etc., HIA.

25. Braithwaite's diary, entries of 11 November and 9 and 10 December 1990.

26. The text of this letter is in Katayev Papers, Box 8, Folder 22, HIA, pp. 6–8.

27. Braithwaite's diary, entry of 11 November 1990; Shevardnadze's remarks on 5 November 1990, Katayev Papers, Box 3, Folder 1, HIA.

28. Yazov's remarks are from the notes of Vitaly Katayev, on 24 August and 5 November 1990, Katayev Papers, Box 3, Folder 1, HIA; Chernyaev, *Sovmestnyi iskhod*, entry of 20 October 1990, p. 882.

29. Odom, *The Collapse of the Soviet Military*, p. 259.

30. Stenogramma zasedania prezidentskogo soveta, 28 September 1990, RGANI, f. 121, op. 3, d. 71, ll. 176, 177–8.

31. The figure discussed at the meeting of the Military Commission of the CC CPSU on 29 October 1990. Katayev Papers, Box 2, Folder 4, HIA; Odom, *The Collapse of the Soviet Military*, pp. 292–7.
32. Katayev's notes at the session of the military commission in the defense department of the CC CPSU, 28 October 1990. Katayev Papers, Box 2, Folder 4, HIA.
33. Alexander Lebed, *Za derzhavu obidno* (Moscow: Moskovskaia Pravda, 1995), pp. 260–1; https://www.youtube.com/watch?v=I0wPT-Ec4NA.
34. The abridged text, only with Gorbachev's speech and answers to questions, was published in *Pravda*, 16 October 1990, and reproduced in MSG SS, vol. 23, pp. 84–95.
35. Grachev, *Gorbachev's Gamble*, p. 274.
36. For more background see Knight, "The KGB, Perestroika, and the Collapse of the Soviet Union," pp. 67–93.
37. Memorandum of conversation, Robert M. Gates and V. I. Kryuchkov, 9 February 1990, KGB Headquarters, Moscow, Scowcroft Collection, Box 21, OA/ID 91128–001, GBPL. Kryuchkov in an interview on 19 May 1999. The Hoover Institution and Gorbachev Foundation Collection interviews on the end of the Cold War, Box 2, Folder 7, p. 26, HIA.
38. Memorandum of conversation, Robert M. Gates and V. I. Kryuchkov, 9 February 1990, KGB Headquarters, Moscow, Scowcroft Collection, Box 21, OA/ID 91128–001, GBPL.
39. Ibid.
40. In his memoirs Gates claimed that Kryuchkov was openly opposing Gorbachev in a meeting with him. The declassified US record of the conversation does not support this claim. Gates, *From the Shadows*, p. 491.
41. Leonid Shebarshin, *Ruka Moskvy: zapiski nachalnika sovetskoi razvedki* (Moscow: Tsentr-100, 1992), pp. 271–4.
42. Braithwaite's diary, entry of 14 December 1990.
43. The data by sociologist Olga Kryshtanovskaia, "Smena vsekh ili smena stilia," *Moscow News* (21 April 1991).
44. Shebarshin, *Ruka Moskvy*, p. 269.
45. Oleg Kalugin, *Spymaster: My Thirty-Two Years in Intelligence and Espionage against the West* (New York: Basic Books, 2009).
46. Shebarshin's interview in *Pravda*, 22 April 1990, reproduced in his *Ruka Moskvy*, p. 316.
47. Ibid, p. 272; Vladimir Kryuchkov, *Lichnoie delo*, vols. 1 and 2 (Moscow: Olimp, 1996), pp. 87–8.
48. Chernyaev, *Sovmestnyi iskhod*, 19 February and 17 March 1990, pp. 919, 929.
49. On this style see Raymond L. Garthoff, *Soviet Leaders and Intelligence: Assessing the American Adversary during the Cold War* (Washington, DC: Georgetown University Press, 2015).
50. Kryuchkov, *Lichnoie delo*, vol. 2, p. 41.
51. The information from Gennady Burbulis, 6 May 2020, by phone.
52. Braithwaite's diary, 11, 22, and 25 December 1990.
53. For discussion of MIC expenditures see Masliukov and Glubokov, "Planirovaniie i finansirovaniie," pp. 105–20; Zasedanie planovoi i biudzhetno-finansovoi komissii, 29 November 1990, GARF, f. 9654, op. 7, d. 881, ll. 63, 84–7. For the background see Julian Cooper, *The Soviet Defence Industry: Conversion and Reform*, Chatham House Papers (London: Bloomsbury Academic, 2000).
54. The best accounts on this program are Hoffman, *The Dead Hand*, and Milton Leitenberg, *The Soviet Biological Weapons Program: A History* (Cambridge, MA: Harvard University Press, 2012).
55. Robert Mosbacher to George Bush, 19 September 1990. Scowcroft Collection, OA-ID 91119-003, GBPL.
56. Stenogramma zasedania prezidentskogo soveta, 28 September 1990. RGANI, f. 121, op. 3, d. 71, ll. 3–14. Katayev Papers, Box 12, Folder 13, HIA. Andrei Kokoshin, "Defense Industry Conversion in the Russian Federation," p. 48; Gaddy, *The Price of the Past*, p. 66.
57. Stenogramma zasedania prezidentskogo soveta, 28 September 1990. RGANI, f. 121, op. 3, d. 71, ll. 50–2; Masliukov and Glubokov, "Planirovaniie i finansirovaniie."

58. Ibid, ll. 82–9; E. P. Velikhov, *Moi put'. Ia na valenkakh poiedu v 35-i god* (Moscow: Sotsproekt, 2009), accessed at https://biography.wikireading.ru/201606.

59. Stenogramma zasedania prezidentskogo soveta, 28 September 1990. RGANI, f. 121, op. 3, d. 71, ll. 105–6; Masliukov and Glubokov, "Planirovaniie i finansirovaniie", ll. 105–6; on the plutonium initiative see the memo of 15 October 1991 in Burns and Hewett Files: USSR, Chronology Files, OA-ID CF01407-013-40, GBPL.

60. Stenogramma zasedania prezidentskogo soveta, 28 September 1990. RGANI, f. 121, op. 3, d. 71, ll. 57–64; Masliukov and Glubokov, "Planirovaniie i finansirovaniie", ll. 57–64. For more about Baklanov's personality and views see O. D. Baklanov, *Kosmos—sud'ba moia. Zapiski iz "Matrosskoi tishiny,"* vol. 1 (Moscow: Obshchestvo sokhraneniia literaturnogo naslediia, 2014), 221, pp. 8–9, 12–14, 24, 221; interview of O. Skvortsov with O. Baklanov, October 2000, in the author's personal files.

61. Stenogramma zasedania prezidentskogo soveta, 28 September 1990. RGANI, f. 121, op. 3, d. 71, ll. 116–18; Masliukov and Glubokov, "Planirovaniie i finansirovaniie", ll. 116–18.

62. On Primakov's autobiographical details see Yevgeny Primakov, *Vstrechi na perekrestkakh* (Moscow: Tsentrpoligraf, 2015), pp. 8–24.

63. Stenogramma zasedania prezidentskogo soveta, 28 September 1990. RGANI, f. 121, op. 3, d. 71, l. 130; Masliukov and Glubokov, "Planirovaniie i finansirovaniie", l. 130.

64. See the American reporting on the event: *Soviet Conversion 1991. Report and Recommendations of an International Working Group on Economic Demilitarization and Adjustment*, ed. John Tepper Marlin, PhD, and Paul Grenier. Colby Papers, MC 113, Box 15, Folder 3. The Seeley Mudd Library, Princeton University.

65. *Soviet Conversion 1991*, pp. 52–3, 55–6.

66. Ibid, p. 57.

67. Ibid, pp. 11–12, 24.

68. Velikhov, *Moi put'*.

69. The first draft, prepared by Vladimir Kudryavtsev and his colleagues from the Institute of State and Law in Moscow, dated 15 June 1990, in GARF, f. 10026, op. 3, d. 411, ll. 1–12; the draft of 22 November 1990 presented by Gorbachev to the Congress of People's Deputies is in GARF, f. 10026, op. 3, d. 411, ll. 33a–33e.

70. MSG SS, vol. 23, pp. 486–7.

71. *Moscow News*, 6 January 1991, p. 6; Medvedev, *Boris Yeltsin*, pp. 406–8.

72. Remnick, *Lenin's Tomb*, pp. 386–7.

73. Dunlop, *The Rise of Russia*, p. 149.

74. The Politburo minutes, 16 November 1990, MSG SS, vol. 23, pp. 426–46.

75. Chernyaev, *Sovmestnyi iskhod*, 15 November 1990, pp. 886–7; MSG SS, vol. 23, pp. 141–2.

76. MSG SS, vol. 23, pp. 176–7; Pavlov, *Upushchen li shans?*, p. 28.

77. On the threat to derail the ratification of treaties on German unification see Zasedaniie voiennoi komissii TsK KPSS, 29 October 1990, Vitaly Katayev's notes, Katayev Papers, Box 2, Folder 4, HIA.

78. Savranskaya and Blanton, *The Last Superpower Summits*, pp. 775–6.

79. MSG SS, vol. 23, pp. 176–7; Savranskaya and Blanton, *The Last Superpower Summits*, pp. 773–80.

80. Chernyaev, *Sovmestnyi iskhod*, 24 November 1990, pp. 887–8.

81. Shakhnazarov's record of his conversation with Gorbachev on 5 December 1990, *V Politburo TsK KPSS*, pp. 658–9.

82. The information to the author from Odd Arne Westad, who at the time worked at the Norwegian Nobel Institute; e-mail of 25 April 2021.

83. A memo to Yeltsin on the situation in Ukraine, prepared for his visit (without authors or a date), AY, f. 6, op. 1, d. 57, ll. 64–73.

84. The text of Yeltsin's speech at the Supreme Soviet of the Ukrainian SSR and other materials, 18–19 November 1990. AY, f. 6, op. 1, d. 57, ll. 110–51; d. 216, ll. 11–45.

85. Solzhenitsyn, "Kak nam obustroit Rossiiu," *Komsomolskaia Pravda* (18 September 1990); the author's interview with Gennady Burbulis, 24 May 2020, by phone.

86. Yevgeny Kozhokin, deputy of Vladimir Lukin, to Andrey Kozyrev (around October 1990), GARF, f. 10026, op. 4, d. 2700, ll. 33–4.

87. The minutes of the Yeltsin consultative council, 24 October 1990, AY, f. 6, op. 1, d. 22, ll. 1–2, 8–11, at https://yeltsin.ru/archive/paperwork/9315; *Komsomolskoie znamia*, 21 November 1990, AY, f. 6, op. 1, d. 57, ll. 110–51.
88. Braithwaite's diary, 20 March 1991.
89. AY, f. 6, op. 1, d. 57, ll. 152–60.
90. Chernyaev, *Sovmestnyi iskhod*, entry of 5 December 1990, p. 890.
91. MSG SS, vol. 23, p. 288; AY, f. 6, op. 1, d. 216, ll. 33–6.
92. The minutes of the Presidential Council, 22 May 1990, RGANI, f. 121, op. 3, d. 56, ll. 67, 70; 30 August 1990, ibid, d. 67, ll. 198–9; Pavlov, *Upushchen li shans?*, p. 4.
93. The memo to Gorbachev, 9 December 1990. AY, f. 6, op. 1, d. 16, ll. 54–6.
94. Sheinis, *Vzlet i padeniie parlamenta*, p. 417.
95. Braithwaite's diary, 17 December 1990.
96. *Chetvertyi s'ezd narodnykh deputatov SSSR, December 17–27 1990. Stenographic report*, vol. 1 (Moscow, 1991), p. 13.
97. The interview with Sazhi Umalatova by Oleg Skvortsov, 15 October 1998.
98. Vorotnikov, *A bylo eto tak*, pp. 464–5; Medvedev, *Boris Yeltsin*, p. 410.
99. The notes of Teimuraz Stepanov-Mamaladze, 21 December 1990, Stepanov-Mamaladze Papers, Box 3, Folder 20, HIA; Shevardnadze's reflections on the "empire" is in Pavel Palazhchenko, "Professia i vremia. Zapiski perevodchika-diplomata," *Znamia* 10 (2020), at https://znamlit.ru/publication.php?id=7755.
100. The televised report on this event is at https://www.youtube.com/watch?v=WnThxagvlPI.
101. Stepanov-Mamaladze's notes on 21 and 22 December 1990, Stepanov-Mamaladze Papers, Box 3, Folder 20, HIA.
102. *Izvestia*, 23 December 1991; Braithwaite's diary, entry of 22 December 1991.
103. D. A. Granin, *Prichudy moiei pamiati* (St Petersburg: Tsentpoligraf, 2010), pp. 134–5.
104. Chernyaev, *Sovmestnyi iskhod*, entry of 21 and 23 December 1990, pp. 891–3.

CHAPTER 7: STANDOFF

1. Thomas Carlyle, *The French Revolution: A History* (London: Modern Library, 2002), p. 537.
2. The author's interview with Condoleezza Rice, Stanford, 23 February 2013. Kirsten Lundberg, "CIA and the Fall of the Soviet Empire: The Politics of 'Getting it Right'," a case study for Ernest May and Philip Zelikow at the Kennedy School of Government, Harvard University, at https://www.cia.gov/library/readingroom/docs/DOC_0005302423.pdf.
3. Condoleezza Rice to Robert Gates, 18 December 1990, Senior Small Group Meeting on Soviet Contingencies, file: USSR Collapse, OA/ID 91119003, Scowcroft Collection, Box 13, GBPL.
4. Gates to Condoleezza Rice, Memorandum to the President, 12 June 1990, OA/ID CF00721, Condoleezza Rice Papers, 1989–1990 Subject Files, Box 2, GBPL.
5. Scowcroft to the President (no date, likely January 1991), OA/ID CF00719-010, Scowcroft Collection, Box 13, GBPL.
6. Interview with James Baker, 11 March 2011, BOHP, p. 29.
7. The original and English translation of this letter are in the Bush Library, College Station, OA/ID 91128-005, GBPL. The letter's idea came from Gorbachev's press secretary, Vitaly Ignatenko, and was drafted by Anatoly Chernyaev; Chernyaev, *Sovmestnyi iskhod*, 24 December 1990, p. 893.
8. Senn, *Gorbachev's Failure in Lithuania*, p. 119.
9. Senn, Op. cit., pp. 127–36.
10. Interview with the KGB colonel Mikhail Golovatov, 13 January 2019, at https://www.rubaltic.ru/article/kultura-i-istoriya/21032019-mikhail-golovatov-u-vilnyusskoy-telebashni-predali-i-nas-i-litovtsev.
11. https://baltnews.lt/vilnius_news/20160408/1015277883.html.
12. Kryuchkov, *Lichnoie delo*, vol. 2, p. 30; Gorbachev, *Zhizn i reformy*, vol. 2, p. 506; Chernyaev, *Sovmestnyi iskhod*, entry of 13 January 1991. Transcript of Shevardnadze's meeting with Ambassador Jack Matlock, 7 January 1991, Katayev Papers, Box 4, Folder 55, HIA.

NOTES to pp. 184–189

13. The notes of Stepanov-Mamaladze, 27 August 1991, Stepanov-Mamaladze Papers, Box 3, Folder 28, HIA; ibid, 3 January 1991, Box 3, Folder 20.
14. Memo, Bush-Gorbachev, 11 January 1991, at https://bush41library.tamu.edu/files/memcons-telcons/1991-01-11-Gorbachev.pdf.
15. See a good review of the press in Bergmane, "French and US Reactions," pp. 258–9; also her " 'This is the End of Perestroika?' International Reactions to the Soviet Use of Force in the Baltic Republics in January 1991," *Journal of Cold War Studies* 22:2 (Spring 2020), pp. 26–57.
16. Chernyaev, *Sovmestnyi iskhod*, entries of 13 and 15 January 1991, pp. 900–2, 903–6; Galina Starovoitova in the BBC's Panorama program, 13 January 1991, from the archives of the BBC, courtesy of Anna Kan.
17. For a summary of the reactions in Moscow see Bergmane, "French and US Reactions," pp. 245–7.
18. Knight, "The KGB, Perestroika, and the Collapse of the Soviet Union," pp. 67–93; Chernyaev, *Sovmestnyi iskhod*, entry of 15 January 1991, pp. 903–6.
19. Gorbachev, *Zhizn i reformy*, vol. 2, pp. 510, 511.
20. Chernyaev, *Sovmestnyi iskhod*, entry of 22 January 1991, p. 909; Braithwaite's diary, 22 and 23 January 1991.
21. *Materialy ob'edinennogo plenuma Tsentralnogo komiteta i Tsentralnoi kontrolnoi komissii KPSS*, 31 January 1991 (Moscow: Izdatelstvo politicheskoi literatury, 1991), pp. 83–4.
22. Deputy General Secretary of the CC CPSU V. Ivashko, a letter, "K partiinym organizatsiiam, vsem kommunistam Vooruzhennykh sil SSSR, voisk KGB, vnutrennikh voisk MVD i zheleznodorozhnykh voisk," 5 February 1991, f. 89, op. 20, d. 32, HIA.
23. The text is in *Raspad SSSR*, vol. 1; vol. 2; the interview with Yeltsin, 13 January 1991, AY, f. 20, no. fono 020.
24. AY, f. 6, op. 1, d. 57, ll. 62–3; d. 59, ll. 16–19; the author's interview with Gennady Burbulis, 24 May 2020, by phone.
25. AY, f. 6, op. 1, d. 22, ll. 112–13, 115–19, 135–9, 156–9.
26. AY, f. 6, op. 1, d. 22, ll. 171–2.
27. The letter to compatriots, 25 December 1990, AY, f. 6, op. 1, d. 59, ll. 1–10.
28. AY, f. 6, op. 1, d. 22, ll. 107–10, 119, 142, 165.
29. Yeltsin's address to the RSFSR Supreme Soviet with his remarks and editing, AY, f. 6, op. 1, d. 19, ll. 213–56.
30. The excerpts of this memo are cited in Yevgenia Albats, *The State Within a State: The KGB and its Hold on Russia—Past, Present, and Future* (New York: Farrar, Straus, Giroux, 1994), pp. 223–4; the memo is also cited in Pikhoia, *Sovetskii Soiuz*, p. 622.
31. Pavlov, *Upushchen li shans?*, pp. 3–8.
32. Ibid, pp. 154, 182.
33. Chernyaev, *Sovmestnyi iskhod*, entry of 19 February 1991, pp. 918–19.
34. Pavlov, *Upushchen li shans?*, p. 106.
35. Recollections of Ruslan Khasbulatov in Nikolai Krotov, *Istoriia sovetskoi bankovskoi reformy 80-h gg. XX v.* vol. 1. *Spetsbanki* (Moscow: Ekonomicheskaia letopis, 2008), p. 423; Pavlov, *Upushchen li shans?*, pp. 130–2.
36. The discussion on the State Bank and the banking legislation on 5 October 1990, GARF, f. 9654, op. 7, d. 302, ll. 61–4, 84–7, 100, 104, 123.
37. Recollections of Gennady Matiukhin in Krotov, *Istoriia sovetskoi*, p. 206.
38. On the failing negotiations on taxes between Pavlov and the Russian government see AY, f. 6, op. 1, d. 16, ll. 54–70; d. 173, l. 61.
39. The papers of the Cabinet of Ministers of the USSR, GARF, f. 5446, op. 163, d. 32, l. 146; d. 35, ll. 116–54.
40. *Kommersant-Vlast* 5 (28 January 1991), at https://www.kommersant.ru/doc/265657. Braithwaite's diary, 25 January 1991.
41. Pavlov, *Upushchen li shans?*, pp. 220–6, 239–40; *Izvestia*, 31 January 1991, p. 1; Petrakov to the British ambassador, Braithwaite's diary, 24 January 1991.

42. On the role of the KGB in the affair see the article of MVD Maj.-Gen. Vladimir Ovchinsky, *Den* 2 (February 1991), p. 2.
43. Braithwaite's diary, entry of 13 February 1991.
44. The minutes of the coordinating advisory council, 26 December 1991, AY, f. 6, op. 1, d. 22, ll. 165–6.
45. Gorbachev, *Zhizn i reformy*, vol. 1, p. 517.
46. The notes of the Politburo meeting, 22 March 1990 and Shakhnazarov's note after his meeting with Gorbachev on 17 May 1990, *V Politburo TsK KPSS*, pp. 581, 595; Chernyaev, *Sovmestnyi iskhod*, entries of 1 September 1990 and 10 March 1991, pp. 870–1, 927.
47. Pikhoia, *Sovetskii Soiuz*, pp. 619–20.
48. Kryuchkov, *Lichnoie delo*, vol. 2, p. 33.
49. The author's interview with Gennady Burbulis, 6 May 2020, by phone.
50. The minutes of the coordinating advisory council on 6 February 1991 and the draft four-part statement. AY, f. 6, op. 1, d. 23, ll. 7–10; d. 57, ll. 174–5.
51. AY, f. 6, op. 1, d. 23, ll. 21–2, 23–4, 29, 110–11.
52. Braithwaite's diary, 14 February 1990; the author's interview with Gennady Burbulis, 24 May 2020, by phone.
53. Sukhanov, *Kak Yeltsin stal prezidentom*, p. 190; information from Rudolf G. Pikhoia, conversation with the author, Moscow, 10 June 2016.
54. Interview with Boris Yeltsin by journalists Sergey Lomakin and Oleg Poptsov, 19 February 1991, at 18:50. Material of Radio Liberty monitoring.
55. The poll of 22 February 1991. Demokraticheskaia Rossiia Papers, Box 2, Folder 10, HIA.
56. Gorbachev, *Zhizn i reformy*, vol. 1, pp. 518, 520–5; MSG SS, vol. 24, pp. 299–339.
57. Pikhoia, *Sovetskii Soiuz*, pp. 625–6.
58. Boldin, *Krushenie piedestala*, pp. 267, 268.
59. Chernyaev, *Sovmestnyi iskhod*, entry of 2 March 1991, pp. 923–5.
60. Khasbulatov, *Poluraspad SSSR*, pp. 124–5, 355; Vladimir Isakov, *Predsedatel soveta respubliki. Parlamentskie dnevniki 1990 goda* (Ekaterinburg: Uralskii rabochii, 1997), pp. 241–2.
61. "Zakopavshyie SSSR," at https://lenta.ru/articles/2016/03/27/miners. On Golikov see https://newtimes.ru/articles/detail/4491; http://vkrizis.ru/obschestvo/ne-stalo-shahtyorskogo-vozhaka-vyacheslava-golikova.
62. Quoted from the anonymous transcript published in the newspaper *Russkaia mysl* (Paris), 15 March 1991; Chernyaev, *Sovmestnyi iskhod*, entry of 10 March 1991, p. 927.
63. The minutes of the coordinating advisory council, 14 March 1991. AY, f. 6, op. 1, d. 24, ll. 3–11, 55–6.
64. Ibid, ll. 59–64.
65. AY, f. 6, op. 1, d. 24, ll. 1–2, 12–13, 29, 40, 42.
66. The record of a conversation with B. N. Yeltsin by four economists from the Hoover Institution, 15 March 1991. From the papers of Mikhail Bernstam, Professor Emeritus of Stanford University.
67. On the NSC arguments see Rice, "Responding to Moscow," 21 January 1991, NSC Files, Condoleezza Rice Papers, Soviet Union/USSR Subject Files, Baltics, GBPL, cited in Bergmane, "French and US Reactions," p. 263.
68. Chernyaev, *My Six Years with Gorbachev*; Matlock, *Autopsy*, pp. 469–72.
69. Chernyaev, *Sovmestnyi iskhod*, entry of 22 February 1991, pp. 919–21; MSG SS, vol. 24, pp. 258–64; https://bush41library.tamu.edu/files/memcons-telcons/1991-02-22-Gorbachev.pdf.
70. MSG SS, vol. 24, pp. 265–98.
71. *The New York Times*, 2 March 1991, at https://www.nytimes.com/1991/03/02/world/after-the-war-the-battleground-death-stalks-desert-despite-cease-fire.html.
72. "Flashback: 1991 Gulf War," 20 March 2003, at http://news.bbc.co.uk/2/hi/middle_east/2754103.stm.
73. Chernyaev's notes, 11 February 1991, Gorbachev Foundation, f. 2, op. 3 (Chernyaev Papers). The exact date of this could be 9 February when Gorbachev, according to Chernyaev, spoke in the Walnut Room about the Gulf War and the Warsaw Pact, *Sovmestnyi iskhod*, pp. 915–16.

74. Chernyaev, *Sovmestnyi iskhod*, entry of 25 February 1991, pp. 921–2.

75. https://bush41library.tamu.edu/files/memcons-telcons/1991-02-23-Kohl.pdf.

76. The author's interview with Condoleezza Rice, Stanford University, 23 February 2013.

77. Scowcroft to Bush (about the end of February 1991), "Coping with the Soviet Union's Internal Turmoil," on file at the National Security Archive.

78. Ibid.

79. The White House, Washington DC, 10 March 1991, on file at the National Security Archive.

80. Matlock, *Autopsy*, pp. 487–8.

81. Chernyaev, *Sovmestnyi iskhod*, entry of 14 March 1991, p. 928. On the growing pessimism about American intentions after their victory in the Gulf see also Pavel Palazhchenko, *My Years with Gorbachev and Shevardnadze*, p. 270.

82. Matlock, *Autopsy*, p. 489. Baker's version of this incident is in his *The Politics of Diplomacy*, pp. 476–7.

83. The record of Gorbachev's talks with James Baker, 15 March 1991, in MSG SS, vol. 25, pp. 40–3, 563–4; Baker, *The Politics of Dipomacy*, p. 476; Palazhchenko, *My Years with Gorbachev and Shevardnadze*, p. 271.

84. The record of Gorbachev's talks with James Baker, 15 March 1991, in MSG SS, vol. 25, p. 564.

85. Ibid, p. 565; Baker, *The Politics of Diplomacy*, p. 476; Palazhchenko, *My Years with Gorbachev and Shevardnadze*, p. 271.

86. Matlock, *Autopsy*, pp. 489–92; Chernyaev, *Sovmestnyi iskhod*, p. 931.

87. Baker, *The Politics of Diplomacy*, p. 477; Proposed Agenda for meeting with the President, 20 March 1991, 2:00. James A. Baker III Papers, Box 115, Folder 8. The Seeley Mudd Library, Princeton University; Bush and Scowcroft, *A World Transformed*, p. 500.

88. Kryuchkov, *Lichnoie delo*, vol. 2, p. 34.

89. Pikhoia, *Sovetskii Soiuz*, p. 631.

90. Bergmane, "French and US Reactions," pp. 287, 289; Beissinger, *Nationalist Mobilization*, p. 387.

91. Matlock, *Autopsy*, p. 477; Braithwaite's diary, 20 March 1991.

92. AY, f. 6, op. 1, d. 61, ll. 1–11. GARF, f. 10026, op. 8, d. 184 and 191.

93. Pikhoia, *Sovetskii Soiuz*, p. 629; also on these fears see Palazhchenko, *My Years with Gorbachev and Shevardnadze*, p. 271.

94. Demokraticheskaia Rossiia Papers, Box 2, Folders 10 and 11, HIA.

95. Vstrecha s vedushchimi ekonomistami strany, 16 March 1991, MSG SS, vol. 25, pp. 60–4, 429–65, 567.

96. Report of "Radio Russia" at 17:40, 22 March 1991, the Foreign Broadcast Information Service (FBIS).

97. Braithwaite's diary, entry of 14 March 1991. *NDI, The Commonwealth of Independent States: Democratic Developments, Issues, and Options* (Washington, DC: January 1992); James Goldgeier and Michael McFaul, *Power and Purpose: U.S. Policy Toward Russia after the Cold War* (Washington, DC: Brookings Institution Press, 2003), pp. 29–30.

98. Chernyaev, *Sovmestnyi iskhod*, entries of 20 and 25 March 1991, pp. 929–30, 931.

99. Pavlov, *Upushchen li shans?*, pp. 161–3, 175–7.

100. On this "plan" see e.g. Khasbulatov, *Poluraspad*, pp. 123, 128.

101. Lukin to Yeltsin, 26 March 1991, AY, f. 6, op. 1, d. 13, ll. 240–1.

102. MSG SS, vol. 25, pp. 129–43; *Nezavisimaia gazeta* (28 March 1991), p. 1.

103. Chernyaev, *Sovmestnyi iskhod*, 29 March 1991, p. 932.

104. Ibid.

105. The notes of Teimuraz Stepanov, 18 March 1991, Stepanov-Mamaladze Papers, Box 3, Folder 25, HIA.

106. This line was formulated by Yeltsin's advisory council before the referendum and confirmed after it. See AY, f. 6, op. 1, d. 13, ll. 1–20. The full text of Yeltsin's report is in *Rossiiskaia gazeta* (31 March 1991), pp. 1–3.

107. The stenographic transcript of the Congress in *Rossiiskaia gazeta* (30 March 1991), pp. 2–5; Vorotnikov, *A bylo eto tak*, pp. 478–9.
108. Alan Cooperman, "Thousands Gather for Manned Rally in Moscow", 8 March 1991, *FBIS-Soviet Politics*. Dunlop Papers, HIA.
109. Pikhoia, *Sovetskii Soiuz*, pp. 421–2; also "A Day of Tension in Moscow," 28 March 1991, *FBIS, AM-Soviet Politics*, Dunlop Papers, HIA; Remnik, *Lenin's Tomb*, pp. 421–2.
110. Braithwaite's diary, 28 March 1991.
111. Gorbachev, *Zhizn i reformy*, vol. 2, pp. 513, 514, 523.
112. Galina Starovoitova at https://youtu.bee/06jiDhmekwl.
113. V. B. Isakov, *Myatezh protiv Yeltsina. Komanda po spaseniiu SSSR* (Moscow: Algoritm EKSMO, 2011), pp. 110–11; Vorotnikov, *A bylo eto tak*, p. 479; Pikhoia, *Sovetskii Soiuz*, pp. 634–5; Gorbachev, *Zhizn i reformy*, vol. 2, p. 520.
114. AY, f. 6, op. 1, d. 14, ll. 175–96.

CHAPTER 8: DEVOLUTION

1. AY, f. 6, op. 1, d. 41, l. 169.
2. Shakhnazarov, *Tsena svobody*, p. 224.
3. The report from the head of planning and the financial-budgetary commission, the Ministry of Finance, and the State Bank to Gorbachev, 21 March 1991, RGANI, f. 121, op. 3, d. 42, ll. 41–6.
4. RGANI, f. 121, op. 3, d. 42.
5. Vadim Medvedev's diary, 23 April 1991, cited in *Soiuz mozhno bylo sokhranit*, p. 259.
6. Gorbachev discussed these demands with Shakhnazarov and other advisors on 8 April 1991, *V Politburo TsK KPSS*, p. 657; Shakhnazarov's memo to Gorbachev on the same day, *Tsena svobody*, p. 522.
7. Gorbachev, *Zhizn i reformy*, vol. 2, p. 529.
8. Chernyaev's note to Gorbachev, 28 March 1991, the Gorbachev Foundation, f. 2, op. 3; Arbatov's note to Yeltsin, 12 April 1991, AY, f. 6, op. 1, d. 41, ll. 165–8.
9. Gorbachev, *Zhizn i reformy*, vol. 2, p. 528.
10. Boris Yeltsin, *Zapiski prezidenta* (Moscow: Ogonyok, 1994), p. 40; Voshchanov, *Yeltsin kak navazhdeniie*, pp. 236–9; Colton, *Yeltsin*, pp. 189, 515.
11. Khasbulatov to Yeltsin, 22 April 1991, AY, f. 6, op. 1, d. 41, ll. 170–1, at https://yeltsin.ru/archive/paperwork/9488.
12. On Gorbachev's plot, Gennady Burbulis to the author, 6 and 24 May 2020, by phone; Shaimiev's remarks at the meeting of the preparatory committee on the Union Treaty, 24 May 1991; *V Politburo TsK KPSS*, pp. 671–2.
13. Shakhnazarov, *Tsena svobody*, pp. 224–5.
14. Burbulis to the Ukrainian oral history project, http://oralhistory.org.ua/interview-ua/445.
15. Pikhoia, *Sovetskii Soiuz*, p. 637.
16. Gorbachev, *Zhizn i reformy*, vol. 2, p. 532; Chernyaev, *Sovmestnyi iskhod*, entry of 9 April 1991, p. 935; see also Braithwaite's diary, 17 and 21 April 1991.
17. Gorbachev, *Zhizn i reformy*, vol. 2, pp. 536–8; Shakhnazarov, *Tsena svobody*, p. 225.
18. On the reasons of the Plenum elites see A. S. Puchenkov, "Avgustovskyi putsch 1991 g.: Vzgliad na sobytiia iz zdaniia TsK (po pokazaniiam ochevidtsev)," *Noveishaia istoriia Rossii* 9:2 (2019), pp. 462–3; Chernyaev, *Sovmestnyi iskhod*, entry of 27 April 1991, p. 937; Gorbachev, *Zhizn i reformy*, vol. 2, pp. 538–9, 540.
19. Braithwaite's diary, 29 April 1991.
20. Khasbulatov, *Poluraspad SSSR*, pp. 156, 157; Shakhnazarov's memo to Gorbachev on 8 April 1991 in *Tsena svobody*, p. 520.
21. A. G. Vishnevsky, *Serp i ruble. Konservativnaia modernizatsiia v SSSR* (Moscow: OGI, 1998), pp. 343–53; Henry Hale, *Patronal Politics: Eurasian Regime Dynamics in Comparative Perspective* (New York: Cambridge University Press, 2014), pp. 54–5.

22. Lukin to Yeltsin, 31 May 1991, GARF, f. 10026, op. 4, d. 2684, ll. 6–7. For the debate between Gorbachev and Yeltsin on the federal tax see *V Politburo TsK KPSS*, p. 672; Yuri Baturin et al., eds., *Epokha Yeltsina. Ocherki politicheskoi istorii* (Moscow: Vagrius, 2001), pp. 135, 137.

23. Marc Garcelon, *Revolutionary Passage: From Soviet to Post-Soviet Russia* (Philadelphia, PA: Temple University Press, 2005), pp. 4, 69, 127–8.

24. Ibid, p. 138; Vladimir Boxer, "Nezabyvaiemyi 1990 ili My iz Kronshtadta," 26 October 2005, at https://polit.ru/article/2005/10/26/demross.

25. Minutes of the Plenary Council of Representatives of the Movement Democratic Russia, 13 April 1991; and the transcript of the all-Russian Conference of Democratic Forces, 14 April 1991. Demokraticheskaia Rossiia Papers, Box 2, Folder 14, HIA.

26. Zaiavleniie koordinatsionnogo soveta dvizheniia Demokraticheskaia Rossiia. Proect. Drafts by Shneider on 8 and 11 April 1991. Demokraticheskaia Rossiia Papers, Box 5, Folder 11, HIA.

27. The transcript of the all-Russian Conference of Democratic Forces, 14 April 1991, Demokraticheskaia Rossiia Papers, Box 2, Folder 14, HIA.

28. Ibid.

29. L. A. Ponomarev, "Pozitsiia dvizheniia Demokraticheskaia Rossiia po voprosu natsional-no-gosudarstvennogo ustroistva," April 1991. Demokraticheskaia Rossiia Papers, Box 6, Folder 4, HIA.

30. Recollections of Vladimir Boxer in September 1991, Demokraticheskaia Rossiia Papers, Box 3, Folder 6, HIA. The minutes of the plenary meeting of Democratic Russia, 27 April 1991, Demokraticheskaia Rossiia Papers, Box 6, Folder 8, HIA; Boxer, "Nezabyvaiemyi 1990."

31. The minutes of the plenary meeting of Democratic Russia, 27 April 1991, Demokraticheskaia Rossiia Papers, Box 6, Folder 8, HIA.

32. Geoghegan, "A Policy in Tension," pp. 787, 794.

33. John Exnicios, former director of the Krieble Institute, interview with David C. Speedie, 14 December 2010, at https://www.carnegiecouncil.org/studio/multimedia/20110208c/index.html, accessed 21 May 2016; Arthur H. Matthews, *Agents of Influence: How the Krieble Institute Brought Democratic Capitalism to the Former Soviet Empire* (Washington, DC: Krieble Institute of the Free Congress Foundation, 1995).

34. Michael McFaul, *From Cold War to Hot Peace: An American Ambassador in Putin's Russia* (New York: Houghton Mifflin Harcourt, 2018), p. 12. The book of interviews was published; see also Sergey Markov and Michael McFaul, *The Troubled Birth of Russian Democracy: Parties, Personalities, and Programs* (Stanford, CA: Hoover Institution Press Publication, 1993).

35. Michael Beschloss and Strobe Talbott, *At the Highest Levels: The Inside Story of the End of the Cold War* (Boston, MA: Little, Brown, 1993), pp. 354–5; the notes of the Shevardnadze-Nixon meeting on 25 March 1991 are in Stepanov's notes, Stepanov-Mamaladze Papers, Box 3, Folder 23, HIA, pp. 37–8.

36. Dimitri K. Simes, *After Collapse: Russia Seeks Its Place as a Great Power* (New York: Simon & Schuster, 1999), the notes, p. 256; telephone conversation between the author and Dimitri Simes, 23 May 2016.

37. On the meeting between Nixon and Gorbachev see "Iz besedy s byvshim prezidentom SShA R. Niksonom," 2 April 1991, MSG SS, vol. 25, pp. 152, 587–8; Palazhchenko, *My Years with Gorbachev and Shevardnadze*, pp. 274–8. No record of the Yeltsin-Nixon meeting is available, on either the American or Russian side. The author's telephone conversation with Dimitri K. Simes, 23 May 2016; Beschloss and Talbott, *At the Highest Levels*, p. 356; Serge Schmemann, "Moscow Journal: In Gorbachev, Nixon Detects a Fellow Scrapper," *The New York Times*, 4 April 1991, at http://www.nytimes.com/1991/04/04/world/moscow-journal-in-gorbachev-nixon-detects-a-fellow-scrapper.html, accessed 20 May 2016.

38. Richard Nixon, "A Superpower at the Abyss," *Time*, 22 April 1991; Monica Crowley, *Nixon in Winter* (New York: Random House, 1998), p. 41, cited in Colton, *Yeltsin*, pp. 190–1.

39. Memorandum of conversation, meeting and dinner with Italian Prime Minister Andreotti, 24 March 1991, GBPL, at https://bush41library.tamu.edu/files/memcons-telcons/1991-03-24-Andreotti.pdf, accessed 19 May 2016.

40. Memorandum of conversation, meeting with Arnold Rüütel, President of Estonia, Oval Office, 29 March 1991, GBPL, at https://bush41library.tamu.edu/files/memcons-telcons/1991-03-29-Ruutel.pdf, accessed 19 May 2016; meeting with Prime of Luxembourg Santer and EC President Delors, 11 April 1991, GBPL at: https://bush41library.tamu.edu/files/memcons-telcons/1991-04-11-Santer.pdf.

41. David Gompert and Ed Hewett to John Helgerson, DDCI, 10 April 1991, Nicholas Burns and Ed Hewett Files, OA/ID CF01486-023, GBPL; 'The Soviet Cauldron,' 23 April 1991, at https://www.cia.gov/library/center-for-the-study-of-intelligence/csi-publications/books-and-monographs/at-cold-wars-end-us-intelligence-on-the-soviet-union-and-eastern-europe-1989-1991/16526pdffiles/SOV91-20177.pdf; on Ermarth's views see Beschloss and Talbott, *At the Highest Levels*, p. 349.

42. Directorate of Intelligence, 29 April 1991, "The Gorbachev Succession," Burns and Hewett Files, OA/ID CF01486-023, GBPL.

43. Burns to Hewett, 30 April 1991, Nicholas Burns and Ed Hewett Files, OA/ID CF01486-023, GBPL; Brent Scowcroft to William H. Webster, 9 May 1991, Scowcroft Collection, Box 13, Soviet collapse, OA/ID 91119-005, GBPL; Bush and Scowcroft, *A World Transformed*, p. 502.

44. Khasbulatov, *Poluraspad SSSR*, pp. 171–2.

45. Kryuchkov, *Lichnoie delo*, vol. 2, pp. 11–12.

46. Demokraticheskaia Rossiia Papers, Box 6, Folder 8, HIA; Sukhanov, *Kak Yeltsin stal prezidentom*, pp. 204–6.

47. Elizabeth Teague, "Boris Yeltsin Introduces his Brain Trust," Report on the USSR, RFE-RL, 12 April 1991.

48. Boxer, "Nezabyvaiemyi 1990."

49. Pikhoia, *Sovetskii Soiuz*, p. 642; the author's interview with Rudolf Pikhoia, a member of Yeltsin's close circle, 5 June 2019, Moscow; Yeltsin, *Zapiski prezidenta*, pp. 46, 47. The electoral materials in Demokraticheskaia Rossiia Papers, Box 5, Folder 5, HIA; Gorbachev, *Zhizn i reformy*, vol. 2, p. 528.

50. Yeltsin's report in *Tretii (vneocherednoi) S'ezd narodnykh deputatov RSFSR, 28 marta–5 aprelia 1991 goda. Stenograficheskii otchet*, vol. 1 (Moscow: Respublika, 1992), pp. 115–27; Tezisy programmy B. N. Yeltsina na post Prezidenta RSFSR. "Vykhod iz krizisa i obnovleniie Rossii," Demokraticheskaia Rossiia Papers, Box 5, Folder 11, HIA.

51. Zasedanie Verkhovnogo Soveta RSFSR. Stenogramma. In: O. Rumyantsev i.a. (ed.), *Iz istorii sozdaniia Konstitutsii Rossiiskoi Federatsii*, vol. 6 (Moscow: 2010), pp. 357–69.

52. Yeltsin in "Who Is Who" program, FBIS, Russian service, Dunlop Papers, Box 9, HIA; Igor Fisunenko, "Kon'iunkturnost ne moie amplua," *Programmy televideniia i radio*, 28, 14–18 July 1991.

53. Round-table of presidential candidates on Soviet TV, 10 and 11 June 1991, FBIS.

54. Matlock, *Autopsy*, pp. 510–11.

55. The early draft program of Yeltsin's visit to the United States (without a date) still did not include a meeting with Bush. GARF, f. 10026, op. 4, d. 2794.

56. The interviews with Gennady Burbulis, 8 February 2011, at https://www.carnegiecouncil.org/studio/multimedia/20110208c/index.html, accessed 21 May 2016; Matthews, *Agents of Influence*, pp. 62, 118. Matlock, *Autopsy*, pp. 509–10.

57. Vladimir Lukin in *The New Times* 23 (1991), p. 6; Liudmila Saraskina, *Alexander Solzhenitsyn* (Moscow: Molodaia gvardiia, 2008), p. 804.

58. Scowcroft to Bush, sometime before 20 June 1991. NSC Files, USSR Chronological Files, June 1991, CF01407-005, GBPL, Box 1, Folder CF01407-005, pp. 1–2.

59. Memorandum of conversation. Meeting with the President of the Russian Republic Boris Yeltsin of the USSR, 20 June 1991, GBPL at: https://bush41library.tamu.edu/files/memcons-telcons/1991-06-20--Yeltsin.pdf.

60. Ibid.

61. Ibid.

62. Bush and Scowcroft, *A World Transformed*, p. 504.

63. Memorandum of telephone conversation with Mikhail Gorbachev, President of the Soviet Union, 21 June 1991, 10:00–10:38, GBPL, at: https://bush41library.tamu.edu/files/

memcons-telcons/1991-06-21-Gorbachev.pdf. For some reason, Bush mentioned Popov's name in conversation, much to Matlock's unhappiness; Matlock, *Autopsy*, pp. 541–3, 545.

64. "Amerika vtoroi raz priznala Yeltsina," *The New Times*, Moscow, no. 26, 1991.

65. The author's interview with Gennady Burbulis, 21 April 2020, by phone; Russian TV "Vesti" 22 June 1991, 23:00, TASS on the results of Yeltsin's visit, 22 June 1991. RFE/RL Research Institute, Dunlop Papers, Box 9, HIA.

66. For the schedule of the event and the brochure with the transcript of all speeches see AY, f. 6, op. 1, d. 84, ll. 1–40, at https://yeltsin.ru/archive/paperwork/10377.

67. Inauguratsiia B. N. Yeltsina, 10 July 1991, at https://www.youtube.com/watch?v=KApj6-RkLz4, accessed 28 May 2017.

68. AY, f. 6, op. 1, d. 84, ll. 21–6.

69. "V Kremlie odnim prezidentom bolshe," *Izvestia*, 11 July 1991, pp. 1, 2; Colton, *Yeltsin*, p. 194.

70. Shakhnazarov, *Tsena svobody*, pp. 168–9.

71. Chernyaev, *Sovmestnyi iskhod*, 23 June and 11 July 1991, pp. 954, 961; Shakhnazarov to Gorbachev, 19 June 1991, in *Tsena svobody*, pp. 539–40.

72. "Analiticheskii material o politicheskikh itogakh vyborov Presidenta RSFSR," 1 July1991, AY, f. 6, op. 1, d. 166, ll. 27–8, at, http://yeltsin.ru/archive/paperwork/18222, accessed 28 May 2017.

73. Stepanov notes, 21 June, 18–21 July 1991, Stepanov-Mamaladze Papers, Box 3, Folder 27, HIA.

74. Shakhnazarov, *Tsena svobody*, p. 256; Chernyaev, *Sovmestnyi iskhod*, 11 July 1991, p. 961.

75. Gorbachev's meeting with González, 8 July 1991, MSG SS, vol. 26; Chernyaev, *Sovmestnyi iskhod*, 9 July 1991, p. 961.

76. Pavlov, *Upushchen li shans?*, pp. 109–10.

77. Matiukhin in Krotov, *Istoriia sovetskoi*, p. 212.

78. Interview with Viktor Ivanenko, at http://ru-90.ru/content/кгб-и-радикальные-перемены-интервью-с-вв-иваненко.

79. Interview of Michael McFaul with Gennady Burbulis, 30 June 1995, Michael McFaul Collection, Box 3, HIA; the author's interview with Gennady Burbulis, 6 May 2020, by phone.

80. AY, f. 6, op. 1, d. 163, ll. 67–75; V. Ivanenko, "Oni mne ne do kontsa doveriali," *Ogonek* 12–13 (24 March–2 April 1992); Tezisy (vystupleniie B. N. Yeltsina); Material k vystupleniiu Prezidenta RSFSR B. N. Yeltsina na soveshchanii rukovodiashchego sostava organov KGB RSFSR (without date, 1991), GARF, f. 10026, op. 4, d. 3411, ll. 64–73; Andrei Przhezdomsky, *Za kulisami putcha. Rossiiskie chekisty protiv razvala organov KGB v 1991 godu* (Moscow: Veche, 2011), p. 59.

81. Leonid Shebarshin, . . . *I zhizni melochnyie sny* (Moscow: Mezhdunarodnyie otnosheniia, 2000), pp. 81–2.

82. Such "cells" were present in nearly all institutions, state agencies, enterprises, and other organizations. *Ukaz Prezidenta RSFSR* 14 (20 July 1991). "O prekrashchenii deiatelnosti organizatsionnykh struktur politicheskikh partii i massovykh obshchestvennykh dvizhenii v gosudarstvennykh organakh, uchrezhdeniiakh i organizatsiiakh RSFSR," *Rossiskaia gazeta* (21 July 1991), p. 1.

83. *Izvestia* (31 July 1991), p. 2.

CHAPTER 9: CONSENSUS

1. On the origins of the "Washington Consensus" see Philip Arestis, "Washington Consensus and Financial Liberalization," and John Williamson, "The Strange History of the Washington Consensus," *Journal of Post Keynesian Economics* 27:2 (Winter 2004–5), pp. 195–206, 251–71; Giovanni Arrighi and Lu Zhang, "Beyond the Washington Consensus: A New Bandung?" https://www.researchgate.net/publication/252076182_BEYOND_THE_WASHINGTON_CONSENSUS_A_NEW_BANDUNG.

2. On the impact of the neoliberalism in Eastern Europe see Ivan Krastev and Stephen Holmes, *The Light That Failed* (New York: Pegasus Books, 2020).

3. Reddaway and Glinski, *The Tragedy of Russia's Reforms*, p. 176.

4. Tobias Rupprecht, "Formula Pinochet: Chilean Lessons for Russian Liberal Reformers during the Soviet Collapse, 1970–2000," *Journal of Contemporary History* 5:1 (2016), pp. 165–8; interview with Vitaly Naishul on 12 February 2011, at http://polit.ru/article/2011/02/14/nayshul; Alfred Kokh's recollections in Alfred Kokh and Igor Svinarenko, *A Crate of Vodka*, trans. Antonina W. Bouis (New York: Enigma Books, 2009), pp. 282–4.

5. Yegor Gaidar, "Otkuda poshli reformatory," interview with Vitaly Leibin, 6 September 2006, at http://polit.ru/article/2006/09/06/gaidar; Vitaly Naishul, "Otkuda sut poshli reformatory," 21 April 2004, at http://polit.ru/article/2004/04/21/vaucher.

6. Yevgeny Yasin, "Reformatory prikhodiat k vlasti," interview with Alfred Kokh and Petr Aven, at http://www.forbes.ru/interview/4615reformatory-prihodyat-k-vlasti-evgenii-yasin. The papers of the Sopron workshop were published as: Merton J. Peck and Thomas J. Richardson, eds., *What Is to Be Done? Proposals for the Soviet Transition to the Market* (New Haven, CT: Yale University Press, 1991).

7. Mikhail Bernstam's conversation with the author, 28 January 2013, Stanford, CA. Bernstam was Gaidar's host at Stanford University.

8. Y. Gaidar, "Dve programmy," *Pravda* (13 September 1990).

9. *The Economy of the USSR: Summary and Recommendations, The IMF, The World Bank, OECD, and EBRD* (Washington, DC: The World Bank, December 1990); *A Study of the Soviet Economy*, vols. 1–3 (Paris: February 1991).

10. The information to the author from Piroska Nagy-Mohacsi, a member of the study team; also her book *The Meltdown of the Russian State: The Deformation and Collapse of the State in Russia* (Cheltenham, UK: Edward Elgar Publishing, 2000), and her paper presented at "The Destruction of the Soviet Economy," an international workshop, LSE, 23 March 2018.

11. "Zakliuchenie IMEMO po dokladu MVF, Vsemirnogo Banka, OESR i EBRR o sostoianii ekonomiki SSSR," 29 January 1991, GARF, f. 5446, op. 163, d. 1290, ll. 9–19; Y. Gaidar, "Vremia nepriiatnykh istin," *Moskovskiie novosti* 3 (20 January 1991), p. 12; Mikhail Bernstam to the author on his conversation with Gaidar in Moscow in March 1991, the interview on 29 January 2013, the Hoover Institution, Stanford University; also an e-mail to the author by Mikhail Bernstam, 25 December 2013.

12. The group included the taxation expert Edward Lazear, former deputy Secretary of the Treasury, Charles McLure, and the theorist of rational expectations, Thomas Sargent. The author's interview with Mikhail Bernstam, 29 January 2013, the Hoover Institution, Stanford University; the private documents from Bernstam's collection.

13. Correspondence with Bernstam, 23 May 2016.

14. Bernstam's notes of the meeting, his personal archive. For an analysis of neoliberal economic doctrine as a "foreign import" accepted by post-communist elites in Poland, see Peter Zeniewski, "Neoliberalism, Exogenous Elites and the Transformation of Solidarity," *Europe-Asia Studies* 63:6 (August 2011), pp. 983–8.

15. A cable from Jack Matlock to General Scowcroft, 071515z, 7 May 1991, Scowcroft Collection, Box 22, OA/ID 91129-002, GBPL.

16. George H. W. Bush, *All the Best: My Life in Letters and Other Writings* (New York: Scribner, 2014), p. 517.

17. Telcon with President Mikhail Gorbachev, 11 May 1991, at https://bush41library.tamu.edu/files/memcons-telcons/1991-05-11-Gorbachev.pdf.

18. Ibid.

19. Doklad V. Pavlova na Verkhovnom Sovete SSSR 22 April 1991, *Izvestia* (23 April 1991), pp. 2–3; *Nezavisimaia gazeta* (31 August 1991), p. 2.

20. Doklad V. Pavlova na Verkhovnom Sovete SSSR 22 April 1991, *Izvestia* (23 April 1991), p. 3; Pavlov, *Upushchen li shans?*, pp. 286, 296.

21. Braithwaite on his lunch with Yavlinsky on 13 May 1991, diary. "Window of Opportunity: Joint Program for Western Cooperation in the Soviet Transformation to Democracy and the Market Economy," 17 June 1991, folder "USSR Chron File; June 1991 [1]," OA/ID CF01407, NSC Files, Burns and Hewett Files, USSR Chronological Files, OA/ID CF01407, GBPL.

22. Primakov, *Vstrechi na perekrestkakh*, pp. 89–90; the author's interview with Grigory Yavlinsky, 24 December 2016, Moscow.

23. Jeffrey J. Sachs, 5 May 1991, "Promoting Economic Reform in the Soviet Union"; Jeffrey Sachs to Ed Hewett, 6 May 1991. OA/ID CF01486–029, NSC Files, Burns and Hewett Files, Subject Files, Box 2, OA/ID CF01486–029, GBPL.

24. Chernyaev, *Sovmestnyi iskhod*, 17 May 1991, p. 942.

25. Ibid, 18 May 1991; Zasedaniie Soveta bezopasnosti, 18 May 1991, *V Politbiuro TsK KPSS*, pp. 668–9.

26. On Blackwill and Zoellick see Beschloss and Talbott, *At the Highest Levels*, p. 385; Goldgeier and McFaul, *Power and Purpose*, pp. 63–4; the author's e-mail correspondence with Dennis Ross on 15 December 2015; Robert Zoellick at http://oralhistory.org.ua/interview-ua/341.

27. On him see, e.g., Boris Fyodorov, *10 bezumnykh let. Pochemu v Rossii ne sostoialis reformy* (Moscow: Kollektsiia Sovershenno Sekretno, 1999), p. 64.

28. The interview with Michael Boskin, 30–31 July 2001, Stanford University, BOHP; the handwritten notes of a meeting of "the Boskin group" with Primakov and Shcherbakov, 30 May 1991, Council of Economic Advisors: Boskin Files, OA/ID CF00756-015, GBPL.

29. Memorandum of conversation. Luncheon meeting between the President and Yevgeny Primakov, 21 May 1991; Scowcroft Collection: Special Separate USSR Notes Files, Box. 22, OA/ID 91129-001, pp. 1–3, GBPL; Beschloss and Talbott, *At the Highest Levels*, pp. 387, 390.

30. Scowcroft's memorandum for the Cabinet: "The U.S. Economic Relationship with the Soviet Union," 31 May 1991. Council of Economic Advisors: Boskin Files: OA-ID CF01113-051, p. 2, GBPL; Bush and Scowcroft, *A World Transformed*, p. 503; Bush, *All the Best*, pp. 521–2; Primakov, *Vstrechi na perekrestkakh*, p. 90.

31. *Raspad SSSR*, vol. 1, pp. 997–8.

32. Chernyaev, *Sovmestnyi iskhod*, 5 June 1991, p. 946; "Nobelevskaia lektsiia," 5 June 1991, in Gorbachev, *Gody Trudnykh Reshenii*, pp. 268–81.

33. Chernyaev, *Sovmestnyi iskhod*, 5 June 1991, p. 947.

34. Braithwaite's diary, 6 and 8 May 1991.

35. See this story in detail in Beschloss and Talbott, *At the Highest Levels*, pp. 362–70; Palazhchenko, *My Years with Gorbachev and Shevardnadze*, p. 286; Komitet po voprosam oborony i gosudarstvennoi bezopasnosti, 23 May 1991, GARF, f. 9654, op. 7, d. 216, ll. 7–61.

36. The materials of the Soviet General Staff used for this paragraph are in the Katayev Papers, Box 5, Folders 8–16, HIA; Chernyaev, *Sovmestnyi iskhod*, 18 May 1991, p. 943.

37. William Safire, "The Grand-Bargain Hunters," *The New York Times* (3 June 1991).

38. News Release, "Hoover Scholars: Soviet Economic Reform Lies with Individual Republics," *Stanford News Service*, 20 June 1991; Beschloss and Talbott, *At the Highest Levels*, p. 376.

39. Matlock, *Autopsy*, pp. 537–9; Braithwaite's diary, 28 May 1991.

40. Brent Scowcroft's memorandum to the secretaries of state, the treasury, defense, agriculture, commerce, OMB, and CEA. "The U.S. Economic Relationship with the Soviet Union," 31 May 1991; Michael Boskin Files, NSC Meeting Files, CF01113-051, GBPL.

41. National Security Council. Meeting on U.S.-Soviet Relations, 3 June 1991, White House Situation Room. NSC Files, Burns Files, Box 2, OA/ID CF01308-005, GBPL.

42. NSC Files, Burns Files, Box 2, OA/ID CF01308-005, GBPL.

43. Ibid, pp. 5–8.

44. Russian translation of the letter from Bush to Gorbachev, 5 June 1991, in the files of Vitaly Katayev, Katayev Papers, Box 4, Folder 58, HIA, pp. 1–8.

45. Braithwaite's diary, 7 June 1991; Primakov, *Vstrechi na perekrestkakh*, pp. 90–1.

46. The author's interview with Grigory Yavlinsky, 24 December 2016, Moscow.

47. Graham Allison and Robert Blackwill, "America's Stake in the Soviet Future," *Foreign Affairs* (Summer 1991), pp. 77–97.

48. Burns and Hewett Files: Subject Files, Box 2, OA/ID CF-1486-019, GBPL. The cover letter and a copy of the program in AY, f. 6, op. 1, d. 160, ll. 10–62, at https://yeltsin.ru/archive/paperwork/13129.

49. *Izvestia* (19 June 1991), p. 1; Burns and Hewett Files: Subject Files, Box 2, OA/ID CF1486-019, GBPL; Beschloss and Talbott, *At the Highest Levels*, p. 401.

50. The transcript of Pavlov's speech is in GARF, f. 9654, op. 7, d. 1334; *Nezavisimaia gazeta* (18 June 1991); Gerashchenko to V. S. Pavlov and A. I. Lukyanov, 12 July 1991, RGAE, f. 2224, op. 32, d. 4006, ll. 28–32, at http://gaidar-arc.ru/file/bulletin-1/DEFAULT/org.stretto.plugins.bulletin.core.Article/file/2571.

51. GARF, f. 9654, op. 7, d. 1334, ll. 77–89, 113–21.

52. The full transcript of Kryuchkov's speech is in GARF, f. 9654, op. 7, d. 1334, ll. 90–110; also his *Lichnoie delo*, vol. 2, pp. 388–91; Pikhoia, *Sovetskii Soiuz*, p. 648.

53. Beschloss and Talbott, *At the Highest Levels*, pp. 394–5.

54. Telephone conversation with Mikhail Gorbachev, 21 June 1991, GBPL, at https://bush-41library.tamu.edu/files/memcons-telcons/1991-06-21-Gorbachev.pdf. On the logic of Gorbachev's political confidence see Chernyaev, *Sovmestnyi iskhod*, 23 June 1991, p. 954.

55. Boris Yeltsin on C-SPAN, 20 June 1991, at https://www.c-span.org/video/?18520-1/president-russian-republic. Meeting with President of the Russian Republic Boris Yeltsin of the USSR, 20 June 1991, p. 5, at https://bush41library.tamu.edu/files/memcons-telcons/1991-06-20-Yeltsin.pdf.

56. Timothy Colton's communication to the author, 25 April 2021; Arnold L. Horelick. "The Future of the Soviet Union: What is in the Western Interest," 16–18 June 1991, p. 20, at https://www.rand.org/pubs/occasional_papers-soviet/OPS022.html. Other participants included Stephen Sestanovich, Stephen Meyer, Frederik Starr, and Robert Legvold. For the conclusion see Opening Session of the London Economic Summit, Monday, 15 July 1991, p. 3, GBPL, at https://bush41library.tamu.edu/files/memcons-telcons/1991-07-15-Mitterrand.pdf.

57. Michael Boskin, 30–31 July 2001, Stanford University, BOHP, p. 20.

58. Memorandum of Conversation. Telcon with Helmut Kohl, 24 June 1991, GBPL, at https://bush41library.tamu.edu/files/memcons-telcons/1991-06-24-Kohl.pdf.

59. Proposed agenda for meeting with the President, 26 June 1991, 1:30 p.m., James A. Baker III Papers (MC 197), Box 115, Folder 8 (White House Meeting Agendas, 1991), Seeley Mudd Library, Princeton University.

60. On Yavlinsky-Allison's tour, see the author's interview with Yavlinsky, 24 December 2016, Moscow; Undated draft letter to Major is in the Burns and Hewett Files: Chronological File, Box 1, OA/ID CF1407-006, GBPL.

61. Interview with Robert Gates, BOHP, p. 91.

62. Braithwaite's diary, 19 July 1991.

63. Jack Matlock, "Gorbachev's Draft Economic Package for G-7," 3 July 1991, Burns and Hewett Files: Subject Files, Box 2, OA/ID CF01486-026, GBPL.

64. Chernyaev, *Sovmestnyi iskhod*, 3 and 7 July 1991, pp. 957, 959. Pavlov's group included Abalkin, Aganbegyan, Y. Yaremenko, V. Martnynov, and O. Ozhereliev, who had diverse, even conflicting views on the reforms. The text of the "letter" produced by this group was sent on 11 July to G-7 leaders. See *V Politburo TsK KPSS*, pp. 680–92.

65. Matlock, "Gorbachev's Draft Economic Package for G-7."

66. GARF, f. 5446, op. 163, d. 47.

67. Documents of 25 June and 6 July 1991 in *V Politburo TsK KPSS*, pp. 678–9; Chernyaev, *Sovmestnyi iskhod*, 7 July 1991, p. 959.

68. The Zaikov commission on the Warsaw Pact political meeting, 6 June 1990, Katayev Papers, Box 3, Folder 1, HIA; recollections of Vladimir Lobov, *Kommersant-Vlast*, 4 April 2005, at https://www.kommersant.ru/doc/560143; Yuli Kvitsinsky, *Vremia i sluchai. Zametki professionala* (Moscow: Olma-press, 1999), pp. 146, 147. For the best-documented study on the Eastern European approaches to NATO at the time see Mary Sarotte, *Not One Inch: America, Russia, and the Making of Post-Cold War Stalemate* (New Haven, CT: Yale University Press, 2021), ch. 4.

69. Chernyaev, *Sovmestnyi iskhod*, 6 July 1991, p. 958; Gorbachev-Kohl conversation (one on one), 5 July 1991, MSG SS, vol. 26, p. 371.
70. Anatoly Chernyaev, *Shest Let s Gorbachevym. Po dnevnikovym zapisiam* (Moscow: Progress-Kultura, 1993), p. 467; Chernyaev, *Sovmestnyi iskhod*, 6 July 1991, p. 958. The remark about "Costa Rica" is omitted from the official Soviet memo, MSG SS, vol. 26, pp. 374–5.
71. Chernyaev, *Sovmestnyi iskhod*, 6 July 1991, p. 958.
72. Telephone conversation with Helmut Kohl, Chancellor of Germany, on 8 July 1991, GBPL, at https://bush41library.tamu.edu/files/memcons-telcons/1991-07-08-Kohl.pdf.
73. John Lloyds, Grigory "Yavlinsky Tries to Warn Off the West," *The Financial Times* (23 July 1991), p. 2; Grigory Yavlinsky, "Soglasie na shans"; Chernyaev, *Sovmestnyi iskhod*, 11 July 1991, p. 962.
74. Gorbachev, *Zhizn i reformy*, vol. 2, pp. 292–4.
75. Gorbachev's Letter of Application, 15 July 1991, Scowcroft Collection, Box 22, OA/ID 91129-001, GBPL.
76. Allison to Bush (via Scowcroft), 12 July 1991, Burns and Hewett Files: Chronological Files, Box 1, OA/ID CF-01407-006, GBPL.
77. Meeting with Manfred Wörner, Secretary-General of NATO, 25 June 1991, Oval Office, GBPL, at https://bush41library.tamu.edu/files/memcons-telcons/1991-06-25-Woerner.pdf.
78. Meeting with Giulio Andrreotti of the Netherlands, 15 July 1991; meeting with Helmut Kohl, 15 July 1991; meeting with Prime Minister Lubbers and EC President Delors, 15 July 1991. Memos and telephone conversations, GBPL.
79. Bush and Scowcroft, *A World Transformed*, pp. 506, 507.
80. Meeting with Prime Minister Kaifu of Japan, 11 July 1991, GBPL, at https://bush41library.tamu.edu/files/memcons-telcons/1991-07-11-Kaifu.pdf.
81. Opening Session of the London Economic Summit, Monday, 15 July 1991, GBPL, p. 3, at https://bush41library.tamu.edu/files/memcons-telcons/1991-07-15-Mitterrand.pdf.
82. Ibid.
83. Second Plenary, London Economic Summit, 16 July 1991, GBPL, at https://bush41library.tamu.edu/files/memcons-telcons/1991-07-16-Mitterrand%20[1].pdf.
84. Mulroney recalled this episode in his conversation with Bush on the day of the coup in Moscow, memo of conversation with Brian Mulroney, 19 August 1991, "Telephone Conversation with Prime Minister Brian Mulroney of Canada, August 19, 1991," GBPL, at http://bushlibrary.tamu.edu/research/pdfs/memcons_telcons/1991-08-19-Mulroney.pdf.
85. Braithwaite's diary, 14 and 16 July 1991; Palazhchenko, *My Years with Gorbachev and Shevardnadze*, p. 296.
86. Vladimir Utkin ("Yuzhmash") at the USSR Supreme Soviet, 23 May 1991, GARF, f. 9654, op. 7, d. 216, ll. 20–1; Yazov in his speech at the Supreme Soviet on 17 June 1991, GARF, f. 9654, op. 7, d. 1334, ll. 76–7; "K voprosu o ratifikatsii dogovora mezhdu SSSR i SShA o sokrashchenii i ogranichenii SNV" (without date), Katayev Papers, Box 6, Folder 22, HIA; Beschloss and Talbott, *At the Highest Levels*, p. 403.
87. Chernyaev, *Sovmestnyi iskhod*, 7 July 1991, p. 960; Palazhchenko, *My Years with Gorbachev and Shevardnadze*, p. 291; Beschloss and Talbott, *At the Highest Levels*, p. 406.
88. "Iz besedy s Prezidentom Frantsii F. Mitteranom," 17 July 1991; "Iz besedy s prezidentom Evropeiskogo banka rekonstruktsii i razvitiia Zhakom Attali," 17 July 1991, MSG SS, vol. 27, pp. 29, 31, 33–6.
89. This paragraph is based on several minutes of this conversation: Savranskaya and Blanton, *The Last Superpower Summits*, pp. 852–3; *V Politburo TsK KPSS*, pp. 693–4 and Chernyaev, *Sovmestnyi iskhod*, 23 July 1991, p. 966.
90. Savranskaya and Blanton, *The Last Superpower Summits*, p. 853.
91. Ibid. The sentence about the "demise of the Soviet Union" is not in the American memcon. Chernyaev, *Sovmestnyi iskhod*, 23 July 1991, p. 966. Chernyaev checked on this phrase with Palazhchenko, who was the Soviet interpreter at the meeting. Palazhchenko, *My Years with Gorbachev and Shevardnadze*, p. 293.
92. Savranskaya and Blanton, *The Last Superpower Summits*, p. 852, *V Politburo TsK KPSS*, p. 695.

93. Beschloss and Talbott, *At the Highest Levels*, p. 407; Chernyaev, *Shest Let s Gorbachevym*, p. 457; Chernyaev, *Sovmestnyi iskhod*, p. 966; Palazhchenko, *My Years with Gorbachev and Shevardnadze*, p. 292.
94. Gorbachev, *Zhizn i reformy*, vol. 2, pp. 296-7.
95. Beschloss and Talbott, *At the Highest Levels*, p. 407.
96. "Beseda s M. Thatcher," 19 July 1991, MSG SS, vol. 27, pp. 89-90; Gorbachev, *Zhizn i reformy*, vol. 2, p. 299; Palazhchenko, *My Years with Gorbachev and Shevardnadze*, pp. 296-7.
97. Recollection of Andrei Kokoshin, then deputy director of the Institute for the US and Canada of the Soviet Academy of Science. Personal communication to the author, Moscow, 25 March 2019.

CHAPTER 10: CONSPIRACY

1. "The Announcement of M. S. Gorbachev on Television," *Izvestia*, 2 August 1991, p. 1.
2. See the transcripts of the Plenum of the CC CPSU, 26 July 1991, GARF, f. P9654, op. 17, d. 1357, ll. 18-25.
3. Otto Latsis, *Tshchatelno splanirovannoe samoubiistvo* (Moscow: Moskovskaia shkola politicheskikh issledovanii, 2001), p. 365. See also the transcripts of the Plenum of the CC CPSU, 25 July 1991, GARF, f. P9654, op. 17, d. 1356, l. 57.
4. Shakhnazarov, *Tsena svobody*, pp. 537-9, 542-3; Shakhnazarov's memo to Gorbachev on 27 July 1991, quoted by Geoghegan, "A Policy in Tension", p. 792.
5. TsDAGO, f. 1, op. 32, d. 2933; Shakhnazarov, *Tsena svobody*, p. 542; *Nezavisimaia gazeta* (20 June 1991), p. 3.
6. Recollections of Yuri Baturin, *Demokratizatsia: The Journal of Post-Soviet Democratization* II:2 (Spring 1994), pp. 212-21; *Soiuz mozhno bylo sokhranit*, pp. 289-301 at: https://www.gorby.ru/userfiles/union_could_be_saved.pdf.
7. Gorbachev, *Zhizn i reformy*, vol. 2, pp. 552, 556. The most detailed analysis of this agreement is in Ignaz Lozo, *Avgustovskii putch 1991 goda. Kak eto bylo* (Moscow: ROSSPEN, 2014), pp. 80-94.
8. Gorbachev, *Zhizn i reformy*, vol. 2, p. 556.
9. Shakhnazarov, *Tsena svobody*, pp. 544-5.
10. "Primernaia protsedura podpisaniia Soiuznogo dogovora," draft from the archive of the Gorbachev Foundation, in *Soiuz mozhno bylo sokhranit*, pp. 302-305 at https://www.gorby.ru/userfiles/union_could_be_saved.pdf.
11. Palazhchenko, *My Years with Gorbachev and Shevardnadze*, p. 298.
12. Braithwaite's diary, 21 June 1991.
13. Baker-Shevardnadze meeting, 29 July 1991, Stepanov notes, Stepanov-Mamaladze Papers, Box 3, Folder 27, HIA.
14. BBC interview with Gennady Yanayev, July 1991 [undated]. Courtesy of Anna Kan. See also Bush, *All the Best*, p. 530.
15. Palazhchenko, *My Years with Gorbachev and Shevardnadze*, p. 299; Savranskaya and Blanton, *The Last Superpower Summits*, p. 804.
16. Bush and Scowcroft, *A World Transformed*, pp. 509-10.
17. "Conversation with J. Bush" (one on one), 30 July 1991, in MSG SS, vol. 27, pp. 156, 159, 164-7; Bush and Scowcroft, *A World Transformed*, p. 511; Chernyaev, *Shest Let s Gorbachevym*, p. 461.
18. "Expanded Bilateral Meeting with Mikhail Gorbachev of the USSR," 30 July 1991, in Memcons—Moscow Summit—7/91, OA/ID CF01756-025, Burns and Hewett Files: Subject Files, Box 1, GBPL.
19. Ibid.
20. See Robert A. Pollard, "Economic Security, and the Origins of the Cold War: Bretton Woods, the Marshall Plan, and American Rearmament, 1944-1950," *Diplomatic History* 9:3 (1985), pp. 274-5.
21. Memorandum of conversation. Meeting with Boris Yeltsin, President of the Republic of Russia, 30 July 1991, GBPL; *Izvestia*, 31 July 1991, p. 2; https://bush41library.tamu.edu/files/memcons-telcons/1991-07-30-Yeltsin.pdf.

22. Beschloss and Talbott, *At the Highest Levels*, pp. 412–13.
23. Gorbachev, *Zhizn i reformy*, vol. 2, p. 308.
24. Ibid, pp. 301–4; Palazhchenko, *My Years with Gorbachev and Shevardnadze*, p. 305; on the Soviet-American condominium see Plokhy, *The Last Empire*, p. 22.
25. Three-on-three meeting with President Mikhail Gorbachev, 31 July 1991, GBPL, at https://bush41library.tamu.edu/files/memcons-telcons/1991-07-31-Gorbachev%20[1].pdf.
26. Palazhchenko, *My Years with Gorbachev and Shevardnadze*, p. 304; Tarmo Vahter, *Estonia: Zharkoie leto 91-go. Avgustovskii putch i vozrozhdenie nezavisimosti* (Tallinn: Eesti Ekspress, 2012), p. 188–191.
27. Three-on-three meeting with President Mikhail Gorbachev, 31 July 1991, GBPL, at https://bush41library.tamu.edu/files/memcons-telcons/1991-07-31-Gorbachev%20[1].pdf.
28. Bush, *All the Best*, pp. 529–30.
29. Beschloss and Talbott, *At the Highest Levels*, p. 415.
30. D. Yazov, "Eto sbalansirovannyi dogovor," *Izvestia* (1 August 1991), p. 2.
31. Matlock, *Autopsy*, pp. 564–5; Gorbachev, *Zhizn i reformy*, vol. 2, p. 304.
32. Matlock, *Autopsy*, pp. 566–7; "Remarks to the Supreme Soviet of the Republic of the Ukraine in Kiev, Soviet Union," 1 August 1991, at https://bush41library.tamu.edu/archives/public-papers/3267.
33. Telephone conversation with Helmut Kohl, 8 July 1991, GBPL, at https://bush41library.tamu.edu/files/memcons-telcons/1991-07-08-Kohl.pdf.
34. CIA, "Gorbachev's Future," 28 May 1991, p. 8, GBPL.
35. Ekonomichni rozrakhunki ta pravovy visnovki scho do vkhozhdeniia Ukraiiny do Soiuzu na umovakh, vyznachenykh proektom dogovoru pro Soiuz suverennykh derzhav (ekspertne zakluchennia), 25 July 1991, TsDAGO, f. 1, op. 32, 2901, ll. 55–6.
36. Meeting with Ukrainian Supreme Soviet Chairman Leonid Kravchuk, 1 August 1991, GBPL, at: https://bush41library.tamu.edu/files/memcons-telcons/1991-08-01-Kravchuk.pdf.
37. Matlock, *Autopsy*, pp. 570–1.
38. Chernyaev, *Sovmestnyi iskhod*, entry of 3 August 1991, p. 969.
39. MSG SS, vol. 27, pp. 208–10; Lozo, *Avgustovskii putsch 1991 goda*, pp. 74, 83.
40. Pavlov, *Upushchen li shans?*, p. 32.
41. Information on the villa and its construction can be found online at https://www.youtube.com/watch?v=pvtLHIxcrOA, accessed 26 April 2021.
42. "Eti dni byli uzhasny," "Foros: 73 chasa pod arestom. Iz dnevnika zheny prezidenta," 3 and 4 August 1991, in *Raisa. Pamiati Raisy Maksimovny Gorbachevoi* (Moscow: Vagrius, 2000), pp. 117–18; V. S. Pavlov, *Avgust iznutri. Gorbachevputch* (Moscow: Delovoi mir, 1993), p. 96.
43. "Eti dni byli uzhasny," 4 August 1991, p. 118.
44. Ibid, 5 and 7 August 1991, pp. 118–19; Taubman, *Gorbachev*, p. 606.
45. "Eti dni byli uzhasny," 6 August 1991, p. 119. The draft of this article was published in M. S. Gorbachev, *Avgustovskii putch. Prichiny i sledstviia* (Moscow: Novosti, 1991), pp. 64–90.
46. "Eti dni byli uzhasny," 8 and 10 August 1991, pp. 119–20; interview with Leonid Kravchuk in *Rozpad Radians'koho Soiuzu*, at http://oralhistory.org.ua/interview-ua/510.
47. "Eti dni byli uzhasny," 18 August 1991, p. 121.
48. "Obrashchenie k prezidentu Rossii B.N. Yeltsinu" (signed on 5 August 1991), *Nezavisimaia gazeta*, 8 August 1991.
49. "Boris Yeltsin: podpisaniie novogo soiuznogo dogovora ne stavit pod somnenie suverenitet respubliki," *Nezavisimaia gazeta* (13 August 1991), p. 1.
50. "Slovo k narodu," *Sovetskaia Rossiia* (23 July 1991).
51. Remnick, *Lenin's Tomb*, pp. 376, 439; Andrei S. Grachev, *Gibel Sovetskogo "Titanika": Sudovoi zhurnal* (Moscow: n.p., 2015), pp. 203–4.
52. This was the version that had been agreed upon in Novo-Ogaryovo on 23 July. Lozo, *Avgustovskii putsch 1991 goda*, pp. 74, 78. In a later interview Oleg Shenin said that Pavlov

leaked the text of the treaty to a journalist who was his friend. See Interview with Oleg Shenin by Oleg Skvortsov, 14 December 1998, p. 18.

53. See one copy in GARF, f. 10036, op. 3, d. 412, p. 132; another was in the archives of the Communist Party of Ukraine, TsDAGO, f. 1, op. 32, d. 2901, ll. 4–20.
54. A. B. Veber, "Podgotovka i proval avgustovskogo putcha," in A. S. Chernyaev, ed., *Dva putcha i raspad SSSR* (Moscow: Gorbachev-fond, 2011), p. 54.
55. Boldin, *Krushenie piedestala*, pp. 13–14; "Vstrecha prezidentov piati respublik," *Izvestia* (14 August 1991), p. 1.
56. Gorbachev, *Zhizn i reformy*, vol. 2, p. 553.
57. Anatoly Adamishin's diary, 24 July 1991, Adamishin Papers, HIA.
58. A. N. Yakovlev to Gorbachev, 30 April 1991, at http://www.alexanderyakovlev.org/f./issues-doc/1024404; "Otkrytoe pismo A. N. Yakovleva kommunistam ob opasnosti revanshizma," 16 August 1991, at http://www.alexanderyakovlev.org/f./issues-doc/1024446, accessed 17 June 2017.
59. The schedule, dated 13 August 1991, is in TsDAGO, f. 1, op. 32, d. 2901, p. 23.
60. "Statia, napisannaia v Forose," Gorbachev, *Avgustovskii putch*, pp. 65, 71–81.
61. "Supreme Soviet Investigation of the 1991 Coup" [the commission headed by Lev Ponomarev, conclusions of hearings on 4 February 1992]. The Suppressed Transcripts: Part 1. *Demokratizatsiya* 3:4 (Fall 1995), pp. 422–4.
62. Kryuchkov, *Lichnoe delo*, vol. 2, pp. 132–47; Boldin, *Krushenie piedestala*, p.12; exploration of Kryuchkov's motives in Lozo, *Avgustovskii putch 1991 goda*, p. 159.
63. Yeltsin, *Zapiski prezidenta*, pp. 72–3; information from the KGB, dated 20 June 1991; Kryuchkov, *Lichnoe delo*, pp. 153–4.
64. Oleg Skvortsov's interview with Valery Boldin, 23 April 1999, in the author's personal archive, courtesy of O. Skvortsov.
65. Oleg Skvortsov's interview with Oleg Baklanov (undated, 1999), in the author's personal archive, courtesy of O. Skvortsov; the author's interview with Oleg Baklanov, 16 April 1997, Moscow.
66. The protocol of interrogation of Oleg Baklanov, 9 September 1991, in Valentin Stepankov, *GKChP: 73 chasa, kotoryie izmenili mir* (Moscow: Vremia, 2011), pp. 36, 37, 39. Oleg Skvortsov's interview with Vladimir Kryuchkov, 7 December 1998, in the author's personal archive, courtesy of O. Skvortsov.
67. Shenin is not mentioned in Stepankov's book, but documents published by *Novaia gazeta* in 2001 indicate that he attended the secret meeting on 5 August. See *Novaia gazeta* 53 (23 July 2001), at http://2001.novayagazeta.ru/nomer/2001/51n/n51n-s15.shtml; Yakovlev, *Sumerki*, p. 614. Oleg Skvortsov's interview with Oleg Shenin, 14 December 1998, in the author's personal archive, courtesy of O. Skvortsov.
68. Stepankov, *GKChP*, pp. 29–30.
69. The two men were deputy heads of the KGB First Main Directorate (foreign intelligence), Major Vladimir Zhizhin and Colonel Alexei Yegorov. Yazov would later order General Pavel Grachev, commander of the Soviet Airborne Troops, to join them to coordinate actions between the KGB and the Army.
70. Stepankov, *GKChP*, pp. 31, 32–3.
71. Interview with Valentin Varennikov, 3 October 2000. Hoover Institution and Gorbachev Foundation Oral History Project, HIA, Box 3, Folder 4, p. 36; V. A. Varennikov, *Nepovtorimoe*, vol. 6 (Moscow: Sovetskii Pisatel, 2001), p. 178.
72. On Pavlov's motives and his open criticism of the Union Treaty see Pavlov, *Avgust iznutri*, pp. 97–8; Pavlov, *Upushchen li shans?*, pp. 16, 34, 237.
73. Oleg Skvortsov's interview with Gennady Yanayev, 25 March 1999. Transcript in the personal archive of the author.
74. Oleg Skvortsov's interview with Valery Boldin, 23 April 1999, pp. 13, 42–3; "GKChP: protsess, kotoryi ne poshel," *Novaia gazeta* 53 (30 July 2001), http://2001.novayagazeta.ru/nomer/2001/53n/n53n-s11.shtml.
75. Stepankov, *GKChP*, pp. 43–4, 52–3.
76. Ibid, p. 53.

77. Raisa's recollections in "Eti dni byli uzhasny," 15 August 1991, p. 121; Shakhnazarov, *Tsena svobody*, p. 263; Stepankov, *GKChP*, p. 64; Gorbachev, *Zhizn i reformy*, vol. 2, p. 557.
78. Gorbachev, *Zhizn i reformy*, vol. 2, pp. 557–8; "Eti dni byli uzhaasny," 18 August 1991, p. 122.
79. Boldin, *Krushenie piedestala*, pp. 16–17; Varennikov, *Nepovtorimoe*, vol. 6, pp. 206–12; Gorbachev, *Zhizn i reformy*, vol. 2, pp. 258–9; Gorbachev, *Avgustovskii putch*, pp. 10–13; Stepankov, *GKChP*, pp. 58–60; Taubman, *Gorbachev*, pp. 608–9.
80. On the attitudes of the KGB personal bodyguards see https://www.youtube.com/watch?v=c1AytxDkErw&t=1205s; Raisa's diary, 18 August 1991.
81. Stepankov, *GKChP*, p. 54; Chernyaev, *Sovmestnyi iskhod*, p. 975.
82. Stepankov, *GKChP*, pp. 72–3, 169–75.
83. Oleg Skvortsov's interview with Gennady Yanayev, 25 March 1999.
84. Lozo, *Avgustovskii putch 1991 goda*, pp. 184–7, 197.
85. On Bessmertnykh see Stepankov, *GKChP*, p. 85.
86. Stepankov, *GKChP*, pp. 83–5, 91–7; Lozo, *Avgustovskii putch 1991 goda*, p. 437. On the reasons for Shenin's non-inclusion in the Emergency Committee see Baklanov in his interview with O. Skvortsov, undated, early 1999. For the texts see *GKChP SSSR. Sbornik opublikovannykh dokumentov (avgust 1991 g)* (Moscow: Samizdat, 2011), pp. 4–8, 14–15, at http://gkchp.sssr.su/gkchp.pdf.
87. Oleg Skvortsov's interview with Oleg Baklanov (undated), 1999. Courtesy of O. Skvortsov.
88. The text of Yanayev's letter to Bush is in OA-ID 9113, Scowcroft Collection, "Dobrynin (Gorbachev) files," GBPL. *GKChP SSSR*, pp. 8–9.
89. The copy of the order is in the file of documents from the Ministry of Defense and the General Staff, provided for the parliamentary commission on the investigation of the GKChP, GARF, f. 9654, op. 7, d. 1360, l. 48; on "no blood spilled" see the deposition of Shaposhnikov to the parliamentary commission of the Russian Supreme Soviet, "The Suppressed Transcripts, Part. 4," *Demokratizatsiya* (Summer 1996), p. 605.
90. Stepankov, *GKChP*, p. 102; Yevgeny Shaposhnikov, *Vybor. Zapiski glavnokomanduiush-chego* (Moscow: 1993), p. 19.

1. AY, f. 6, op. 1, d. 135, ll. 95–9.
2. Adamishin's diary, 18 August 1991, Adamishin Papers, HIA.
3. Ibid, 18 and 20 August 1991, Adamishin Papers, HIA.
4. Interview with Yelena Bonner on Radio Liberty, 15 August 2001, at http://archive.svoboda.org/programs/hr/2001/hr.081501.asp.
5. The notebook of Stepanov-Mamaladze, 19 August 1991, Stepanov-Mamaladze Papers, Box 3, Folder 28, HIA.
6. Masha Lipman, "Life Without Lies: One Year after the Death of Fear," *Washington Post*, 16 August 1992.
7. Victoria Bonnell, Ann Cooper, and Grigory Freidin, eds., *Russia at the Barricades: Eyewitness Accounts of the August 1991 Coup* (Armonk, NY: M. E. Sharpe, 1994), p. 93.
8. Interview with Bonner on Radio Liberty, 15 August 2001, at http://archive.svoboda.org/programs/hr/2001/hr.081501.asp.
9. On Lukin see "Syn komissara," *Itogi* 13 (28 March 2011); the author's interview with Vladimir Lukin, 30 June 2017, Moscow.
10. Yeltsin, *Zapiski prezidenta*, pp. 67, 70; Voshchanov, *Yeltsin kak navazhdenie*, pp. 259–61.
11. Naina Yeltsina, *Lichanaia zhizn* (the excerpts from the memoirs), at https://www.business-gazeta.ru/article/348365; Gennady Burbulis, interview by journalist Andrei Karaulov, 23 August 1991, Karaulov, *Vokrug Kremlia*, pp. 303–4.
12. Stepankov, *GKChP*, pp. 106–7; Ruslan Khasbulatov, *Poluraspad SSSR*, p. 290; Burbulis in Karaulov, *Vokrug Kremlia*.
13. Lozo, *Avgustovskii putch 1991 goda*, pp. 202–3; Gennady Burbulis's recollections in "Meltdown," *Foreign Affairs*, 20 June 2011, at http://foreignpolicy.com/2011/06/20/meltdown; Ruslan Khasbulatov, ed. Richard Sakwa, *The Struggle for Russia: Power and*

Change in the Democratic Revolution (London: Routledge, 1993), pp. 141–2; the author's interview with Vladimir Lukin, Moscow, 30 June 2017.

14. Lozo, *Avgustovskii putch 1991 goda*, p. 207. A video recording of Yeltsin's speech is at https://www.youtube.com/watch?v=-zXChf5tEMI&t=336s.

15. Yeltsin, *Zapiski prezidenta*, p. 87. On Gamsakhurdia's compliance see GARF, f. 9654, op. 7, d. 1360 (the materials of the Ministry of Defense of the USSR), ll. 118–21. On Lithuania and Moldova see GARF, f. 9654, op. 7, d. 1360, ll. 83–4, 99–100.

16. V. A. Yadov, "O nekotorykh prichinakh putcha i ego porazheniia s tochki zreniia massovogo soznaniia i obshchestvennogo mneniia," GARF, f. 9654, op. 7, d. 1363; Yeltsin's appeal to the Patriarch on 19 August 1991 is in Demokraticheskaia Rossiia Papers, Box 2, Folder 21, HIA.

17. Collins from the US Embassy in Moscow to the Secretary of State, a ciphered cable on 19 August 1991, 16:32Z, NSC Files; White House Situation Room cables during the coup, GBPL.

18. American Embassy on 21 August 1991, 18:57Z, NSC Files; White House Situation Room, GBPL.

19. Bush and Scowcroft, *A World Transformed*, pp. 518–19; Baker, *The Politics of Diplomacy*, pp. 514–16; interview with Robert Gates, BOHP, p. 85; Beschloss and Talbott, *At the Highest Levels*, pp. 429–30.

20. Bush, *All the Best*, p. 533.

21. Memo of conversations on 19 August 1991, the Bush Library. The Bush-Mitterrand conversation took place at 6:50 a.m., at https://bush41library.tamu.edu/files/memcons-telcons/1991-08-19-Mitterrand.pdf, accessed 15 January 2018; for redacted versions of the Bush-Kohl conversation see https://bush41library.tamu.edu/files/memcons-telcons/1991-08-19-Kohl.pdf.

22. "First Statement on Soviet Coup," 19 August 1991, at http://www.c-spanvideo.org/program/20705-1. Memo of conversation with Toshiki Kaifu, 19 August 1991, GBPL, at https://bush41library.tamu.edu/files/memcons-telcons/1991-08-19-Kaifu.pdf.

23. Telephone conversations with John Major and Ruud Lubbers, 19 August 1991, GBPL, at https://bush41library.tamu.edu/files/memcons-telcons/1991-08-19-Major%20[1].pdf, and https://bush41library.tamu.edu/files/memcons-telcons/1991-08-19-Lubbers.pdf.

24. "Telephone Conversation with Prime Minister Brian Mulroney of Canada, August 19, 1991," GBPL, at http://bushlibrary.tamu.edu/research/pdfs/memcons_telcons/1991-08-19-Mulroney.pdf.

25. Kryuchkov, *Lichnoe delo*, pp. 53–7.

26. Yeltsin, *Zapiski prezidenta*, pp. 74, 76–8, 88.

27. Shebarshin, *Ruka Moskvy*, pp. 279–80; Stepankov, *GKChP*, p. 129.

28. For Kravchuk's version of this episode, see Plokhy, *The Last Empire*, pp. 143–156, 158; Stepankov, *GKChP*, pp. 119–21. Kravchuk's speech broadcast on 19 August 1991 at 9 p.m. on the "Vremia" program, at https://www.youtube.com/watch?v=WEtj2JRRM8M.

29. On these plans see Stepankov, *GKChP*, pp. 113–16; Voshchanov, *Yeltsin kak navazhdenie*, p. 254.

30. Shebarshin, *Ruka Moskvy*, p. 280; Yanayev, interview with O. Skvortsov, 25 March 1999; Baklanov, interview with O. Skvortsov (n.d.), p. 41. The copies in the author's personal archive. Courtesy of O. Skvortsov.

31. Stepankov, *GKChP*, pp. 116–17.

32. Chernyaev, *Shest Let s Gorbachevym*, p. 485.

33. Nevzorov's comments on 21 August 1991 are at https://www.youtube.com/watch?v=zE-R60-TIY0, accessed 25 April 2021. Prokhanov's recollections are online at http://izbor-skiy-club.livejournal.com/552743.html, accessed 12 August 2017.

34. Stepankov, *GKChP*, pp. 127–30; Lozo, *Avgustovskii putch 1991 goda*, pp. 280–2.

35. Y. Gaidar's conversation with his friend, journalist Viktor Yaroshenko (transcript from tape), 22 August 1991, *Vestnik Evropy* 46 (2016); Anna Ostapchuk, "Politicheskaia elita v moment perevorota," interview with B. Grushin, *Nezavisimaia gazeta*, 31 August 1991, p. 2; Victoria Bonnell and Gregory Freidin, "Televorot: The Role of Television Coverage in Russia's August 1991 Coup", *Slavic Review* 52:4 (Winter 1993), pp. 810–38.

36. Shebarshin, *Ruka Moskvy*, p. 256; Lozo's interview with Shebarshin in Lozo, *Avgustovskii putch 1991 goda*, p. 289. On the role of the media during the coup see Mikhail Berger, "Fakt, kotoryi nashol Interfaks," *Izvestia*, 31 August 1991; "Kak pressa pobedila GKChP," part 2, https://www.svoboda.org/a/27926336.html.

37. Stepankov, *GKChP*, pp. 154–5; Boris Yeltsin, *The Struggle for Russia* (New York: Crown, 1994), p. 75.

38. Yeltsin, *Zapiski prezidenta*, pp. 93–4; the description of Moscow streets is from Adamishin's diary, 20 August 1991, Adamishin Papers, HIA; Stepankov, *GKChP*, p. 144.

39. Bonnell, Cooper, and Freidin, *Russia at the Barricades*, pp. 74, 87. On the KGB predictions of the coup's fallout see Stepankov, *GKChP*, pp. 31–2; interview with Bonner on Radio Liberty, 15 August 2001, at http://archive.svoboda.org/programs/hr/2001/hr.081501.asp.

40. A copy of the telegram from Rodric Braithwaite to the FCO, from the files at the National Security Archive, Washington, DC. Courtesy of Sir Rodric Braithwaite and Svetlana Savranskaya.

41. NSC files, cables from the US Embassy, 19 August 1991, 1914Z, 1120Z, 18:01 EDT. NSC Files; White House Situation Room, GBPL. Collins's conclusions are in 1914Z, OA-ID, CF01723-011-4; the interview with James Collins in *The Ambassadorial Series*, compiled and edited by the Monterey Initiative in Russian Studies. Middlebury Institute of International Studies, 10 May 2021, p. 28, at https://www.middlebury.edu/institute/sites/www.middlebury.edu.institute/files/2021-05/Ambassadorial%20Series%20Transcripts_0.pdf?fv=lToKNLlx.

42. On Shevardnadze's appeal, the US Embassy cable of 19 August 1991, sent at 1930Z, 17223-007-16; on Sobchak see the US Embassy cable of 19 August 1991, 1852Z, 1991, CF01723-007-7. NSC Files; White House Situation Room, GBPL.

43. Interview with V. N. Samsonov, 18 August 2011, at http://www.online812.ru/2011/08/22/004.

44. Vladimir Putin in the film *Delo Sobchaka* (2019), directed by Ksenia Sobchak, at https://www.youtube.com/watch?v=Ra1kPqcxsAM.

45. Starovoitova's account of her activities during the coup on 2 October 1991, at https://www.youtube.com/watch?v=S30wA6JWVCU; recollections of Starovoitova's son Platon Borshchevsky, Hove, UK, 16 March 2017.

46. Galina Starovoitova, interview with Andrei Karaulov, 22 May 1991, in Karaulov, *Vokrug Kremlia*, pp. 97–8; Starovoitova on the BBC, 19 and 20 August 1991. Courtesy of Anna Kan and the BBC archives.

47. The cable from Collins to the Secretary of State, 19 August 1991, 1642Z, 1991, OA-ID CF01723-001-5-7. NSC Files; White House Situation Room, GBPL.

48. The BBC, 20 August 1991 broadcast. Courtesy of Anna Kan.

49. Gennady Burbulis, interview with Andrei Karaulov, 18 August 1991, in Karaulov, *Vokrug Kremlia*, p. 294.

50. Margaret Thatcher, *The Downing Street Years* (New York: HarperCollins, 1993), p. 513. Starovoitova online at https://www.youtube.com/watch?v=S30wA6JWVCU; also the footage from the BBC on 19 August 1991. Courtesy of Anna Kan; also https://www.bbc.com/russian/media-37145656.amp.

51. Paul Nathanson, the Center for Democracy, on the activities of the Center during the coup, 27 August 1991, The Center for Democracy records, Box 15, Folder "SU: coup articles", 1 of 2, HIA; Andrei Kozyrev, "Stand by Us!" *The Washington Post*, 21 August 1991, p. A21.

52. NSC Files, the White House Situation Room Files, CIA intelligence support cable for Monday, 19 August 1991, 1005Z, 1991, OA-ID CF01723-01-0028-29, GBPL.

53. Baker, *The Politics of Diplomacy*, p. 519.

54. Gates, *From the Shadows*, pp. 521–2; Beschloss and Talbott, *At the Highest Levels*, p. 432. Plokhy, *The Last Empire*, p. 105.

55. "Telecon with President Boris Yeltsin of Republic of Russia, USSR," 20 August 1991, GBPL, at https://bush41library.tamu.edu/files/memcons-telcons/1991-08-19-Yeltsin.pdf. http://bushlibrary.tamu.edu/research/pdfs/memcons_telcons/1991-08-19—Yeltsin.pdf; Bush and Scowcroft, *A World Transformed*, pp. 527–8.

56. Yeltsin, *Zapiski prezidenta*, pp. 93–4.

57. On Gorbachev and his family during the coup see Raisa's diary in Gorbachev, *Zhizn i reformy*, vol. 2, pp. 563–8; "Eti dni byli uzhasny," pp. 124–8; Chernyaev, *Sovmestnyi iskhod*, pp. 978–9; Taubman, *Gorbachev*, pp. 610–11.
58. For the English translation see Curzio Malaparte, *Coup d'Etat: The Technique of Revolution* (New York: E. P. Dutton, 1932). The document "About Some Axioms of Emergency Situation," prepared by the KGB, was found by the investigation in a safe of Yanayev's, "The Suppressed Transcripts: Part 1," *Demokratizatsiya* 3:4 (Fall 1995), p. 438.
59. Ostapchuk, "Politicheskaia elita v moment perevorota," p. 2; GARF, f. 9654, op. 7, d. 1363.
60. The telephone conversation between George H. W. Bush and the President of Turkey, Turgut Özal, 19 August 1991, GBPL, at https://bush41library.tamu.edu/files/memcons-telcons/1991-08-19-Ozal.pdf.
61. "'Perevorot,' Beseda E. Gaidara i V. Yaroshenko 22 avgusta 1991 g.," *Vestnik Evropy* 46 (2016), at http://magazines.russ.ru/vestnik/2016/46-47/perevorot.html.
62. GARF, f. 9654, op. 7, d. 1359, ll. 10–15. For different and conflicting notes of this session in the files of the GKChP investigation, see Stepankov, *GKChP*, pp. 140–1.
63. The explanatory note by V. Shcherbakov to the deputies of the Supreme Soviet of the USSR (a copy of which he also sent to Gorbachev on 22 August 1991); see GARF, f. 9654, op. 7, d. 1359, ll. 10–19.
64. "'Perevorot.' Beseda E. Gaidara i V. Yaroshenko 22 avgusta 1991 g."; Yegor Gaidar, *V dni porazhenii i pobed* (Moscow: Vagrius, 1996), pp. 72–3; the text of the "analysis-proclama-tion" of the Gaidar Institute, published on 20 August 1991, is at http://gaidar-arc.ru/file/bulletin-1/DEFAULT/org.stretto.plugins.bulletin.core.Article/file/4155.
65. Stepankov, *GKChP*, p. 203; GARF, f. 9654, op. 7, d. 1363, l. 115.
66. Andrei Grachev, *Gibel Sovetskogo "Titanika." Sudovoi zhurnal* (Moscow: Prozaik, 2018), p. 203.
67. The footage of the events in Leningrad is from Sergey Loznitsa, "Sobytie," at https://www.youtube.com/watch?v=VF4MJJm2bh0.
68. Gosnell's cable to the State Department, 20 August 1991, 1959Z, NSC Files, the White House Situation Room Files, GBPL.
69. Prokhanov's recollections about the coup at http://izborskiy-club.livejournal.com/552743.html; *Komsomolskaia Pravda*, 3 September 1991, p. 4; Mikhail Leontiev, "Russkii kapital: ne na smert' a na zhizn," *Nezavisimaia gazeta*, 22 August 1991, p. 4. For more on the role of women, Afgantsy, and businessmen see Dunlop, *The Rise of Russia*, pp. 222–5. On Shevardnadze, see the cable of the US Embassy on 20 August 1991, 1524Z, NSC Files, the White House Situation Room Files, GBPL; the notes of Stepanov-Mamaladze, 20 August 1991, Stepanov-Mamaladze Papers, Box 3, Folder 28, HIA.
70. The MVD report: "Ob obstanovke v strane za 20 avgusta 1991 goda," GARF, f. 9654, op. 7, d. 1345, ll. 114–16; Harvey Balzer, "Ordinary Russians? Rethinking August 1991," *Demokratizatsiya* 13:2 (Spring 2005), pp. 193–218.
71. Stepankov, *GKChP*, p. 196; Lozo, *Avgustovskii putch 1991 goda*, pp. 222–3.
72. Primakov's testimony is cited in Stepankov, *GKChP*, p. 191; Primakov, *Vstrechi na perekrestkakh*, p. 99; Yanayev's interview by O. Skvortsov, 25 March 1999, in the author's personal files. Courtesy of O. Skvortsov. Cable from the US Embassy to the State Department, 20 August 1991, 1158Z, NSC Files, the White House Situation Room Files, GBPL.
73. Stepankov, *GKChP*, pp. 207–8.
74. Lozo, *Avgustovskii putch 1991 goda*, pp. 242–5; Yevgeny Savostianov, "V avguste 91-go," in A. I. Muzykantskii, E. V. Savostianov, et al. (eds.), *Avgust 1991. Konets KPSS. Vospominaniia uchastnikov sobytii* (Moscow: Edinaia Kniga, 2006), p. 10.
75. The recollections of Sergey Yushenkov in Muzykantskii, Savostianov, et al., *Avgust 1991*, pp. 61–7.
76. Lebed, *Za derzhavu obidno*, pp. 389–91, 396–7, 398–9; Alexander Korzhakov, *Boris Yeltsin—ot rassveta do zakata* (Moscow: Interbuk, 1997), p. 53.
77. Quoted from the interview in the film by David Satter, *The Age of Delirium*, at https://www.youtube.com/watch?v=TOiW0EqU6yo; Stepankov, *GKChP*, pp. 216–17, 225–6.

78. The author's interview with Gennady Burbulis, 24 May 2020, by phone; Ivanenko at http://ru-90.ru/content/кгб-и-радикальные-перемены-интервью-с-вв-иваненко; Satter, *The Age of Delirium*, at https://www.youtube.com/watch?v=TOiW0EqU6yo. On the Russian KGB officials see "The Suppressed Transcripts: Part 1," *Demokratizatsiya* 3:4 (Fall 1995), p. 425.

79. Yeltsin, *The Struggle for Russia*, pp. 82, 85; Korzhakov, *Boris Yeltsin—ot rassveta do zakata*, p. 56.

80. Information of Rodric Braithwaite to the author, 20 April 2021; on Rostropovich see *Nezavisimaia gazeta*, 22 August 1991, p. 6; on Shevardnadze see the notes by Stepanov, 21 August 1991, Stepanov-Mamaladze Papers, Box 3, Folder 28, HIA.

81. Yegor Gaidar's interview on 22 August 1991 with the journalist Viktor Yaroshenko; see '"Perevorot." Beseda E. Gaidara i V. Yaroshenko 22 avgusta 1991 g." *Vestnik Evropy* 46 (2016), at http://magazines.russ.ru/vestnik/2016/46-47/perevorot.html. On the time of the assault, an "Alfa" group veteran confirmed it in the film by Satter, *The Age of Delirium*, at https://www.youtube.com/watch?v=TOiW0EqU6yo.

82. On the expectations and preparations at the US Embassy, see the cable from Collins to the State Department, 21 August 1991, 0124Z, NSC Files, the White House Situation Room Files, GBPL; Baker, *The Politics of Diplomacy*, p. 521.

83. Korzhakov, *Boris Yeltsin—ot rassveta do zakata*, pp. 54–5; Yeltsin, *The Struggle for Russia*, pp. 84, 93.

84. Stepankov, *GKChP*, 156.

85. This episode is in Yevgeny Shaposhnikov, *Vybor*, pp. 34–5.

86. Lozo, *Avgustovskii putch 1991 goda*, p. 223; Stepankov *GKChP*, pp. 238–9.

87. Lozo, *Avgustovskii putch 1991 goda*, p. 231.

88. Stepankov, *GKChP*, p. 210; Lozo, *Avgustovskii putch 1991 goda*, p. 229.

89. Vadim Bakatin, *Izbavlenie ot KGB* (Moscow: Novosti, 1992), p. 55; interview with Oleg Shenin by O. Skvortsov, 14 December 1998.

90. Lozo, *Avgustovskii putch 1991 goda*, pp. 239–43.

91. Stepankov, *GKChP*, p. 239; Gennady Gudkov, "KGB protiv GKChP," at http://echo.msk.ru/blog/gudkov/2040242-echo, accessed 20 August 2017.

92. Gaidar in '"Perevorot"'; The author's interview with Gennady Burbulis, 28 April 2020, by phone.

93. Stepankov, *GKChP*, pp. 255–7, 260.

94. Yeltsin, *The Struggle for Russia*, p. 101.

95. Vladislav Achalov, *Mera vozdeistviia—rasstrel*, vol. 2: *Ya skazhu Vam pravdu* (Moscow: Knishnyi Mir, 2010), p. 44; Pugo's note in Stepankov, *GKChP*, p. 312.

96. Shenin in interview with O. Skvortsov, 14 December 1998, Moscow.

97. Shcherbakov's letter to Gorbachev on 21 August 1991; the declaration of the Council of Ministers of the USSR, 21 August 1991: GARF, f. 9654, op. 7, d. 1359, ll. 21–3, 140.

98. GARF, f. 10026, op. 1, d. 569, l. 39.

99. Ibid, ll. 1–3; Braithwaite's diary, 21 and 23 August 1991. The cables from Polish ambassador Stanisław Ciosek at http://www.gorby.ru/userfiles/shifrogrammy.pdf, accessed 28 April 2018.

100. Uncorrected stenogram of the Extraordinary Session of the RSFSR Supreme Soviet, 21 August 1991, GARF, f. 10026, op. 1, d. 569, ll. 1–3.

101. GARF, f. 10026, op. 1, d. 569, l. 7; Naina Yeltsina, *Lichnaia zhizn* (Moscow: Sindbad, 2017), p. 212; Yeltsin, *The Struggle for Russia*, p. 103.

102. Yeltsin to the RSFSR Supreme Soviet on 21 August 1991, GARF, f. 10023, op. 1, d. 569, l. 7; Gerd Stricker, ed., *Russkaia pravoslavnaia tserkov v sovetskoie vremia*, vol. 1 (Moscow: Propylei, 1995).

103. GARF, f. 10026, op. 1, d. 569, l. 7.

104. GARF, f. 10026, op. 1, d. 569, ll. 7–8.

105. Bakatin, *Izbavlenie ot KGB*, p. 16

106. GARF, f. 10026, op. 1, d. 569, l. 8.

107. Lozo, *Avgustovskii putch 1991 goda*, p. 250.

NOTES to pp. 306-315

108. Braithwaite's diary, 21 August 1991; on the invitation of CNN see the recollections of Georgy Urushadze at http://www.bbc.com/russian/features-37119374?post_id=974438 595911674_1168146229874242#, accessed 15 July 2016.
109. Telephone conversation with President Boris Yeltsin, 21 August 1991, at 8:30 a.m., GBPL, at https://bush41library.tamu.edu/files/memcons-telcons/1991-08-21-Yeltsin%20[1].pdf.
110. Stepankov, *GKChP*, pp. 274, 276–9. Gorbachev believed that the ringleaders had come to press him into submission, *Zhizn i reformy*, vol. 2., p. 571. For the note from Lukyanov and Ivashko see also the photograph from the site of the Gorbachev Foundation: http://www.gorby.ru/putsch/21_avgusta.
111. Plokhy, *The Last Empire*, pp. 125, 128.
112. Raisa's diary in Gorbachev, *Zhizn i reformy*, vol. 2, p. 569, as well as his own reflections on p. 571; Stepankov, *GKChP*, pp. 270–1. Gorbachev's ire against the junta ringleaders is also cited as the main motive by Gorbachev's biographer, William Taubman, communication to the author, 16 April 2018.
113. Stepankov, *GKChP*, pp. 275–6.
114. Memo of conversation, Bush and Gorbachev, 21 August 1991, 12:19–12:31 p.m., 1991, GBPL, at https://bush41library.tamu.edu/files/memcons-telcons/1991-08-21-Gorbachev.pdf.
115. Gorbachev, *Zhizn i reformy*, vol. 2, p. 570; Stepankov, *GKChP*, pp. 279–81; Taubman, *Gorbachev*, p. 613.
116. Chernyaev, *Shest Let s Gorbachevym*, p. 489.
117. Stepankov, *GKChP*, pp. 281–3; see also Anatoly Lukyanov, *Avgust 91-go. A byl li zagovor?* (Moscow: Algoritm-Eksmo, 2010), pp. 50–75.
118. From Raisa's diary in Gorbachev, *Zhizn i reformy*, vol. 2, p. 573; Stepankov, *GKChP*, pp. 285–7.
119. MSG SS, vol. 27, pp. 232–3; Taubman, *Gorbachev*, pp. 614–16, 619.
120. Taubman, *Gorbachev*, pp. 616–17, 619; Starovoitova at http://oralhistory.org.ua/interview-ua/566; on Popov and the crowd's response see American Embassy cable on 22 August 1991, 1509Z, NSC Files, the White House Situation Room Files, GBPL.

CHAPTER 12: DEMISE

1. Telephone conversation with Boris Yeltsin, President of the Russian Republic, USSR, 9:20–9:31 p.m. EST, 21 August 1991, GBPL, at https://bush41library.tamu.edu/files/memcons-telcons/1991-08-21-Yeltsin%20[2].pdf.
2. The NSC Files; the White House Situation Room Files, 025-15, GBPL.
3. On the expected Communist revanche, see the author's conversation with Rudolf Pikhoia, 15 September 2018, Moscow.
4. Yeltsin's decrees are in *Raspad SSSR*, vol. 1, pp. 836–46.
5. MSG SS, vol. 27, pp. 234–5. Shakhnazarov mistakenly claims that those appointments were made on 24 August 1991, *Tsena svobody*, p. 279.
6. Gorbachev's press conference at http://www.gorby.ru/putsch/22_avgusta; Chernyaev, *Shest Let s Gorbachevym*, pp. 488–9.
7. Muzykantskii, E. V. Savostianov, et al., *Avgust 1991*, p. 56; Braithwaite's diary, 22 August 1991.
8. Igor Kharichev, "Sobytiia v tempe Allegro Molto," in Muzykantskii, Savostianov, et al., *Avgust 1991*, p. 36.
9. The transcript of the session of the Supreme Soviet of the RSFSR, 22 and 23 August 1991, GARF, f. 10026, op. 1, d. 569, ll. 114–18, 142, 156–7; the author's conversation with Rudolf Pikhoia, 15 September 2018, Moscow.
10. The author's interview with Vladimir Lukin, 30 June 2017, Moscow.
11. Ibid; an excerpt from Shebarshin's notes from 22 August 1991, *Ruka Moskvy*, pp. 287–9.
12. Yeltsin, *The Struggle for Russia*, p. 106.
13. GARF, f. 9654, op. 7, d. 1360, ll. 50–4.
14. Vladimir Lukin shared the news about nuclear controls to Ambassador Strauss on 24 October 1991. Strauss's cable to Baker, 24 October 1991 at 1417Z, 1991. Courtesy of Svetlana Savranskaya, National Security Archive.

NOTES to pp. 315–321

15. Shaposhnikov, *Vybor*, p. 65, Shebarshin, *Ruka Moskvy*, pp. 291–3.
16. This note is reproduced in Muzykantskii, Savostianov, et al., *Avgust 1991*, p. 98.
17. The document is reproduced in ibid, p. 89.
18. Ibid, pp. 16–24, 90–2.
19. Chernyaev, *Shest Let s Gorbachevym*, p. 492.
20. Puchenkov, "Avgustovskyi putsch 1991 g.," pp. 472–3; Onikov, *KPSS*, p. 160; Granin, *Prichudy moiei pamiati*, pp. 391–4.
21. Transcripts of the session of the Supreme Soviet of the RSFSR, 23 August 1991, GARF, f. 10026, op. 1, d. 569, ll. 156–7, and d. 2919.
22. "O zasedanii Kabineta Ministrov v tot ponedelnik," *Izvestia*, 23 August 1991. The unredacted copy of the notes, countersigned by other witnesses, is in GARF, f. 9654, op. 7, d. 1358, ll. 7–11. "Vstrecha s deputatami rossiiskogo parlamenta," 23 August 1991, MSG SS, vol. 27, pp. 264–70.
23. "Vstrecha s deputatami rossiiskogo parlamenta," pp. 273–4; "Gorbachev's Speech to Russians," *The New York Times*, 24 August 1991, pp. 6–7.
24. "Gorbachev's Speech to Russians," p. 7; the working notes of Stepanov-Mamaladze Papers, 23 August 1991, HIA.
25. Shakhnazarov, *Tsena svobody*, pp. 278–9; Chernyaev, *Shest Let s Gorbachevym*, p. 492.
26. Gennady Burbulis in Pyotr Aven and Alfred Kokh, *Revoliutsia Gaidara. Istoriia reform 90-kh iz pervykh ruk* (Moscow: Alpina, 2013), p. 50; the author's interview with Gennady Burbulis, 24 May 2020, by phone.
27. Braithwaite's diary, 24 August 1991, "From the diaries of Sergey Sergeyevich Dmitriev," *Otechestvennaia istoriia* (January–February 2001), p. 167.
28. On Zhirinovsky during the coup see: https://www.youtube.com/watch?v=pUhuzD7WVQ8; Alexei Pankin's interview with Zhirinovsky in August 2016 at https://www.nnov.kp.ru/radio/26570/3586043.
29. Prokhanov's recollections about the August days are at https://www.nnov.kp.ru/radio/26570/3586043. Nevzorov's comments are at https://www.youtube.com/watch?v=zE-R60-TIY0.
30. Stepankov, *GKChP*, pp. 306–7, 311.
31. Bergmane, "French and US Reactions," p. 326; Kristina Spohr Readman, *Germany and the Baltic Problem After the Cold War: The Development of a New Ostpolitik, 1989–2000* (London: Routledge, 2004), pp. 30–1.
32. Bergmane, "French and US Reactions," p. 285; Voshchanov, *Yeltsin kak navazhdenie*, pp. 287–9.
33. Vahter, *Estonia*, pp. 283–7, 196–8.
34. Braithwaite's diary, 23 August 1991.
35. *Raspad SSSR*, vol. 1, pp. 879, 880.
36. Vahter, *Estonia*, p. 305; Voshchanov, *Yeltsin kak navazhdeniie*, pp. 283–4.
37. Vahter, *Estonia*, pp. 305, 306–7.
38. Spohr Readman, *Germany and the Baltic Problem*, 36; Bergmane, "French and US Reactions," pp. 320–1; Braithwaite's diary, 23 and 26 August 1991.
39. Interview with Vladimir Grinev at http://oralhistory.org.ua/interview-ua/239; interview with Yevgeny Marchuk at http://oralhistory.org.ua/interview-ua/428.
40. Ciphered telegrams from the Transcarpathian Military District to the Ministry of Defense, 20 August 1991 at 15:50 and 18:00, and on 21 August 1991 at 01:45 a.m., GARF, f. 9654, op. 7, d. 1360, ll. 93, 109, 137; Levko Lukianenko in the oral history project about Ukraine's independence at *Rozpad Radians'koho Soiuzu*, http://oralhistory.org.ua/interview-ua.
41. Interview with Vladimir Grinev at http://oralhistory.org.ua/interview-ua/239; interview with Yevgeny Marchuk at http://oralhistory.org.ua/interview-ua/428.
42. The author's interview with Gennady Burbulis, 24 May 2020, by phone.
43. Interview with Vladimir Grinev at http://oralhistory.org.ua/interview-ua/239, accessed 10 October 2019; Plokhy, *The Last Empire*, pp. 162, 164.
44. Tsypko at the political round table of the Congress of the Compatriots in Moscow, 28 August 1991, GARF, f. 9654, op. 7, d. 2756, ll. 87, 98, 122, 133.

45. Hurenko in Georgy Kasianov, *Ukraina 1991–2007. Ocherki noveishei istorii* (Kiev: Nash Chas, 2008), p. 35; interview with Lukianenko in *Rozpad Radians'koho Soiuzu*.

46. Interview with Lukianenko in *Rozpad Radians'koho Soiuzu*; Solchanyk, "Kravchuk and the Coup"; interview with John Stepanchuk in *Rozpad Radians'koho Soiuzu*, at http://oralhistory.org.ua/interview-ua/315; Plokhy, *The Last Empire*, pp. 165–7, at http://static.rada.gov.ua/site/postanova_eng/Rres_Declaration_Independence_rev12.htm.

47. Interview with Leonid Kravchuk in *Rozpad Radians'koho Soiuzu*, at http://oralhistory.org.ua/interview-ua/510; interview with Grinev, *Rozpad Radians'koho Soiuzu*, at http://oralhistory.org.ua/interview-ua/239; Plokhy, *The Last Empire*, p. 168; Kasianov, *Ukraina 1991–2007*, pp. 36–7.

48. Ivan Drach in Vera Kuznetsova, "Rossiia: shag k imperii. Novyie gosudarstvenniki zanimaiut mesto starykh?" *Nezavisimaia gazeta*, 27 August 1991, p. 3; Plokhy, *The Last Empire*, p. 169.

49. Interview with Leonid Kravchuk in *Rozpad Radians'koho Soiuzu*, at http://oralhistory.org.ua/interview-ua/510; interview with Nikolai Bagrov, at http://oralhistory.org.ua/interview-ua/372.

50. "Verkhovnyi Sovet SSSR. Vneocherednaia sessiya," *Bulletin* 2 of the joint session (Sovet Soiuza and Sovet Natsionalnostei), 26 August 1991, pp. 31–41, 63–4 at, http://sten.vs.sssr.su/12/6/2.pdf.

51. Ibid, pp. 69–71, at http://sten.vs.sssr.su/12/6/2.pdf.

52. Sobchak, *Khozhdenie vo vlast*. On the Baltics: American Consul in Leningrad to the State Department, 22 August 1991, 1616Z, GBPL.

53. "Verkhovnyi Sovet SSSR. Vneocherednaia sessiia," *Bulletin* 2, 26 August, 1991, pp. 81–4, at http://sten.vs.sssr.su/12/6/2.pdf; Bill Keller, "Collapse of an Empire," *The New York Times*, 27 August 1991, at http://www.nytimes.com/1991/08/27/world/soviet-turmoil-collapse-empire-soviet-politicians-agree-union-dying-but-there-no.html?pagewanted=all&mcubz=1

54. "Press sekretar prezidenta ofitsial'no zaiavliaet," *Rossiiskaia gazeta*, 27 August 1991.

55. Solzhenitsyn, "Kak nam obustroit Rossiiu," at http://www.lib.ru/PROZA/SOLZHENICYN/s_kak_1990.txt.

56. See Lukin's correspondence with Alexander Solzhenitsyn on 20 March 1992, at https://rg.ru/17/07/13/rossijskomu-politiku-vladimiru-lukinu-ispolnilos-80-let.html.

57. GARF, f. 9654, op. 7, d. 2756, ll. 87, 98, 119–60.

58. The author's interviews with Gennady Burbulis, 21 April and 24 May 2020. Alexander Drozdov, a friend of Burbulis, called the declaration "a trial balloon." The author's interview with Drozdov on 24 March 2020.

59. Pavel Voshchanov, "Kak ia ob'iavlial voinu Ukraine," *Novaia gazeta*, 23 October 2003; also his *Yeltsin kak navazhdenie*, p. 290.

60. "'Krizis mozhet stat neperenosimym.' Zaiavleniie politsoveta dvizheniia demokraticheskikh reform," *Izvestia*, 29 August 1991; Vera Kuznetsova, "Metamorfozy eltsinskoi natsional-politiki. Na oblomkakh rukhnuvshikh struktur vlasti," *Nezavisimaia gazeta*, 31 August 1991; Voshchanov, *Yeltsin kak navazhdenie*, pp. 293–4.

61. Interview with Leonid Kravchuk at http://oralhistory.org.ua/interview-ua/510.

62. Vladimir Kovalenko, "Golovokruzheniie Rossii ot uspekhov," *Nezavisimaia gazeta*, 3 September 1991, p. 5. The author's conversation with Rudolf Pikhoia, Moscow, 15 September 2018.

63. "Rossiia i Ukraina dogovorilis," *Izvestia*, 29 August 1991, p. 2; the author's interview with Lukin, 30 July 1991, Moscow; "Verkhovnyi Sovet SSSR," *Bulletin* 9, 29 August 1991, p. 6; Plokhy, *The Last Empire*, pp. 180–1.

64. Stankevich on Ukraine to Braithwaite, Braithwaite's diary, 27 June 1991; the author's interview with Lukin, 30 June 2017, Moscow; Voshchanov, "Kak ia ob'iavlial voinu Ukraine"; Adamishin's diary, 22, 23, 24 September 1991, HIA; Duygu Bazoglu Sezer, "Balance of Power in the Black Sea in the Post-Cold War Era: Russia, Turkey, and Ukraine," in *Crimea: Dynamics, Challenges, and Prospects*, ed. Maria Drohobycky (London: Rowman & Little Brown, 1995), p. 167.

65. Gorbachev on Kruchina in *Zhizn i reformy*, vol. 1, p. 228; Stepankov, *GKChP*, pp. 300–4.

66. Khlebnikov, *Godfather of the Kremlin*, pp. 60–6.
67. On Bocharov's scheme see his memo of 26 August 1991, GARF, f. 10036, op. 10, d. 3, ll. 5–6. He resigned on 1 October 1991, *Rossiiskaia gazeta*, 2 October 1991, p. 1; M. A. Bocharov, "Vremia vseobshchego ocharovania, i razocharovaniia," in Krotov, *Ocherki istorii*, pp. 482–3.
68. Spravka to the committee for foreign affairs and international trade, 1 September 1991, GARF, f. 10026, op. 4, d. 2687, ll. 24–6; V. A. Rayevsky from the Ministry of Finance to Yuri Luzhkov, 15 October 1991; Ivan Silayev on the state of monetary circulation, mid-October, GARF, f. 5446, op. 63, d. 41, ll. 40, 43–5.
69. Khlebnikov, *Godfather of the Kremlin*, pp. 58, 75.
70. "Razgovor s synom," *Moskoskiie Novosti* 36 (8 September 1991); Arkady Ostrovsky, *The Invention of Russia: The Journey from Gorbachev's Freedom to Putin's War* (London: Atlantic Books, 2015), pp. 136–8.
71. Mikhail Leontiev, "Russkii kapital. Ne na smert', a na zhizn'," *Nezavisimaia gazeta*, 22 August 1991, p. 4; Gaddy, *The Price of the Past*, p. 87; also Borovoy's interviews on the Russian radio station "Mayak" on 25 August 1991, RFE/RL Research Institute; and "Posledniaia ekspropriatsiia," *Literaturnaia gazeta*, 2 October 1991, p. 5, Dunlop Papers, Box 2, Folder Post-Coup (5), HIA.
72. Adamishin's diary, 7 and 9 October 1991; Gaddy, *The Price of the Past*, p. 87.
73. "Biografiia Mikhaila Khodorkovskogo," at https://khodorkovsky.ru/bio; see also Mikhail Khodorkovsky, Leonid Nevzlin, *Chelovek s rublem* (Moscow: MENATEP-inform, 1992).
74. M. Khodorkovsky, "Bunt Bankirov," *Nezavisimaya gazeta*, 14 September 1991; Matiukhin in Krotov, *Ocherki istorii*, pp. 213–14, 230–1.
75. Adamishin's diary, 14 October 1991, Adamishin Papers, HIA.
76. Ibid, 31 October 1991.
77. Derluguian, *Bourdieu's Secret Admirer*, p. 304; Vadim Volkov, *Violent Entrepreneurs: The Use of Force in the Making of Russian Capitalism* (Ithaca, NY: Cornell University Press, 2002).
78. Shakhnazarov, *Tsena svobody*, p. 281.
79. *Raspad SSSR*, vol. 1, p. 859.
80. Recollection of Gerashchenko and Andrei Zverev, the Russian official who was appointed to replace him, in Krotov, *Ocherki istorii* pp. 178, 181–2, 193; Leontiev, "Russkii kapital," Ne na smert, a na zhizn," *Nezavisimaia gazeta*, 22 August 1991, p. 4; and his "Putchisty vozvrashchaiutsia," *Nezavisimaia gazeta*, 31 August 1991, p. 3; "'Krizis mozhet stat neperenosimym,'" *Izvestia*, 29 August 1991, p. 3.
81. Rasporiazheniie Prezidenta RSFSR, 28 and 31 August 1991, in *Raspad SSSR*, vol. 1, pp. 863, 876.
82. Adamishin's diary, 5 September 1991, Adamishin Papers, HIA; GARF, f. 10026, op. 4, d. 2705, l. 64.
83. Adamishin's diary, 5 September 1991, Adamishin Papers, HIA.
84. *Izvestia*, 29 August 1991, p. 2; "Osnovnyie polozheniia strategii vneshneekonomicheskoi politiki v skladyvaiushcheisia ekonomicheskoi i politicheskoi situatsii," a memorandum to the Committee for foreign and economic relations of the Supreme Soviet of the RSFSR, 29 August 1991, GARF, f. 10026, op. 4, d. 2705, l. 64.
85. The author's interview with Grigory Yavlinsky, 19 December 2016, Moscow.
86. MSG SS, vol. 28, pp. 11–12, 523.
87. Ibid, pp. 12, 13, 15, 20, 22.
88. Braithwaite's diary, 1 September 1991; Adamishin's diary, 31 August 1991, Adamishin Papers, HIA.
89. "Vneocherednoi Piatyi S'ezd narodnykh deputatov SSSR," *Bulletin* 1, p. 2.
90. Medvedev, *V komande Gorbacheva*, p. 141.
91. Yuri Shcherbak at the Congress, afternoon session, 2 September 1991, *Bulletin* 1, p. 7.
92. *Bulletin* 2, 2 September 1991, p. 13; *Bulletin* 5, 4 September 1991, p. 9.
93. *Bulletin* 2, 2 September 1991, pp. 6–7, 14; *Bulletin* 3, 3 September 1991, p. 22. The text of the Declaration is in *Izvestia*, 6 September 1991, p. 1.
94. *Bulletin* 3, 3 September 1991, p. 20; *Bulletin* 4, 4 September 1991, pp. 13–14.

95. Braithwaite's diary, 10 September 1991; Medvedev, *V komande Gorbacheva*, p. 141; Nikolai Ryzhkov in his interview with Michael McFaul, 30 September 1992, McFaul Collection, HIA.
96. Boris Pankin, *Sto oborvannykh dnei* (Moscow: Sovershenno sekretno, 1993), p. 238.
97. "Savisaar's remarks at the State Council," Gorbachev MSG SS, vol. 28, pp. 106–7; Vahter, *Estonia*, p. 352.
98. "Zasedanie Gosudarstvennogo Soveta SSSR", 6 September 1991, Gorbachev MSG SS, vol. 28, pp. 109–10; B. Pankin, "O priznanii nezavisimosti Latvii, Litvy, i Estonii," *Izvestia*, 7 September 1991, p. 4.
99. Andrei S. Grachev, *Dalshe bez menia. Ukhod prezidenta* (Moscow: Progress-Kultura, 1994), p. 64. Grachev removed this analogy in the English-language translation of his book.

CHAPTER 13: CACOPHONY

1. Braithwaite's diary, 23 August 1991; Adamishin's diary, 26–28 August 1991, esp. pp. 16–17, Anatoly Adamishin Papers, HIA.
2. The notes of Stepanov-Mamaladze, 28 August 1991, Stepanov-Mamaladze Papers, Box 3, Folder 28, HIA.
3. Pankin, *Sto oborvannykh dnei*, pp. 17, 20–1; Yeltsin, *Zapiski prezidenta*, p. 138; also his *The Struggle for Russia*, p. 107.
4. Pankin, *Sto oborvannykh dnei*, pp. 20–1, 31–9.
5. Ibid, pp. 36–41; the interview with Boris Pankin in *Rozpad Radians'koho Soiuzu*, at http://oralhistory.org.ua/interview-ua/557.
6. Pankin, *Sto oborvannykh dnei*, pp. 43–5.
7. Ibid, pp. 60–3; Braithwaite's diary, 1 September 1991.
8. MSG SS, vol. 28, pp. 15, 48.
9. "Vystupleniie I. Silayeva," MSG SS, vol. 28, pp. 487–9.
10. MSG SS, vol. 28, pp. 112–16, 117, 119.
11. Bakatin, *Izbavleniie ot KGB* (Moscow: Novosti, 1992), p. 116.
12. Pankin, *Sto oborvannykh dnei*, pp. 48–9, 72–3; Braithwaite's diary, 30 August 1991.
13. Pankin, *Sto oborvannykh dnei*, pp. 49, 71.
14. Pankin, *Sto oborvannykh dnei*, p. 78; *Izvestia*, 10 September 1991, p. 1.
15. Braithwaite's diary, 10 September 1991; Notes of Stepanov-Mamaladze, 10–11 September 1991, Stepanov-Mamaladze Papers, Box 3, Folder 29, HIA.
16. MSG SS, vol. 28, pp. 142–5, 147; Baker, *The Politics of Diplomacy*, p. 529.
17. MSG SS, vol. 28, pp. 130–7, 176–9, 554–5, 567.
18. MSG SS, vol. 28, p. 219.
19. MSG SS, vol. 28, pp. 151, 170.
20. Gorbachev's conversation with Horst Köhler, 12 September 1991, MSG SS, vol. 28, pp. 226–7.
21. Bush and Scowcroft, *A World Transformed*, pp. 536–7.
22. Ibid, pp. 536–8; Beschloss and Talbott, *At the Highest Levels*, pp. 440–1. Bush's conversations with Kohl on 26 and 27 August 1991, Scowcroft Collection, Presidential Telcons and Memcons, OA-ID 91113-001, GBPL.
23. William Safire, "After the Fall," *The New York Times*, 29 August 1991.
24. https://www.armscontrol.org/factsheets/Ukraine-Nuclear-Weapons.
25. Bush's talk with Landsbergis, 31 August 1991, GBPL, at https://bush41library.tamu.edu/files/memcons-telcons/1991-08-31-Landsbergis.pdf.
26. Bush and Scowcroft, *A World Transformed*, pp. 538–9.
27. Kate Geoghegan, "The Specter of Anarchy, the Hope of Transformation: The Role of Non-State Actors in the U.S. Response to Soviet Reform and Disunion, 1981–1996," PhD Thesis, University of Virginia, December 2015, p. 257.
28. Baker, *The Politics of Diplomacy*, pp. 524–5.
29. The notes of Stepanov-Mamaladze, 28 August 1991, Stepanov-Mamaladze Papers, Box 3, Folder 28, HIA; Baker, *The Politics of Diplomacy*, p. 525.

30. https://www.c-span.org/video/?21026-1/state-department-news-briefing. Diana Villiers Negroponte, *Master Negotiator: The Role of James A. Baker III at the End of the Cold War* (New York: Archway Publications, 2020), p. 198.
31. Graham Allison and Robert Blackwill, "On with the Grand Bargain," *The Washington Post*, 27 August 1991.
32. A cable from Major to Bush on 22 August 1991; Scowcroft's draft of Bush's response to Major, 22 August 1991, the Bush Library, the NSC Files: Burns and Hewett Files, USSR Chron Files, OA-ID CF01407, GBPL.
33. Bush and Scowcroft, *A World Transformed*, p. 540; Baker, *The Politics of Diplomacy*, p. 526.
34. Memorandum from Brent Scowcroft to POTUS, "Developments in the USSR," 5 September 1991. NSC Files, Burns and Hewett Files, GBPL.
35. Quoted in Bush and Scowcroft, *A World Transformed*, p. 541.
36. Ibid, p. 542; interview with Brent Scowcroft, 10–11 August 2000, BOHP, pp. 51–2.
37. "Key points in Secretary Baker's meetings in the USSR and the Baltics, September 11–16, 1991," NSC Files, Burns and Hewett Files, USSR Chron Files, OA-ID C1407-009-22, GBPL.
38. Pankin, *Sto oborvannykh dnei*, pp. 85–7, 91–2.
39. MSG SS, vol. 28, pp. 201–2; "Key points in Secretary Baker's meetings," C1407-009-23; Baker, *The Politics of Diplomacy*, pp. 527–8.
40. The Center for Democracy Papers, Box 15, folder: SU: Cuba, HIA. "Key points in Secretary Baker's meetings"; conversation with the Secretary of State J. Baker, 11 September 1991, MSG SS, vol. 28, pp. 192–9; Baker, *The Politics of Diplomacy*, pp. 527–8.
41. Pankin, *Sto oborvannykh dnei*, pp. 93–5. The reconstruction of what happened is based on Baker, *The Politics of Diplomacy*, pp. 528–9; "Key points in Secretary Baker's meetings"; Pankin, *Sto oborvannykh dnei*, p. 94; Plokhy, *The Last Empire*, pp. 203–4.
42. Baker, *The Politics of Diplomacy*, p. 528.
43. "Key points in Secretary Baker's meetings"; Baker, *The Politics of Diplomacy*, p. 528.
44. Baker, *The Politics of Diplomacy*, p. 534; Bakatin, *Izbavlenie ot KGB*, p. 105.
45. "Key points in Secretary Baker's meetings," pp. 3, 4; Baker, *The Politics of Diplomacy*, p. 530.
46. "Key points in Secretary Baker's meetings," p. 9; Baker, *The Politics of Diplomacy*, pp. 530–1.
47. Interview with Robert Zoellick, Box 173, Series 12, Folder 8, JAB, Seeley Mudd Library, Princeton, NJ. The notes of Stepanov-Mamaladze, 12 September 1991, Stepanov-Mamaladze Papers, Box 3, Folder 29, HIA.
48. Baker, *The Politics of Diplomacy*, pp. 535–6.
49. "Key points in Secretary Baker's meetings," pp. 10–11; Baker, *The Politics of Diplomacy*, pp. 536–8.
50. The memorandum of 18 February 1992 to the NSC from the CIA and State Department, "Defining American Interests in Kazakhstan." A document from the National Security Archive, courtesy of Svetlana Savranskaya.
51. "Key points in Secretary Baker's meetings," p. 12; Baker, *The Politics of Diplomacy*, pp. 536–9.
52. Baker, *The Politics of Diplomacy*, p. 932.
53. Protokol zasedania Koordinatsionnogo Soveta dvizheniia "Demokraticheskaia Rossiia," 5 September 1991, Demokraticheskaia Rossiia papers, Box 6, Folder 5, HIA.
54. On this feeling see Alexander Yakovlev, conversation with Baker, 13 September 1991, at http://www.alexanderyakovlev.org/fond/issues-doc/1024458, accessed 20 August 2018; Vladimir Pastukhov, "Rossiiskoie demokraticheskoie dvizhenie: put k vlasti," *Polis*, 1–2 (1992), pp. 8–16.
55. The minutes of the Council of the movement Demokraticheskaia Rossiia Papers, 14 September 1991, Box 6, Folder 5, HIA, pp. 1–2.
56. Ibid., pp. 20–6.
57. Ibid, pp. 28, 32–3.
58. Ibid, pp. 145–6.
59. Ibid, pp. 115–25.
60. Ibid, pp. 68, 81, 83, 108–12.

61. "Zaiavleniie Demokraticheskogo Kongressa i Mezhparlamentskoi konferentsii demokrat-icheskikh fraktsii, 7 September 1991, Bishkek, Box 6, Folder 5, Demokraticheskaia Rossiia Papers, HIA, pp. 87, 88.

62. Dmitry Furman, "Perestroika glazami moskovskogo gumanitariia," at http://dmitriy-furman.ru/?page_id=3657.

63. The minutes, pp. 94–5, 97–8.

64. Ibid, pp. 160–2.

65. The minutes of the State Council, 16 September 1991, MSG SS, vol. 28, pp. 251, 270–1, 491–4.

66. Ibid, p. 265.

67. Ibid, p. 263.

68. Ibid, pp. 264–5, 278, 494–502.

69. MSG SS, vol. 28, pp. 269–71, 279, 320.

70. AY, f. 6, op. 1, d. 163, at https://yeltsin.ru/archive/paperwork/18109.

71. MSG SS, vol. 28, pp. 321–2.

72. MSG SS, vol. 28, p. 323.

73. MSG SS, vol. 28, pp. 262, 245.

74. MSG SS, vol. 28, pp. 272, 311–12; Shushkevich in *Rozpad Radians'koho Soiuzu*, at http://oralhistory.org.ua/interview-ua/455.

75. 'Beseda s ministrom finansov SShA N. Brady," 19 September 1991, MSG SS, vol. 28, pp. 357–66.

76. Nicholas F. Brady, Memorandum to the President, 21 September 1991, Burns and Hewett Files; USSR Chron Files, OA-ID, CF01407-009-76/79, GBPL.

77. Interview with G. E. Burbulis by Oleg Moroz, *Literaturnaia gazeta* 45 (1991); http://www.ru-90.ru/content/переломный-момент-истории-интервью-с-гэ-бурбулисом; recol-lections of Alexander Shokhin in Pyotr Aven and Kokh, *Revoliutsia Gaidara*, pp. 119, 120.

78. The author's interview with Gennady Burbulis, 24 May 2020, by phone.

79. Ibid.

80. Interview of Andrei Karaulov with Gennady Burbulis, *Nezavisimaia gazeta*, 5 September 1991, p. 7; the author's interview with Gennady Burbulis, 24 May 2020, by phone.

81. The biography of Igor Nit and the essence of his theory is at http://realism2002.narod.ru/biography.html. Yakov Feygin, "Reforming the Cold War State: Economic Thought, Internationalization, and the Politics of Soviet Reform, 1955–1985," PhD Dissertation, University of Pennsylvania, 2017.

82. By that time the group included Edward Lazear, Charles McLure, Thomas Sargent, Annelise Anderson, and Judy Shelton. Mikhail Loginov, "V naibolshei stepeni gotova k reformam," interview with Mikhail Bernstam, *Rossiiskaia gazeta*, 9 May 1991, pp. 1, 2; *Reforma bez shoka. Vybor sotsialno-priemlemykh reshenii. Vyschii Ekonomichestkii Sovet pri Prezidiume Verkhovnogo Soveta Rossii.* (Moscow-San Francisco. "Za ekonom-icheskuiu gramotnost," 1992); the author's interviews with Mikhail Bernstam, Stanford, 21 December 2012.

83. Yelena Penskaia, "Pamiati Evgeniia Saburova," *Russkii zhurnal*, 23 June 1991, at http://www.litkarta.ru/dossier/penskaya-saburov.

84. Saburov published the first draft of his program, co-authored with Alexander Granberg, in *Kommersant*, 9 September 1991, p. 9, at http://www.ru-90.ru/content/переломный-момент-истории-интервью-с-гэ-бурбулисом.

85. "Perelomnyi moment istorii," interview with G. E. Burbulis at http://www.ru-90.ru/content/переломный-момент-истории-интервью-с-гэ-бурбулисом; Recollections of Alexander Shokhin in Aven and Kokh, *Revoliutsia Gaidara*, pp. 119, 120; Braithwaite's diary, 16 October 1991.

86. Yegor Gaidar, *V dni porazhenii* (Moscow: Vagrius, 1996), p. 263.

87. Vladimir Mashits in Aven and Kokh, *Revoliutsia Gaidara*, p. 183.

88. Gaidar, *V dni porazhenii*, pp. 264–6.

89. Gaidar's team consisted of Vladimir Mashits, Andrei Nechaev, Alexei Golovkov, Konstantin Kagalovsky, and Andrei Vavilov.

90. Yavlinsky also joined the race by advising Gorbachev on economic reform: MSG SS, vol. 28, p. 366; Gaidar, *V dni porazhenii*, p. 275.

91. Gaidar, *V dni porazhenii*, pp. 249–50, 261; Mikhail Bernstam also admits this peculiarity of Gaidar's approach as a great advantage over other competitors. The e-mail information from Bernstam to the author, 25 December 2013.

92. Gaidar, *V dni porazhenii*, p. 253.

93. "Shans dlia Rossii—shans dlia vsekh," *Nezavisimaia gazeta*, 28 September 1991, p. 4; Rudiger Dornbusch, "Monetary Problems of Post-Communism: Lessons from the End of the Austro- Hungarian Empire," *Weltwirtschaftliches Archiv*, 1992, Bd. 128, H. 3.

94. Gaidar, *V dni porazhenii*, pp. 267–74. For this conviction in the mind of Burbulis see "Zapiski o novoi Rossii. Tri konsensusa. Gennady Burbulis vspominaet," *Vestnik Evropy* 46–7 (2016).

95. The full text of memorandum remains unpublished. The quotations from the documents are borrowed from an investigative journalist, Oleg Moroz, who apparently had access to the document in the papers of Yegor Gaidar (personal communications to Moroz, 28–30 September 2019); http://www.relga.ru/Environ/WebObjects/tgu-www.woa/wa/Main?textid=5130&level1=main&level2=articles.

96. "Perelomnyi moment istorii," interview with G. E. Burbulis at http://www.ru-90.ru/content/переломный-момент-истории-интервью-с-гэ-бурбулисом.

97. "Soveshchanie v Orekhovoi komnate po problemam Soiuznogo dogovora," 20 September 1991, MSG SS, vol. 28, pp. 375–6.

98. Quotations from Oleg Moroz, "Yeltsin vybiraet napravleniie dvizheniia," http://litresp.ru/chitat/ru/%D0%9C/moroz-oleg-pavlovich/eljcin-protiv-gorbacheva-gorbachev-protiv-eljcina/33.

99. Burbulis, in Aven and Kokh, *Revoliutsia Gaidara*, p. 54. On the cultural and political functions of the Russian banya see Ethan Pollock, *Without the Banya We Would Perish: The History of the Russian Bathhouse* (New York: Oxford University Press, 2019).

100. Burbulis in Aven and Kokh, *Revoliutsia Gaidara*, pp. 54, 55; "Zapiski o novoi Rossii. Tri konsensusa. Gennady Burbulis vspominaet," *Vestnik Evropy* 46–7 (2016).

101. Plokhy, *The Last Empire*, p. 279.

102. *Pravda Ukrainy*, 2, 3 and 4 October 1991.

103. The full text of Kravchuk's address in *Pravda Ukrainy*, 3 October 1991.

104. "Meeting with Leonid Kravchuk, Ukrainian Supreme Soviet Chairman," 25 September 1991, at http://bushlibrary.tamu.edu/research/pdfs/memcons_telcons/1991-09-25-Kravchuk.pdf. Scowcroft at http://oralhistory.org.ua/interview-ua/352.

105. Scowcroft to Bush, Memo on meeting with Leonid Kravchuk, 25 September 1991, pp. 1–2, 4–5, Scowcroft Collection, GBPL.

106. "Meeting with Leonid Kravchuk, Ukrainian Supreme Soviet Chairman," 25 September 1991, at <http://bushlibrary.tamu.edu/research/pdfs/memcons_telcons/1991-09-25-Kravchuk.pdf.

107. Bush and Scowcroft, *A World Transformed*, p. 543.

108. Ibid, p. 542; interview 2 with Brent Scowcroft, 10–11 August 2000, BOHP, p. 54.

109. Bush and Scowcroft, *A World Transformed*, p. 545.

110. Villiers Negroponte, *Master Negotiator*, p. 201; Bush's conversation with the Secretary-General of NATO Manfred Wörner, 27 September 1991, at https://bush41library.tamu.edu/files/memcons-telcons/1991-09-27-Woerner.pdf.

111. Bush and Scowcroft, *A World Transformed*, p. 545.

112. Chernyaev, *Sovmestnyi iskhod*, 27 September 1991, pp. 989–91.

113. MSG SS, vol. 28, pp. 420–32; Pankin, *Sto oborvannykh dnei*, p. 193.

114. Chernyaev, *Sovmestnyi iskhod*, 27 September 1991, pp. 989–91; "Julius Ceasar," the Big Soviet Encyclopedia, at http://bse.sci-lib.com/article120367.html.

115. "Harvard Discussion with Kravchuk on Nuclear Weapons," Philip Zelikow's memo to Graham Allison, Robert Blackwill, Al Carnesale, Ashton Carter, Bill Hogan, 27 September 1991. Courtesy of Svetlana Savranskaya, the National Security Archive.

116. Plokhy, *The Last Empire*, pp. 208–9.

117. See the estimate of Ukrainian nuclear capacities and problems by the Ukrainian experts on 2 February 1993, at https://nsarchive2.gwu.edu/Nuclear-Weapons-and-Ukraine/ Doc-32-Ukraine-Foreign-Ministry-report-nuclear-policy-alternatives-1993-02-02.pdf; also the Ukrainian experts' estimate on 21 February 1993, at https://nsarchive2.gwu.edu/ Nuclear-Weapons-and-Ukraine/Doc-36-Ukraine-Foreign-Ministry-consequences-not-joining-NPT-1993-04-21.pdf.

118. Press conference of Kravchuk on 4 October 1991, *Pravda Ukrainy*, 8 October 1991.

CHAPTER 14: INDEPENDENCE

1. Memcon, meeting with Alexander Yakovlev, 10 November 1991, Burns and Hewett files; USSR: Chronology Files, OA-ID CF01407-14-35, GBPL.

2. The date of the meeting is in *Soyuz mozhno bylo sokhranit*, p. 362.

3. Shakhnazarov, *Tsena svobody*, pp. 284–5.

4. Shakhnazarov at the extraordinary session of the Supreme Soviet of the RSFSR, GARF, f. 10026, op. 1, d. 569, l. 19; Shakhnazarov, *Tsena svobody*, p. 285.

5. Shakhnazarov, *Tsena svobody*, p. 285.

6. Boris Yeltsin, *Midnight Diaries* (New York: Public Affairs, 2000), pp. 253–4.

7. *Izvestia*, 2 October 1991, p. 1; *Rossiiskaia gazeta*, 2 October 1991; "Kto pravopreemnik byvshego SSSR?" *Izvestia*, 3 October 1991, p. 1; MSG SS, vol. 28, p. 589.

8. *Nezavisimaia gazeta*, 12 October 1991, p. 3.

9. A. Tsypko, "Drama rossiiskogo vybora," *Izvestia*, 1 October 1991, p. 5.

10. Vitaly Portnikov, "Nezavisimost RSFSR. Mirazh ili politicheskaia avantiura," *Nezavisimaia gazeta*, 15 October 1991, p. 4.

11. Adamishin's diary, 6 October 1991, Adamishin Papers, HIA; Vitaly Portnikov, "Leonid Kravchuk: Rossiia khochet stat Sovetskim Soiuzom," *Nezavisimaia gazeta*, 9 October 1991, p. 3.

12. Chernyaev, "Sovmestnyi iskhod," 7 October 1991, p. 996; Valery Soldatenko, *Rossiia—Krym—Ukraina. Opyt vzaimootnosheniy v gody revoliutsii i grazhdanskoi voiny* (Moscow: ROSSPEN, 2018), pp. 78–80.

13. Burbulis in interview in *Novoie Vremia* 45 (1991); also his "Minnoie pole vlasti."

14. *Nezavisimaia gazeta*, 1 October 1991, p. 1.

15. Adamishin on 30 September, 2 and 3 October 1991, Adamishin Papers, HIA. *Nezavisimaia gazeta*, 10 October 1991, pp. 1, 2.

16. Shakhnazarov, *Tsena svobody*, pp. 287–9; MSG SS, vol. 28, pp. 436–8.

17. Chernyaev, *Sovmestnyi iskhod*, 6 October 1991, p. 994; Braithwaite's diary, 7 October 1991.

18. Memcon, Bush-Gorbachev conversation, 6 October 1991, Burns and Hewett Files, CFO-1407-10-20, GBPL; Chernyaev, *Sovmestnyi iskhod*, 6 October 1991, pp. 995–6.

19. Gates, *From the Shadows*, p. 530.

20. Bush and Scowcroft, *A World Transformed*, p. 547; "Telecom with Boris Yeltsin, President of the Republic of Russia," 18 October 1991, at http://bushlibrary.tamu.edu/ research/pdfs/memcons_telcons/1991-10-08-Yeltsin.pdf.

21. "Telecom with Boris Yeltsin, President of the Republic of Russia," 8 October 1991, at http://bushlibrary.tamu.edu/research/pdfs/memcons_telcons/1991-10-08-Yeltsin.pdf.

22. Yeltsin's notes on 8 October 1991, AY, f. 6, op. 1, d. 163, l. 46, at https://yeltsin.ru/archive/ paperwork/18099, accessed 5 July 2020.

23. Grachev, *Dalshe bez menia*, pp. 48–9. The transcript of the State Council, 11 October 1991, RGANI, f. 121, d. 103, ll. 2–11; *Nezavisimaia gazeta*, 9 October 1991, p. 3.

24. RGANI, f. 121, d. 103, ll. 12–20, 21–8.

25. Ibid, ll. 44, 47–8.

26. Ibid.

27. Ibid, ll. 48–9, 95–6.

28. AY, f. 6, op. 1, d. 91, ll. 43–7, at https://yeltsin.ru/archive/paperwork/10434.

29. Chernyaev, *Sovmestnyi iskhod*, 12 October 1991, pp. 997–9.

30. Adamishin's diary, 19 October 1991, Adamishin Papers, HIA.

31. AY, f. 6, op. 1, d. 91, ll. 39–42; 104, ll. 1–4, at https://yeltsin.ru/archive/paperwork/10434/; *Nezavisimaia gazeta*, 15 October 1991, p. 1; Braithwaite's diary, 16 October 1991.

32. Burbulis and Vladimir Lopukhin in Aven and Kokh, *Revoliutsia Gaidara*, pp. 56, 183; Yeltsina, *Lichnaia zhizn*, p. 215.

33. Burbulis in Aven and Kokh, *Revoliutsia Gaidara*, p. 56; On the Gaidar family roots see an interview with Ariadna Bazhov-Gaidar, his mother, https://www.womanhit.ru/psychology/family/655439-ariadna-bazhovagaydar-tri-izvestnyih-familii-soshlis-vodnom-klubke.html.

34. On the honor, Bernstam's recollections about Gaidar, 12 March 2013, Stanford, CA; Gaidar, *V dni porazhenii*, p. 277.

35. Burbulis in Aven and Kokh, *Revoliutsia Gaidara*, p. 57.

36. Mikhail Bernstam, "Prolegomenon, part 4," the comments on his personal documents. Courtesy of Mikhail Bernstam.

37. Braithwaite's diary, 16 October 1991.

38. Telephone conversation with Boris Yeltsin, President of the Republic of Russia, 25 August 1991, GBPL, at https://bush41library.tamu.edu/files/memcons-telcons/1991-10-25-Yeltsin.pdf.

39. Stenographic report of Yeltsin's speech with his handwritten remarks, 28 October 1991, AY, f. 6, op. 1, d. 84, ll. 41–133; 134–5.

40. *Piatyi (vneocherednoi) S'ezd narodnykh deputatov RSFSR, October 1991. Bulletin* no. 13, p. 24; *Bulletin* no. 14, pp. 8, 14–15 (Moscow, 1991); http://pravo.gov.ru/proxy/ips/?docbody=&prevDoc=102016271&backlink=1&&nd=102012920; and http://pravo.gov.ru/proxy/ips/?docbody=&prevDoc=102017933&backlink=1&&nd=102012915.

41. Braithwaite's diary, 19 November 1991.

42. The author's interview with Mikhail Bernstam, 6 February 2013, Stanford University; *The Financial Times*, 21 October 1991, p. 7.

43. The author's interview with Mikhail Bernstam, 6 February 2013.

44. A copy of the document is in the personal collection of Mikhail Bernstam. Courtesy of Bernstam. The author's interview with Mikhail Bernstam, 6 February 2013, Stanford University.

45. This scenario draws on the comments of Mikhail Bernstam in his personal collection of documents. Courtesy of Bernstam; the author's interview with Mikhail Bernstam, 6 February 2013, Stanford University.

46. V. Portnikov, "Yeltsin obsuzhdal s voiennymi vozmozhnost iadernogo udara po Ukraine," *Nezavisimaia gazeta*, 24 October 1991; Andrei Kozyrev, *Firebird: The Elusive Fate of Russian Democracy* (Pittsburgh, PA: University of Pittsburgh Press, 2019), p. 77; Yegor Gaidar, *Anatomiia putcha*, at http://ru-90.ru/content/гайдар-ет-крах#_ftn74.

47. The author's interview with Mikhail Bernstam on 6 February 2013.

48. Alexander, Shokhin in Aven and Kokh, *Revoliutsia Gaidara*, p. 121.

49. Ukaz Prezidenta RSFSR o liberalizatsii vneshneekonomicheskoi deiatelnosti na territorii RSFSR, 15 November 1991, no. 213, at http://www.consultant.ru/document/cons_doc_LAW_143; Stenograma zasedaniia pravitelstva RSFSR, 28 November 1991, at http://ru-90.ru/content/стенограмма-заседания-правительства-рсфср-28-ноября-1991-года.

50. Stenographic record of the meeting of the Russian government, 15 November 1991, at http://ru-90.ru/content/заседания-правительства-рсфср-15-ноября-1991-года-0.

51. The author's interview with Mikhail Bernstam, 6 February 2013.

52. "Ekonomicheskaia situatsiia v Rossii—1991 god." Materialy k prezidentskomu konsultativnomy sovetu Yeltsina, 22 October 1991, at https://yeltsin.ru/archive/paperwork/10590; http://ru-90.ru/content/заседания-правительства-рсфср-15-ноября-1991-года-0.

53. Shokhin in Aven and Kokh, *Revoliutsia Gaidara*, p. 121; the author's interview with Alexander Drozdov, 24 April 2020.

54. "Gathering Storm," NSC Files, Burns Files: the USSR Chron Files, OA-ID CF01498-008, GBPL.

55. Ibid; also US Embassy cable 221538Z, NSC Files, Burns Files: the USSR Chron Files, OA-ID CF01498-008, GBPL.

56. Interview with Brent Scowcroft, 10–11 August 2000, BOHP, pp. 50, 53.

57. The US Embassy cable 221538Z, NSC Files, Burns Files: the USSR Chron Files, OA-ID CF01498-008, GBPL. On the "betrayal" by the intelligentsia see Vladislav Zubok, *Dmitrii Likhachev. Zhizn i vek* (St Petersburg: Vita Nova, 2016), pp. 457–8.
58. "Mikhail Gorbachev: nuzhna revoliutsiia umov," interview with Gorbachev by Len Karpinsky, *Moskovskiie Novosti*, 3 November 1991, p. 4. Shakhnazarov's memo to Gorbachev on 29 October 1991, *Tsena svobody*, pp. 296, 565–6.
59. From the diary of V. A. Medvedev, 21 October 1991, in *Soiuz mozhno bylo sokhranit*, pp. 383–4.
60. *Izvestia*, 21 October 1991, p. 1.
61. Pankin, *Sto oborvannykh dnei*, pp. 200–2, 211–13. "Points for Pankin: Middle East," 22 October 1991, James A. Baker III Papers, Box 176, Folder 27, Seeley Mudd Library, Princeton University.
62. Bush and Scowcroft, *A World Transformed*, pp. 410, 548.
63. Mary Dejevsky, "Yeltsin Moves to Wrest Power from Gorbachev," *The London Times*, 29 October 1991; Stanislav Kondrashov, "Zemletriasenie na Smolenskoi ploshchadi," *Izvestia*, 2 November 1991, pp. 1, 12; "Sud'ba sotrudnikov MIDa reshaetsia v eti dni," *Izvestia*, 3 November 1991, p. 1; Adamishin's diary, 14 November 1991, Adamishin Papers HIA; Andrei Kozyrev to Yeltsin and Burbulis, "Ob imushchestve MID SSSR," 13 November 1991, GARF, f. 10026, op. 4, d. 1277, ll. 175–6.
64. Pankin, *Sto oborvannykh dnei*, p. 233. Luncheon meeting with President Gorbachev, 29 October 1991, 12:30–1:15 p.m., GBPL, at https://bush41library.tamu.edu/files/memcons-telcons/1991-10-2-Gorbachev%20[1].pdf.
65. Plokhy, *The Last Empire*, p. 237; meeting on Soviet debt, 5 November 1991, WHORM, CO165, 306788 Russia, GBPL.
66. Pankin, *Sto oborvannykh dnei*, pp. 234–6.
67. Shakhnazarov's record of the Gorbachev-Yeltsin talk, 2 November 1991, *V Politburo TsK KPSS*, pp. 713–14.
68. The stenographic record of the State Council, 4 November 1991, GARF, f. 121, op. 3, d. 107, ll. 254–88; the memcon of Gorbachev with Deputy Secretary of Defense Donald Atwood, 5 November 1991, CF01407–012, GBPL.
69. Pankin, *Sto oborvannykh dnei*, pp. 240, 245; GARF, f. 121, op. 3, d. 107, l. 282.
70. Stepanov's notes, 5 November 1991, Stepanov-Mamaladze Papers, Box 3, Folder 30, HIA.
71. The stenographic record of the State Council, 4 November 1991, GARF, f. 121, op. 3, d. 107, ll. 121–31.
72. GARF, f. 121, op. 3, d. 107, ll. 141–206; the stenographic record of the State Council, 14 November 1991, GARF, f. 121, op. 3, d. 114, ll. 184–99.
73. Yeltsin disclosed this fact on 11 December 1991 in his confidential briefing with Russian parliamentarians. AY, f. 6, op. 1, d. 104, l. 97, at https://yeltsin.ru/archive/paperwork/10637.
74. Bakatin, *Izbavleniie ot KGB*, pp. 62–3; interview with Viktor Ivanenko at: http://ru-90.ru/content/кгб-и-радикальные-перемены-интервью-с-вв-иваненко.
75. Interview with Ivanenko at http://ru-90.ru/content/кгб-и-радикальные-перемены-интервью-с-вв-иваненко.
76. *V Politburo TsK KPSS*, p. 722; Grachev, *Dalshe bez menia*, pp. 144–6.
77. Chernyaev, *Sovmestnyi iskhod*, 17 November 1991, pp. 1,021–3; Shakhnazarov, *Tsena svobody*, pp. 169, 176; Pankin, *Sto oborvannykh dnei*, p. 251; Grachev, *Dalshe bez menia*, pp. 149–51.
78. *V Politburo TsK KPSS*, p. 723; the stenographic report of the State Council, 14 November 1991, GARF, f. 121, op. 3, d. 114, ll. 132–5.
79. *Raspad SSSR*, vol. 1, pp. 965–6.
80. "O formirovanii sistemy gosrezervov RSFSR," 25 November 1991, at https://yeltsin.ru/archive/act/33772; *V Politburo TsK KPSS*, p. 717; the decree of the State Council, 14 November 1991, *Raspad SSSR*, vol. 1, pp. 966–70.
81. http://ru-90.ru/content/заседания-правительства-рсфср-15-ноября-1991-года-0; Gaidar, *V dni porazhenii*, p. 314.

82. Plokhy, *The Last Empire*, p. 230; the author's interview with Gennady Burbulis, 24 May 2020, by phone. For the background see Roman Solchanyk, *Ukraine and Russia: The Post-Soviet Transition* (New York: Roman and Littlefield, 2001); Serhii Plokhy, *The Lost Kingdom: The Quest for Empire and the Making of the Russian Nation* (New York: Basic Books, 2017).
83. On the Ukrainian regionalism see Nataliya Kibita, *Soviet Economic Management under Khrushchev. The Sovnarkhoz Reform* (London: Routledge, 2015); "Why Isn't Ukraine Authoritarian?" 11 July 2019, at https://huri.harvard.edu/news/why-isnt-ukraine-authoritarian-asks-nataliya-kibita.
84. Shakhnazarov to Gorbachev on 8 October 1991, in *Tsena svobody*, pp. 560–1; Yegor Gaidar, *Krakh*, at http://ru-90.ru/content/гайдар-ет-крах.
85. N. Mikhalchenko and V. Andrushchenko, *Belovezhie. L. Kravchuk. Ukraina* (Kiev: Ukrainskii tsentr dukhovnoi kultury, 1996), pp. 73–5.
86. Philip Zelikow's memo, 5 November 1991, OA-ID CF1407-013, GBPL.
87. Andrew Wilson, *Ukrainian Nationalism in the 1990s: A Minority Faith* (Cambridge: Cambridge University Press, 1997); Paul Stepan Pirie, *History, Politics, and National Identity in Southern and Eastern Ukraine*, PhD thesis, School of Slavonic and East European Studies, University of London, 1998.
88. Shakhnazarov, *Tsena svobody*, p. 561.
89. For the background see Gwendolyn Sasse, *The Crimea Question: Identity, Transition, and Conflict* (Cambridge, MA: Harvard University Press, 1998), pp. 159–64.
90. *Pravda Ukrainy*, 12 October 1991; on Kravchuk's address see *Krymskaia Pravda*, 26 October 1991.
91. The interview with Nikolai Bagrov, *Krymskaia Pravda*, 30 October 1991. On Bagrov's interest in backing Kravchuk see Galina Starovoitova, at http://oralhistory.org.ua/interview-ua/566; also the interview with Nikolai Bagrov at http://oralhistory.org.ua/interview-ua/372.
92. *Krymskaia Pravda*, 13 and 16 November 1991.
93. Interview with Galina Starovoitova for the project *Rozpad Radians'koho Soiuzu*, at http://oralhistory.org.ua/interview-ua/566.
94. Braithwaite's diary, 17 November 1991; Adamishin's diary, 3 December 1991, Adamishin Papers, HIA.
95. Braithwaite's diary, 6 November 1991.
96. The stenographic report of the State Council, 25 November 1991, RGANI, f. 121, op. 3, d. 122, ll. 6–7, 16, 21–34; Chernyaev, *Sovmestnyi iskhod*, 26 November 1991, p. 1,027; Grachev, *Dalshe bez menia*, p. 165.
97. The stenographic report of the State Council, 25 November 1991, GARF, f. 121, op. 3, d. 114, ll. 105–8; the decree of the State Council on 27 November 1991, in *Raspad SSSR*, vol. 1, p. 986.
98. The stenographic report of the State Council, 25 November 1991, GARF, f. 121, op. 3, d. 114, l. 50–59.
99. Ibid, ll. 48–51.
100. The decision of the Council of Republics of the Supreme Soviet of the USSR, 28 November 1991, *Raspad SSSR*, vol. 1, pp. 997–8; the stenographic record of the meeting of the Russian government on 28 November 1991, GARF, f. A-259, op. 1, d. 5284, l. 63, at http://ru-90.ru/content/стенограмма-заседания-правительства-рсфср-28-ноября-1991-года.
101. https://bush41library.tamu.edu/files/memcons-telcons/1991-11-30-Yeltsin.pdf.
102. The stenographic record of the meeting of the Russian government, 28 November 1991, at http://ru-90.ru/content/стенограмма-заседания-правительства-рсфср-28-ноября-1991-года.
103. Ibid.
104. http://ru-90.ru/content/заседания-правительства-рсфср-15-ноября-1991-года-0; http://ru-90.ru/content/стенограмма-заседания-правительства-рсфср-28-ноября-1991-года.
105. http://ru-90.ru/content/стенограмма-заседания-правительства-рсфср-28-ноября-1991-года.

106. The background of the Chechen-Russian conflict is in John B. Dunlop, *Russia Confronts Chechnya: Roots of a Separatist Conflict* (Cambridge, 1998); Carlotta Gall & Thomas de Waal, *Chechnya: Calamity in the Caucasus* (New York: New York University Press, 1998); Gail Lapidus, 'Contested Sovereignty: The Tragedy of Chechnya', *International Security* 23:3 (Summer 1998), pp. 5–49.

107. For more details see Plokhy, *The Last Empire*, pp. 246–8; Adamishin's diary, 22 November 1991, Adamishin Papers, HIA.

108. http://ru-90.ru/content/стенограмма-заседания-правительства-рсфср-28-ноября-1991-года.

109. Meeting on Soviet Debt, 5 November 1991, WHORM, CO165, 306788 Russia, GBPL; Goldgeier and McFaul, *Power and Purpose*, pp. 68–9; the author's interview with Grigory Yavlinsky, 25 December 2016, Moscow.

110. Gaidar, *V dni porazhenii*, p. 318.

111. Goldgeier and McFaul, *Power and Purpose*, p. 71; Braithwaite's diary, 16 November 1991; Mulford in Goldgeier and McFaul, *Power and Purpose*, p. 70; http://ru-90.ru/content/стенограмма-заседания-правительства-рсфср-28-ноября-1991-года.

112. http://ru-90.ru/content/стенограмма-заседания-правительства-рсфср-28-ноября-1991-года. See similar advice from Georgy Arbatov to Yeltsin, AY, f. 6, op. 1, d. 160, l. 98.

113. Chernyaev, *Sovmestnyi iskhod*, 3 December 1991, pp. 1030–1.

114. Philip Zelikow's memo, 4 November 1991, Burns and Hewett Files; Ed Hewett to Brent Scowcroft, 8 November 1991, Chron USSR files, OA-ID CF1407-013 and CF1407-012, GBPL

115. Goldgeier and McFaul, *Power and Purpose*, p. 47; Nicholas Burns to Ed Hewett and David Gompert, 22 November 1991, Burns and Hewett Files. Chron USSR files. OA-ID CF 01407-012-37, GBPL.

116. Interview with Brent Scowcroft, 10–11 August 2000, Washington DC, BOHP, p. 52. The summary from a memo of Nicholas Burns to Ed Hewett and David Gompert, 22 November 1991, Burns and Hewett Files. Chron USSR files. OA-ID CF 01407-012-37, GBPL; Baker, *The Politics of Diplomacy*, pp. 560–1.

117. Goldgeier and McFaul, *Power and Purpose*, p. 35.

118. Plokhy, *The Last Empire*, p. 284; Kasianov, *Ukraina 1991–2007*, p. 37; *Pravda Ukrainy*, 30 November 1991.

119. Meeting with Alexander Yakovlev, 19 November 1991, Burns and Hewett Files; USSR: Chronology Files, OA-ID CF01407-14-35, 36, GBPL.

120. *Pravda Ukrainy*, 30 October 1991; Mikhalchenko and Andrushchenko, *Belovezhie*, p. 89; *Nezavisimaia gazeta*, 28 November 1991, p. 4; Aleksei Plotitsyn, "Posmotrim pravde v glaza," ibid, p. 5; Vitaly Portnikov, "Konets imperii," 30 November 1991, p. 1.

121. Mikhail Gorbachev, *Dekabr-91: Moia pozitsiia* (Moscow: Novosti, 1992), p. 57.

122. Conversation with President Mikhail Gorbachev of the USSR, 30 November 1991, GBPL, at http://bushlibrary.tamu.edu/research/pdfs/memcons_telcons/1991-11-30-Gorbachev.pdf.

123. Telegram from Strauss to Bush, 20 October 1991, on file at the National Security Archive, courtesy of Svetlana Savranskaya; Bush's conversation with Mulroney, 30 November 1991, GBPL, at https://bush41library.tamu.edu/files/memcons-telcons/1991-11-30-Mulroney.pdf.

124. Telephone conversation with Boris Yeltsin, President of the Republic of Russia, 30 November 1991, GBPL, at https://bush41library.tamu.edu/files/memcons-telcons/1991-11-30-Yeltsin.pdf.

125. Mikhalchenko and Andrushchenko, *Belovezhie*, pp. 89–90; Leonid Kravchuk in *Rozpad Radians'koho Soiuzu* at http://oralhistory.org.ua/interview-ua/510.

126. Chernyaev, *Sovmestnyi iskhod*, pp. 1,030–1; telephone conversation with President Leonid Kravchuk of Ukraine on 3 December 1991, GBPL, at https://bush41library.tamu.edu/files/memcons-telcons/1991-12-03-Kravchuk.pdf.

127. Starovoitova in her interview to *Rozpad Radians'koho Soiuzu*, at http://oralhistory.org.ua/category/interview-ua/page/3.

CHAPTER 15: LIQUIDATION

1. Kravchuk cited in Mikhalchenko and Andrushchenko, *Belovezhie*, p. 91; also Plokhy, *The Last Empire*, pp. 401–2.

2. V. A. Rayevsky to the State Council, 18 November 1991, the Archive of the Central Bank, at http://gaidar-arc.ru/file/bulletin-1/DEFAULT/org.stretto.plugins.bulletin.core. Article/file/757.

3. Interview with Galina Starovoitova for the Ukrainian project *Rozpad Radians'koho Soiuzu*, at http://oralhistory.org.ua/category/interview-ua/page/3.

4. The author's interview with Lukin, 30 June 2017; interview with Starovoitova for the Ukrainian project *Rozpad Radians'koho Soiuzu*; Gaidar, "Za riumkoi takie voprosy ne reshalis," at, https://www.svoboda.org/a/3547434.html.

5. The author's interview with Gennady Burbulis, 6 May 2020, by phone.

6. Gaidar, "Za riumkoi takie voprosy ne reshalis."

7. https://yeltsin.ru/archive/act/33830.

8. Stanislav Shushkevich, *Moia zhizn, krusheniie i voskreshenie SSSR* (Moscow: ROSSPEN, 2012), pp. 192–3; Vyacheslav Kebich, *Iskushenie vlast'iu. Iz zhisni premier-ministra* (Minsk: Paradoks, 2008), pp. 187–8.

9. Shushkevich, *Moia zhizn*, pp. 12–13, 70–1.

10. Ibid, pp. 199–200.

11. Ibid, p. 200; Leonid Kravchuk, *Maemo te, shcho maemo: Spohady i rozdumy*, (Kyiv: Stolittia, 2002) pp. 129–30; Plokhy, *The Last Empire*, pp. 303–5;

12. Shushkevich, *Moia zhizn*, pp. 199–200; the author's interview with Gennady Burbulis, 6 May 2020, by phone.

13. Kebich, *Iskushenie vlast'iu*, pp. 199–200; Gaidar, *V dni porazhenii*, pp. 324–5; Gaidar, "Za riumkoi takie voprosy ne reshalis," https://www.svoboda.org/a/3547434.html. Kozyrev omitted the episode from his memoirs, *Firebird*, pp. 47–8.

14. Shushkevich, *Moia zhizn*, p. 200; Kebich, *Iskushenie vlast'iu*, p. 200.

15. Kravchuk, "Da Ukrainu prosto prinudili vziat Krym," 9 September 2016, at https://republic.ru/posts/73137.

16. Interview with Galina Starovoitova for the Ukrainian project *Rozpad Radians'koho Soiuzu*, at http://oralhistory.org.ua/category/interview-ua/page/3; Kravchuk, "Da Ukrainu prosto prinudili vzyat Krym."

17. The recollection of journalists cited in *Soyuz mozhno bylo sokhranit*, pp. 503–4.

18. Yeltsin, *Zapiski prezidenta*, pp. 143–4, 146, 147.

19. Kozyrev, *Firebird*, pp. 128–9.

20. Leonid Kravchuk, *Ostanni dni imperii* (Kiev: Dovira, 1994), pp. 17, 20; Kebich, *Iskushenie vlast'iu*, pp. 202–3; Plokhy, *The Last Empire*, pp. 310–12, 315.

21. Korzhakov, *Boris Yeltsin—ot rassveta do zakata*, p. 128; Yegor Gaidar, *Vlast i sobstvennost. Smuty i instituty. Gosudarstvo i evoliutsiia* (St Petersburg: Norma, 2009), pp. 123–4.

22. Kebich, *Iskushenie vlast'iu*, p. 206.

23. Kozyrev, *Firebird*, pp. 49–50.

24. Telephone conversation with President Yeltsin of the Republic of Russia, 8 December 1991, GBPL, http://bushlibrary.tamu.edu/research/pdfs/memcons_telcons/1991-12-08-Yeltsin.pdf.

25. Ibid; Shaposhnikov, *Vybor*, pp. 125–7.

26. Allen Weinstein to Paul Nathanson, 9 December 1991, The Center for Democracy Papers, Box 18, HIA.

27. The copy of the full text of the economic coordination memorandum with signatures is in The Center for Democracy Papers, Box 18, HIA. The abridged version of the document was published in *Rossiiskaia gazeta*, 10 December 1991, at https://yeltsin.ru/day-by-day/1991/12/10/8722; Kravchuk, *Ostanni dni imperii*, p. 33; Gaidar, *V dni porazhenii*, pp. 321, 327.

28. Gaidar, "Za riumkoi takie voprosy ne reshalis." Shakhrai and Burbulis shared this view. Burbulis to the author, 28 April 2020, by phone; Kravchuk, "Da Ukrainu prosto prinudili vziat Krym."

29. The declaration of the Committee of the Constitutional Supervision of the USSR, 11 December 1991, in *Raspad SSSR*, vol. 1, pp. 1,033–4; Stepanov's notes, 8, 9, 10 December 1991, Stepanov-Mamaladze Papers, Box 3, Folder 31. HIA.

30. Gaidar, "Za riumkoi takie voprosy ne reshalis"; Taubman, *Gorbachev*, p. 635.

31. Taubman, *Gorbachev*, p. 634; Nazarbayev's recollections in *Soyuz mozhno bylo sokhranit*, pp. 507–8; Shakhnazarov *V Politburo TsK KPSS*, p. 732; Kravchuk, *Ostanni dni imperii*, p. 29.

32. Chernyaev, *Sovmestnyi iskhod*, 10 and 11 December 1991, pp. 1034–6; Stepanov's notes, 4 December 1991, Stepanov-Mamaladze Papers, Box 3, Folder 31. HIA.

33. Bakatin, *Izbavleniie ot KGB*, p. 133.

34. Kozyrev, *Firebird*, p. 51; Shaposhnikov, *Vybor*, pp. 128, 137; Volkogonov's memo to Yeltsin, 10 December 1991, at https://yeltsin.ru/archive/paperwork/10464; Yeltsin's theses for the military conference, 11 December 1991, at https://yeltsin.ru/archive/paperwork/10462.

35. Shaposhnikov, *Vybor*, p. 137; Chernyaev, *Sovmestnyi iskhod*, 11 December 1991, pp. 1,035–6.

36. Nazarbayev's recollections, *Soyuz mozhno bylo sokhranit*, p. 507.

37. Stepanov's notes, 4 December 1991, Stepanov-Mamaladze Papers, Box 3, Folder 31. HIA.

38. Kozyrev, *Firebird*, p. 56; Starovoitova at http://oralhistory.org.ua/category/interview-ua/page/3.

39. Stenographic report on Yeltsin's meeting with parliamentary factions, 11 December 1991, at Yeltsin's speech at the RSFSR Supreme Soviet on 12 December 1991, at https://yeltsin.ru/archive/paperwork/10637/https://yeltsin.ru/archive/paperwork/10401.

40. Yeltsin's decree to appoint Shakhrai, 12 December 1991, at https://yeltsin.ru/archive/act/33804; Shakhnazarov, *Tsena svobody*, p. 283.

41. The author's interview with Gennady Burbulis, 6 May 2020, by phone.

42. *Izvestia*, 12 December 1991, p. 2.

43. Chernayev, *Sovmestnyi iskhod*, 12 December 1991, p. 1,036; Vitaly Tretiakov's interview with Mikhail Gorbachev, *Nezavisimaia gazeta*, 12 December 1991, p. 5.

44. The author's interview with Gennady Burbulis, 21 April 2020, by phone.

45. Ibid.

46. The author's interview with Francis Fukuyama, 19 February 2013, Stanford, CA; Burns quoted in Plokhy, *The Last Empire*, p. 323.

47. Bush and Scowcroft, *A World Transformed*, pp. 556–7.

48. Proposed Agenda for meeting with the President, 4 and 10 December 1991, James A. Baker III Papers, Box 115, Folder 8, Seeley Mudd Library, Princeton, NJ.

49. Baker, *The Politics of Diplomacy*, pp. 562–3; Villiers Negroponte, *Master Negotiator*, pp. 206–7.

50. "America and the Post-Coup Soviet Union," at https://www.c-span.org/video/?23366-1/post-coup-soviet-union.

51. "Telephone conversation with President Boris Yeltsin of Russia," 13 December 1991, GBPL, at http://bushlibrary.tamu.edu/research/pdfs/memcons_telcons/1991-12-13-Yeltsin.pdf.

52. Baker, *The Politics of Diplomacy*, pp. 564–5.

53. Summary of Baker-Kozyrev talk; handwritten notes taken at 16 December 1991 meeting with Foreign Minister Kozyrev, Moscow. NSC Files, Burns and Hewett Files, USSR Chronological File, 16 December 1991, OA/ID CFO 1407-016. GBPL; Baker, *The Politics of Diplomacy*, pp. 565–7.

54. Summary of Baker-Yeltsin talks. NSC Files, Burns-Hewett Files, USSR Chronological File, 16 December 1991, OA/ID CFO 1407-016, GBPL; Baker, *The Politics of Diplomacy*, pp. 569–71.

55. Baker's handwritten notes of 16 December 1991, Meeting with Yeltsin. James A. Baker III Papers, Box 176, Folder 28, Seeley Mudd Library, Princeton, NJ. Baker gave a slight spin to his notes in his memoirs and eluded the fact that Gorbachev was no longer in nuclear command. Baker, *The Politics of Diplomacy*, p. 572.

56. Kozyrev in Aven and Kokh, *Revoliutsia Gaidara*, p. 273.

57. Jim Collins from the US Embassy in Moscow to the NSC, 6 December 1991, NSC Files, Burns and Hewett Files; USSR: Chronological Files, OA-ID CF01407-16, pp. 11–17, GBPL.

58. Memorandum of David Mulford to Michael Boskin, Robert Zoellick, Ed Hewett et al., 10 December 1991, NSC Files, Burns and Hewett Files; USSR: Chronological Files, OA-ID CF01407-16, pp. 2–5, GBPL.

59. The Russian records on the meeting with economists on 12–13 December 1991 is at https://yeltsin.ru/archive/paperwork/13145; economic checklist for Yeltsin, 15 December 1991, James A. Baker III Papers, Box 176, Folder 28, Seeley Mudd Library, Princeton University; Mikhail Bernstam, e-mail to the author, 9 August 2020.

60. Interview with Andrei Kozyrev in Aven and Kokh, *Revoliutsia Gaidara*, p. 274; Burbulis to the author, 24 May 2021, by phone.

61. More on this program in Spohr, *Post Wall, Post Square*, pp. 471–7.

62. Baker, *The Politics of Diplomacy*, pp. 567, 577; Stepanov-Mamaladze notes, 17 December 1991, Stepanov-Mamaladze Papers, Box 3, Folder 31, HIA.

63. "Telephone conversation with President Boris Yeltsin of Russia," 13 December 1991, GBPL, at http://bushlibrary.tamu.edu/research/pdfs/memcons_telcons/1991-12-13-Yeltsin.pdf; Bush and Scowcroft, *A World Transformed*, p. 557.

64. Baker, *The Politics of Diplomacy*, p. 565; Palazhchenko, *Professia i vremia*, p. 359; the author's communication with Pavel Palazhchenko, 21 March 2021.

65. Baker, *The Politics of Diplomacy*, pp. 573–4.

66. Interview with Galina Starovoitova in the Ukrainian project "*Rozpad Radyan'skoho Soyuzu*," at http://oralhistory.org.ua/category/interview-ua/page/3. The date of the conversation is disputed. Starovoitova indicated it was 19 December 1991. Chernyaev dated the meeting as 15 December 1991, *Sovmestnyi iskhod*, p. 1,037; on Galina Starovoitova's vote see the author's correspondence with her son Platon and her sister Olga, 19 May 2021, by phone.

67. Gorbachev on Starovoitova at http://starovoitova.ru/?p=62.

68. http://ru-90.ru/content/стенограмма-заседания-правительства-рсфср-28-ноября-1991-года.

69. Adamishin's diary, 10, 12, 13, 19, 20, 22 December 1991, Adamishin Papers, HIA.

70. Ibid, 22 December 1991; Kozyrev, *Firebird*, pp. 61–2; Stepanov's notes, 18 December 1991, Stepanov-Mamaladze Papers, Box 3, Folder 31, HIA; Yeltsin's decree on the MID, 18 December 1991, at https://yeltsin.ru/archive/act/33824.

71. Interview with Georgy Kunadze, 2 December 2017, at https://www.svoboda.org/a/28886758.html; Stepanov's notes, 19 December 1991, Stepanov-Mamaladze Papers, Box 3, Folder 31, HIA.

72. The decrees are available at https://yeltsin.ru/archive/act/33826/; https://yeltsin.ru/archive/act/33832; https://yeltsin.ru/archive/act/33823/; https://yeltsin.ru/archive/act/33822; https://yeltsin.ru/archive/act/33825; *Raspad SSSR*, vol. 1, pp. 1,064–7; Kozyrev, *Firebird*, p. 56; Yakovlev, *Sumerki*, p. 507.

73. Braithwaite's diary, 19 December 1991; Kozyrev, *Firebird*, p. 57.

74. Braithwaite's diary, 20 December 1991; Kozyrev, *Firebird*, pp. 57–8; Yeltsin's letter on the UN to the US government, 20 December 1991, WHORM, CO 165, 320925, GBPL; *Nezavisimaia gazeta*, 19 December 1991, p. 3.

75. Baker, *The Politics of Diplomacy*, p. 583.

76. Kozyrev, *Firebird*, pp. 59–61; *Raspad SSSR*, vol. 1, p. 1,049.

77. Kozyrev, *Firebird*, pp. 60–1.

78. For a very detailed description of Gorbachev's last days in power see Conor O'Clery, *Moscow, December 25, 1991: The Last Day of the Soviet Union* (Dublin: Transworld, 2011).

79. Yakovlev, *Sumerki*, p. 506.

80. Yeltsin, *Zapiski prezidenta*, p. 151; Yakovlev, *Sumerki*, p. 507.

81. Yakovlev, *Sumerki*, pp. 507–9.

82. Ibid, p. 509.

83. The text of the speech is in Gorbachev, *Zhizn i reformy*, vol. 1, pp. 6–7.

84. O'Clery, *Moscow, December 25, 1991*, pp. 76–7, 133–5, 201–2.

85. Ibid, pp. 26–7.

86. Ibid, pp. 203–4; for the text of Gorbachev's farewell address, see http://www.nytimes.com/1991/12/26/world/end-of-the-soviet-union-text-of-gorbachev-s-farewell-address.html?pagewanted=all; interview with Igor Malashenko, 28 February 2018, at https://thebell.io/mozhno-lyubit-mozhno-nenavidet-no-smeyatsya-nad-tsarem-neslyhanno-the-bell-publikuet-ne-vyhodivshee-ranshe-intervyu-igorya-malashenko.

87. Chernyaev, *Sovmestnyi iskhod*, p. 1,045.

88. Shakhnazarov, *Tsena svobody*, p. 350; Stepanov's notes, 25 December 1991, Stepanov-Mamaladze Papers, Box 3, Folder 31, HIA.

89. O'Clery, *Moscow, December 25, 1991*, pp. 231–4; Shaposhnikov, *Vybor*, diary entry of 25 December 1991.

90. Bush, *All the Best*, p. 543; Bush and Scowcroft, *A World Transformed*, pp. 559–62, 564; Palazhchenko, *My Years with Gorbachev and Shevardnadze*, pp. 364–6; "Telcon with Mikhail Gorbachev, President of the Soviet Union," 25 December 1991, GBPL, at http://bushlibrary.tamu.edu/research/pdfs/memcons_telcons/1991-12-25-Gorbachev.pdf. On 'the stroke of a pen' see Colin L. Powell, *My American Journey* (New York: Ballantine Books, 2003), p. 546.

91. Plokhy, *The Last Empire*, pp. 381–2.

92. Bush and Scowcroft, *A World Transformed*, p. 563.

93. "Address to the Nation on the Commonwealth of Independent States," 25 December 1991, https://bush41library.tamu.edu/archives/public-papers/3791.

94. Kozyrev, *Firebird*, p. 58.

CONCLUSION

1. Shakhnazarov, *Tsena svobody*, p. 212.

2. Steven Solnick, *Stealing the State* (Cambridge, MA: Harvard University Press, 1998), p. 4.

3. The Russian and Eastern European elites are contrasted in Krastev and Holmes, *The Light That Failed*.

4. Braithwaite's diary, 1 January 1992.

5. Westad, *The Cold War: A Global History* (London: Allen Lane, 2017), p. 616.

6. Strobe Talbott, *The Great Experiment: The Story of Ancient Empires, Modern States, and the Quest for a Global Nation* (New York: Simon & Schuster, 2008), p. 275. Talbott's comments at the conference "U.S. Presidents Confront Russia: A Century of Challenge, 1917–2017," Miller Center for Public Affairs, University of Virginia, 10 December 2017 (the author's notes).

7. Spohr, *Post Wall, Post Square*, pp. 467–70.

8. Adam Tooze, *Crashed: How a Decade of Financial Crises Changed the World* (London: Viking, 2018).

9. The quote comes from the memoirs of Massimo d'Azeglio, *I miei ricordi* (Florence: Barbera, 1898), p. 5.

10. https://data.worldbank.org/indicator/SP.DYN.LE00.IN?locations=RU; Nataliya Romashevskaya, "Poverty Trends in Russia: A Russian Perspective," in Jeni Klugman, ed., *Poverty in Russia: Public Policy and Private Responses* (Washington, DC: The World Bank, 1997), pp. 119–21.

11. Spohr, *Post Wall, Post Square*, p. 481.

12. The first snapshot of this rethinking is in Eric Shiraev and Vladislav Zubok, *Anti-Americanism in Russia: From Stalin to Putin* (New York: Palgrave Press, 2000); also Vladislav Zubok, "Russia and the West: Twenty Difficult Years," in Geir Lundestad (ed.), *International Relations Since the End of the Cold War: New and Old Dimensions* (London: Oxford University Press, 2013), pp. 209–28. See also the declassified conversations between Yeltsin and President Clinton at https://clinton.presidentiallibraries.us/items/show/57569.

13. On this hotly contested topic see Mary Elise Sarotte, "A Broken Promise? What the West Really Told Moscow about NATO Expansion," *Foreign Affairs* 93:5 (September/October 2014);

https://networks.h-net.org/node/28443/discussions/6590537/h-diploissf-policy-roundtable-xii-1-nato-expansion-retrospect.

14. Graham Allison, *Destined for War: Can America and China Escape Thucydides's Trap?* (Boston, MA: Mariner Books, 2017).

15. https://www.nytimes.com/interactive/2018/11/18/world/asia/china-rules.html; https://www.nytimes.com/interactive/2018/11/25/world/asia/china-economy-strategy.html.

16. On these and other inquiries see Krastev and Holmes, *The Light That Failed*.

17. Artemy Kalinovsky, "The Gorbachev Predicament: How Obama's Political Challenges Resemble Gorbachev's," *Foreign Affairs*, 19 January 2011, at https://www.foreignaffairs.com/articles/2011-01-19/gorbachev-predicament.

SELECTED BIBLIOGRAPHY

PRIMARY SOURCES

The Russian Federation

Arkhiv Prezidentskogo Tsentra B. N. Yeltsina (AY) at: https://yeltsin.ru/archive/
Rossiiskii Gosudarstvennyi Arkhiv Noveishei Istorii (RGANI), Moscow
    Materialy Prezidentskogo Soveta SSSR, f. 121, op. 3
    Materialy Gosudarstvennogo Soveta SSSR, f. 121, op. 3
    Materialy Soveta Federatsii SSSR, f. 121, op. 3
State Archive of the Russian Federation (GARF), Moscow
    The Council of Ministers of the USSR, f. R5446, op. 163
    The Supreme Soviet of the RSFSR, f. 10026, op. 4
    The Supreme Soviet of the USSR, f. 9654, op. 7, 10
The Archive of Alexander N. Yakovlev at https://www.alexanderyakovlev.org/fond/issues/73229
The Archive of the Gorbachev Foundation
The Archive of Yeltsin Center

Ukraine

Tsentralny Derzhavnyi Archiv gromadyanskikh obiedinenii (TsDAGO), Kiev
    Materialy Obshchego Otdela Kommunisticheskoi Partii Ukrainy, f. 1, op. 32

United Kingdom

The Archives of St Antony's College, Oxford
    The Anatoly Chernyaev Papers. The Politburo notes

United States

George H. W. Bush Presidential Library (GBPL)
    Brent Scowcroft Collection
    Council of Economic Advisors
        Michael Boskin Files
    Memcons and Telcons
    NSC Files
        Nicholas Burns Files
        Nicholas Burns and Ed Hewett Files
        Condoleezza Rice Papers
    WHORM Files

SELECTED BIBLIOGRAPHY

Hoover Institution Library & Archives (HIA), Stanford, CA
  A. L. Adamishin Papers
  Democratic Russia (Demokraticheskaia Rossiia) Papers
  John Dunlop Papers
  Hoover Institution and Gorbachev Foundation Collection
  Vitaly Katayev Papers
  Michael McFaul Collection
  Russian Archives project, Fond 89
  Teimuraz Stepanov-Mamaladze Papers
  The Center for Democracy (Allen Weinstein) Papers
  Zelikow and Rice Papers
Mikhail S. Bernstam personal papers, Stanford University (now at the University of Notre Dame)
National Security Archive (NSA), George Washington University, Washington, DC
  Russian and East European Archival Documents Database (READD-RADD Collection)
Seeley G. Mudd Library (SML), Princeton University
  James A. Baker III Papers (JAB)
  Colby Papers
  Council of Foreign Relations meeting records
  Don Oberdorfer Papers

Published Documents

Allison, Graham, and Grigory Yavlinsky. *Window of Opportunity: The Grand Bargain for Democracy in the Soviet Union.* New York: Pantheon Books, 1991.
Gorbachev, Mikhail. *Perestroika: New Thinking for Our Country and the World.* New York: HarperCollins, 1987.
Materialy ob'edinennogo plenuma Tsentralnogo komiteta i Tsentralnoi kontrolnoi komissii KPSS. Moscow: Izdatelstvo politicheskoi literatury, 1991.
Raspad SSSR: Dokumenty i fakty (1986–1992 gg.), vol. 1 (Moscow: Walters Kluwer, 2009)
Rumyantsev, O. G., ed., *Iz istorii sozdaniia Konstitutsii Rossiiskoi Federatsii. Konstitutsionnaia komissiia: stenogrammy, materialy, dokumenty (1990–1993).* Moscow: Wolters Kluwer. Fond Konstitutsionnykh reform, 2008–10.
Sobraniie Sochinenii Mikhaila Sergeyevich Gorbacheva, vols. 1–28. Moscow: Ves Mir, 2008–18.
"Supreme Soviet Investigation of the 1991 Coup: The Suppressed Transcripts," part I: *Demokratizatsiya* 3 no. 4 (Fall 1995): 411–50; (Winter 1996), 109–38; (Fall 1996), 603–22.
V Politburo TsK KPSS . . . Po zapisiam A. Chernyaeva, V. Medvedeva, G. Shakhnazarova. 1985–1991. Moscow: Gorbachev-Fond, 2010.
2-a sessia Verkhovnogo Soveta RSFSR. Bulleten № 1. Sovmestnoe zasedanie Soveta Respubliki I Soveta Natsionalnostey. 3 sept. 1990. Stenografichesky otchet. Vol. 1. Moscow: Izdanie Verkhovnogo Soveta SSSR, 1991.
4-y s'ezd narodnykh deputatov SSSR. 17–27 ec. 1990. Stenografichesky otchet. Vol. 1. Moscow: Izdanie Verhovnogo Soveta SSSR, 1991.

Memoirs and Published Diaries

Abalkin, Leonid. *Neispolzovannyi shans. Poltora goda v pravitelstve.* Moscow: Izdatelstvo politicheskoi literatury, 1991.
Adamishin, Anatoly. *V raznyie gody. Vneshnepoliticheskie ocherki.* Moscow: Ves Mir, 2016.
Adamishin, Anatoly, and Richard Schifter. *Human Rights, Perestroika, and the End of the Cold War.* Washington, DC: United States Institute of Peace Press, 2009.
Aven, Pyotr, and Alfred Kokh, Revoliutsia Gaidara. Istoriia reform 90-kh iz pervykh ruk (Moscow: Alpina, 2013)
Bakatin, Vadim. *Izbavlenie ot KGB.* Moscow: Novosti, 1992.

SELECTED BIBLIOGRAPHY

Baker, James A. *The Politics of Diplomacy: Revolution, War, and Peace, 1989–1992*. New York: G. P. Putnam's Sons, 1995.

Baklanov, Oleg. *Kosmos—sud'ba moia. Zapiski iz "Matrosskoi tishiny,"* vol. 1. Moscow: Obshchestvo sokhraneniia literaturnogo naslediia, 2014.

Boldin, Valery. *Krushenie piedestala. Shtrikhi k portretu M.S. Gorbacheva*. Moscow: Respublika, 1995.

Bush, George, and Brent Scowcroft. *A World Transformed*. New York: Knopf, 1998.

Chernyaev, Anatoly. *Shest Let s Gorbachevym. Po dnevnikovym zapisiam*. Moscow: Progress-Kultura, 1993.

Chernyaev, Anatoly. *My Six Years with Gorbachev*. Moscow: Progress, 1993.

Chernyaev, Anatoly. *Sovmestnyi iskhod. Dnevnik dvukh epokh 1972–1991 gody*. Moscow: ROSSPEN, 2008.

Fyodorov, Boris. *10 bezumnykh let. Pochemu v Rossii ne sostoialis reformy*. Moscow: Kollektsiia Sovershenno Sekretno, 1999.

Gates, Robert M. *From the Shadows: The Ultimate Insider's Story of Five Presidents and How They Won the Cold War*. New York: Simon & Schuster, 1996.

Gorbachev, Mikhail. *Zhizn i reformy*, vols. 1 and 2. Moscow: Novosti, 1995.

Gorbacheva, Raisa. *I Hope*. New York: HarperCollins, 1991.

Granin, D. A. *Prichudy moei pamiati*. St Petersburg: Tsentpoligraf, 2010.

Isakov, Vladimir. *Predsedatel soveta respubliki. Parlamentskie dnevniki 1990 goda*. Ekaterinburg: Uralskii rabochii, 1997.

Kalugin, Oleg. *Spymaster: My Thirty-Two Years in Intelligence and Espionage against the West*. New York: Basic Books, 2009.

Khasbulatov, Ruslan. *Poluraspad SSSR. Kak razvalili sverkhderzhavu*. Moscow: Yauza Press, 2011.

Kokh, Alfred, and Igor Svinarenko. *A Crate of Vodka*, trans. Antonina W. Bouis. New York: Enigma Books, 2009.

Kozhokin, Yevgeny. "Mysli o pervom S'ezde narodnykh deputatov RSFSR," in O. G. Rumyantsev, ed., *Iz istorii sozdaniia Konstitutsii Rossiiskoi Fedratsii*, vol. 6. Moscow: Wolters Kluwer. Fond Konstitutsionnykh reform, 2010, pp. 820–3.

Kozyrev, Andrei. *Firebird: The Elusive Fate of Russian Democracy*. Pittsburgh, PA: University of Pittsburgh Press, 2019.

Kryuchkov, Vladimir. *Lichnoie delo*, vols. 1 and 2. Moscow: Olimp, 1996.

Lebed, Alexander. *Za derzhavu obidno*. Moscow: Moskovskaia Pravda, 1995.

Lieven, Anatol, and Victor Kogan-Jasnyi. *Baltiiskoie otrazheniie. Vospominania o nekotorykh sobytiiakh 1988–93 gg*. Moscow: Grazhdanskaia preemstvennost, 2016.

Ligachev, Yegor. *Inside Gorbachev's Kremlin*, introduction by Stephen F. Cohen. New York: Westview Press, 1996.

Matlock, Jack. *Autopsy on an Empire*. New York: Random House, 1995.

Onikov, Leon. *KPSS: anatomiia raspada*. Moscow: Respublika, 1996.

Palazhchenko, Pavel. *My Years with Gorbachev and Shevardnadze: The Memoir of a Soviet Interpreter*. University Park, PA: Pennsylvania State University Press, 1997.

Pankin, Boris. *Sto oborvannykh dnei*. Moscow: Sovershenno sekretno, 1993.

Pavlov, Valentin. *Upushchen li shans? Finansovyi kliuch k rynku*. Moscow: Terra, 1995.

Petrakov, Nikolai. *Russkaia ruletka. Ekonomicheskii eksperiment tsenoiu 150 millionov zhiznei*. Moscow: Ekonomika, 1998.

Prokofiev, Yuri. *Do i posle zapreta KPSS. Pervyi sekretar MGK KPSS vspominaet*. Moscow: Algoritm, Eksmo, 2005.

Ryzhkov, Nikolai. *Perestroika: Istoriia predatelstv*. Moscow: Novosti, 1993.

Ryzhkov, Nikolai. *Desiat' let velikikh potriasenii*. Moscow: Kniga. Prosveshcheniie. Miloserdiie, 1996.

Sakharov, Andrei. *Trevoga i nadezhda. Vol. 2. Stat'i, pis'ma, vystupleniia, interview, 1986–1989*. Moscow: Vremia, 2006.

Sell, Louis. *From Washington to Moscow: US-Soviet Relations and the Collapse of the USSR*. Durham, NC: Duke University Press, 2016.

SELECTED BIBLIOGRAPHY

Shakhnazarov, Georgy. *Tsena svobody*. Moscow: Rossika Zevs, 1993.

Shebarshin, Leonid. *Ruka Moskvy: zapiski nachalnika sovetskoi razvedki*. Moscow: Tsentr-100, 1992.

Sitarian, S. A. *Uroki budushchego*. Moscow: Ekonomicheskaia gazeta, 2010.

Sukhanov, Lev. *Kak Yeltsin stal prezidentom. Zapiski pervogo pomoshchnika*. Moscow: Eksmo, 2011.

Vorotnikov, Vitaly. *A bylo eto tak . . . Iz dnevkika chlena Politbiuro TsK KPSS*. Moscow: Sovet veteranov knigoizdaniia, 1995.

Yakovlev, Alexandr N. *Sumerki*. Moscow: Materik, 2005.

Yeltsin, Boris. *Prezidentskiy marafon. Razmyshleniya, vospominaniya, vpechatleniya*. Moscow: AST, 2000.

Yeltsin, Boris. *The Struggle for Russia*. New York: Crown Books, 1994.

Zotov, M. S. *Ia—bankir. Ot Stalina do Putina*. Moscow: RUSAKI, 2004.

Unpublished Memoirs and Diaries

Adamishin, Anatoly, *Diaries*

Braithwaite, Rodric, *Diary*

Stepanov-Mamaladze, Teimuraz, *Diary and Notes*

Interviews, Conversations, and E-mails

James A. Baker III, Washington, 2013

Oleg Baklanov, Moscow, 1997

Mikhail Bernstam, Stanford, 2013–20

Michael Boskin, Stanford, 2013

Rodric Braithwaite, London, 2014–19

Gennady Burbulis, by phone, 2020

Anatoly Chernyaev, Moscow, 1995–2001

Alexander Drozdov, Moscow, 2020

Francis Fukuyama, Stanford, 2013

Mikhail Gorbachev, Moscow, 1995

Andrei Kokoshin, Moscow, 2019

Yevgeny Kozhokin, Moscow, 2017

Vladimir Lukin, Moscow, 2017

Jack Matlock, Washington, 2007–14

Michael McFaul, Stanford, 2013

William Odom, Washington, 2000–1

Pavel Palazhchenko, Moscow, 2021

Alexei Pankin, Moscow, 2020

Rudolf Pikhoia, Moscow, 2018

Condoleezza Rice, Stanford, 2013

George Schultz, Stanford, 2013

Georgy Shakhnazarov, Moscow, Oslo, Jachranka, 1995–2000

Eduard Shevardnadze, Tbilisi, 1999

Strobe Talbott, Charlottesville, 2017

Sergey Tarasenko, Moscow i.a., 1998–2001

Grigory Yavlinsky, Moscow, 2016

Philip Zelikow, Charlottesville, 2017

Robert B. Zoellick, Washington, 1998; Charlottesville, 2017

Andrei B. Zubov, Moscow, 2017

Unpublished and Published Interviews

Collection of interviews by Oleg Skvortsov, Institute of General History, Moscow

Collection of interviews by the Gorbachev Foundation–Stanford University project, HIA

Karaulov, Andrei. *Vokrug Kremlia*. Moscow: Slovo, 1993

SELECTED BIBLIOGRAPHY

Ryzhkov, Nikolai. "Esli by Andropov dol'she prozhil," at https://lenta.ru/articles/2020/04/23/35/?f-bclid=IwAR00Uocg8CZYJyrQgxdnZo8jkbqY_t8dBXEAOX7IVM3JbvyuRXJ3VvHs2NQ

Volsky, Arkady. "Chetyre genseka," *Kommersant*, no. 169, 12 September 2006, at: https://www.kommersant.ru/doc/704123

SECONDARY SOURCES

Books

Adomeit, Hannes. *Imperial Overstretch: Germany in Soviet Policy from Stalin to Gorbachev*. Baden-Baden: Nomos, 1998.

Albats, Yevgenia. *The State within a State*. New York: Farrar, Straus and Giroux, 1999.

Andreiev Nikolai. *Zhizn Gorbacheva*. Moscow, MA: Dobroie delo, 2016.

Aron, Leon. *Boris Yeltsin: A Revolutionary Life*. New York: HarperCollins, 2000.

Bakatin, Vadim, *Izbavlenie ot KGB*. Moscow: Novosti, 1992.

Balzer, Harvey, ed. *Five Years that Shook the World: Gorbachev's Unfinished Revolution*. Boulder, CO: Westview Press, 1991.

Beissinger, Mark R. *Nationalist Mobilization and the Collapse of the Soviet State*. Cambridge: Cambridge University Press, 2002.

Beschloss, Michael R., and Strobe Talbott. *At the Highest Levels: The Inside Story of the End of the Cold War*. Boston: Little, Brown, 1993.

Bozo, Frédéric. *Mitterrand, the End of the Cold War, and German Unification*. Oxford: Berghahn Books, 2010.

Breslauer, George W. *Gorbachev and Yeltsin as Leaders*. New York: Cambridge University Press, 2002.

Brown, Archie. *The Gorbachev Factor*. Oxford and New York: Oxford University Press, 1996.

Brown, Archie. *Seven Years that Changed the World: Perestroika in Perspective*. Oxford: Oxford University Press, 2007.

Brown, Archie. *The Rise and Fall of Communism*. New York: HarperCollins, 2009.

Brudny, Yitzhak M. *Reinventing Russia: Russian Nationalism and the Soviet State, 1953–1991*. Cambridge, MA: Harvard University Press, 1998.

Bunce, Valerie. *Subversive Institutions: The Design and the Destruction of Socialism and the State*. Cambridge: Cambridge University Press, 1999.

Cohen, Stephen F., and Katrina van den Heuvel. *Voices of Glasnost: Interviews with Gorbachev's Reformers*. New York: W. W. Norton, 1989.

Colton, Timothy J. *Yeltsin: A Life*. New York: Basic Books, 2011.

Cox, Michael, ed. *Rethinking the Soviet Collapse: Sovietology, the Death of Communism and the New Russia*. London: Pinter, 1998.

Crowley, Monica. *Nixon in Winter*. New York: Random House, 1998.

Daniels, Robert. *The Rise and Fall of Communism in Russia*. New Haven, CT: Yale University Press, 2007.

Derluguian, Georgi M. *Bourdieu's Secret Admirer in the Caucasus: The World-System Biography*. Chicago, IL: Chicago University Press, 2005.

Dobbs, Michael. *Down with Big Brother: The Fall of the Soviet Empire*. New York: Alfred A. Knopf, 1997.

Dunlop, John. *The Rise of Russia and the Fall of the Soviet Empire*. Princeton, NJ: Princeton University Press, 1993.

Ellman, Michael, and Vladimir Kontorovich. *The Destruction of the Soviet Economic System: An Insider's History*. London: Routledge, 1998.

English, Robert D. *Russia and the Idea of the West: Gorbachev, Intellectuals, and the End of the Cold War*. New York: Columbia University Press, 2000.

Foglesong, David S. *The American Mission and the "Evil Empire."* New York: Cambridge University Press, 2007.

Fowkes, Ben. *The Disintegration of the Soviet Union: A Study in the Rise and Triumph of Nationalism*. London: Macmillan, 1997.

Furman, Dmitry. *Nashi Desiat Let. Politicheskii protsess v Rossii s 1991 po 2001 god*. Moscow-St Petersburg: Letnii Sad, 2001.

SELECTED BIBLIOGRAPHY

Gaidar, Yegor. *Collapse of an Empire: Lessons for Modern Russia*, trans. Antonina W. Bouis. Washington, DC: Brookings Institution, 2007.

Gaidar, Yegor. *V dni porazhenii i pobed*. Moscow: Vagrius, 1996.

Garcelon, Marc. *Revolutionary Passage: From Soviet to Post-Soviet Russia*. Philadelphia, PA: Temple University Press, 2005.

Garthoff, Raymond L. *Soviet Leaders and Intelligence: Assessing the American Adversary during the Cold War*. Washington, DC: Georgetown University Press, 2015.

Goldgeier, James, and Michael McFaul. *Power and Purpose: U.S. Policy Toward Russia after the Cold War*. Washington, DC: Brookings Institution Press, 2003.

Grachev, Andrei S. *Gorbachev*. Moscow: Vagrius, 2001.

Grachev, Andrei S. *Gorbachev's Gamble: Soviet Foreign Policy and the End of the Cold War*. Cambridge: Polity, 2008.

Hahn, Gordon M. *Russia's Revolution from Above, 1985–2000: Reform, Transition and Revolution in the Fall of the Soviet Communist Regime*. New Brunswick, NJ: Transaction, 2002.

Hoffman, David E. *The Oligarchs: Wealth and Power in the New Russia*. New York: Public Affairs, 2011.

Hoffman, David E. *The Dead Hand: The Untold Story of the Cold War Arms Race and its Dangerous Legacy*. New York: Anchor Books, 2010.

Johnson, Juliet. *A Fistful of Rubles: The Rise and Fall of the Soviet Banking System*. Ithaca, NY: Cornell University Press, 2000.

Kotkin, Stephen. *Armageddon Averted: The Soviet Collapse, 1970–2000*. New York: Oxford University Press, 2008 (updated edition).

Kotkin, Stephen, and Jan Tomasz Gross. *Uncivil Society: 1989 and the Implosion of the Communist Establishment*. New York: Modern Library, 2009.

Kotz, David M., and Fred Weir. *Revolution from Above: The Demise of the Soviet System*. New York: Routledge, 1997.

Krotov, Nikolai. *Istoriia sovetskoi bankovskoi reformy 80-h gg. XX v. vol. 1. Spetsbanki*. Moscow: Ekonomicheskaia letopis, 2008.

Lévesque, Jacques. *The Enigma of 1989: The USSR and the Liberation of Eastern Europe*, trans. Keith Martin. Berkeley, CA: University of California Press, 1997.

Lewin, Moshe. *The Soviet Century*. London: Verso, 2005.

Lukin, Alexander. *The Political Culture of Russian "Democrats."* Oxford: Oxford University Press, 2000.

Marples, David R. *The Collapse of the Soviet Union, 1985–1991*. New York: Pearson Education Ltd, 2004.

Matthews, Arthur H. *Agents of Influence: How the Krieble Institute Brought Democratic Capitalism to the Former Soviet Empire*. Washington, DC: Krieble Institute of the Free Congress Foundation, 1995.

Medvedev, Roy. *Boris Yeltsin. Narod i vlast v kontse XX veka. Iz nabliudenii istorika*. Moscow: Vremia, 2011.

Medvedev, Vadim. *V komande Gorbacheva: vzgliad iznutri*. Moscow: Bylina, 1994.

Miller, Chris. *The Struggle to Save the Soviet Economy: Mikhail Gorbachev and the Collapse of the USSR*. Chapel Hill, NC: University of North Carolina Press, 2016.

Mlechin, Leonid. *Yuri Andropov. Posledniaia nadezhda rezhima*. Moscow: Tsentrpoligraph, 2008.

Morgan, Michael Cotey, *The Final Act: The Helsinki Accords and the Transformation of the Cold War*. Princeton, NJ: Princeton University Press, 2018.

Oberdorfer, Don. *From the Cold War to a New Era: The United States and the Soviet Union, 1983–1991*. Baltimore, MD: Johns Hopkins University Press, 1998.

O'Clery, Conor. *Moscow, December 25, 1991: The Last Day of the Soviet Union*. New York: Random House, 2012.

O'Connor, Kevin, *Intellectuals and Apparatchiks: Russian Nationalism and the Gorbachev Revolution*. New York: Lexington Books, Rowman & Littlefield, 2006.

Odom, William. *The Collapse of the Soviet Military*. New Haven, CT, and London: Yale University Press, 1998.

SELECTED BIBLIOGRAPHY

Ostrovsky, Alexander. *Glupost ili izmena? Rassledovaniie gibeli SSSR*. Moscow: Krymskii most, 2011.

Ostrovsky, Arkady. *The Invention of Russia: The Rise of Putin and the Invention of Fake News*. London: Penguin, 2017.

Park, Andrus. *End of an Empire? A Conceptualization of the Soviet Disintegration Crisis, 1985–1991*. Tartu, Estonia: University of Tartu Press, 2009.

Pikhoia, Rudolph. *Sovetskii Soiuz: istoriia vlasti. 1945–1991*. Moscow: RAGS, 1998.

Pleshakov, Constantine. *There Is No Freedom Without Bread! 1989 and the Civil War That Brought Down Communism*. New York: Farrar, Straus, and Giroux, 2009.

Plokhy, Serhii. *The Last Empire: The Final Days of the Soviet Union*. New York: Basic Books, 2014.

Pryce-Jones, David. *The War That Never Was: The Fall of the Soviet Empire, 1985–91*. London: Weidenfeld and Nicolson, 1995.

Radchenko, Sergey. *Unwanted Visionaries: The Soviet Failure in Asia at the End of the Cold War*. New York: Oxford University Press, 2014.

Reddaway, Peter, and Dmitri Glinski. *The Tragedy of Russia's Reforms: Market Bolshevism against Democracy*. Washington, DC: United States Institute of Peace, 2001.

Remnick, David. *Lenin's Tomb: The Last Days of the Soviet Empire*. New York: Random House, 1993.

Sakwa, Richard. *Gorbachev and his Reforms, 1985–1990*. London: Philip Allan, 1990.

Savranskaya, Svetlana, Thomas Blanton, and Vladislav Zubok, eds. *Masterpieces of History: The Peaceful End of the Cold War in Europe, 1989*. Budapest: Central European University Press, 2010.

Savranskaya, Svetlana, and Thomas Blanton, eds. *The Last Superpower Summits: Reagan, Gorbachev and Bush at the End of the Cold War*. Budapest: Central European University Press, 2016.

Senn, Alfred. *Gorbachev's Failure in Lithuania*. New York: St. Martin's Press, 1995.

Service, Robert. *The End of the Cold War, 1985–1991*. London: Macmillan, 2015.

Sheinis, Viktor. *Vlast i zakon. Politika i konstitutsii v Rossii v XX–XXI vekakh*. Moscow: Mysl, 2014.

Sheinis, Viktor. *Vzlet i padeniie parlamenta: Perlomnyie gody v rossiiskoi politike (1985–1991)*. Moscow Carnegie Center, Fond INDEM, 2005.

Simes, Dimitri K. *After Collapse: Russia Seeks Its Place as a Great Power*. New York: Simon & Schuster, 1999.

Solnick, Steven. *Stealing the State: Control and Collapse in Soviet Institutions*. Cambridge, MA: Harvard University Press, 1998.

Spohr, Kristina. *Post Wall, Post Square: Rebuilding the World After 1989*. New York: William Collins, 2019.

Spohr, Kristina Readman. *Germany and the Baltic Problem After the Cold War: The Development of a New Ostpolitik, 1989–2000*. London: Routledge, 2004.

Stepankov, Valentin. *GKChP: 73 chasa, kotorye izmenili mir*. Moscow: Vremia, 2011.

Stepankov, Valentin, and E. Lisov. *Kremlevskii zagovor*. Moscow: Ogonek, 1992

Strayer, Robert. *Why Did the Soviet Union Collapse? Understanding Historical Change*. New York: M. E. Sharpe, Inc., 1998.

Suny, Ronald Grigor. *The Revenge of the Past: Nationalism, Revolution, and the Collapse of the Soviet Union*. Stanford, CA: Stanford University Press, 1993.

Sutela, Pekka. *Economic Thought and Economic Reform in the Soviet Union*. Cambridge: Cambridge University Press, 1991.

Talbott, Strobe. *The Great Experiment: The Story of Ancient Empires, Modern States, and the Quest for a Global Nation*. New York: Simon & Schuster, 2008.

Taubman, William. *Gorbachev: His Life and Times*. New York: Simon & Schuster, 2017.

Tinguy, Anne de, ed. *The Fall of the Soviet Empire*. New York: Columbia University Press, 1998.

Tolz, Vera, and Iain Elliot, eds. *The Demise of the USSR: From Communism to Independence*. London: Palgrave Macmillan, 1995.

Vahter, Tarmo. *Estonia: Zharkoie leto 91-go. Avgustovskii putch i vozrozhdenie nezavisimosti*. Tallinn: Eesti Ekspress, 2012.

SELECTED BIBLIOGRAPHY

Volkov, Vadim. *Violent Entrepreneurs: The Use of Force in the Making of Russian Capitalism.* Ithaca, NY: Cornell University Press, 2002.

Walker, Edward W. *Dissolution: Sovereignty and the Breakup of the Soviet Union.* New York: Rowman & Littlefield, 2003.

Watson, William E. *The Collapse of Communism in the Soviet Union.* Westport, CT: Greenwood, 1998.

Westad, Odd Arne. *The Cold War: A Global History.* London: Allen Lane, 2017.

Wilson, James. *The Triumph of Improvisation: Gorbachev's Adaptability, Reagan's Engagement, and the End of the Cold War.* Ithaca, NY: Cornell University Press, 2015.

Woodruff, David. *Money Unmade: Barter and the Fate of Russian Capitalism.* Ithaca, NY: Cornell University Press, 1999.

Yurchak, Alexei. *Everything Was Forever, Until It Was No More: The Last Soviet Generation.* Princeton, NJ: Princeton University Press, 2006.

Zaal, von, Yuliya. *KSZE-Prozess und Perestroika in der Sowjetunion: Demokratisierung, Werteumbruch und Auflösung.* Munich: Oldenburg Wissenschaftsverlag, 2014.

Zelikow, Philip, and Condoleezza Rice. *Germany Unified and Europe Transformed: A Study in Statecraft.* Cambridge, MA: Harvard University Press, 1997.

Zezina, M. R., O. G. Malysheva, F. V. Malkhozova, and R. G. Pikhoia. *Chelovek peremen. Issledovaniie politicheskoi biografii B. N. Yeltsina.* Moscow: Novyi Khronograf, 2011.

Zubok, Vladislav M. *A Failed Empire: The Soviet Union in the Cold War from Stalin to Gorbachev.* Chapel Hill, NC: University of North Carolina Press, 2009.

Zubok, Vladislav M. *Zhivago's Children: The Last Russian Intelligentsia.* Cambridge, MA: Belknap Press, 2009.

Zubok, Vladislav M. *The Idea of Russia: The Life and Work of Dmitry Likhachev.* London: I. B. Tauris, 2016.

Articles

Bonnell, Victoria, and Gregory Freidin. "Televorot: The Role of Television Coverage in Russia's August 1991 Coup," *Slavic Review* 52:4 (Winter 1993), pp. 810–38.

Brown, Archie. "The National Question, the Coup, and the Collapse of the Soviet Union," in Alastair Kocho-Williams, ed., *The Twentieth-Century Russia Reader.* New York: Routledge, 2011, pp. 291–310.

Brubaker, R. "Nationhood and the National Question in the Soviet Union and Post-Soviet Eurasia: An Institutionalist Account," *Theory and Society* 23 (1994), pp. 47–78.

Cohen, Stephen F. 'Was the Soviet System Reformable?' *Slavic Review* 63:3 (2004), pp. 459–88.

Dunlop, John B. "The August 1991 Coup and its Impact on Soviet Politics," *Journal of Cold War Studies* 5:1 (2003), pp. 94–127.

Evangelista, Matthew. "Norms, Heresthetics, and the End of the Cold War," *Journal of Cold War Studies* 3:1 (Winter 2001), pp. 5–35.

Geoghegan, Kate. "A Policy in Tension: The National Endowment for Democracy and the U.S. Response to the Collapse of the Soviet Union," *Diplomatic History* 42:5 (2018), pp. 771–801.

Hanson, Stephen E. "Gorbachev: The Last True Leninist Believer?" in Daniel Chirot, ed., *The Crisis of Leninism and the Decline of the Left: The Revolutions of 1989.* Seattle, WA: University of Washington Press, 1991.

Kramer, Mark. "The Reform of the Soviet System and the Demise of the Soviet State," *Slavic Review* 63:3 (2004), pp. 505–12.

Kramer, Mark. "The Demise of the Soviet Bloc," *Europe-Asia Studies* 63:9 (November 2011), pp. 1,535–90.

Lieven, Dominic. "Western Scholarship on the Soviet Regime," *Journal of Contemporary History* 29:2 (1994).

Muiznieks, Nils R. "The Influence of the Baltic Popular Movements on the Process of Soviet Disintegration," *Europe-Asia Studies* 47:1 (1995), pp. 3–25.

Pravda, Alex. "The Collapse of the Soviet Union 1990–1991," in *The Cambridge History of the Cold War,* vol. III. Cambridge: Cambridge University Press, 2010.

509

SELECTED BIBLIOGRAPHY

Rey, Marie-Pierre. "'Europe is our common home': A Study of Gorbachev's Diplomatic Concept," *Cold War History* 4:2 (2004), pp. 33–65.

Rowley, David. "Interpretations of the End of the Soviet Union: Three Paradigms," *Kritika* 2:2 (2001), pp. 395–426.

Scarborough, Isaac. "(Over)determining Social Disorder: Tajikistan and the Economic Collapse of Perestroika," *Central Asian Survey* 35:3 (2016), pp. 439–63.

Shlykov, Vitaly. "Chto pogubilo Sovetskii Soiuz? Amerikanskaia razvedka o sovetskykh voiennykh dokhodakh," *Voennyi vestnik* 8 (2001), pp. 2–40.

Shlykov, Vitaly. "Chto pogubilo Sovetskii Soiuz? Genshtab i ekonomika," *Voennyi vestnik* 9 (2002), pp. 5–191.

Soiuz mozhno bylo sokhranit: Belaia kniga: Dokumenty i fakty o politike M. S. Gorbacheva po reformirovaniiu i sokhraneniiu mnogonatsional'nogo gosudarstva. Moscow: Izdatel'stvo AST, 2007. For an electronic copy at the site of the Gorbachev Foundation, see https://www.gorby.ru/userfiles/union_could_be_saved.pdf.

Taylor, Brian D. "The Soviet Military and the Disintegration of the USSR," *Journal of Cold War Studies* 5:1 (2003), pp. 17–66.

Tuminez, Astrid S. "Nationalism, Ethnic Pressures, and the Breakup of the Soviet Union," *Journal of Cold War Studies* 5:4 (Fall 2003), pp. 81–136.

Wallander, Celeste A. "Western Policy and the Demise of the Soviet Union," *Journal of Cold War Studies* 5:4 (2003), pp. 137–77.

Zlotnik, Marc. "Yeltsin and Gorbachev: The Politics of Confrontation," *Journal of Cold War Studies* 5:1 (2003), pp. 128–64.

Zubok, Vladislav. "With His Back Against the Wall: Gorbachev, Soviet Demise, and German Reunification," *Cold War History* 14:4 (2014), pp. 619–45.

Zubok, Vladislav. "Gorbachev, German Reunification, and Soviet Demise," in Frederic Bozo, Andreas Roedder, and Mary Sarotte, eds., *German Unification: A Multinational History.* New York: Routledge, 2016, pp. 88–108.

Zubok, Vladislav. "The Collapse of the Soviet Union," in Juliana Furst, Silvio Pons, and Mark Selden, eds., *The Cambridge History of Communism*, vol. III, *Endgames? Late Communism in Global Perspective, 1968 to the Present.* Cambridge: Cambridge University Press, 2017.

Zubok, Vladislav. "The Soviet Union and China in the 1980s: Reconciliation and Divorce," *Cold War History* 17:2 (Spring 2017), pp. 121–41.

Zubok, Vladislav. "Intelligentsia as a Liberal Concept in Soviet History, 1945–1991," in Riccardo Cucciolla, ed., *Dimensions and Challenges of Russian Liberalism: Historical Drama and New Prospects.* Cham, Switzerland: Springer, 2019, pp. 45–62.

Zweynert, Joachim. "Economic Ideas and Institutional Change: Evidence from Soviet Economic Discourse, 1987–1991," *Europe-Asia Studies* 58:2 (2006), pp. 169–92.

Dissertations

Bergmane, Una. "French and US Reactions Facing the Disintegration of the USSR: The Case of the Baltic States (1989–1991)," Sciences Po, Paris, 2016.

Cucciolla, Riccardo. "The Crisis of Soviet Power in Central Asia: The Uzbek 'Cotton Affair' (1975–1991)," PhD Dissertation, IMT School for Advanced Studies, Lucca, 2017.

Geoghegan, Kate. "The Specter of Anarchy, the Hope of Transformation: The Role of Non-State Actors in the U.S. Response to Soviet Reform and Disunion, 1981–1996," University of Virginia, Charlottesville, 2015.

Scarborough, Isaac. "The Extremes it Takes to Survive: Tajikistan and the Collapse of the Soviet Union, 1985–1992," London School of Economics and Political Sciences, 2018.

INDEX

INDEX

Armenia, 153, 176, 198
  boycott of Union referendum (1991), 200
  earthquake (1988), 55, 95
  see also Nagorny Karabagh
Army, Soviet
  Afgantsy (veterans of Afghanistan), 296,
    298, 299, 302
  anti-Gorbachev rallies in Moscow, 163, 204
  arms control cuts, 159, 262
  attitudes during junta rule, 298–9, 301
  in the Baltic republics, 183, 318
  and the Commonwealth of Independent
    States, 419
  demoralized by Gorbachev's zigzags, 185
  and economic liberalization, 373, 374–5
  and ethnic-nationalist conflicts, 104–5,
    161–2
  fears of anti-Gorbachev coup, 111, 114,
    141, 209
  in Moscow during junta rule, 277–8,
    282–3, 298–9
  not fully in control, 183, 403
  oath of allegiance to the Soviet Union,
    403, 404, 407
  reactions to its withdrawal from Eastern
    Europe, 159–60, 161, 163, 216
  retreat from East Germany and Eastern
    Europe, 124, 159–60, 181, 344, 381
  and the Soviet Union's dissolution, 402–3,
    404, 407, 409
  taken over by Yeltsin's Russia, 358, 389,
    407
  threat of partitioning, 381
  voting for Yeltsin, 283, 449
  see also MIC
Åslund, Anders, 415
Attali, Jacques, 251–2, 340
Aven, Pyotr, 391
Azerbaijan, 156, 176, 200, 268, 374, 381
  Armenian pogroms in, 54, 56
  use of Soviet troops in (1990), 104–5
  see also Nagorny Karabagh

Baghirov, Kamran, 54
Bagrov, Nikolai, 385, 386
Bakatin, Vadim, 175, 308, 338
  as candidate for Russia's presidency, 216
  criticism by Gorbachev, 152
  dismissed by Yeltsin, 418–19
  as head of the KGB, 314, 316, 346, 407
  and Lithuania's secession, 113
  pro-Americanism, 346
Baker, James, 50, 110–11, 153, 161, 236, 419
  advising Gorbachev, 96, 198–9, 201, 380
  on Baltic independence and policies,
    199, 347

and the coup in Moscow, 284, 292, 300
dangers of Soviet break-up, 342–3
engaged in Soviet politics, 198, 199
and the five principles, 243, 344, 347,
  394, 412
friendship with Shevardnadze, 143, 258,
  284, 346–7, 392, 415
on Grand Bargain, 239, 244
and the Gulf crisis, 143
on handling Yeltsin and the Russian
  factor, 199, 260
at the Moscow summit (July 1991), 258,
  261
negotiating Gorbachev's safe retirement, 41
negotiating safety of Soviet nuclear
  weapons, 411, 413
Princeton speech on "post-Soviet Union"
  (December 1991), 411
private views on Soviet collapse, 415–16
supporting Russian democracy, 347, 392,
  415
on Ukraine, 392
on US recognition of post-Soviet states,
  413, 416, 419–20
visits to the collapsing Soviet Union:
  September 1991, 344–8; December
  1991, 412–14, 415–16
on Yeltsin-Gorbachev rivalry, 345–6
Baklanov, Oleg, 168, 169, 171
  on arms reductions, 251
  in junta of August 1991, 270, 277, 301–2,
    303
  seeing Yeltsin before the emergency, 286
  trip to Foros, 306
balance of trade, Soviet, 17–18, 23, 390
Balcerowicz, Leszek, 128, 132, 235; *see also*
  Poland, economic reforms
Baltic republics (Lithuania, Latvia, Estonia)
  as beneficiaries of the Soviet collapse, 438
  bloodshed in January 1991, 183–5
  at the Congress of People's Deputies, 76
  disputed issues, 261, 334
  during junta rule in Moscow, 284, 305
  fear of independence reversal, 332, 334
  gaining sovereignty, 318–19, 334, 342
  Gorbachev's pledge not to use force, 96,
    184
  and Kaliningrad region, 347
  national mobilization, 85
  Nazi-Soviet pact (1939) 57, 76, 85
  "people's fronts," 55, 56, 57, 60, 449
  rejection of Soviet commitments, 347
  and republican "self-accounting," 56, 59
  Russian-speaking minorities, 182–3, 186,
    200, 261, 319, 347
  Soviet military and assets in, 327, 347, 381

INDEX

INDEX

during junta rule in August 1991, 281, 282, 299

on Gorbachev, 282, 311, 317, 365

idea of a union of Slavic republics, 173

and the KGB, 165, 226, 227, 299, 303, 354, 382, 407

at meeting of Slavic leaders in Viskuli, 398, 400–1

and Russia's primacy in the post-Soviet space, 264–7

and Russia's strategy of reforms, 355–6, 357–8, 372

shutdown of the Party apparatus, 315

and Ukraine, 327, 383, 400, 401

and the West, 82–3, 221, 222, 409–10, 436

Western help, 221, 222, 409–10, 415

on Yeltsin's grandstanding, 415

and Yeltsin's presidential campaign, 212, 216–17, 218

as Yeltsin's strategist, 150, 186, 191, 216–17, 353–5

Burns, Nicholas, 377–8, 410, 425

Bush administration

American recognition of Russia and Ukraine, 262

dilemma of Gorbachev vs republics, 181, 433

project "Russia's freedom," 433

viewing Soviet Union as an "evil empire," 425, 433

Bush, Barbara, 119

Bush, George H. W., 50, 83

against financial help to Soviet Union, 122, 236–7, 239–41, 244, 245, 343, 353

arms reduction talks, 238, 251, 261–2, 368

and the Baltic case, 95–6, 114, 172, 195, 213, 258–62, 284, 341–2

and changes in Eastern Europe, 92, 93, 94–5

Christmas 1991 call from Gorbachev, 424–5

contacts with Yeltsin, 214, 222, 260, 293, 311, 368

fear of military coup in Moscow, 258–9, 341, 378, 392

and German unification, 110, 118

and Gorbachev's safe retirement, 416, 420

humanitarian aid/food assistance to the USSR, 345, 353, 368, 380, 415

intelligence on Soviet crisis, 215, 258, 262, 378, 378

pressures on inside the US, 341, 360, 393, 394, 395–6

reacting to Soviet Union's demise, 341, 410, 424, 425

reacting to junta in Moscow, 283–4, 292–3, 307, 311

recognition of Russia (RSFSR), 404

sanctions on the USSR (1991), 195, 198

and Soviet role in the Gulf crisis, 143–4, 172, 195

strategy regarding Soviet collapse, 197, 199–200, 341–4, 368

supporting and steering Gorbachev, 111–12, 113–14, 121, 172, 198, 199–200, 221, 222, 233–4, 240, 249, 252–3, 259, 261, 285, 338, 342, 393, 394, 434

support of the post-Soviet union of republics, 262, 263, 368

and Ukraine's independence, 262–3, 359, 360–1, 392, 393, 395–6

US leadership in NATO and G-7, 245, 249–50, 251

at the US-Soviet summits: 1989, 95–6; 1990, 118–19, 143–4; 1991, 258–62

Cabinet of Ministers (USSR), 171, 172, 205, 211, 224

during emergency rule, 294, 298, 302, 316

liquidation of, 316, 331, 332, 364

Camdessus, Michel, 368

Carpendale, Andrew, 342, 343, 410–11

Castro, Fidel, 238, 399

Ceaușescu, Nicolae, 90, 91, 97

Celeste, Richard, 169

Center for Democracy, Washington DC, 291–2; see also Weinstein, Allen

Central Asia (republics)

dependence on Russia, 332, 381, 408

and Islamic fundamentalism, 347, 408

joins the Commonwealth, 411

Soviet republics of, 114, 131, 152, 158, 208, 257, 315

withdrawal of Soviet weapons, 161

Yeltsin's attitude towards, 201

CFE (Treaty on the Conventional Forces in Europe), 159, 161, 163, 250, 412

Ratification of, 238, 344

Charter of Paris (1990), 172

Chebrikov, Viktor, 20, 27, 58, 88

Chechnya, 74, 131, 208, 389, 435, 436, 403

Cheney, Richard, 92, 220, 221

advocating break-up of Soviet Union, 239, 342, 344, 361, 392

Chernenko, Konstantin, 20

Chernobyl nuclear catastrophe, 25, 44, 364, 397, 405

financial consequences, 25

Chernomyrdin, Viktor, 157, 327

514

INDEX

Chernovol, Vyacheslav, 385

Chernyaev, Anatoly, 21, 34, 40, 66, 87, 110, 135, 149, 157, 165, 261
attempting to resign as Gorbachev's aide, 185
attitude to Yeltsin's "Russia," 103, 224
connections to democratic opposition, 207
in Crimea with Gorbachev, August 1991, 273, 274, 275, 287, 293, 309
on demise of Gorbachev's leadership, 148, 177, 188, 224, 370
and dismantling of Soviet statehood, 309, 334
estimate of Soviet collapse, 423
and German unification, 110, 116, 118, 124
on Gorbachev's clinging to the Party and Soviet system, 155, 237, 317
and Gorbachev's last days in power, 378, 406
on Gorbachev's place in history, 193
as Gorbachev's speechwriter, 225, 237, 245, 266
on Lithuania crisis, 112
on nationalism and separatism, 59, 74
radicalization, 87
on Russian attitudes to Gorbachev, 201, 224
on Russian democracy and statehood, 203
on Ukraine and Crimea, 367
and the Union Treaty, 190, 257
on US attitudes to Gorbachev, 197, 198–9, 23
on US conduct, 143, 235, 254
Westernism and reliance on the United States, 116, 118–19, 144, 254

China, People's Republic of, 60, 408, 420
impact on Soviet reforms, 41, 61, 229
recognition of Russia, 420
reforms as a possible road for the USSR, 158, 175
Sino-Soviet summit (May 1989), 60
Tiananmen Square crackdown, 61, 84–5, 90, 93, 96, 108, 152, 184, 204, 292, 438
Western investments, 434, 438
in US-Soviet relations, 261

CIA (Central Intelligence Agency)
analysis of the Soviet crisis, 93, 182, 215, 245, 378
and the August 1991 coup, 271, 283–4, 292
briefing Bush and Scowcroft on Soviet affairs, 215, 258, 259, 262, 378
intelligence sources in Moscow, 245, 377

as a model for the reformed KGB, 346, 382
in Soviet officials' imagination, 165
pro-Yeltsin bias in, 292, 378

CIS (Commonwealth of Independent States), 400, 406, 407, 408, 409, 425
Alma-Ata conference, 416, 417, 419–20
borders between members, 405
as cover for Soviet Union's dissolution, 436
declaration of, 401–2, 404
extra-legal nature of, 400, 405–6, 419
fictional joint control over Soviet nukes, 220
nuclear controls, 401, 404, 413
and the Soviet Army, 404
see also Viskuli

civil war, specter/fear of, 108, 113, 147, 149, 151, 153, 154, 164, 174, 195–6, 269, 276, 282, 301, 314, 333, 405, 406, 416, 430
prospect in Ukraine, 320, 393, 405
see also Yugoslavia

Clinton, Bill, 426, 434

CMEA (Council for Mutual Economic Assistance), 47
crisis and dissolution, 246

CNN, 121, 143, 152, 196, 204
covering Gorbachev's farewell speech, 422–3
during emergency rule, 283, 288
invited to fly to Crimea to rescue Gorbachev, 306

COCOM (Coordinating Committee for Multilateral Export Controls), 45, 159

Colby, William, 169

Cold War
"defeat" of the Soviet Union, 411, 433
perceived end of, 43–4, 50, 92, 95–6, 143, 148, 252, 405, 433
Western policies in, 44–5, 158, 259

Collins, James, 283, 289, 290

Colton, Timothy, 244

"Common European Home" (Gorbachev's vision of Europe), 48, 50, 89, 94, 97, 109, 110, 173, 249, 275

Commonwealth of Independent States *see* CIS

Communist Party *see* Party, the

Conference on Security and Cooperation in Europe *see* CSCE

Congress of People's Deputies (RSFSR):
May–June 1990, 116–18; March 1991, 203–5; May 1991, 216; October 1991, 373
approving the RSFSR presidency, 191, 205, 216

INDEX

granting Yeltsin extraordinary powers for reforms, 373

standoff between Yeltsin and Gorbachev, 203–5

Congress of People's Deputies (USSR), 36
electing Gorbachev as President, 107–8
election and convocation of, 70
last straw for Gorbachev to stay in power, 406, 421
reformed out of existence, 256, 331, 332–4, 348
sessions: May–June 1989, 74–8; December 1989, 175–8; March 1990, 107–8; September 1991, 332–4

Constitution of the Soviet Union
breached by Yeltsin during emergency rule, 306, 311–12
and Commonwealth accords, 400, 410
debates on confederation, 59, 99, 120, 134, 135, 429
defended by Yeltsin and Russian democrats, 283
defied by RSFSR Congress, 204
eroded and abrogated, 264, 332, 333–4, 348, 370
Novo-Ogaryovo Joint Declaration, 208, 209
and reforms of political system (1988), 35–6
and reforms of ruling structures (1990), 107, 108
respected by hardliners and junta (1990–91), 156, 270, 277, 288
and "socialist democracy," 33
troika deals with Yeltsin and Nazarbayev: July 1991, 256–7; September 1991, 331

Constitutional Assembly, Russian (1918), 333, 379

Cooperatives, Law on, 32, 63, 397

cooperatives, Soviet, 18, 113, 129, 130, 166, 168
as profiteers, 79, 80, 81, 111, 126, 189
taxation of, 127, 189
see also Cooperatives, Law on

Coordinating Committee for Multilateral Export Controls

Cossiga, Francesco, 418, 422

Council for Mutual Economic Assistance see CMEA

Council of Federation (1990–91), 108,

Crimea
annexed by Russia (2014), 2, 437
autonomy within Ukrainian republic, 70, 385
Gorbachev on vacation in, 34, 38, 40, 41, 87, 134, 265–6, 273, 306

Kravchuk's diplomacy towards, 385–6, 389
and Ukraine referendum (December 1991), 395
and Ukraine's insecurity, 363
Ukrainian-Russian dispute over, 324, 325, 326, 327, 351, 384, 394, 400

CSCE (Conference on Security and Cooperation in Europe), 172

Cuadra, Sergio de la, 230, 415

Cuba, 96, 119, 239
abrogation of Soviet assistance to, 344, 345

Czechoslovakia, 48, 93
plans to join NATO, 161
"Prague Spring" (1968), 34
Soviet invasion of (1968), 47, 59, 97, 112, 115, 184

Darman, Richard, 239

De Michelis, Gianni, 145

Delors, Jacques, 133, 249, 410

Dementey, Nikolai, 266, 315

Demirchan, Karen, 54

Democratic Russia (DR), 101, 115, 140, 164, 189
absence of economic strategy, 348, 349–50, 354
against Gorbachev and the Soviet government, 105, 152, 176, 184, 234
against the Union Treaty, 201, 267
backing Baltic independence, 86, 115, 184–5, 213, 290
backing Ukraine's sovereignty, 117, 211
"common democratic space," 333, 343, 351
"dark forces" of reaction, 140–1, 243
declarations of human rights, 333, 339
and economic liberalization, 150–1, 229
gatherings and rallies, 150, 153, 184, 194, 202, 210–11, 317, 348–5
mass base, 211
pro-Western moods, 339, 348–50
and RSFSR parliament, 117, 131
and shutdown of the Party in Moscow, 315
supported by American NGOs, 202, 212–13
supporting and criticizing Yeltsin, 202–3, 216, 333, 349, 371
unprepared for state work, 348, 350
weakness of, 430

"democrats of the first wave," 9, 73, 76, 117, 348, 350; see also intelligentsia

Deng Xiaoping, 16, 60, 61, 295, 434

diamonds, Soviet, 111, 127, 137, 330, 370, 376, 388, 390, 391

INDEX

Dienstbier, Jiří, 340
Diuk, Nadia, 212
Doguzhiev, Vitaly, 295, 302, 304
Dole, Robert, 220
Dornbusch, Rudiger, 231, 356, 414
Dudayev, Dzhokhar, 389
Dumas, Roland, 340, 419
Durdinets, Valery, 392

East Germany (German Democratic
    Republic), 49, 91, 92, 93
Eastern Europe, 3, 15, 18, 43, 47–8, 89, 433
    collapse of trade with the USSR, 246, 247
    illiberal trend in, 438s
    nationalism in, 52
    and neoliberal economics, 230
    peaceful revolutions in, 94, 306
    plans to join NATO, 161, 246–7
    as priority for the West over Russia, 433,
        434
    prospect of violence in, 48–9
    rejection of "Finlandization," 247
    as US strategic priority after 1989, 239,
        245, 284
    withdrawal of Soviet forces from, 159–61,
        327
    see also Soviet bloc; Warsaw Treaty
        Organization; CMEA
EBRD (European Bank for Reconstruction
    and Development), 249, 251, 340
economic treaty among post-Soviet
    republics
    talks on, 346, 357, 367–8, 369, 370
    and Ukraine, 367, 370, 373, 383, 386, 400
    Yeltsin's zigzags on, 357, 369, 370, 373
economy, Soviet, 16, 23
    blows to, 24, 25, 26
    collapse of the central state, 327, 329–30
    crisis, 4, 126
    crisis of supply, 62, 424
    de-centralization of, 27–8, 30
    IMF-World Bank study of, 231
    joint-stock companies, 157
    loss of state control over export, 111, 113,
        166, 207, 374–5
    "nationalization" by RSFSR, 120,
    political liberalization, 78–9
    populist policies, 126, 129, 146, 201, 231,
        232, 327
    price liberalization, 128, 132, 373, 374–6,
        383
    privatization, 129, 132, 156–7, 234, 326–9
    protectionist reaction to crisis of, 207
    reform programs in 1991, 348
    subsidies, 18, 99, 201, 327, 372, 377, 357,
        367, 395, 419

and Western economists, 126, 231, 233,
    235, 356, 372, 354–5, 373, 374–8, 415
    see also finances, Soviet; inflation
EEC see European Economic Community
elites, Russia's (after 1991), and decline of
    liberal Westernism, 435–6
Emergency Committee (State Committee
    for the State of Emergency; GKChP;
    junta)
    assurances to the West, 276, 277, 292
    and bureaucratic class, 294, 295, 296, 297,
        304
    consequences of its failure, 303–4, 320
    and curfew in Moscow, 298
    delegation to Crimea, 273–4, 275, 276, 303
    disagreement and disintegration, 297,
        301–3, 307
    economic crisis, 272, 280, 294, 302
    and Gorbachev's absence, 275, 287, 290
    and Gorbachev's "treason" 318
    lack of economic strategy, 294
    lack of legitimacy, 273, 275, 285, 286–8,
        290, 291, 293, 294, 295–6, 304, 305
    logistics, 269–72
    and the media, 279–80, 286, 287, 287–8,
        297, 298
    "Operation Thunder," 297, 301, 302
    and the Party, 276–7
    plans for Yeltsin, 286, 288–9
    popular resistance to, 289, 296, 297, 300,
        302
    popular initial acceptance of, 1, 320
    reactions in the West, 272, 274, 280–1,
        287, 289, 292
    repentance of members, 303
    and republican/regional elites, 283, 286,
        297, 306
    shock effect of, 278, 280–1
    tipping point for, 294, 302
    unready to use violence, 285
emergency legislation, 108, 146, 259
    wasted by Gorbachev, 171–3, 174, 201
entrepreneurs, Russian
    against the junta, 296–7, 296, 328
    and the collapse of the Soviet state, 327–9
    and Party money, 157, 326
    as promoters of liberalization, 204, 225,
        327, 328, 349
Erb, Richard, 414
Ermarth, Fritz, 182, 214
Estonia, 77, 389
    Russia's recognition of sovereignty,
        318–19
    and Russian democrats, 291
    separatism of, 59, 112–13
    see also Baltic republics

517

INDEX

EU *see* European Union
European Bank for Reconstruction and
　　Development *see* EBRD
European Economic Community, 47, 102,
　　122, 190, 249, 340
European Union, 133, 340
　　exclusion of Russia, 436

Fahd bin Abdulaziz Al Saud, King of Saudi
　　Arabia, 145
Falin, Valentin, 118
Federal Reserve System, 188, 222, 229, 351,
　　353
Filshin, Gennady, 189
finances, Soviet, 17, 30–1, 111
　　budget deficit, 62, 63, 80, 242
　　debts and dependence on Western
　　　　credits, 111, 116, 139, 161, 170, 194,
　　　　233, 234, 294
　　dualism of, 30–1, 32, 128, 129, 130
　　fear of Western sanctions, 272, 274, 285,
　　　　293, 295, 304
　　food imports (as a Soviet problem), 18
　　gold reserves, 111, 127, 338, 353, 412
　　loss of revenues, 126–7, 412
　　manipulations with cashless money, 129
　　printing money, 237, 330, 358, 370, 376,
　　　　387, 397
　　ruble zone during the collapse, 358,
　　　　369–70, 405, 419
　　Soviet bankruptcy, 110, 237, 242, 246,
　　　　293, 294, 327, 338, 390
　　taken under Russia's control, 376–7,
　　　　387–8
　　see also foreign debts and credits, Soviet;
　　　　Goznak; inflation; Ministry of Finance
Fischer, Stanley, 235
Fisunenko, Igor, 218, 219
Fokin, Vitold, 263, 351, 369, 370, 399
　　at meeting of Slavic leaders in Viskuli,
　　　　399, 400, 401, 405
foreign debts and credits, Eastern European,
　　15–16, 17, 48, 93, 340
foreign debts and credits, Soviet, 17, 25, 48
　　denial of credits, 111, 242, 294, 338, 340,
　　　　353
　　restructuring of, 249, 340
　　Russia takes over, 390–1, 404
　　Western pressure to pay, 353
foreign investments in the USSR, 246
Foreign Ministry, Russian 226, 380, 418,
　　426; *see also* Kozyrev, Andrei
foreign trade, Soviet
　　collateralized by gold, 353
　　halted for lack of credit, 111, 294
　　impact of de-centralization, 90

Friedman, Milton, 229, 232
Frolov, Ivan, 35
Fukuyama, Francis, 410
Furman, Dmitry, 45, 81
Fyodorov, Boris, 457
Fyodorov, Svyatoslav 73

G-7
　　competition among Soviet actors to get
　　　　money from, 352
　　internal coordination, 343
　　and Soviet debts/financial chaos, 390–1
　　summits: Houston, 1990, 122, 231, 232;
　　　　London, 1991, 234, 238, 246, 248,
　　　　249–54
　　and Western Sherpas, 247, 338, 340, 353
Gaidar, Masha, 295
Gaidar, Yegor, 231, 371, 406
　　and the "500 Days," 231
　　abolition of state monopoly on currency
　　　　regulation, 374
　　absence of financial reserves, 390–1, 414
　　decree on price liberalization, 373, 374–6;
　　　　other decrees, 398
　　drafting the Commonwealth accords,
　　　　400, 405
　　and failing central governance, 356, 375,
　　　　376
　　IMF-World Bank study of Soviet
　　　　economy, 232
　　macroeconomic theory, 231, 355, 356,
　　　　371, 373
　　at meeting of Slavic leaders in Viskuli,
　　　　398–402
　　partnership with Burbulis, 355–6
　　on preventing war with Ukraine, 405
　　produces strategy of reforms for Yeltsin,
　　　　355–8
　　reactions to emergency rule, 231, 288,
　　　　295, 300, 303
　　reforms postponed, 383
　　in the Russian "government of reforms,"
　　　　376, 377
　　on seizing financial and economic assets
　　　　and controls, 376, 398
　　social consequences of reforms, 435
　　his team of economists, 295, 398
　　Western lack of assistance, 390–1, 414,
　　　　434
　　and Yeltsin, 295, 371–2, 431
Gamsakhurdia, Zviad, 91, 198, 283, 415
Gandhi, Rajiv, 63
Garcelon, Marc, 210
Garrison, Jim, 83
Gates, Robert, 50, 92, 163–4, 181, 245
　　and the coup in Moscow, 283, 292

INDEX

INDEX

lionized by the West, 95, 119, 148, 340, 415

losing popularity at home, 2, 24, 80, 88, 105, 125, 205, 310

loss of power instruments, 314–15, 407–8, 417

and military industries, 64–6, 167–9, 251

and NATO, 110–12, 118, 124, 247

Nine Plus One talks, 206–10, 218, 234–5, 240, 241, 255–7, 258, 266, 315; *see also* Union Treaty

Nobel Peace Prize, 148, 173, 184

non-use of force and legalism, 43, 47, 54, 55, 61, 105, 183–5, 196, 203, 322, 406, 428

and nuclear arms, 44, 262

and nuclear controls, 275, 314–15, 378, 413–14, 408, 417, 419, 421, 424

and the Party apparatus, 27, 40–1, 66–7, 71, 72, 107, 123, 135, 155, 157–8, 209, 225, 255

and the Party's destruction, 315, 316

place in history, 193, 422

political isolation, 378, 379, 387, 417

popular anger against, 115, 121, 191, 193–4

and the post-August 1991 provisional government, 312, 322, 331; *see also* State Council

reading and theorizing by, 34, 38, 66–7, 68, 106, 135, 266

rejection of junta members, 274, 306, 307–8

reliance on intelligentsia, 46, 54, 55, 56, 72

reliance on KGB, 165, 166, 197, 199, 222, 243, 265, 268, 269

reliance on US leadership, 45–6, 196, 197, 198–9, 233, 252, 258, 260

resigns as Party head, 318

return to Moscow after junta's collapse, 309–10

and Russia's economic reform, 378–9

and Russia's sovereignty, 99, 117–18

and the Russian Communist Party, 100, 124, 136, 155, 193, 225

and Russian liberals, 105, 150, 152, 184, 217, 234, 378, 417

and Russian opposition and separatism, 100, 204–5, 417

and the Russian presidency, 219, 224

and the Ryzhkov government, 134, 136, 140

and Shevardnadze's resignation, 177

and "socialist democracy," 27, 28, 35–6, 60, 61, 67, 225, 428

on Soviet nationalities, 51, 53–4

on Stalin and terror, 34–5, 57

as a struggling world statesman, 247, 248, 255, 260–1, 262, 337, 339–40, 379–80

terms of retirement, 420–2

"turn to the right," 154, 171–3, 174, 192, 260,

on Ukrainian independence and sovereignty, 321, 370, 393–4, 395

and Ukrainian separatism, 256, 257, 258, 263, 393–4, 395

Union presidency, 106–8, 171, 174, 257, 266, 282

Union Treaty, 85, 135, 138, 170–1

US-Soviet summits, 44, 96, 118–19, 182, 253

US economic support, 119, 144, 235

vacation in August 1991, 265–6

verbosity, 1, 105–6, 202, 261, 353

and Vilnius bloodshed (January 1991), 183–4, 185

and Yeltsin, 39, 117–18, 119, 133, 137–8, 148–9, 201, 223, 357, 379, 382, 387

and Yeltsin's anti-Party decrees, 265

Gorbacheva, Irina, 265, 307, 310

Gorbacheva, Raisa, 26, 104, 105, 109, 118, 119, 177, 251, 264, 270, 410

decision to go on vacation in August 1991, 265

her fear and breakdown, 307, 308, 309, 310, 378

as an intellectual partner of Mikhail, 19–20, 34

during isolation in Zaria, 273, 274, 293, 307

and the Soviet Cultural Foundation, 100

on the Union Treaty, 266–7

Gorbunovs, Anatolijs, 57, 185, 319

Gosnell, Jack, 296

Gosplan, 18, 28, 31, 88, 175, 230

Gospriemka see State Inspection

Goznak, 330, 376, 387–8

Grachev, Andrei, 267, 335

Grachev, Pavel, 281, 298, 407, 413

Grand Bargain (private proposal of Western assistance to Soviet reforms, 1991), 235, 236, 238, 239–40, 241, 243–4, 245, 248

compared to the Marshall Plan of 1947, 235, 240, 340

Granin, Daniil, 316

Greenspan, Alan, 353

Grinev, Vladimir, 321, 322, 331

Gromov, Boris, 175, 216, 267

Gromyko, Andrei, 20, 27, 28, 45

GRU, 92, 253, 299

INDEX

INDEX

Kennan, George, 6, 411

Kerensky, Alexander, 138

KGB (Committee for State Security), USSR, 13, 14, 16, 27, 33, 66, 67, 71, 83, 86, 143, 155, 163–70, 175, 213, 232, 301, 316, 399, 417
   on American engagement in Russian politics, 212–13
   broken up and demoralized, 378, 382
   commercial activities, 127–8, 157, 189, 327–8, 437
   division and hesitancy during the emergency, 283, 299, 299, 302
   Gorbachev's encirclement in Zaria, 274, 292, 293
   headquarters spared in August 1991, 313–14
   logistics of the coup, 271, 272, 273–4, 287, 290
   merged with the police forces, 418
   and nationalist movements, 52, 74, 76, 86, 92, 164
   not acting on the oath to the Soviet Union, 402
   obedience to leadership of, 165–6
   and prospects of social unrest, 152, 153, 155, 227
   protection of leadership, 118, 166, 265, 274, 307, 382
   and Russian nationalism, 216
   and Russian politics, 115, 117, 164, 186, 219, 227, 299, 455
   split over the Union Treaty, 271
   supporting Yeltsin, 71, 149, 227, 449
   suspected attempt on Yeltsin's life, 147
   tapping communications, 165, 213, 221–2, 257, 269
   "turn to the right," 154
   see also KGB, Russian

KGB, Russian, 137, 149, 150, 226, 299; *see also* KGB, USSR

Khasbulatov, Ruslan, 131–2, 146, 193, 227, 327, 373
   during the junta's rule, 281, 282, 295, 304–5
   and Gorbachev, 204, 209–10, 211
   and the victory of Russian democracy, 306, 311, 313

Khlebnikov, Paul, 327

Khodorkovsky, Mikhail, 328–9

Khrushchev, Nikita, 22, 30, 34, 44, 45, 57, 65, 66, 79, 389, 431
   and Crimea, 327
   lessons for Gorbachev, 31, 38, 420, 427

Kirkland, Lane, 202, 220

Kissinger, Henry, 66, 220

Kobets, Konstantin, 299

Kohl, Helmut, 45, 90, 110, 196
   financial support to Gorbachev, 116, 144, 145, 244, 249, 250, 339–40
   reaction to the coup in Moscow, 284, 287
   on separatism in the USSR, 114, 341
   and Soviet troops in East Germany, 124, 284, 381
   Soviet-German accords (1990), 124
   special relations with Gorbachev, 110, 112, 121, 246, 416
   on Yugoslavia, 261

Köhler, Horst, 340

Kolosovsky, Andrei, 404–5, 412, 413

Komplektov, Viktor, 292

Komsomol, entrepreneurship of, 157, 327–8

Koppel, Ted, 422, 423, 424

Korea, Republic of, 208

Korzhakov, Alexander ("Sasha"), 149, 282, 315, 358, 403

Kovalev, Sergey, 339

Kozyrev, Andrei, 238, 291, 319, 356, 367, 377, 394–5, 400, 414, 417
   and the destruction of the Union, 367–8
   during junta rule, 283, 290–2
   ensuring Russia's status as Soviet successor state, 412, 419, 420
   expectation of Western help, 222, 292, 414, 426
   at meeting of Slavic leaders in Viskuli, 398, 400, 402, 403
   as Russian Foreign Minister, 226
   takeover of the Ministry of Foreign Affairs of the USSR, 336, 380, 412, 417
   and US leadership, 220, 221, 404–5, 408, 413

Kravchenko, Leonid, 298

Kravchuk, Antonina, 266

Kravchuk, Leonid, 86, 359, 360, 360, 383
   and Crimea's separatism, 385–6
   defying Gorbachev, 265, 266, 351–2, 394
   during emergency rule, 283, 286, 307, 308
   and economic relations with Russia, 352, 361, 369, 370
   growing confidence, 201, 256, 265, 320, 359
   as a leader of Ukraine's independence, 320–2, 351, 359
   at meeting of Slavic leaders in Viskuli, 396, 398–405
   Nine Plus One talks, 255–6, 315, 326, 352, 369, 370
   partnership with Yeltsin, 173–4, 325
   and the post-Soviet confederation, 263, 266, 361, 364, 383

INDEX

presidential race in Ukraine, 256, 326, 359, 360, 364, 384–6

referendum on independence, 322, 393, 397

trip to Canada and the United States (September 1991), 359–61, 363

on Ukraine's nuclear arms, 363, 367, 392, 401

and Ukrainian-American diaspora, 359, 360

and Ukrainian-Russian conflict, 325–6

worries about dominant Russia, 174, 263

Kremlin, the

as Gorbachev's presidential residence, 130, 168, 177, 184, 224

seized by Yeltsin, 407–8, 413, 419, 420–1, 424

and Yeltsin's demands and empowerment, 120, 137–8, 219, 223, 224

Krenz, Egon, 93

Krieble, Robert, 212, 217, 220, 291

Kruchina, Nikolai, 157, 315, 326, 327–8

Kryuchkov, Vladimir, 66, 88–9, 108, 113, 115, 130, 143, 193, 215, 256, 327

and American agents of influence, 165

arrest, 309

on the bloodshed in Vilnius (January 1991), 183

calculations for Russia's role, 286

enjoying Gorbachev's trust, 151, 261, 269

fear of Western sanctions, 285

and Grand Bargain, 235–6, 242

insinuating and goading Gorbachev, 148, 165, 187, 254, 269

plotting to introduce emergency, 200, 221

on political reforms, 163–4

reading of intelligence, 269–70

reluctance to use force, 284, 288–9, 297, 302, 303

as a ringleader of a junta, 164, 269–71, 272, 273, 274, 275, 276, 285–7, 288–9

trip to Foros, 305, 306, 307–8

on the Union referendum, 191, 200

and the Union Treaty, 269, 430

on Western financial policies, 164, 165–6, 168, 177, 190, 290, 294, 301–2, 303

and Yeltsin, 226, 286–7, 288

see also KGB, USSR

Kryzhanovsky, Pyotr, 396

Kunadze, Georgy, 418

Kuwait, 142–3, 196

Kuzbass, 79, 193, 211, 216, 218, 297; see also workers

Kvitsinsky, Yuly, 247, 336

Landsbergis, Vytautas, 58, 76, 112, 114, 182, 184, 186, 282, 342

Latin America

as a mirror for Soviet troubles, 247, 248, 249, 435

as a testing-ground for neoliberalism, 230–1, 249

Latvia, 114, 185

gaining sovereignty, 318–19

national referendum on independence (1991), 200

see also Baltic republics

Lavrov, Kirill, 147

Lavrov, Sergey, 336–7

Lebed, Alexander, 297, 298, 305

legal succession from the Soviet Union to Russia, 212, 264, 350

British advice on, 419

and financial institutions, 376–7

Russian-Ukrainian dispute over, 367, 401

Western consent to, 369, 413, 419, 426

Yeltsin's dilemma on, 366, 373

Lenin, Vladimir, 16, 29, 35, 36, 72, 219, 293, 329, 333, 337, 343, 373, 375, 379

construction of the Soviet Union, 51, 400, 403

his cult debunked, 72

his reforms, 428

Levada, Yuri, 217

Lieven, Dominic, 68

Ligachev, Yegor, 20, 23, 29, 39, 40, 106, 107, 112, 115, 123–4

Likhachev, Dmitry, 75, 99, 108, 333

Lincoln, Abraham, 193

Lithuania

assassination of customs officers (July 1991), 261

bloodshed in January 1991, 182–3, 290

separatism (1989–90), 89, 104, 112

Soviet economic sanctions against, 113, 115

suspends independence declaration, 123

see also Baltic republics

Lobov, Vladimir, 262

Lubbers, Ruud, 249, 284

Lugar, Richard, 411

Lukianenko, Levko, 320, 321

Lukin, Vladimir, 313

concept of Russia inside a Union, 174, 207

excluded from the Viskuli talks, 398

relations with the United States, 220, 221

resistance to the junta, 281

as supporter of the Union Treaty, 207, 209

and territories and borders of Russia, 173–4, 324, 325

INDEX

INDEX

conflict in Transnistria, 436
separatism and violence in, 153, 262, 283, 350
Mosbacher, Robert, 144, 220, 221
Moscow
attitudes to preservation of the Union, 202
as capital of the Soviet Union and the RSFSR, 124, 134, 137, 145, 219
as center of the defense industries, 65, 169–70
as controller of Union economic assets, 52, 157–8
envy and enmity toward, 73–4, 76–7, 120–1, 139, 150
as hotbed of Westernism and liberalism, 80, 86, 97, 99, 101, 105, 117, 128, 178, 184, 186, 194, 197, 210, 217
living standards deteriorating under Gorbachev, 62
power struggle in, 150, 152, 202, 203–204, 207
as Soviet-Russian media hub, 72, 76, 105, 117, 135
supporting market reforms, 135
supporting Yeltsin, 71, 138, 201, 217
as symbol of colonial domination, 58
under control of Democratic Russia, 115, 152
Movement for Democracy and Reforms, 225, 280; see also Shevardnadze, Eduard
Mulford, David C., 239, 353, 390, 414
Müllerson, Rein, 319
Mulroney, Brian, 122, 250, 422
on the coup in Moscow, 285
on recognition of the Balts and Ukraine, 341, 359
Murashov, Arkady, 150, 348, 349–50; see also Democratic Russia; MDG
Mutalibov, Ayaz, 351, 419
Myasnikov, Georgy, 100

Nabiyev, Rahmon, 419
Nagorny Karabagh, conflict over, 54–5, 358, 389, 436
Naishul, Vitaly, 230–1
Najibullah, Mohammad, 345
Nakasone, Yasuhiro, 66
National Democratic Institute (NDI), 213
National Endowment for Democracy (NED), Washington DC, 202, 212, 291
lobbying for Ukraine's independence, 342
National Security Council (NSC), 83, 164, 181, 343
contingency group on the Soviet Union, 181, 377–8

nationalism
as anti-systemic force, 4
in Azerbaijan (1990), 104–5, 162, 184
Azeri-Armenian conflict, 54–5
in the Baltic republics (1988), 56
in Georgia and Abkhazia (1988–89), 74, 91
in Kazakhstan (1986), 53
nationalists, Russian 99, 100, 146, 267
and collapse of the Soviet state, 317–18
and emergency rule, 287
hating Gorbachev, 107
NATO, 97, 124
cooperation council (NACC), 413
declaration to reform itself (1990), 122, 123
and Eastern European countries, 161, 246–7
expansion and Russia's reaction, 436, 437
humanitarian aid to the Soviet Union, 346, 411
and junta rule in Moscow, 284, 300
non-enlargement "pledge," 110
Russia's request to join, 410, 413
and Soviet military withdrawal, 159, 160
Nazarbayev, Nursultan, 109, 175, 176, 209, 241, 283, 381
excluded from meeting of Slavic leaders, 400, 404, 408
as Gorbachev's unsteady ally, 257, 258, 331, 332, 352, 408
soliciting US recognition, 347
worries about Russia's dominance, 325, 347–8
and Yeltsin, 268, 323, 338, 408
Nazi-Soviet pact (1939), 57, 76, 85, 86, 112, 320
Gorbachev's concealment of original, 421
see also Baltic republics
Németh, Miklós, 91
Nevzorov, Alexander, 287, 318
New Economic Policy (NEP), 16, 27
"new political thinking," 43–4, 46
"new world order," 247
of the Bush administration, 143, 411
crisis of, discussed, 438, 439
for Gorbachev, 43, 46, 116, 197, 237, 260, 261
place of Russia in, 434
and the Soviet military, 160
and Yeltsin and Russian democrats, 150, 291, 411
Nicaragua, 96
Nine Plus One talks see Novo-Ogaryovo; Union Treaty; Gorbachev, Mikhail

INDEX

ban on rallies, 202, 203
Cabinet, 246, 294–5
concept of conservative reforms, 187–8, 242
concept for the RSFSR government, 226
concern for Western banks and profiteers, 189–90, 272
demanding emergency rule, 242
exit from junta, 298
on Grand Bargain, 236, 241–2
participation in the junta and sickness, 272, 287, 294–5, 298
as Prime Minister of the USSR, 175–6, 187–90, 202, 234
public hatred of, 189
and Soviet bankruptcy, 272
on the Union Treaty, 272, 295, 478
view of Gorbachev, 187
perestroika, 22, 31, 34, 50, 55, 59, 62, 66, 67, 71, 181, 187, 194, 266, 399, 415
declared extinct, 184, 317, 328
in need of Western support, 116
Pérez de Cuéllar, Javier, 277, 426
Petrakov, Nikolai, 108, 128, 142, 149, 154
and the "500 Days," 133–6, 146, 147
in Andropov's group of economists, 422
program of market transition (1990), 128–9, 130, 132, 142, 429
on republics' separatism, 129, 130, 134
Pikhoia, Rudolf, 155
Pinochet, Augusto, 230, 288, 295, 300
Pipes, Richard, 212
Plekhanov, Yuri, 274, 275, 306, 307, 309
Plokhy, Serhii, 307, 359, 383, 385, 393
Poland, 17, 90, 91, 340, 381, 395, 408
economic reforms ("the Balcerowicz Plan"), 128, 129
impact on political movements in the Soviet Union, 141, 193, 194, 294
see also Solidarity
Politburo, 155, 192
and German unification, 116
and Gorbachev's reforms, 34, 36, 37, 38, 41, 46, 49, 54, 55, 57, 58, 61, 64, 71, 72
as institution in decline, 36, 69, 79, 107, 123, 155, 224
reformers and Gorbachev loyalists added to, 40, 41, 88
political liberalization, 35, 38, 40–1; see also Constitution
Polozkov, Ivan, 117, 123, 155, 156, 171, 192, 205, 209, 225
Ponomarev, Lev, 212
Popov, Gavriil, 73, 105, 115, 116, 225, 310
demanding Ukraine's territories, 325
elected Mayor of Moscow, 219

fearful of dictatorship, 194, 202, 299–300
shutdown of the Party apparatus, 315
soliciting Western food aid to Moscow, 346
suspected conspiracy against Gorbachev, 221–2, 243
Portnikov, Vitaly, 366–7
Powell, Colin, 258–9, 361
Presidential Council (1990), 108–9, 172, 193
presidential elections in RSFSR (June 1991), 215–19
price reform under Gorbachev
buying panics, 131, 146
delayed, 63
overdue, 31, 130–1
Primakov, Yevgeny, 135, 243, 251, 308, 332
during emergency rule, 297
as Gorbachev's emissary, 143–4, 234
in Gorbachev's provisional government, 338
and Grand Bargain, 235, 236–7
and the Gulf war, 143–4, 196
as head of foreign intelligence, 382, 407, 418
joins the democratic opposition, 304
on export of arms, 168–9
privatization see economy
Prokhanov, Alexander, 267, 287, 296
Prokofiev, Yuri, 146, 202, 224–5, 276, 315
provisional government: 1917, 138, 144, 197, 349, 366; after August 1991 see State Council
Prunskienė, Kazimira, 115, 183
public opinion and polls, 124, 135, 138, 192, 217, 283, 430
during emergency rule, 294
on growing anarchy, 171
in Moscow on the Commonwealth accords, 409
reaction to Gorbachev's resignation, 422
in Ukraine, 359, 384
Pugo, Boris, 57, 175, 193, 242, 256, 327
commits suicide, 303
in the junta, 287, 298
Putin, Vladimir, 2, 290, 432, 436–7

Qian Qichen, 96

Radio Liberty, 283, 296
Rappaport, Bruce, 167
Rasputin, Valentin, 99, 100, 130
Reagan, Ronald, 17, 37, 44
and Gorbachev, 44, 49, 50
pressure on Soviet economy, 44–5
Referendum (1 December 1991) on Ukraine's independence see Ukraine

527

INDEX

INDEX

INDEX

as RSFSR prime minister, 226, 310, 338, 352

"saving" Gorbachev in Crimea, 306, 308–9

and Soviet foreign debts, 390

Simes, Dimitri K, 213

Sitaryan, Stepan, 35, 442

Slavsky, Yefim, 26

Sliunkov, Nikolai, 99

Snegur, Mircea, 419

Sobchak, Anatoly, 78, 108, 128, 225, 268
  on Baltic and Ukraine's independence, 323, 325, 334, 386
  commercial activities, 329
  during emergency rule, 281, 289–90, 296,
  elected mayor of Leningrad (St Petersburg), 219
  as Gorbachev's uncertain ally, 332, 346

"socialist democracy," 15, 21, 27, 28, 33–6, 42, 60–2, 77, 101, 158, 225, 428
  in Gorbachev's new Party program, 255

Sokurov, Alexander, 217å

Solidarity (Polish movement), 15
  impact on Ukrainian nationalists, 85
  as a model for Russian democrats, 73, 151, 193, 194, 202
  round table and elections, 86, 90, 211

Solzhenitsyn, Alexander, 66, 100, 232, 333
  influence on Yeltsin, 150, 220
  on the union of three Slavic nations, 173, 324, 327

Soros, George, 147, 230

Soviet bloc, 17–18, 90, 96–7

Soviet collapse
  causes of, 3–6, 9, 397–8, 427–9
  estimates about, 2, 135, 181
  explanations of, 3–7
  historical alternatives, 428
  and mass disillusionment in Russia, 435, 437
  parallels with Western decline, 438
  place in history, 439
  Western media's narrative, 423
  see also Soviet Union; Soviet Union, dissolution of

Soviet identity crumbling, 82–3, 84, 87

Soviet Union (Union of Soviet Socialist Republics; USSR)
  as a confederation, 51, 58–9, 135, 208–9
  conference in Alma-Ata, 416, 417, 419–20
  exit law for republics, 60, 107, 113
  founding Treaty of 1922, 400, 405
  fragility and resilience of, 432
  Gorbachev's resignation
  Joint Declaration of April 1991, 209

meltdown of executive power, 303, 316, 331, 332, 364

name discarded, 208

perceived death of, 348, 400–2, 425

Russian nationalism, 51–2, 156, 219, 267

as sovereign legal entity, 319

Union Treaty, 264, 269; see also Union Treaty

Western humanitarian and food aid to, 345, 353, 368, 380, 412, 415

see also legal succession; Soviet Union, dissolution of

Soviet Union, dissolution of
  changing Russian perceptions of, 435, 437
  declaration of, 400–2
  fear and insecurity of initiators, 402–3
  informing the US government on, 403–5
  meeting of Slavic leaders in Viskuli, 397, 398–405
  and public apathy, 409, 422, 424
  ratification and popular reactions to, 409
  in Western imagination, 423, 425, 433, 437
  Western surprise and verdict, 410, 415–16

Soyuz, 171, 172, 243

Spohr, Kristina, 434, 435

Stalin, Joseph, 21, 30, 34, 35, 40, 43, 75, 243, 246, 249, 266, 269, 280, 295, 339, 348, 359, 389, 403, 425

Stankevich, Sergey, 73, 105, 313–14, 325, 366, 398

Starovoitova, Galina, 73, 86–7, 120
  advising Yeltsin, 191, 217, 386, 292, 391
  advocating Western help to Yeltsin during the coup, 290, 291
  assassinated (1998), 417
  demanding Gorbachev's resignation, 184, 290
  demanding Gorbachev's return during junta days, 290
  excluded from the talks in Viskuli, 401
  on foreign debts, 391
  on Gorbachev's missed opportunities, 310, 416–17
  on inevitability of the Soviet Union's break-up, 87, 291
  and the Soviet Union's abrupt dissolution, 416–17
  on Ukraine's independence, 386, 396, 398, 400–1

START (Strategic Arms Reduction Treaty), 238, 250, 251, 253, 258, 261–2, 412
  ratification in the Union's Supreme Soviet, 343

INDEX

State Bank, 18, 32, 79, 188, 237, 242
  and commercial banks, 328
  during the emergency rule, 304
  loss of revenues, 391, 412–13
  and monetary liberalization, 32, 33, 128
  role after economic liberalization, 374
  and "swap" operations, 111
  taken over by Yeltsin's government, 329–30, 383, 387
  see also Gerashchenko, Viktor
State Committee for the State of Emergency *see* Emergency Committee
State Council (provisional government after August 1991), 331, 334, 337, 346, 351–3, 355, 356, 358, 369–70, 376, 377, 380–3, 386, 387, 388, 391, 406, 417
State Enterprises, Law on, 27–9, 63, 189, 397
State Inspection (*Gospriemka*), 24
Stepanov-Mamaladze, Teimuraz, 55, 80, 82, 91, 97, 118, 119, 123, 160, 316, 416, 422
Stoltenberg, Thorvald, 240
Stolypin, Pyotr, 187–8, 266, 427
Strategic Arms Reduction Treaty *see* START
Strategic Defense Initiative *see* SDI
Strauss, Robert, 341, 394
Sukhanov, Lev, 83–4, 192
Summers, Larry, 229
Sununu, John, 393
Supreme Soviet (RSFSR), 101, 131, 193
  Gorbachev's explanations to, 316–17
  ratifies the dissolution of the USSR, 409
  and Russian presidency, 191
  in session during emergency rule, 282, 304–6
  split over Yeltsin's separatism and radicalism, 193
  "war of laws" with the USSR Supreme Soviet, 145–6, 397
  as "the White House," symbol of Russian democracy, 297, 298, 300, 304, 310
Supreme Soviet (USSR)
  absence during emergency rule, 295–6, 304
  "closed" session on Soviet crisis, 242
  controlled and disabled by republics, 331, 409
  curbing populist allocations of, 129
  in Gorbachev's political reforms, 78
  as the last representative institution of the Union, 222–3, 333
  populism and economic interests in, 77, 78–9, 80, 126–7

push for a strong hand, 171
  and the Union Treaty, 256, 257
  upstaged by the RSFSR parliament, 205
Sviridov, Georgy, 147

Talbott, Strobe, 1, 416, 434
Tarasenko, Sergey, 119, 144, 416
Tatarstan, 201, 208, 210
Taubman, William, 21, 26–7, 33, 38, 60–1, 94, 133, 142, 310
taxation, Soviet
  on cooperatives, 33
  federal tax, 134, 133, 134, 210, 256, 257, 266
  Pavlov's reforms, 188–9
  and republics' non-payment, 174, 188, 206, 327
  on state enterprises, 78, 130
Ter-Petrosian, Levon, 419
Thatcher, Margaret, 37, 80, 94, 122
  calls Yeltsin during the coup, 291
  and Grand Bargain, 238–9, 254–5
Thurmond, Strom, 220
Tikhonov, Nikolai, 23
Tocqueville, Alexis de, 43, 68, 141
travel abroad and cultural shock, Soviet, 81, 82
Travkin, Nikolai, 83, 366, 406
Treaty on the Conventional Forces in Europe *see* CFE
triumphalism, Western, 2
Trump, Donald, 438–9
Tsereteli, Zurab, 415, 416
Tsypko, Alexander, 72, 324, 366
Tucker, Robert C., 266
Tudjman, Franjo, 370
Tuleyev, Aman, 216
Tusk, Donald, 2

Ukraine, 25–6
  Act of Independence (1991), 321–2
  claim on Union's assets, 332, 383, 391
  and Crimea *see* Crimea
  declaration of sovereignty (1990), 120, 263, 320, 321, 385, 399, 400
  and Donbass, 263, 324, 325, 330, 352, 363, 367, 384, 386, 392, 363, 384, 386, 394
  economic assets on its territory, 256, 321
  economic dependence on RSFSR, 352, 330, 384, 405
  fears of dominant Russia, 191
  and Gorbachev-Yeltsin rivalry, 256, 320, 384
  and Gorbachev's provisional government, 331

INDEX

as a mediator of Gorbachev-Yeltsin
"settlement," 420–1
and non-Russian nationalism, 53–4
and Russian nationalism, 99
supports Russian liberals and
"democracy," 203
on Ukraine's independence, 393
Yakovlev, Vladimir, 328
Yakovlev, Yegor, 184, 225, 307, 328
as head of Soviet television, 423
Yanayev, Gennady, 175, 246, 256
background, 258
charming Bush, 258, 262, 284
fear and denial, 297–8
Gorbachev's choice as Vice-President of
the USSR, 176, 265
as the junta's figurehead, 274, 275, 276,
277, 280, 281, 282, 284, 285
press conference on August 19, 1991,
287–8
snubbed and scorned, 176, 263
and the Soviet economy, 294
Yankelevich, Tatiana, 281, 289
Yaremenko, Yuri, 168, 169
Yaroshenko, Viktor, 141–2, 146, 157, 159
Yavlinsky, Grigory, 132
and "400 Days of Confidence," 132, 139
and the "500 Days," 132–4, 146, 147
argues to preserve the Union, 355, 367,
369–70, 388
criticism of, 354
gloomy forecasts, 194–5
and Grand Bargain, 235–7, 240–1, 248
reform proposals before August 1991,
234–5
reform proposals post-August 1991, 338,
351
refusal to go to G-7 meeting in London,
234
as RSFSR deputy Prime Minister, 132,
147
solicits Western help after the coup, 363
supports Yeltsin-Gaidar reforms, 388
as top Soviet economist after August
1991, 331, 340, 345, 346, 352, 363, 419
and Washington Consensus, 330
Yavorivsky, Vladimir, 321
Yazov, Dmitry, 108, 115, 141, 143, 151, 162,
193, 215, 246, 256, 327
against the use of force, 277, 278, 301,
302, 303
and arms reductions, 161, 163, 251, 262
arrested, 309
introduces troops to Moscow, 277–8, 301
in the junta, 271–2, 273, 274, 277
on Lithuania crisis, 112, 113, 183

plot to introduce an emergency rule, 221,
271
and the Soviet Army in crisis, 160, 162
trip to Crimea to see Gorbachev, 306–8
withdraws troops from Moscow, 302,
303
Yazova, Emma, 301
Yeltsin, Boris, 7, 36, 38–9
admiring and emulating the United
States, 84, 222, 225, 233
advisory circle, 150, 186, 190, 194
against Western assistance to Gorbachev,
243–4
antics, theatrics, and swagger 217,
259–60, 281, 306, 382, 387, 391, 399,
401, 415, 422, 424
appropriation of Soviet economic assets,
120, 137, 218, 221, 316, 376, 38
and autonomies within the RSFSR,
135–6, 191, 201, 208, 256
birthday party (1991), 192
celebrates US recognition of Russia, 426
and Central Asian republics, 201, 268,
395, 407–8, 412
and Chechnya, 389–90
and Commonwealth of Independent
States, 401, 404, 408, 409
and confederation "from below," 171,
173, 186, 195, 207, 221, 268
contacts with Bush, 83–4, 221, 259–60,
291–2, 307, 311, 368–9, 388, 390,
404–5, 411–12
courage, 292–3, 300–1
and Crimea, 174, 386, 401
deciding alone on economic reforms in
Russia, 195, 358, 372–3
decrees on destroying the Party, 227–8,
316
desire to join NATO, 410, 413
discontent with Western policies after
1991, 435, 437
economic populism, 147, 201, 218, 226,
395
economic reforms, 132, 133, 134, 146,
147, 148, 166, 241, 352, 355
economic treaty with republics, 357, 369,
370, 373
effect on Russians, 39, 99, 102, 149,
193–4, 217–18, 219
ejection from the Politburo (1987), 39,
elected Chairman of the RSFSR Supreme
Soviet, 118
elected in Moscow (1989), 71
elected President of the RSFSR, 219
elected to the Supreme Soviet of the
USSR, 76

INDEX